Psychology
R 150.3 PSY

PSYCHOLOGY BASICS

MAGILL'S CHOICE

PSYCHOLOGY BASICS

Volume 1

Abnormality: Psychological Models—
Learning Disorders

Editor

Nancy A. Piotrowski, Ph.D.
University of California, Berkeley

SALEM PRESS
Pasadena, California
Hackensack, New Jersey

Copyright © 2005, by SALEM PRESS, INC.
All rights in this book are reserved. No part of this work may be used or reproduced in any manner whatsoever or transmitted in any form or by any means, electronic or mechanical, including photocopy, recording, or any information storage and retrieval system, without written permission from the copyright owner except in the case of brief quotations embodied in critical articles and reviews. For information address the publisher, Salem Press, Inc., P.O. Box 50062, Pasadena, California 91115.

∞ The paper used in these volumes conforms to the American National Standard for Permanence of Paper for Printed Library Materials, Z39.48-1992 (R1997).

The essays in this work originally appeared in *Magill's Encyclopedia of Social Science: Psychology*, 2003; new material has been added.

Library of Congress Cataloging-in-Publication Data
Psychology basics / editor, Nancy A. Piotrowski.— Rev. ed.
    p. cm. — (Magill's choice)
Includes bibliographical references and index.
    ISBN 1-58765-199-8 (set : alk. paper) — ISBN 1-58765-200-5 (v. 1 : alk. paper) — ISBN 1-58765-201-3 (v. 2 : alk. paper)
    1. Psychology—Encyclopedias.   I. Piotrowski, Nancy A. II. Series
BF31.P765 2004
150'.3—dc22

2004016637

Second Printing

FRANKLIN TOWNSHIP PUBLIC LIBRARY
485 De MOTT LANE
SOMERSET, NJ 08873
732-873-8700

PRINTED IN THE UNITED STATES OF AMERICA

TABLE OF CONTENTS

Publisher's Note

The first edition of *Psychology Basics*, drawn from the six-volume *Survey of Social Science: Psychology* (1993), has been a popular, accessible, and affordable source of information about important theories and issues in this dynamic field. Since the publication of *Psychology Basics* in 1998, the larger set has undergone a substantial redesign, revision, and update as the four-volume *Magill's Encyclopedia of Social Science: Psychology* (2003), which was named a 2004 Outstanding Reference Source by RUSA. Essays in the two-volume *Psychology Basics, Revised Edition*, are taken from this award-winning work.

This revised title in the Magill's Choice series features 127 essays. One-third of these topics did not appear in the previous edition of *Psychology Basics*. The remaining two-thirds have the same or similar titles but were either newly commissioned for the revision of the larger encyclopedia or feature both updated text—bringing them in line with the most recent edition of the American Psychiatric Association's *Diagnostic and Statistical Manual of Mental Disorders: DSM-IV-TR* (2000)—and new "Sources for Further Study" sections that offer the latest editions and scholarship. Additions to the *Revised Edition* include new top matter, tailored subheadings guiding readers through the text, photographs and medical drawings, helpful lists of diagnostic criteria from the DSM-IV-TR, and two appendices: a Biographical List of Psychologists with brief profiles of major figures in the field, both past and present, and an annotated Web Site Directory for support groups, organizations, and on-line sources of information on this field. As a result, *Psychology Basics, Revised Edition*, supersedes the previous *Psychology Basics* and should prove to be even more valuable.

Arranged in an A-Z format, *Psychology Basics, Revised Edition*, highlights theories and concepts in the following areas:

- aging
- childhood and adolescence
- cognition
- conditioning
- consciousness
- depression
- development
- diagnosis
- emotions
- experimentation
- intelligence
- language
- learning
- memory
- methodology
- motivation
- origin and definition of psychology
- personality
- psychobiology
- psychopathology
- psychotherapy

- sensation and perception
- sexuality
- social psychology

- stress
- thought
- treatments

Entries range from four to eight pages in length. Every entry begins with standard information for "Type of psychology" and "Fields of study." An abstract briefly defines the subject, summarizing its importance to psychology, and "Key concepts" lists five to ten of the most important issues to be discussed in the essay that follows. The text of each article offers a clear and concise discussion of the topic. An entry on a mental illness addresses its cause, diagnosis, treatment, and impact. An entry on a theory or school examines its origin, history, and current status. Informative, descriptive subheadings divide the text. All terminology is explained, and context is provided to make the information accessible to general readers. Every entry includes a bibliography of secondary sources with annotations discussing their content and value; for this revision, all bibliographies have been updated from the 2003 source set. Every essay is signed by the author and concludes with a list of cross-references to related articles within *Psychology Basics, Revised Edition*. At the end of volume 2 are a Glossary of crucial terms with concise definitions, the Biographical List of Psychologists, the Web Site Directory, a Categorized List of Entries divided into thirty-seven subjects, and a comprehensive Index.

We wish to express our thanks to the Editor, Nancy A. Piotrowski, Ph.D., of the University of California, Berkeley; her insightful Introduction can be found at the beginning of volume 1. We also thank the contributors—academicians from psychology, medicine, and other disciplines in the social and life sciences—for sharing their expertise with general readers; a list of their names and affiliations follows.

CONTRIBUTORS

Christopher M. Aanstoos
State University of West Georgia

Richard Adler
University of Michigan—Dearborn

Mark B. Alcorn
University of Northern Colorado

Jeffrey B. Allen
University of Mississippi

Tara Anthony
Syracuse University

Richard P. Atkinson
Fort Hays State University

Bryan C. Auday
Gordon College

Stephen M. Auerbach
Virginia Commonwealth University

Stephen R. H. Beach
University of Georgia

Donald G. Beal
Eastern Kentucky University

Brett L. Beck
Bloomsbury University

Susan E. Beers
Sweet Briar College

Tanja Bekhuis
TCB Research

Mary Brabeck
Boston College

Lillian J. Breckenridge
Oral Roberts University

T. L. Brink
Crafton Hills College

Dennis Bull
Dallas Theological Seminary

Joan Bartczak Cannon
University of Lowell

Paul J. Chara, Jr.
Northwestern College

Judith M. Chertoff
Baltimore-Washington Institute for Psychoanalysis

Rebecca M. Chesire
University of Hawaii—Manoa

James R. Deni
Appalachian State University

Thomas E. DeWolfe
Hampden-Sydney College

Ronna F. Dillon
Southern Illinois University

Robert J. Drummond
University of North Florida

Christopher A. Duva
Eastern Oregon University

Carolyn Zerbe Enns
Cornell College

Lawrence A. Fehr
Widener University

Margaret M. Frailey
American Association of Counseling and Development

Robin Franck
Southwestern College

Cynthia McPherson Frantz
Amherst College

Donna Frick-Horbury
Appalachian State University

Lisa Friedenberg
*University of North Carolina
at Asheville*

R. G. Gaddis
Gardner-Webb College

Albert R. Gilgen
University of Northern Iowa

Virginia L. Goetsch
West Virginia University

Doyle R. Goff
Lee College

Sanford Golin
University of Pittsburgh

Diane C. Gooding
University of Wisconsin—Madison

Laurence Grimm
University of Illinois at Chicago

Lonnie J. Guralnick
Western Oregon State College

Regan A. R. Gurung
University of Wisconsin—Green Bay

Ruth T. Hannon
Bridgewater State College

Carol A. Heintzelman
Millersville University

James Taylor Henderson
Wingate College

Lindsey L. Henninger
Independent Scholar

Oliver W. Hill, Jr.
Virginia State University

Robert A. Hock
Xavier University

David Wason Hollar, Jr.
Rockingham Community College

Sigmund Hsiao
University of Arizona

Timothy L. Hubbard
Eastern Oregon State College

Loring J. Ingraham
George Washington University

Tiffany A. Ito
University of Southern California

Jay W. Jackson
*Indiana University—Purdue University,
Fort Wayne*

Robert Jensen
California State University, Sacramento

Eugene R. Johnson
Central Washington University

William B. King
Edison Community College

Debra A. King-Johnson
Clemson University

Terry J. Knapp
University of Nevada, Las Vegas

Gabrielle Kowalski
Cardinal Stritch University

R. Eric Landrum
Boise State University

Kevin T. Larkin
West Virginia University

Joseph C. LaVoie
University of Nebraska at Omaha

Leon Lewis
Appalachian State University

Martha Oehmke Loustaunau
New Mexico State University

Deborah R. McDonald
New Mexico State University

David S. McDougal
*Plymouth State College of the University
System of New Hampshire*

Linda Mealey
College of St. Benedict

Norman Miller
University of Southern California

Todd Miller
University of St. Thomas

Robin Kamienny Montvilo
Rhode Island College

Brian Mullen
Syracuse University

Donald J. Nash
Colorado State University—Lamar

Elizabeth M. McGhee Nelson
Christian Brothers University

John W. Nichols
Tulsa Junior College

Steve A. Nida
Franklin University

Cynthia O'Dell
Indiana University Northwest

Amy L. Odum
University of New Hampshire

Janine T. Ogden
Marist College

Randall E. Osborne
Phillips University

Gerard O'Sullivan
Felician College

Vicky Phares
University of South Florida

Nancy A. Piotrowski
University of California, Berkeley

Anthony R. Pratkanis
University of California, Santa Cruz

Frank J. Prerost
Midwestern University

Timothy S. Rampey
Victoria College

Lillian M. Range
University of Southern Mississippi

Loretta A. Rieser-Danner
Pennsylvania State University, Ogontz

Denise S. St. Cyr
New Hampshire Technical College

Frank A. Salamone
Iona College

Rosemary Scheirer
Chestnut Hill College

Rebecca Lovell Scott
College of Health Sciences

Felicisima C. Serafica
The Ohio State University

Matthew J. Sharps
California State University, Fresno

R. Baird Shuman
*University of Illinois at Urbana-
Champaign*

Sanford S. Singer
University of Dayton

Virginia Slaughter
University of Queensland

Lesley A. Slavin
Virginia Commonwealth University

Sheldon Solomon
Skidmore College

Frank J. Sparzo
Ball State University

Sharon Wallace Stark
Monmouth University

Michael A. Steele
Wilkes University

Joseph E. Steinmetz
Indiana University, Bloomington

Richard G. Tedeschi
University of North Carolina at Charlotte

Linda R. Tennison
College of Saint Benedict
Saint John's University

Harry A. Tiemann, Jr.
Mesa State College

Derise E. Tolliver
DePaul University

Marlene E. Turner
San Jose State University

Susana P. Urbina
University of North Florida

Lois Veltum
University of North Dakota

Scott R. Vrana
Purdue University

John F. Wakefield
University of North Alabama

Elaine F. Walker
Emory University

Mary L. Wandrei
Marquette University

Daniel L. Wann
Murray State University
University of Kansas

Jennifer A. Sanders Wann
Murray State University

Allyson M. Washburn
Institute on Aging/Jewish Home

Ann L. Weber
University of North Carolina
at Asheville

Michael Wierzbicki
Marquette University

April Michele Williams
Drury University

Karen Wolford
State University of New York, Oswego

Edelgard Wulfert
State University of New York, Albany

Frederic Wynn
County College of Morris

Ling-Yi Zhou
University of St. Francis

PSYCHOLOGY
BASICS

INTRODUCTION

Many different ideas may come to mind when people hear the word "psychology." For some, word associations may be first: psychic, psychedelic, psychotic, psychogenic, psychosomatic, psychopath—words that have associations to psychology in one way or another. Others might think of concepts, such as the psyche, referring to the self and the soul. They may think of getting psyched, or prepared for action, with psyched up being good and psyched out being bad. Some may think about Alfred Hitchcock's classic 1960 film *Psycho*, a story about a murderous and odd man—which, sadly, added stigma to the tragedy of mental illness and suffering by reinforcing stereotypes of the mentally ill as violent and dangerous individuals.

When people think of psychology, they often think of clinicians, such as those portrayed on television and in films or heard on the radio—people who work with or otherwise counsel the troubled and mentally ill. Ideas about Sigmund Freud and his theories of the id, ego, and superego are also common associations with the field. Still others will ponder whether psychology is really about consciousness, the mind, psyche, or brain—and wonder how these entities are different and similar. Somewhat less frequently, people might think not about human psychology but instead about rats running mazes, pigeons operating machinery, monkeys using sign language, salivating dogs and ringing bells, and even the mating habits of ducks and other animals. A few people might see psychology as related to machines, for indeed there is psychology involved in the design of artificial intelligence systems and in the interface shared by humans and machines, such as when hands type on a computer, fly a plane, or perform microsurgery with the use of virtual reality-type cameras. All these examples reflect psychology and its research.

Indeed, what people think of when they hear the word "psychology" can vary widely by their personal experience. For some, their first exposure to the term may be through an elective course taken in high school or college. Others may first encounter it in their jobs, when they learn that there may be business value in considering psychological angles to advertising, product development, sales, or business organization management. Similarly, others may learn about it in careers such as medicine or law, when they find that it can enhance performance or improve communication with clients, colleagues, and trainees. Artists might approach the field as a means of learning more about creativity and how to foster it. Some may come to know psychology through a personal or family crisis, possibly through exposure to a counselor or self-help book. Others may learn about the concept through films, songs, current events, or advertising portraying psychological principles or themes.

Most commonly, though, psychology is recognized as the study of human behavior. The field is advanced by the work of many individuals applying the principles of psychology in diverse settings for the purposes of teaching, research, clinical work, organizational management, administration, advocacy, data analysis, and consultation. Psychologists work in many different settings, such as universities, colleges, clinics, forensics units, the armed services, social service agencies, hospitals, research groups, laboratories, government bodies, businesses, wilderness areas, and even space. The work of psychologists has far-reaching effects for diverse peoples and in diverse settings, contributing much in terms of practical solutions to both the large and small questions of daily life.

Psychology has deep roots in applications related to military defense, medicine, and teaching. In terms of military defense, psychology assisted the U.S. government with organizational decisions determining job assignments in the early 1900's via its development of intelligence testing strategies. As a result of creating ways of ranking soldiers for assignment from very basic to very complex work tasks, increases in efficiency were gained. Principles of psychology are also useful for the military in terms of fostering cohesion among soldiers, training and teaching them what they need to know in an efficient manner, and helping soldiers (and their families) deal with the stresses of active military duty. Additionally, the field has made contributions to understanding the psychological aspects of warfare, such as persuading one's enemies to provide information and debriefing those who have been prisoners of war.

The roots of psychology in medicine are obvious. Basic applications began as the treatment of those who were considered ill, feebleminded, or possessed by spirits. With regard to spirituality, there should be no surprise in finding a strong historical thread linking psychology and religion when it comes to healing. This link spans at least from William James's classic book *The Varieties of Religious Experience* (1902) to current efforts in the field examining spirituality as it relates to illness, healing, diagnosis, resilience against stress, and various types of group support. Historically, those not cured by other methods of medicine were usually sent to healers of the mind and spirit. At some point, psychologists were enlisted to help count and categorize such individuals. As the field developed, methods such as behavioral pharmacology grew in prominence with the discovery of new drugs to treat mental disorders. More recently, the effect of psychology in the treatment and prevention of stress-related, lifestyle-related, chronic, and terminal health problems has been noteworthy. As examples, psychological interventions related to stress management have been found useful for preventing heart disease and stroke. Obesity is often treated with behavioral interventions designed to modify lifestyle from a biopsychosocial perspective. Chronic pain is often addressed with cognitive interventions for pain perception and management. Even conditions such as cancer may be better managed with psychological interventions such as group support, family therapy, and mood-enhancing interventions that facilitate adherence to medical interventions for the body.

With regard to teaching, psychology has played a large role in the structure and design of academic settings, the development of educational curricula, achievement and intelligence testing, and career advisement and placement. It has also touched practices such as preschool for young children, the learning of new career skills later in life, retraining after injuries to the body or brain, and behavioral learning (such as how one might learn to shoot a basketball or play the piano). More recently, studies have examined Internet-based learning and how it differs from face-to-face learning. Whether online learning formats can be effective and whether the socialization aspects of learning can take place online are some of the questions pursued.

In the United States, psychology has gained a foothold in government, with psychologists being elected and appointed to public offices and serving in high-level decision-making bodies. One example is the placement of psychologists in the National Institutes of Health (NIH), where they have been able to influence government spending related to research, health care, and problem prevention on many fronts. In 1995, an office was established in the NIH called the Office of Behavioral and Social Science Research (OBSSR), with a designated role of advancing behavioral science knowledge and applications in the activities fostered and otherwise supported by the NIH.

As these many examples illustrate, psychology has become a diverse field. In looking to the future, it is clear that the role of psychology in the workplace and in international communications and relationships will expand. Notable growth has been seen, for instance, in the numbers of studies examining cultural differences among groups defined in terms of age, gender, ethnicity, race, sexual orientation, socioeconomic status, and other markers of culture. Pick virtually any area of psychological study and look at the number of references for cultural variation or differences since the mid-twentieth century, and it will be easy to spot a trend of increasing publications by year over time. This trend has been inspired by a desire to create better understanding among different cultures, as well as to assist efforts in providing more culturally appropriate and culturally sensitive training, education, and medical care. No doubt, this area of study will increase in importance as the field of psychology continues to evolve and as humans, as a group, continue to understand the ideas of conflict and cooperation as we approach nearly seven billion in number.

I hope that these volumes on psychology allow the diversity and capability of this vibrant and valuable field to shine. I also hope that it encourages its readers to be inspired, curious, and mindful observers of human behavior more and more each day, as there is much to be learned.

Nancy A. Piotrowski, Ph.D.
University of California at Berkeley

ABNORMALITY
PSYCHOLOGICAL MODELS

TYPE OF PSYCHOLOGY: Psychopathology; psychotherapy
FIELDS OF STUDY: Behavioral and cognitive models; evaluating psychotherapy; humanistic-phenomenological models; models of abnormality

Abnormal behavior is typically defined as behavior that is harmful to the self or others or that is dysfunctional. Three models of abnormality stress medical or biological roots; psychological aspects, such as unconscious conflicts, inappropriate learning, blocking of full development, or maladaptive thoughts; and social and cultural context.

KEY CONCEPTS
- behavioral model
- cognitive model
- humanistic model
- medical model
- psychoanalytic model
- sociocultural model

Prehistoric humans believed that evil spirits, witchcraft, the full moon, or other supernatural forces caused mental disorders. In modern times, people have more naturalistic ideas. The models of abnormality can be divided into three types: medical, psychological, and cultural. Medical models hold that mental disorders take on a psychological appearance, but the underlying problems are physical in nature. Psychological models hold that mental disorders are caused and then maintained by a person's past and present life experiences, which can result in inner conflicts, learned responses that are problematic, blocked efforts to grow and achieve self-actualization, or pessimistic, distorted thinking. Cultural models stress the sociocultural context of stress.

MEDICAL MODELS OF ABNORMALITY
Medical or biological models of abnormality stem back to Greek physician Hippocrates (c. 470-c. 377 B.C.E.), who proposed that psychological disorders are caused by body-fluid imbalances. Greeks believed that the uterus could move around a woman's body, attaching itself at different places and causing the symptoms of hysteria, a disorder in which a person has physical symptoms without the usual organic causes.

The medical model gained support when people realized that some bizarre behaviors were due to brain damage or other identifiable physical causes. For example, people with scars in certain areas of the brain may have seizures. Also, people who contract the sexually transmitted disease syphilis, which is caused by microorganisms, can develop aberrant behavior ten to twenty years after the initial infection. Syphilis moves through the body and attacks different organs, sometimes the brain.

In modern times, biological researchers use research techniques to explore the brain chemistries of mentally disturbed people. They suspect that changes in the workings of neurotransmitters may contribute to many psychological disorders. For example, depression can be associated with abnormally low levels of norepinephrine and serotonin.

The medical model of abnormality is pervasive and can be seen in the language that is often used to describe mental problems. In this language, a patient is diagnosed with a mental disorder. This illness requires treatment that might include hospitalization and therapy to relieve symptoms and produce a cure.

The medical model ushered in humane treatment for people who hitherto had been persecuted as agents of the devil. Some of the advances in treatment for psychological problems include antipsychotic medication, which can reduce hallucinations and help a person with schizophrenia avoid hospitalization; lithium, which can moderate the debilitating mood extremes of bipolar disorder; antidepressants, which can relieve the chronic pain of depression; and antianxiety drugs, which can relieve the acute stress of anxiety disorders. These kinds of advances help the day-to-day lives of many people.

Also, the medical model has focused research attention on the genetic inheritance of mental illness. One way to study the genetic basis of behavior is to compare identical twins with fraternal twins. An identical twin of a schizophrenic who was adopted into an entirely different family and never even met the other twin is still twice as likely to be schizophrenic as a person identified randomly from the general population. Another way to study the genetic basis of behavior is to compare adopted children to their adoptive parents and to their biological parents. Using these types of research, scientists have implicated heredity in a number of mental disorders, including schizophrenia, depression, and alcoholism.

However, it may not be appropriate to view all psychological disorders in medical terms. Some disorders can be directly tied to life experiences. Also, the medical model has promoted the idea that people who behave abnormally are not responsible for their actions. They are mentally sick, therefore not in control of themselves. Some people disagree with this notion. In *The Myth of Mental Illness* (1961), American psychiatrist Thomas Szasz argued that mental illness is a socially defined, relative concept that is used to cast aside people who are different. In 1987 Szasz charged psychologists, psychiatrists, and other mental health professionals with being too quick to guard society's norms and values and too slow to take care of the people who are in some way different. Further, Szasz claimed that the label "sick" invites those with problems to become passively dependent on doctors and drugs rather than relying on their own inner strengths.

PSYCHOLOGICAL MODELS OF ABNORMALITY

The psychological model of abnormality also stems from ancient Greece. In the second century C.E., the Greek physician Galen described a patient whose symptoms were caused either by an inflammation of the uterus or by something about which she was troubled but which she was not willing to discuss. He tested these two hypotheses and concluded that the patient's problem was psychological in origin.

The psychological model gained support when French physician Jean-Martin Charcot (1825-1893) used hypnosis to distinguish hysterical paralysis (with no organic cause) from neurologically based paralysis. When Charcot hypnotized patients, those with hysterical paralysis could use their supposedly paralyzed body part. One of his students, Austrian physician Sigmund Freud (1856-1939), expanded this approach. Freud and others believed that mental disorders usually begin with a traumatic event in childhood and can be treated with psychotherapy, a form of "talking cure." Today, there are four main psychological models of abnormality: psychoanalytic, behavioral, humanistic, and cognitive.

PSYCHOANALYTIC MODEL. A psychoanalytic model, stemming from Freud, emphasizes the role of parental influences, unconscious conflicts, guilt, frustration, and an array of defense mechanisms that people use, unconsciously, to ward off anxiety. According to this view, people develop psychological problems because they have inner conflicts intense enough to overwhelm their normal defenses.

Freud thought that all people have some aspects of their personality that are innate and self-preserving (the id), some aspects of their personality that are learned rules or conscience (the superego), and some aspects of their personality that are realistic (the ego). For example, the id of a person who is hungry wants to eat immediately, in any manner, regardless of the time or social conventions. However, it may be time to meet with the supervisor for an important review. The superego insists on meeting with the supervisor right now, for as long as necessary. The ego may be able to balance personal needs and society's requirements by, for example, bringing bagels for everyone to the meeting with the supervisor. People must somehow harmonize the instinctual and unreasoning desires of the id, the moral and restrictive demands of the superego, and the rational and realistic requirements of the ego.

Conflicts between the id, ego, and superego may lead to unpleasant and anxious feelings. People develop defense mechanisms to handle these feelings. Defense mechanisms can alleviate anxiety by staving off the conscious awareness of conflicts that would be too painful to acknowledge. A psychoanalytic view is that everyone uses defense mechanisms, and abnormality is simply the result of overblown defense mechanisms.

Some of the most prominent defense mechanisms are repression, regression, displacement, reaction formation, sublimation, and projection. In repression, a person forgets something that causes anxiety. For example, a student who genuinely forgets her meeting with her professor about a make-up test has repressed the appointment. In regression, a person reverts back to activities and feelings of a younger age. For example, a toddler who reclaims his old discarded bottle when a new baby sister comes on the scene is regressing. In displacement, a person has very strong feelings toward one person but feels for some reason unable to express them. Subsequently, she finds herself expressing these feelings toward a safer person. For example, a person who is extremely angry with her boss at work may keep these feelings to herself until she gets home but then find herself very angry with her husband, children, and pets. In reaction formation, people have very strong feelings that are somehow unacceptable, and they react in the opposite way. For example, a person who is campaigning against adult bookstores in the community may be secretly fascinated with pornography. In sublimation, a person rechannels energy, typically sexual energy, into socially acceptable outlets. For example, a woman who is attracted to the young men in swimsuits at the pool may decide to swim one hundred laps. In projection, people notice in others traits or behaviors that are too painful to admit in themselves. For example, a person who is very irritated by his friend's whining may have whining tendencies himself that he cannot admit. All defense mechanisms are unconscious ways to handle anxiety.

The psychoanalytic model opened up areas for discussion that were previously taboo and helped people to understand that some of their motivations are outside their own awareness. For example, dissociative disorders occur when a person's thoughts and feelings are dissociated, or separated, from conscious awareness by memory loss or a change in identity. In dissociative identity disorder, formerly termed multiple personality, the individual alternates between an original or primary personality and one or more secondary or subordinate personalities. A psychoanalytic model would see dissociative identity disorder as stemming from massive repression to ward off unacceptable impulses, particularly those of a sexual nature. These yearnings increase during adolescence and adulthood, until the person finally expresses them, often in a guilt-inducing sexual act. Then, normal forms of repression are ineffective in blocking out this guilt, so the person blocks the acts and related thoughts entirely from consciousness by developing a new identity for the dissociated bad part of self.

The psychoanalytic model views all human behavior as a product of mental or psychological causes, though the cause may not be obvious to an outside observer or even to the person performing the behavior. Psychoanalytic influence on the modern perspective of abnormality has been enormous. Freudian concepts, such as Freudian slips and unconscious motivation, are so well known that they are now part of ordinary language and culture. However, the psychoanalytic model has been criticized because it is not verifiable, because it gives complex explanations when simple and straightforward ones are sufficient, because it cannot be proven wrong (lacks disconfirmability), and because it was based mainly on a relatively small number of upper-middle-class European patients and on Freud himself.

BEHAVIORAL MODEL. A behavioral model, or social-learning model, stemming from American psychologists such as John B. Watson (1878-1958) and B. F. Skinner (1904-1990), emphasizes the role of the environment in developing abnormal behavior. According to this view, people acquire abnormal behavior in the same ways they acquire normal behavior, by learning from rewards and punishments they either experience directly or observe happening to someone else. Their perceptions, expectations, values, and role models further influence what they learn. In this view, a person with abnormal behavior has a different reinforcement history from that of others.

The behavioral model of abnormality stresses classical conditioning, operant conditioning, and modeling. In classical conditioning, a child might hear a very loud sound immediately after entering the elevator. Thereafter, this child might develop a phobia of elevators and other enclosed spaces. In operant conditioning, a mother might give the child a cookie to keep him quiet. Soon, the child will notice that when he is noisy and bothersome, his mother gives him cookies and will develop a pattern of temper tantrums and other conduct disorders. In modeling, the person might notice that her mother is very afraid of spiders. Soon, she might develop a phobia of spiders and other small creatures.

The behavioral model advocates a careful investigation of the environmental conditions in which people display abnormal behavior. Behaviorists pay special attention to situational stimuli, or triggers, that elicit the abnormal behavior and to the typical consequences that follow the abnormal behavior. Behaviorists search for factors that reinforce or encourage the repetition of abnormal behaviors.

The behavioral model helped people realize how fears become associated with specific situations and the role that reinforcement plays in the origin and maintenance of inappropriate behaviors. However, this model ignores the evidence of genetic and biological factors playing a role in some disorders. Further, many people find it difficult to accept the view of human behavior as simply a set of responses to environmental stimuli. They argue that human beings have free will and the ability to choose their situation as well as how they will react.

HUMANISTIC MODEL. A humanistic model, stemming from American psychologist Carl Rogers (1902-1987) and others, emphasizes that mental disorders arise when people are blocked in their efforts to grow and achieve self-actualization. According to this view, the self-concept is all-important and people have personal responsibility for their actions and the power to plan and choose their behaviors and feelings.

The humanistic model stresses that humans are basically good and have tremendous potential for personal growth. Left to their own devices, people will strive for self-actualization. However, people can run into roadblocks. Problems will arise if people are prevented from satisfying their basic needs or are forced to live up to the expectations of others. When this happens, people lose sight of their own goals and develop distorted self-perceptions.

They feel threatened and insecure and are unable to accept their own feelings and experiences. Losing touch with one's own feelings, goals, and perceptions forms the basis of abnormality. For example, parents may withhold their love and approval unless a young person conforms to their standards. In this case, the parents are offering conditional positive regard. This causes children to worry about such things as, "What if I do not do as well on the next test?", "What if I do not score in the next game?", and "What if I forget to clean my room?" In this example, the child may develop generalized anxiety disorder, which includes chronically high levels of anxiety. What the child needs for full development of maximum potential, according to the humanistic view, is unconditional positive regard.

American psychologist Abraham Maslow (1908-1970) and other humanistic theorists stress that all human activity is normal, natural, rational, and sensible when viewed from the perspective of the person who is performing the behavior. According to this model, abnormality is a myth. All abnormal behavior would make sense if one could see the world through the eyes of the person who is behaving abnormally.

The humanistic model has made useful contributions to the practice of psychotherapy and to the study of consciousness. However, the humanistic model restricts attention to immediate conscious experience, failing to recognize the importance of unconscious motivation, reinforcement contingencies, future expectations, biological and genetic factors, and situational influences. Further, contrary to the optimistic self-actualizing view of people, much of human history has been marked by wars, violence, and individual repression.

COGNITIVE MODEL. A cognitive model, stemming from American psychologists Albert Ellis and Donald Meichenbaum, American psychiatrist Aaron Beck, and others, finds the roots of abnormal behavior in the way people think about and perceive the world. People who distort or misinterpret their experiences, the intentions of those around them, and the kind of world where they live are bound to act abnormally.

The cognitive model views human beings as thinking organisms that decide how to behave, so abnormal behavior is based on false assumptions or unrealistic situations. For example, Sally Smith might react to getting fired from work by actively searching for a new job. Sue Smith, in contrast, might react to getting fired from work by believing that this tragedy is the worst possible thing that could have happened, something that is really awful. Sue is more likely than Sally to become anxious, not because of the event that happened but because of what she believes about this event. In the cognitive model of abnormality, Sue's irrational thinking about the event (getting fired), not the event itself, caused her abnormal behavior.

Beck proposed that depressed people have negative schemas about themselves and life events. Their reasoning errors cause cognitive distortions. One cognitive distortion is drawing conclusions out of context, while ignoring other relevant information. Another cognitive distortion is overgeneralizing, drawing a general rule from one or just a few isolated incidents and applying the conclusion broadly to unrelated situations. A third cognitive distortion is dwelling on negative details, while ignoring positive aspects. A fourth cognitive distortion is thinking in an all-or-nothing way. People who think this way categorize experiences as either completely good or completely bad, rather than somewhere in between the two extremes. A fifth cognitive distortion is having automatic thoughts, negative ideas that emerge quickly and spontaneously, and seemingly without voluntary control.

The cognitive and behavioral models are sometimes linked and have stimulated a wealth of empirical knowledge. The cognitive model has been criticized for focusing too much on cognitive processes and not enough on root causes. Some also see it as too mechanistic.

The cognitive model proposes that maladaptive thinking causes psychological disorders. In contrast, the psychoanalytic model proposes that unconscious conflicts cause psychological disorders; the humanistic model proposes that blocking of full development causes psychological disorders; and the behavioral model proposes that inappropriate conditioning causes psychological disorders. These psychological models of abnormality stress the psychological variables that play a role in abnormal behavior.

SOCIOCULTURAL MODELS OF ABNORMALITY

A sociocultural model of abnormality emphasizes the social and cultural context, going so far as to suggest that abnormality is a direct function of society's criteria and definitions for appropriate behavior. In this model, abnormality is social, not medical or psychological. For example, early Greeks revered people who heard voices that no one else heard because they interpreted this phenomenon as evidence of divine prophecy. In the Middle Ages, people tortured or killed people who heard voices because they interpreted this same proclivity as evidence of demonic possession or witchcraft. Today, people treat those who hear voices with medicine and psychotherapy because this symptom is viewed as evidence of schizophrenia.

Social and cultural context can influence the kinds of stresses people experience, the kinds of disorders they are likely to develop, and the treatment they are likely to receive. Particularly impressive evidence for a social perspective are the results of a well-known study, "On Being Sane in Insane Places" (1973), by American psychologist David Rosenhan. Rosenhan arranged for eight normal people, including himself, to arrive at eight different psychiatric hospitals under assumed names and to complain of hearing voices repeating innocuous words such as "empty," "meaningless," and "thud." These pseudopatients responded truthfully to all other questions except their names. Because of this single symptom, the hospital staff diagnosed all eight as schizophrenic or manic-depressive and hospitalized them. Although the pseudopatients immediately stopped reporting that they heard voices and asked to be released, the hospitals kept them from seven to fifty-two days, with an average of nineteen days. When discharged, seven of the eight were diagnosed with schizophrenia "in remission," which implies that they were still schizophrenic but simply did not show signs of the illness at the time of release. The hospital staff, noticing that these people took notes, wrote hospital chart entries such as "engages in writing behaviors." No staff member detected that the pseudopatients were normal people, though many regular patients suspected as much. The context in which these pseudopatients behaved (a psychiatric hospital) controlled the way in which others interpreted their behavior.

Particularly impressive evidence for a cultural perspective comes from the fact that different types of disorders appear in different cultures. Anorexia nervosa, which involves self-starvation, and bulimia nervosa, which involves binge eating followed by purging, primarily strike middle- and upper-class women in Westernized cultures. In Western cultures, women may feel particular pressure to be thin and have negatively distorted images of their own bodies. Amok, a brief period of brooding followed by a violent outburst that often results in murder, strikes Navajo men and men in Malaysia, Papua New Guinea, the Philippines, Polynesia, and Puerto Rico. In these cultures, this disorder is frequently triggered by a perceived insult. Pibloqtoq, a brief period of extreme excitement that is often followed by seizures and coma lasting up to twelve hours, strikes people in Arctic and Subarctic Eskimo communities. The person may tear off his or her clothing, break furniture, shout obscenities, eat feces, and engage in other acts that are later forgotten. As researchers examine the frequency and types of disorders that occur in different societies, they note some sharp differences not only between societies but also within societies as a function of the age and gender of the individuals being studied.

The sociocultural model of abnormality points out that other models fail to take into account cultural variations in accepted behavior patterns. Understanding cross-cultural perspectives on abnormality helps in better framing questions about human behavior and interpretations of data. Poverty and discrimination can cause psychological problems. Understanding the context of the abnormal behavior is essential.

The medical, psychological, and sociocultural models of abnormality represent profoundly different ways of explaining and thus treating people's problems. They cannot be combined in a simple way because they often contradict one another. For example, a biological model asserts that depression is due to biochemistry. The treatment, therefore, is medicine to correct the imbalance. In contrast, a behavioral model asserts that depression is learned. The treatment, therefore, is changing the rewards and punishers in the environment so that the person unlearns the old, bad habits and learns new, healthy habits.

One attempt to integrate the different models of abnormality is called the diathesis-stress model of abnormality. It proposes that people develop disorders if they have a biological weakness (diathesis) that predisposes them to the disorder when they encounter certain environmental conditions (stress). The diathesis-stress approach is often used to explain the development of some forms of cancer: a biological predisposition coupled with certain environmental conditions. According to this model, some people have a predisposition that makes them vulnerable to a disorder such as schizophrenia. They do not develop schizophrenia, however, unless they experience particularly stressful environmental conditions.

It is unlikely that any single model can explain all disorders. It is more probable that each of the modern perspectives explains certain disorders and that any single abnormal behavior has multiple causes.

SOURCES FOR FURTHER STUDY

Alloy, Lauren B., Neil S. Jacobson, and Joan Acocella. *Abnormal Psychology: Current Perspectives.* 8th ed. Boston: McGraw-Hill, 1999. This comprehensive textbook discusses the medical (biological), psychodynamic (psychoanalytic), and cognitive models of abnormality.

American Psychiatric Association. *Diagnostic and Statistical Manual of Mental Disorders: DSM-IV-TR.* Rev. 4th ed. Washington, D.C.: Author, 2000. This listing of all psychological disorders includes for each a description, associated features and disorders, prevalence, course, and differential diagnosis. It is revised every five to ten years as new information becomes available.

Gotlib, I. H., and C. L. Hammen. *Psychological Aspects of Depression: Toward a Cognitive-Interpersonal Integration.* New York: John Wiley & Sons, 1992. This book provides a summary of the symptoms of depression as well as theoretical explanations.

Gottesman, Irving I. *Schizophrenia Genesis: The Origins of Madness.* New York: W. H. Freeman, 1991. Gottesman, an active researcher in the field of schizophrenia, wrote this book for nonprofessionals interested in schizophrenia and included first-person accounts written by people diagnosed with schizophrenia.

Kesey, Ken. *One Flew over the Cuckoo's Nest.* New York: Viking, 1962. This novel, and the 1975 film on which it is based, made the point that psychiatric diagnosis and treatment can be used to control behavior considered undesirable in a hospital and yet healthy from other perspectives.

Rosenhan, David L. "On Being Sane in Insane Places." *Science* 179 (1973): 250-258. The original report of a classic study of the effect that context has on perceptions of behavior.

Lillian M. Range

SEE ALSO: Psychoanalytic Psychology.

ADOLESCENCE
COGNITIVE SKILLS

TYPE OF PSYCHOLOGY: Developmental psychology
FIELDS OF STUDY: Adolescence; cognitive development

Adolescence brings the potential for logical and theoretical reasoning, systematic problem solving, and acquisition of abstract concepts; adolescent cognitive skills are reflected in social and personality development as well as in learning and problem-solving behavior.

KEY CONCEPTS
- concrete operations stage
- developmental approach
- egocentrism
- formal operations stage
- hypothetical-deductive reasoning
- imaginary audience
- information-processing approach
- personal fable
- psychometric approach

Psychologists approach the study of adolescent cognitive skills from three perspectives: the psychometric, the developmental, and the information-processing. The psychometric approach focuses on defining and measuring intellectual skills. Psychometric research typically involves studies of performance on intelligence tests. The developmental approach seeks to identify the types of cognitive skills that are unique to the adolescent years. This approach has been heavily influenced by the cognitive stage theory of Swiss psychologist Jean Piaget. The information-processing approach examines the characteristics of memory and problem solving. It views adolescent cognitive skills as parameters that determine how the brain stores and analyzes information.

PSYCHOMETRIC APPROACH
In the psychometric view, adolescence is a period of cognitive stability. Intelligence quotient (IQ) scores show little change during adolescence. Although IQ scores often fluctuate during early childhood, scores generally stabilize about age eight. It is common to find temporary periods of instability in IQ scores after age eight, such as at the onset of puberty or during other stressful times, but dramatic and long-term score changes are rare. According to this perspective, adolescence does not bring significant changes in cognitive skills.

Theory and research on cognitive skills began with the development of modern intelligence tests, such as Alfred Binet's 1916 test; however, the intelligence-testing, or psychometric, approach has contributed little to an understanding of adolescent cognitive skills. Intelligence tests are best suited to the study of individual differences, or how people compare to others of their age. It is difficult to use intelligence testing to compare and contrast cognitive skills at different ages.

Intelligence tests also are used to study the stability of intellectual level and the likelihood it will change in later years. Research indicates, however, that intelligence test scores in adolescence generally are similar to scores during childhood, although scores may fluctuate during childhood as a function of changes in factors such as diet, socioeconomic status, and education. Again, the psychometric approach seems poorly suited to the study of adolescent cognitive skills.

DEVELOPMENTAL APPROACH

The developmental approach seeks to identify the cognitive skills of adolescence and to contrast them with the skills found at other ages. This approach addresses both the qualities of thought and the process of change. In 1958 Piaget and his coworker Barbel Inhelder published *The Growth of Logical Thinking from Childhood Through Adolescence*, a detailed account of Piaget's four stages of cognitive development. In addition to proposing that specific cognitive skills emerge in each stage, he proposes that the move from one stage to the next is largely maturational.

This statement may be confusing. Clearly, sixteen-year-olds must "know more" than eight-year-olds, and adolescents have the capacity to learn school subjects beyond the grasp of elementary school children. The psychometric approach, however, is not designed to contrast the nature of cognitive skills at different ages. Intelligence tests are scored by comparing a specific person to other people of the same age. A score of 100 at age eight means that a person performs similarly to the average eight-year-old; a score of 100 at age eighteen means that a person performs similarly to the average eighteen-year-old. IQ score is expected to remain the same if the person matures at a relatively normal rate.

Two of Piaget's stages are of particular importance to the study of adolescence: the concrete operational stage (ages seven to twelve) and the formal operational stage (ages twelve and up). During the concrete operational stage, children acquire basic logical concepts such as equivalence, seriation, and part-whole relations. Children also master reversibility, a skill allowing them mentally to restore a changed object or situation to its original state. With reversibility, children can recognize that a small glass of juice poured into a taller and thinner glass may look like more juice but is actually the same amount. During concrete operations, children can think logically as long as their reasoning is in reference to tangible objects.

The formal operational stage follows the concrete operational stage and is the final stage of cognition, according to Piaget. Beginning at adolescence, thinking becomes more logical, more abstract, more hypothetical, and more systematic. Unlike their concrete operational counterparts, formal thinkers can study ideologies, generate a variety of possible outcomes to an action, and systematically evaluate alternative approaches to a problem. Formal thinkers also are better able to adopt a new course of action when a particular strategy proves unsuccessful. In the Piagetian model, adolescents are compared to scientists as they utilize hypothetical-deductive reasoning to solve problems. Although children during the concrete operational stage would solve problems by trial and error, adolescents could be expected to develop hypotheses and then systematically conclude which path is best to follow in order to solve the problem.

INFORMATION-PROCESSING APPROACH

The information-processing approach provides additional information about these child/adolescent contrasts. According to John Flavell, cognitive growth is the acquisition of increasingly sophisticated and efficient problem-solving skills. For example, adolescents can hold more information in memory than children, which enhances their ability to solve complex problems. Improvements in memory reflect more than changes in capacity. Adolescents are better able to develop associations between words and ideas, which in turn facilitates remembering them. Part of their improvement is a result of the fact that adolescents know more than children. Adolescents also are better able to think abstractly and develop hypotheses. These skills in part reflect improvements in generalization, identifying similarities between previous situations and new ones. Changes in thinking and hypothesizing also enable adolescents to generate a wider variety of problem-solving strategies, which enhances their performance. Finally, adolescents know more about the nature of thought and memory. This metacognition, or ability to "think about thinking," increases the planning in their problem-solving behavior.

Information-processing research has helped explain some of the inconsistencies that appear in Piagetian research. According to Piagetian theory, people are located within particular cognitive stages and will reason at those levels of maturity in all problem-solving situations. Why, then, do most people show features of several stages, depending on the type of problem presented? According to information-processing research, variability in performance across different problem types is to be expected. The more one knows, the easier it is to use efficient cognitive processes. People will appear more cognitively mature performing tasks about which they are knowledgeable.

APPLICATION OF RESEARCH

The research on adolescent thinking has been applied to the study of learning, personality, and social behavior during adolescence. For example, research on adolescent cognition has influenced the development of both curricula and teaching methods at the middle-school and high-school levels. As individuals who are entering the stage of formal thinking, adolescents are better equipped to handle abstract topics such as geometry and physics. Their emerging ability to consider systematically the effects of several factors when solving a problem make adolescents good candidates for laboratory science courses.

Some applications of research on adolescent cognitive skills are the subject of much debate, however; ability tracking is a case in point. Psychometric research indicates that intellectual functioning becomes relatively stable in preadolescence. From this point onward, children continue to perform at the same level relative to their age-mates on standardized measures such as IQ tests. The stability of test performance has been used to support the creation and maintenance of ability tracks beginning in the middle-school years. Proponents of tracking maintain that ability grouping, or tracking, enables teachers to challenge more able students without frustrating less capable students. Opponents of tracking maintain that less able students benefit from both the academic challenges and the competent role models provided by superior students in ungrouped classrooms. In fact, critics of tracking charge that the level at which performance stabilizes actually results from subtle differences in how teachers interact with their students, differences often based on inaccurate assumptions about student potential. Perhaps students with low test scores, many of whom are poor or minority students, perform poorly because people expect them to be less capable.

ADOLESCENTS AND SOCIAL COGNITION

Although Piaget primarily limited his research of adolescent reasoning to mathematical and scientific concepts, he did consider the role that formal operations play in the adolescent's social life. David Elkind continued research in this area by noting that features of formal thinking are reflected in adolescent personality characteristics. According to Elkind, the ability to think abstractly and hypothetically enables adolescents to develop their own idealistic, theoretical views of the world. The ability to distinguish between reality and theory, however, can lead to disillusionment and the recognition that adolescents' idols have "feet of clay." Elkind identified an adolescent egocentrism that he equates with the heightened self-consciousness of adolescence. This egocentrism demonstrates itself in two types of social thinking—personal fable and imaginary audience.

In personal fable, young adolescents see themselves as unique and special. Personal fable may lead adolescents to take unnecessary risks because they believe they are so different from others: "I can drink and drive." "Only other people get pregnant." Personal fable also makes adolescents believe that no one else can understand how they feel or offer any useful suggestions: "No one has ever had a problem like mine." In imaginary audience, adolescents believe that "everyone" is watching them. Elkind sees this self-consciousness as an application of hypothetical thinking: "If my characteristics are so obvious to me, they must also be obvious to everyone else."

NEURAL BASIS OF ADOLESCENT COGNITION

Interest has been growing in the prospect of uniting brain and cognitive development during adolescence. With the use of magnetic resonance imaging (MRI), researchers now have a better understanding of how the adolescent brain actually functions. A surprising discovery is the fact that there are changes in the structure of the brain that appear relatively late in child development. Of special note during the teenage years is the second wave of synapse formation just before puberty, along with a pruning back during adolescence. It had already been known that prior to birth and during the first months after birth there was an overproduction of connections, but it was not known that a second spurt occurred. This time of rapid development of synapses followed by the pruning of connections determines the cells and connections that will be "hardwired." From studies of growth patterns of the developing brain, it has also been found that fiber systems which influence language learning and associative thinking develop more rapidly just before puberty and for a short period of time just after puberty. Changes in the prefrontal cortex increase the adolescent's potential to reason with more accuracy, show more control over impulses, and make more effective judgments. Even the cerebellum is still developing into adolescence. Although commonly associated with physical coordination, the cerebellum also plays a role in processing mental tasks, such as higher thought, decision making, and social skills. In summary, it is now known that an important part of the growth of the brain is happening just before puberty and well into adolescence.

Lillian J. Breckenridge

Cognitive changes also affect social behavior by inducing changes in social cognitive development. Social cognition refers to an individual's understanding of people and of interactions among people. According to Piaget, changes in cognition are reflected in the way people think about themselves and other people. The thinking of preadolescents (seven to eleven years) begins to focus less on the obvious features of objects, events, and people. They are better able to translate patterns of behavior into psychological characteristics, such as concluding that a particular person is "nice" or "rude." They are becoming less egocentric, better able to appreciate that people have different points of view. It is not surprising, then, that they are better able to see the world from the perspective of another person. As they enter formal operations (eleven or twelve years and older), adolescents are able to think in more logical and abstract ways. These changes are reflected in their ability to describe people in abstract terms, such as "cooperative" or "uncoordinated," and compare people along psychological dimensions.

Robert Selman has observed that changes in social cognition occur in stages that closely parallel Piaget's stages of cognitive development. According to Selman's research, most concrete operational preadolescents (ages ten to twelve) recognize the existence of different points of view. Many of them, however, have difficulty evaluating conflicting perspectives or understanding how perspectives relate to membership in different social groups. As adolescents become more fully formal operational (twelve to fifteen years and older), they become able to understand the relationship between another person's perspective and their membership in social systems. For example, the difference between two people's points of view may reflect their membership in different racial or ethnic groups. Progress through Selman's stages also is influenced by social experiences. In other words, it is possible for a person to mature intellectually and to become less egocentric without becoming skillful at adopting others' points of view.

FORMAL OPERATIONS CONTROVERSY

Piaget believed that formal operational thought, entered between eleven and fifteen years of age, was a fourth and final stage of cognitive development, although he did say that adults are quantitatively more knowledgeable than adolescents. Some experts argue that young adults demonstrate a fifth, postformal stage that is different from adolescent thinking. Postformal thought is characterized by an understanding that the correct answer to a problem requires reflective thinking that may vary from one situation to another. Truth is viewed as an ongoing, never-ending process. Critics of this view argue that research evidence is lacking to document this as a qualitatively more advanced stage than formal operational thought.

Research has called into question the link between adolescence and the stage of formal operational thought. It is estimated that only one in three young adolescents is a formal operational thinker. Many adolescents think in ways characteristic of concrete operations or use formal thinking only part of the time. In fact, even many adults have not mastered formal operations. Critics argue that individual differences and cultural experiences may play a greater role in determining formal operations than Piaget envisioned.

Piagetian theory has been notoriously difficult to evaluate. Research indicates that performance on Piagetian tasks depends on understanding the instructions, being able to attend to the relevant aspects of the problems, and being interested in the problems themselves. Adolescents who perform best on formal operational tasks are often those with interests in the natural sciences—an unlikely finding if cognitive change is largely maturational.

Adolescents who do use formal operations may experience development in two phases, one early and the other during late adolescence. The initial stage is primarily assimilation and involves the incorporation of new information into existing knowledge. Rather than using hypothetical-deductive thinking, adolescents at this point may simply be consolidating their concrete operational thinking. They tend to perceive their world in subjective and idealistic terms. During the later phase, adolescents are more likely to accommodate, restoring intellectual balance after a cognitive upheaval occurs.

Although the popularity of Piagetian theory has declined, it remains one of the most influential theories in developmental psychology. In fact, it was Piagetian theory that led information-processing psychologists to become interested in cognitive development. In a summation, understanding adolescent cognitive skills requires some familiarity with all perspectives, in spite of their respective weaknesses. Each has made a unique historical contribution to current views of cognition.

SOURCES FOR FURTHER STUDY

Byrnes, James P. *Minds, Brains, and Learning: Understanding the Psychological and Educational Relevance of Neuroscientific Research.* New York: Guilford Press, 2001. Provides a stimulus for rethinking assumptions regarding the connection between mental and neural processes. The author challenges some of Piaget's ideas on formal operational thought. Gives a clear and readable overview of current neuroscientific work, especially for those relatively new to the field.

Elkind, David. *The Child's Reality: Three Developmental Themes.* Hillsdale, N.J.: Lawrence Erlbaum, 1978. Discusses the ways in which adolescent cognitive skills are reflected in personality and in social behavior. Excellent presentations on egocentrism, ideologies, personal fable, and imaginary audience.

Flavell, John, Patricia Mill, and Scott Miller. *Cognitive Development.* Rev. ed. Englewood Cliffs, N.J.: Prentice-Hall, 2001. Presents theory and research on cognitive development from an information-processing approach. Discusses relationship between information-processing and Piagetian theory. An excellent effort to compare and contrast these two perspectives.

Ginsburg, Herbert, and Sylvia Opper. *Piaget's Theory of Intellectual Development.* Englewood Cliffs, N.J.: Prentice-Hall, 1988. In its latest edition, this now classic work contains an updated presentation of Piaget's theory of cognitive development, including a detailed analysis of formal operational thinking.

Kuhn, D. "Adolescence: Adolescent Thought Processes." In *Encyclopedia of Psychology,* edited by Alan E. Kazdin. New York: Oxford University Press, 2000. This is an outstanding reference source for cognitive development in general. Kuhn provides a good evaluation of Piaget's work.

Muuss, R. E. "Social Cognition: Robert Selman's Theory of Role Taking." *Adolescence* 17, no. 67 (1982): 499-525. Discusses the relationship between adolescent cognitive skills and the ability to adopt another person's point of view. Includes an overall summary of Robert Selman's model of social cognitive development.

Pruitt, David B., ed. *Your Adolescent: Emotional Behavioral and Cognitive Development from Early Adolescence Through the Teen Years.* New York: Harper-

Collins, 2000. Written with the parent in mind, this resource covers a wide range of concerns and issues. It is published by the American Academy of Child and Adolescent Psychiatry and complements a similar book written for the childhood years. The approach is more practical than scholarly.

Lisa Friedenberg; updated by Lillian J. Breckenridge

SEE ALSO: Adolescence: Sexuality; Cognitive Development: Jean Piaget; Identity Crises; Learning.

ADOLESCENCE
SEXUALITY

TYPE OF PSYCHOLOGY: Developmental psychology
FIELD OF STUDY: Adolescence

Adolescent sexuality examines the physical, psychological, and behavioral changes that occur as the individual leaves childhood, acquires sexual maturity, and incorporates the various aspects of sexuality into his or her identity.

KEY CONCEPTS
- contraception
- development of sexual identity
- levels of sexual activity
- psychological effects
- puberty

Perhaps no single event during the adolescent years has as dramatic or widespread effects as the realization of sexuality. The lives of both boys and girls become wrapped in this new dimension. Adolescence is a time of sexual exploration and experimentation, of sexual fantasies and sexual realities, of incorporating sexuality into one's identity. These processes determine adolescents' comfort with their own emerging sexuality as well as with that of others. Adolescents are also beginning to be involved in intimate relationships, a context in which sexual activity often occurs.

In recent decades, many of the milestones by which adulthood is defined and measured—full-time employment, economic independence, domestic partnership/marriage, and childbearing—are attained at later ages in people's lives than they were in earlier generations, while puberty begins at earlier ages. Thus, adolescents face many years between the onset of puberty, fertility, and the natural intensification of sexual feelings and the achievement of committed relationships and economic independence. As a result, young people have sexual intercourse earlier in life, and there are greater percentages of adolescents who are sexually experimenting at every age level, a greater number of acts of premarital intercourse, and a greater number of sexual partners before marriage.

PHYSICAL CHANGES

Adolescence is the life stage between childhood and adulthood. Its age limits are not clearly specified, but it extends roughly from age twelve to the late teens, when physical growth is nearly complete. Puberty, a term often confused with adolescence, occurs at the end of childhood and lasts from two to four years. It is the period of adolescence during which an individual reaches sexual maturity.

Human beings grow most rapidly at two times during their lives: before they are six months old and during adolescence. The second period of accelerated growth is often referred to as the adolescent growth spurt. Adolescents grow both in height and weight, with the increase in height occurring first. As they gain weight, the amount and distribution of fat in their bodies changes, and the proportion of bone and muscle tissue increases. In girls, the adolescent growth spurt usually begins between the ages of nine and eleven and reaches a peak at an average of twelve and a half years. Then growth slows and usually ceases completely between the ages of fifteen and eighteen. The growth spurt in boys generally begins about two years later than it does in girls and lasts for a longer time. It begins between the ages of eleven and fourteen, reaches a peak at about age fifteen, and slowly declines until the age of nineteen or twenty.

The teenager's body grows at differing rates, so that at times adolescents look a bit awkward. Big feet and long legs are the early signs of a changing body, but even these changes do not occur at the same time. First the hands and feet grow, then the arms and legs; only later do the shoulders and chest grow to fit the rest of the developing body. Changes in body proportion become obvious. The trunk widens in the hips and shoulders, and the waistline narrows. Boys tend to broaden mostly in the shoulders, girls in the hips.

Puberty is chiefly characterized by sexual development. Sexual development can be best understood by examining the maturation of primary and secondary sex characteristics. Primary sex characteristics are the physiological features of the sex organs. For males, these organs are the penis and the testes; for females, they are the ovaries, uterus, clitoris, and vagina. Secondary sex characteristics are not directly related to the sexual organs but nevertheless distinguish a mature male from a mature female. Examples of secondary sex characteristics are the male beard and the female breasts.

In girls, the onset of breast development is usually, but not always, the first sign that puberty has begun. This typically occurs between the ages of ten and eleven but can occur as late as ages thirteen and fourteen. There is simultaneous development of the uterus and vagina, with enlargement of the labia and clitoris. Menarche (the first menstrual period), although perhaps the most dramatic and symbolic sign of a girl's changing status, occurs relatively late in puberty, after the growth spurt has reached its peak velocity. The first menstrual periods tend to be irregular, and ovulation (the release of a mature egg) does not usually begin until a year or so after menarche. Onset age of menarche has decreased as body weight has increased in the modern era, with girls on average reaching menarche at ten and a half to eleven years of age.

The first noticeable change in boys is usually growth of the testes and scrotum. The growth of the genitals begins, on average, about the age of twelve and is completed, on average, by about the age of fifteen. Boys generally become capable of ejaculation about a year after the penis begins to grow. These first emissions may occur as a result of nocturnal emissions, the

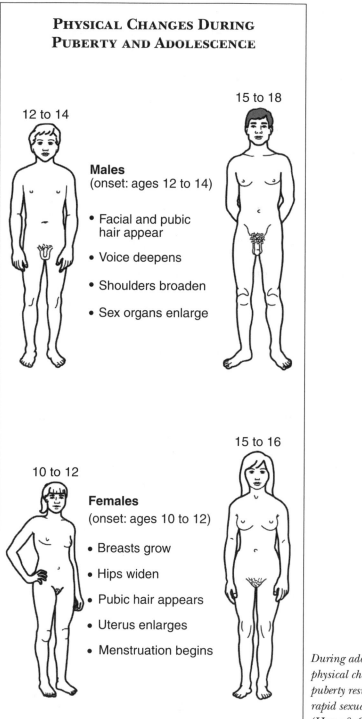

PHYSICAL CHANGES DURING PUBERTY AND ADOLESCENCE

15 to 18

12 to 14

Males
(onset: ages 12 to 14)

- Facial and pubic hair appear
- Voice deepens
- Shoulders broaden
- Sex organs enlarge

15 to 16

10 to 12

Females
(onset: ages 10 to 12)

- Breasts grow
- Hips widen
- Pubic hair appears
- Uterus enlarges
- Menstruation begins

During adolescence, the physical changes of puberty result in relatively rapid sexual development. (Hans & Cassidy, Inc.)

ejaculation of semen during sleep. Nocturnal emissions are a normal phase of development and are frequently caused by sexual excitation in dreams or by some type of physical condition, such as a full bladder or even pressure from pajamas.

As the bodies of adolescents become more adult, their interest in sexual behavior increases sharply. They must learn the necessary behavior to satisfy that interest, and they must face the issue of a mature gender identity. This includes the expression of sexual needs and feelings and the acceptance or rejection of sex roles. The onset of dating and the beginning of physical intimacies with others can provoke frustration and anxiety. As this unfamiliar territory is explored, the adolescent is often very underinformed and overly self-conscious. Conflicting sexual values and messages are frequently encountered, accentuating the problem of integrating sexual drives with other aspects of the personality.

PSYCHOLOGICAL ADJUSTMENT

Adolescents are acutely aware of the rapid changes taking place in their bodies. How they react to such changes greatly affects how they evaluate themselves; it is in this manner that physical and psychological development are related.

Physical changes may cause psychological discomfort. Adolescents are particularly concerned about whether they are the "right" shape or size and whether they measure up to the "ideal" adolescent. Rapid growth, awkwardness, acne, voice changes, menarche, and other developments may produce emotional distress. Therefore, it is not surprising that the timing of physical and sexual maturity may have an important influence on psychosocial adjustment. Adolescents are generally concerned about anything that sets them apart from their peers. Being either the first or last to go through puberty can cause considerable self-consciousness.

In general, boys who mature early have a distinct advantage over those who mature late. They tend to be more poised, easygoing, and good-natured. They are taller, heavier, and more muscular than other boys their age. They are also more likely to excel in sports, achieve greater popularity, and become school leaders. The ideal form for men in American society, as represented by the media, is that of the postpubescent male. Therefore, early entry into puberty draws boys closer to the male "ideal." In contrast, late-maturing boys not only are smaller and less well developed than others in their age group but also are not as interested in dating. When they do become interested in intimacy, they often lack social skills; they are more likely to feel inadequate, anxious, and self-conscious. These personality characteristics tend to persist into early adulthood, although they may become less marked and often disappear as time goes by.

For girls, early maturation appears to be a mixed blessing. Girls who mature early grow taller, develop breasts, and go through menarche as much as six years before some of their peers. Their larger size and more adult physique may make them feel conspicuous and awkward, while at the same time they may be popular with boys and experience more dating opportunities. They also may have to deal with parents and other caregivers who have reacted to their early sexual development by being overly restrictive. The beauty ideal for women in American society, as portrayed by the media, is that of a prepubescent female. Changes in body fat related to puberty thus may lead to body image problems, as entry into puberty increases the distance from the beauty ideal just as girls become most interested in it. As with boys, the consequences of early and late maturation decrease over time. However, either early or late start of menarche seems significantly more difficult to deal with than if more typical.

SEXUAL BEHAVIOR

Sexual maturation has other psychological consequences as well. In particular, patterns of sexual behavior change tremendously with the arrival of sexual maturity. As adolescents' bodies become more adult, their interest in sexual behavior increases sharply; as they explore their sexual identities, they develop a sexual script, or a stereotyped pattern for how individuals should behave sexually.

The sexual script for boys is frequently different from the sexual script for girls. As a result, boys and girls generally think differently about sex. This discrepancy can cause problems and confusion for adolescents as they struggle with their sexual identities. For boys, the focus of sexuality may be sexual conquest, to the point that young men who are nonexploitative or inexperienced may be labeled with negative terms such as "sissy." Boys are more likely than girls to see intercourse as a way of establishing their maturity and of achieving social status. As a consequence, boys are more likely to have sex with someone who is a relative stranger, to have more sexual partners, and to disassociate sex from love and emotional intimacy.

Adolescent girls are much more likely than adolescent boys to link sexual intercourse with love. The quality of the relationship between the girl and her partner is a very important factor. Most girls would agree that sexual intercourse is acceptable if the two people are in love and that is not acceptable if they are not in a romantic relationship. Consequently, girls are less likely than boys to list pleasure, pleasing their partner, and relieving sexual tension as reasons for having sex.

During the past several decades, attitudes toward sexual activity have changed dramatically. Views regarding premarital sex, extramarital sex, and specific sexual acts are probably more open and permissive today than they have been at any other time in recent history. Young people are exposed to sexual stimuli on television and in magazines and motion pictures to a greater extent than ever before. Effective methods of birth control have lessened the fear of pregnancy. All these changes have given the adolescent more freedom. At the same time, the rise of acquired immunodeficiency syndrome (AIDS) in the late 1970's, the sharp increases in AIDS cases among heterosexual teenagers in the 1990's, and the increased concern over antibiotic-resistant gonorrhea and other sexually transmitted diseases have only produced more conflict, since guidelines for "appropriate behavior" are less clear-cut than they were in the past. In some families, the divergence between adolescent and parental standards of sexual morality is great.

Research specifically directed toward the exploration of adolescent sexuality was not seriously undertaken until the 1950's and 1960's. Even then, the few studies that were conducted handled the topic delicately and focused on attitudes rather than behavior. When behavior was emphasized, age at first intercourse was generally selected as the major variable. Later studies have been more detailed and expansive; however, a paucity of research in this area still exists.

In *Facing Facts* (1995), Debra W. Haffner categorizes adolescent sexuality into three stages; early, middle, and late. In early adolescence (ages nine to thirteen for girls, eleven to fifteen for boys) experimenting with sexual behavior is common, although sexual intercourse is usually limited. A 1994 national telephone survey of ninth- to twelfth-grade students found that nearly all had engaged in kissing; more than 70 percent had engaged in touching above the waist and more than 50 percent below the waist; 15 percent had engaged in mutual masturbation. This time period is characterized by the beginning of the process of separating from the family and becoming more influenced by peers. During middle adolescence (thirteen to sixteen for girls, fourteen to seventeen for boys) sexual experimentation is common, and many adolescents have first intercourse during this stage of life. Of ninth- through twelfth-grade students, 50 percent report having had sexual intercourse, with percentages from 38 percent of ninth-graders to 65 percent of twelfth-graders. A slightly higher percentage of young men than young women reported having had sexual intercourse. In late adolescence (women sixteen and older; men seventeen and older), the process of physical maturation is complete. There is autonomy from family as well as from the peer group as adult roles are defined. Sexuality often becomes associated with commitment and planning for the future.

Awareness of sexual orientation often emerges in adolescence. Margaret Rosario and her colleagues conducted a study of fourteen- to twenty-one-year-old lesbian, gay, and bisexual youths which found that the average age at which girls were certain of being gay was approximately 16 and the average age for boys was 14.6, with the majority reporting a history of sexual activity with both sexes.

Boys appear to initiate intercourse earlier than girls, but girls catch up by the late teens. The timing of puberty is important for boys, while for girls, social controls exert a greater influence than the onset of puberty. Girls who are academically engaged, with higher self-esteem, and with interests outside the dating culture are more likely to delay the onset of sexual activity. For both boys and girls, dual-parent families, higher socioeconomic status, parental supervision, and close relationships with parents are all associated with delayed onset of sexual activity.

Contraceptive use among adolescents continues to increase. Two-thirds of adolescents report using some method of contraceptive, usually condoms, the first time they have sexual intercourse. The older they are at first intercourse, the more likely they are to use a contraceptive as well. Programs that improve teen access to contraceptives have not produced increased rates of sexual activity but do increase condom use.

Social concerns such as teenage pregnancy, sexually transmitted diseases, and sex education have focused attention on the need to understand clearly the dynamics of adolescent sexuality. This awareness should continue to encourage broader perspectives for the study of teenage sexual behavior and produce detailed knowledge of sexuality as it occurs in the adolescent experience.

Sources for Further Study

Alan Guttmacher Institute. *Sex and America's Teenagers.* New York: Author, 1994. The report of a study conducted by the Alan Guttmacher Institute on teenage sexual activity in the 1990's. It is presented in written and graphical forms and provides a good look at adolescent sexuality.

Bell, Ruth, et al. *Changing Bodies, Changing Lives: A Book for Teens on Sex and Relationships.* 3d ed. New York: Random House, 1998. Written specifically for a teenage audience. Teens from around the United States were surveyed in order to determine the book's contents, and they share their unique perspectives on sexuality. This is perhaps one of the best resources available for teens.

Columbia University Health Education Program. *The Go Ask Alice Book of Answers: A Guide to Good Physical, Sexual, and Emotional Health.* New York: Owl Books, 1998. Inspired by Columbia's award-winning and hugely popular Web site, this book is packed with straightforward, nonjudgmental, comprehensive answers to the toughest, most embarrassing questions teens and adults have about sexual, emotional, and physical health.

Madaras, Lynda, with Area Madaras. *The "What's Happening to My Body?" Book for Girls: A Growing Up Guide for Parents and Daughters.* 3d rev. ed. New York: Newmarket, 2000. Written especially for adolescents and their parents. The author is a leading sex educator, and she is joined by her daughter. The primary focus is on female puberty; however, topics such as sexual feelings and sexual intercourse are also discussed. Well written, with illustrations that enhance the text.

Madaras, Lynda, with Dane Saavedra. *The "What's Happening to My Body?" Book for Boys: A Growing Up Guide for Parents and Sons.* 3d rev. ed. New York: Newmarket, 2000. Written by a leading sex educator with the assistance of an adolescent boy. The book deals primarily with male puberty but includes information about sexual feelings and sexual intercourse. A very useful and informative book, written in a conversational style.

Rosario, Margaret, et al. "The Psychosexual Development of Urban Lesbian, Gay, and Bisexual Youths." *The Journal of Sex Research* 33, no. 2 (1996): 113-126. Fills one of the gaps left by general reference sources that often treat adolescent sexuality as strictly heterosexual in nature. Provides current information on alternative sexuality choices made by adolescents.

Strasburger, Victor C., and Robert T. Brown. *Adolescent Medicine: A Practical Guide.* 2d ed. Philadelphia: Lippincott-Raven, 1998. This book addresses the physical and psychosocial problems of teenagers that physicians are most likely to treat. The emphasis is on practical information. Applied diagnostic and treatment guidelines cover conditions such as asthma, diabetes mellitus, developmental problems, headaches, sexually transmitted diseases and pregnancy, depression, and eating disorders.

Doyle R. Goff; updated by Cynthia O'Dell

SEE ALSO: Adolescence: Cognitive Skills; Drives; Homosexuality; Identity Crises.

Affiliation and Friendship

Type of psychology: Social psychology
Fields of study: Interpersonal relations; social motives

Affiliation is the tendency to seek the company of others; people are motivated to affiliate for several reasons, and affiliation also meets many human needs. Friendship is an important close relationship based on affiliation, attraction, and intimacy.

Key concepts
- affiliation
- attraction
- communal relationship
- complementarity
- consensual validation
- exchange relationship
- propinquity
- proselytize
- social comparison

Affiliation is the desire or tendency to be with others of one's own kind. Many animal species affiliate, collecting in groups, flocks, or schools to migrate or search for food. Human affiliation is not controlled by instinct but is affected by specific motives. One motivation for affiliation is fear: People seek the company of others when they are anxious or frightened. The presence of others may have a calming or reassuring influence. Research in 1959 by social psychologist Stanley Schachter indicated that fear inducement leads to a preference for the company of others. Further work confirmed that frightened individuals prefer the company of others who are similarly frightened, rather than merely the companionship of strangers. This preference for similar others suggests that affiliation is a source of information as well as reassurance.

Social Comparison Theory

The value of obtaining information through affiliating with others is suggested by social comparison theory. Social comparison is the process of comparing oneself to others in determining how to behave. According to Leon Festinger, who developed social comparison theory in 1954, all people have beliefs, and it is important to them that their beliefs be correct. Some beliefs can be objectively verified by consulting a reference such as a dictionary or a standard such as a yardstick. Others are subjective beliefs and cannot be objectively verified. In such cases, people look for consensual validation—the verification of subjective beliefs by obtaining a consensus among other people—to verify their beliefs. The less sure people are of the correctness of a belief, the more they rely on social comparison as a source of verification.

The more people there are who agree with one's opinion about something, the more correct one feels in holding that opinion.

INFLUENCES ON AFFILIATION

Beyond easing fear and satisfying the need for information or social comparison, mere affiliation with others is not usually a satisfactory form of interaction. Most people form specific attractions for other individuals, rather than being satisfied with belonging to a group. These attractions usually develop into friendship, love, and other forms of intimacy. Interpersonal attraction, the experience of preferring to interact with specific others, is influenced by several factors. An important situational or circumstantial factor in attraction is propinquity. Propinquity refers to the proximity or nearness of other persons. Research by Festinger and his colleagues has confirmed that people are more likely to form friendships with those who live nearby, especially if they have frequent accidental contact with them.

Further research by social psychologist Robert Zajonc indicated that propinquity increases attraction because it increases familiarity. Zajonc found that research subjects expressed greater liking for a variety of stimuli merely because they had been exposed to those stimuli more frequently than to others. The more familiar a person is, the more predictable that person seems to be. People are reassured by predictability and feel more strongly attracted to those who are familiar and reliable in this regard.

Another important factor in attraction and friendship is physical attractiveness. According to the physical attractiveness stereotype, most people believe that physically attractive people are also good and valuable in other ways. For example, physically attractive people are often assumed to be intelligent, competent, and socially successful. Attraction to physically attractive persons is somewhat modified by the fear of being rejected. Consequently, most people use a matching principle in choosing friends and partners: They select others who match their own levels of physical attractiveness and other qualities.

Matching implies the importance of similarity. Similarity of attitudes, values, and background is a powerful influence on interpersonal attraction. People are more likely to become friends if they have common interests, goals, and pastimes. Similar values and commitments are helpful in establishing trust between two people. Over time, they choose to spend more time together, and this strengthens their relationship.

Another factor in interpersonal attraction is complementarity, defined as the possession of qualities that complete or fulfill another's needs and abilities. Research has failed to confirm that "opposites attract," as attraction appears to grow stronger with similarities, not differences, between two people. There is some evidence, however, that people with complementary traits and needs will form stronger relationships. For example, a person who enjoys talking will have a compatible relationship with a friend or partner who enjoys listening. Their needs are different but not opposite—they complete each other.

FRIENDSHIP

Friendship begins as a relationship of social exchange. Exchange relationships involve giving and returning favors and other resources, with a short-term emphasis on maintaining fairness or equity. For example, early in a relationship, if one person does a favor for a friend, the friend returns it in kind. Over time, close friendships involve shifting away from an exchange basis to a communal basis. In a communal relationship, partners see their friendship as a common investment and contribute to it for their mutual benefit. For example, if one person gives a gift to a good friend, he or she does not expect repayment in kind. The gift represents an investment in their long-term friendship, rather than a short-term exchange.

Friendship also depends on intimate communication. Friends engage in self-disclosure and reveal personal information to each other. In the early stages of friendship, this is immediately reciprocated: One person's revelation or confidence is exchanged for the other's. As friendship develops, immediate reciprocity is not necessary; long-term relationships involve expectations of future responses. According to psychologist Robert Sternberg, friendship is characterized by two experiences: intimacy and commitment. Friends confide in each other, trust each other, and maintain their friendship through investment and effort.

COMFORT IN A GROUP

Theories of affiliation explain why the presence of others can be a source of comfort. In Schachter's classic 1959 research on fear and affiliation, university women volunteered to participate in a psychological experiment. After they were assembled, an experimenter in medical attire deceived them by explaining that their participation would involve the administration of electrical shock. Half the subjects were told to expect extremely painful shocks, while the others were assured that the shocks would produce a painless, ticklish sensation. In both conditions, the subjects were asked to indicate where they preferred to wait while the electrical equipment was being set up. Each could indicate whether she preferred to wait alone in a private room, preferred to wait in a large room with other subjects, or had no preference.

The cover story about electrical shock was a deception; no shocks were administered. The fear of painful shock, however, influenced the subjects' preferences: Those who expected painful shocks preferred to wait with other subjects, while those who expected painless shocks expressed no preference. Schachter concluded that (as the saying goes) misery loves company. In a later study, subjects were given the choice of waiting with other people who were not research subjects. In this study, subjects who feared shock expressed specific preference for others who also feared shock: Misery loves miserable company.

The social comparison theory of affiliation explains the appeal of group membership. People join groups such as clubs, organizations, and churches to support one another in common beliefs or activities and to provide one another with information. Groups can also be a source of pressure to conform. One reason individuals feel pressured to conform with group behavior is that they assume the group has better information than they have. This is termed informational influence. Cohesive groups—groups with strong member loyalty and commitment to membership—can also influence members to agree in the absence of information. When a member conforms with the group because he or she does not want to violate the group's standards or norms, he or she has been subjected to normative influence.

FACTORS IN FRIENDSHIP

Studies of interpersonal attraction and friendship have documented the power of circumstances such as propinquity. In their 1950 book *Social Pressures in Informal Groups*, Leon Festinger, Stanley Schachter, and Kurt Back reported the friendship preferences of married students living in university housing. Festinger and his colleagues found that the students and their families were most likely to form friendships with others who lived nearby and with whom they had regular contact. Propinquity was a more powerful determinant of friendship than common background or academic major. Propinquity appears to act as an initial filter in social relationships: Nearness and contact determine the people an individual meets, after which other factors may affect interpersonal attraction.

The findings of Festinger and his colleagues can be applied by judiciously

People are more likely to become friends if they share interests, goals, and pastimes. (CLEO Photography)

choosing living quarters and location. People who wish to be popular should choose to live where they will have the greatest amount of contact with others: on the ground floor of a high-rise building, near an exit or stairwell, or near common facilities such as a laundry room. Zajonc's research on the power of mere exposure confirms that merely having frequent contact with others is sufficient to predispose them to liking.

Mere exposure does not appear to sustain relationships over time. Once people have interacted, their likelihood of having future interactions depends on factors such as physical attractiveness and similarity to one another. Further, the quality of their communication must improve over time as they engage in greater self-disclosure. As friends move from a tit-for-tat exchange to a communal relationship in which they both invest time and resources, their friendship will develop more strongly and satisfactorily.

LOVE

Research on love has identified a distinction between passionate love and companionate love. Passionate love involves intense, short-lived emotions and sexual attraction. In contrast, companionate love is calmer, more stable, and based on trust. Companionate love is strong friendship. Researchers assert that if passionate love lasts, it will eventually calm down and become transformed into companionate love.

Researcher Zick Rubin developed a scale to measure love and liking. He found that statements of love involved attachment, intimacy, and caring. Statements of liking involved positive regard, judgments of similarity, trust, respect, and affection. Liking or friendship is not simply a weaker form of love but a distinctive combination of feelings, beliefs, and behaviors. Rubin found that most dating couples had strong feelings of both love and liking for each other; however, follow-up research confirmed that the best predictor of whether partners were still together later was how much they had liked—not loved—each other. Liking and friendship form a solid basis for love and other relationships that is not easily altered or forgotten.

RESEARCH

Much early research on affiliation and friendship developed from an interest in social groups. After World War II, social scientists were interested in identifying the attitudes and processes that unify people and motivate their allegiances. Social comparison theory helps to explain a broad range of behavior, including friendship choices, group membership, and proselytizing. Festinger suggested that group membership is helpful when one's beliefs have been challenged or disproved. Like-minded fellow members will be equally motivated to rationalize the challenge. In their 1956 book *When Prophecy Fails*, Festinger, Henry Riecken, and Schachter document the experience of two groups of contemporary persons who had attested a belief that the world would end in a disastrous flood. One group was able to gather and meet to await the end, while the other individuals, mostly college students, were scattered and could not assemble. When the world did not end as predicted, only those in the group context were able to rationalize their predicament, and they proceeded to proselytize, spreading the word to "converts." Meanwhile, the scattered members, unable to rationalize their surprise, lost faith in the prophecy and left the larger group.

Research on propinquity combined with other studies of interpersonal attraction in the 1960's and 1970's. Friendship and love are challenging topics to study because they cannot be re-created in a laboratory setting. Studies of personal relationships are difficult to conduct in natural settings; if people know they are being observed while they talk or date, they behave differently or leave the scene. Natural or field studies are also less conclusive than laboratory research because it is not always clear which factors have produced the feelings or actions that can be observed.

Friendship has not been as popular a topic in relationships research as romantic love, marriage, and sexual relationships. Some research has identified gender differences in friendship: Women communicate their feelings and experiences with other women, while men's friendships involve common or shared activities. Developmental psychologists have also identified some age differences: Children are less discriminating about friendship, identifying someone as a friend who is merely a playmate; adults have more complex ideas about friendship forms and standards.

As research on close relationships has gained acceptance, work in communication studies has contributed to the findings of social psychologists. Consequently, more is being learned about the development and maintenance of friendship as well as the initial attractions and bonds that encourage people's ties to others.

Sources for Further Study

Festinger, Leon, Stanley Schachter, and Kurt Back. *Social Pressures in Informal Groups.* Stanford, Calif.: Stanford University Press, 1963. This classic work documents the authors' research on housing and friendship preferences and ties work on friendship to theories of group structure and function.

Hendrick, Clyde, and Susan Hendrick. *Close Relationships: A Sourcebook.* Thousand Oaks, Calif.: Sage, 2000. A wide-ranging sourcebook of current theory, research, and practical application of the psychology of friendship.

_____. *Liking, Loving, and Relating.* 2d ed. Pacific Grove, Calif.: Brooks/Cole, 1992. The Hendricks provide a thorough review of the processes of affiliation and interpersonal attraction. They include a discussion of issues in relationships, such as separation and divorce, blended families, changing sex roles, and dual-career couples.

Yager, Jan. *Friendshifts: The Power of Friendship and How It Shapes Our Lives.* 2d ed. Stamford, Conn.: Hannacroix Creek Books, 1999. A practical book on the structures and sustenance of friendships.

Ann L. Weber

See also: Attraction Theories; Groups.

Aggression

Type of psychology: Biological bases of behavior; emotion; personality; psychopathology

Fields of study: Aggression; biology of stress; childhood and adolescent disorders; coping; critical issues in stress; personality disorders; stress and illness

Aggression is an emotional response to frustration that often leads to angry and destructive actions directed against individuals, animals, or such organizations as corporate bureaucracies, social and religious groups, or governments.

Key concepts
- anger
- defensive aggression
- frustration
- hostility
- offensive aggression
- predatory aggression
- regression
- social immaturity
- socialization
- stress
- tantrum

Aggression, as the term is applied to humans, occurs as an emotional reaction to dissatisfactions and stress resulting in behaviors that society considers antagonistic and destructive. The term as used in common parlance has broad meanings and applications. In psychological parlance, however, aggression generally refers to an unreasonable hostility directed against situations with which people must cope or think they must cope. On a simple and relatively harmless level, people may demonstrate momentary aggressive behavior if they experience common frustrations such as missing a bus, perhaps reacting momentarily by stamping a foot on the ground or swearing. The moment passes, and no one is hurt by this sort of aggression, which most people demonstrate with fair frequency as they deal with frustration in their daily lives.

People with tattered self-images may direct their aggression toward themselves, possibly in the form of expressing or thinking disparaging things about themselves or, in extreme cases, harming themselves physically, even to the point of suicide. Such internalized forms of aggression may remain pent up for years in people who bear their frustrations silently. Such frustrations may eventually erupt into dangerous behavior directed at others, leading to assaults, verbal or physical abuse, and, in the most extreme cases, to massacres. Such was the case when Timothy McVeigh blew up the Alfred P.

Murrah Federal Building in Oklahoma City on April 19, 1995, as an act of civil protest, killing 167 people, none of whom he knew.

Infants and young children make their needs known and have them met by crying or screaming, which usually brings them attention from whoever is caring for them. Older children, basing their actions on these early behaviors, may attempt to have their needs met by having tantrums, or uncontrolled fits of rage, in an effort to achieve their ends. In some instances, adults who are frustrated, through regression to the behaviors of infancy or early childhood, have tantrums that, while disconcerting, frequently fail to succeed in anything more than emphasizing their social immaturity. Socialization demands that people learn how to control their overt expressions of rage and hostility.

TYPES OF AGGRESSION

Hugh Wagner, a behavioral psychologist concerned with the biology of aggression, has identified three types: offensive aggression, defensive aggression, and predatory aggression. Offensive aggression occurs when the aggressor initiates aggressive behavior against one or more nonaggressors. The response to offensive aggression is likely to be defensive aggression that generally takes the form of self-defense.

Predatory aggression differs from offensive or defensive aggression, although it is basically a form of offensive aggression. It is characterized by, for example, such phenomena as the lurking of predatory animals that make themselves as inconspicuous as possible until their prey is within striking distance. They then pounce on the prey with the intention of killing it as quickly as they can so that they can eat it. Among humans, hunters are examples of predatory aggressors, although not all modern hunters consume their prey.

BIOLOGICAL ROOTS OF AGGRESSION

Although aggressive acts are usually triggered by environmental factors, laboratory research suggests that aggression has biological roots. Various experiments point to the fact that the three basic types of aggression are controlled by different mechanisms in the midbrain. It has been demonstrated in laboratory animals that offensive aggression has intimate connections to neurons in the ventral tegmental area of the midbrain. When lesions occur in this section of the brain, offensive aggression decreases markedly or disappears altogether, although defensive and predatory aggression are not affected.

Conversely, when parts of the anterior hypothalamus are stimulated, offensive behavior increases, and attack may ensue. The brain appears in these experiments to be programmed in such a way that defensive aggression is controlled by the periaqueductal gray matter (PAG) found in the midbrain. So specialized are the neural activities of the midbrain that defensive aggression involving perceived threats emanates from a different part of the brain than defensive aggression that involves an actual attack. Acid-based amino

> ## DSM-IV-TR CRITERIA FOR INTERMITTENT EXPLOSIVE DISORDER
> **(DSM CODE 312.34)**
>
> Several discrete episodes of failure to resist aggressive impulses resulting in serious assaultive acts or destruction of property
>
> Degree of aggressiveness expressed during episodes grossly out of proportion to any precipitating psychosocial stressors
>
> Aggressive episodes not better accounted for by another mental disorder and not due to direct physiological effects of a substance or general medical condition

neurons from the medial hypothalamus are known to trigger defensive aggression.

Alcoholic intake often intensifies aggressive behavior because alcohol reduces the inhibitions that the cerebral cortex controls while stimulating the neural pathways between the medial hypothalamus and the PAG. Although alcohol does not increase aggressive behavior in all humans, many people react aggressively when they consume alcoholic beverages.

AGGRESSION AND BODY CHEMISTRY
In most species, including humans, males are more aggressive than females. This is thought to be because of the testosterone levels present in varying degrees in males. The higher the testosterone level, the more aggressive the male. Aggressive behavior that threatens the welfare of the species is often controlled in humans by medication that reduces the testosterone levels and pacifies aggressive men.

It is notable that young men tend to be considerably more aggressive than older males, presumably because as men age, their testosterone levels decrease considerably. Prisons are filled with young men unable to control their aggressions sufficiently to stay out of trouble with the law. Many of these prisoners mellow into relatively benign older men, not because prison has reformed them but because their body chemistry has undergone significant changes through the years.

At one time, aggressive behavior was controlled by electric shock therapy (which is used at present in some extreme cases) or by the more drastic surgical procedure known as lobotomy. Lobotomies often left people in virtually catatonic states from which they could never emerge. Drugs and psychiatric treatment have replaced most of the more devastating procedures of the nineteenth and twentieth centuries.

ROAD RAGE AND AIR RAGE
Two of the most common forms of offensive aggression in modern society are road rage and air rage. Road rage, which generally occurs on crowded,

multilane highways, is often committed by otherwise civilized individuals who, when behind the wheel of a car that weighs more than a ton, become irrational. If someone cuts them off in traffic, drives slowly in the lane ahead of them, or commits some other perceived roadway insult, perpetrators of road rage may bump the rear of car ahead of them, pass the car and shoot at the offending driver, or force the offending driver off the road and onto the shoulder, where a fight or a shooting may occur.

Air rage is somewhat different. Some people who have been flying for long periods in cramped airplane conditions, often passing through several time zones, may suffer from disorientation. Often this feeling is intensified by the consumption of alcohol before or during the flight. Such people, if refused another drink or if asked to return to their seats and buckle their seat belts, may strike out at flight attendants or at fellow passengers.

AGGRESSION IN ANIMALS

Although humans exhibit aggression in its most subtle and complicated forms, other species of animals also manifest aggressive behaviors. Most animals will fight if they are attacked because self-defense and self-preservation are inherent in most species. Within their own social constructs, some animals will attack those outside their group, even those of the same species, although few animals turn on their own species to nearly the extent that humans do. Carnivorous animals exhibit aggressiveness in preying on other animals as food sources, the large overpowering the small, the swift overtaking the slow, the strong killing and consuming the weak. Most animals also aggressively defend the areas in which they forage and build their nests or dens.

The less aggressive species of animals have been domesticated by humans as sources of food, notably poultry, cattle, and fish. More aggressive animals are sometimes used in sports such as bullfighting or cockfighting. In these instances, the animals are taught aggressive behaviors that are not instinctive in most of them. They are trained to perform, and satisfactory performance on their parts is rooted in aggression.

AGGRESSION AND PROCREATION

Aggressive behavior in nearly all species is rooted in sexuality. The male is usually more aggressive than the female. The sexual act is fundamentally an act of male aggression. Males during their sexual prime maintain the high levels of testosterone that assure the continuance of their species but that also result in aggressive, sometimes antisocial behavior.

The offensive aggression of one species, such as the predatory birds that feed on newborn turtles in the Galápagos Islands, evokes defensive aggressive behavior on the part of those seeking to protect their young and to assure the continuance of their species. The species that demonstrates defensive aggression in a situation of this sort may demonstrate offensive aggression in pursuing and attacking a weaker species. All of these aggressions among nonhumans are, in the final analysis, directed at preserving the species.

CAN HUMAN AGGRESSION BE CONTROLLED?

Aggression is so inherent in nearly every species that it is doubtful that it can ever be fully controlled, nor would it be desirable to control it. When aggression among humans reaches the point of threatening the social fabric, however, steps must be taken to control or, at least, to redirect it. The adolescent male who wants to beat everyone up probably is suffering from extreme anger. It may be possible to redirect this anger, which is a form of energy, into more socially acceptable channels. It may also be possible to control elements in the environment—home life, being bullied at school, being rejected by peers—in such ways as to reduce the anger and resentment that have led to aggressive behavior.

The management of aggression through psychotherapy and medication may prove effective. The aggressive individual, however, may resist the treatment that could succeed in controlling the socially unacceptable aggressive behavior in which he or she engages. Attempts to control aggression often run counter to the very nature of human beings as they pass through the various developmental stages of their lives.

SOURCES FOR FURTHER STUDY

Anderson, Daniel R., et al. *Early Childhood Television Viewing and Adolescent Behavior.* Boston: Blackwell, 2001. Of particular relevance to those interested in aggression are chapters 6 ("Aggression") and 9 ("Self-Image: Role Model Preference and Body Image"). The five coauthors of this valuable study seek to explore the roots of aggression in teenagers in terms of their exposure to violence through television viewing in their formative years.

Archer, John, and Kevin Browne. *Human Aggression: Naturalistic Approaches.* New York: Routledge, 1989. The approach is that of the social psychologist who is much concerned with environmental factors affecting aggression. A worthwhile book for the beginner.

Blanchard, Robert J., and Caroline D. Blanchard, eds. *Advances in the Study of Aggression.* New York: Academic Press, 1984. Dan Olweus's chapter, "Development of Stable Aggressive Reaction Patterns in Males," and John Paul Scott's chapter, "Advances in Aggression Research: The Future," are particularly compelling. The book as a whole is well constructed, although it may be more appropriate for those experienced in the field than to beginners.

Englander, E. K. *Understanding Violence.* Mahwah, N.J.: Lawrence Erlbaum, 1997. The author presents a panoramic view of violence and human aggression, condensing effectively the major research in the field over the previous half century.

Feshbach, Seymour, and Jolanta Zagrodzka, eds. *Aggression: Biological, Developmental, and Social Perspectives.* New York: Plenum Press, 1997. This comprehensive collection, although somewhat specialized, covers the two major factors in aggression (the biological roots and social determinants) thoroughly and accurately, interpreting recent research in the field extremely well.

Hoffer, Eric. *The True Believer: Thoughts on the Nature of Mass Movements.* New York: Perennial Library, 1989. One of the most compelling and readable accounts of mass movements and their relation to aggressive behavior in individuals.

Lesko, Wayne A. *Readings in Social Psychology: General, Classic, and Contemporary Selections.* 4th ed. Boston: Allyn & Bacon, 2000. Chapter 11, "Aggression," is clear and forthright. A desirable starting point for those who are not experienced in the field.

Lorenz, Konrad. *On Aggression.* 1963. Translated by Marjorie Kerr Wilson. Reprint. New York: Routledge, 2002. This classic and revolutionary study posits a killer instinct in both animals and humans.

Scott, John Paul. *Aggression.* Chicago: University of Chicago Press, 1975. Although it is somewhat outdated, this book remains especially valuable for its chapters on the physiology of aggression (chapter 3) and on the social causes of aggression (chapter 5). The book is well written and easily understandable for those who are new to the field.

Wagner, Hugh. *The Psychobiology of Human Motivation.* New York: Routledge, 1999. Chapter 7 focuses on aggression and explores possible biological origins of the three types of aggression (offensive, defensive, and predatory) that Wagner employs in making his classifications.

R. Baird Shuman

SEE ALSO: Domestic Violence; Emotions; Hormones and Behavior; Stress: Behavioral and Psychological Responses.

Aging

Cognitive Changes

TYPE OF PSYCHOLOGY: Cognition; intelligence and intelligence testing; learning; memory; psychopathology; sensation and perception

FIELDS OF STUDY: Aging; behavioral and cognitive models; cognitive processes; social perception and cognition; thought

Behavioral scientists have become increasingly interested in studying the cognitive changes that occur in the elderly across time. Studies have been conducted in order to assist individuals in their adjustment to aging as well as to unlock the secrets of the aging process itself.

KEY CONCEPTS
- attention
- cognition
- environmental influences
- information processing
- learning
- long-term memory
- mild cognitive impairment (MCI)
- pacing of instruction
- sensoriperceptual changes
- short-term memory

Cognitive changes refer to those changes which occur in overall mental functions and operations. Cognition encompasses all mental operations and functions, including attention, intelligence, memory, language and speech, perception, learning, concept formation, thought, problem solving, spatial and time orientation, and motor/behavior control. Psychologists have worked to define and measure various areas of cognitive functioning, even though there has been no consensus about these areas. Understanding the progression of cognitive functioning requires an understanding of brain structure and those human functions emanating from the brain and its fullest human potentiality, the mind. There is considerable debate within the scientific community about what type of cognitive functions actually exist as well as the nature of the mental mechanisms that are necessary to understand cognitive functioning.

A common belief is that cognitive abilities decline markedly in older individuals. More and more, however, this idea is being shown to be exaggerated. Studies attest that the diminishment of cognitive skills with age may not be significant, especially before the age of about seventy-five. Aging has been found to have different effects on long-term and short-term memory processes. The capacity of short-term memory (which is quite limited in all age groups) remains essentially the same for people as they age. Long-term memory, however, does show a decline. This decline can be minimized by various strategies; the use of mnemonic devices is very effective, as is taking extra time in learning and remembering.

Both biological and environmental factors have been studied in regard to aging and cognition. An environment that induces apathy or depression has been found to have a lowering effect on cognitive abilities. Environments that provide stimuli to interest the individual can reduce cognitive decline. Moreover, at least one study has found that providing challenging stimuli can even reverse cognitive declines that have been observed. There is a tremendous range of aging effects from individual to individual, with some showing virtually no changes and others showing serious decay of functions. It should be noted that this discussion concerns cognition in healthy individuals; diseases such as Alzheimer's disease and Parkinson's disease and events such as strokes (cardiovascular accidents) have effects on memory that are considered separately from the normal effects of aging.

Modern research on cognitive changes caused by aging emphasizes the information-processing capabilities of individuals as reflected in memory capacities. Memory is a basic psychological function upon which higher-level psychological processes such as speech, learning, concept formation, and problem solving are based. Lester Sdorow describes the brain's information-processing capacities as the human being's active acquisition of information about the world. Sensory stimuli are transmitted to the brain, where replicas of the external world are stored briefly in the sensory registry (one second for visual stimuli and four seconds for auditory memory). Information is then transferred to short-term memory for about twenty seconds, unless it is actively rehearsed, then into long-term memory, where it is potentially retained for a lifetime.

INFORMATION PROCESSING AND MEMORY

Information processing is a view of cognitive development that is based on the premise that complex cognitive skills develop as the product of the integration of a hierarchy of more basic skills obtained through life experience and learning. According to this view, prerequisite skills are mastered and form the foundation for more and more complex skills.

Information-processing theories emerged as psychologists began to draw comparisons between the way computers operate and the way humans use logic and rules about the world as they develop. Humans use these rules for processing information. New rules may be added and old rules modified throughout childhood and adulthood as more information is obtained from worldly interactions. The cognitive changes that occur throughout adult life, as more useful and accurate rules are learned, are every bit as important as the cognitive advances that occurred during childhood, as long as the basic rules acquired in childhood were not distorted by aberrant experiences. Each advance refines the ability to process information. Elizabeth F.

Loftus points out that the terms "cognition" and "information processing" have supplanted the term "thinking" among modern cognitive scientists. Similar efforts have been made to redefine other human abilities such as problem solving (by H. A. Simon) and intelligence (by Robert Sternberg) in order to describe greater specificity of function.

Researchers have spent much time and effort defining and redefining memory constructs, although theorists remain in the early stages of understanding memory. Much debate has focused on naturalistic versus laboratory methodologies, with few resolutions as to how the results of both can contribute to a permanent knowledge base of memory.

The mediation school of thought suggests theoretical mechanisms of encoding, retention, and retrieval to explain memory functioning. Consequently, concerted efforts have been made to attribute memory changes across the life span to the specific deterioration of such mechanisms. Researchers continue to debate the importance, even existence, of such constructs. Similarly, the dichotomy of long-term versus short-term memory continues to be debated. In order to test the empirical validity of such theories, constructs must be able to be disproved if false, and these metaphorical constructs have proved difficult or impossible to test because of their abstract nature.

The greatest controversy in memory research focuses on laboratory versus naturalistic experiments; some researchers, such as M. R. Banaji and R. G. Crowder, state that naturalistic experiments have yielded no new principles and no new methods of memory research and should be abandoned. Others, such as H. P. Bahrick, claim that the naturalistic approach has provided in ten years what the laboratory has not in a hundred years. Banaji and Crowder criticize naturalistic experiments for their lack of control and thus their lack of generalizability. Confining a study to a specific population in a contrived laboratory setting, however, does not seem to generalize any further. S. J. Ceci and Urie Bronfenbrenner emphasize the need to focus on the process of understanding, whatever that process might be. As Endel Tulving notes, the polemics that have ensued from this debate are not going to advance the science of memory. He concludes that there is no reason to believe that there is only one correct way of studying memory.

INFORMATION PROCESSING IN THE ELDERLY

Learning, memory, and attention are all aspects of cognition. Learning is the acquisition of information, skills, and knowledge, measured by improvement in responses. Memory involves retaining and retrieving information for later use. Attention is the mechanism by which individuals process information. Cognition is how sensory input is transformed, stored, and retrieved from memory.

Major stages of information-processing models of learning and memory include registration (input), storage (retention), and retrieval (process input for response). Attention is a major component of registration in that fo-

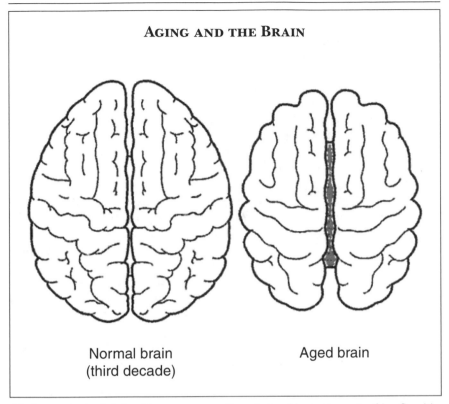

AGING AND THE BRAIN

Normal brain
(third decade)

Aged brain

The human brain shrinks with age as nerve cells are lost and brain tissue atrophies. Cognitive changes in the elderly can range from mild forgetfulness to dementia. (Hans & Cassidy, Inc.)

cusing on stimuli and processing of information begin at this stage. Environmental influences, age-related sensoriperceptual changes, and pacing of instruction affect the processing of information.

Environmental influences can produce negative responses from the elderly because older adults are less comfortable in unfamiliar settings or with unfamiliar people and have difficulty performing multiple tasks. Additionally, the ability to block out extraneous information and to focus on multiple instructions decreases with age.

Sensoriperceptual changes include age-related vision deficits such as altered color perception as a result of yellowing of the eye lens, difficulty seeing at various distances as a result of presbyopia, difficulty adjusting from light to dark, and decreased peripheral vision and depth perception. Sensorineural hearing loss affects the ability to hear high-frequency sounds and consonants and hinders communication. Also, excessive noise interferes with the ability to hear in the elderly.

Pacing of instruction includes both the time it takes to present and the amount of information presented. With age, there is slowing of physiological and psychological responses. Reaction time increases. Studies have shown that the elderly learn more efficiently when they are able to learn and respond at their own pace.

STUDIES IN AGE-RELATED COGNITION

In examining cognitive changes in aging populations, aside from the theoretical debates, researchers have reported that cognitive processes progressively decline as chronological age advances. Studies have tended to describe the cognitive declines as gradual and general, rather than being attributable to discrete cognitive losses in specific areas of functioning.

Several studies have supported the existence of age-related cognitive decline, while other studies dispute the severity of such declines. Research interest is increasing in the areas of identifying factors related to cognitive decline and interventions to abate them. Under the direction of Ronald C. Petersen and Michael Grundman, the National Institute on Aging is studying whether daily doses of vitamin E or donepezil can prevent those with mild cognitive impairment from developing Alzheimer's disease. Other studies are investigating cholinesterase inhibitors and anti-inflammatory agents as a means of slowing the progression of mild cognitive impairment.

Psychologists who studied memory change identified diminished memory capacity in the elderly as attributable to a number of processes, such as slowed semantic access and a reduced ability to make categorical judgments. Other researchers concluded that older subjects were slower in mental operations but were not less accurate. Some researchers hypothesized that slower speed tied up processing functions, resulting in apparent memory impairment. Still others hypothesized that older adults have more trouble with active memory tasks because of increased competition for a share of memory processing resources, whereas others linked the aged's poor performance on working memory tasks to an actual deficiency in processing resources. Finally, some researchers concluded that older adults might simply have less mental energy to perform memory tasks. These studies accept gradual memory decline, or a slowing of processing, as a normal by-product of aging.

There are some who believe that mild cognitive impairment is a neurological disorder. This belief stems from the identification of atrophy of the left medial lobe and small medial temporal lobe, low parietal/temporal perfusion, and asymmetry of the brain as revealed by computed tomography. One study identified those with small hippocampi as prone to developing Alzheimer's disease. Additionally, electroencephalogram tracings of the brains of patients with mild cognitive impairment and patients with Alzheimer's disease showed similarities.

R. A. Hock, B. A. Futrell, and B. A. Grismer studied eighty-two elderly persons, from sixty to ninety-nine years of age, who were living independently. These normal adults were tested on a battery of eight tasks that were selected to reflect cognitive functioning, particularly measuring primary and secondary memory, memory for nonverbal material, span of attention, the capacity to divide attention among competing sources of stimulation, and two motor tasks requiring psychomotor integrity. This study found a gradual, progressive decline in cognitive functioning but found that the decline did not reach statistically significant levels. The decline was general, suggesting that it may have been a function of reduced attention rather than more discrete losses. This finding appears to be consistent with the notion that crystallized intellectual or abstract processes are well maintained across time. There were suggestions that speed of information processing is a sensitive measure of the aging process.

It is possible, however, that the tasks selected for this study did not discriminate between younger and older aging adults because the tasks may be more reliable for assessing brain injuries and psychologically impaired persons, who were not included in the population studied. Consequently, further studies on the same cognitive tasks with impaired aged adults would be necessary to see if the same relationships and conclusions would apply. Individuals with impaired cognitive functioning offer a unique opportunity to determine if the brain continues to show the same propensity to function as a unitary, global system as is observed with individuals who experience the normal aging process.

Although the brain does exhibit localization of functions, with specialization of certain brain cells for specific functions, its overall mode of operation is as a total unit. The brain has an exceptional capacity to compensate for the loss of some specific functions and continue the rest of its mental operations. This capacity or flexibility in brain function has been termed equipotentiation. Further studies of individuals with brain impairments will help to show how the brain attempts to carry out its overall functions when more specific impairments have been sustained. When cognitive disorders result in faulty information processing, actual observable changes may occur in a person's daily behavior. The previously neat person, for example, may neglect personal hygiene. The person who previously exhibited exceptional verbal abilities may speak in a socially inappropriate manner. The staid conservative businessperson may act impulsively or even make unreasonable decisions about personal finances and may show impaired social judgment.

MILD COGNITIVE IMPAIRMENT

Studies of cognitive changes across the life span must distinguish between normal gradual change in the elderly and change that is associated with disordered functioning. Studies must also respect the complexity of the human brain. Morton Hunt notes that cognitive scientists have concluded that there may be 100 billion neurons in the interior of the brain. Each of these neurons may be interconnected to hundreds of others by anywhere from one thousand to ten thousand synapses, or relay points. This may enable the average healthy person to accumulate five hundred times as much information as is contained in the entire *Encyclopedia Britannica,* or 100 trillion bits of information. The circuitry in one human brain is probably sixty times the complexity of the entire United States telephone system. Given this complexity, even the daily estimated loss of 100,000 brain cells from the aging process may leave human beings capable of sound cognitive functioning well into old age.

"Mild cognitive impairment" is a term used to describe isolated memory losses without changes in activities of daily living. There is some support for the theory that mild cognitive impairment represents a transitional stage between normal aging and Alzheimer's disease and may be a precursor to Alzheimer's disease. A significant proportion of patients with mild cognitive impairment do not progress to Alzheimer's disease. One research study followed a group of mildly cognitively impaired patients and reported they developed Alzheimer's disease at a rate of 10 percent to 15 percent per year, while individuals without mild cognitive impairment developed Alzheimer's disease at a rate of 1 percent to 2 percent per year. Individuals who have a memory problem but do not meet clinical criteria for Alzheimer's disease are considered to have mild cognitive impairment with memory loss. This is an important group for Alzheimer's disease research because up to 40 percent of those who are mildly cognitively impaired develop Alzheimer's disease within three years. One study supported that those who carried the gene apolipoprotein E-4 (APOE-4) were more likely to develop Alzheimer's disease. Studies involving molecular brain activity have contributed to understanding normal and abnormal memory activities. Another study linked poor performance on a memory test that provided cues to help participants at time of recall indicated a cognitive decline. To date, there are no treatments to prevent or manage mild cognitive impairment. Therefore, awareness, understanding the implications, and early identification are important in management and education about mild cognitive impairment.

Paul Baltes notes that it used to be considered "common knowledge" that cognitive abilities decline with age, but today this view is highly debatable. When the effects of disease and injury are separated out in studies of the healthy elderly, no drastic decline in cognitive ability is found. This conclusion may be one reason that studies of cognition and aging have begun to make a distinction regarding intelligence. The distinction is between crystallized intelligence, involving the accumulation of facts and knowledge, which holds up with age, and fluid intelligence, which is the rapid processing of new information, a function that appears particularly associated with the young and vulnerable to the effects of age or disease. Studies of neurologically healthy aging adults have revealed no consistent evidence of a reduced ability to learn. Studies have further shown that very little practice may be required to improve substantially an elderly person's ability to perform some cognitive tasks, reflecting a motivational factor. Studies of mentally active persons in their eighties have concluded that loss of cognitive ability stemmed more from intellectual apathy or boredom than from actual physical deterioration.

John Darley and his colleagues concluded that on average, the decline of intellectual capability with age is slight and probably does not occur before age seventy-five. When declines do occur, they do not occur equally across cognitive functions. Vocabulary and verbal skills may actually improve with age, whereas skills involving spatial visualization and deductive reasoning are more likely to diminish. In general, verbal skills and accumulated knowledge are maintained with aging, while tasks that require quick responses are more susceptible to aging.

SOURCES FOR FURTHER STUDY

Bahrick, H. P. "A Speedy Recovery from Bankruptcy for Ecological Memory Research." *American Psychologist* 46, no. 1 (1991): 76-77. This article addresses the controversy between those who favor naturalistic memory studies and those who favor strict experimental studies; Bahrick favors the naturalistic approach.

Banaji, Mahzarin R., and Robert G. Crowder. "The Bankruptcy of Everyday Memory." *American Psychologist* 44, no. 9 (1989): 1185-1193. This article addresses the controversy between naturalistic and experimental research; the authors favor more controlled experimental approaches.

Ceci, S. J., and Urie Bronfenbrenner. "On the Demise of Everyday Memory." *American Psychologist* 46, no. 1 (1991): 27-31. Addresses the naturalistic versus experimental memory study issue, offering a balanced perspective and inviting scientific inquiry regardless of the type of methodology.

Craik, Fergus I. M., and Timothy Salthouse, eds. *The Handbook of Aging and Cognition.* 2d ed. Mahwah, N.J.: Lawrence Erlbaum, 2000. A collection of review essays on all aspects of the aging brain.

Friedrich, M. J. "Mild Cognitive Impairment Raises Alzheimer Disease Risk." *Journal of the American Medical Association* 282 (1999): 621-622. Discusses link between cognitive impairment and developing Alzheimer's disease.

Lindsay, Heather. "Delaying Treating Mild Cognitive Impairment." *Clinical Psychiatry News* 27 (1999): 18. Addresses consequences of not treating mild cognitive impairment early.

Loftus, Elizabeth F. *Memory: Surprising New Insights into How We Remember and Why We Forget.* New York: Ardsley House, 1988. Discusses the development of the cognitive sciences in seeking greater specificity for human abilities such as thinking and memory.

Park, Denise, and Norbert Schwarz, eds. *Cognitive Aging: A Primer.* Philadelphia: Psychology Press, 2000. Upper-level college and graduate text covers all aspects of cognition in aging brains at an introductory level.

Petersen, Ronald. "Mild Cognitive Impairment or Questionable Dementia?" *Archives of Neurology* 57 (2000): 643-644. Differentiates between mild cognitive impairment and dementia.

Petersen, Ronald C., et al. "Mild Cognitive Impairment: Clinical Characterization and Outcome." *Archives of Neurology* 56 (1999): 303-308. Speaks of symptoms and consequences of untreated mild cognitive impairment.
Shah, Yogesh, Eric Tangalos, and Ronald Petersen. "Mild Cognitive Impairment: When Is It a Precursor to Alzheimer's Disease?" *Geriatrics* 55 (2000): 62-67. Discusses relationship between memory decline, mild cognitive impairment, and Alzheimer's disease.

Robert A. Hock; updated by Sharon Wallace Stark

SEE ALSO: Alzheimer's Disease; Dementia; Memory; Parkinson's Disease.

ALZHEIMER'S DISEASE

TYPE OF PSYCHOLOGY: Cognition; memory; psychopathology
FIELDS OF STUDY: Aging; cognitive processes; depression; interpersonal
    relations; social perception and cognition; thought

Alzheimer's disease (AD) is the most frequent cause of dementia. Dementia is the loss of cognitive and social abilities to the degree that they interfere with activities of daily living (ADLs). AD is an irreversible and gradual brain disorder known to occur with aging.

KEY CONCEPTS
- activities of daily living (ADLs)
- cognitive function
- cognitive impairment
- dementia
- memory loss
- motor function
- neurofibrillary fibers
- plaques

Alzheimer's disease (AD) and dementia are not a normal part of aging. Diseases that affect the brain such as genetic, immunologic, and vascular abnormalities cause AD. A defect in connections between the brain's cells causes gradual death of brain cells. AD advances progressively, from mild forgetfulness to a severe loss of mental function. It results in memory loss, behavior and personality changes, deterioration in thinking abilities, difficulty speaking (aphasia), declining motor function (apraxia), and difficulty recognizing objects (agnosia).

Forgetfulness and loss of concentration are early symptoms that may not be readily identified because they are considered normal signs of aging. Forgetfulness and loss of concentration may also result from use of drugs or alcohol, depression, fatigue, grief, physical illness, impaired vision, or hearing loss. The symptoms of AD usually occur after sixty years of age but may occur as early as forty. Symptoms often begin with recent memory loss, confusion, poor judgment, and personality changes. In later stages of AD, ADLs such as dressing and eating are affected. Eventually, AD sufferers are completely dependent on others for ADLs. They become so debilitated that they become bedridden, at which time other physical problems develop. Seizures may occur late in AD.

PREVALENCE AND IMPACT
AD accounts for 50 to 75 percent of all dementias. AD prevalence increases from 1 percent at age sixty-five to between 20 and 35 percent by age eighty-five. On average, AD sufferers may live from eight to twenty years following diagnosis. According to the World Health Organization (WHO), the num-

ber of people worldwide aged sixty-five years and older will reach 1.2 billion by 2025 and will exceed 2 billion by 2050. Of these, an estimated 22 million individuals will be afflicted with AD worldwide. The Alzheimer's Association speculates that if a preventive is not found, AD will be diagnosed in 14 million Americans by the middle of the twenty-first century.

A study done in 1998 revealed that African Americans and Latino Americans might have a higher overall risk of AD. Socioeconomic status, health care, level of education, and culture may also influence the diagnosis of AD. Another study in 1998 estimated that the annual economic burden created by the cost of caring for a patient with mild AD is $18,000, for a patient with moderate AD $30,000, and for a patient with severe AD $36,000. More than half of AD patients are cared for at home, with almost 75 percent of their care provided by family and friends. In 2002 the Alzheimer's Association estimated that approximately $33 billion is lost annually by American businesses as a result of AD. Time taken by caregivers of AD sufferers accounts for $26 billion, and $7 billion is spent for health issues and long-term care related to AD. Additionally, AD costs the United States more than $100 billion annually.

HISTORY

AD is named after a German physician, Dr. Alois Alzheimer, who in 1906 found plaques and neurofibrillary tangles in the brain of a mentally disturbed woman. Today, these plaques and tangles in the brain are considered hallmarks of AD.

There is also evidence that ancient Greeks and Romans recognized the disease, as there are writings dating from their time that appear to describe symptoms of AD. In the sixteenth century, playwright and poet William Shakespeare wrote that old age is a "second childishness and mere oblivion." In the past, terms such as "senility" and "hardening of the arteries" were commonly used to describe dementia. Until recently, AD was considered an inevitable consequence of aging. Beginning in the last quarter of the twentieth century, researchers discovered more about AD.

RISK FACTORS

The major risk factors for AD are age and family history. Other possible risk factors include a serious head injury and lower socioeconomic status. There is speculation that genetics, environmental influences, weight, educational level, and blood pressure and blood cholesterol levels are factors that may increase the risk for AD.

CAUSES

There are no definitive causes of AD. Some that have been identified include lesions caused by plaque, inflammation in brain cells, oxidative stress effects on brain cells, genetic factors, beta amyloid protein and senile plaques, tau protein and neurofibrillary tangles, estrogen effects on brain neurotransmitters, dysfunction in brain cell communication, autoimmune responses, viruses, and vessel anomalies.

PLAQUE. In AD, plaques develop in the areas of the brain that regulate memory and other cognitive functions. These plaques are deposits of beta-amyloid (a protein fragment from a larger protein called amyloid precursor protein, APP) intermingled with portions of neurons and with nonnerve cells such as microglia (cells that surround and digest damaged cells or foreign substances) and astrocytes (glial cells that support and nourish neurons). Plaques are found in the spaces between the brain's nerve cells. Researchers do not know whether amyloid plaques cause AD or are a by-product of the AD process.

AD consists of abnormal collections of twisted threads found inside nerve cells. The chief component is a protein called tau. In the central nervous system, tau proteins bind and stabilize brain cells' support structure by forming tubules that guide nutrients and molecules from the cells to the ends of the axon. Tau normally holds together connector pieces of the tubule tracks. In AD, tau threads twist around each other and form neurofibrillary tangles. Support to the cell is lost, causing cell death and leading to dementia.

GENETIC FACTORS IN AD DEVELOPMENT. Two types of AD have been identified: familial AD (FAD), which follows an inheritance pattern, and sporadic AD. The *Diagnostic and Statistical Manual of Mental Disorders* (4th ed., 1994, DSM-IV) describes AD as early-onset (younger than sixty-five years) or late-onset (sixty-five years and older). Only 5 to 10 percent of AD cases are early onset. Some forms of early-onset AD are inherited and often progress faster than late-onset AD.

ESTROGEN. Estrogen use has been associated with a decreased risk of AD and enhanced cognitive functioning. Its antioxidant and anti-inflammatory effects enhance the growth of processes of neurons for memory function. This has created intense interest in the relationship between estrogen, memory, and cognitive function in humans.

AUTOIMMUNE SYSTEM. The body's immune system may attack its own tissues and produce antibodies against essential cells. Some researchers postulate that aging neurons in the brain trigger an autoimmune response that causes AD. Antibodies have been identified in the brains of those with Alzheimer's disease.

VIRUSES. The discovery of slow-acting viruses that cause some brain disorders has resulted in some researchers believing that a virus may cause AD. As of 2002, no virus had been identified in the brains of those with AD.

VESSEL ANOMALIES. Defects in brain blood vessels such as cerebroarteriosclerosis or problems in the blood-brain barrier (which guards against foreign bodies or toxic agents in the blood stream from entering the brain) have not been identified as causes of AD.

GROWTH FACTORS. Some researchers believe that a decline in growth factors or an increase in factors that are toxic to neuronal cells causes AD. Researchers are investigating introducing naturally occurring nerve

DSM-IV-TR CRITERIA FOR DEMENTIA OF THE ALZHEIMER'S TYPE

Development of multiple cognitive deficits manifested by both memory impairment (impaired ability to learn new information or recall previously learned information) and one or more of the following cognitive disturbances:

- aphasia (language disturbance)
- apraxia (impaired ability to carry out motor activities despite intact motor function)
- agnosia (failure to recognize or identify objects despite intact sensory function)
- disturbance in executive functioning (planning, organizing, sequencing, abstracting)

Cognitive deficits each cause significant impairment in social or occupational functioning and represent significant decline from previous level of functioning

Course characterized by gradual onset and continuing cognitive decline

Cognitive deficits not due to any of the following:

- other central nervous system conditions causing progressive deficits in memory and cognition (such as cerebrovascular disease, Parkinson's disease, Huntington's disease, subdural hematoma, normal-pressure hydrocephalus, brain tumor)
- systemic conditions known to cause dementia (such as hypothyroidism, vitamin B or folic acid deficiency, niacin deficiency, hypercalcemia, neurosyphilis, HIV infection)
- substance-induced conditions

Deficits do not occur exclusively during course of a delirium

Disturbance not better accounted for by another Axis I disorder (such as Major Depressive Episode, Schizophrenia)

Code based on presence or absence of clinically significant behavioral disturbance:

- Without Behavioral Disturbance (DSM code 294.10): Cognitive disturbance not accompanied by any clinically significant behavioral disturbance
- With Behavioral Disturbance (DSM code 294.10): Cognitive disturbance accompanied by clinically significant behavioral disturbance (such as wandering, agitation)

Specify with Early Onset (onset at age sixty-five years or younger) or with Late Onset (onset after age sixty-five) growth factor (NGF) into the brain to stimulate brain cell growth in rats.

CHEMICAL DEFICIENCIES. AD brains have lower levels of neurotransmitters responsible for cognitive functions and behavior. Acetylcholine is a neurotransmitter that is found in lower levels in the AD brain than in normally functioning brains. Scientists have seen slight, temporary cognitive improvement when acetylcholine levels in AD patients have been increased.

ENVIRONMENT. Metals such as aluminum and zinc have been found in brain tissue of people with AD. Researchers are studying these and other environmental factors to discover their relationship to AD development.

DIAGNOSIS

There is no single reliable biological test to diagnose AD; therefore, criteria to assist primary care providers in diagnosing AD have been established to differentiate between AD and other forms of dementia. One such guideline has been established by the Agency for Health Care Policy and Research (AHCPR). Any positive response to six identified areas warrants a workup for dementia. New diagnostic tools and criteria make it possible for health care providers to make a positive clinical diagnosis of AD with around 90 percent accuracy.

Diagnostic criteria for AD includes dementia, history, physical and mental examinations consistent with AD, normal blood tests, and medications that are not the cause of dementia. Brain imaging study—computed tomography (CT) or magnetic resonance imaging (MRI)—is normal or shows brain atrophy.

A medical history provides information about mental or physical conditions, prescription drugs, and family health history. A physical examination evaluates nutritional status, blood pressure, and pulse. A neurological examination evaluates for neurological disorders. The Mini-Mental State Examination (MMSE) and Addenbrooke's Cognitive Examination (ACE) are instruments used to evaluate AD.

Blood and urine tests evaluate for other causes of dementia. Psychiatric evaluation assesses mood and emotional factors that mimic dementia. A neuropsychological assessment evaluates memory, sense of time and place, and ability to understand, communicate, and do simple calculations.

MRI and CT scans of the brain assess for the possibility of other potential causes of dementia, such as stroke, Huntington's disease, or Parkinson's disease.

Early diagnosis of AD is important to determine the proper treatment and to detect underlying diseases such as depression, drug interactions, vitamin deficiencies, or endocrine problems. These diseases may be reversible if detected early. A definitive diagnosis of AD can only be confirmed on autopsy.

FOUR STAGES OF AD

Early-stage AD is recognized when one exhibits recent memory loss, mild aphasia, avoidance of the unfamiliar, difficulty writing, and necessity for reminders to perform ADLs such as dressing, washing, brushing one's teeth, and combing one's hair. Apathy and depression are common.

Middle-stage AD is recognized when one exhibits routine recent memory loss, moderate aphasia, getting lost in familiar surroundings, repetitive actions, apraxia, mood and behavior disturbances, and necessity for reminders and help with ADLs.

Late-stage AD is recognized when one misidentifies familiar people and places, is bradykinesic (exhibits slowness of movement and general muscle rigidity), frequently falls, has more frequent mood and behavior disturbances, and needs help with all ADLs.

Terminal-stage AD is recognized when one has no association to past or present, is mute or enunciates few coherent words, is oblivious to surroundings, has little spontaneous movement, is dysphagic (has difficulty swallowing), exhibits passive mood and behavior, and needs total care.

DSM-IV divides Alzheimer's disease into subtypes that represent the predominant features of the clinical presentation: with delirium, with delusions, with depressed mood, and uncomplicated. "With behavioral disturbance" can also be used to indicate the presence of difficulties such as wandering or combativeness.

TREATMENT

The principal goal of treatment is to slow AD progression, provide a safe environment, maintain function as long as possible, and provide emotional support for the patient and family through social services and support groups. However, the treatment of dementia varies according to the stage of the disease and is focused on management of symptoms because no cure exists. It is of utmost importance to educate the patient and family about AD, its course, ramifications, and treatment options. Treatment includes both patient and caregivers. In early stages of AD, patients and their families may need counseling to deal with a sense of loss; be made aware of support groups, respite care, and other social services that are available to them; and be introduced to legal considerations in making decisions about future care needs such as medical and financial powers of attorney and a living will. As more supervision is required, caregivers need to be aware of physical dangers that can result from memory loss, such as fires from unattended stoves or burning cigarettes, malnutrition from "forgetting" to eat and difficulty swallowing, increased risk for falls related to confusion, disorientation, and declining motor function as well as issues about driving related to poor motor and cognitive function. Caregivers should also be aware of the patient's finances, to assist in paying and recording bills and planning for future care needs. During late-stage AD, the family may need assistance in preparing for the patient's death. Hospice care should be discussed, as it provides for physical care and comfort for the patient and emotional support for the family.

PHARMACEUTICAL THERAPY

Pharmaceutical agents used to slow the progression of AD include acetyl-cholinesterase inhibitors (tacrine, donepezil, rivastigmine, and galanta-mine). These agents block the breakdown of neurotransmitters in the brain and are used to lessen symptoms of mild to moderate AD. Their action extends cognitive function and improves behavioral symptoms for twelve months up to two years. Vitamin E or selegiline delays the progression of AD. Estrogen has been associated with a decreased risk of AD and enhanced cognitive functioning. Its antioxidant and anti-inflammatory effects enhance the growth of neuron processes for memory function. Ginkgo biloba has provided moderate cognitive improvement with few ill effects. Delusions and hallucinations often develop in moderately impaired patients. In the absence of agitation or combativeness, the best treatment is reassurance and distraction. Delusions and hallucinations accompanied by agitation and combativeness can be treated with low doses of antipsychotic or antidepressant medications. Medications may also be used to control wandering, anxiety, insomnia, and depression.

COMPLICATIONS

People with AD do not die from AD but from complications that result from the disease. The most common cause of death in AD is pneumonia. Difficulty swallowing increases the risk of inhaling foods and liquids into the lungs, which then may cause aspiration and pneumonia. The risk of falling is increased by disorientation, confusion, and declining motor function. Falls can lead to fractures and head injuries. Surgical intervention and immobilization also present risks for additional life-threatening complications in the elderly. Memory loss may result in fires from unattended stoves or burning cigarettes or malnutrition from "forgetting" to eat.

PREVENTION

Studies have supported that regular use of nonsteroidal anti-inflammatory drugs (NSAIDs) such as ibuprofen (Advil, Motrin, Nuprin), naproxen sodium (Aleve), and indomethacin (Indocin) may reduce AD risk by 30 to 60 percent.

Researchers are also studying the antioxidant affects of vitamin E and selegiline hydrochloride in preventing brain damage caused by toxic free radicals to slow the rate of progression of AD. Studies of estrogen replacement therapy in menopausal women showed a reduced risk of developing AD by 30 to 40 percent. In 2002, a synthetic form of beta-amyloid protein (AN-1792) vaccine was being investigated in clinical trials.

RESEARCH FOR THE FUTURE

The National Institutes of Health's Alzheimer's Disease Prevention Initiative was organized to investigate pharmacological interventions and to identify factors that will assist in early recognition of AD and delay the development of AD. A collaborative association with federal and private agencies has allowed for diverse investigations that include biologic and epidemiologic research; instrument development to identify high-risk individuals, facilitating clinical trials; and researching alternate strategies to treat behavioral disturbances in AD patients.

New drugs to reduce symptoms of AD are being studied in clinical trials. Other research is being done to identify factors related to patients' and caregivers' coping and stress as well as support mechanisms in dealing with progressive nature of AD.

SOURCES FOR FURTHER STUDY

Hamdy, Ronald, James Turnball, and Joellyn Edwards. *Alzheimer's Disease: A Handbook for Caregivers.*New York: Mosby, 1998. Causes, symptoms, stages, and treatment options for AD are discussed.

Karlin, Nancy, J. Paul, A. Bell, and Jody L. Noah. "Long-Term Consequences of the Alzheimer's Caregiver Role: A Qualitative Analysis." *American Journal of Alzheimer's Disease* (May/June, 2001): 177-182. Examines caregivers' adaptation to the role of caregiver, caregiver burden and coping, social support issues, and positive and negative experiences created by unplanned changes brought on by AD.

Leon, J., C. Cheng, and P. Neumann. "Alzheimer's Disease Care: Costs and Potential Savings." *Health Affiliates* (November/December, 1998): 206-216. Identifies the economic impact of caring for and treating those with AD.

Mace, M., and P. Rabins. *The Thirty-Six-Hour Day: A Family Guide to Caring for Persons with Alzheimer Disease, Related Dementing Illnesses, and Memory Loss in Later Life.* Baltimore: Johns Hopkins University Press, 1999. Discusses what dementia is, physical and psychological problems, effects on caregivers, financial and legal issues, and long-range care planning for AD sufferers.

Powell, L., and K. Courtice. *Alzheimer's Disease: A Guide for Families and Caregivers.* Cambridge, Mass.: Perseus, 2001. Provides information about early signs, tests, diagnosis, and treatment research for AD. Also provides insight into the emotional aspects experienced by caregivers, with advice on communication, safety, and long-term care issues for AD suffers.

St. George-Hyslop, Peter H. "Piecing Together Alzheimer's." *Scientific American* (December, 2000): 76-83. Good description of AD, symptoms, support, and research in the quest for a cure.

Terry, R., R. Katzman, K. Bick, and S. Sisodia. *Alzheimer Disease.* 2d ed. Philadelphia: Lippincott Williams & Wilkins, 1999. An in-depth review of hereditary links, signs and symptoms, diagnosis, and treatment for AD.

Sharon Wallace Stark

SEE ALSO: Aging: Cognitive Changes; Brain Structure; Dementia; Parkinson's Disease.

Amnesia and Fugue

TYPE OF PSYCHOLOGY: Psychopathology
FIELD OF STUDY: Coping

The inability to totally or partially recall or identify a past experience is called amnesia. A fugue is an extensive escape from life's problems that involves an amnesiac state and actual flight from familiar surroundings. During a fugue, a new partial or entire identity may be assumed. Both fugue and amnesia involve the concept of dissociation.

KEY CONCEPTS
- behavioral explanation
- continuous amnesia
- dissociation
- dissociative disorders
- generalized amnesia
- localized amnesia
- psychodynamic explanation
- psychogenic amnesia
- selective amnesia

Amnesia involves the failure to recall a past experience because of an anxiety that is associated with the situation. Fugue states take place when a person retreats from life's difficulties by entering an amnesic state and leaving familiar surroundings. During a fugue state, a person may assume a new partial or whole personality. Although amnesia may be caused by organic brain pathology, attempts to cope with anxiety can produce amnesia and fugue. The concept of dissociation refers to the ability of the human mind to split from conscious awareness. Through dissociation, a person can avoid anxiety and difficulty in managing life stresses. When stress and anxiety overwhelm a person, the mind may split from a conscious awareness of the troubling situations. When this takes place, the individual automatically loses memory of the event and may physically leave the stressful situation through a fugue state.

Amnesia and fugue are two of the dissociative disorders recognized by the American Psychiatric Association. The dissociative disorders are methods of avoiding anxiety through the process of pathological dissociation. In addition to amnesia and fugue, the dissociative disorders include dissociative identity disorder and depersonalization disorder. In the former, a person develops a number of alter identities. This disorder was previously called multiple personality disorder. Depersonalization disorder involves a process in which individuals suddenly feel that their bodies or senses of self have changed dramatically.

AMNESIA TYPES

Another term for dissociative amnesia is psychogenic amnesia. This conveys the concept that the amnesia is not due to organic brain pathology. Individuals developing psychogenic or dissociative amnesia often encounter a traumatic event or extreme stress that overloads their coping abilities. Four different types of psychogenic or dissociative amnesia can be identified. Localized amnesia is seen when a person cannot remember anything about a specific event. This is often seen after a person experiences a very traumatic event, such as a serious accident, and then does not recall what happened. The second type of amnesia is called selective amnesia and occurs when only some parts of a certain time period are forgotten. Infrequently, generalized amnesia takes place, and the person forgets his or her entire life history. The fourth type of dissociative amnesia is the continuous type. This form of amnesia is seen when a person does not remember anything beyond a certain point in the past.

DIAGNOSIS

It is difficult to report reliable data on the prevalence of dissociative disorders, but it appears that women are diagnosed with the dissociative disorders at a rate five times that of men.

To make the diagnosis of dissociative amnesia, a doctor must identify a disturbance in memory that involves the appearance of one or more episodes of inability to recall important personal information that is usually of a traumatic or stressful nature. The memory loss must be too extensive to be explained by ordinary forgetfulness. When people develop dissociative amnesia, they may not be able to remember their own names or the identities of relatives, but they retain a number of significant abilities. In psychogenic or dissociative amnesia, basic habits and skills remain intact. Thus, the person is still able to read a book, drive a car, and recognize familiar objects. The memories that are lost revolve around life events and autobiographical information.

The diagnosis of dissociative fugue requires sudden, unexpected travel away from the home or customary place of work. Together with this travel, the person is unable to recall the past. During the fugue, the person shows confusion about personal identity or assumes a new one. The person's activities at the time of the fugue can vary extensively, from short-term involvement in new interests to traveling to distant locations and assuming a new identity and work roles. The fugue can last for days, weeks, or even years. At some point, the individual will leave the fugue state and be in a strange place without awareness of the events that took place during the dissociative period. When a fugue state is taking place, the person appears normal to others and can complete complex tasks. Usually, the activities selected by the person are indicative of a different lifestyle from the previous one.

The diagnosis of dissociative amnesia and fugue can be controversial because it often depends upon self-reports. The possibility that a person is fak-

DSM-IV-TR CRITERIA FOR AMNESIA AND FUGUE

DISSOCIATIVE AMNESIA (DSM CODE 300.12)

Predominant disturbance is one or more episodes of inability to recall important personal information, usually of a traumatic or stressful nature, too extensive to be explained by ordinary forgetfulness

Disturbance not occurring exclusively during the course of Dissociative Identity Disorder, Dissociative Fugue, Post-traumatic Stress Disorder, Acute Stress Disorder, or Somatization Disorder and not due to direct physiological effects of a substance or a neurological or other general medical condition

Symptoms cause clinically significant distress or impairment in social, occupational, or other important areas of functioning

DEPERSONALIZATION DISORDER (DSM CODE 300.6)

Persistent or recurrent experiences of feeling detached from, and as if an outside observer of, one's mental processes or body (such as feeling in a dream)

During depersonalization experience, reality testing remains intact

Depersonalization causes clinically significant distress or impairment in social, occupational, or other important areas of functioning

Experience not occurring exclusively during the course of another mental disorder, such as Schizophrenia, Panic Disorder, Acute Stress Disorder, or another Dissociative Disorder, and not due to direct physiological effects of a substance or general medical condition

DISSOCIATIVE FUGUE (DSM CODE 300.13)

Predominant disturbance is sudden, unexpected travel away from home or one's customary place of work, with inability to recall one's past

Confusion about personal identity or assumption of new identity (partial or complete)

Disturbance not occurring exclusively during course of Dissociative Identity Disorder and not due to direct physiological effects of a substance or general medical condition such as temporal lobe epilepsy

Symptoms cause clinically significant distress or impairment in social, occupational, or other important areas of functioning

DISSOCIATIVE IDENTITY DISORDER (DSM CODE 300.14)

Presence of two or more distinct identities or personality states, each with its own relatively enduring pattern of perceiving, relating to, and thinking about the environment and self

At least two of these identities or personality states recurrently take control of person's behavior

Inability to recall important personal information too extensive to be explained by ordinary forgetfulness

Disturbance not due to direct physiological effects of a substance (such as blackouts or chaotic behavior during alcohol intoxication) or general medical condition (such as complex partial seizures); in children, symptoms not attributable to imaginary playmates or other fantasy play ing the symptoms must be considered. Objective diagnostic measures for these disorders do not exist. The possibility of malingering or fabricating the symptoms must be considered in arriving at a diagnosis of dissociative amnesia and fugue.

When diagnosing dissociative amnesia and fugue, a number of other disorders and conditions have to be excluded. A number of medical conditions such as vitamin deficiency, head trauma, carbon monoxide poisoning, and herpes encephalitis can produce similar symptoms. Amnesia can also be found in conjunction with alcoholism and the use of other drugs.

POSSIBLE CAUSES

Normal dissociation is often differentiated from pathological dissociation. Normal dissociation can be an adaptive way to handle a traumatic incident. It is commonly seen as a reaction to war and civil disasters. In normal dissociation, the person's perception of the traumatic experience is temporarily dulled or removed from the conscious mind. Pathological dissociation is an extreme reaction of splitting the anxiety-provoking situation from consciousness.

There exist a limited number of research studies that seek to explain the causes of dissociation in certain individuals and predict what persons are vulnerable to the development of dissociative amnesia or fugue during periods of trauma or overwhelming stress. The psychodynamic explanation emphasizes the use of repression as a defense against conscious awareness of the stressful or traumatic event. Entire chunks of the person's identity or past experiences are split from the conscious mind as a way to avoid painful memories or conflicts. According to this explanation, some individuals are vulnerable to the use of dissociation because of their early childhood experiences of trauma or abuse. With the early experience of abuse, the child learns to repress the memories or engage in a process of self-hypnosis. The hypnotic state permits the child to escape the stress associated with the abuse or neglect. The abused child feels a sense of powerlessness in the face of repeated abuse and splits from this conscious awareness. This isolation of the stressful event leads to the development of different memory processes from those found in normal child development.

A behavioral explanation for the likely development of dissociation as a means to cope with stressful events focuses on the rewarding aspects of dissociative symptoms. The child learns to role-play and engage in selective attention to recognize certain environmental cues that provide rewards. Stressful circumstances are blocked out and disturbing thoughts ignored. Eventually, this process expands into a tendency to assume new roles and block out stressful situations.

The dissociative disorders appear to be influenced by sociocultural factors which are dependent upon social attitudes and cultural norms. Acceptance and toleration of the symptoms associated with dissociative disorders depend upon prevailing societal attitudes. Over time, cultures vary in the acceptance of dissociative symptoms and the manifestation of amnesia and fugue states. For example, historical reports of spirit possession can be interpreted as the experience of a fugue state.

TREATMENT

The symptoms associated with dissociative amnesia and fugue usually spontaneously disappear over time. As the experience of stress begins to lessen, the amnesia and fugue often disappear. When providing treatment for these individuals, it is important that caregivers provide a safe environment which removes them from the possible sources of stress. Some persons are hospitalized for this reason. The institutional setting allows them to regain comfort away from the traumatizing or stress-producing situation. Occasionally the memory loss can be retrieved through the use of specific medications. One such medication is sodium amytal, which can be used during an interview process that attempts to restore the lost memories. Hypnosis is also used as a means to put the person in a receptive state for questions that may overcome the amnesia.

Hypnosis is also used in the treatment of fugue states. The goal when using hypnosis is to access important memories that may have triggered the fugue. Medications are sometimes used with patients who have a history of fugue. Antianxiety medications, called benzodiazepines, have been utilized with individuals showing dissociative fugue. The medication helps to alleviate the feelings of worry and apprehension.

Because amnesia does not typically interfere with a person's daily functioning, few specific complaints about the lack of memory take place. Individuals may complain about other psychological symptoms but not the amnesia. Consequently, treatment often does not focus on the lost memories. Some of the associated symptoms that occur with amnesia include depression and stress due to a fugue state. Treatment is often directed toward alleviating the depression and teaching a person stress management techniques.

SOURCES FOR FURTHER STUDY

Lewis, D., C. Yeager, Y. Swica, J. Pincus, and H. Lewis. "Objective Documentation of Child Abuse and Dissociation in Twelve Murderers." *American Journal of Psychiatry* 154 (1997): 1703-1710. This research study reports on the relationship between early child abuse and later dissociation. The article investigated a unique sample of murderers in coming to its conclusions.

Lowenstein, R. "Psychogenic Amnesia and Psychogenic Fugue." In *Review of Psychiatry*, edited by A. Tasman and S. Goldfinger. New York: American Psychiatric Press, 1991. Provides a review of the scientific investigations into the causes of psychogenic amnesia and fugue.

Lynn, S., and J. Rhue. *Dissociation: Clinical and Theoretical Perspectives.* New York: Guilford Press, 1994. This volume comprises a number of chapters written by experts in the study of dissociation. The contributors place great emphasis on the role of trauma in producing vulnerability for dissociation as a defense in adulthood.

Michelson, L, and W. Ray. *Handbook of Dissociation: Theoretical, Empirical, and Clinical Perspectives.* New York: Plenum Press, 1996. Provides an extensive explanation of dissociation with multiple examples. It is written for a reader who needs detailed research and clinical information.

Putnam, F. *Dissociation in Children and Adolescents.* New York: Guilford Press, 1997. This is a useful book for information on the manifestation of normal dissociation in children and teenagers and how normal dissociation can evolve into pathological dissociation, which signals the development of the dissociative disorders.

Sackeim, H., and W. Vingiano. "Dissociative Disorders." In *Adult Psychopathology and Diagnosis,* edited by S. Turner and M. Hersen. New York: John Wiley & Sons, 1984. The importance of treating other psychological symptoms is discussed in this chapter. Persons with dissociative disorders often show depression that should receive treatment.

Sadovsky, R. "Evaluation of Patients with Transient Global Amnesia." *American Family Physician* 57 (1998): 2237-2238. One of the medical conditions that has symptoms similar to those of dissociative amnesia is transient global amnesia. This article, which is written for physicians, provides the specifics for making a differential diagnosis.

Tulving, E. "What Is Episodic Memory?" *Current Directions in Psychological Science* 2 (1993): 67-70. This article is useful for understanding the different forms of memory loss that are seen in dissociative amnesia.

Tutkun, H., V. Sar, L. Yargic, and T. Ozpulat. "Frequency of Dissociative Disorders Among Psychiatric Inpatients in a Turkish University Clinic." *American Journal of Psychiatry* 155 (1998): 800-805. The dissociative disorders vary in incidence across countries. This article provides information concerning the reasons for the differences between cultural groups.

Frank J. Prerost

SEE ALSO: Brain Structure; Memory; Memory: Animal Research.

ANALYTIC PSYCHOLOGY

JACQUES LACAN

TYPE OF PSYCHOLOGY: Personality

FIELDS OF STUDY: Classic analytic themes and issues; humanistic-phenomenological models; personality theory; psychodynamic and neoanalytic models; thought

Lacan, a pioneering psychoanalyst who emphasized the relationship between language and the unconscious, radically reinterpreted Freud in light of philosophy and structuralist linguistics. Lacan's theories of the unconscious (that it is "structured like a language") and the mirror phase have significantly reshaped the discourse of psychoanalysis and cultural theory.

KEY CONCEPTS

- desire
- falsifying character of the ego
- imaginary
- imaginary misidentification/*méconnaissance*
- *jouissance*
- lack/manque
- little object *a*/*objet petit a*
- mirror stage
- real
- symbolic

According to Freudian psychoanalysis, desire is biological and driven by sexual force, or libido. Jacques Lacan (1901-1981), on the other hand, regarded desire as a drive for an original ontological unity which can never be achieved because of the psychic split resulting from what he called "the mirror stage" as well as the Freudian Oedipal phase. Desire emerges from this split or "lack" which it tries, continually, to fill. Desire expresses itself through language.

Lacan believed that his form of psychoanalysis was not a departure from, but a return to, the original principles of Freudian analysis. Lacan's readers have long complained about the difficulty of his prose, which is characterized by a seeming lack of linearity and an often impenetrable style. Many of Lacan's commentators have likened his discursive style to a rebus or puzzle, designed to communicate the idea that no "truth" about psychic life can ever be wholly and fully expressed through language because the psyche is always split against itself, and language is the result of absence and difference.

THE MIRROR STAGE

Central to Lacanian psychoanalysis is the celebrated mirror stage. Lacan argues that a child's ego only begins to emerge in the ages between six months and eighteen months, when the child first sees its own reflection in a mirror. This experience is illusory, according to Lacan, because the child's actual experience of its own body is never that of a clearly delineated whole in the child's full control. Lacan's observations on the so-called mirror stage relied heavily upon the earlier work of the American psychologist and philosopher James Mark Baldwin (1861-1934).

Desire emerges from the perceived distance between the actual or lived experience of the child's own body and the reflection it first sees in the mirror. The child envies the perfection of the mirror image or the mirroring response of its parents, says Lacan, and this lack, or manque, is permanent because there will always be a gap or existential distance between the subjective experience of the body and the complete image in the mirror, or the apparent wholeness of others.

Desire begins at the mirror stage in the psychic development of the young child. The apparent completeness of the reflected image gives the otherwise helpless child a sense of mastery over its own body, but this sense of self-mastery is as illusory as it is frustrating. Lacan urged his fellow psychoanalysts to reassess their focus on the patient's ego and turn their attention back to the unconscious because of what he termed "the falsifying character of the ego." Lacan argued that psychoanalysis should "return to Freud" and abandon its fascination with the ultimately untrustworthy ego of the patient.

Lacan believed that his theory of the "mirror stage" answered two fundamental questions raised by Sigmund Freud's 1914 essay, "On Narcissism": What "psychical action" takes place to bring the ego into being? If one is not a narcissist from the earliest stages of life, what causes narcissism to emerge? According to Lacan, the mechanism of the mirror stage answers both of these questions.

THE OEDIPUS COMPLEX

Lacan, like Freud, believed that individuals are socialized by passing through the three stages of the Oedipus complex: seduction, the "primal scene," and the castration phase, the last of which Lacan reconfigured as the "Father's 'No'." In the so-called seduction phase, the child is attracted to the original object of desire, which is the body of the mother. In the "primal scene" or "primal stage" the child witnesses the father having sexual intercourse with the mother, and this is followed by the "castration phase," wherein the father restricts the child's access to the mother under threat of castration. The "Law of the Father" or "Father's 'No'" causes the child to redirect desire from the mother to what Lacan calls the "Other"—a hypothetical "place" in the unconscious which allows the individual to later project desire onto other persons—other, that is, than the mother.

Lacan holds that there are three "registers" in the child's psychosexual development: the imaginary, the symbolic, and the real. These correspond—somewhat—to the Freudian oral, anal, and genital stages and are related, indirectly, to the three stages of the Oedipus complex.

At the level of the imaginary, the pre-Oedipal infant inhabits a world without clear subject-object distinctions. The child thinks that it is coextensive with the mother's body. While the child perceives the mother's body as nurturing and pleasurable, it also entertains fantasies that the mother's body might overwhelm and destroy it. This yields alternating fantasies of incorporation and assault, whereby the child is both blissful in its identification with the body of the mother and frightfully aggressive toward it. At this stage in its development, the child inhabits a world of images. The mirror stage is the most important moment of imaginary misidentification, or *méconnaissance*.

It is the father who disrupts the closed dyadic relationship between mother and child, according to Lacan. The father signifies what Lacan calls "the Law" or the "Law of the Father," which is always, in the first instance, the incest taboo. The child's intensely libidinal relationship with its mother's body is opened to the wider world of family and society by the figure of the father. The father's appearance divides the child from the mother's body and drives the child's desire for its mother into the unconscious. Therefore "the Law" and unconscious desire for the mother emerge at the same time, according to Lacanian psychoanalysis.

The child's experience of the father's presence is also its first experience of sexual difference, and with it comes the dim awareness that there is someone else other than the mother in its world. The "Father's 'No'" deflects the child's desire from the mother to what Lacan calls the "Other." Lacan identified the "Other" as a hypothetical place in the unconscious which can be projected onto human counterparts by subjects. Lacan held that the "Other" is never fully grasped because the nature of desire is such that its object is always beyond its reach.

LANGUAGE AND THE SYMBOLIC

This is the point at which the child enters the register of the symbolic. It is at this stage, according to Lacan, that the child also enters the "language system." Absence, lack, and separation characterize the language system, according to Lacan, because language names things which are not immediately present ("signifieds") and substitutes words ("signifiers") for them. This is also the beginning of socialization, says Lacan. Just as the child realizes that sexual identity is the result of an originary difference between mother and father, it comes to grasp that language itself is an unending chain of "differences," and that the terms of language are what they are only by excluding one another. Signs always presuppose the absence of the objects they signify—an insight which Lacan inherited from structuralist anthropology and linguistics.

The loss of the precious object that is the mother's body drives desire to seek its satisfaction in incomplete or partial objects, none of which can ever fully satisfy the longing bred by the loss of the maternal body. People try vainly to settle for substitute objects, or what Lacan calls the "object little *a*." Lacan's thinking was heavily influenced by structuralist thinkers such as the anthropologist Claude Lévi-Strauss (b. 1908) and linguists Ferdinand de Saussure (1857-1913) and Roman Jakobson (1896-1982). Lacan's chief claim, based upon his readings of Saussure and Jakobson, is that the unconscious is "structured like a language." Lacan refashioned Freud's terminology of psychic condensation and displacement by translating them into what Lacan believed to be their equivalent rhetorical terms: metaphor and metonymy. Metaphor works by condensing two separate images into a single symbol through substitution, while metonymy operates by association— using a part to represent the whole (such as "crown" for "king") or using contiguous elements (such as "sea" and "boat").

The presence of the father teaches the child that it must assume a predefined social and familial role over which it exercises no control—a role which is defined by the sexual difference between mother and father, the exclusion of the child from the sexual relationship which exists between the mother and the father, and the child's relinquishment of the earlier and intense bonds which existed between itself and the mother's body. This situation of absence, exclusion, and difference is symbolized by the phallus, a universal signifier or metonymic presence which indicates the fundamental lack or absence which lies at the heart of being itself—the *manque à être*, as Lacan calls it.

THE REAL AND JOUISSANCE

Finally, Lacan posits a register called "the real"—not the empirical world but the ineffable realm of constancy beyond the field of speech. According to Lacan, the "reality" which is given to consciousness is no more and no less than an amalgam of the imaginary (the specular and imagistic world of the rationalizing ego, with all of its self-delusions, defenses, and falsifications) and the symbolic (the meaningful social world of language). Lacan resists defining the real in any explicit or easily codifiable way. In his later work in the 1960's Lacan discussed the register of the real in light of his work on *jouissance*, a term which is loosely translated as "enjoyment" but which is much more complex.

According to Lacan, *jouissance* is any experience which is too much for the organism to bear. More often than not it is experienced as suffering—an unbearable pain which is experienced as a kind of satisfaction by the unconscious drives. According to Lacan, this is what lies at the heart of the Freudian "repetition compulsion," namely an unconscious, and unconsciously satisfying, wish to suffer. Healthy human life is about the regulation of *jouissance*. Children's bodies are prone to overexcitation and overstimulation because they are full of *jouissance*, which is slowly drained from the body of the child after its encounter with the "Law of the Father" and its entry into the register of the symbolic. Portions of *jouissance* linked to especially intense bodily memories from childhood can become "caught" or centered in the body and manifest as symptoms. Lacan reconfigured Freud's theory of castration by redefining it as the loss of *jouissance* from the body. More broadly,

Lacan says that the entry into language itself is castration because it introduces the idea of lack or absence into the world.

LACANIAN CLINICAL PRACTICE

For Lacan, human subjects construct themselves through language. One of the chief goals of Lacanian clinical practice is to create a space wherein the patient can experience and release *jouissance* through speech without the disintegration of the his or her sense of self. The analyst will then determine where a patient lies on a diagnostic continuum—neurotic (obsessional or hysteric), perverse, or psychotic.

Psychotic patients, according to Lacanian analysis, are most greatly disconnected at the level of language, or the symbolic. The Lacanian analyst works with the disjointed speech of the psychotic to allow him or her to live within and to express, through language, the world of signifiers without significant discontinuity.

The perverse patient, on the other hand, is often drawn to a fetish object. The fetish object is a compliant one, and it allows the patient to experience *jouissance* without having to relive the experience of castration which was attendant upon the "Father's 'No.'" The perverse patient engages in an act of substitution, whereby a complicit object grants a sense of release—a real or simulated experience of *jouissance*—while allowing him or her to avoid the painful sense of separation from the Other, or the presymbolic mother.

The obsessional neurotic fears loss of control. Obsessional neurotics struggle to control and contain the upwelling of desire and the accompanying experience of *jouissance*. The obsessional neurotic speaks the language of mastery and order and attempts to exercise control well beyond his or her purview. The analyst is sensitive to dichotomizing tendencies in the patient's speech (order and disorder, right and wrong). According to Lacan, the patient's fantasy is that the upwelling of *jouissance* will alienate those around him or her and leave havoc in its wake. The analyst works with the obsessional neurotic to help the patient meet his or her needs without limiting defenses—to experience and speak desire without the fear of losing self-control.

Hysterics experience a deep and debilitating sense of lack which leads to a feeling of alienation from the Other. Once the hysteric obtains the imaginary object of the mother's desire, he or she wishes to be rid of it—sometimes almost violently. The goal of Lacanian analysis when working with hysterics is to move them beyond the dichotomy of having/not having, to help them to achieve satisfactory levels of comfort with themselves, and to find a neutral space where the sense of lack is not all-consuming.

THE CASE OF AIMÉE

Lacan's early work on paranoia dealt with the case of a patient he called Aimée (Marguerite Anzieu) who was arrested by the Paris police in the attempted stabbing of a famous actress, Huguette Duflos. Lacan first encountered Aimée in 1931 at Sainte-Anne's Hospital, where he had begun his clinical training as a *légiste medicale,* or forensic psychiatrist, four years earlier. Lacan's patient, the subject of numerous press accounts and much public speculation, had come to believe that her young son was about to be murdered by Duflos. One night Aimée attended a play which featured the famous Parisian actress and suddenly lunged from the crowd of theatergoers, brandishing a knife. Aimée was promptly arrested and given over to Lacan's care.

Lacan conducted an exhaustive number of analytic interviews with Aimée. Lacan was able to reconstruct the trajectory of Aimée's descent into what he termed self-punishment paranoia. Aimée both feared and admired Duflos, and she came to believe that the actress—really her ideal image of the actress—posed a danger to her and to her young child. Duflos's ideal image was the object of Aimée's intense hatred as well as her excessive fascination, writes Lacan, and in attacking Duflos the deluded woman was really punishing herself.

In one especially striking memory, Aimée recalled (falsely) reading an article in a newspaper in which the actress told an interviewer that she was planning to kill Aimée and her young son. Aimée therefore regarded her attack on Duflos as an act of preemptive self-defense based upon a misrecognition. Aimée finally found the real punishment she unconsciously craved (her *jouissance*) in her public humiliation, arrest, and confinement.

Lacan was struck by the relationship between memory (or, in this case, false memory) and identity. One sees in Lacan's early analysis of Aimée many of the most significant elements of his psychoanalytic theory, including the mirror stage, the imaginary, *jouissance* and its role in paranoia, and the power of misidentification.

Lacan's detailed analysis of "the case of Aimée" in his 1932 doctoral thesis, *De la psychose paranoiaque dans les rapports avec la personnalité* (paranoid psychosis and its relations to the personality), laid the groundwork for much of his later work on the nature of identity, the genesis of narcissism, the power of the image, and the fundamentally social character of personality. From 1933 onward, Lacan was known as a specialist in the diagnosis and treatment of paranoia. His densely textured doctoral dissertation was widely circulated among artists and poets identified with the Surrealist movement, and Lacan wrote regularly for *Minotaure,* a Surrealist review published between 1933 and 1939 by Albert Skira. Many of Lacan's interpreters regard his work with philosopher Alexandre Kojève (1902-1968) as a theoretical turning point and the genesis of his thinking on the psychological significance of lack, loss, and absence.

In 1936 Lacan presented his paper "Le Stade du miroir" (the mirror stage) at the fourteenth International Psychoanalytical Congress, held at Marienbad in August of 1936 under the chairmanship of the preeminent British psychoanalyst Ernest Jones. It is in this seminal essay, since lost, that Lacan outlined his theory of the mirror stage. His theory of self-mastery through mimicry, in which the young child responds to its prematuration or defenselessness by identifying with images outside itself, was influenced by the anthropological insights of Roger Caillois (1913-1978).

Lacan's radical revision of psychoanalysis, which he regarded as a "return to Freud," led to his eventual ejection from the Société Française de Psychanalyse (SFP) in 1963. Lacan founded a new school, first called the École Française de Psychanalyse and then later the École Freudienne de Paris (EFP). Lacan dissolved the EFP in 1980 and died a year later, leaving behind a body of work which continues to influence psychoanalytic studies, philosophy, and literary and cultural theory.

Sources for Further Study

Dor, Joel. *Introduction to the Reading of Lacan: The Unconscious Structured Like a Language*. New York: Other Press, 1998. A clearly written and accessible introduction. Includes a useful bibliography.

Evans, Dylan. *An Introductory Dictionary of Lacanian Psychoanalysis*. New York: Routledge, 1996. Evans defines more than two hundred technical terms in their historical contexts.

Fink, Bruce. *A Clinical Introduction to Lacanian Psychoanalysis: Theory and Technique*. Cambridge, Mass.: Harvard University Press, 1997. A practicing psychoanalyst clearly introduces Lacan in theory and in clinical practice. Includes an extensive bibliography.

Lacan, Jacques. *Écrits: A Selection*. Translated by Bruce Fink. New York: W. W. Norton, 2002. Lacan's selections from his "writings"—really transcriptions of his lectures and seminars. An important collection of seminal works.

Leader, Darian, and Judy Groves. *Introducing Lacan*. New York: Toten Books, 1995. A concise, clearly written, and entertaining introduction to Lacan's most important concepts. Written by Leader, a practicing Lacanian analyst, for the general reader and wittily illustrated by Groves.

Muller, John P., and William J. Richardson. *Lacan and Language: A Reader's Guide to "Écrits."* New York: International Universities Press, 1982. One of the earliest and most comprehensive introductions to Lacan's work, coauthored by a practicing analyst and a philosopher with psychoanalytic training.

Gerard O'Sullivan

SEE ALSO: Language; Psychoanalytic Psychology; Psychoanalytic Psychology and Personality: Sigmund Freud.

ANALYTICAL PSYCHOLOGY
CARL JUNG

TYPE OF PSYCHOLOGY: Personality
FIELD OF STUDY: Psychodynamic and neoanalytic models

Analytical psychology is one of the most complex theories of personality. It attempts to improve on Sigmund Freud's work by deemphasizing sexual instincts and the abnormal side of human nature. Three of its more significant contributions are the notions of psychological types, the concept of the collective unconscious, and the depiction of the unconscious self as the most critical structure within the psyche.

KEY CONCEPTS
- anima and animus
- archetypes
- collective unconscious
- conscious ego
- persona
- personal unconscious
- self
- shadow

Carl Gustav Jung (1875-1961) founded analytical psychology, perhaps the most complex major theory of personality. It includes the presentation and analysis of concepts and principles based on numerous disciplines within the arts and sciences. Because this complexity is combined with Jung's often awkward writing, the task of mastering his theory is a challenge even for experts in the field of personality. His key contribution was taking the study of psychology beyond the claims made by Sigmund Freud (1856-1939). Jung's emphasis on adult development and personality types and his willingness to break with strict Freudian teachings were major contributions within the history of psychology in general and personality in particular.

Jung's theory can best be understood by examining the key structures he proposes and the dynamics of personality. Jung divides the personality, or psyche, into three levels: At the conscious level, there is the conscious ego. The conscious ego lies at the center of consciousness. In essence, it is the conscious mind—one's identity from a conscious perspective. It is particularly important to the person whose unconscious self is not yet fully developed. As the unconscious self begins to develop, the importance of the conscious ego will diminish.

Beneath the conscious ego is the personal unconscious. This level involves material that has been removed from the consciousness of the person. This information may leave consciousness through forgetting or repression. Because the personal unconscious is close to the surface, which is consciousness, items in it may be recalled at a later date. The personal unconscious is similar to Freud's notion of the preconscious. Material within the personal unconscious is grouped into clusters called complexes. Each complex contains a person's thoughts, feelings, perceptions, and memories concerning particular concepts. For example, the mother complex contains all personal and ancestral experiences with the concept of mother. These experiences can be both good and bad.

The deepest level of the psyche is called the collective unconscious. This level contains the memory traces that have been passed down to all humankind as a function of evolutionary development. It includes tendencies to behave in specific ways, such as living in groups or using spoken language. While each individual has his or her own personal unconscious, all people share the same collective unconscious. The key structures within the collective unconscious that determine how people behave and respond to their environment are labeled archetypes. Each archetype enables people to express their unique status as human beings.

Carl Jung.
(Library of Congress)

ARCHETYPES

Archetypes are divided into major and minor archetypes. The major archetypes include the persona, animus, anima, shadow, and self. The persona is one's public personality, which one displays in order to be accepted by society. One's goal is to balance the needs of the persona with the desire to express one's true self. In contrast to the persona, the shadow represents the dark side of the psyche. It includes thoughts and feelings which the person typically does not express because they are not social. These cognitions can be held back on either a conscious or an unconscious level. The anima represents the feminine aspects of males, while the animus represents the masculine aspects of females. These archetypes have come about as a function of centuries of interactions between males and females. They have the potential to improve communication and understanding between males and females. Finally, the most important psychic structure in Jung's theory is the self. It is the archetype which provides the whole psyche with a sense of unity and stability. The major goal of each person's life is to optimize the development of the self.

PSYCHIC STRUCTURES AND PERSONALITIES

In an effort to optimize the development of the self, each person develops his or her own psychological type. Each type (Jung conceived of eight types) consists of a combination of a person's basic attitude and basic function. Jung's two attitudes are extroversion and introversion. These terms follow societal stereotypes, with the extrovert being outgoing and confident and the introvert being hesitant and reflective. These attitudes are combined with four basic functions, or ways of relating to the world. These functions are thinking, feeling, sensing, and intuiting, which are consistent with a general societal view of these terms. Jung used the possible combination of the attitudes and functions to form the eight possible psychological types. Each person is thought to have dominance within one of the available types.

In addition to providing key psychic structures, Jung provides personality dynamics. He claimed that each person is endowed with psychic or libidinal energy. Unlike Freud, however, Jung did not view this energy as strictly sexual. Rather, he perceived it as life-process energy encompassing all aspects of the psyche. According to Jung, this energy operates according to two principles of energy flow: equivalence and entropy. The principle of equivalence states that an increase in energy within one aspect of the psyche must be accompanied by a decrease in another area. For example, if psychic energy is increasing in the unconscious self, it must decrease elsewhere, such as in the conscious ego. The principle of entropy states that when psychic energy is unbalanced, it will seek a state of equilibrium. For example, it would not be desirable to have the majority of one's psychic energy located in the conscious ego. The energy needs of the other levels of consciousness must also be met.

Jung's psychic structures, along with his views on the dynamics of personality, have provided psychologists with a wealth of information to consider, many complexities to address, and numerous possible ways to apply his ideas to human development and personality assessment.

REALIZATION OF SELF

Jung made significant contributions to knowledge of areas such as human development and personality assessment. In terms of human development, Jung emphasized that personality development occurs throughout the life of the person. This was critical in that Freud's theory, the dominant theory at that time, emphasized the first five years of life in examining personality development. The overall goal of the person in Jung's approach to development is the realization of the self, which is a long and difficult process. Unlike Freud, Jung was particularly interested in development during the adulthood years. He emphasized the changes that occur beginning at the age of thirty-five or forty. He believed that this was often a time of crisis in the life of the person. This notion of a midlife crisis (which Jung experienced himself) has continued to be the source of significant theoretical and empirical claims.

Jung believed that the concept of a crisis during middle age was necessary and beneficial. Often, a person has achieved a certain level of material success and needs to find new meaning in life. This meaning can be realized by shifting from the material and physical concerns of youth to a more spiritual and philosophical view of life. The person seeks gradually to abandon the emphasis on the conscious ego which is dominant in youth. A greater balance between the unconscious and conscious is pursued. If this is successfully achieved, the person can reach a state of positive psychological health that Jung labels individuation. Perhaps the key to the midlife years in Jung's theory is that these are the years in which the person is attempting to discover the true meaning of life. Finally, Jung stated that religion can play an important role in life during the midlife and old-age years. During the midlife years, a sense of spirituality rather than materialism is important in personality development; looking at the possibility of life after death can be positive for the older adult.

ASSESSMENT TECHNIQUES

Jung made use of several interesting assessment techniques in addressing the problems of his patients. Like Freud, Jung was an advocate of the case-study method. He believed that much could be learned through an in-depth analysis of the problems of his patients. In his cases, Jung made extensive use of dream analysis. Jung maintained that dreams serve many purposes. They can be used to address and resolve current conflicts or to facilitate the development of the self. Dreams can therefore be oriented toward the future. While Freud focused his analysis on individual dreams, Jung would examine a group of dreams in order to uncover the problems of the patient. This examination of multiple dreams was viewed by Jung as a superior approach to gaining access to the deeper meanings of dreams, which could often be found in the collective unconscious.

Another important assessment device used by Jung which continues to have applications today is the word-association test. In this test, a person responds to a stimulus word with whatever comes to mind. Jung originally worked with a group of one hundred stimulus words and would focus on issues such as the response word given by the patient, the length of time it took the patient to respond, the provision of multiple responses, the repetition of the stimulus word, and the absence of a response. These and other factors could be used to establish the existence of an underlying neurosis as well as specific conflicts and complexes.

SPLIT WITH FREUD

The development of Jung's analytical psychology can be traced to the development of his relationship with Sigmund Freud and the subsequent split that occurred between the two theorists. In 1906 Jung published a book which concerned the psychoanalytic treatment of schizophrenia. He sent a copy of this book to Freud, who was thoroughly impressed by Jung's work. Jung became one of the strongest Freudian advocates from 1907 to 1912. During this time he collaborated with Freud and was viewed by many within psychoanalytic circles as the heir apparent to Freud. Jung had, in fact, been elected president of the prestigious International Psychoanalytic Association. In 1913 and 1914, however, he abandoned Freud and his psychoanalytic theory. Three basic problems led to this split. The first was Freud's emphasis on sexuality. Jung believed that while sexual instincts did exist, they should not be emphasized at the expense of other relevant aspects of the psyche. Second, Jung believed that Freud overemphasized abnormality. He maintained that Freud appeared to have little to say about the normal aspects of human nature. Finally, unlike Freud, Jung wished to emphasize the biology of the species rather than the biology of the individual.

The split between Freud and Jung was important for practical as well as theoretical reasons. Jung was rejected for a period of time by other analytically oriented thinkers because of his split with Freud. In addition, the break with Freud led Jung to experience a mental crisis which lasted for several years. This combination of factors eventually led Jung to conclude that he must develop his own view of the psyche, along with appropriate treatment techniques.

While the challenges encountered by Jung in his life were difficult to overcome, they clearly played a major role in his ability to develop the most complex theory of personality ever formulated. His key concepts and psychic structures, including the collective unconscious, personal unconscious, archetypes, self, and personality typology, continue to be among the most interesting theoretical contributions in the history of personality psychology.

Sources for Further Study

Brome, Vincent. *Jung: Man and Myth.* New York: Granada, 1980. This is a sound biography of Jung and discussion of his work. Perhaps its main advantage is that it provides an analysis which is fair to both Jung and his critics.

Freud, Sigmund, and C. G. Jung. *The Freud/Jung Letters.* Edited by William McGuire. Cambridge, Mass.: Harvard University Press, 1988. Provides a unique analysis of the development of the relationship between Freud and Jung. Accurately portrays the promise of unity and collaboration within the relationship in its early years, beginning around 1907, and exposes the problems that eventually led to the Freud/Jung split, which was complete by 1914. Provides a context for examining the remainder of Jung's work and the personal problems that he was to encounter following his split with Freud.

Hannah, Barbara. *Jung, His Life and Work: A Biographical Memoir.* Wilmette, Ill.: Chiron, 1997. This positive biographical view of Jung is provided by a Jungian analyst who was a friend and colleague of Jung for three decades. While it may not be as objectively written as other accounts, it has the advantage of being written by a scholar who had firsthand knowledge of many of Jung's ideas.

Jung, C. G. *Memories, Dreams, Reflections.* 1963. Reprint. New York: Vintage Books, 1989. Jung's autobiography. It thoroughly portrays the evolution of his thinking, including all those factors that were critical to his theoretical conceptions. Essential reading for anyone interested in gaining further insights into Jung and his work, even though his writing is often difficult to follow.

_____. *Psychological Types.* Rev. ed. London: Routledge, 1989. Provides both an overview of the basic principles of Jung's theory and an analysis of the derivation of the attitudes and functions that yield his psychological types. Particularly important to those who are interested in the derivation of Jung's view of typology.

Noll, Richard. *The Jung Cult: Origins of a Charismatic Movement.* New York: Free Press, 1997. Noll suggests that Jung's theories spawned not so much a psychology as a religious cult, based in nineteenth century occultism, neopaganism, and social Darwinism. Highly controversial.

Shamdasani, Sonu. *Cult Fictions: C. G. Jung and the Founding of Analytical Psychology.* New York: Routledge, 1998. A rebuttal to Noll's deconstruction of the "Jung Cult." Presents an accurate history of the foundation of analytical psychology both during and after Jung's life.

Lawrence A. Fehr

See also: Abnormality: Psychological Models; Analytical Psychotherapy; Dreams; Personality Theory; Psychoanalytic Psychology.

ANALYTICAL PSYCHOTHERAPY

TYPE OF PSYCHOLOGY: Psychotherapy
FIELD OF STUDY: Psychodynamic therapies

Analytical psychotherapy is associated with the theory and techniques of Carl Jung. Similar to other psychodynamic therapies, it stresses the importance of discovering unconscious material. Unique to this approach is the emphasis on reconciling opposite personality traits that are hidden in the personal unconscious and the collective unconscious.

KEY CONCEPTS
- collective unconscious
- compensatory function
- confession
- education
- elucidation
- method of active imagination
- method of amplification
- personal unconscious
- transference
- transformation

Analytical psychotherapy is an approach to psychological treatment pioneered by Carl Jung (1875-1961), a Swiss psychoanalyst. A follower of Sigmund Freud (1856-1939), Jung was trained in the psychoanalytic approach, with its emphasis on the dark, inaccessible material contained in the unconscious mind. Freud was fond of Jung and believed that he was to be the heir to the legacy Freud had begun. Jung began to disagree with certain aspects of Freud's theory, however, and he and Freud parted ways bitterly in 1914.

Jung's concept of the structure of personality, on which he based his ideas of psychotherapy, was obviously influenced by Freud and the psychoanalytic tradition, but he added his own personal and mystical touches to its concepts. Jung believed that the personality consists of the ego, which is one's conscious mind. It contains the thoughts, feelings, and perceptions of which one is normally aware. Jung also proposed a personal unconscious that contains events and emotions of which people remain unaware because of their anxiety-provoking nature. Memories of traumatic childhood events and conflicts may reside in the personal unconscious. Jung's unique contribution to personality theory is the idea of a collective unconscious. This consists of memories and emotions that are shared by all humanity. Jung believed that certain events and feelings are universal and exert a similar effect on all individuals. An example would be his universal symbol of a shadow, meaning the evil, primitive nature that resides within everyone. Jung believed that although people are aware of the workings of the conscious ego, it is the unavailable material contained in the personal unconscious and collective unconscious that has the greatest influence on one's behavior.

Jung's analytical psychotherapy was a pioneering approach during the very early era of psychological treatment. He conformed to the beliefs of other psychodynamic therapists, such as Freud and Alfred Adler (1870-1937), in the importance of discovering unconscious material. The psychoanalysts would be followed by the behavioral school's emphasis on environmental events and the cognitive school's focus on thoughts and perceptions. Psychoanalysis brought a prominence to psychology it had not known previously.

PERSONALITY AND THE UNCONSCIOUS MIND

Jung believed that emotional problems originate from a one-sided development of personality. He believed that this is a natural process and that people must constantly seek a balance of their traits. An example might be a person who becomes overly logical and rational in his behavior and decision making, while ignoring his emotional and spontaneous side. Jung believed this one-sided development eventually would lead to emotional difficulty and that one must access the complementary personality forces that reside in the unconscious. Even psychotherapists must be aware that along with their desire to help others, they have complementary darker desires that are destructive to others. Jung believed that emotional problems are a signal that one is becoming unbalanced in one's personality and that this should motivate one to develop more neutral traits.

The process of analytical psychotherapy, as in most psychodynamic approaches, is to make the patient conscious or aware of the material in his or her unconscious mind. Jung believed that if the conscious mind were overly logical and rational, the unconscious mind, to balance it, would be filled with equally illogical and emotional material. To access this material, Jung advocated a free and equal exchange of ideas and information between the analyst and the patient. Jung did not focus on specific techniques as did Freud, but he did believe that the unconscious material would become evident in the context of a strong, trusting therapeutic relationship. Although the patient and analyst have equal status, the analyst serves as a model of an individual who has faced her or his unconscious demons.

STAGES OF ANALYTIC PSYCHOTHERAPY

Analytic psychotherapy proceeds in four stages. The first stage is that of confession. Jung believed that it is necessary for the patient to tell of his or her conflicts and that this is usually accompanied by an emotional release. Jung did not believe that confession is sufficient to provide a cure for one's ills, however, nor did he believe (unlike Freud) that an intellectual understanding of one's difficulties is adequate. The patient must find a more neutral ground in terms of personality functioning, and this can only be accomplished by facing one's unconscious material.

The second stage of psychotherapy is called elucidation, and it involves becoming aware of one's unconscious transferences. Transference is a process in which a patient transfers emotions about someone else in his or her life onto the therapist; the patient will behave toward the therapist as he or she would toward that other person. It is similar to meeting someone who reminds one of a past relationship; for no apparent reason, one might begin to act toward the new person the same way one did to the previous person. Jung believed that these transferences to the analyst give a clue about unconscious material. A gentle, passive patient might evidence hostile transferences to the therapist, thus giving evidence of considerable rage that is being contained in the unconscious.

The third stage of analytic psychotherapy consists of education. The patient is instructed about the dangers of unequal personality development and is supported in his or her attempts to change. The overly logical business executive may be encouraged to go on a spontaneous vacation with his family with few plans and no fixed destinations. The shy student may be cajoled into joining a debate on emotional campus issues. Jung believed in the value of experiencing the messages of one's unconscious.

The final stage of psychotherapy, and one that is not always necessary, is that of transformation. This goes beyond the superficial encouragements of the previous stages and attempts to get the patient to delve deeply into the unconscious and thereby understand who he or she is. This process of understanding and reconciling one's opposites takes considerable courage and exploration into one's personal and cultural past. It is a quest for one's identity and purpose in life that requires diligent work between the analyst and patient; the result is superior wisdom and a transcendent calm when coping with life's struggles.

ANALYTIC TECHNIQUES

Jung developed several techniques aimed at uncovering material hidden in the unconscious. Like Freud, Jung believed that the content of dreams is indicative of unconscious attitudes. He believed that dreams have a compensatory function; that is, they are reflections of the side of personality that is not displayed during one's conscious, everyday state. The sophisticated librarian may have dreams of being an exotic dancer, according to Jung, as a way of expressing the ignored aspects of personality.

Jung gives an example of the compensatory aspects of dreams when describing the recollections of a dutiful son. The son dreamed that he and his father were leaving home, and his father was driving a new automobile. The father began to drive in an erratic fashion. He swerved the car all over the road until he finally succeeded in crashing the car and damaging it very badly. The son was frightened, then became angry and chastised his father for his behavior. Rather than respond, however, his father began to laugh until it became apparent that he was very intoxicated, a condition the son had not previously noticed. Jung interpreted the dream in the context of the son's relationship with his father. The son overly idealized the father, while refusing to recognize apparent faults. The dream represented the son's latent anger at his father and his attempt to reduce him in status. Jung indicated to the young man that the dream was a cue from his unconscious that he should evaluate his relationship with his father with a more balanced outlook.

AMPLIFICATION METHOD

Jung employed the method of amplification for interpreting dreams. This technique involved focusing repeatedly on the contents of the dream and giving multiple associations to them. Jung believed that the dream often is basically what it appears to be. This differs dramatically from Freudian interpretation, which requires the patient to associate dream elements with childhood conflicts.

The amplification method can be applied to a dream reported by a graduate student in clinical psychology. While preparing to defend his dissertation, the final and most anxiety-provoking aspect of receiving the doctorate, the student had a dream about his oral defense. Before presenting the project to his dissertation committee that was to evaluate its worth (and seemingly his own), the student dreamed that he was in the bathroom gathering his resources. He noticed he was wearing a three-piece brown suit; however, none of the pieces matched. They were different shades of brown. Fortunately, the pieces were reversible, so the student attempted to change them so they would all be the same shade. After repeated attempts he was unable to get all three pieces of the suit to be the same shade of brown. He finally gave up in despair and did not appear for his defense. With a little knowledge about the student, an analytical therapist would have an easy time with the meaning of this dream. This was obviously a stressful time in the young man's life, and the dream reflected his denied anxiety. In addition, the student did not like brown suits; to him, a brown suit that did not match was even more hideous. It is apparent that he was unhappy and, despite his best attempts to portray confidence, the budding clinician was afraid that he was going to "look stupid." Jung would have encouraged him to face these fears of failure that were hidden in his unconscious.

ACTIVE IMAGINATION

A final application of analytical psychotherapy stems from Jung's method of active imagination. Jung believed that unconscious messages could come not only from dreams but also from one's artistic productions. He encouraged his patients to produce spontaneous, artistic material. Some patients sketched, while others painted, wrote poetry, or sang songs. He was interested in the symbols that were given during these periods, and he asked his clients to comment on them. Jung believed that considerable material in the unconscious could be discovered during these encounters. He also talked with his patients about the universal meanings of these symbols (as in his idea of the collective unconscious), and they would attempt to relate this material to the their own cultural pasts.

Many modern therapies, such as art, music, and dance therapy, draw heavily from this idea that one can become aware of unconscious and emotional material through association involving one's artistic productions. These therapists believe, as did Jung, that patients are less defensive during these times of spontaneous work and, therefore, are more likely to discover unconscious material.

CONTRIBUTIONS TO PSYCHOLOGY

Analytical psychotherapy is not considered a mainstream approach to psychotherapy, but it does have a small group of devoted followers. Some of Jung's techniques have been adapted into other, more common approaches. Many therapists agree with Jung's deemphasis on specific techniques in favor of a focus on the establishment of a supportive therapy relationship. Jung moved away from the stereotypical analyst's couch in favor of face-to-face communication between doctor and patient. Many psychotherapists endorse Jung's belief that the analyst and patient should have relatively equal status and input. Jung also reduced the frequency of meeting with his patients from daily (as Freud recommended) to weekly, which is the norm today.

Jung's analytical approach changed the focus of psychotherapy from symptom relief to self-discovery. He was interested not only in patients with major problems but also in those who were dissatisfied with their mundane existences. These people were usually bright, articulate, and occupationally successful.

Jung's most lasting contributions probably have been his insights into the polarity of personality traits. The Myers-Briggs Type Indicator, based on Jungian personality descriptions, is one of the most widely used personality tests in business and industry. Jung also believed that personality changes throughout one's life, and he encouraged a continual evaluation of oneself. The idea of a midlife crisis, a period when one reevaluates personal and occupational goals, is a product of Jung's theory. He believed that individuals continually should strive to achieve a balance in their personality and behavior.

SOURCES FOR FURTHER STUDY

Bishop, Paul, ed. *Jung in Contexts: A Reader.* New York: Routledge, 2000. A collection of essays written between 1980 and 2000 on the evolution and theory of Jungian analytic psychology.

Hall, Calvin Springer, Gardner Lindzey, and John Campbell. *Theories of Personality.* 4th ed. New York: John Wiley & Sons, 1998. This is a classic text in personality theory and application, and it gives a detailed description of Jung's theory. Recommended for the serious student of Jung.

Hall, Calvin Springer, and Vernon J. Nordby. *A Primer of Jungian Psychology.*

New York: New American Library, 1973. This paperback attempts to provide a comprehensive treatment of Jung's ideas. It is intended for the beginning student of Jung.

Hergenhahn, B. R., and Matthew Olsen. *Personality Theories: An Introduction.* 5th ed. Upper Saddle River, N.J.: Prentice Hall, 1998. Engler's chapter on Jung and his psychotherapy is easy to read and contains a good balance between theory and practical application.

Jung, C. G. *Man and His Symbols.* 1961. Reprint. New York: Laureleaf Books, 1997. Jung's own summary of his theories on dreams and dream analysis, aimed at a lay reader.

Mathers, Dale. *An Introduction to Meaning and Purpose in Analytical Psychology.* Philadelphia: Taylor & Francis, 2001. A guide aimed at therapists, counselors, and other mental health professionals, explaining the basic premises of analytical psychology.

Samuels, Andrew. *Jung and the Post-Jungians.* New York: Routledge, 1986. A comprehensive overview of both Jung's thought and the developments of his followers.

Stevens, Anthony. *Jung: A Very Short Introduction.* New York: Oxford University Press, 2001. A concise overview of Jung's analytical psychology theories, written by a prominent Jungian.

Brett L. Beck

SEE ALSO: Abnormality: Psychological Models; Analytical Psychology: Carl Jung; Dreams; Psychoanalytic Psychology.

Animal Experimentation

Type of psychology: Psychological methodologies
Fields of study: Experimental methodologies; methodological issues

Psychologists study animals and animal behavior as well as humans; sometimes the goal is to understand the animal itself, and sometimes it is to try to learn more about humans. Because there are many biological and psychological similarities between humans and other animals, the use of animal models can be extremely valuable, although it is sometimes controversial.

Key concepts
- analogy
- applied research
- basic research
- biopsychology
- ethology
- homology
- Institutional Animal Care and Use Committees
- invasive procedures
- learning theory
- situational similarity

Prior to the general acceptance of Charles Darwin's evolutionary theory in the late nineteenth century, animals were considered to be soulless machines with no thoughts or emotions. Humans, on the other hand, were assumed to be qualitatively different from other animals because of their abilities to speak, reason, and exercise free will. This assumption made it unreasonable to try to learn about the mind by studying animals.

After Darwin, however, people began to see that, even though each species is unique, the chain of life is continuous, and there are similarities as well as differences among species. As animal brains and human brains are made of the same kinds of cells and have similar structures and connections, it was reasoned, the mental processes of animals must be similar to the mental processes of humans. This new insight led to the introduction of animals as psychological research subjects around the year 1900. Since then, animal experimentation has taught much about the brain and the mind, especially in the fields of learning, memory, motivation, and sensation.

Psychologists who study animals can be roughly categorized into three groups. Biopsychologists, or physiological psychologists, study the genetic, neural, and hormonal controls of behavior, for example, eating behavior, sleep, sexual behavior, perception, emotion, memory, and the effects of drugs. Learning theorists study the learned and environmental controls of behavior, for example, stress, stimulus-response patterns, motivation, and the effects of reward and punishment. Ethologists and sociobiologists concentrate on animal behavior in nature, for example, predator-prey interactions, mating and parenting, migration, communication, aggression, and territoriality.

REASONS FOR USING ANIMAL SUBJECTS

Psychologists study animals for a variety of reasons. Sometimes they study the behavior of a particular animal in order to solve a specific problem. They may study dogs, for example, to learn how best to train them as watchdogs, chickens to learn how to prevent them from fighting one another in henhouses, and wildlife to learn how to regulate populations in parks, refuges, or urban areas. These are all examples of what is called applied research.

Most psychologists, though, are more interested in human behavior but study animals for practical reasons. A developmental psychologist, for example, may study an animal that has a much shorter life span than humans so that each study takes a much shorter time and more studies can be done. Animals may also be studied when an experiment requires strict controls; researchers can control the food, housing, and even social environment of laboratory animals but cannot control such variables in the lives of human subjects. Experimenters can even control the genetics of animals by breeding them in the laboratory; rats and mice have been bred for so many generations that researchers can special-order from hundreds of strains and breeds and can even obtain animals that are as genetically identical as identical twins.

Another reason psychologists study animals is that there are fewer ethical considerations as compared to research with human subjects. Physiological psychologists and neuropsychologists, in particular, may utilize invasive procedures (such as brain surgery or hormone manipulation) that would be unethical to perform on humans. Without animal experimentation, these scientists would have to do all their research on human victims of accident or disease, a situation which would reduce the number of research subjects dramatically as well as raise additional ethical considerations.

A number of factors make animal research applicable for the study of human psychology. The first factor is homology. Animals that are closely related to humans are likely to have similar physiology and behavior because they share the same genetic blueprint. Monkeys and chimpanzees are the animals most closely related to humans and thus are homologically most similar. Monkeys and chimpanzees make the best subjects for psychological studies of complex behaviors and emotions, but because they are expensive and difficult to keep, and because there are serious ethical considerations when using them, they are not used when another animal would be equally suitable.

The second factor is analogy. Animals that have a similar lifestyle to humans are likely to have some of the same behaviors. Rats, for example, are social animals, as are humans; cats are not. Rats also show similarity to humans in their eating behavior (which is one reason rats commonly live

The study of animals, particularly primates, has taught researchers much about human beings. (Adobe)

around human habitation and garbage dumps); thus, they can be a good model for studies of hunger, food preference, and obesity. Rats, however, do not have a similar stress response to that of humans; for studies of exercise and stress, the pig is a better animal to study.

The third factor is situational similarity. Some animals, particularly domesticated animals such as dogs, cats, domestic rabbits, and some birds, adapt easily to experimental situations such as living in a cage and being handled by humans. Wild animals, even if reared from infancy, may not behave normally in experimental situations. The behavior of a chimpanzee that has been kept alone in a cage, for example, may tell something about the behavior of a human kept in solitary confinement, but it will not necessarily be relevant to understanding the behavior of most people in typical situations.

By far the most common laboratory animal used in psychology is *Rattus norvegicus*, the Norwegian rat. Originally the choice of the rat was something of a historical accident. Because the rat has been studied so thoroughly over the past century, it is now often the animal of choice so that comparisons can be made from study to study. Fortunately, the rat shares many features with humans. Other animals frequently used in psychological research include pigeons, mice, hamsters, gerbils, cats, monkeys, and chimpanzees.

SCIENTIFIC VALUE

One of the most important topics for which psychologists use animal experimentation is the study of interactive effects of genes and the environment on the development of the brain and subsequent behavior. These studies can only be done using animals as subjects because they require individuals with a relatively short life span that develop quickly, invasive procedures to measure cell and brain activity, or the manipulation of major social and environmental variables in the life of the subject.

In the 1920's, E. C. Tolman and Robert Tryon began a study of the inheritance of intelligence using rats. They trained rats to run a complex maze and then, over many generations, bred the fastest learners with one another and the slowest learners with one another. From the beginning, offspring of the "bright" rats were substantially faster than offspring of the "dull" rats. After only seven generations, there was no overlap between the two sets, showing that "intelligence" is at least partly genetic and can be bred into or out of animals, just as size, coat color, or milk yield can be.

Subsequent work with selectively bred bright versus dull rats, however, found that the bright rats would only outperform the dull rats when tested on the original maze used with their parents and grandparents; if given a different task to measure their intelligence, the bright rats were no brighter than the dull rats. These studies were the first to suggest that intelligence may not be a single attribute that one either has much or little of; there may instead be many kinds of intelligence.

Traditionally, intelligence quotient (IQ) tests measure two kinds of intelligence: one related to verbal skills and one related to spatial skills. Newer theories and tests attempt to address the possibility that there are dozens of different kinds of intelligence. The newer tests may help to identify special talents that may otherwise go unrecognized, undeveloped, and unrewarded in people who are not especially good at tasks measured by the more traditional tests. The new theories of multiple intelligences are also being used in the field of artificial intelligence to develop computer and robotic systems which utilize less sequential processing and more parallel systems or netlike processing, more like the human brain.

BRAIN STUDIES

Another series of experiments that illustrates the role of animal models in the study of brain and behavior is that developed by David Hubel and Torsten Wiesel, who study visual perception (mostly using cats). Hubel and Wiesel were able to study the activity of individual cells in the living brain. By inserting a microelectrode into a brain cell of an immobilized animal and flashing visual stimuli in the animal's visual field, they could record when the cell responded to a stimulus and when it did not.

Over the years, scientists have used this method to map the activities of cells in several layers of the visual cortex, the part of the brain that processes visual information. They have also studied the development of cells and the cell connections, showing how early experience can have a permanent effect on the development of the visual cortex. Subsequent research has demonstrated that the environment has major effects on the development of other areas of the brain as well. The phrase "use it or lose it" has some accuracy when it comes to development and maintenance of brain connections and mental abilities.

HARLOW'S EXPERIMENTS

Perhaps the most famous psychological experiments on animals were those by Harry Harlow in the 1950's. Harlow was studying rhesus monkeys and breeding them in his own laboratory. Initially, he would separate infant monkeys from their mothers. Later, he discovered that, in spite of receiving adequate medical care and nutrition, these infants exhibited severe behavioral symptoms: They would sit in a corner and rock, mutilate themselves, and scream in fright at the approach of an experimenter, a mechanical toy, or another monkey. As adolescents, they were antisocial. As adults, they were psychologically ill-equipped to deal with social interactions: Male monkeys were sexually aggressive, and females appeared to have no emotional attachment to their own babies. Harlow decided to study this phenomenon (labeled "maternal deprivation syndrome") because he thought it might help to explain the stunted growth, low life expectancy, and behavioral symptoms of institutionalized infants which had been documented earlier by René Spitz.

Results of the Harlow experiments profoundly changed the way psychologists think about love, parenting, and mental health. Harlow and his colleagues found that the so-called mothering instinct is not very instinctive at all but rather is learned through social interactions during infancy and adolescence. They also found that an infant's attachment to its mother is based not on its dependency for food but rather on its need for "contact comfort." Babies raised with both a mechanical "mother" that provided milk and a soft, cloth "mother" that gave no milk preferred the cloth mother for clinging and comfort in times of stress.

Through these experiments, psychologists came to learn how important social stimulation is, even for infants, and how profoundly lack of such stimulation can affect mental health development. These findings played an important role in the development of staffing and activity requirements for foundling homes, foster care, day care, and institutions for the aged, disabled, mentally ill, and mentally retarded. They have also influenced social policies which promote parent education and early intervention for children at risk.

LIMITATIONS AND ETHICAL CONCERNS

However, there are drawbacks to using animals as experimental subjects. Most important are the clear biological and psychological differences between humans and nonhuman animals; results one gets in a study using nonhuman animals simply may not apply to humans. In addition, animal subjects cannot communicate directly with the researchers; they are unable to express their feelings, motivations, thoughts, and reasons for their behavior. If a psychologist must use an animal instead of a human subject for ethical or practical reasons, the scientist will want to choose an animal that is similar to humans in the particular behavior being studied. Three factors can create similarity between animal and human behavior; each of these three must be considered.

For the same reasons that animals are useful in studying psychological processes, however, people have questioned the moral justification for such use. As it is now realized that vertebrate animals can feel physical pain, and that many of them have thoughts and emotions as well, animal experimentation has become politically controversial.

Psychologists generally support the use of animals in research. The American Psychological Association (APA) identifies animal research as an important contributor to psychological knowledge. The majority of individual psychologists would tend to agree. In 1996, S. Plous surveyed nearly four thousand psychologists and found that fully 80 percent either approved or strongly approved of the use of animals in psychological research. Nearly 70 percent believed that animal research was necessary for progress in the field of psychology. However, support dropped dramatically for invasive procedures involving pain or death. Undergraduate students majoring in psychology produced largely similar findings. Support was less strong among newer psychologists than older and was also less strong in women than in men.

Some psychologists would like to see animal experimentation in psychology discontinued. An animal rights organization called Psychologists for the Ethical Treatment of Animals (PSYETA), established in 1981, is highly critical of the use of animals as subjects in psychological research and has strongly advocated improving the well-being of those animals that currently are used through publication of the *Journal of Applied Animal Welfare Science*. PSYETA is also a strong advocate for the developing field of human-animal studies, in which the relationship between humans and animals is explored. Companion animals (pets) can have a significant impact on psychological and physical health and can be used as a therapeutic tool with, for example, elderly people in nursing homes and emotionally disturbed youths. In this field of study, animals are not the subjects of the experiment; rather it is the relationship between humans and animals that is the topic of interest.

REGULATIONS

In response to such concerns, the U.S. Congress amended the Animal Welfare Act in 1985 so that it would cover laboratory animals as well as pets.

(Rats, mice, birds, and farm animals are specifically excluded.) Although these regulations do not state specifically what experimental procedures may or may not be done on laboratory animals, they do set standards for humane housing, feeding, and transportation. Later amendments were added in 1991 in an effort to protect the psychological well-being of nonhuman primates.

In addition, the Animal Welfare Act requires that all research on warm-blooded animals (except those listed above) be approved by a committee before it can be carried out. Each committee (called an Institutional Animal Care and Use Committee, or IACUC) is composed of at least five members and must include an animal researcher; a veterinarian; someone with an area of expertise in a nonresearch area, such as a teacher, lawyer, or member of the clergy; and someone who is unaffiliated with the institution where the experimentation is being done who can speak for the local community. In this way, those scientists who do animal experiments are held accountable for justifying the appropriateness of their use of animals as research subjects.

The APA has its own set of ethical guidelines for psychologists conducting experiments with animals. The APA guidelines are intended for use in addition to all local, state, and federal laws that apply, including the Animal Welfare Act. In addition to being a bit more explicit in describing experimental procedures that require special justification, the APA guidelines require psychologists to have their experiments reviewed by local IACUCs and do not explicitly exclude any animals. About 95 percent of the animals used in psychology are rodents and birds (typically rats, mice, and pigeons), which are currently not governed by the Animal Welfare Act. It seems likely that federal regulations will change to include these animals at some point in the future, and according to surveys, the majority of psychologists believe that they should be. Finally, psychologists are encouraged to improve the living environments of their animals and consider nonanimal alternatives for their experiments whenever possible.

Alternatives to animal experimentation are becoming more widespread as technology progresses. Computer modeling and bioassays (tests using biological materials such as cell cultures) cannot replace animal experimentation in the field of psychology, however, because computers and cell cultures will never exhibit all the properties of mind that psychologists want to study. At the same time, the use of animals as psychological research subjects will never end the need for study of human subjects. While other animals may age, mate, fight, and learn much as humans do, they will never speak, compose symphonies, or run for office. Animal experimentation continues to have an important, though limited, role in psychological research.

Sources for Further Study

Fox, Michael Allen. *The Case for Animal Experimentation.* Berkeley: University of California Press, 1986. Although the author is philosophically in favor of most animal experimentation, he gives a clear and thorough discussion of the entire context of animal experimentation from both sides. Includes sections on animal rights, similarities and differences between human and nonhuman subjects, the role of methodological considerations and replicability in scientific progress, and alternatives to animal testing. The author specifically addresses some of the uglier behavioral studies on animals, including some by Harry Harlow.

Gross, Charles G., and H. Philip Zeigler, eds. *Motivation.* Vol. 2 in *Readings in Physiological Psychology.* New York: Harper & Row, 1969. Although there are dozens of newer collections of articles in the area of physiological psychology, this one does a particularly good job of covering the broad diversity of topics in the field. In addition, all the work represented in this particular collection came from animal studies. This or a similar collection can be consulted for illustration of many specific methodologies used in research with animals.

Miller, Neal E. "The Value of Behavioral Research on Animals." *American Psychologist* 40 (April, 1985): 423-440. Good discussion of advances in the behavioral sciences that came from animal studies, including studies on effects of early experience on the brain and behavior, drug effects, eating disorders, and diseases of aging. Also includes some discussion of applied studies which benefit nonhuman species.

National Academy of Sciences and the Institute of Medicine. Committee on the Use of Animals in Research. *Science, Medicine, and Animals.* Washington, D.C.: National Academy Press, 1991. This thirty-page pamphlet answers commonly asked questions about the use of animals in biomedical research. Although not focusing specifically on psychology, it does address research in psychomedical areas such as brain research and drug addiction.

National Research Council. *Guide for the Care and Use of Laboratory Animals.* Washington, D.C.: National Academy Press, 1996. The primary reference on animal care and use for researchers, the Guide covers specific legal regulations regarding institutional responsibilities; animal housing and environment; veterinary care; and facility requirements. Also available online at http://www.nap. edu/readingroom/books/labrats/

Psychologists for the Ethical Treatment of Animals. http://www.psyeta.org. Informative page for this animal rights organization. Provides links to the table of contents of the journals they publish as well as full-text access to some articles.

Linda Mealey; updated by Linda R. Tennison

SEE ALSO: Behaviorism; Conditioning; Emotions; Hunger; Imprinting; Instinct Theory; Memory: Animal Research; Pavlovian Conditioning.

ANXIETY DISORDERS

TYPE OF PSYCHOLOGY: Psychopathology
FIELDS OF STUDY: Anxiety disorders; behavioral and cognitive models;
    psychodynamic and neoanalytic models

*Anxiety is a central concept in many different schools of psychology, and there are
many widely varying theories concerning it; theories of anxiety often have spawned approaches to treating anxiety disorders.*

KEY CONCEPTS
- ego
- libido
- operant conditioning
- Pavlovian conditioning
- phobia
- preparedness
- repression
- three-systems approach
- two-factor theory
- vicarious transmission

The concept of anxiety is one of the most often-used and loosely defined
concepts in psychology. It can be used to describe a temporary state ("He
seems anxious today") or an enduring personality trait ("He is an anxious
person"). It is used to assign cause ("He stumbled over the words in his
speech because he was anxious") and to describe an effect ("Having to give a
speech makes him anxious"). It is seen as the result of discrete objects or situations, such as snakes or heights, or as evolving from basic existential problems such as the trauma of birth or the fear of death. All major theories in
psychology in some way confront anxiety.

Because of its preeminence in the field of psychology, there are many different theories about the nature and origin of anxiety disorders. The two
most important and influential viewpoints on anxiety are the Freudian and
the behavioral viewpoints. Although these theories attempt to explain many
anxiety disorders, an examination of how they apply to phobias presents a
good indication of how they work. A phobia can be defined as an anxiety disorder involving an intense fear of a particular thing (such as horses) or situation (such as heights).

FREUDIAN APPROACH
Sigmund Freud, who said that understanding anxiety "would be bound to
throw a flood of light on our whole mental existence," had two theories of
anxiety, an early one, in 1917, and a later one, in 1926. In the early theory, libido (mental energy, often equated with sexual drive) builds up until it is
discharged by some pleasurable activity. Sometimes the energy cannot be

discharged, for example, when the sexual object is not attainable or is morally unacceptable. This undischarged energy is anxiety and remains even when its original, unacceptable object is repressed or eliminated from conscious awareness. This anxiety may attach itself to an otherwise harmless object, resulting in a phobia. This theory is best illustrated in one of Freud's most famous cases, that of "Little Hans," a five-year-old who developed a phobia of horses. Freud believed that Little Hans had a sexual desire for his mother and wanted his father dead so that he could have his mother to himself. This desire for his mother and hatred of his father were unacceptable impulses and so were repressed from consciousness, resulting in anxiety. This anxiety attached itself to horses, Freud thought, because the black blinders and muzzle of the horse symbolized his father's glasses and mustache.

In Freud's first theory, repression causes anxiety. In psychoanalytic theory, repression is a defense mechanism that keeps unacceptable thoughts and impulses from becoming conscious. In the later theory, the relationship between them has changed: Anxiety causes repression. In this theory, anxiety acts as a signal to the ego (in Freud's theory, the rational, conscious part of the mind) that a forbidden impulse (such as Little Hans's desire for his mother) is trying to force its way into consciousness. This signal alerts the ego to try to repress the unwanted impulse. If the ego cannot successfully repress the forbidden impulse, it may try to transfer the forbidden impulse to an irrelevant object (horses, in Little Hans's case). This object can arouse all the emotions associated with the forbidden impulse, including the signal anxiety. In this way, it becomes a phobic object.

TWO-FACTOR THEORY

One influential behavioral approach to anxiety is O. Hobart Mowrer's two-factor theory. It uses the principles of Pavlovian learning—in which two stimuli are presented, one after the other, and the response to the first changes because of the response automatically elicited by the second stimulus—and operant conditioning—learning in which a behavior increases or decreases depending on whether the behavior is followed by reward or punishment—to explain fear and phobic avoidance, respectively. Fear is acquired through Pavlovian conditioning when a neutral object or situation is paired with something painful or punishing. For example, involvement in an automobile crash can result in a fear of driving. At this point, operant learning principles take over to explain phobic avoidance. In operant learning, any action that leads to a reward is likely to be repeated. The person who is anxious about driving might avoid driving. Because this avoidance is rewarded by reduced anxiety, the person is more likely to avoid driving in the future. Continued avoidance makes it harder to get back behind the wheel again.

Many problems were found with two-factor theory, and many modifications have been made to it. Two problems will be discussed here to illustrate these changes. First, the theory predicts that people will be likely to fear things that are most often associated with pain. There are very few people in modern society, however, who are phobic of electrical sockets and end tables, even though almost everyone has received a shock from the former and stubbed a toe on the latter. On the other hand, many people are afraid of snakes and spiders, even if they have never been bitten by one. This has been explained through the concept of preparedness: Human evolutionary history has prepared people to learn that some things—such as reptiles, insects, heights, darkness, and closed spaces—are dangerous. These things are "easy" to learn to fear, and they account for a large proportion of phobias. On the other hand, human evolutionary ancestors had no experience with electric sockets or guns, so people today are not prepared to become phobic of these objects, even though they cause much more pain in modern society than do snakes or spiders.

Two-factor theory states that in order for something to cause fear, it must be paired with a painful or punishing experience. People, however, sometimes become phobic of objects or situations with which they have never had a bad experience. Indeed, many people who have never seen a live snake are afraid of snakes. Thus, there must be other ways in which fear is acquired. One of these is vicarious transmission: Seeing someone act afraid of something can lead to acquiring that fear. For example, whether an infant becomes afraid of being in a high place depends on whether its mother is smiling or has an expression of fear on her face. In an ingenious set of experiments, Susan Mineka and her colleagues showed that vicarious transmission of fear is influenced by preparedness. She showed that rhesus monkeys that watched a videotape of other monkeys acting afraid of a snake became afraid of snakes themselves. Monkeys that watched other monkeys act afraid of rabbits, however, did not become afraid of rabbits because they were not evolutionarily prepared to fear rabbits. Human beings also can acquire fear by being told that something is dangerous. A child can learn to avoid running in front of oncoming cars by being told not to do this by his or her parents; he or she does not have to be hit by a car or watch someone get hit in order to acquire this information.

TREATING ANXIETY

All theories of anxiety disorders attempt to explain and organize what is known about fear and anxiety. Some of the theories, including the ones described here, also have been applied in developing treatments for anxiety disorders. As might be expected, clinical psychologists with very different ideas about the cause of anxiety will recommend very different treatments to eliminate it.

In the case of Little Hans, Freud thought that his anxiety about horses was caused by repressed sexual impulses toward his mother and hatred of his father. From this, it follows that these repressed impulses would need to be brought out into the open and resolved before his anxiety about horses

DSM-IV-TR CRITERIA FOR GENERALIZED ANXIETY DISORDER
(DSM CODE 300.02)

Excessive anxiety and worry (apprehensive expectation), occurring more days than not for at least six months, about a number of events or activities (such as work or school performance)

Person finds it difficult to control worry

Anxiety and worry associated with three or more of the following symptoms, with at least some present more days than not for previous six months (only one item required in children):

- restlessness or feeling keyed up or on edge
- being easily fatigued
- difficulty concentrating or mind going blank
- irritability
- muscle tension
- sleep disturbance (difficulty falling or staying asleep, or restless unsatisfying sleep)

Focus of anxiety and worry not confined to features of Axis I disorder

Anxiety and worry do not occur exclusively during Post-traumatic Stress Disorder

Anxiety, worry, or physical symptoms cause clinically significant distress or impairment in social, occupational, or other important areas of functioning

Disturbance not due to direct physiological effects of a substance or general medical condition and does not occur exclusively during a mood disorder, psychotic disorder, or pervasive developmental disorder

---

would diminish. This was the basic goal of the psychoanalytic therapy Freud recommended for Hans.

On the other hand, if Hans's parents had taken him to a behaviorally oriented therapist, the therapist would have assumed that the child's fear stemmed from a fright he suffered in the presence of a horse. In fact, Freud stated that the phobia began when Hans saw a horse fall while pulling a bus. Further, the therapist would assume that now Hans was rewarded for avoiding horses by anxiety reduction and by getting extra attention from his parents. Treatment would involve having the boy gradually think about, look at, and even pet horses, and it would include being rewarded for approaching (rather than avoiding) horses.

Given these vastly different theories and treatments, a question arises as to which one is right. The theoretical issues are still debated, but it is clear that treatments based on a behavioral model of anxiety are much more successful in reducing fear than are treatments based on the theories of Freud or his followers.

COGNITIVE THEORIES

Cognitive theories of anxiety also illustrate how theory is applied to develop a treatment. There are many different cognitive models of anxiety, but all are similar in that they assume that there is a cognitive cause of the fear state. This cognitive step is sometimes called an irrational belief. A cognitive theorist might explain Little Hans's fear in the following way: Hans is afraid of horses because he has some irrational belief that horses are dangerous. The specific belief might be "The horse will bite me" or "The horse might get spooked and run into me" or even "Horses have germs, and if I go near one, I'll catch its germs and get sick." The theory assumes that anxiety will stop when the irrational belief is eliminated. Thus, a cognitive therapist would first carefully question Hans to find out the specific irrational belief causing his fear. Once that is determined, the therapist would use persuasion, logical reasoning, and evidence to try to change the belief. (Little Hans was used here only to continue with the same example. A therapist probably would not try to reason with a five-year-old, and a different treatment would be used. Cognitive therapies are more commonly used with adults.)

PHYSIOLOGICAL THEORIES

Physiological theories of anxiety are increasing in importance. As with behavioral, psychodynamic, and cognitive theories, there are many physiological theories. They differ with respect to the brain areas, pathways, or chemicals implicated in anxiety. It is likely that many physiological theories contain an element of truth. Anxiety is a complex state, involving multiple interacting parts of the nervous system, and it will take much additional research to develop a complete model of the brain's role in anxiety.

One physiological variable that has been integrated into many theories of anxiety is the panic attack. This is a sudden and usually short-lived attack that includes trouble with breathing, heart palpitations, dizziness, sweating, and fear of dying or going crazy. These attacks appear purely physiological in that they seem to come "out of the blue" at first; however, psychological factors determine whether they progress into a full-blown disorder. People can become anxious about having panic attacks, and this added anxiety leads to more attacks, producing panic disorder. Some people become afraid of having an attack in a place where they will be unable to cope or receive help. These people may progressively avoid more and more places. This is known as agoraphobia, which at its worst can result in people who are afraid to leave their homes.

The development of physiological theories also illustrates an important point in the relationship between theory and therapy. Thus far, it has been stressed that theories of anxiety help determine treatment. This relationship also works in reverse: Success or failure of treatments adds information used in theory development. This is most clear in physiological theories. For example, the physiological mechanisms of different types of anxiety-reducing tranquilizers have been investigated to provide clues as to how the brain is involved in anxiety.

IMPACT ON FIELD OF PSYCHOLOGY

Just as most theories in psychology have a view of anxiety, anxiety is an important concept in many areas of psychology. Obviously, anxiety is very important in the fields of psychopathology and psychotherapy. It also has been very important in learning theory; experiments with conditioned fear have advanced knowledge about Pavlovian and operant conditioning. Anxiety is also an important trait in theories of personality, and it figures in theories of motivation. It might be said that anxiety is everywhere in psychology.

Theoretical developments in anxiety have been incorporated into other areas of psychology. For example, in the early 1960's, Peter Lang described fear and anxiety as being composed of three systems—that is, there are three systems in which fear is expressed: verbal (saying "I'm anxious"), behavioral (avoiding or running away from a feared object), and physiological (experiencing an increase in heart rate or sweating). An important point in understanding the three systems of fear is that the systems do not always run along parallel tracks. A person may speak of being anxious about the condition of the world environment without any physiological arousal. Alternatively, a boy's heart might pound at the sight of a snake in the woods, but he reports no fear and does not run away in the presence of his friends. Describing fear in a three-systems framework presents an important challenge to any theory of anxiety. An adequate theory must explain why the three systems sometimes give the same information and sometimes do not. The three-systems approach not only has been very influential in anxiety theory and research but also has been applied to many other areas of psychology, such as studying emotion, stress, and pain. This approach is an important concept in behavioral formulations of anxiety, stating that anxiety has behavioral, physiological, and verbal components and that they do not necessarily provide the same information.

Another major challenge for theories of anxiety is to begin to integrate different positions. The present theories are not all mutually exclusive. The fact that a behavioral theory of anxiety has some validity does not mean that cognitive approaches are wrong. Also, psychological theories need to be integrated with physiological theories that describe brain activity during anxiety. Although theory and research in anxiety has a long and fruitful history, there is much work to be done, and many important developments lie ahead.

SOURCES FOR FURTHER STUDY

Antony, Martin M., Susan M. Orsillo, and Lizabeth Roemer, eds. *Practitioner's Guide to Empirically Based Measures of Anxiety*. Plenum Press, 2001. Reviews more than two hundred instruments for measuring adult anxiety. Aimed at mental health professionals.

Barlow, David H. *Anxiety and Its Disorders*. 2d ed. New York: Guilford Press, 2001. The author, one of the leaders in the field of anxiety research, presents his integrative theory of anxiety. The book also describes assessment and treatment of anxiety and includes a separate chapter on each recognized anxiety disorder. The book's intended audience is graduate students and professionals in psychology, but it is very well written and worth the effort for anyone interested in an up-to-date and comprehensive presentation of anxiety disorders.

Freud, Sigmund. "Analysis of a Phobia in a Five-Year-Old Boy." In *The Standard Edition of the Complete Psychological Works of Sigmund Freud,* edited by James Strachey. Vol. 10. London: Hogarth Press, 1955. Originally published in 1909, this is Freud's description of the case of Little Hans, the most famous patient in the history of anxiety disorders. Freud is an excellent writer, and he presents many vivid details in this case history, making it interesting to read.

_____. "Inhibition, Symptoms, and Anxiety." In *The Standard Edition of the Complete Psychological Works of Sigmund Freud,* edited by James Strachey. Vol. 20. London: Hogarth Press, 1959. In this paper, originally published in German in 1926, Freud describes his revised theory of anxiety. The paper covers a wide range of topics (including a redescription of Little Hans) and is not as readable as the initial presentation of the case. It is, however, an interesting illustration of the change in Freud's thinking about anxiety.

Marks, Isaac Meyer. *Living with Fear: Understanding and Coping with Anxiety.* 2d ed. New York: McGraw-Hill, 2001. This is a work written for the general public by Britain's foremost authority on fear and anxiety. It is accessible and provides a good introduction to theory and treatment of anxiety.

Stein, Dan J., and Eric Hollander, eds. *Textbook of Anxiety Disorders*. Washington, D.C.: American Psychiatric Press, 2002. An up-to-date clinical guide to anxiety and its treatment.

Tuma, A. Hussain, and Jack D. Maser, eds. *Anxiety and the Anxiety Disorders.* New York: Lawrence Erlbaum, 1985. This thousand-page book contains forty-three chapters of high quality, with most of the leaders in the field of anxiety represented. Every important theoretical approach to anxiety is covered. There are two hundred pages of references, an author index, and a subject index, making it easy to find information on specific topics.

Scott R. Vrana

SEE ALSO: Abnormality: Psychological Models; Amnesia and Fugue; Conditioning; Multiple Personality; Obsessive-Compulsive Disorder; Pavlovian Conditioning; Phobias.

Attachment and Bonding in Infancy and Childhood

TYPE OF PSYCHOLOGY: Developmental psychology
FIELDS OF STUDY: Infancy and childhood; interpersonal relations

Bonding and attachment are two theoretical constructs that psychologists have used to describe and explain the intense emotional tie that develops between a caregiver and child. Research has helped psychologists to explain the development of several common social behaviors in infancy and to use individual differences in infant behavior to predict aspects of later development.

KEY CONCEPTS
- approach behaviors
- attachment behaviors
- avoidance
- felt security
- resistance
- separation protest
- signalling behaviors
- "strange situation"
- stranger anxiety

Bonding refers to the development of an emotional tie of the mother to the infant. This biologically based process is believed to occur in mothers shortly after the birth of an infant, a time period during which the mother's intense emotional response is triggered by contact with her newborn. The existence of such a bond is then evidenced in the mother's behavior. Attachment, on the other hand, refers to a relationship between the caregiver and infant that develops over the infant's first year of life; the quality of the attachment is apparent in the behavior of the infant.

Evidence for the biologically based bonding process has been inconsistent. In contrast, there exists considerable scientific evidence to support the notion of attachment. Thus, the remainder of this discussion will focus on the development of the attachment relationship.

The work of British psychiatrist John Bowlby played an important role in the acceptance and understanding of the notion of mother-infant attachment. Bowlby argued that the behaviors of infants are not random and that, in fact, some of the behaviors exhibited most commonly by infants actually serve a single goal. Specifically, he argued that the infant behaviors of crying, babbling, smiling, clinging, non-nutritional sucking, and following all play an important role in bringing the infant into close contact with the caregiver. He believed that, for the infant, seeking and maintaining proximity to the caregiver are essential for survival because the infant is dependent upon the caregiver for food, shelter, and protection. Thus, the infant's behavior is organized and goal-directed. During early infancy, however, this goal is neither understood nor learned by the infant. Rather, humans are born with a biological predisposition to engage in certain behaviors that aid in the maintenance of proximity to the caregiver. Thus, the goal of maintaining proximity is built into the human infant, as are some initial behaviors that serve the function of achieving that goal. With further development, the infant becomes more aware of the goal, and therefore his or her behaviors become more intentional.

The infant's emotional state is also believed to play an important role in attempts to seek and maintain proximity to the caregiver. That is, the infant's behavior is dependent upon his or her sense of emotional security. For example, as long as a child is in the immediate presence of the attachment figure, or within easy reach, the child feels secure and may then attend to important developmental tasks such as exploration of the environment, using the mother as a secure base from which to explore. Upon the threat of loss of the attachment figure, however, the infant may lose that sense of security and may exhibit attachment behaviors designed to increase the proximity of the attachment figure. Thus, the infant's attempts to seek or maintain proximity to the caregiver are determined by how secure he or she feels with the caregiver in a specific environment.

The attachment relationship and the infant's sense of security develop over the period of infancy. Bowlby has described four phases in the development of the attachment to the caregiver. In phase one, the newborn shows limited discrimination among people and therefore exhibits no preferential or differential behaviors, thus behaving in a friendly manner toward all people. In phase two, the eight- to twelve-week-old infant shows the ability to discriminate the caregiver from others but exhibits no preferential behavior toward the caregiver. In phase three, which generally appears at approximately seven or eight months of age, the infant clearly discriminates the caregiver from other people and begins to show preferential treatment toward him or her. For example, the infant begins to follow a departing mother, greets mother upon her return, and uses her as a base from which to explore an unfamiliar environment. Furthermore, during phase three, the infant begins to treat strangers with caution and may withdraw from a stranger. In phase four, the child maintains a "goal-directed partnership" with the caregiver, a more complex relationship in which the child is acquiring some insight into the caregiver's own feelings and motives, and thus interacts with the caregiver as a partner. This final phase is not apparent in most children until after age two.

PATTERNS OF INFANT-MOTHER ATTACHMENT

During the second half of the first year of life (after about eight months of age), infants begin to show very clear attempts at exploration when their mothers are present. In fact, research reported by Mary Ainsworth in the mid-1970's suggests that once an infant is able to crawl, he or she does not always remain close to the mother. Instead, the child begins to move away from the mother, more carefully exploring objects and people. From time to time he or she returns to her, as if to check her whereabouts or to check in with her. If the mother moves away, however, or if the infant is frightened by some event, he or she will either approach the mother or will signal to bring the mother in closer proximity. For example, the infant often fusses, cries, and clings to the caregiver at the first sign of the caregiver's possible departure, a response known as separation protest. At about the same time, infants begin to express stranger anxiety or stranger wariness by fussing and crying when an unfamiliar person enters the room or approaches.

Ainsworth designed a special laboratory technique, known as the "strange situation," that allows direct observation of the interactions between the behaviors associated with exploration, attachment, separation protest, and stranger anxiety. This situation places an infant in an unfamiliar setting with a stranger, both in the presence and in the absence of the mother. The procedure consists of a series of three-minute episodes (the process lasts a total of about twenty minutes) in which the child is exposed to an unfamiliar playroom containing a set of age-appropriate toys. During the initial episodes, the mother remains in the playroom with the infant. Mother and infant are then joined in the playroom by a female stranger, who first talks to the mother, then approaches the baby. Next, the mother leaves the room, and the baby and stranger are left alone together. Mother then returns and the stranger leaves, so that the baby is reunited with the mother. Following this episode, the baby is left alone in the room, then joined by the stranger; finally, the mother again returns and the stranger leaves.

This strange situation, therefore, exposes a child to three potentially upsetting experiences: separation from the caregiver, contact with a stranger, and unfamiliar surroundings. The episodes are arranged in such a way that they present a series of stressful experiences to the infant and thus present an opportunity to observe not only the infant's immediate response to a stranger and to separation from the mother but also his or her ability to derive comfort from the mother and to use her as a secure base for exploration.

Ainsworth has reported that, while there are many similarities in infant responses to this strange situation, there are also important individual differences. In her initial study of twelve-month-old infants and their mothers, Ainsworth reported three distinct patterns of responding to the events of the strange situation, and the validity of these behavior patterns has been demonstrated by much additional research.

A majority of the infants exhibited active exploration of the new environment and the available toys when their mothers were present. Some of these infants showed distress during the first separation from mother, and by the second separation, the majority of these infants expressed distress. Upon reunion with their mother, they actively sought contact with her and were easily comforted by her, showing considerable signs of positive emotion but very little, if any, signs of negative emotion. Furthermore, these infants frequently returned to play and exploration after a period of contact with their mother. In general, then, these infants used their mothers as a secure base from which to explore the novel environment, exhibited appropriate attachment behaviors following her departure, and were easily comforted by the mother upon her return. Ainsworth suggested that this pattern of behavior reflects a secure attachment relationship.

A second group of infants showed a very different pattern of behavior. This minority group showed no evidence of distress during separation. They did sometimes show distress when left alone in the playroom but were easily comforted by the returning stranger. Furthermore, this group actually avoided or ignored their mothers when they returned. In essence, the mothers were treated very much as were the strangers. These infants showed virtually no signs of separation protest or stranger anxiety and exhibited very few attachment behaviors. Ainsworth suggested that this pattern of behavior reflects an insecure, avoidant attachment relationship.

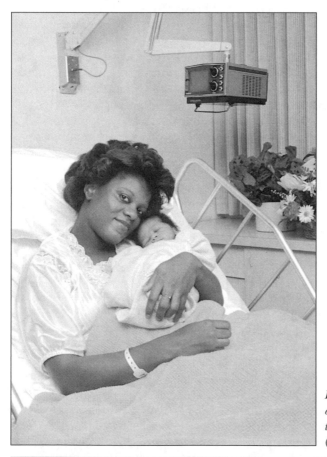

Bonding is an emotional and physiological process that begins at birth.
(Digital Stock)

Finally, a third group of children were extremely distressed upon separation yet, despite their obvious separation and stranger anxiety, resisted comfort from their mothers. Their behavior suggested an angry ambivalence—they objected to being left alone, but they refused to be consoled when reunited with their mothers. This group of infants often exhibited distress upon first entering the unfamiliar room with their mothers, and they rarely left her side to explore the toys or the environment, either before or after separation, suggesting a lack of a sense of security. Ainsworth suggested that this behavior pattern reflects an insecure, resistant, or ambivalent attachment relationship.

It is important to note that Ainsworth's research was done in the United States in the 1970's. Follow-up work has demonstrated that various sociocultural factors can influence the patterns of attachment behavior seen in the "strange situation." For instance, studies done in North Germany in the 1980's revealed that as many as 60 percent of babies in that culture were classified as insecure-avoidant because of their lack of distress at separation from their mothers in the strange situation test. In contrast, studies of attachment carried out in Japan in the 1980's and 1990's indicate that up to 40 percent of Japanese infants are classified as insecure-ambivalent in the strange situation due to their tendency to cling to their mothers throughout the procedure. These differing cross-cultural patterns imply that the wider sociocultural context influences how mothers and infants interact: North German mothers expect their infants to be relatively self-sufficient and confident, even during short separations such as those characteristic of the "strange situation" procedure. Japanese mothers, on the other hand, expect their infants to be upset when they are out of close proximity, and in daily practice are unlikely to leave their infants alone even for short periods. These cross-cultural variations in patterns of attachment highlight the importance of considering mother-infant attachment in context.

The development of these distinct patterns of attachment is believed to be the result of the history of interaction between the caregiver and infant. Specifically, attachment theory suggests that responsive and consistent caregiving results in a secure mother-infant attachment, unresponsive caregiving results in an avoidant attachment, and inconsistent caregiving results in a - resistant/ambivalent attachment. The "avoidant" mother has been described as cold and disliking physical contact with the infant, who responds by acting aloof and avoiding social interaction. The "resistant" mother, on the other hand, has been described as unpredictable, sometimes responding but sometimes not, and the infant often responds with anger and ambivalence.

As the infant matures, the specific behaviors that indicate the existence of the attachment relationship may change. The research evidence strongly suggests, however, that such individual differences in the quality of the mother-infant attachment relationship are predictive of later behavior. For example, infants who exhibit secure attachment patterns at one year of age have been found to be more cooperative with adults, to show greater enthusiasm for learning, to be more independent, and to be more popular with their peers during the preschool years. Thus, the quality of the mother-infant attachment relationship may have long-range effects. This does not mean that the child's future is determined solely by the quality of the attachment relationship. The evidence indicates that certain negative consequences of an insecure attachment relationship may be overcome by changes in the nature of the child's important relationships.

ATTACHMENT IN NONHUMAN PRIMATES

The existence of a mother-infant attachment relationship has been recognized for many years. For most of those years, however, psychologists explained the development of this attachment by way of traditional learning theory. That is, behaviorists argued that the infant-mother attachment develops because mothers are associated with the powerful, reinforcing event of being fed. In this way, the mother becomes a conditioned reinforcer. This reinforcement theory of attachment, however, came into question as a result of the work of Harry and Margaret Harlow in the early 1960's.

The Harlows' work was not with human infants but with infant rhesus monkeys. They removed newborn monkeys from their mothers at birth and raised them in the laboratory with two types of artificial or surrogate mothers. One surrogate mother was made of terrycloth and could provide "contact comfort." The other surrogate mother was made of wire. A feeding bottle was attached to one of the substitute mothers for each of the monkeys. Half of the monkeys were fed by the wire mother; the other half were fed by the cloth mother. This allowed the Harlows to compare the importance of feeding to the importance of contact comfort for the monkeys.

In order to elicit attachment behaviors, the Harlows introduced some frightening event, such as a strange toy, into the cages of the young monkeys. They expected that if feeding were the key to attachment, then the frightened monkeys should have run to the surrogate mother that fed them. This was not the case, however: All the young monkeys ran to their cloth mothers and clung to them, even if they were not fed by them. Only the cloth mothers were able to provide security for the frightened monkeys. The Harlows concluded that a simple reinforcement explanation of attachment was inaccurate and that the contact comfort, not the food, provided by a mother plays a critical role in the development of attachment.

This research provided the impetus for the development of Bowlby's ethological account of attachment. Since that time, research by Mary Ainsworth and Alan Sroufe, as well as many others, has provided important information for the continuing development of understanding of the complex relationship between caregivers and infants.

BIBLIOGRAPHY

Ainsworth, Mary D. Salter, Mary C. Blehar, Everett Waters, and S. Wall. *Patterns of Attachment*. Hillsdale, N.J.: Lawrence Erlbaum, 1978. Outlines, in general terms, the development of John Bowlby's attachment theory. Describes in detail the procedures and scoring techniques for the strange situation and describes the patterns of behavior associated with the secure, avoidant, and resistant attachments. Discusses the antecedents of individual differences in the attachment relationship.

Bowlby, John. *Attachment and Loss.* 2d ed. 3 vols. New York: Penguin Books, 1991. Examines the theoretical foundation of the attachment construct and discusses attachment behavior. Outlines the development, maintenance, and function of attachment in both humans and animals.

Cassidy, Jude, and Phillip R. Shaver, eds. *Handbook of Attachment: Theory, Research, and Clinical Applications.* New York: Guilford Press, 1999. A comprehensive collection of papers on modern attachment theory, including chapters on atypical attachment and implications for mental health.

Crittenden, Patricia McKinsey, and Angelika Hartl Claussen, eds. *The Organization of Attachment Relationships: Maturation, Culture, and Context.* New York: Cambridge University Press, 2000. A collection of papers examining important influences on attachment in infancy, childhood, and adulthood.

Loretta A. Rieser-Danner; updated by Virginia Slaughter

SEE ALSO: Affiliation and Friendship; Development; Gender-Identity Formation; Imprinting.

Attention-Deficit Hyperactivity Disorder (ADHD)

Type of psychology: Psychopathology
Field of study: Childhood and adolescent disorders

Attention-deficit hyperactivity disorder is one of the most common disorders of childhood and adolescence, but it is also one of the most disturbing and debilitating conditions that a child or adolescent can experience. Research into this disorder has identified its primary causes; however, it remains difficult to treat effectively.

Key concepts
- impulsivity
- inattention
- overactivity
- treatment

Attention-deficit hyperactivity disorder (ADHD) is one of the most extensively studied behavior disorders that begin in childhood. Thousands of articles and books have been published on the subject. There are a number of reasons this disorder is of such interest to researchers and clinicians. The two primary reasons are, first, that ADHD is a relatively common disorder of childhood, and second, that there are numerous problems associated with ADHD, including lower levels of intellectual and academic performance and higher levels of aggressive and defiant behavior. (Although ADHD usually persists into adulthood, it is most commonly regarded as a childhood disorder.)

In national and international studies of childhood emotional and behavioral disorders, ADHD has been found to be relatively common among children. Although prevalence estimates range from 1 percent to 20 percent, most researchers agree that between 3 percent and 7 percent of children could be diagnosed as having ADHD. The revised fourth edition of the *Diagnostic and Statistical Manual of Mental Disorders* (DSM-IV-TR), published by the American Psychiatric Association in 2000, describes the diagnostic criteria for ADHD. In order to receive the diagnosis of ADHD according to DSM-IV-TR, a child must show abnormally high levels of inattention, hyperactivity-impulsivity, or both when compared with peers of the same age. The DSM-IV-TR lists two sets of behavioral symptoms characteristic of ADHD. The first list contains nine symptoms of inattention such as "often has difficulty sustaining attention in tasks or play activities," while the second list contains nine symptoms of hyperactivity-impulsivity such as "often talks excessively" and "often has difficulty awaiting turn." In order to be diagnosed with ADHD, a child must exhibit six to nine symptoms from at least one of the lists. Although many of these behaviors are quite common for most children at some point in their lives, the important point to consider in the diagnosis of ADHD is that these behaviors must be in excess of the levels of behaviors most frequently exhibited by children of that age and that the behaviors must cause functional impairment in at least two settings (for instance, at home and at school). Additionally, it is expected that these behaviors have been excessive for at least six months and that some of the problem behaviors were present by the time the child was seven years old.

Boys tend to outnumber girls in the diagnosis of ADHD, with the male: female ratio estimated at 2:1 to 9:1, depending on the source. ADHD boys tend to be more aggressive and antisocial than ADHD girls, while girls are more likely to display inattentive symptoms of ADHD than boys.

ASSOCIATED PROBLEMS

There are a number of additional problems associated with ADHD, including the greater likelihood of ADHD boys exhibiting aggressive and antisocial behavior. Although many ADHD children do not show any associated problems, many ADHD children show deficits in both intellectual and behavioral functioning. For example, a number of studies have found that ADHD children score an average of seven to fifteen points below other children on standardized intelligence tests. It may be, however, that this poorer performance reflects poor test-taking skills or inattention during the test rather than actual impairment in intellectual functioning. Additionally, ADHD children tend to have difficulty with academic performance and scholastic achievement. It is assumed that this poor academic performance is a result of inattention and impulsiveness in the classroom. When ADHD children are given medication to control their inattention and impulsiveness, their academic productivity has been shown to improve.

ADHD children have also been shown to have a high number of associated emotional and behavioral difficulties. As mentioned earlier, ADHD boys tend to show higher levels of aggressive and antisocial behavior than ADHD girls and normal children. Additionally, it is estimated that up to 50 percent of ADHD children have at least one other disorder. Many of these problems are related to depression and anxiety, although many ADHD children also have severe problems with temper tantrums, stubbornness, and defiant behavior. It is also estimated that up to 50 percent of ADHD children have impaired social relations; that is, they do not get along with other children. That there are many problems associated with ADHD may be part of the reason that researchers have been so intrigued by this disorder.

Researchers must understand a disorder before they can attempt to treat it. There are a variety of theories on the etiology of ADHD, but most researchers now believe that there are multiple factors that influence its development. It appears that many children have a biological predisposition toward ADHD; in other words, they may have a greater likelihood of developing ADHD as a result of genetic factors. This predisposition is exacerbated by a variety of factors, such as complications during pregnancy, neurological disease, exposure to toxins, family adversity, and inconsistent parental discipline. Although a very popular belief is that food additives or sugar can cause ADHD, there has been almost no scientific support for these claims. As so many factors have been found to be associated with the development of ADHD, it is not surprising that numerous treatments have been developed for the amelioration of its symptoms. Although numerous treatment methods have been developed and studied, ADHD remains a difficult disorder to treat effectively.

DRUG THERAPIES

Treatments of ADHD can be broken down into roughly two categories: medication and behavioral or cognitive-behavioral treatment with the individual ADHD child, parents, or teachers. Traditional psychotherapy and play therapy have not been found to be effective in the treatment of ADHD. Stimulant medications have been used in the treatment of ADHD since 1937. The most commonly prescribed stimulant medications are methylphenidate (Ritalin), pemoline (Cylert), and dextroamphetamine (Dexedrine). Behavioral improvements caused by stimulant medications include those in impulse control and improved attending behavior. Overall, approximately 75 percent of ADHD children on stimulant medication show behavioral improvement, and 25 percent show either no improvement or decreased behavioral functioning. The findings related to academic performance are mixed. It appears that stimulant medications can help the ADHD child with school productivity and accuracy but not with overall academic achievement. In addition, although ADHD children tend to show improvement while they are on a stimulant medication, there are rarely any long-term benefits to the use of such medications. In general, stimulant medication can be seen as only a short-term management tool.

Antidepressant medications (such as imipramine and Prozac) have also been used with ADHD children. These medications are sometimes used when stimulant medication is not appropriate (for example, if the child has motor or vocal tics). Antidepressant medications, like stimulant medications, appear to provide only short-term improvement in ADHD symptoms. Overall, the use or nonuse of medications in the treatment of ADHD should be carefully evaluated by a qualified physician (such as a psychiatrist). If the child is started on medication for ADHD, the safety and appropriateness of the medication must be monitored continually throughout its use.

BEHAVIOR THERAPIES

Behavioral and cognitive-behavioral treatments have been used with ADHD children, with parents, and with teachers. Most of these techniques attempt to provide the child with a consistent environment in which on-task behavior is rewarded (for example, the teacher praises the child for raising his or her hand and not shouting out an answer), and in which off-task behavior is either ignored or punished (for example, the parent has the child sit alone in a chair near an empty wall, a "time-out chair," after the child impulsively throws a book across the room). In addition, cognitive-behavioral treatments try to teach ADHD children to internalize their own self-control by learning to "stop and think" before they act.

One example of a cognitive-behavioral treatment, which was developed by Philip Kendall and Lauren Braswell, is intended to teach the child to learn five "steps" that can be applied to academic tasks as well as social interactions. The five problem-solving steps that children are to repeat to themselves each time they encounter a new situation are the following: Ask "What am I supposed to do?"; ask "What are my choices?"; concentrate and focus in; make a choice; and ask "How did I do?" (If I did well, I can congratulate myself; if I did poorly, I should try to go more slowly next time.) In each therapy session, the child is given twenty plastic chips at the beginning of the session. The child loses a chip each time he or she does not use one of the steps, goes too fast, or gives an incorrect answer. At the end of the session, the child can use the chips to purchase a small prize; chips can also be stored in a "bank" in order to purchase an even larger prize in the following sessions. This treatment approach combines the use of cognitive strategies (the child learns self-instructional steps) and behavioral techniques (the child loses a desired object, a chip, for impulsive behavior).

Overall, behavioral and cognitive-behavioral treatments have been found to be relatively effective in the settings in which they are used and at the time they are being instituted. Like the effects of medication, however, the effects of behavioral and cognitive-behavioral therapies tend not to be long-lasting. There is some evidence to suggest that the combination of medication and behavior therapy can increase the effectiveness of treatment. In the long run, however, no treatment of ADHD has been found to be truly effective, and in a majority of cases, the disorder persists into adulthood.

HISTORY AND CHANGING DIAGNOSTIC CRITERIA
Children who might now be diagnosed as having ADHD have been written about and discussed in scientific publications since the mid-1800's. Attention to ADHD began in the United States after an encephalitis epidemic in 1917. Because the damage to the central nervous system caused by the disease led to poor attention, impulsivity, and overactivity in children who survived, researchers began to look for signs of brain injury in other children who had similar behavioral profiles. By the 1950's, researchers began to refer to this disorder as "minimal brain damage," which was then changed to "minimal brain dysfunction" (MBD). By the 1960's, however, the use of the term MBD was severely criticized because of its overinclusiveness and nonspecificity. Researchers began to use terms that more specifically characterized children's problems, such as "hyperkinesis" and "hyperactivity."

The *Diagnostic and Statistical Manual of Mental Disorders* (DSM), is the primary diagnostic manual used in the United States. In 1968, the second edition, called DSM-II, presented the diagnosis of "Hyperkinetic Reaction of Childhood" to characterize children who were overactive and restless. By

DSM-IV-TR CRITERIA FOR ATTENTION-DEFICIT HYPERACTIVITY DISORDER (ADHD)

Manifested as inattention or hyperactivity-impulsivity

INATTENTION

Six or more of the following symptoms, persisting for at least six months to a degree maladaptive and inconsistent with developmental level:

- often fails to give close attention to details or makes careless mistakes in schoolwork, work, or other activities
- often has difficulty sustaining attention in tasks or play activities
- often does not seem to listen when spoken to directly
- often does not follow through on instructions and fails to finish school work, chores, or duties in the workplace (not due to oppositional behavior or failure to understand instructions)
- often has difficulty organizing tasks and activities
- often avoids, dislikes, or is reluctant to engage in tasks that require sustained mental effort (such as schoolwork or homework)
- often loses things necessary for tasks or activities (such as toys, school assignments, pencils, books, tools)
- often easily distracted by extraneous stimuli
- often forgetful in daily activities

HYPERACTIVITY-IMPULSIVITY

Six or more of the following symptoms, persisting for at least six months to a degree maladaptive and inconsistent with developmental level:

Hyperactivity
- often fidgets with hands or feet or squirms in seat
- often leaves seat in classroom or in other situations in which remaining seated is expected
- often runs about or climbs excessively in situations in which it is inappropriate (in adolescents or adults, may be limited to subjective feelings of restlessness)
- often has difficulty playing or engaging in leisure activities quietly
- often "on the go" or often acts as if "driven by a motor"
- often talks excessively

Impulsivity
- often blurts out answers before questions have been completed
- often has difficulty awaiting turn
- often interrupts or intrudes on others

Some hyperactive-impulsive or inattentive symptoms cause impairment present before age seven

Some impairment from the symptoms present in two or more settings, such as school and home

Clear evidence of clinically significant impairment in social, academic, or occupational functioning

Symptoms do not occur exclusively during the course of a pervasive developmental disorder, schizophrenia, or other psychotic disorder and are not better accounted for by another mental disorder (mood disorder, anxiety disorder, dissociative disorder, personality disorder)

DSM code based on type:

- Attention-Deficit/Hyperactivity Disorder, Predominantly Inattentive Type (DSM code 314.00): Inattention, but not hyperactivity-impulsivity during the previous six months
- Attention-Deficit/Hyperactivity Disorder, Predominantly Hyperactive-Impulsive Type (DSM code 314.01): Hyperactivity-impulsivity but not inattention during the previous six months
- Attention-Deficit/Hyperactivity Disorder, Combined Type (DSM code 314.01): Both inattention and hyperactivity-impulsivity during the previous six months

1980, when the third edition (DSM-III) was published, researchers had begun to focus on the deficits of attention in these children, so two diagnostic categories were established: "Attention Deficit Disorder with Hyperactivity (ADD with H)" and "Attention Deficit Disorder without Hyperactivity (ADD without H)." After the publication of DSM-III, many researchers argued that there were no empirical data to support the existence of the ADD without H diagnosis. In other words, it was difficult to find any children who were inattentive and impulsive but who were not hyperactive. For this reason, in 1987, when the revised DSM-III-R was published, the only diagnostic category for these children was "Attention-Deficit Hyperactivity Disorder (ADHD)."

With the publication of the fourth version of the manual, the DSM-IV, in 1994, three distinct diagnostic categories for ADHD were identified: ADHD Predominantly Hyperactive-Impulsive Type, ADHD Predominantly Inattentive Type, and ADHD Combined Type. The type of ADHD diagnosed is dependent upon the number and types of behavioral symptoms a child exhibits. Six of nine symptoms from the Hyperactivity-Implusivity list but fewer than six symptoms from the Inattention list lead to a diagnosis of ADHD Predominantly Hyperactive-Impulsive Type. Six of nine symptoms from the Inattention list but fewer than six symptoms from the Hyperactivity-Implusivity list lead to a diagnosis of ADHD Predominantly Inattentive Type. A child who exhibits six of nine behavioral symptoms simultaneously from both lists receives a diagnosis of ADHD Combined Type.

While the diagnostic definition and specific terminology of ADHD will undoubtedly continue to change throughout the years, the interest in and commitment to this disorder will likely continue. Children and adults with

ADHD, as well as the people around them, have difficult lives to lead. The research community is committed to finding better explanations of the etiology and treatment of this common disorder.

SOURCES FOR FURTHER STUDY

Barkley, Russell A. "Attention-Deficit Hyperactivity Disorder." In *Treatment of Childhood Disorders*, edited by E. J. Mash and R. A. Barkley. 2d ed. New York: Guilford Press, 1998. This chapter provides a thorough discussion of different treatments for ADHD children, including stimulant medication, antidepressant medication, behavior therapy, parent training, teacher training, and cognitive-behavioral therapy. Each treatment modality is discussed in a fair and objective manner, and empirical research is provided to support the conclusions given.

_____. *Attention-Deficit Hyperactivity Disorder: A Handbook for Diagnosis and Treatment*. 2d ed. New York: Guilford Press, 1998. Provides comprehensive discussion of nearly all aspects of ADHD, including assessment, diagnosis, and treatment. Also notable for a thorough discussion of ADHD in older adolescents and adults. This excellent and comprehensive book is written by one of the leading researchers in the investigation of ADHD.

Kendall, Philip C. "Attention-Deficit Hyperactivity Disorder." In *Childhood Disorders*. Hove, East Sussex, England: Psychology Press, 2000. A volume in the series Clinical Psychology, A Modular Course. A succinct but thorough discussion of ADHD, including current research on cognitive and neuropsychological performance of children with the disorder.

Wender, Paul H. *ADHD: Attention-Deficit Hyperactivity Disorder in Children and Adults*. New York: Oxford University Press, 2000. A comprehensive overview of ADHD history, diagnosis, treatment. Discusses strengths associated with ADHD as well as problems associated with the disorder.

Wodrich, David L. *Attention-Deficit/Hyperactivity Disorder: What Every Parent Wants to Know*. 2d ed. Baltimore: Paul H. Brookes, 2000. A book aimed at the general public, containing practical advice and clear descriptions of ADHD and related disorders, as well as resources for treatment.

Vicky Phares; updated by Virginia Slaughter

SEE ALSO: Cognitive Behavior Therapy; Drug Therapies; Learning Disorders.

ATTRACTION THEORIES

TYPE OF PSYCHOLOGY: Social psychology
FIELD OF STUDY: Interpersonal relations

Theories of interpersonal attraction attempt to specify the conditions that lead people to like, and in some cases love, each other. Attraction is a two-way process, involving not only the person who is attracted but also the attractor.

KEY CONCEPTS
- equity theory
- matching phenomenon
- mere exposure
- physical attractiveness stereotype
- proximity
- reciprocity
- reinforcement model
- social exchange theory

Relationships are central to human social existence. Personal accounts by people who have been forced to endure long periods of isolation serve as reminders of people's dependence on others, and research suggests that close relationships are the most vital ingredient in a happy and meaningful life. In short, questions dealing with attraction are among the most fundamental in social psychology.

The major theories addressing interpersonal attraction have a common theme: reinforcement. The principle of reinforcement is one of the most basic notions in all of psychology. Put simply, it states that behaviors that are followed by desirable consequences (often these take the form of rewards) tend to be repeated. Applied to interpersonal relations, this principle suggests that when one person finds something rewarding in an interaction with another person (or if that person anticipates some reward in a relationship that has not yet been established), then the person should desire further interaction with that other individual. In behavioral terms, this is what is meant by the term "interpersonal attraction," which emerges in everyday language in such terms as "liking" or, in the case of deep involvement, "loving." Appropriately, these theories, based on the notion that individuals are drawn to relationships that are rewarding and avoid those that are not, are known as reinforcement or reward models of interpersonal attraction.

The first and most basic theory of this type was proposed in the early 1970's by Donn Byrne and Gerald Clore. Known as the reinforcement-affect model of attraction ("affect" means "feeling" or "emotion"), this theory proposes that people will be attracted not only to other people who reward them but also to those people whom they associate with rewards. In other words, a person can learn to like others through their connections to experiences that are positive for that individual. It is important to recognize that a major implication here is that it is possible to like someone not so much because of that person himself or herself but rather as a consequence of that person's merely being part of a rewarding situation; positive feelings toward the experience itself get transferred to that other person. (It also follows that a person associated with something unpleasant will tend to be disliked.) This is called indirect reinforcement.

For example, in one experiment done during the summer, people who evaluated new acquaintances in a cool and comfortable room liked them better than when in a hot and uncomfortable room. In another, similar, study subjects rating photographs of strangers gave more favorable evaluations when in a nicely furnished room than when they were in a dirty room with shabby furniture. These findings provide some insight into why married couples may find that their relationship benefits from a weekend trip away from the children or a romantic dinner at a favorite restaurant; the pleasant event enhances their feelings for each other.

There are other models of interpersonal attraction that involve the notion of rewards but consider the degree to which they are offset by the costs associated with a relationship. Social exchange theory suggests that people tend to evaluate social situations. In the context of a relationship, a person will compare the costs and benefits of beginning or continuing that relationship. Imagine, for example, that Karen is considering a date with Dave, who is kind, attractive, and financially stable but fifteen years older. Karen may decide that this relationship is not worth pursuing because of the disapproval of her mother and father, who believe strongly that their daughter should be dating a man her own age. Karen's decision will be influenced by how much she values the approval of her parents and by whether she has dating alternatives available.

A third model of attraction, equity theory, extends social exchange theory. This approach suggests that it is essential to take into account how both parties involved in a relationship assess the costs and benefits. When each person believes that his or her own ratio of costs to benefits is fair (or equitable), then attraction between the two tends to be promoted. On the other hand, a relationship may be placed in jeopardy if one person thinks that the time, effort, and other resources being invested are justified, while the other person does not feel that way.

Considering the rewards involved in the process of interpersonal attraction provides a useful model but one that is rather general. To understand attraction fully, one must look more specifically at what people find rewarding in relationships. Social psychological research has established some definite principles governing attraction that can be applied within the reward framework.

FACTORS OF ATTRACTION

The first determinant of attraction, reciprocity, is probably fairly obvious, as it most directly reflects the reinforcement process; nevertheless, it is a pow-

Determinants of attraction include reciprocity and proximity. (CLEO Photography)

erful force: People tend to like others who like them. There are few things more rewarding than genuine affection, support, concern, and other indicators that one is liked by another person.

The second principle, proximity, suggests that simple physical closeness tends to promote attraction. Research has confirmed what many people probably already know: People are most likely to become friends (or romantic partners) with others with whom they have worked, grown up, or gone to school. Other studies have shown that people living in dormitories or apartments tend to become friends with the neighbors who live closest to them. Simply being around people gives an individual a chance to interact with them, which in turn provides the opportunity to learn who is capable of providing the rewards sought in a relationship.

It seems, however, that there is yet another force at work, a very basic psychological process known as the mere exposure phenomenon. Research has demonstrated consistently that repeated exposure to something new tends to increase one's liking for it, and examples of the process are quite common in everyday life. It is not uncommon, for example, for a person to buy a new tape or compact disc by a favorite musical artist without actually having heard the new material, only to be disappointed upon listening to it. The listener soon discovers, however, that the album "grows" on him or her and finds himself or herself liking it quite a bit after hearing it a few times. Such occurrences probably involve the mere exposure phenomenon. In short, familiarity breeds liking, and physical closeness makes it possible for that familiarity to develop.

BEAUTY AND ROMANCE

Generally speaking, the same factors that promote the development of friendships also foster romantic attraction. The third principle of attraction, physical attractiveness, is somewhat of an exception, however, as it is more powerful in the romantic context.

In a classic study published by Elaine Hatfield Walster and her associates in 1966, first-year men and women at the University of Minnesota were randomly paired for dates to a dance. Prior to the date, these students had provided considerable information about themselves, some of it through personality tests. During the evening, each person individually completed a questionnaire that focused primarily on how much that person liked his or her date, and the participants were contacted for follow-up six months later. Despite the study of complex facts about attraction, such as what kinds of personality traits within a couple promote it, the only significant factor in this experiment's results was physical appearance. For both sexes, the better-looking the partner, the more the person liked his or her date, the stronger was the desire to date the person again, and the more likely the individual was actually to do so during the next six months.

The potent effect of physical attractiveness in this study sparked much interest in this variable on the part of researchers over the next decade or so. The earliest studies determined rather quickly that both men and women, given the opportunity to select a date from among several members of the opposite sex, almost invariably would select the most attractive one. In real-life dating, however, there is usually the chance that the person asking another out might be turned down. When later experiments began building the possibility of rejection into their procedures, an interesting effect emerged, one that has been termed the "matching phenomenon." People tend to select romantic partners whose degree of attractiveness is very similar to their own.

Other research revealed that physically attractive people are often judged favorably on qualities other than their appearance. Even when nothing is known but what the person looks like, the physically attractive individual is thought to be happier, more intelligent, and more successful than someone who is less attractive. This finding is referred to as the "physical attractiveness stereotype," and it has implications that extend the role of appearance well beyond the matter of dating. Studies have shown, for example, that work (such as a writing sample) will be assessed more favorably when produced by an attractive person than when by someone less attractive, and that a cute child who misbehaves will be treated more leniently than a homely one. What is beautiful is also good, so to speak. Finally, one may note that physical attractiveness fits well with the reward model: It is pleasant and reinforcing both to look at an attractive person and to be seen with him or her, particularly if that person is one's date.

The last principle of attraction, similarity, is the most important one in long-term relationships, regardless of whether they are friendships or romances. An extremely large body of research has demonstrated consistently that the more similar two people are, especially attitudinally, the more they will like each other. It turns out that the old adage, "opposites attract," is simply false. (Note that the matching phenomenon also reflects similarity.) A friend or spouse who holds attitudes similar to one's own will provide rewards by confirming that one's own feelings and beliefs are correct; it is indeed reinforcing when someone else agrees.

EVOLUTIONARY THEORIES OF ATTRACTION

Evolutionary psychologists have provided an important new way to look at why individuals are attracted to others. Borrowing from the basic theorizing of the English biologist Charles Darwin, psychologists are paying increasing attention to the information provided by both physical and social features of living creatures. Everyone is influenced by what people look like; they form impressions of others before they even hear them speak. People often use the appearance and behavior of others to make a variety of judgments about them. These judgments are made quickly and unconsciously and are fairly resistant to change. What sort of impressions are formed? What aspects of a person are focused upon? Evolutionary psychology has some answers to these questions.

Specifically, evolutionary psychologists suggest that the attractiveness of a person's body serves as a valuable and subtle indicator of social behavior, social relationship potential, fitness, reproductive value, and health. Evolutionary psychologists place heavy emphasis on clearly observable features of human bodies and do not focus as much on internal, unobservable aspects of personality such as kindness or trustworthiness. There is a growing body of research that supports these ideas. For example, significant relationships were found between attractiveness and measures of mental health, social anxiety, and popularity, so the idea behind evolutionary theory does seem to be relevant.

Most work studying how body characteristics relate to attractiveness has focused on a single factor, such as the face, although many features of the body can influence attractiveness. Faces are often the first part of a person that is looked at. Furthermore, the face is almost always clearly visible (except for those of women in cultures that forbid it). Social psychologists have shown that people often make quick judgments about others based on their faces, and more than 80 percent of studies on judging attractiveness have focused on the face alone. The sex, age, and past experiences of the perceiver, specific facial features such as large lips for women and strong jaws for men, body and facial symmetry, and specific body ratios such as the waist-to-hip ratio (WHR, the number attained by dividing the waist measurement by the circumference of the hips) all influence judgments of attractiveness. Consistent with this idea are findings that some standards of attractiveness are consistent across time and cultures. For example, people with symmetrical faces—those whose eyes and ears appear to be of equal size and equal distances apart—are preferred over people who do not have symmetrical faces.

FEMALE SHAPELINESS

Another example of a body characteristic that is tied to attractiveness from an evolutionary perspective is women's WHR. Around the world, men prefer women with lower WHRs (between 0.7 and 0.8). Evolutionary psychology research emphasizes the importance of WHRs as a major force in social perception and attraction because shape is a very visible sign of the location of fat stores. This consequently signals reproductive potential and health. Low WHRs do indeed directly map onto higher fertility, lower stress levels, and resistance to major diseases. For example, women with WHRs of 0.8 are almost 10 percent more likely to get pregnant than women with WHRs around 0.9.

Although not as much research has focused on the female breast as a signaler of reproductive fitness, a variety of studies suggest that it is also an important factor, although the evidence is mixed. Some studies support the commonly held stereotype that men prefer larger breasts, although others seem to show no such preference. In contrast, some studies have showed that small and medium breasts are preferred to larger breasts, but much of this work focused either on the bust or on WHRs, not both together. Unfortunately, methodological restrictions and poor stimulus materials limit the generalizability of most previous work using WHRs and other bodily features. For example, many studies used line drawings of figures or verbal descriptions of figures instead of pictures of real people. Research is currently under way to provide clearer tests of evolutionary psychology theories of attraction.

The most consistently documented finding on the evolutionary basis of attraction relates to gender differences in human mate choice. Consistent with Darwin's ideas that humans are naturally programmed to behave in ways to ensure that their genes will be passed on to future generations (ensuring survival), evidence indicates that men tend to prefer young, healthy-looking mates, as these characteristics are associated with the delivery of healthy babies. An examination of the content of more than eight hundred personal advertisements found that men stressed attractiveness and youth in mates more than did women, a finding supported by marriage statistics throughout the twentieth century. Women have been shown to place more emphasis on a prospective mate's social status and financial status, and these traits are often related to being able to take good care of children. The fact that women in Western societies are achieving higher economic positions, however, would suggest that this pattern of preferences may change in time.

HISTORICAL DEVELOPMENT

Although it would seem to be of obvious importance, physical appearance as a determinant of romantic attraction was simply neglected by researchers until the mid-1960's. Perhaps they mistakenly assumed the widespread existence of an old ideal that one should judge someone on the basis of his or her intrinsic worth, not on the basis of a superficial characteristic. Nevertheless, when the Minnesota study discussed earlier produced a physical attractiveness effect so strong as to eliminate, or at least obscure, any other factors related to attraction in the context of dating, social psychologists took notice. In any science, surprising or otherwise remarkable findings usually tend to stimulate additional research, and such a pattern definitely describes the course of events in this area of inquiry.

By around 1980, social psychology had achieved a rather solid understanding of the determinants of attraction to strangers, and the field began turning more of its attention to the nature of continuing relationships. Social psychologist Zick Rubin had first proposed a theory of love in 1970, and research on that topic flourished in the 1980's as investigators examined such topics as the components of love, different types of love, the nature of love in different kinds of relationships, and the characteristics of interaction in successful long-term relationships. Still other lines of research explored how people end relationships or attempt to repair those that are in trouble.

People view relationships with family, friends, and lovers as central to their happiness, a research finding that is totally consistent with common experience. One need only look at the content of motion pictures, television programs, song lyrics, novels, and poetry, in which relationships, particularly romantic ones, are so commonly a theme, to find evidence for that point. Nearly half of all marriages end in divorce, however, and the lack of love in the relationship is usually a precipitating factor. Whatever social psychology can teach people about what determines and maintains attraction can help improve the human condition.

Sources for Further Study

Berscheid, Ellen, and Harry T. Reis. "Attraction and Close Relationships." In *The Handbook of Social Psychology*, Vol. 2, edited by Daniel T. Gilbert, Susan T. Fiske, and Gardner Lindsey. 4th ed. Boston: McGraw-Hill, 1998. An in-depth review of theories of attraction and a good summary of research findings.

Berscheid, Ellen, and Elaine Hatfield Walster. *Interpersonal Attraction*. 2d ed. Reading, Mass.: Addison-Wesley, 1978. Presents a solid overview of the psychology of attraction. Directed toward the reader with no background in social psychology, the book is quite readable. It is highly regarded and frequently cited within the field. Clever illustrations feature many cartoons.

Buss, David M. *Evolutionary Psychology: The New Science of the Mind*. Boston: Allyn & Bacon, 1999. A readable book about the ways in which evolutionary science can help the study of social behavior. Good sections on mating strategies and the factors determining attraction.

Duck, Steve. *Relating to Others*. Chicago: Dorsey Press, 1988. Deals briefly with the traditional work on interpersonal attraction but is most notable for being devoted primarily to reviewing the research on personal relationships, which became important in the 1980's. Covers such topics as developing and maintaining relationships, exclusivity in relationships, and repairing and ending them.

Hatfield, Elaine, and Susan Sprecher. *Mirror, Mirror: The Importance of Looks in Everyday Life*. Albany: State University of New York Press, 1986. A thorough and readable review of all the different effects of personal appearance. Explores how judgments of attractiveness are made and addresses the effects of beauty across the entire life span. Nicely supported with effective photographs and illustrations.

Langlois, Judith H., et al. "Maxims or Myths or Beauty? A Meta-analytic and Theoretical Review." *Psychological Bulletin* 126, no. 3 (2000): 390-423. Provides a wonderful resource by reviewing many articles that look at the factors that predict attractiveness. Also uses the evolutionary approach to explain some of the findings.

Myers, David G. *Social Psychology*. 6th ed. New York: McGraw-Hill, 1999. This popular social psychology textbook features an unusually good chapter on interpersonal attraction. Offers a solid survey of the research relating to the principles of attraction and provides good coverage of work on love. The author's engaging writing style makes this an excellent starting point for further exploration of the topic.

Steve A. Nida; updated by Regan A. R. Gurung

SEE ALSO: Affiliation and Friendship.

AUTISM

TYPE OF PSYCHOLOGY: Psychopathology
FIELD OF STUDY: Childhood and adolescent disorders

Aspects of autism, a poorly understood, nonschizophrenic psychosocial disorder, include great social unresponsiveness, speech and language impairment, ritualistic play activity, and resistance to change. The causes of and treatments for autism have not been conclusively determined, although behavior therapy is a promising alternative.

KEY CONCEPTS
- affective
- cognitive
- dopamine
- echolalia
- electroencephalogram (EEG)
- epileptic seizure
- norepinephrine
- schizophrenia
- secretin
- serotonin

The modern term "autism" was originated by Leo Kanner in the 1940's. In "Autistic Disturbances of Affective Contact" (1943), he described a group of autistic children; he viewed them as much more similar to one another than to schizophrenics, with whom they generally had been associated. Until that time, the classical definition for autism (still seen in some dictionaries) was "a form of childhood schizophrenia characterized by acting out and withdrawal from reality." Kanner believed that these children represented an entirely different clinical psychiatric disorder. He noted four main symptoms associated with the disease: social withdrawal or "extreme autistic aloneness"; either muteness or failure to use spoken language "to convey meaning to others"; an "obsessive desire for maintenance of sameness"; and preoccupation with highly repetitive play habits, producing "severe limitation of spontaneous activity." Kanner also noted that autism—unlike other types of childhood psychoses—began in or near infancy and had both cognitive and affective components.

Over the years, several attempts have been made to establish precise diagnostic criteria for autism. Among the criteria given in the American Psychiatric Association's *Diagnostic and Statistical Manual of Mental Disorders* (rev. 4th ed., 2000, DSM-IV-TR) are pervasive lack of responsiveness to other people; gross deficits in language development; if speech is present, peculiar patterns (such as echolalia and pronoun reversals); bizarre reaction to environmental aspects (resistance to change); and the absence of any symptoms of schizophrenia. These criteria are largely a restatement of Kanner's viewpoint.

The prevalence of autism is generally estimated at between 3 to 9 percent of the population of the United States. Study of the sex distribution shows that it is 2.5 to 4 times as common in males as in females. The causes of autism have not been conclusively determined, although the possibilities are wide-ranging and said to be rooted in both biology and environment. As an example of the latter, one of the most widely cited causes has been vaccination, particularly the mumps, measles, and rubella (MMR) vaccine that is given at approximately eighteen months of age and often corresponds with the earliest detected symptoms of autism. Still, researchers in the United States and Europe have determined that this vaccine does not cause autism, based on the fact that vaccination rates held steady throughout the 1990's at almost 97 percent of children, yet the rate of autism diagnosis increased sevenfold during the same time period.

Possible physiological causes include genetics (siblings of autistic children are two hundred times more likely than the general population to be diagnosed with autism themselves), neurochemistry (abnormal levels of the neurotransmitters norepinephrine, serotonin, and dopamine have been established in children with autism as well as their relatives), low birth weight, older mothers, and brain abnormalities such as reduction of tissue in the cerebellum and enlarged ventricles in the cerebrum.

Largely because of Kanner's original sample (now known to have been atypical), many people believe that autistic children come from professional families. Subsequent studies have indicated that this is not so. Rather, autistic children come from families within a wide socioeconomic range, and more than 75 percent of them score in the moderately mentally retarded range on intelligence tests prior to or in the absence of effective treatment.

The behavior that characterizes the autistic personality strongly suggests that the disorder is related to other types of neurologic dysfunction. Identified neurological correlations include soft neurologic signs (such as poor coordination), seizure disorders (such as phenylketonuria), abnormal electroencephalograms, and unusual sleep patterns. This emphasis on neurologic—or organic—explanations for autism is relatively new; autism was previously thought to be an entirely emotional disorder.

The difficulties that autistic children show in social relationships are exhibited in many ways. Most apparent is a child's failure to form social bonds. For example, such youngsters rarely initiate any interactions with other children. Moreover, unlike nonautistic children, they do not seek parental company or run to parents for solace when distressed. Many sources even point to frequent parental statements that autistic children are not as "cuddly" as normal babies and do not respond to their mothers or to affectionate actions. Autistic children avoid direct eye contact and tend to look through or past other people. In addition, autistic children rarely indulge in any cooperative play activities or strike up close friendships with peers.

Sometimes speech does not develop at all. When speech development does occur, it is very slow and may even disappear again. Another prominent

DSM-IV-TR Criteria for Autism

Autistic Disorder (DSM code 299.00)

Six or more criteria from three lists

1) Qualitative impairment in social interaction, manifested by at least two of the following:
- marked impairment in use of multiple nonverbal behaviors (eye-to-eye gaze, facial expression, body postures, gestures)
- failure to develop peer relationships appropriate to developmental level
- lack of spontaneous seeking to share enjoyment, interests, or achievements with others
- lack of social or emotional reciprocity

2) Qualitative impairments in communication, manifested by at least one of the following:
- delay in, or total lack of, development of spoken language, not accompanied by attempts to compensate through alternative modes of communication such as gesture or mime
- in individuals with adequate speech, marked impairment in ability to initiate or sustain conversation
- stereotyped and repetitive use of language or idiosyncratic language
- lack of varied, spontaneous make-believe play or social imitative play appropriate to developmental level

3) Restricted, repetitive, and stereotyped patterns of behavior, interests, and activities, manifested by at least one of the following:
- preoccupation with one or more stereotyped and restricted patterns of interest abnormal in either intensity or focus
- apparently inflexible adherence to specific, nonfunctional routines or rituals
- stereotyped and repetitive motor mannerisms (hand or finger flapping, complex whole-body movements)
- persistent preoccupation with parts of objects

Delays or abnormal functioning in at least one of the following areas, with onset prior to age three:
- social interaction
- language as used in social communication
- symbolic or imaginative play

Symptoms not better explained by Rett's Disorder or Childhood Disintegrative Disorder speech pathology in autism is either immediate or delayed repetition of something heard but simply parroted back (such as a television commercial), phenomena called immediate and delayed echolalia, respectively. Yet another problem seen is lack of true language comprehension, shown by the fact that an autistic child's ability to follow instructions is often dependent on situational cues. For example, such a child may understand the request to come and eat dinner only when a parent is eating or sitting at the dinner table.

Behavior denoting resistance to change is often best exemplified by rigid and repetitive play patterns, the interruption of which results in tantrums and even self-injury. Some autistic children also develop very ritualistic preoccupations with an object or a schedule. For example, they may become extremely distressed with events as minor as the rearrangement of furniture in a particular room at home.

TREATMENT

Autistic children can be very frustrating to both parents and siblings, disrupting their lives greatly. Often, individuals with autism also cause grief and guilt feelings in parents. According to Mary Van Bourgondien, Gary Mesibov, and Geraldine Dawson, this can be ameliorated by psychodynamic, biological, or behavioral techniques. These authors point out that all psychodynamic therapy views autism as an emotional problem, recommending extensive psychotherapy for the individual with autism and the rest of the family. In contrast, biological methodology applies psychoactive drugs and vitamins. Finally, behavioral therapy uses the axioms of experimental psychology, along with special education techniques that teach and reinforce appropriate behavior.

Psychodynamic approaches are based on the formation of interpersonal relationships between the child and others. One example of these is holding therapy, which involves the mother holding the child for long periods of time so that a supposedly damaged bond between the two can be mended. Floor time, joining the child in his or her activities, is a more active method of establishing a bond with a child. However, both of these methods lack empirical verification of their effectiveness.

Biological methods, on the other hand, involve affecting how the brain receives and processes information. Sensory integration is favored by occupational therapists from the perspective that the nervous system is attempting to regain homeostasis, causing the individual to behave oddly. The approach, an attempt to meet the sensory needs through a "sensory diet" of activities throughout the day, is not supported by scientific research and is not even implemented in an agreed-upon fashion by all of its practitioners. Auditory integration training (AIT) works in the same way as sensory integration with regard to the sensation of sound but is not generally accepted by professionals as being effective. Drug therapies include antiseizure medications, tranquilizers, stimulants, antidepressants, and antianxiety medications that have varying results. One of the most controversial drug therapies is the injection of the hormone secretin, which reportedly causes remarkable improvements in the symptoms of some children but no change in others. Dietary interventions include megadoses of vitamins and minerals that could have very harmful side effects and are not reliably beneficial. Some parents also follow a gluten-free and casein-free regimen with their children, effectively eliminating all milk and wheat products from their diets. Only anecdotal evidence exists of the effectiveness of this and other special diets.

The last category of therapies, behavioral or skill-based techniques, is the most empirically supported. The Treatment and Education of Autistic and Related Communication Handicapped Children (TEACCH) program emphasizes modification of the environment to improve the adaptive functioning of the individual given his or her unique characteristics and teaching others to accommodate autistic children at their particular level of functioning. In contrast, applied behavior analysis programs, such as those advocated by Norwegian psychologist Ivar Lovaas, involve manipulating the environment only for the initial purpose of shaping an individual's skills toward more normal functioning, with the eventual goal of mainstreaming the child with his or her typically developing peers in the regular education setting, an outcome that is estimated to be more likely for children whose treatment begins by two or three years of age.

CHANGING PERCEPTIONS OF AUTISM

It is widely reported that autistic children, as defined by Kanner in the 1940's, were at first perceived as victims of an affective disorder brought on by their emotionally cold, very intellectual, and compulsive parents. The personality traits of these parents, it was theorized, encouraged such children to withdraw from social contact with them, and then with all other people.

In the years that have followed, additional data—as well as conceptual changes in medicine and psychology—have led to the belief that autism, which may actually be a constellation of disorders that exhibit similar symptoms, has a biological basis that may reside in subtle brain and hormone abnormalities. These concepts have been investigated and are leading to definitive changes in the therapy used to treat individual autistic children. Although no general treatment or unifying concept of autism has developed, promising leads include modalities that utilize drugs which alter levels of serotonin and other neurotransmitters, as well as examination of patients by nuclear magnetic resonance and other techniques useful for studying the brain and the nervous system.

The evolution of educational methodology aimed at helping individuals with autism has also been useful, aided by legislation aimed at bringing severely developmentally disabled children into the mainstream. Some cities and states have developed widespread programs for educating autistic people of all ages. Instrumental here has been the development of the National Society for Autistic Children, which has focused some of its efforts on dealing with autistic adolescents and adults.

Combined therapy, biological intervention, and educational techniques have helped autistic persons and their families to cope, have decreased behavior problems in autists, have enhanced the scholastic function of a number of these people, and have produced hope for autistic adults, once nearly all institutionalized.

SOURCES FOR FURTHER STUDY

Herin, L. Juane, and Richard L. Simpson. "Interventions for Children and Youth with Autism: Prudent Choices in a World of Exaggerated Claims and Empty Promises. Part I: Intervention and Treatment Option Review." *Focus on Autism and Other Developmental Disabilities* 13 (1998): 194-211. Covers the specific interventions from the psychodynamic, biological, and behavioral categories and gives an overview of the research support for each.

Kalat, James W. *Biological Psychology.* 8th ed. Belmont, Calif.: Thomson Wadsworth, 2004. A basic text that explains the role of physiological factors in behavior.

Kaye, James A., Maria del Mar Melero-Montes, and Hershel Jick. "Mumps, Measles, and Rubella Vaccine and the Incidence of Autism Recorded by General Practitioners: A Time-Trend Analysis." *British Medical Journal* 322 (2001): 460-463. Describes evidence refuting the hypothesis that the MMR vaccination causes autism.

Lonsdale, Derrick, and Raymond J. Shamberger. "A Clinical Study of Secretin in Autism and Pervasive Developmental Delay." *Journal of Nutritional and Environmental Medicine* 10 (2000): 271-280. Describes an experiment to measure the effectiveness of secretin injections for alleviating the symptoms of autism.

Lovaas, Ivar, and Tristam Smith. "Intensive Behavioral Treatment for Young Autistic Children." In *Advances in Clinical Child Psychology,* edited by B. B. Lahey and A. E. Kazdin. New York: Plenum Press, 1988. A detailed description of ABA therapy and specific research findings relating to the topic.

Maurice, Catherine, Gina Green, and Stephen C. Luce, eds. *Behavioral Intervention for Young Children with Autism: A Manual for Parents and Professionals.* Austin, Tex.: Pro-Ed, 1996. Edited by the mother of two children who were diagnosed with autism and successfully treated with behavior therapy, it provides clear guidance for parents embarking on a search for effective treatment methods for their children and the professionals who are helping them. Included is information on the effectiveness of various treatments, funding behavior therapy, working with educators and other professionals, and what is involved in behavior therapy.

Murray, John B. "Psychophysiological Aspects of Autistic Disorders: Overview." *Journal of Psychology* 130 (1996): 145-158. Covers the symptoms and potential causes of autism.

Sundberg, Mark L., and James W. Partington. *Teaching Language to Children with Autism or Other Developmental Disabilities.* Pleasant Hill, Calif.: Behavior Analysts, 1998. Gives technical guidelines on applied behavior analysis techniques used to teach the different components of language in a skill-based intervention.

Van Bourgondien, Mary E., Gary B. Mesibov, and Geraldine Dawson. "Pervasive Developmental Disorders: Autism." In *The Practical Assessment and Management of Children with Disorders of Development and Learning,* edited by Mark L. Wolraich. Chicago: Year Book Medical Publishers, 1987. Succinctly and clearly describes autism, including its definition, incidence, etiologies and pathophysiologies, assessment and findings, and management. Also included are 133 useful references. Although technically written, the article is nevertheless very useful to the beginning reader.

Sanford S. Singer; updated by April Michele Williams

SEE ALSO: Abnormality: Psychological Models; Language; Schizophrenia: Background, Types, and Symptoms; Schizophrenia: Theoretical Explanations.

BEHAVIORISM

DATE: Founded in 1912
TYPE OF PSYCHOLOGY: Learning
FIELDS OF STUDY: Behavioral and cognitive models; experimental methodologies; instrumental conditioning; methodological issues; nervous system; Pavlovian conditioning; thought

Behaviorism uses the methods of natural science to search for relationships between behavior and the observable social and physical environment. The focus on observable and measurable behavior-environment relationships distinguishes behaviorism from other psychological perspectives that rely on unobservable and hypothetical explanations such as the mind, ego, the self, and consciousness.

KEY CONCEPTS
- classical conditioning
- operant behavior
- operant conditioning
- punisher
- reflex
- reinforcer
- stimulus control

Behaviorism was founded in 1912 by the American psychologist John Broadus Watson (1878-1958). Watson's position was formed as a reaction to the contemporary focus of psychology on consciousness and the method of research known as introspection, which he considered to be highly subjective. Using the research of the Russian Nobel Prize-winning physiologist Ivan Petrovich Pavlov (1849-1936), Watson argued that psychology could become a natural science only by truly adopting the methods of science. For him, psychological study must have an empirical, objective subject matter and that the events to be investigated as possible causes of behavior must also be described objectively and verified empirically through experimental research. This latter point meant that introspection would have to be abandoned, for it was unscientific. Watson therefore presented the goals of psychology as the prediction and control of behavior rather than as the understanding of the mind and consciousness.

Watson's behaviorism was an extension of Pavlov's discovery of the conditioning of stimulus-response reflexive relationships. The term "reflex" refers to the connection between some environmental event, or stimulus, and the response that it elicits. The response is involuntary—inborn or unlearned—and relatively simple. In addition, no prior learning is necessary for the response to occur when the stimulus is presented. What Pavlov had already demonstrated experimentally was how previously neutral parts of the environment could become effective in stimulating or eliciting an animal's salivation response. By repeatedly pairing a bell with food powder, which elicited salivation, and then presenting the bell alone, Pavlov showed that the bell by itself could then elicit salivation. This process, termed classical conditioning (the process is also known as Pavlovian or respondent conditioning), in turn offered Watson an explanation for behavior that relied on observable elements, thus eliminating the need to use unobservable and hypothetical mental explanations.

Watson's significant contribution resulted from his attempt to show how Pavlov's discovery of the conditioning process with animals could also explain the behavior of human beings. Watson assumed that human behavior and the behavior of animals were both governed by the same laws of nature. Given this assumption, the objective methods of study that were appropriate for the scientific study of nonhuman animals were therefore appropriate for the study of human beings as well. Watson demonstrated the application of these methods in the famous but ethically controversial case study of "Little Albert." In this study, Watson and his graduate student, Rosalie Rayner, showed how human emotional responses could come to be conditioned to previously neutral environmental stimuli. "Little Albert" was eleven months old at the time of the study, which Watson and Rayner began by showing that Albert initially approached and smiled when he was shown a live rat. At a time when the rat was not present, Watson struck a metal bar with a hammer. Albert then flinched and began to cry. Next, the rat and the loud, unexpected sound were presented together on seven occasions. On these occasions, Albert reacted to the sound of the hammer striking the metal bar, withdrawing from the rat, moving away from the sound, whimpering, and then crying. Finally, the rat alone was shown to Albert. Now, when only the rat was placed before Albert, he would instantly move away from the rat, whimper, and then cry. Watson and Rayner had demonstrated through the process of classical conditioning that the once-neutral object, the rat, would now produce, or elicit, a strong emotional response.

Watson attempted to present an objective, behavioristic account of the full range of human behavior in *Behaviorism* (1924), written for a popular audience. In that book, Watson proposed that the stimulus-response reflex was the essential building block of all human behaviors. A collection of separate elemental reflexive responses, unlearned and as-yet unconditioned, could become integrated into a complex habit through the regular presentation of the appropriate stimuli by the physical and social environment by parents, siblings, teachers, and others. The result would be, in Watson's words, "habits, such as tennis, fencing, shoe-making, mother-reactions, religious reactions, and the like." The process by which these habits were formed was presumably the conditioning process discovered by Pavlov. In addition to such "habits," Watson attempted to show that the conditioning of neutral environmental stimuli to existing reflexive responses could also account for thinking and the personality.

B. F. Skinner and Radical Behaviorism

A very different form of behaviorism came from the work of the American psychologist Burrhus Frederic Skinner (1904-1990). Skinner, too, focused his research on behavior. He also continued to search for lawful relationships between behavior and the environment. Skinner's thinking began with an acceptance of the stimulus-response approach of Watson, but Skinner ultimately took behaviorism in a different direction. The first presentation of Skinner's approach was in *The Behavior of Organisms* (1938). In this book, he described the methods and results of systematic research that demonstrated the key points of what was later to become known as radical behaviorism: Stimulus-response relationships, or reflexes, include only a narrow range of behavior; classical, or Pavlovian, conditioning could not account for the development of new behavior or the complexity of human behavior; behavior does show lawful relationships with the environment; the consequences immediately following a behavior determine the future strength of that behavior; new behavior can be acquired by the process of shaping (from existing behavior, elemental forms can be strengthened by consequences which follow the step-by-step approximations until the new behavior is present); once acquired, behavior is maintained by a particular arrangement of environmental consequences; and certain events are present when a behavior is strengthened. Often, one of those antecedent events is, by design, especially correlated with the behavior and the consequence that makes that behavior stronger in the future. At a later time, the presence of that antecedent event by itself will make the behavior more likely to occur.

Skinner named the process that he used to investigate these behavior-environment relationships operant conditioning. He called the behavior in this process operant behavior because it operates or acts on the environment. In operating, or acting, on the environment, the behavior produces consequences, or changes, in the environment. Consequences in turn affect the behavior for the future. Skinner was able to detect this relationship between present consequences to the behavior and their later effect on behavior by the method that he used for his research. This method, used initially with rats and later with pigeons, allowed him to observe and measure the behavior of interest continuously and over long periods of time. Not only was the behavior observed at the time that the consequence to it occurred, but it was also observed continuously subsequent to the consequence.

Skinner observed two effects of consequences on the future strength of behavior. Some consequences resulted in stronger behavior (reinforced the behavior), while other consequences resulted in weaker behavior (punished the behavior). For Skinner and his followers, the consequent events to behavior that serve as reinforcers or punishers are defined only in terms of their effects on the future strength of some behavior. Events or things in themselves are not reinforcers or punishers. For example, a harsh command to a learner in the classroom ("Sit down and get to work!") is assumed by many teachers to "punish" wandering around the room and inattentiveness to seatwork. In countless instances, however, the teacher's consequence serves only to strengthen or maintain the learner's wandering and inattentiveness. In this case, the teacher's remarks function as a reinforcer, irrespective of what the teacher believes.

Skinner also showed that once a behavior had been acquired and was maintained, the occurrence of the behavior could be made more or less probable by the presentation or removal of events that preceded the behavior. These antecedent events—for example, the ringing of a telephone—have been reliably present when one picks up the telephone and says "Hello." If one picks up the telephone and says "Hello" when the telephone has not rung, the voice of another person responding to the greeting is extremely unlikely. The term for this process is "stimulus control," defined as the effect that events preceding a behavior can have on the likelihood of that behavior occurring. Stimulus control comes about because of the presence of particular events when a behavior is reinforced.

THE CAUSES OF BEHAVIOR

For Skinner, the causes of behavior lie in humans' genetic endowment and the environment in which they live. The specific ways in which the environment causes behavior can be seen in the experimentally derived principles noted previously.

Skinner's approach differs sharply from most psychological theories that put the causes of behavior inside the person. Skinner believed that these internal causes were either not scientific explanations but actually behaviors themselves in need of explanation or were explanations taken from disciplines other than psychology.

Skinner regarded the "mind" as an unscientific explanation because of its status as an inference from the behavior that it was supposed to explain. While psychological theory has, since the 1970's, redefined the "mind" in two broad ways, Skinner noted that the redefining did not solve the problems posed by the requirements of science. On one hand, mental processes have become cognitive processes, a metaphor based on computer operations. Humans are said to "process" information by "encoding, decoding, storing, and retrieving" information. However, all these hypothesized activities remain inferences from the behavior that they are said to explain. There is no independent observation of these hypothetical activities.

On the other hand, the mind has been translated to mean the brain, which can be studied scientifically. Thus, the physiology of the brain is thought to explain behavior. Neither Skinner nor other radical behaviorists deny the role of the brain in a complete understanding of behavior. However, psychology and brain physiology look for the causes of behavior at different levels of observation. Psychology is viewed as a separate discipline with its own methods of scientific investigation leading to the discovery of distinct psychological explanations for behavior. In addition, research results suggest that rather than brain physiology explaining behavior, changes in the brain and changes in behavior appear to result from changes in the environment. Changes in behavior are correlated with changes in the brain, but changes at both levels appear to be the result of the environment.

Thoughts and feelings are also considered to be causes of behavior. One thinks about talking with a friend and then goes to the telephone and dials the friend's number. These two people talk together on the telephone regularly because they feel affection for each other. The "thinking" or "feeling" referred to as causes for the actions involved in dialing the telephone and talking with each other are themselves viewed as responses in need of explanation. What gave rise to thinking in early development, and what now makes thoughts of this particular friend so strong? How have feelings of affection become associated with this friend? From the radical behaviorist perspective, both the thoughts and the feeling are explained by the principles of operant or classical conditioning.

RADICAL BEHAVIORISM AND COMPLEX HUMAN BEHAVIOR

Some of the facts of human experience include talking, thinking, seeing, problem solving, conceptualizing, and creating new ideas and things. A common point of view holds that behaviorism either rejects or neglects these aspects of human experience. However, a fuller reading of Skinner's works reveals that he offered a serious examination of these topics and demonstrated that behavioral principles could account for their presence in the repertoire of human behavior.

For example, Skinner's examination of verbal behavior resulted in *Verbal Behavior* (1957). In this book, he showed that behavioral principles were capable of explaining the acquisition and continuation of behaviors such as talking, reading, and thinking. Basic processes such as imitation, reinforcement, shaping, and stimulus control were all shown to have likely roles in the various aspects of verbal behavior.

Behaviorism's analysis of verbal behavior is directly related to the more complex forms of human behavior, often referred to as higher mental processes. For example, radical behaviorism views thinking as an activity derived from talking out loud. Parents and teachers encourage children to talk to themselves, initially by encouraging whispering, then moving the lips as in speaking but without making sounds. What results, then, is talking privately, "in our own heads." In a similar fashion, a parent asks a child to "think before you act" and a teacher asks learners to "think through" the solution to a problem in mathematics or ethics. The social environment thus encourages people to think, often shows them how to do so, and then reinforces them for doing so when the overt results of their thinking are praised or given high scores.

More complex behavior-environment relationships such as those found in concept formation have also been analyzed in terms of the principles of behaviorism. The term "concept" is defined as a characteristic that is common to a number of objects that are otherwise different from one another.

People are said to have concepts in their heads which produce the behaviors they observe. A radical behavioral analysis, however, views concepts as the appropriate response to the common characteristic. The appropriate response has been reinforced only when it occurs in the presence of the specific characteristic. For example, a child is said to understand the concept of "red" when the child reliably says "red" in response to the question "What color are these objects?" in the presence of a red hat, red fire truck, red tomato, and red crayon.

APPLICATIONS OF THE PRINCIPLES OF BEHAVIORISM

The behaviorism of Watson has resulted in applications in psychology and many other disciplines. The most notable form of application of Watson's behaviorism is the psychological treatment known as systematic desensitization. This treatment was created by South African psychiatrist Joseph Wolpe (1915-1997). Systematic desensitization was designed to reverse the outcome of the classical conditioning process in which extremely intense negative emotional responses, such as fear or anxiety, are elicited by everyday aspects of the environment. This outcome is referred to as a phobia. The treatment first requires training in relaxation. The second component of treatment takes a person through a hierarchy of steps beginning with a setting very distant from the feared stimulus and ending with the problem setting. At each step, the individual is asked to note and in some manner signal the experiencing of fear or anxiety and then is instructed to relax. Movement through the hierarchy is repeated until the person can experience each step, including the one that includes the feared stimulus, and report feeling relaxed at every step. This treatment has been employed in both the clinic and in real-life settings. Systematic desensitization has been shown to be an effective intervention for fears associated with, for example, dental treatment and flying, as well as the intense anxiety that accompanies social phobia and panic disorder.

Applied behavior analysis is the field of application that has arisen out of Skinner's behavioral principles. Applied behavior analysis was introduced first in educational settings. Applications in education have occurred at every level from preschool to university classrooms. Equally important has been repeated successful application to learners with autism, severe and profound delays in behavioral development, and attention deficit disorder, with and without hyperactive behavior. The application of behavioral principles has been shown to be effective across behaviors, settings, individuals, and teachers.

Applications of behavioral principles have also been shown to be effective in reducing behaviors that pose a threat to public health, including smoking, overeating, essential hypertension, and domestic violence. Finally, behavioral principles have found application in the arena of public safety. For example, researchers using techniques based on Skinner's science of behavior have increased seat belt usage by automobile drivers.

SOURCES FOR FURTHER STUDY

Alberto, Paul A., and Anne C. Troutman. *Applied Behavior Analysis for Teachers.* 5th ed. Upper Saddle River, N.J.: Prentice-Hall, 1999. A readable introduction to applied behavior analysis principles and methods for use in the classroom.

Baum, William J. *Understanding Behaviorism: Science, Behavior, and Culture.* New York: HarperCollins College Publishers, 1994. Written by a well-known radical behaviorist. A thorough review of Skinner's behaviorism in relation to philosophy of science and in its societal implications.

Johnson, Kent R., and T. V. Joe Layng. "Breaking the Structuralist Barrier: Literacy and Numeracy with Fluency." *American Psychologist* 47, no. 11 (1992): 1475-1490. Demonstrates the application of Skinner's principles to the design of maximally effective academic curricula for children and adults. Accessible reading that does not require a background in statistics.

Pierce, W. David, and Carl D. Cheney. *Behavior Analysis and Learning.* 3d ed. Mahwah, N.J.: L. Erlbaum Associates, 2004. An excellent introduction at the college level to basic Skinnerian principles and experimental methods for basic behavioral research.

Skinner, B. F. *About Behaviorism.* New York: Alfred A. Knopf, 1974. Skinner's analysis of thinking, perceiving, emotions, and the self.

_____. *Walden Two.* 1948. Reprint. New York: Macmillan, 1990. A fictional account of the application of behavioral principles in a utopian community.

Watson, John B. *Behaviorism.* 1924. Reprint. New Brunswick, N.J.: Transaction, 1998. Early principles of behaviorism in the words of its founder.

Robert Jensen

SEE ALSO: Conditioning; Habituation and Sensitization; Learned Helplessness; Learning; Pavlovian Conditioning; Phobias; Radical Behaviorism: B. F. Skinner; Reflexes; Thought: Study and Measurement.

BIPOLAR DISORDER

TYPE OF PSYCHOLOGY: Biological bases of behavior; psychopathology; psychotherapy

FIELDS OF STUDY: Biological treatments; depression

Knowledge about bipolar disorder, a serious mental illness that is characterized by depressive episodes and manic episodes, has grown extensively since the 1970's. Advanced neurobiological research and assessment techniques have shown the biochemical origins and genetic element of this disorder. Recent research indicates the ways in which stress may play a role in precipitating recurrence of episodes.

KEY CONCEPTS
- diathesis-stress model
- lithium carbonate
- mania
- melatonin
- neurotransmitter
- psychotic symptoms
- seasonal affective disorder (SAD)

Although mood fluctuations are a normal part of life, individuals with bipolar affective disorder experience extreme mood changes. Bipolar affective disorder, or bipolar disorder (also called manic-depressive disorder), has been identified as a major psychiatric disorder characterized by dramatic mood and behavior changes. These changes, ranging from episodes of high euphoric moods to deep depressions, with accompanying behavioral and personality changes, are devastating to the victims of the disorder and perplexing to the loved ones of those affected. Prevalence rates have been estimated at about 1.6 (0.8 to 2.6) percent of the American population. The disorder is divided fairly equally between males and females. Clinical psychiatry has been effective in providing biochemical intervention in the form of lithium carbonate to stabilize or modulate the ups and downs of this illness. However, lithium treatment has only been effective for approximately 70 percent of those to whom it is administered. Mood-stabilizing anticonvulsant medications such as Depakote, Tegretol, and Lamictal, are showing promise in helping some people who were formerly referred to as lithium nonresponders. Psychotherapy is seen by most practitioners as a necessary adjunct to medication.

SYMPTOMS

In the manic phase of a bipolar episode, the individual may experience inappropriately good moods, or "highs," or may become extremely irritable. During a manic phase, the person may overcommit to work projects and meetings, social activities, or family responsibilities in the belief that he or she can accomplish anything; this is known as manic grandiosity. At times,

DSM-IV-TR Criteria for Bipolar I Disorder

Bipolar I Disorder, Single Manic Episode (DSM code 296.0x)

Only one Manic Episode and no past Major Depressive Episodes

Manic Episode not better accounted for by Schizoaffective Disorder and not superimposed on Schizophrenia, Schizophreniform Disorder, Delusional Disorder, or Psychotic Disorder Not Otherwise Specified

Specify mixed if symptoms meet criteria for Mixed Episode

Specify for current or most recent episode: Severity/Psychotic/Remission Specifiers; with Catatonic Features; with Postpartum Onset

Bipolar I Disorder, Most Recent Episode Hypomanic (DSM code 296.40)

Currently or most recently in Hypomanic Episode

Previously at least one Manic Episode or Mixed Episode

Symptoms cause clinically significant distress or impairment in social, occupational, or other important areas of functioning

Episodes not better accounted for by Schizoaffective Disorder and not superimposed on Schizophrenia, Schizophreniform Disorder, Delusional Disorder, or Psychotic Disorder Not Otherwise Specified

Specify: Longitudinal Course Specifiers (with and Without Interepisode Recovery); with Seasonal Pattern (applies only to pattern of Major Depressive Episodes); with Rapid Cycling

psychotic symptoms such as delusions, severe paranoia, and hallucinations may accompany a manic episode. These symptoms may lead to a misdiagnosis of another psychotic disorder such as schizophrenia. However, skilled clinicians can make a differential diagnosis between schizophrenia and bipolar disorder.

The initial episode of bipolar disorder is typically one of mania or elation, although in some people a depressive episode may signal the beginning of the disorder. Episodes of bipolar disorder can recur rapidly—within hours or days—or may have a much slower recurrence rate, even of years. The duration of each episode, whether it is depression or mania, varies widely among individuals but normally remains fairly consistent for each individual.

TYPES

According to the *Diagnostic and Statistical Manual of Mental Disorders: DSM-IV-TR* (rev. 4th ed., 2000), the diagnostic manual of the American Psychiatric Association, there are several types of bipolar disorder, which are categorized according to the extent of severity, the types of the symptoms, and the duration of the symptoms. Bipolar I disorder is characterized by alternating periods of mania and depression. At times, severe bipolar disorder may be accompanied by psychotic symptoms such as delusions and hallucinations. For this reason, Bipolar I disorder is also considered a psychotic disorder. Bipolar II disorder is characterized by alternating episodes of a milder form of mania (known as hypomania) and depression. Cyclothymia is a form of bipolar disorder in which hypomania alternates with a low-level, chronic depressive state. Seasonal affective disorder (SAD) is characterized by alternating mood episodes that vary according to seasonal patterns; the mood changes are thought to be related to changes in the amount of sunlight and accompanying effects on the levels of hormone melatonin. In the Northern Hemisphere, the typical pattern is associated with manic symptoms in the spring and summer and depression in the fall and winter. Manic episodes often have a shorter duration than the depressive episodes. Bipolar disorder must be differentiated from depressive disorders, which include major depression (unipolar depression) and dysthymia, a milder but chronic form of depression.

CAUSES

The causes of bipolar disorder are not fully understood, but genetic factors play a major role. Approximately 80 percent of individuals with bipolar disorder have a relative with some form of mood disorder, whether bipolar disorder or depression. It is not uncommon to see families in which several

---

DSM-IV-TR CRITERIA FOR BIPOLAR II DISORDER
(DSM CODE 296.89)

Presence or history of one or more Major Depressive Episodes

Presence or history of at least one Hypomanic Episode

No Manic Episodes or Mixed Episodes

Mood symptoms not better accounted for by Schizoaffective Disorder and not superimposed on Schizophrenia, Schizophreniform Disorder, Delusional Disorder, or Psychotic Disorder Not Otherwise Specified

Symptoms cause clinically significant distress or impairment in social, occupational, or other important areas of functioning

Specify for current or most recent episode: Hypomanic (currently or most recently in Hypomanic Episode) or Depressed (currently or most recently in Major Depressive Episode)

Specify for current or most recent Major Depressive Episode (only if the most recent type of mood episode): Severity/Psychotic/Remission Specifiers; Chronic; with Catatonic Features; with Melancholic Features; with Atypical Features; with Postpartum Onset

Specify: Longitudinal Course Specifiers (with and Without Interepisode Recovery); with Seasonal Pattern (applies only to pattern of Major Depressive Episodes); with Rapid Cycling

generations are affected by bipolar disorder. Serotonin, norepinephrine, and dopamine, brain chemicals known as neurotransmitters that regulate mood, arousal, and energy, respectively, may be altered in bipolar disorder.

A diathesis-stress model has been proposed for some psychosomatic disorders such as hypertension and ulcers. This model has also been applied to bipolar disorder. In a diathesis-stress model, there is a susceptibility (the diathesis) for the disorder. An individual who has a diathesis is at risk for the disorder but may not show signs of the disorder unless there is sufficient stress. In this model, a genetic or biochemical predisposition toward the disorder (the bipolar diathesis) may lie dormant until stress triggers the emergence of the illness. The stress may be psychosocial, biological, neurochemical, or a combination of these factors.

A diathesis-stress model can also account for some of the recurrent episodes of mania in bipolar disorder. Investigators suggest that positive life events, such as the birth of a baby or a job promotion, as well as negative life events, such as divorce or the loss of a job, may trigger the onset of episodes in individuals with bipolar disorder. Stressful life events and the social rhythm disruptions that they cause can have adverse effects on a person's circadian rhythms. Circadian rhythms are normal biologic rhythms that govern such functions as sleeping and waking, body temperature, and oxygen consumption. Circadian rhythms affect hormonal levels and have significant effects on both emotional and physical well-being. For those reasons, many clinicians encourage individuals with bipolar disorder to work toward maintaining consistency in their social rhythms.

More recently, investigators have compared the course of bipolar disorder to kindling, a process in which epileptic seizures increase the likelihood of further seizures. According to the kindling hypothesis, triggered mood episodes may leave the individual's brain in a sustained sensitized state that makes the person more vulnerable to further episodes. After a while, external factors are less necessary for a mood episode to be triggered. Episode sensitization may also account for rapid-cycling states, in which the individual shifts from depression to mania over the course of a few hours or days.

IMPACT

The impact of bipolar disorder is considerable. Some believe that the illness puts people on an "emotional roller coaster" in which their ups and downs are so severe that resulting behavior can have its own disastrous consequences. For example, people suffering from episodes of mania sometimes use drugs, alcohol, money, or sex to excess, then later have to deal with an additional set of problems and trauma brought about by their behavior and impulsiveness.

Organizations such as the National Alliance for the Mentally Ill (NAMI) and support groups such as the Depressive and Manic Depressive Association (DMDA) have provided a way for people with bipolar disorder to share their pain as well as to triumph over the illness. Many people have found comfort in knowing that others have suffered from the mood shifts, and they can draw strength from one another. Family members and friends can be the strongest supporters and advocates for those who have bipolar disorder or other psychiatric illnesses. Many patients have credited their families' constant, uncritical support, in addition to competent effective treatment including medications and psychotherapy, with pulling them through the devastating effects of the illness.

TREATMENT APPROACHES

Medications have been developed to aid in correcting the biochemical imbalances thought to be part of bipolar disorder. Lithium carbonate is usually effective for approximately 70 percent of those who take it. Many brilliant and successful people have reportedly suffered from bipolar disorder and have been able to function successfully with competent and responsible treatment. Some people who have taken lithium for bipolar disorder, however, have complained that it robs them of their energy and creativity and said that they actually miss the energy associated with manic phases of the illness. This perceived loss, some of it realistic, can be a factor in relapse associated with lithium noncompliance.

Other medications have been developed to help those individuals who are considered lithium nonresponders or who find the side effects of lithium intolerable. Anticonvulsant medications, such as Depakote (valproic acid), Tegretol (carbamazepine), and Lamictal (lamotrigine), which have been found to have mood-stabilizing effects, are often prescribed to individuals with bipolar disorder. During the depressive phase of the disorder, electroconvulsive (shock) therapy (ECT) has also been administered to help restore the individual's mood to a normal level. Phototherapy is particularly useful for individuals who have SAD. Psychotherapy, especially cognitive-behavioral therapy or interpersonal social rhythm therapy, is viewed by most practitioners as a necessary adjunct to medication. Indeed, psychotherapy has been found to assist individuals with bipolar disorder in maintaining medication compliance.

Local mental health associations are able to recommend psychiatric treatment by board-certified psychiatrists and licensed psychologists who specialize in the treatment of mood disorders. Often, temporary hospitalization is necessary for complete diagnostic assessment, initial mood stabilization, and intensive treatment, medication adjustment, or monitoring of an individual who feels suicidal. As many as 15 percent of those with bipolar disorder commit suicide. This frightening reality makes early intervention, relapse prevention, and treatment of the disorder necessary to prevent such a tragic outcome.

SOURCES FOR FURTHER STUDY

Goldberg, J., and Martin Harrow, eds. *Bipolar Disorders: Clinical Course and Outcome.* Washington, D.C.: American Psychiatric Press, 1999. This edited volume summarizes recent research regarding the course and outcome of bipolar disorder. Chapters are written by experts in the field.

Goodwin, Frederick K., and Kay R. Jamison. *Manic Depressive Illness.* New York: Oxford University Press, 1990. This comprehensive book on bipolar disorder provides information on diagnosis, theories regarding the etiology of the disorder, and treatment options.

Jamison, Kay R. *An Unquiet Mind.* New York: A. A. Knopf, 1995. An insightful first-person account of a psychiatrist's experience with bipolar disorder. Offers descriptions of mania as well as depression and discusses relevant issues such as the genetic basis of the disorder.

Johnson, Sheri L., and John E. Roberts. "Life Events and Bipolar Disorder: Implications from Biological Theories." *Psychological Bulletin* 117, no. 3 (1995): 434-449. This theoretical article was written for psychologists but is readily accessible to laypeople. The authors review research and accounts for ways in which life events, both positive and negative ones, may trigger the onset of episodes in individuals with bipolar disorder.

Diane C. Gooding and Karen Wolford

SEE ALSO: Anxiety Disorders; Attention-Deficit Hyperactivity Disorder (ADHD); Clinical Depression; Depression; Drug Therapies; Madness: Historical Concepts; Obsessive-Compulsive Disorder; Personality Disorders; Schizophrenia: Background, Types, and Symptoms; Schizophrenia: Theoretical Explanations.

Brain Structure

Type of psychology: Biological bases of behavior
Fields of study: Biological influences on learning; nervous system;
  thought

Different areas of the brain have specialized functions that control activities ranging from basic biological processes to complex psychological operations. Understanding the distinctive features of different neurological areas provides insight into why people and other animals act, feel, and think as they do.

Key concepts
- cerebral cortex
- cerebral hemispheres
- forebrain
- hindbrain
- lobes
- midbrain
- neural tube
- neurons

About two weeks after conception, a fluid-filled cavity called the neural tube begins to form on the back of the human embryo. This neural tube will sink under the surface of the skin, and the two major structures of the central nervous system (CNS) will begin to differentiate. The top part of the tube will enlarge and become the brain; the bottom part will become the spinal cord. The cavity will persist through development and become the fluid-filled central canal of the spinal cord and the four ventricles of the brain. The ventricles and the central canal contain cerebrospinal fluid, a clear plasmalike fluid that supports and cushions the brain and also provides nutritive and eliminative functions for the CNS. At birth the average human brain weighs approximately 12 ounces (350 grams), a quarter of the size of the average adult brain, which is about 3 pounds (1,200 to 1,400 grams). Development of the brain in the first year is rapid, with the brain doubling in weight in the first six months.

The development of different brain areas depends on intrinsic and extrinsic factors. Internally, chemicals called neurotrophins promote the survival of neurons (the basic cells of the nervous system that are specialized to communicate electrochemically with one another) and help determine where and when neurons will form connections and become diverse neurological structures. Externally, diverse experiences enhance the survival of neurons and play a major role in the degree of development of different neurological areas. Research has demonstrated that the greater the exposure a child receives to a particular experience, the greater the development of the neurological area involved in processing that type of stimulation. While this phenomenon occurs throughout the life span, the greatest impact of environmental stimulation in restructuring and reorganizing the brain occurs in the earliest years of life.

Experience can alter the shape of the brain, but its basic architecture is determined before birth. The brain consists of three major subdivisions: the hindbrain (rhombencephalon, or "parallelogram-brain"), the midbrain (mesencephalon, or "midbrain"), and the forebrain (prosencephalon, or "forward brain"). The hindbrain is further subdivided into the myelencephalon ("marrow-brain") and the metencephalon ("after-brain"), while the forebrain is divided into the diencephalon ("between-brain") and the telencephalon ("end-brain"). To visualize roughly the locations of these brain areas in a person, one can hold an arm out, bend the elbow 90 degrees, and make a fist. If the forearm is the spinal cord, where the wrist enlarges into the base of the hand corresponds to the hindbrain, with the metencephalon farther up than the myelencephalon. The palm of the hand, enclosed by the fingers, would be the midbrain. The fingers would be analogous to the forebrain, with the topmost surface parts of the fingers being the telencephalon.

One can take the analogy a step further. If a fist is made with the fingers of the other hand and placed next to the fist previously made, each fist would represent the two cerebral hemispheres of the forebrain, with the skin of the fingers representing the forebrain's cerebral cortex, the six layers of cells that cover the two hemispheres. Finally, like close-fitting gloves, the meninges cover the cortex. The three layers of the meninges play a protective and nutritive role for the brain.

The more advanced the species, the greater the development of the forebrain in general and the cortex in particular. The emphasis here is placed on a neuroanatomical examination of the human brain, beginning with a look at the hindbrain and progressing to an investigation of the cerebral cortex. The terms "anterior" ("toward the front") and "posterior" ("toward the back") will be used frequently in describing the location of different brain structures. Additionally, the words "superior" ("above") and "inferior" ("below") will be used to describe vertical locations.

THE HINDBRAIN

As the spinal cord enters the skull, it enlarges into the bottommost structure of the brain, the medulla (or medulla oblongata). The medulla controls many of the most basic physiological functions for survival, particularly breathing and the beating of the heart. Reflexes such as vomiting, coughing, sneezing, and salivating are also controlled by the medulla. The medulla is sensitive to opiate and amphetamine drugs, and overdoses of these drugs can impair its normal functioning. Severe impairment can lead to a fatal shutdown of the respiratory and cardiovascular systems.

Just above the medulla lie the pons, parts of the reticular formation, the raphe system, and the locus coeruleus. All these structures play a role in arousal and sleep. The pons plays a major role in initiating rapid eye move-

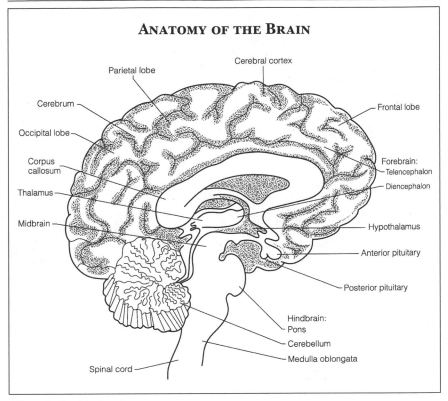

ANATOMY OF THE BRAIN

Cerebral cortex
Parietal lobe
Cerebrum
Occipital lobe
Corpus callosum
Thalamus
Midbrain
Frontal lobe
Forebrain:
Telencephalon
Diencephalon
Hypothalamus
Anterior pituitary
Posterior pituitary
Hindbrain:
Pons
Cerebellum
Medulla oblongata
Spinal cord

(Hans & Cassidy, Inc.)

ment (REM) sleep. REM sleep is characterized by repeated horizontal eye movements, increased brain activity, and frequent dreaming. The reticular system (sometimes called the reticular activating system, or RAS) stretches from the pons through the midbrain to projections into the cerebral cortex. Activation of the reticular system, by sensory stimulation or thinking, causes increases in arousal and alertness in diverse areas of the brain. For the brain to pay attention to something, there must be activation from the reticular formation. The raphe system, like the reticular system, can increase the brain's readiness to respond to stimuli. However, unlike the reticular formation, the raphe system can decrease alertness to stimulation, decrease sensitivity to pain, and initiate sleep. Raphe system activity is modulated somewhat by an adjacent structure called the locus coeruleus. Abnormal functioning of this structure has been linked with depression and anxiety.

The largest structure in the metencephalon is the cerebellum, which branches off from the base of the brain and occupies a considerable space in the back of the head. The cerebellum's primary function is the learning and control of coordinated perceptual-motor activities. Learning to walk, run, jump, throw a ball, ride a bike, or perform any other complex motor activity causes chemical changes to occur in the cerebellum that result in the construction of a sort of program for controlling the muscles involved in the particular motor skills. Activation of specific programs enables the performance of particular motor activities. The cerebellum is also involved in other types of learning and performance. Learning language, reading, shifting attention from auditory to visual stimuli, and timing (such as in music or the tapping of fingers) are just a few tasks for which normal cerebellar functioning is essential. People diagnosed with learning disabilities often are found to have abnormalities in the cerebellum.

THE MIDBRAIN

The superior and posterior part of the midbrain is called the tectum. There are two enlargements on both sides of the tectum known as the colliculi. The superior colliculus controls visual reflexes such as tracking the flight of a ball, while the inferior colliculus controls auditory reflexes such as turning toward the sound of a buzzing insect. Above and between the colliculi lies the pineal gland, which contains melatonin, a hormone that greatly influences the sleep-wake cycle. Melatonin levels are high when it is dark and low when it is light. High levels of melatonin induce sleepiness, which is one reason that people sleep better when it is darker. Another structure near the colliculi is the periaqueductal gray (PAG) area of the ventricular system. Stimulation of the PAG helps to block the sensation of pain.

Beneath the tectum is the tegmentum, which includes some structures involved in movement. Red nucleus activity is high during twisting movements, especially of the hands and fingers. The substantia nigra smooths out movements and is influential in maintaining good posture. The characteristic limb trembling and posture difficulties of Parkinson's disease are attributable to neuronal damage in the substantia nigra.

THE FOREBRAIN

Right above the midbrain, in the center of the brain, lies the thalamus, which is the center of sensory processing. All incoming sensory information, except for the sense of smell, goes to the thalamus first before it is sent on to the cerebral cortex and other areas of the brain. Anterior to and slightly below the thalamus is the hypothalamus. Hypothalamic activity is involved in numerous motivated behaviors such as eating, drinking, sexual activity, temperature regulation, and aggression. Its activity occurs largely through its regulation of the pituitary gland, which is beneath the hypothalamus. The pituitary gland controls the release of hormones that circulate in the endocrine system.

SUBCORTICAL STRUCTURES. Numerous structures lie beneath the cerebral cortex in pairs, one in each hemisphere. Many of these structures are highly interconnected with one another and are therefore seen to be part of a system. Furthermore, most of the subcortical structures can be categorized as belonging to one of two major systems. Surrounding the thalamus is one system called the basal ganglia, which is most prominently involved in movements and muscle tone. The basal ganglia deteriorate in Parkinson's and Huntington's diseases, both disorders of motor activity. The three major structures of the basal ganglia are the caudate nucleus and putamen, which form the striatum, and the globus pallidus. The activities of the basal ganglia extend beyond motor control. The striatum, for instance, plays a significant role in the learning of habits as well as in obsessive-compulsive disorder, a disorder of excessive habits. In addition, disorders of memory, attention, and emotional expression (especially depression) frequently involve abnormal functioning of the basal ganglia.

The nucleus basalis, while not considered part of the basal ganglia, nevertheless is highly interconnected with those structures (and the hypothalamus) and receives direct input from them. Nucleus basalis activity is essential for attention and arousal.

The other major subcortical system is the limbic system. The limbic system was originally thought to be involved in motivated or emotional behaviors and little else. Later research, however, demonstrated that many of these structures are crucial for memory formation. The fact that people have heightened recall for emotionally significant events is likely a consequence of the limbic system's strong involvement in both memory and motivation or emotion.

Two limbic structures are essential for memory formation. The hippocampus plays the key role in making personal events and facts into long-term memories. For a person to remember information of this nature for more than thirty minutes, the hippocampus must be active. In people with Alzheimer's disease, deterioration of the hippocampus is accompanied by memory loss. Brain damage involving the hippocampus is manifested by amnesias, indecisiveness, and confusion. The hippocampus takes several years to develop fully. This is thought to be a major reason that adults tend to remember very little from their first five years of life, a phenomenon called infantile amnesia.

The second limbic structure that is essential for learning and memory is the amygdala. The amygdala provides the hippocampus with information about the emotional context of events. It is also crucial for emotional perception, particularly in determining how threatening events are. When a person feels threatened, that person's amygdala will become very active. Early experiences in life can fine-tune how sensitive a person's amygdala will be to potentially threatening events. A child raised in an abusive environment will likely develop an amygdala that is oversensitive, predisposing that person to interpret too many circumstances as threatening. Two additional limbic structures work with the amygdala in the perception and expression of threatening events, the septal nuclei and the cingulate gyrus. High activity in the former structure inclines one to an interpretation that an event is not threatening. Activity in the latter structure is linked to positive or negative emotional expressions such as worried, happy, or angry looks.

Other major structures of the limbic system include the olfactory bulbs and nuclei, the nucleus accumbens, and the mammillary bodies. The olfactory bulbs and nuclei are the primary structures for smell perception. Experiencing pleasure involves the nucleus accumbens, which is also often stimulated by anything that can become addictive. The mammillary bodies are involved in learning and memory.

CORTICAL LOBES. The most complex thinking abilities are primarily attributable to the thin layers that cover the two cerebral hemispheres—the cortex. It is this covering of the brain that makes for the greatest differences between the intellectual capabilities of humans and other animals. Both hemispheres are typically divided into four main lobes, the distinct cortical areas of specialized functioning. There are, however, many differences among people, not only in the relative size of different lobes but also in how much cerebral cortex is not directly attributable to any of the four lobes.

The occipital lobe is located at the back of the cerebral cortex. The most posterior tissue of this lobe is called the striate cortex because of its distinctive striped appearance. The striate cortex is also called the primary visual cortex because it is there that most visual information is eventually processed. Each of the layers of this cortical area is specialized to analyze different features of visual input. The synthesis of visual information and the interpretation of that result involve other lobes of the brain. The occipital lobe also plays the primary role in various aspects of spatial reasoning. Activities such as spatial orientation, map reading, or knowing what an object will look like if rotated a certain amount of degrees all depend on this lobe.

Looking down on the top of the brain, a deep groove called the central sulcus can be seen roughly in the middle of the brain. Between the central sulcus and the occipital lobe is the parietal lobe. The parietal lobe's predominate function is the processing of the bodily sensations: taste, touch, temperature, pain, and kinesthesia (feedback from muscles and joints). A parietal band of tissue called the postcentral gyrus that is adjacent to the central sulcus (posterior and runs parallel to it) contains the somatosensory cortex in which the surface of the body is represented upside down in a maplike fashion. Each location along this cortical area corresponds to sensations from a different body part. Furthermore, the left side of the body is represented on the right hemisphere and vice versa. Damage to the right parietal cortex usually leads to sensory neglect of the left side of the body—the person ignores sensory input from that side. However, damage to the left parietal cortex causes no or little sensory neglect of the right side of the body.

The parietal lobe is involved with some aspects of distance sensation. The posterior parietal lobe plays a role in the visual location of objects and the bringing together of different types of sensory information, such as coordinating sight and sound when a person looks at someone who just called his or her name. Some aspects of the learning of language also engage the operation of the parietal cortex.

On the sides of each hemisphere, next to the temples of the head, reside the temporal lobes. The lobes closest to the ears are the primary sites of the interpretation of sounds. This task is accomplished in the primary auditory cortex, which is tucked into a groove in each temporal lobe, called a lateral sulcus. Low-frequency sounds are analyzed on the outer part of this sulcus; higher-pitched sounds are represented deeper inside this groove. Closely linked with auditory perception are two other major functions of the temporal lobe: language and music comprehension. Posterior areas, particularly Wernicke's area, play key roles in word understanding and retrieval. More medial areas are involved in different aspects of music perception, especially the planum temporale.

The temporal cortex is the primary site of two important visual functions. Recognition of visual objects is dependent on inferior temporal areas. These areas of the brain are very active during visual hallucinations. One area in this location, the fusiform gyrus, is very active during the perception of faces and complex visual stimuli. A superior temporal area near the conjunction of the parietal and occipital lobes is essential for reading and writing.

The temporal lobe is in close proximity to, and shares strong connections with, the limbic system. Thus, it is not surprising that the temporal lobe plays a significant role in memory and emotions. Damage to the temporal cortex leads to major deficits in the ability to learn and in maintaining a normal emotional balance.

The largest cerebral lobe, comprising one-third of the cerebral cortex, is the frontal lobe. It is involved in the greatest variety of neurological functions. The frontal lobe consists of several anatomically distinct and functionally distinguishable areas that can be grouped into three main regions. Starting at the central sulcus (which divides the parietal and frontal lobes) and moving toward the anterior limits of the brain, one finds, in order, the precentral cortex, the premotor cortex, and the prefrontal cortex. Each of these areas is responsible for different types of activities.

In 1870 German physicians Gustav Fritsch and Eduard Hitzig were the first to stimulate the brain electrically. They found that stimulating different regions of the precentral cortex resulted in different parts of the body moving. Subsequent research identified a "motor map" that represents the body in a fashion similar to the adjacent and posteriorly located somatosensory map of the parietal lobe. The precentral cortex, therefore, can be considered the primary area for the execution of movements.

The premotor cortex is responsible for planning the operations of the precentral cortex. In other words, the premotor cortex generates the plan to pick up a pencil, while the precentral cortex directs the arm to do so. Thinking about picking up the pencil, but not doing so, involves more activity in the premotor cortex than in the precentral cortex. An inferior premotor area essential for speaking was discovered in 1861 by Paul Broca and has since been named for him. Broca's area, usually found only in the left hemisphere, is responsible for coordinating the various operations necessary for the production of speech.

The prefrontal cortex is the part of the brain most responsible for a variety of complex thinking activities, foremost among them being decision making and abstract reasoning. Damage to the prefrontal cortex often leads to an impaired ability to make decisions, rendering the person lethargic and greatly lacking in spontaneous behavior. Numerous aspects of abstract reasoning, such as planning, organizing, keeping time, and thinking hypothetically, are also greatly disturbed by injuries to the prefrontal cortex.

Research with patients who have prefrontal disturbances has demonstrated the important role of this neurological area in personality and social behavior. Patients with posterior prefrontal damage exhibit many symptoms of depression: apathy, restlessness, irritability, lack of drive, and lack of ambition. Anterior abnormalities, particularly in an inferior prefrontal region called the orbitofrontal area, result in numerous symptoms of psychopathy: lack of restraint, impulsiveness, egocentricity, lack of responsibility for one's actions, and indifference to others' opinions and rights.

The prefrontal cortex also contributes to the emotional value of decisions, smell perception, working memory (the current ability to use memory), and the capacity to concentrate or shift attention. Children correctly diagnosed with attention-deficit hyperactivity disorder (ADHD) often have prefrontal abnormalities.

HEMISPHERIC DIFFERENCES. The two cerebral hemispheres are connected by a large band of fibers called the corpus callosum and several small connections called commissures. In the early 1940's, American surgeon William van Wagenen, in order to stop the spread of epileptic seizures from crossing from one hemisphere to the other, performed the first procedure of cutting the 200 million fibers of the corpus callosum. The results were mixed, however, and it was not until the 1960's that two other American surgeons, Joe Bogen and P. J. Vogel, decided to try the operation again, this time also including some cutting of commissure fibers. The results reduced or stopped the seizures in most patients. However, extensive testing by American psychobiologist Roger Sperry and his colleagues demonstrated unique behavioral changes in the patients, called split-brain syndrome. Research with split-brain syndrome and less invasive imaging techniques of the brain, such as computed tomography (CT) and positron-emission tomography (PET) scans, has demonstrated many anatomical and functional differences between the left and right hemispheres.

The degree of differences between the two cerebral hemispheres varies greatly, depending on a number of factors. Males develop the greatest lateralization—differences between the hemispheres—and develop the differences soonest. Those with a dominant right hand have greater lateralization than left- or mixed-handers. Therefore, when there is talk of "left brain versus right brain," it is important to keep in mind that a greater degree of difference exists in right-handed males. A minority of people, usually left-handers, show little differences between the left and right hemi-spheres.

The right hemisphere (RH) tends to be larger and heavier than the left hemisphere (LH), with the greatest difference in the frontal lobe. Con-versely, several other neurological areas have been found to be larger in the LH: the occipital lobe, the planum temporale, Wernicke's area, and the Sylvian fissure. An interesting gender difference in hemispheric operation is that the LH amygdala is more active in females, whereas the RH amygdala is more active in males.

The left-brain/right-brain functional dichotomy has been the subject of much popular literature. While there are many differences in operation be-tween the two hemispheres, many of these differences are subtle, and in many regards both hemispheres are involved in the psychological function in question, only to different degrees.

The most striking difference between the two hemispheres is that the RH is responsible for sensory and motor functions of the left side of the body, and the LH controls those same functions for the body's right side. This contralateral control is found, to a lesser degree, for hearing and, due to the optic chiasm, not at all for vision.

In the domain of sound and communication, the LH plays a greater role in speech production, language comprehension, phonetic and semantic analysis, visual word recognition, grammar, verbal learning, lyric recitation, musical performance, and rhythm keeping. A greater RH contribution is found in interpreting nonlanguage sounds, reading Braille, using emo-tional tone in language, understanding humor and sarcasm, expressing and interpreting nonverbal communication (facial and bodily expressions), and perceiving music. Categorical decisions, the understanding of metaphors, and the figurative aspects of language involve both hemispheres.

Regarding other domains, the RH plays a greater role in mathematical operations, but the LH is essential for remembering numerical facts and the reading and writing of numbers. Visually, the RH contributes more to men-tal rotation, facial perception, figured/ground distinctions, map reading, and pattern perception. Detail perception draws more on LH resources. The RH is linked more with negative emotions such as fear, anger, pain, and sadness, while positive affect is associated more with the LH. Exceptions are that schizophrenia, anxiety, and panic attacks have been found to be related more to increases in LH activity.

SUMMARY

It has been estimated that the adult human brain contains 100 billion neu-rons, forming more than 13 trillion connections with one another. These connections are constantly changing, depending on how much learning is occurring and on the health of the brain. In this dynamic system of different neurological areas concerned with diverse functions, the question arises of how a sense of wholeness and stability emerges. In other words, where is the "me" in the mind? While some areas of the brain, such as the frontal lobe, appear more closely linked with such intimate aspects of identity as planning and making choices, it is likely that no single structure or particular function can be equated with the self. It may take the activity of the whole brain to give a sense of wholeness to life. Moreover, the self is not to be found anyplace in the brain itself. Instead, it is what the brain does—its patterns of activity—that defines the self.

SOURCES FOR FURTHER STUDY

Goldberg, Stephen. *Clinical Neuroanatomy Made Ridiculously Simple.* Miami: MedMaster, 2000. One of a series of books intended to help students in the medical professions by presenting an abbreviated version of various medical subjects. The use of mnemonic devices, humor, and case studies makes the book accessible to a college-educated audience.

Hendleman, Walter J. *Atlas of Functional Neuroanatomy.* Boca Raton, Fla.: CRC Press, 2000. Presents a visual tour of the brain through drawings, photographs, and computer-generated illustrations. Three-dimensional images of the brain can be observed by using the accompanying CD-ROM.

Kalat, James W. *Biological Psychology.* 8th ed. Belmont, Calif.: Thomson Wadsworth, 2004. A top-selling book in the area of physiological psychology. While intended for college students, this engaging, easy-to-read text is accessible to general audiences. Two chapters contain excellent overviews of brain anatomy and functioning.

Ornstein, Robert. *The Right Mind: Making Sense of the Hemispheres.* New York: Harcourt Brace, 1997. The author who helped popularize the left-brain/right-brain dichotomy in *The Psychology of Consciousness* (1972) reexamines the functioning of the two hemispheres in this book. The result is an easy-to-read, entertaining view of hemispheric lateralization that dispels many myths about differences in hemispheric functioning.

Ornstein, Robert, and Richard F. Thompson. *The Amazing Brain.* Boston: Houghton Mifflin, 1991. One of the best introductory books about the brain, written with a light and humorous touch. The lay reader will enjoy the accessibility of the text, the excellent (and unique) sketches, and the fanciful flare the authors use in examining a complicated subject.

Paul J. Chara, Jr.

SEE ALSO: Animal Experimentation; Consciousness; Consciousness: Altered States; Endocrine System; Hormones and Behavior; Memory; Memory: Animal Research; Nervous System; Neuropsychology.

Case-Study Methodologies

Type of psychology: Psychological methodologies
Field of study: Descriptive methodologies

Case-study methodologies include a number of techniques for studying people, events, or other phenomena within their natural settings. Typically, case studies involve careful observations made over an extended period of time in situations where it is not possible to control the behaviors under observation. The results and interpretation of the data are recorded in narrative form.

Key concepts
- extraneous variable
- independent variable
- laboratory setting research
- naturalistic observation
- quasi-experiments

According to social scientist Robert Yin, case-study research is one of the most frequently misunderstood methods used to study behaviors. Yin, in his book *Case Study Research: Design and Methods* (1984), points out that misconceptions have come about because of the limited coverage that case-study research receives in the average textbook on research methods. In addition, most texts typically confuse the case-study approach with either qualitative research methods or specific types of quasi-experimental designs (experiments that do not allow subjects to be assigned randomly to treatment conditions).

Yin defines a case study as a method for studying contemporary phenomena within their natural settings, particularly when the behaviors under study cannot be manipulated or brought under the experimenter's control. Thus, unlike studies that are performed in the sometimes rigidly sterile laboratory setting (in which phenomena are studied in an artificial environment with rigorous procedures in place to control for outside influences), the case-study approach collects data where the behaviors occur, in real-life contexts. Although behavior in natural settings can lead to a wealth of data waiting to be mined, case-study methodology also has its drawbacks. Someone using this approach needs to recognize that the lack of control over extraneous variables can compound the difficulty associated with trying to identify the underlying variables that are causing the behaviors. Extraneous variables can be defined as those that have a detrimental effect on a research study, making it difficult to determine if the result is attributable to the variable under study or to some unknown variable not controlled for. Despite this concern, case-study methods are seen as valuable research tools to help unlock the mysteries behind events and behaviors. The approach has been used by psychologists, sociologists, political scientists, anthropologists, historians, and economists, to name a few.

HISTORY OF CASE STUDIES

Long before the scientific community began to formalize the procedures associated with conducting case studies, scientists, philosophers, and physicians were studying phenomena in their natural contexts by making direct observations and later systematically recording them. Although it is difficult to pinpoint how long this method has been used, there are a number of documented cases dating back to the second and third centuries. Galen, a leading physician in Rome in the second century, spent five years as a surgeon to the gladiators in the Roman Colosseum. During this time, he made painstaking observations correlating head injuries that the gladiators received with loss of intellectual abilities. In a sense, this was a prelude to the case study of today.

Psychology has been heavily influenced by the natural sciences. Since the natural sciences gave birth to the scientific method—a particular technique for gaining knowledge which includes the testing of hypotheses in ways that can be verified—it is not surprising that psychology adopted a modified version of the scientific method that could be applied to the study of people and other organisms. It soon became apparent, however, that not all situations lend themselves to study by an experiment. Thus, it was important for alternative methodologies to be developed and used. The case study is an outgrowth of this quest to find alternative methods for studying complex phenomena.

DESIGN TYPES AND PURPOSES

Yin suggests that case-study designs vary according to two distinct dimensions. One dimension accounts for the number of "cases" being studied: the presence of either single- or multiple-case designs. A second dimension allows for case studies to be either "holistic" (studying the entire unit of analysis as a single global entity) or "embedded" (allowing multiple units of analysis to be studied for the purpose of understanding their interworkings). According to Yin, this classification system leaves the researcher with a choice among four different design types: single-case (holistic) design, single-case (embedded) design, multiple-case (holistic) design, and multiple-case (embedded) design. Choosing among these designs involves the kinds of research questions that the researcher is attempting to answer.

Case-study methods are initiated for a variety of reasons, one of which is to serve as a vehicle for exploratory research. As a new research area begins to develop, the initial uncharted territory is sometimes best studied (particularly when the research questions are ill-defined) using a case-study method to determine which direction should be pursued first. This method has therefore been commonly misperceived as being able to contribute only in a limited exploratory capacity; however, the case study can, and should, be used not only to help focus initial research questions but also to describe and explain behaviors. As Yin makes clear, both "how" questions and "why" questions can be answered by this approach.

EXPERIMENTS VERSUS CASE STUDIES

A frequently asked question is, "When should one choose to conduct a case study, rather than an experiment?" To answer this question, it is important to understand some basic differences between case-study methods and experimental designs. Experiments allow the researcher to manipulate the independent variables (those under the control of the experimenter) that are being studied.

For example, in a study to determine the most effective treatment approach for severe depression, subjects could be randomly assigned to one of three different treatments. The treatments are under the control of the researcher in the sense that he or she determines who will get a particular treatment and exactly what it will be. On the other hand, case studies are used in situations where the variables cannot be manipulated. Experiments typically, although not exclusively, are performed in a laboratory setting. Case studies occur in naturalistic settings, a research environment in which, in contrast to laboratory research, subjects are studied in the environment in which they live, with little or no intervention on the part of the researcher. Experiments are characterized as having rigorous control over extraneous variables. Case studies typically lack such control. Experiments place a heavy emphasis on data-analysis procedures that use numbers and statistical testing. Case studies emphasize direct observation and systematic interviewing techniques, and they are communicated in a narrative form. Experiments are designed so that they can be repeated. Case studies, by their very nature, can be quite difficult to repeat.

SINGLE-CASE VERSUS MULTIPLE-CASE STUDIES

One of Yin's dimensions for classifying case studies involves single-case versus multiple-case studies. In some instances, only a single-case study is necessary or at times even possible; this is true when a unique case comes along that presents a valuable source of information. For example, a social scientist wanting to explore the emotional impact of a national tragedy on elementary-school children might choose to study the *Challenger* space shuttle disaster or the World Trade Center attacks, as a single-case study.

Eminent Russian psychologist Aleksandr Luria, in his book *The Mind of a Mnemonist: A Little Book About a Vast Memory* (1968), has, in a most engaging style, described a single-case (holistic) study. The case involved a man by the name of Shereshevskii (identified in the book as subject "S") who possessed an extraordinary memory. Luria began to observe "S" systematically in the 1920's, after "S" had asked him to test his memory. Luria was so astounded by the man's ability to study information for brief periods of time and then repeat it back to him without an error that he continued to observe and test "S" over the following thirty years. Luria was convinced that this man possessed one of the best memories ever studied.

Because of the nature of the phenomenon—an unusually vast memory—and the fact that this man was capable of performing memory feats never before witnessed, a single-case (holistic) study was begun. When studying rare phenomena, as in this instance, it is not possible to find the number of subjects typically required for an experiment; thus, the case-study approach presents the best alternative. Over the ensuing thirty years, Luria carefully documented the results of literally hundreds of memory feats. In some instances, Luria presented "S" with a list of words to memorize and asked him to recall them immediately. At other times, without any forewarning, Luria asked "S" to recall words from lists given more than fifteen years before. In most of these instances, "S" recalled the list with only a few errors. Luria commented on much more than the results of these memory tests; he also carefully studied the personality of "S." Luria wanted to understand him as a whole person, not only as a person with a great memory. Closely involved with his subject, Luria personally gave the instructions and collected the data. Whereas the data from the memory tasks provided some degree of objectivity to the study, most of the information came from the subjective observations and judgments made by Luria himself. The study was reported in a book-length narrative.

Hawthorne Studies

A second example involves a case study that was part of a larger group known as the Hawthorne studies, conducted at the Western Electric Company, near Chicago, in the 1920's. One particular study, called the Bank Wiring Observation Room Study, was initiated to examine the informal social interactions that occur within a small group of employees in an industrial plant.

A group of fourteen men was moved to a self-contained work room that simulated the plant environment; a psychologist was assigned to observe the behavior of the group. No manipulation of any variables occurred; there was only passive observation of the employees' behavior. As might be expected, the presence of the observer discouraged many of the men from behaving as they normally would if someone were not present. The men were suspicious that the psychologist would inform their supervisor of any behaviors that were not allowed on the job. After a month passed, however, the men became accustomed to the observer and started to behave as they normally did inside the plant. (One should note the length of time needed to begin observing "normal" work behaviors; most experiments would have been terminated long before the natural behaviors surfaced.) The informal social interactions of this group were studied for a total of eight months.

This study was significant in that it exposed a number of interesting social phenomena that occur in a small division at work. One finding was that informal rules were inherent in the group and were strictly enforced by the group. For example, workers always reported that the same number of units were assembled for that day, regardless of how many were actually assembled. This unspoken rule came from a group that had considerable influence over the rate of production. Also, despite a company policy that forbade an employee to perform a job he was not trained to do, men frequently rotated job assignments to counteract the boredom that typically occurs in this kind of work.

This study was important because it systematically observed the naturally occurring relationships and informal social interactions that exist in an industrial setting. The case-study method proved to be very effective in bringing this information to light.

CASE STUDY CRITICISMS

Over the years, case-study methods have not received universal acceptance, which can be seen in the limited exposure that they receive in social science textbooks on methodology; it is not uncommon for a textbook to devote only a few paragraphs to this method. This attitude is attributable in part to some of the criticisms raised about case-study designs. One criticism is that this technique lends itself to distortions or falsifications while the data are being collected. Because direct observation may rely on subjective criteria, in many instances based on general impressions, it is alleged that this data should not be trusted. A second criticism is that it is difficult to draw cause-and-effect conclusions because of the lack of control measures to rule out alternative rival hypotheses. Third, the issue of generalization is important after the data have been collected and interpreted. There will often be a question regarding the population to which the results can be applied.

In the second half of the twentieth century, there appears to have been a resurgence of the use of case-study methods. Part of the impetus for this change came from a reactionary movement against the more traditional methods that collect data in artificial settings. The case-study method plays a significant role in studying behavior in real-life situations, under a set of circumstances that would make it impossible to use any other alternative.

SOURCES FOR FURTHER STUDY

Baker, Therese L. *Doing Social Research*. 3d ed. New York: McGraw-Hill, 1998. Gives the reader a general introduction to field research, observational studies, data collection methods, survey research, and sampling techniques as well as other topics which will help the reader evaluate "good" field experiments from those that are poorly constructed.

Berg, Bruce L. *Qualitative Research Methods for the Social Sciences*. 4th ed. Boston: Allyn & Bacon, 2000. Discusses a field strategy used by anthropologists and sociologists to study groups of people; in addition, discusses the ethical issues that arise while conducting research. Looks at the dangers of covert research and provides the guidelines established by the National Research Act.

Griffin, John H. *Black Like Me*. Reprint. New York: Signet, 1996. This excellent book, first published in 1962, is a narrative of the author's experiences traveling around the United States observing how people react to him after he takes on the appearance of a black man. This monumental field study, which contributed to an understanding of social prejudice, provides the reader with an excellent example of the significance of and need for conducting field research.

Luria, Aleksandr R. *The Mind of a Mnemonist: A Little Book About a Vast Memory.* 1968. Reprint. Cambridge, Mass: Harvard University Press, 1988. A fascinating case study, written by a founder of neuropsychology and one of the most significant Russian psychologists. Directed toward a general audience. The case study focuses on his subject, Shereshevskii (subject "S"), and his extraordinary memory.

Singleton, Royce, Jr., et al. *Approaches to Social Research.* 3d ed. New York: Oxford University Press, 1999. This well-written text discusses various aspects of field experimentation, such as how to select a research setting and gather information, how to get into the field, and when a field study should be adopted. The chapter on experimentation can be used to contrast "true" experiments with field studies.

Spradley, James. *Participant Observation.* New York: International Thompson, 1997. A guide to constructing and carrying out a participant observation study, from a chiefly anthropological perspective.

Yin, Robert K. *Case Study Research: Design and Methods.* 3d ed. Thousand Oaks, Calif.: Sage, 2003. This volume is perhaps the finest single source on case-study methods in print. Yin shows the reader exactly how to design, conduct, analyze, and even write up a case study. Approximately forty examples of case studies are cited with brief explanations. Not highly technical.

Bryan C. Auday

SEE ALSO: Animal Experimentation; Experimentation: Independent, Dependent, and Control Variables; Survey Research: Questionnaires and Interviews.

CLINICAL DEPRESSION

TYPE OF PSYCHOLOGY: Psychopathology
FIELD OF STUDY: Depression

Clinical depression is an emotional disorder characterized by extreme sadness or a loss of ability to experience pleasure. Its clinical features also include symptoms that are cognitive (for example, low self-worth), behavioral (for example, decreased activity level), and physical (for example, fatigue). Depression is a frequently diagnosed disorder in both inpatient and outpatient mental health settings.

KEY CONCEPTS
- anhedonia
- Beck Depression Inventory (BDI)
- Children's Depression Inventory (CDI)
- cognitive therapy for depression
- dysphoria
- dysthymic disorder
- helplessness
- monoamine oxidase inhibitors (MAOIs)
- tricyclics

Clinical depression is a severe emotional disorder that is characterized by four classes of symptoms: emotional, cognitive, behavioral, and physical. The major emotional symptoms, at least one of which is necessary for the diagnosis of depression, are dysphoria (extreme sadness or depressed mood) and anhedonia (lack of capacity to experience pleasure). Depressed individuals also experience cognitive symptoms. They may have feelings of worthlessness or excessive or inappropriate guilt. Some may have recurrent thoughts of death or suicidal ideation; others actually attempt suicide or create a specific plan for doing so. Behavioral symptoms of depression may include either restlessness or agitation, diminished ability to think or concentrate, and indecisiveness. Depressed individuals also experience several physical symptoms. They become easily fatigued, experience a loss or gain in appetite, show significant weight loss or gain, and experience sleep disturbances, such as insomnia (an inability to fall asleep) or hypersomnia (excessive sleepiness).

PREVALENCE

Depression is one of the more commonly experienced mental disorders. For example, in 1985, psychologists John Wing and Paul Bebbington examined research that used psychological tests to measure the prevalence of (or lifetime risk for) depression in the general population. They found that estimates of the prevalence of depression generally ranged from about 5 to 10 percent. Interestingly, all the studies examined by Wing and Bebbington agreed that depression was more common in women than in men. Estimates of the prevalence of depression ranged from 2.6 to 4.5 percent in men and from 5.9 to 9.0 percent in women.

Depression is also related to other characteristics. Risk for depression increases with age. The evidence is clear that depression is more common in adults and the elderly than in children or adolescents. Interest in childhood depression has increased since the early 1970's, however, and the number of children and adolescents who have been diagnosed as depressed has increased since that time. Depression is also related to socioeconomic status. In general, people who are unemployed and who are in lower income groups have higher risks for depression than others. This may be a result of the higher levels of stress experienced by individuals in lower-income groups. Finally, family history is related to depression. That is, clinical depression tends to run in families. This is consistent with both biological and psychological theories of depression.

Psychologists face several difficulties when attempting to determine the prevalence of depression. First, the symptoms of depression range in severity from mild to severe. It may not always be clear at which point these symptoms move from the mild nuisances associated with "normal" levels of sadness to significant symptoms associated with clinical depression. Since the early 1970's, clinical psychologists have devoted an increased amount of attention to depressions that occur at mild to moderate levels. Even though these milder depressions are not as debilitating as clinical depression, they produce significant distress for the individual and so warrant attention. In 1980 the term "dysthymic disorder" was introduced to describe depressions which, although mild to moderate, persist chronically.

Another complication in determining the prevalence of depression is that it may occur either as a primary or as a secondary problem. As a primary problem, depression is the initial or major disorder which should be the focus of clinical intervention. On the other hand, as a secondary problem, depression occurs in reaction to or as a consequence of another disorder. For example, many patients experience such discomfort or distress from medical or mental disorders that they eventually develop the symptoms of depression. In this case, the primary disorder and not depression is usually the focus of treatment.

TREATMENT APPROACHES

There are several major approaches to the treatment of clinical depression, each focusing on one of the four classes of symptoms of depression. Psychoanalytic therapists believe that the cause of depression is emotional: underlying anger that stems from some childhood loss and that has been turned inward. Psychoanalysts therefore treat depression by helping the patient to identify the cause of the underlying anger and to cope with it in an effective manner.

Psychiatrist Aaron T. Beck views depression primarily as a cognitive disorder. He holds that depressives have negative views of self, world, and future, and that they interpret their experiences in a distorted fashion so as to support these pessimistic views. A related cognitive model of depression is that of Martin E. P. Seligman. He argues that depression results from the perception that one is helpless or has little or no control over the events in one's life. Seligman has shown that laboratory-induced helplessness produces many of the symptoms of depression. Cognitive therapy for depression, which Beck described in 1979, aims at helping depressed patients identify and then change their negative and inaccurate patterns of thinking.

Behavioral therapists view depression as the result of conditioning. Psychologist Peter Lewinsohn suggests that depression results from low amounts of reinforcement. His behavioral therapy for depression aims at increasing reinforcement levels, through scheduling pleasant activities and improving the patient's social skills.

Biologically oriented therapies exist as well. Two classes of antidepressant medications, monoamine oxidase inhibitors (MAOIs) and tricyclics, are effective both in treating clinical depression and in preventing future episodes of depression. Electroconvulsive (shock) therapy (ECT) has also been found to be effective in treating severe depression. Although the reasons the biological treatments work have not been conclusively identified, it is thought that they are effective because they increase the activity or amounts of norepinephrine and serotonin, two neurotransmitters which are important in the transmission of impulses in the nervous system.

DEPRESSION MEASURES

In 1983, Eugene Levitt, Bernard Lubin, and James Brooks reported the results of the National Depression Survey, which attempted to determine the prevalence and correlates of depression in the general population. They interviewed more than 3,000 people, including 622 teenagers, who were randomly selected to be a representative sample of the entire United States' population. Subjects completed a brief self-report measure of depression and answered questions concerning their age, occupation, education, religion, and other variables.

Levitt, Lubin, and Brooks found that slightly more than 3 percent of the population was experiencing depression that was severe enough to warrant clinical intervention and so could be termed clinical depression. This figure is similar to that found by other investigators. In addition, Levitt, Lubin, and Brooks found that depression was related to sex, age, occupational status, and income. Depression was higher for subjects who were female, older, lower in occupational status, and either low or high in income (earning less than $6,000 or more than $25,000).

One of the most widely used measures of depression is the Beck Depression Inventory (BDI). Beck introduced this test in 1961 to assess the severity of depression in individuals who are known or suspected to have depression. The BDI has twenty-one items, each concerning a symptom of depression

DSM-IV-TR CRITERIA FOR MAJOR DEPRESSION

MAJOR DEPRESSIVE EPISODE

Five or more of the following symptoms present during the same two-week period and representing a change from previous functioning:

- depressed mood or loss of interest or pleasure (at least one); does not include symptoms clearly due to a general medical condition, mood-incongruent delusions, or hallucinations
- depressed mood most of the day, nearly every day, as indicated by either subjective report or observation made by others; in children and adolescents, can be irritable mood
- markedly diminished interest or pleasure in all, or almost all, activities most of the day, nearly every day, as indicated by either subjective account or observation made by others
- significant weight loss (when not dieting) or weight gain or decrease/increase in appetite nearly every day; in children, consider failure to make expected weight gains
- insomnia or hypersomnia nearly every day
- psychomotor agitation or retardation nearly every day observable by others, not merely subjective feelings of restlessness or being slowed down
- fatigue or loss of energy nearly every day
- feelings of worthlessness or excessive or inappropriate guilt (which may be delusional) nearly every day, not merely self-reproach or guilt about being sick
- diminished ability to think or concentrate, or indecisiveness, nearly every day, either by subjective account or as observed by others
- recurrent thoughts of death (not just fear of dying), recurrent suicidal ideation without a specific plan, or suicide attempt or specific plan for committing suicide

Criteria for Mixed Episode not met

Symptoms cause clinically significant distress or impairment in social, occupational, or other important areas of functioning

(for example, weight loss, suicidal thinking) which is rated for severity. The BDI can be self-administered or can be completed by an interviewer.

Since its introduction, the BDI has become one of the most widely used measures of depression for both research and clinical purposes. Many studies have shown that the BDI is an accurate and useful measure of depression. For example, BDI scores have been found to be related to both clinicians' ratings of the severity of a patient's depression and clinical improvements during the course of treatment for depression as well as being able to discrimi-

Symptoms not due to direct physiological effects of a substance or general medical condition

Symptoms not better accounted for by bereavement, persist for longer than two months, or characterized by marked functional impairment, morbid pre-occupation with worthlessness, suicidal ideation, psychotic symptoms, or psychomotor retardation

MAJOR DEPRESSIVE DISORDER, SINGLE EPISODE (DSM CODE 296.2X)

Presence of single Major Depressive Episode

Major Depressive Episode not better accounted for by Schizoaffective Disorder and not superimposed on Schizophrenia, Schizophreniform Disorder, Delusional Disorder, or Psychotic Disorder Not Otherwise Specified

No Manic Episodes, Mixed Episodes, or Hypomanic Episodes, unless all manic-like, mixed-like, or hypomanic-like episodes are substance- or treatment-induced or due to direct physiological effects of a general medical condition

Specify for current or most recent episode: Severity/Psychotic/Remission Specifiers; Chronic; with Catatonic Features; with Melancholic Features; with Atypical Features; with Postpartum Onset

MAJOR DEPRESSIVE DISORDER, RECURRENT (DSM CODE 296.3X)

Presence of two or more Major Depressive Episodes; with an interval of at least two consecutive months in which criteria not met for Major Depressive Episode

Major Depressive Episodes not better accounted for by Schizoaffective Disorder and not superimposed on Schizophrenia, Schizophreniform Disorder, Delusional Disorder, or Psychotic Disorder Not Otherwise Specified

No Manic Episodes, Mixed Episodes, or Hypomanic Episodes, unless all manic-like, mixed-like, or hypomanic-like episodes are substance- or treatment-induced or due to direct physiological effects of a general medical condition

Specify for current or most recent episode: Severity/Psychotic/Remission Specifiers; Chronic; with Catatonic Features; with Melancholic Features; with Atypical Features; with Postpartum Onset

Specify: Longitudinal Course Specifiers (with and Without Interepisode Recovery); with Seasonal Pattern

nate between the diagnosis of clinical depression and other conditions.

Psychologist Maria Kovacs developed the Children's Depression Inventory (CDI) by modifying the BDI for use with children. Similar in format to the BDI, the CDI contains twenty-eight items, each of which concerns a symptom of depression that is rated for severity. Research has supported the utility of the CDI. CDI ratings have been found to be related to clinicians' ratings of childhood depression. CDI scores have also been found to discriminate children hospitalized for depression from children hospitalized for other disorders. The CDI (along with other measures of childhood depression) has contributed to psychology's research on and understanding of the causes and treatment of childhood depression.

DEPRESSION RESEARCH

Many research projects since the 1970's have examined the effectiveness of cognitive and behavioral treatments of depression. Beck and his colleagues have demonstrated that cognitive therapy for depression is superior to no treatment whatsoever and to placebos (inactive psychological or medical interventions which should have no real effect but which the patient believes have therapeutic value). In addition, this research has shown that cognitive therapy is about as effective as both antidepressant medications and behavior therapy. Similarly, Lewinsohn and others have shown the effectiveness of behavior therapy on depression by demonstrating that it is superior to no treatment and to placebo conditions.

One of the most important studies of the treatment of depression is the Treatment of Depression Collaborative Research Program, begun by the National Institute of Mental Health (NIMH) in the mid-1980's. Members of a group of 250 clinically depressed patients were randomly assigned to one of four treatment conditions: interpersonal psychotherapy, cognitive behavioral psychotherapy, tricyclic antidepressant medication, and placebo medication. Treatment was presented over sixteen to twenty sessions. Patients were assessed by both self-report and a clinical evaluator before treatment, after every fourth session, and at six-, twelve-, and eighteen-month follow-ups after the end of treatment.

This study found that patients in all four treatment conditions improved significantly over the course of therapy. In general, patients who received antidepressant medication improved the most, patients who received the placebo improved the least, and patients who received the two forms of psychotherapy improved to an intermediate degree (but were closer in improvement to those receiving antidepressant medication than to those receiving the placebo). This study also found that, for patients in general, there was no significant difference between the effectiveness rates of the antidepressant medication and the two forms of psychotherapy.

For severely depressed patients, however, antidepressant medication and interpersonal psychotherapy were found to be more effective than other treatments; for less severely depressed patients, there were no differences in effectiveness across the four treatment conditions.

THEORIES

Clinical depression is one of the most prevalent psychological disorders. Because depression is associated with an increased risk for suicide, it is also one of the more severe disorders. For these reasons, psychologists have devoted much effort to determining the causes of depression and developing effective treatments.

Theories and treatments of depression can be classified into four groups: emotional, cognitive, behavioral, and physical. In the first half of the twentieth century, the psychoanalytic theory of depression, which emphasizes the role of the emotion of anger, dominated clinical psychology's thinking about the causes and treatment of depression. Following the discovery of the first antidepressant medications in the 1950's, psychologists increased their attention to physical theories and treatments of depression. Since the early 1970's, Beck's and Seligman's cognitive approaches and Lewinsohn's behavioral theory have received increased amounts of attention. By the 1990's, the biological, cognitive, and behavioral theories of depression had all surpassed the psychoanalytic theory of depression in terms of research support for their respective proposed causes and treatments.

Another shift in emphasis in psychology's thinking about depression concerns childhood depression. Prior to the 1970's, psychologists paid relatively little attention to depression in children; classical psychoanalytic theory suggested that children had not yet completed a crucial step of their psychological development that psychoanalysts believed was necessary for a person to become depressed. Thus, many psychologists believed that children did not experience depression or that, if they did become depressed, their depressions were not severe. Research in the 1970's demonstrated that children do experience depression and that, when depressed, children exhibit symptoms similar to those of depressed adults. Since the 1970's, psychologists have devoted much effort to understanding the cause and treatment of childhood depression. Much of this work has examined how the biological, cognitive, and behavioral models of depression, originally developed for and applied to adults, may generalize to children.

Another shift in psychology's thinking about depression concerns the attention paid to mild and moderate depressions. Since the 1960's, clinical psychology has been interested in the early detection and treatment of minor conditions in order to prevent the development of more severe disorders. This emphasis on prevention has influenced the field's thinking about depression. Since the early 1970's, psychologists have applied cognitive and behavioral models of depression to nonpatients who obtain high scores on measures of depression. Even though these individuals are not clinically depressed, they still experience significant distress and so may benefit from the attention of psychologists. By using cognitive or behavioral interventions with these individuals, psychologists may prevent the development of more severe depressions.

SOURCES FOR FURTHER STUDY

Beck, Aaron T., A. J. Rush, B. F. Shaw, and G. Emery. *Cognitive Therapy of Depression.* 1979. Reprint. New York: Guilford Press, 1987. Summarizes the cognitive theory of depression and describes how this model can be applied in the treatment of depressed patients.

Beutler, Larry E., John F. Clarkin, and Bruce Bongar. *Guidelines for the System-*

atic Treatment of the Depressed Patient. New York: Oxford University Press, 2000. Summarizes the state of research and extracts treatment principles that can be applied by mental health professionals from a wide range of theoretical backgrounds.

Blazer, Dan. *Depression in Late Life*. 3d ed. New York: Springer, 2002. A comprehensive review of the treatment of depression among the elderly. Covers epidemiology, pharmacology, depression and cognitive impairment, unipolar and bipolar disorders, bereavement, and existential depression.

Hammen, Constance. *Depression*. New York: Psychology Press, 1997. A modular course presenting research-based information on the diagnosis and treatment of depression. Written for students and mental health professionals.

Lewinsohn, Peter M., Rebecca Forster, and M. A. Youngren. *Control Your Depression*. Rev. ed. New York: Simon & Schuster, 1992. A self-help book for a general audience. Describes Lewinsohn's behavioral therapy, which has been found to be an effective treatment for depression.

Nezu, Arthur M., George F. Ronan, Elizabeth A. Meadows, and Kelly S. McClure, eds. *Practitioner's Guide to Empirically Based Measures of Depression*. New York: Plenum Press, 2000. Reviews and compares more than ninety measures of depression in terms of requirements, suitability, costs, administration, reliability, and validity.

Seligman, Martin E. P. *Helplessness: On Depression, Development, and Death*. 1975. Reprint. San Francisco: W. H. Freeman, 1992. Seligman explains the learned helplessness theory of depression, describing his early research and comparing the symptoms of laboratory-induced helplessness to those of clinical depression.

Michael Wierzbicki

See also: Bipolar Disorder; Cognitive Behavior Therapy; Cognitive Therapy; Depression; Diagnosis; Drug Therapies; Mood Disorders; Suicide.

COGNITIVE BEHAVIOR THERAPY

TYPE OF PSYCHOLOGY: Psychotherapy
FIELD OF STUDY: Behavioral therapies

A number of approaches to therapy fall within the scope of cognitive behavior therapy. These approaches all share a theoretical perspective that assumes that internal cognitive processes, called thinking or cognition, affect behavior; that this cognitive activity may be monitored; and that desired behavior change may be effected through cognitive change.

KEY CONCEPTS
- behavior therapy
- cognition
- cognitive restructuring
- cognitive therapy
- depression

The cognitive behavior therapies are not a single therapeutic approach but rather a loosely organized collection of therapeutic approaches that share a similar set of assumptions. At their core, cognitive behavior therapies share three fundamental propositions: Cognitive activity affects behavior; cognitive activity may be monitored and altered; and desired behavior change may be effected through cognitive change.

The first of the three fundamental propositions of cognitive behavior therapy suggests that it is not the external situation which determines feelings and behavior but rather the person's view or perception of that external situation that determines feelings and behavior. For example, if one has failed the first examination of a course, one could appraise it as a temporary setback to be overcome or as a horrible loss. While the situation remains the same, the thinking about that situation is radically different in the two examples cited. Each of these views will lead to significantly different emotions and behaviors.

The third cognitive behavioral assumption suggests that desired behavior change may be effected through cognitive change. Thus, while cognitive behavior theorists do not reject the notion that rewards and punishment (reinforcement contingencies) can alter behavior, they are likely to emphasize that there are alternative methods for behavior change, one in particular being cognitive change. Many approaches to therapy fall within the scope of cognitive behavior therapy as it is defined above. While these approaches share the theoretical assumptions described above, a review of the major therapeutic procedures subsumed under the heading of cognitive behavior therapy reveals a diverse amalgam of principles and procedures, representing a variety of theoretical and philosophical perspectives.

RATIONAL THERAPIES
Rational-emotive therapy, developed by psychologist Albert Ellis, is regarded by many as one of the premier examples of the cognitive behavioral ap-

proach; it was introduced in the early 1960's. Ellis proposed that many people are made unhappy by their faulty, irrational beliefs, which influence the way they interpret events. The therapist will interact with the patient, attempting to direct him or her to more positive and realistic views. Cognitive therapy, pioneered by Aaron T. Beck, has been applied to such problems as depression and stress. For stress reduction, ideas and thoughts that are producing stress in the patient will be questioned; the therapist will get the patient to examine the validity of these thoughts. Thought processes can then be restructured so the situations seem less stressful. Cognitive therapy has been found to be quite effective in treating depression, as compared to other therapeutic methods. Beck held that depression is caused by certain types of negative thoughts, such as devaluing the self or viewing the future in a consistently pessimistic way.

Rational behavior therapy, developed by psychiatrist Maxie Maultsby, is a close relative of Ellis's rational-emotive therapy. In this approach, Maultsby combines several approaches to include rational-emotive therapy, neuropsychology, classical and operant conditioning, and psychosomatic research; however, Maultsby was primarily influenced by his association with Albert Ellis. In this approach, Maultsby attempts to couch his theory of emotional disturbance in terms of neuropsychophysiology and learning theory. Rational behavior therapy assumes that repeated pairings of a perception with evaluative thoughts lead to rational or irrational emotive and behavioral reactions. Maultsby suggests that self-talk, which originates in the left hemisphere of the brain, triggers corresponding right-hemisphere emotional equivalents. Thus, in order to maintain a state of psychological health, individuals must practice rational self-talk that will, in turn, cause the right brain to convert left-brain language into appropriate emotional and behavioral reactions.

Rational behavior therapy techniques are quite similar to those of rational-emotive therapy. Both therapies stress the importance of monitoring one's thoughts in order to become aware of the elements of the emotional disturbance. In addition, Maultsby advocates the use of rational-emotive imagery, behavioral practice, and relaxation methods in order to minimize emotional distress.

SELF-INSTRUCTIONAL TRAINING

Self-instructional training was developed by psychologist Donald Meichenbaum in the early 1970's. In contrast to Ellis and Beck, whose prior training was in psychoanalysis, Meichenbaum's roots are in behaviorism and the behavioral therapies. Thus Meichenbaum's approach is heavily couched in behavioral terminology and procedures. Meichenbaum's work stems from his earlier research in training schizophrenic patients to emit "healthy speech." By chance, Meichenbaum observed that patients who engaged in spontaneous self-instruction were less distracted and demonstrated superior task performance on a variety of tasks. As a result, Meichenbaum emphasizes the critical role of "self-instructions"—simple instructions such as "Relax. . . Just attend to the task"—and their noticeable effect on subsequent behavior.

Meichenbaum developed self-instructional training to treat the deficits in self-instructions manifested in impulsive children. The ultimate goal of this program was to decrease impulsive behavior. The way to accomplish this goal, as hypothesized by Meichenbaum, was to train impulsive children to generate verbal self-commands, to respond to their verbal self-commands, and to encourage the children to self-reinforce their behavior appropriately.

The specific procedures employed in self-instructional training involve having the child observe a model performing a task. While the model is performing the task, he or she is talking aloud. The child then performs the same task while the model gives verbal instructions. Subsequently, the child performs the task while instructing himself or herself aloud, then while whispering the instructions. Finally, the child performs the task covertly. The self-instructions employed in the program included questions about the nature and demands of the task, answers to these questions in the form of cognitive rehearsal, self-instructions in the form of self-guidance while performing the task, and self-reinforcement. Meichenbaum and his associates have found that this self-instructional training program significantly improves the task performance of impulsive children across a number of measures.

Systematic Rational Restructuring

Systematic rational restructuring is a cognitive behavioral procedure developed by psychologist Marvin Goldfried in the mid-1970's. This procedure is a variation on Ellis's rational-emotive therapy; however, it is more clearly structured than Ellis's method. In systematic rational restructuring, Goldfried suggests that early social learning experiences teach individuals to label situations in different ways. Further, Goldfried suggests that emotional reactions may be understood as responses to the way individuals label situations, as opposed to responses to the situations themselves. The goal of systematic rational restructuring is to train patients to perceive situational cues more accurately.

The process of systematic rational restructuring is similar to systematic desensitization, in which a subject is to imagine fearful scenes in a graduated order from the least fear-provoking to the most fear-provoking scenes. In systematic rational restructuring, the patient is asked to imagine a hierarchy of anxiety-eliciting situations. At each step, the patient is instructed to identify irrational thoughts associated with the specific situation, to dispute them, and to reevaluate the situation more rationally. In addition, patients are instructed to practice rational restructuring in specific real-life situations.

Stress Inoculation

Stress inoculation training incorporates several of the specific therapies already described. This procedure was developed by Meichenbaum. Stress inoculation training is analogous to being inoculated against disease. That is, it prepares patients to deal with stress-inducing events by teaching them to use coping skills at low levels of the stressful situation and then gradually to cope with more and more stressful situations. Stress inoculation training involves three phases: conceptualization, skills acquisition and rehearsal, and application and follow-through.

In the conceptualization phase of stress inoculation training, patients are given an adaptive way of viewing and understanding their negative reactions to stressful events. In the skills-acquisition and rehearsal phase, patients learn coping skills appropriate to the type of stress they are experiencing. With interpersonal anxiety, a patient might develop skills that would make the feared situation less threatening (for example, learning to initiate and maintain conversations). The patient might also learn deep muscle relaxation to lessen tension. In cases of anger, patients learn to view potential provocations as problems that require a solution rather than as threats that require an attack. Patients are also taught to rehearse alternative strategies for solving the problem at hand.

The application and follow-through phase of stress inoculation training involves the patients practicing and applying the coping skills. Initially, patients are exposed to low levels of stressful situations in imagery. They practice applying their coping skills to handle the stressful events, and they overtly role-play dealing with stressful events. Next, patients are given homework assignments that involve gradual exposure to actual stressful events in his or her everyday life. Stress inoculation training has been effectively applied to many types of problems. It has been used to help people cope with anger, anxiety, fear, pain, and health-related problems (for example, cancer and hypertension). It appears to be suitable for all age levels.

PROBLEM-SOLVING THERAPY

Problem-solving therapy, as developed by psychologists Thomas D'Zurilla and Marvin Goldfried, is also considered one of the cognitive behavioral approaches. In essence, problem-solving therapy is the application of problem-solving theory and research to the domain of personal and emotional problems. Indeed, the ability to solve problems is seen as the necessary and sufficient condition for emotional and behavioral stability. Problem solving is, in one way or another, a part of all psychotherapies.

Cognitive behavior therapists have taught general problem-solving skills to patients with two specific aims: to alleviate the particular personal problems for which patients have sought therapy and to provide patients with a general coping strategy for personal problems.

The actual steps of problem solving that patients are taught to carry out systematically are as follows. First, it is necessary to define the dilemma as a problem to be solved. Next, a goal must be selected which reflects the ultimate outcome a patient desires. The patient then generates a list of many different possible solutions, without evaluating their potential merit (a kind of brainstorming). Now the patient evaluates the pros and cons of each option in terms of the probability that it will meet the goal selected and its practicality, which involves considering the potential consequences to oneself and to others of each solution. The possible solutions are ranked in terms of desirability and practicality, and the highest one is selected. Next, the patient tries to implement the solution chosen. Finally, the patient evaluates the therapy, assessing whether the solution alleviated the problem and met the goal, and, if not, what went wrong—in other words, which of the steps in problem solving needs to be redone.

Problem-solving therapies have been used to treat a variety of target behaviors with a wide range of patients. Examples include peer relationship difficulties among children and adolescents, examination and interpersonal anxiety among college students, relapse following a program to reduce smoking, disharmony among family members, and the inability of chronic psychiatric patients to cope with interpersonal problems.

SELF-CONTROL THERAPY

Self-control therapy for depression, developed by psychologist Lynn Rehm, is an approach to treating depression which combines the self-regulatory notions of behavior therapy and the cognitive focus of the cognitive behavioral approaches. Essentially, Rehm believes that depressed people show deficits in one or some combination of the following areas: monitoring (selectively attending to negative events), self-evaluation (setting unrealistically high goals), and self-reinforcement (emitting high rates of self-punishment and low rates of self-reward). These three components are further broken down into a total of six functional areas.

According to Rehm, the varied symptom picture in clinically depressed patients is a function of different subsets of these deficits. Over the course of therapy with a patient, each of the six self-control deficits is described, with emphasis on how a particular deficit is causally related to depression, and on what can be done to remedy the deficit. A variety of clinical strategies are employed to teach patients self-control skills, including group discussion, overt and covert reinforcement, behavioral assignments, self-monitoring, and modeling.

STRUCTURAL PSYCHOTHERAPY

Structural psychotherapy is a cognitive behavioral approach that derives from the work of two Italian mental health professionals, psychiatrist Vittorio Guidano and psychologist Gianni Liotti. These doctors are strongly persuaded by cognitive psychology, social learning theory, evolutionary epistemology, psychodynamic theory, and cognitive therapy. Guidano and Liotti suggest that for an understanding of the full complexity of an emotional disorder and subsequent development of an adequate model of psychotherapy, an appreciation of the development and the active role of an individual's knowledge of self and the world is critical. In short, in order to understand a patient, one must understand the structure of that person's world.

Guidano and Liotti's therapeutic process utilizes the empirical problem-solving approach of the scientist. Indeed, the two suggest that therapists should assist patients in disengaging themselves from certain ingrained beliefs and judgments and in considering them as hypotheses and theories subject to disproof, confirmation, and logical challenge. A variety of behavioral experiments and cognitive techniques are used to assist the patient in assessing and critically evaluating his or her beliefs.

OTHER THERAPIES

As can be seen, the area of cognitive behavior therapy involves a wide collection of therapeutic approaches and techniques. The approaches described here are but a representative sample of possible cognitive behavioral approaches. Also included within this domain are anxiety management training, which comes from the work of psychologist Richard Suinn, and personal science, from the work of psychologist Michael Mahoney.

The cognitive behavioral approaches are derived from a variety of perspectives, including cognitive theory, classical and operant conditioning approaches, problem-solving theory, and developmental theory. All these approaches share the perspective that internal cognitive processes, called thinking or cognition, affect behavior, and that behavior change may be effected through cognitive change.

These approaches have several other similarities. One is that all the approaches see therapy as time-limited. This is in sharp distinction to the traditional psychoanalytic therapies, which are generally open-ended. The cognitive behavior therapies attempt to effect change rapidly, often with specific, preset lengths of therapeutic contact. Another similarity among the cognitive behavior therapies is that their target of change is also limited. For example, in the treatment of depression, the target of change is the symptoms of depression. Thus, in the cognitive behavioral approaches to treatment, one sees a time-limited focus and a limited target of change.

EVOLUTION

Cognitive behavior therapy evolved from two lines of clinical and research activity. First, it derives from the work of the early cognitive therapists (Albert Ellis and Aaron Beck); second, it was strongly influenced by the careful empirical work of the early behaviorists.

Within the domain of behaviorism, cognitive processes were not always seen as a legitimate focus of attention. In behavior therapy, there has always been a strong commitment to an applied science of clinical treatment. In the behavior therapy of the 1950's and 1960's, this emphasis on scientific methods and procedures meant that behavior therapists focused on events that were directly observable and measurable. Within this framework, behavior was seen as a function of external stimuli which determined or were reliably associated with observable responses. Also during this period, there was a deliberate avoidance of such "nebulous" concepts as thoughts, cognitions, or images. It was believed that these processes were by their very nature vague, and one could never be confident that one was reliably observing or measuring these processes.

By following scientific principles, researchers developed major new treatment approaches which in many ways revolutionized clinical practice (among them are systematic desensitization and the use of a token economy). During the 1960's, however, several developments within behavior therapy had emphasized the limitations of a strict conditioning model to understanding human behavior.

In 1969, psychologist Albert Bandura published his influential volume *Principles of Behavior Modification*. In this book, Bandura emphasized the role of internal or cognitive factors in the causation and maintenance of behavior. Following from the dissatisfaction of the radical behavioral approaches to understanding complex human behavior and the publication of Bandura's 1969 volume, behavior therapists began actively to seek and study the role of cognitive processes in human behavior.

SOURCES FOR FURTHER STUDY

D'Zurilla, Thomas J., and Arthur M. Nezu. "Social Problem-Solving in Adults." In *Advances in Cognitive-Behavioral Research and Therapy*, edited by Philip C. Kendall. Vol. 1. New York: Academic Press, 1982. An excellent summary of problem-solving therapy. As indicated by its title, the Kendall book in which this article appears also contains other informative articles dealing with cognitive behavior therapy.

Goldfried, Marvin R. "The Use of Relaxation and Cognitive Relabeling as Coping Skills." In *Behavioral Self-Management: Strategies, Techniques, and Outcomes*, edited by Richard B. Stuart. New York: Brunner/Mazel, 1977. A description of systematic rational restructuring by Marvin Goldfried, who developed the technique; reveals its similarities to and differences from rational-emotive therapy.

Maultsby, Maxie C., Jr. *Rational Behavior Therapy*. Englewood Cliffs, N.J.: Prentice-Hall, 1984. An excellent summary of rational behavior therapy, as developed by Maultsby; discusses self-talk and its emotional and behavioral consequences.

Meichenbaum, Donald. *Cognitive Behavior Modification*. New York: Plenum Press, 1979. A well-written introduction to Meichenbaum's approaches, with clear examples of the applications of self-instructional training to impulsive children and schizophrenic patients.

_____. *Stress Inoculation Training*. New York: Pergamon Press, 1985. This short training manual presents a clear, useful overview of stress inoculation training, along with a detailed account of the empirical research completed in testing the approach.

Donald G. Beal

SEE ALSO: Cognitive Social Learning: Walter Mischel; Cognitive Therapy.

COGNITIVE DEVELOPMENT
JEAN PIAGET

TYPE OF PSYCHOLOGY: Developmental psychology
FIELD OF STUDY: Cognitive development

Piaget, in one of the twentieth century's most influential development theories, proposed a sequence of maturational changes in thinking: From the sensorimotor responses of infancy, the child acquires symbols. Later, the child begins relating these symbols in such logical operations as categorizing and quantifying. In adolescence, abstract and hypothetical mental manipulations become possible.

KEY CONCEPTS
- concrete operations stage
- conservation
- egocentric
- formal operations stage
- operations
- preoperational stage
- schema (*pl.* schemata)
- sensorimotor stage

Jean Piaget (1896-1980), a Swiss psychologist, generated the twentieth century's most influential and comprehensive theory of cognitive development. Piaget's theory describes how the maturing child's interactions with the environment result in predictable sequences of changes in certain crucial understandings of the world about him or her. Such changes occur in the child's comprehension of time and space, quantitative relationships, cause and effect, and even right and wrong. The child is always treated as an actor in his or her own development.

Advances result from the active desire to develop concepts, or schemata, which are sufficiently similar to the real world that this real world can be fitted or assimilated into these schemata. Schemata can be defined as any process of interpreting an object or event, including habitual responses, symbols, or mental manipulations. When a schema ("Cats smell nice") is sufficiently discrepant from reality ("That cat stinks"), the schema itself must be accommodated or altered ("That catlike creature is a skunk").

For children everywhere, neurologically based advances in mental capacity introduce new perceptions that make the old ways of construing reality unsatisfactory and compel a fundamentally new construction of reality—a new stage of development. Piaget conceptualizes four such stages: sensorimotor (in infancy), preoperational (the preschool child), concrete operational (the school-age child), and formal operational (adolescence and adulthood).

SENSORIMOTOR STAGE

In the sensorimotor stage, the infant orients himself or herself to objects in the world by consistent physical (motor) movements in response to those sensory stimuli that represent the same object (for example, the sight of a face, the sound of footsteps, or a voice all represent "mother"). The relationship between motor responses and reappearing objects becomes progressively more complex and varied in the normal course of development. First, reflexes such as sucking become more efficient; then sequences of learned actions that bring pleasure are repeated (circular reactions). These learned reactions are directed first toward the infant's own body (thumb sucking), then toward objects in the environment (the infant's stuffed toy).

The baby seems to lack an awareness that objects continue to exist when they are outside the range of his or her senses. When the familiar toy of an infant is hidden, he or she does not search for it; it is as if it has disappeared from reality. As the sensorimotor infant matures, the infant becomes convinced of the continuing existence of objects that disappear in less obvious ways for longer intervals of time. By eighteen months of age, most toddlers have achieved such a conviction of continuing existence, or object permanence.

PREOPERATIONAL STAGE

In the preoperational stage, the preschool child begins to represent these permanent objects by internal processes or mental representations. Now the development of mental representations of useful objects proceeds at an astounding pace. In symbolic play, blocks may represent cars and trains. Capable of deferred imitation, the child may pretend to be a cowboy according to his or her memory image of a motion-picture cowboy. The most important of all representations are the hundreds of new words the child learns to speak.

As one might infer from the word "preoperational," this period, lasting from about age two through ages six or seven, is transitional. The preschool child still lacks the attention, memory capacity, and mental flexibility to employ his or her increasing supply of symbolic representations in logical reasoning (operations). It is as if the child remains so focused upon the individual frames of a motion picture that he or she fails to comprehend the underlying plot. Piaget calls this narrow focusing on a single object or salient dimension "centration." The child may say, for example, that a quart of milk he or she has just seen transferred into two pint containers is now "less milk" because the child focuses upon the smaller size of the new containers. Fido is seen as a dog, not as an animal or a mammal. The child uncritically assumes that other people, regardless of their situation, share his or her own tastes and perspectives. A two-year-old closes his eyes and says, "Now you don't see me, Daddy." Piaget calls this egocentrism.

CONCRETE OPERATIONS STAGE

The concrete operations stage begins at age six or seven, when the school-age child becomes capable of keeping in mind and logically manipulating several concrete objects at the same time. The child is no longer the prisoner of the momentary appearance of things. In no case is the change more evident than in the sort of problem in which a number of objects (such as twelve black checkers) are spread out into four groups of three. While the four-year-old, preoperational child would be likely to say that now there are more checkers because they take up a larger area, to the eight-year-old it is obvious that this transformation could easily be reversed by regrouping the checkers. Piaget describes the capacity to visualize the reversibility of such transformations as "conservation." This understanding is fundamental to the comprehension of simple arithmetical manipulations. It is also fundamental to a second operational skill: categorization. To the concrete-operational child, it seems obvious that while Rover the dog can for other purposes be classified as a household pet, an animal, or a living organism, it will still be a "dog" and still be "Rover." A related skill is seriation: keeping in mind that an entire series of objects can be arranged along a single dimension, such as size (from smallest to largest). The child now is also capable of role-taking, of understanding the different perspective of a parent or teacher. No longer egocentric (assuming that everyone shares one's own perspective and cognitively unable to understand the different perspective of another), the child becomes able to see himself or herself as others see him or her and to temper the harshness of absolute rules with a comprehension of the viewpoints of others.

FORMAL OPERATIONS STAGE

The formal operational stage begins in early adolescence. In childhood, logical operations are concrete ones, limited to objects that can be visualized, touched, or directly experienced. The advance of the early adolescent into formal operational thinking involves the capacity to deal with possibilities that are purely speculative. This permits coping with new classes of problems: those involving relationships that are purely abstract or hypothetical or that involve the higher-level analysis of a problem by the systematic consideration of every logical (sometimes fanciful) possibility. The logical adequacy of an argument can be examined apart from the truth or falsity of its conclusions.

Concepts such as "forces," "infinity," or "justice," nowhere directly experienced, can now be comprehended. Formal operational thought permits the midadolescent or adult to hold abstract ideals and to initiate scientific investigations.

ILLUSTRATING STAGE DEVELOPMENT

Piaget was particularly clever in the invention of problems which illustrate the underlying premises of the child's thought. The crucial capability that signals the end of the sensorimotor period is object permanence, the child's conviction of the continuing existence of objects that are outside the range of his or her senses. Piaget established the gradual emergence of object permanence by hiding from the child familiar toys for progressively longer periods of time, with the act of hiding progressively less obvious to the child. Full object permanence is not considered achieved until the child will search for a familiar missing object even when he or she could not have observed its being hidden.

The fundamental test of concrete operational thought is conservation. In a typical conservation task, the child is shown two identical balls of putty. The child generally affirms their obvious equivalence. Then one of the balls of putty is reworked into an elongated, wormlike shape while the child watches. The child is again asked about their relative size. Younger children are likely to say that the wormlike shape is smaller, but the child who has attained conservation of mass will state that the size must still be the same. Inquiries concerning whether the weights of the differently shaped material (conservation of weight) are the same and whether they would displace the same amount of water (conservation of volume) are more difficult questions, generally not answerable until the child is older.

STANDARDIZED TESTS

Since Piaget's original demonstrations, further progress has necessitated the standardization of these problems with materials, questions, procedures, and scoring so clearly specified that examiners can replicate one another's results. Such standardization permits the explanation of the general applicability of Piaget's concepts. Standardized tests have been developed for measuring object permanence, egocentricity, and role-taking skills. The Concept Assessment Kit, for example, provides six standard conservation tasks for which comparison data (norms) are available for children in several widely diverse cultures. The relative conceptual attainments of an individual child (or culture) can be measured. Those who attain such basic skills as conservation early have been shown to be advanced in many other educational and cognitive achievements.

IMPLICATIONS FOR EDUCATION

Piaget's views of cognitive development have broad implications for educational institutions charged with fostering such development. The child is viewed as an active seeker of knowledge. This pursuit is advanced by his or her experimental engagement with problems which are slightly more complex than those problems successfully worked through in the past. The teacher is a facilitator of the opportunities for such cognitive growth, not a lecturer or a drillmaster. The teacher provides physical materials that can be experimentally manipulated. Such materials can be simple: Blocks, stones, bottle caps, and plastic containers all can be classified, immersed in water, thrown into fire, dropped, thrown, or balanced. Facilitating peer relationships and cooperation in playing games is also helpful in encouraging social role-taking and moral development.

Because each student pursues knowledge at his or her own pace and in his or her own idiom, great freedom and variety may be permitted in an essentially open classroom. The teacher may nudge the student toward cognitive advancement by presenting a problem slightly more complex than that already comprehended by the student. A student who understands conservation of number may be ready for problems involving the conservation of length, for example. The teacher, however, does not reinforce correct answers or criticize incorrect ones. Sequencing is crucial. The presentation of knowledge or skill before the child is ready can result in superficial, uncomprehended verbalisms. Piaget does not totally reject the necessity of the inculcation of social and cultural niceties (social-arbitrary knowledge), the focus of traditional education. He would maintain, however, that an experimentally based understanding of physical and social relationships is crucial for a creative, thoughtful society.

FINESSING PIAGET'S RESEARCH

Piaget hypothesized sequences of age-related changes in ways of dealing with reality. His conclusions were based on the careful observation of a few selected cases. The voluminous research since Piaget's time overwhelmingly supports the sequence he outlined. The process almost never reverses. Once a child understands the conservation of substance, for example, his or her former conclusion that "Now there is more" seems to the child not simply wrong but absurd. Even within a stage, there is a sequence. Conservation of mass, for example, precedes conservation of volume.

Post-Piagetian research has nevertheless led to a fine-tuning of some of Piaget's conclusions and a modification of others. Piaget believed that transitions to more advanced cognitive levels awaited neurological maturation and the child's spontaneous discoveries. Several researchers have found that specific training in simplified and graded conservation and categorization tasks can lead to an early ripening of these skills. Other research has called into question Piaget's timetable. The fact that, within a few months of birth, infants show subtle differences in their reactions to familiar versus unfamiliar objects suggests that recognition memory for objects may begin earlier than Piaget's age for object permanence. If conservation tasks are simplified—if all distraction is avoided, and simple language and familiar materials are used—it can be shown that concrete operations also may begin earlier than Piaget thought. Formal operations, on the other hand, may not begin as early or be applied as universally in adult problem solving as suggested by Piaget's thesis. A significant percentage of older adolescents and adults fail tests for formal operations, particularly in new problem areas.

More basic than readjustments of his developmental scheduling is the reinterpretation of Piaget's stages. The stage concept implies not only an invariant sequence of age-related changes but also developmental discontinuities involving global and fairly abrupt shifts in an entire pattern or structure. The prolonged development and domain-specific nature of many operational skills, however, suggest a process that is neither abrupt nor global. An alternative view is that Piaget's sequences can be understood as the results of continuous improvements in attention, concentration, and memory. Stages represent only transition points on this continuous dimension. They are more like the points of a scale on a thermometer than the stages of the metamorphosis of a caterpillar into a moth.

PIAGET'S IMPACT

Even with the caveat that his stages may reflect, at a more fundamental level, an underlying continuum, Piaget's contributions can be seen as a great leap forward in approximate answers to one of humankind's oldest riddles: how human beings know their world. The eighteenth century philosopher Immanuel Kant described certain core assumptions, such as quantity, quality, and cause and effect, which he called "categories of the understanding." Human beings make these assumptions when they relate specific objects and events to one another—when they reason. Piaget's work became known to a 1960's-era American psychology that was dominated by B. F. Skinner's behavioral view of a passive child whose plastic nature was simply molded by the rewards and punishments of parents and culture. The impact of Piaget's work shifted psychology's focus back to a Kantian perspective of the child as an active reasoner who selectively responds to aspects of culture he or she finds relevant. Piaget himself outlined the sequence, the pace, and some of the dynamics of the maturing child's development of major Kantian categories. Such subsequent contributions as Lawrence Kohlberg's work on moral development and Robert Selman's work on role-taking can be viewed as an elaboration and extension of Piaget's unfinished work. Piaget, like Sigmund Freud, was one of psychology's pivotal thinkers. Without him, the entire field of developmental psychology would be radically different.

SOURCES FOR FURTHER STUDY

Piaget, Jean. *The Psychology of the Child.* Translated by Helen Weaver. New York: Basic Books, 2000. Piaget's seminal presentation of his theories on children's cognitive development from infancy to adolescence.

Scholnik, Ellin Kofsky, ed. *Conceptual Development: Piaget's Legacy.* Hillsdale, N.J.: Lawrence Erlbaum, 1999. A collection of papers presented at the centenary of Piaget's birth at the Jean Piaget Society's annual symposium, assessing his legacy and effect on the understanding of children's cognitive development.

Serulnikov, Adriana. *Piaget for Beginners.* New York: Writers and Readers, 2000. A condensed overview of Piaget's theories for the general public. Part of the well-known For Beginners series.

Singer, Dorothy G., and Tracey A. Robinson. *A Piaget Primer: How a Child Thinks.* Rev. ed. New York: Plume, 1996. An introduction to Piaget's theories aimed at educators, child psychologists, and parents, using examples and illustrations from classic children's literature and popular children's television programming.

Smith, Lesley M., ed. *Critical Readings on Piaget.* New York: Routledge, 1996. A collection of essays assessing Piaget's theories and their impact, all originally published between 1990 and 1995. A follow-up to the same editor's *Piaget: Critical Assessments* (1992), which covered the period 1950 to 1990.

Thomas E. DeWolfe

SEE ALSO: Adolescence: Cognitive Skills; Cognitive Psychology; Development; Language; Moral Development.

Cognitive Psychology

Type of psychology: Cognition
Fields of study: Cognitive processes; thought

Cognitive psychology is concerned with the scientific study of human mental activities involved in the acquisition, storage, retrieval, and use of information. Among its wide concerns are perception, memory, reasoning, problem solving, intelligence, language, and creativity; research in these areas has widespread practical applications.

Key concepts
- artificial intelligence
- cognitive behavioral therapy
- cognitive science
- episodic memory
- long-term memory
- metamemory
- prospective memory
- semantic memory
- short-term memory
- working memory

Cognitive psychology is that branch of psychology concerned with human mental activities. A staggering array of topics fit under such a general heading. In fact, it sometimes seems that there is no clear place to end the catalog of cognitive topics, as mental operations intrude into virtually all human endeavors. As a general guideline, one might consider the subject matter of cognitive psychology as those mental processes involved in the acquisition, storage, retrieval, and use of information.

Among the more specific concerns of cognitive psychologists are perception, attention, memory, and imagery. Studies of perception and attention might be concerned with how much of people's vast sensory experience they can further process and make sense of, and how they recognize incoming information as forming familiar patterns. Questions regarding the quality of memory include how much information can be maintained, for how long, and under what conditions; how information is organized in memory and how is it retrieved or lost; and how accurate the memory is, as well as what can be done to facilitate a person's recall skills. Cognitive researchers concerned with imagery are interested in people's ability to "see" in their minds a picture or image of an object, person, or scene that is not physically present; cognitive researchers are interested in the properties of such images and how they can be manipulated.

In addition to these concerns, there is great interest in the higher-order processes of planning, reasoning, problem solving, intelligence, language, and creativity. Cognitive psychologists want to know, for example, what steps are involved in planning a route to a destination or a solution to a problem, and what factors influence people's more abstract ability to reason. They seek to understand the importance of prior knowledge or experience, to discover which strategies are effective, and to see what obstacles typically impede a person's thinking. They are interested in the relationships between language and thought and between creativity and intelligence.

The following exchange is useful in illustrating some of the topics important to cognitive psychologists. Imagine that "Jacob" and "Janet" are two children on a busy playground:

> JACOB: Do you want to play some football?
>
> JANET: Sure! Tell me where the ball is and I'll go get it.
>
> JACOB: The football's in my locker in the equipment room. Go back in the building. Go past our classroom, turn right at the water fountain, and it's the second door on your left. My locker is number 12, and the combination is 6-21-13.
>
> JANET: Okay, it'll just take me a couple of minutes. [As she runs to get the ball, Janet repeats over and over to herself, "12; 6, 21, 13. . . ."]
>
> JACOB: [*shouting*] The football field's being watered; meet me in the gym.

Even such a simple encounter involves and depends upon a rich assortment of cognitive skills. At a basic level, Jacob and Janet have to be aware of each other. Their sensory systems allow the detection of each other, and their brains work on the raw data (information) from the senses in order to perceive or interpret the incoming information. In this case, the data are recognized as the familiar patterns labeled "Jacob" and "Janet." During the course of the brief conversation, the children must also attend to (concentrate on) each other, and in doing so they may be less attentive to other detectable sights and sounds of their environment.

This scenario illustrates the use of more than one type of memory. Janet stores the locker number and combination in short-term memory (STM), and she maintains the information by rehearsing it. After Janet retrieves the ball and redirects her attention to choosing teams for the football game, she may forget this information. Jacob does not need to rehearse his combination continually to maintain it; rather, his frequent use of his combination and the meaningfulness of this information have helped him to store it in long-term memory (LTM). If someone later asks Janet where she got the football, she will retrieve that information from her episodic LTM. Episodic memory holds information about how things appeared and when they occurred; it stores things that depend on context. The language comprehension of the children also illustrates another type of LTM. Semantic LTM, or semantic memory, holds all the information they need in order to use language; it includes not only words and the symbols for them, their meaning and what they represent but also the rules for manipulating them. When Janet hears the words "football," "water fountain," and "locker," she effortlessly retrieves their meanings from LTM. Furthermore, metamemory, an understanding of the attributes of one's own memories, is demonstrated. Janet knows to rehearse the combination to prevent forgetting it.

Jacob probably employed mental imagery and relied on a cognitive map in order to direct Janet to the equipment room. From his substantial mental representation of the school environment, Jacob retrieved a specific route, guided by a particular sequence of meaningful landmarks. In addition to their language capabilities and their abilities to form and follow routes, a number of other higher-level mental processes suggest something of the intelligence of these children. They appear to be following a plan that will result in a football game. Simple problem solving is demonstrated by Janet's calculation of how long it will take to retrieve the football and in Jacob's decision to use the gym floor as a substitute for the football field.

THEORETICAL AND METHODOLOGICAL APPROACHES

To understand cognitive psychology, one must be familiar not only with the relevant questions—the topic matter of the discipline—but also with the approach taken to answer these questions. Cognitive psychologists typically employ an information-processing model to help them better understand mental events. An assumption of this model is that mental activities (the processing of information) can be broken down into a series of interrelated stages and scientifically studied. A general comparison can be made between the information processing of a human and a computer. For example, both have data input into the system, humans through their sense organs and computers via the keyboard. Both systems then translate and encode (store) the data. The computer translates the keyboard input into electromagnetic signals for storage on a disk. People oftentimes translate the raw data from their senses to a linguistic code which is retained in some unique human storage device (for example, a piercing, rising-and-falling pitch may be stored in memory as "baby's cry"). Both humans and computers can manipulate the stored information in virtually limitless ways, and both can later retrieve information from storage for output. Although there are many dissimilarities between how computers and humans function, this comparison accurately imparts the flavor of the information-processing model.

In addition to constructing computational models that specify the stages and processes involved in human thought, cognitive psychologists use a variety of observational and experimental methods to determine how the mind works. Much can be learned, for example, from the study of patients with neuropsychological disorders such as the progressive dementias, including Alzheimer's disease. The "lesion," or brain injury, study is the oldest and most widely used technique to study brain function. Examining what happens when one aspect of cognition is disrupted can reveal much about the operation of the remaining mechanisms.

Behavioral studies—in contrast to "lesion" studies—examine cognitive function in healthy subjects, using a variety of experimental methods developed throughout the twentieth century. One of the continuing challenges of cognitive psychology is the construction of experiments in which observable behaviors accurately reveal mental processes. Researchers bring volunteers into the laboratory and measure, for example, the time it takes for subjects to judge whether a word they are shown had appeared in a list of words they had earlier studied.

Other researchers study human cognition in more naturalistic settings called field studies. In one such study, the average score of grocery shoppers on a paper-and-pencil arithmetic test was 59 percent, but their proficiency in the supermarket on analogous tasks reached ceiling level (98 percent). Much of what is done in the laboratory could be thought of as basic research, whereas field approaches to the study of cognition could be characterized as applied research.

APPLIED RESEARCH IN COGNITIVE PSYCHOLOGY

For many psychologists, the desire to "know about knowing" is sufficient reason to study human cognition; however, there are more tangible benefits. Examples of these widespread practical applications may be found in the fields of artificial intelligence, law, and in the everyday world of decision making.

Artificial intelligence (AI) is a branch of computer science that strives to create a computer capable of reasoning, processing language, and, in short, mimicking human intelligence. While this goal has yet to be obtained in full, research in this area has made important contributions. The search for AI has improved the understanding of human cognition; it has also produced applied benefits such as expert systems. Expert systems are computer programs that simulate human expertise in specific domains. Such programs have been painstakingly developed by computer scientists who have essentially extracted knowledge in a subject area from a human expert and built it into a computer system designed to apply that knowledge. Expert systems do not qualify as true artificial intelligence, because, while they can "think," they can only do so very narrowly, on one particular topic.

A familiar expert system is the "chess computer." A computerized chess game is driven by a program that has a vast storehouse of chess knowledge and the capability of interacting with a human player, "thinking" about each game in which it is involved. Expert systems are also employed to solve problems in law, computer programming, and various facets of industry. A medical expert system has even been developed to consult interactively with patients and to diagnose and recommend a course of treatment for infectious diseases.

The cognitive research of Elizabeth Loftus and her colleagues at the University of Washington demonstrates the shortcomings of human long-term memory. This research is relevant to the interpretation of eyewitness testimony in the courtroom. In one study, Loftus and John Palmer showed their subjects films of automobile accidents and asked them to estimate the speeds of the cars involved. The critical variable was the verb used in the question to the subjects. That is, they were asked how fast the cars were going when they "smashed," "collided," "bumped," "hit," or "contacted" each other. Interestingly, the stronger the verb, the greater was the speed estimated. One interpretation of these findings is that the nature of the "leading question" biased the answers of subjects who were not really positive of the cars' speeds. Hence, if the question employed the verb "smashed," the subject was led to estimate that the cars were going fast. Any astute attorney would have no trouble capitalizing on this phenomenon when questioning witnesses to a crime or accident.

In a second experiment, Loftus and Palmer considered a different explanation for their findings. Again, subjects saw filmed car accidents and were questioned as to the speeds of the cars, with the key verb being varied as previously described. As before, those exposed to the verb "smashed" estimated the fastest speeds. In the second part of the experiment, conducted a week later, the subjects were asked additional questions about the accident, including, "Did you see any broken glass?" Twenty percent of the subjects reported seeing broken glass, though none was in the film. Of particular interest was that the majority of those who made this error were in the group that had been exposed to the strongest verb, "smashed."

Loftus and Palmer reasoned that the subjects were melding actual information that they had witnessed with information from another source encountered after the fact (the verb "smashed" presented by the questioner). The result was a mental representation of an event that was partly truth and partly fiction. This interpretation has implications for the evaluation of eyewitness testimony. Before testifying in court, a witness will likely have been questioned numerous times (and received many suggestions as to what may have taken place) and may even have compared notes with other witnesses. This process is likely to distort the originally experienced information.

Consider next the topic of decision making, an area of research in cognitive psychology loaded with practical implications. Everyone makes scores of decisions on a daily basis, from choosing clothing to match the weather to selecting a college or a career objective. Psychologists Amos Tversky and Daniel Kahneman are well known for their research on decision making and, in particular, on the use of heuristics. Heuristics are shortcuts or rules of thumb that are likely, but not guaranteed, to produce a correct decision. It would seem beneficial for everyone to appreciate the limitations of such strategies. For example, the availability heuristic often leads people astray when their decisions involve the estimating of probabilities, as when faced with questions such as, Which produces more fatalities, breast cancer or diabetes? Which are more numerous in the English language, words that begin with k or words that have k as the third letter? Experimental subjects typically, and incorrectly, choose the first alternative. Kahneman and Tversky's research indicates that people rely heavily on examples that come most easily to mind—that is, the information most available in memory. Hence, people overestimate the incidence of breast-cancer fatalities because such tragedies get more media attention relative to diabetes, a more prolific but less exotic killer. In a similar vein, words that begin with *k* come to mind more easily (probably because people are more likely to organize their vocabularies by the initial sounds of the words) than words with *k* as the third letter, although the latter, in fact, outnumber the former. One's decision making will doubtless be improved if one is aware of the potential drawbacks associated with the availability heuristic and if one is able to resist the tendency to estimate probabilities based upon the most easily imagined examples.

COGNITIVE CONTEXTS

The workings of the human mind have been pondered throughout recorded history. The science of psychology, however, only dates back to 1879, when Wilhelm Wundt established the first laboratory for the study of psychology in Leipzig, Germany. Although the term was not yet popular, Wundt's primary interest was clearly in cognition. His students laboriously practiced the technique of introspection (the careful attention to, and the objective reporting of, one's own sensations, experiences, and thoughts), as Wundt hoped to identify through this method the basic elements of human thought. Wundt's interests remained fairly popular until around 1920. At that time, John B. Watson, a noted American psychologist and behaviorist, spearheaded a campaign to redefine the agenda of psychology. Watson was convinced that the workings of the mind could not be objectively studied through introspection and hence mandated that the proper subject matter for psychologists should be overt, observable behaviors exclusively. In this way, dissatisfaction with a method of research (introspection) led to the abandonment of an important psychological topic (mental activity).

In the 1950's, a number of forces came into play that led to the reemergence of cognitive psychology in the United States. First, during World War II, considerable research had been devoted to human-factors issues such as human skills and performance within, for example, the confines of a tank or cockpit. After the war, researchers showed continued interest in human attention, perception, decision making, and so on, and they were influenced by a branch of communication science, known as information theory, that dealt abstractly with questions of information processing. The integration of these two topics resulted eventually in the modern information-processing model, mentioned above.

Second, explosive gains were made in the field of computer science. Of particular interest to psychology were advances in the area of artificial intelligence. It was a natural progression for psychologists to begin comparing computer and brain processes, and this analogy served to facilitate cognitive research.

Third, there was growing dissatisfaction with behavioral psychology as defined by Watson and with its seeming inability to explain complex psychological phenomena. In particular, Noam Chomsky, a well-known linguist, proposed that the structure of language was too complicated to be acquired via the principles of behaviorism. It became apparent to many psychologists that to understand truly the diversity of human behavior, internal mental processes would have to be accepted and scientifically studied.

Working memory emerged as an important theoretical construct in the 1980's and 1990's. Everyday cognitive tasks—such as reading a newspaper article or calculating the appropriate amount to tip in a restaurant—often involve multiple steps with intermediate results that need to be kept in mind temporarily to accomplish the task at hand successfully. "Working memory" refers to the system or mechanism underlying the maintenance of task-relevant information during the performance of a cognitive task. As the "hub of cognition," working memory has been called "perhaps the most significant achievement of human mental evolution." According to Alan Baddeley, working memory comprises a visuospatial sketchpad; a phonological loop, concerned with acoustic and verbal information; a central executive that is involved in the control and regulation of the system; and an episodic buffer that combines information from long-term memory with that from the visuospatial sketchpad and the phonological loop. Prospective memory is also emerging as an important domain of research in cognitive psychology. This type of memory involves the intention to carry out an action in the future: for instance, to pick up dry cleaning after work.

Cognitive psychology is now a vibrant subdiscipline that has attracted some of the finest scientific minds. It is a standard component in most undergraduate and graduate psychology programs. More than half a dozen academic journals are devoted to its research, and it continues to pursue answers to questions that are important to psychology and other disciplines as well. The cognitive perspective has heavily influenced other subfields of psychology. For example, many social psychologists are interested in social cognition, the reasoning underlying such phenomena as prejudice, altruism, and persuasion. Some clinical psychologists are interested in understanding the abnormal thought processes underlying problems such as depression and anorexia nervosa. A subspecialty—cognitive behavioral therapy—treats mental illness using methods that attempt to directly treat these abnormal thoughts.

The burgeoning field of cognitive science represents a union of cognitive psychology, neuroscience, computer science, linguistics, and philosophy. Cognitive scientists are concerned with mental processes but are particularly interested in establishing general, fundamental principles of information processing as they may be applied by humans or machines. Their research is often heavily dependent on complex computer models rather than experimentation with humans. With fast-paced advances in computer technology, and the exciting potential of expertise shared in an interdisciplinary fashion, the field of cognitive science holds considerable promise for answering questions about human cognition.

SOURCES FOR FURTHER STUDY

Ashcraft, Mark H. *Human Memory and Cognition.* 2d ed. New York: Harper-Collins College, 1994. A fine textbook, geared for college students who have had some background in psychology but accessible to the inquisitive layperson. Ashcraft writes informally and provides chapter outlines and summaries, a glossary of key terms, and suggested supplemental readings. Perception and attention, memory, language, reasoning, decision making, and problem solving are all well covered.

Baddeley, Alan D. "The Cognitive Psychology of Everyday Life." *British Journal of Psychology* 72, no. 2 (1981): 257-269. An interesting journal article in which Baddeley describes his research conducted outside the laboratory environment. Considers such practical topics as absentmindedness, alcohol effects, and the effectiveness of saturation advertising. A must for those who question the ecological validity (the real-life applicability) of cognitive research.

Berger, Dale E., Kathy Pezdek, and William P. Banks, eds. *Applications of Cognitive Psychology.* Hillsdale, N.J.: Lawrence Erlbaum, 1987. Five chapters each on three topics: educational applications, teaching of thinking and problem solving, and human-computer interactions. The chapters range in sophistication and accessibility, so this book should appeal to readers of diverse backgrounds. Includes helpful name and subject indexes.

Hochberg, Julian. *Perception and Cognition at Century's End.* San Diego, Calif.: Academic Press, 1998. This book reviews research findings over the preceding half-century in broad areas of perception and other aspects of cognitive functioning.

Kahneman, Daniel, Paul Slovic, and Amos Tversky, eds. *Judgment Under Uncertainty: Heuristics and Biases.* New York: Cambridge University Press, 1987. A comprehensive source on heuristics and decision making with an easy-to-understand introductory chapter by the editors. A four-chapter section is devoted to the availability heuristic, and there is an interesting chapter on probabilistic reasoning in clinical medicine.

Kendler, Howard H. *Historical Foundations of Modern Psychology.* Chicago: Dorsey Press, 1987. A well-written account of the emergence of cognitive psychology and the contributions of other disciplines such as linguistics, engineering, and computer science. Approachable for the layperson; provides a fine historical backdrop. It is of limited use, beyond review, for the upper-level college student.

Miyake, Akira, and Priti Shah, eds. *Models of Working Memory: Mechanisms of Active Maintenance and Executive Control.* New York: Cambridge University Press, 1999. This volume compares and contrasts existing models of working memory. It does so by asking each contributor to address the same comprehensive set of important theoretical questions on working memory. The answers to these questions provided in the volume elucidate the emerging general consensus on the nature of working memory among different theorists and crystallize incompatible theoretical claims that must be resolved in future.

Pinker, Steven. *How the Mind Works.* New York: W. W. Norton, 1997. Pinker, one of the world's leading cognitive scientists, discusses what the mind is, how it evolved, and how it allows one to see, think, feel, laugh, interact, enjoy the arts, and ponder the mysteries of life. He explains the mind by "reverse-engineering" it—figuring out what natural selection designed it to accomplish in the environment in which humans evolved.

Sternberg, Robert J., and Talia Ben-Zeev. *Complex Cognition: The Psychology of Human Thought.* New York: Oxford University Press, 2001. Reviews of the key concepts and research findings within the field of cognitive psychology. The authors offer a synthesis of the two dominant approaches in cognitive studies—normative reference and "bounded rationality"—combining the best elements of each to present an inclusive new theory that emphasizes multiple points of view, including both the objective and subjective views of the self and others.

Wells, Gary L., and Elizabeth F. Loftus, eds. *Eyewitness Testimony: Psychological Perspectives.* New York: Cambridge University Press, 1984. A fourteen-chapter source with heavy consideration of laboratory research and references to courtroom cases as well. There is nice coverage of research on children as witnesses as well as on "earwitness" testimony and the use of hypnosis as a memory aid.

Mark B. Alcorn; updated by Allyson M. Washburn

SEE ALSO: Cognitive Development: Jean Piaget; Language; Logic and Reasoning.

Cognitive Social Learning
Walter Mischel

Type of psychology: Personality
Fields of study: Behavioral and cognitive models; personality theory

Mischel's social learning theory presents a cognitive-social alternative to traditional personality theories. He posits that behavior is determined by a complex interaction of situational and cognitive variables and cannot be predicted from a few widely generalized traits. Consistent features in behavior result from cognitive person variables, defined as acquired and relatively stable modes of information processing.

Key concepts
- construction competencies
- encoding strategy
- expectancies
- person variable
- personal construct
- personality trait
- prototype
- stimulus value

Psychologist Walter Mischel developed a cognitive social learning approach to personality that presents a serious challenge to traditional theories and their central tenet that behavior can be predicted from a few widely generalized traits. In his influential book *Personality and Assessment* (1968), Mischel reviewed the literature on personality traits. Personality traits can be defined as a stable disposition to behave in a given way over time and across situations. Although Mischel found impressive consistencies for some attributes, such as intelligence, the vast majority of behavior patterns were not consistent, even in highly similar situations. Mischel concluded that behavior is largely determined by situational variables that interact in complex ways with individual modes of information processing. Stable features in behavior result from acquired cognitive person variables (relatively stable individual differences that influence how people interact with their world).

Person Variables

Cognitive and behavioral construction competencies represent the first of the person variables. Mischel terms them "competencies" to emphasize that they represent potentials—that is, what people *can* do, rather than what they do. Referring to their "constructive" quality implies that people do not passively store but actively construct their experiences by transforming and synthesizing incoming information in novel ways. Another of these person variables involves encoding strategies and personal constructs. People encode information and classify events in personalized, unique ways. For different individuals, traitlike constructs such as intelligence or honesty may therefore have some overlapping features but may also have many idiosyncratic ones. This explains why two people can witness and process the same event but interpret it differently. Both people only attend to stimuli consistent with their own personal construct systems and ignore discrepant information.

Mischel maintains that besides knowing people's potentials and how they construct events, to predict behavior people must also know their expectations. One type, termed stimulus-outcome expectancies, develops when people form associations between two events and begin to expect the second event as soon as the first occurs. For example, if a child learns to associate parental frowning with being scolded, any angry face alone may instill anxiety.

A second type, termed response-outcome expectancies, refers to learned "if-then rules," in which specific actions will result in certain outcomes. Outcome expectancies can have a significant influence on what people do. When expectations are inconsistent with reality, they can lead to dysfunctional behavior. Expecting relief from alcohol, when drinking actually leads to multiple problems, illustrates this point.

Subjective stimulus values—subjective values or worth that a person attributes to an object or event—are another type of person variable. In spite of holding identical outcome expectancies, people may behave differently if they do not attribute equal value to this outcome. For example, many believe that practice makes perfect, but not everyone values achievement. Furthermore, the worth of a given outcome often depends on its context. Even an avid skier might cancel a ski trip on an icy, stormy winter day.

Self-regulatory systems and plans are yet another kind of person variable. Besides being affected by external rewards and punishments, people are capable of regulating their own behavior. They set goals and mediate self-imposed consequences, depending on whether they meet their own standards. These self-regulatory processes produce individual differences in behavior independently from the effects of extrinsically imposed conditions.

More recently, Mischel and his colleagues have proposed that people also classify events based on cognitive prototypes. These are analogous to templates, and they contain only the best or most typical features of a concept. Although prototypes facilitate the classification of input information, they carry with them the danger of stereotyping. Anyone who, for example, has mistaken a woman business executive for the secretary can appreciate the problem resulting from inaccurate classification.

In summary, with the concept of person variables, Mischel can explain behavioral consistency and at the same time take into account the environment as an important determinant of human actions. In psychologically strong situations, person variables play a minimal role (at a church service, for example, all people behave similarly). In psychologically weak situations (such as a cocktail party), however, individual differences are pronounced because there are no consistent cues to signal what behaviors are deemed appropriate. Therefore, whether or how much cognitive dispositions influence behavior varies with the specific situation.

DISPOSITIONAL AND SITUATIONAL VARIABLES

Despite a widespread tendency among people to describe themselves and others in traitlike terms (intelligent, friendly, aggressive, domineering, and so forth), research has shown that a person's behavior cannot be predicted from a few broadly generalized personality traits. This does not mean that behavior is totally inconsistent, but that dispositions alone are insufficient to explain consistency and that dispositional, as well as situational, variables need to be taken into account for a complete analysis.

To separate the effects of person and situation variables on behavior, Mischel and his colleagues conducted a series of experiments. In one study, the experimenters assessed adolescents' dispositions toward success or failure. Weeks later they had them solve skill-related tasks and, regardless of their actual performance, gave one group success, a second group failure, and a third group no feedback on their performance. Then the adolescents had to choose between a less desirable reward, one for which attainment was independent of performance on similar tasks, and a preferred reward, for which attainment was performance-dependent. In both bogus feedback conditions, the situational variables had a powerful effect and completely overrode preexisting dispositions toward success or failure. Adolescents who believed they had failed the tasks more often selected the noncontingent reward, while those who believed they had succeeded chose the contingent reward. For subjects in the no-feedback condition, however, the preexisting expectancy scores were highly accurate predictors of their reward choices. This study illustrates how dispositions emerge under weak situational cues but play a trivial role when the setting provides strong cues for behavior. Therefore, Mischel (1973) considers it more meaningful to analyze "behavior-contingency units" that link specific behavior patterns to those conditions in which they are likely to occur, rather than looking only at behavior. In other words, instead of labeling people "aggressive," it would be more useful to specify under what conditions these people display aggressive behaviors. Such precise specifications would guard against an oversimplified trait approach and highlight the complexities and idiosyncrasies of behavior as well as its interdependence with specific stimulus conditions.

SELF-CONTROL

Mischel and his colleagues also have conducted extensive research on self-control. Their work has been summarized in an article published in 1989 in the journal *Science*. In several experiments, the researchers attempted to clarify why some people are capable of self-regulation, at least in some areas of their lives, while others fail in such attempts. They found enduring differences in self-control as early as the preschool years. In one study, for example, they showed young children pairs of treats, one less and one more desirable (for example, two versus five cookies or one versus two marshmallows). The children were told that the experimenter would leave the room and that they could obtain the more valuable treat if they waited until he or she returned. They could also ring the bell to bring the experimenter back sooner, but then they would receive the lesser treat. During the waiting period, which lasted a maximum of fifteen minutes, the children were unobtrusively observed. Later, the children's strategies to bridge the waiting period were analyzed. It became apparent that self-control increased when the children used behavioral or cognitive strategies to bridge the delay, such as avoiding looking at the rewards, distracting themselves with singing, playing with their fingers, or cognitively transforming the rewards (for example, thinking of marshmallows as clouds). Interestingly, a follow-up study more than ten years later revealed that those preschool children who had displayed more self-control early were socially and academically more competent, more attentive, more verbal, and better able than their peers to cope with stress as adolescents. In a related study, the length of delay time in preschool proved to be correlated with the adolescents' Scholastic Aptitude Test (SAT) scores, suggesting that greater self-control is related to superior academic achievement.

These studies provide an excellent illustration of how cognitive person variables sometimes can have very stable and generalized effects on behavior. The early acquisition of effective cognitive and behavioral strategies to delay gratification had a positive influence on the children's long-term adjustment. Thus, self-control fulfills the requirements of a "personality disposition" in Mischel's sense, because it constitutes an important mediating mechanism for adaptive social behavior throughout the life cycle.

Although the examples presented above lend support to Mischel's theory, one might argue that children's behavior under the constraints of a research setting is artificial and may not reflect what they normally do in their natural environment. While this argument is plausible, it was not supported in a later study with six- to twelve-year-old children in a summer residential treatment facility. Observing children under naturalistic circumstances in this facility led to comparable results. Children who spontaneously used effective cognitive-attentional strategies for self-regulation showed greater self-control in delay situations and were better adjusted than their peers.

An unanswered question is how best to teach children effective information-processing skills. If these skills acquire dispositional character and influence overall adjustment, their attainment would indeed be of vital importance to healthy development.

EVOLUTION OF RESEARCH

Until the late 1960's, the field of personality psychology was dominated by trait and state theories. Their central assumption, that people have traits that produce enduring consistencies in their behavior, went unchallenged for many years. The widespread appeal of these trait assumptions notwithstanding, since the late 1960's personality and social psychologists have been entangled in the "person-situation debate," a controversy over whether the presumed stability in behavior might be based more on illusion than reality. While doubts about the existence of traits were already raised in the middle of the twentieth century, the work of Walter Mischel was instrumental in bringing the controversy into the forefront of academic psychology. In reviewing a voluminous body of literature, Mischel showed in 1968 that virtually all so-called trait measures, except intelligence, change substantially over time and even more dramatically across situations. Traits such as honesty, assertiveness, or attitudes toward authority typically showed reliability across situations of .20 to .30. This means that if the correlation of behavior presumably reflecting a trait in two different situations is .30, less than one-tenth (.30 × .30 = .09, or 9 percent) of the variability in the behavior can be attributed to the trait. Mischel therefore concluded that perceptions of behavioral stability, while not arbitrary, are often only weakly related to the phenomenon in question.

FUNCTIONAL ANALYSIS

There is consensus, however, that human actions show at least some degree of consistency, which is evidenced most strongly by the sense of continuity people experience in their own selves. How can people reconcile the inconsistency between their own impressions and the empirical data? Mischel's cognitive social learning perspective presents one possible solution to this dilemma. Rather than trying to explain behavior by a few generalized traits, Mischel has shifted the emphasis to a thorough examination of the relationship between behavior patterns and the context in which they occur, as the following example illustrates. Assume that parents are complaining about their child's demanding behavior and the child's many tantrums. After observing this behavior in various situations, a traditional personality theorist might conclude that it manifests an underlying "aggressive drive." In contrast, a social learning theorist might seek to identify the specific conditions under which the tantrums occur and then change these conditions to see if the tantrums increase or decrease. This technique, termed "functional analysis" (as described in Mischel in 1968), systematically introduces and withdraws stimuli in the situation to examine how the behavior of interest changes as a function of situational constraints.

The controversy sparked by Mischel's work has not been completely resolved. Few psychologists today, however, would assume an extreme position and either argue that human actions are completely determined by traits or advocate a total situation-specificity of behavior. As with so many controversies, the truth probably lies somewhere in the middle.

SOURCES FOR FURTHER STUDY

Lieber, Robert M., and Michael D. Spiegler. *Personality: Strategies and Issues.* 7th ed. Monterey, Calif.: Brooks/Cole, 1996. Chapter 21 presents a readable synopsis of Mischel's cognitive social-learning theory and reviews the concept of person variables, Mischel's work on delay of gratification, and his position on the interaction of emotion and cognition. Highly recommended as an easy introduction to Mischel's work.

Mischel, Harriet N., and Walter Mischel, eds. *Readings in Personality.* New York: Holt, Rinehart and Winston, 1973. Presents a collection of papers by different authors on some of the central topics and viewpoints in personality psychology. Provides in-depth analyses of various trait, state, and social theories of personality. Several chapters by Walter Mischel present his views on social learning, personality, and his empirical work on self-control.

Mischel, Walter. *Personality and Assessment.* 1968. Reprint. Mahwah, N.J.: Lawrence Erlbaum, 1996. Classic exposition of Mischel's early work, containing a compelling critique of traditional trait and state approaches to personality. Discusses issues relevant to the assessment and modification of maladaptive social behavior. Should be available in many public and all university libraries.

_____. "Toward a Cognitive Social Learning Reconceptualization of Personality." *Psychological Review* 80, no. 4 (1973): 252-283. Written in response to the many reactions Mischel's 1968 book provoked in the research community. Clarifies several common misunderstandings of Mischel's position (for example, the situation-specificity issue) and gives a thorough presentation of his five personality variables. No specialized knowledge in psychology or personality theory is necessary for the reader to be able to follow the author's main arguments.

Mischel, Walter, Yuichi Shoda, and Monica L. Rodriguez. "Delay of Gratification in Children." *Science* 244, no. 4907 (1989): 933-938. Presents an excellent, brief summary of Mischel's work on self-control and delay of gratification spanning almost two decades. Discusses a number of stable individual differences in information-processing and strategic behaviors used by preschool children that were predictive of adult social adjustment.

Edelgard Wulfert

SEE ALSO: Cognitive Behavior Therapy; Cognitive Psychology; Cognitive Therapy; Learning; Personal Constructs: George A. Kelly; Social Learning: Albert Bandura.

COGNITIVE THERAPY

TYPE OF PSYCHOLOGY: Psychotherapy
FIELD OF STUDY: Cognitive therapies

Cognitive therapy holds that emotional disorders are largely determined by cognition, or thinking, that cognitive activity can take the form of language or images, and that emotional disorders can be treated by helping patients modify their cognitive distortions. Treatment programs based on this model have been highly successful with depression, panic disorder, generalized anxiety disorder, and other emotional problems.

KEY CONCEPTS
- arbitrary inference
- automatic thoughts
- cognitive specificity hypothesis
- cognitive triad
- schemata
- selective abstraction

Cognitive therapy, originally developed by Aaron T. Beck (born in 1921), is based on the view that cognition (the process of acquiring knowledge and forming beliefs) is a primary determinant of mood and behavior. Beck developed his theory while treating depressed patients. He noticed that these patients tended to distort whatever happened to them in the direction of self-blame and catastrophe. Thus, an event interpreted by a normal person as irritating and inconvenient, for example, the malfunctioning of an automobile, would be interpreted by the depressed patient as another example of the utter hopelessness of life. Beck's central point is that depressives draw illogical conclusions and come to evaluate negatively themselves, their immediate world, and their future. They see only personal failings, present misfortunes, and overwhelming difficulties ahead. It is from these cognitions that all the other symptoms of depression derive.

It was from Beck's early work with depressed patients that cognitive therapy was developed. Shortly thereafter, the concepts and procedures were applied to other psychological problems, with notable success.

AUTOMATIC THOUGHTS AND SCHEMATA

Two concepts of particular relevance to cognitive therapy are the concepts of automatic thoughts and schemata. Automatic thoughts are thoughts that appear to be going on all the time. These thoughts are quite brief—only the essential words in a sentence seem to occur, as in a telegraphic style. Further, they seem to be autonomous, in that the person made no effort to initiate them, and they seem plausible or reasonable to the person (although they may seem far-fetched to somebody else). Thus, as a depressed person is giving a talk to a group of business colleagues, he or she will have a variety of thoughts. There will be thoughts about the content of the material. There is also a second stream of thoughts occurring. In this second channel, the person may experience such thoughts as: "This is a waste of time," or "They think I'm dumb." These are automatic thoughts.

Beck has suggested that although automatic thoughts are occurring all the time, the person is likely to overlook these thoughts when asked what he or she is thinking. Thus, it is necessary to train the person to attend to these automatic thoughts. Beck pointed out that when people are depressed, these automatic thoughts are filled with negative thoughts of the self, the world, and the future. Further, these automatic thoughts are quite distorted, and finally, when these thoughts are carefully examined and modified to be more in keeping with reality, the depression subsides.

The concept of schemata, or core beliefs, becomes critical in understanding why some people are prone to having emotional difficulties and others are not. The schema appears to be the root from which the automatic thoughts derive. Beck suggests that people develop a propensity to think crookedly as a result of early life experiences. He theorizes that in early life, an individual forms concepts—realistic as well as unrealistic—from experiences. Of particular importance are individuals' attitudes toward themselves, their environment, and their future. These deeply held core beliefs about oneself are seen by Beck as critical in the causation of emotional disorders. According to cognitive theory, the reason these early beliefs are so critical is that once they are formed, the person has a tendency to distort or view subsequent experiences to be consistent with these core beliefs. Thus, an individual who, as a child, was subjected to severe, unprovoked punishment from a disturbed parent may conclude "I am weak" or "I am inferior." Once this conclusion has been formulated, it would appear to be strongly reinforced over years and years of experiences at the hands of the parent. Thus, when this individual becomes an adult, he or she tends to interpret even normal frustrations as more proof of the original belief: "See, I really am inferior." Examples of these negative schemata or core beliefs are "I am inferior," "I am unlovable," and "I cannot do anything right." People holding such core beliefs about themselves would differ strongly in their views of a frustrating experience from those people who hold a core belief such as "I am capable."

Another major contribution of cognitive therapy is Beck's cognitive specificity hypothesis. Specifically, Beck has suggested that each of the emotional disorders is characterized by its own patterns of thinking. In the case of depression, the thought content is concerned with ideas of personal deficiency, impossible environmental demands and obstacles, and nihilistic expectations. For example, a depressed patient might interpret a frustrating situation, such as a malfunctioning automobile, as evidence of his or her own inadequacy: "If I were really competent, I would have anticipated this problem and been able to avoid it." Additionally, the depressed patient might react to the malfunctioning automobile with "This is too much, I cannot take it anymore." To the depressed patient, this would simply be another example of the utter hopelessness of life.

PATTERNS OF THOUGHT

While the cognitive content of depression emphasizes the negative view of the self, the world, and the future, anxiety disorders are characterized by fears of physical and psychological danger. The anxious patient's thoughts are filled with themes of danger. These people anticipate detrimental occurrences to themselves, their family, their property, their status, and other intangibles that they value.

In phobias, as in anxiety, there is the cognitive theme of danger; however, the "danger" is confined to definable situations. As long as phobic sufferers are able to avoid these situations, they do not feel threatened and may be relatively calm. The cognitive content of panic disorder is characterized by a catastrophic interpretation of bodily or mental experiences. Thus, patients with panic disorder are prone to regard any unexplained symptom or sensation as a sign of some impending catastrophe. As a result, their cognitive processing system focuses their attention on bodily or psychological experience. For example, one patient saw discomfort in the chest as evidence of an impending heart attack.

The cognitive feature of the paranoid reaction is the misinterpretation of experience in terms of mistreatment, abuse, or persecution. The cognitive theme of the conversion disorder (a disorder characterized by physical complaints such as paralysis or blindness, of which no underlying physical basis can be determined) is the conviction that one has a physical disorder. As a result of this belief, the patient experiences sensory or motor abnormalities that are consistent with the patient's faulty conception of organic pathology.

CHANGING THE PATIENT'S MIND

The goal of cognitive therapy is to assist the patient to evaluate his or her thought processes carefully, to identify cognitive errors, and to substitute more adaptive, realistic cognitions. This goal is accomplished by therapists helping patients to see their thinking about themselves (or their situation) as similar to the activity of a scientist—that they are engaged in the activity of developing hypotheses (or theories) about their world. Like a scientist, the patient needs to "test" his or her theory carefully. Thus, patients who have concluded that they are "worthless" people would be encouraged to test their "theories" rigorously to determine if this is indeed accurate. Further, in the event that the theories are not accurate, patients would be encouraged to change their theories to make them more consistent with reality (what they find in their experience).

A slightly different intervention developed by Beck and his colleagues is to help the patient identify common cognitive distortions. Beck originally identified four cognitive distortions frequently found in emotional disorders: arbitrary inference, selective abstraction, overgeneralization, and magnification or minimization. These were later expanded to ten or more by Beck's colleagues and students.

Arbitrary inference is defined as the process of drawing a conclusion from a situation, event, or experience when there is no evidence to support the conclusion or when the conclusion is contrary to the evidence. For example, a depressed patient on a shopping trip had the thought, "The sales-clerk thinks I am a nobody." The patient then felt sad. On being questioned by the psychologist, the patient realized that there was no factual basis for this thought.

Selective abstraction refers to the process of focusing on a detail taken out of context, ignoring other, more salient features of the situation, and conceptualizing the whole experience on the basis of this element. For example, a patient was praised by friends about the patient's child-care activities. Through an oversight, however, the patient failed to have her child vaccinated during the appropriate week. Her immediate thought was "I am a failure as a mother." This idea became paramount despite all the other evidence of her competence.

Overgeneralization refers to patients' patterns of drawing a general conclusion about their ability, their performance, or their worth on the basis of a single incident. For example, a student regards his poor performance on the first examination of the semester as final proof that he "will never make it in college." Magnification and minimization refer to gross errors in evaluation. For example, a person, believing that he has completely ruined his car (magnification) when he sees that there is a slight scratch on the rear fender, regards himself as "good for nothing." In contrast, minimization refers to minimizing one's achievements, protesting that these achievements do not mean anything. For example, a highly successful businesswoman who was depressed concluded that her many prior successes "were nothing. . . simply luck." Using the cognitive distortions, people are taught to examine their thoughts, to identify any distortions, and then to modify their thoughts in order to eliminate the distortions.

THERAPEUTIC TECHNIQUES

In terms of the therapeutic process, the focus is initially on the automatic thoughts of patients. Once patients are relatively adept at identifying and modifying their maladaptive automatic thoughts, the therapy begins to focus on the maladaptive underlying beliefs or schemata. As previously noted, these beliefs are fundamental beliefs that people hold about themselves. These beliefs are not as easy to identify as the automatic thoughts. Rather, they are identified in an inferential process. Common patterns are observed; for example, the person may seem to be operating by the rule "If I am not the best _____, then I am a failure," or "If I am not loved by my spouse or mate, then I am worthless." As in the case of the earlier cognitive work with automatic thoughts, these beliefs are carefully evaluated for their adaptability or rationality. Maladaptive beliefs are then modified to more adaptive, realistic beliefs.

A variety of techniques have been developed by cognitive therapists for modifying maladaptive cognitions. One example of these techniques is self-monitoring. This involves the patient's keeping a careful hour-by-hour record of his or her activities, associated moods, or other pertinent phenomena. One useful variant is to have the patient record his or her mood on a simple zero-to-one-hundred scale, where zero represents the worst he or she has ever felt and one hundred represents the best. In addition, the patient can record the degree of mastery or pleasure associated with each recorded activity.

A number of hypotheses can be tested using self-monitoring, such as "It does not do any good for me to get out of bed," "I am always miserable; it never lets up," and "My schedule is too full for me to accomplish what I must." By simply checking the self-monitoring log, one can easily determine if one's miserable mood ever ceases. A careful examination of the completed record is a far better basis for judging such hypotheses than is the patient's memory of recent events, because his or her recollections are almost always tainted by the depression.

As therapy progresses and patients begin to experience more elevated moods, the focus of treatment becomes more cognitive. Patients are instructed to observe and record automatic thoughts, perhaps at a specific time each evening, as well as recording when they become aware of increased dysphoria. Typically, the thoughts are negative self-referents ("I am worthless" or "I will never amount to anything"), and initially, the therapist points out their unreasonable and self-defeating nature. With practice, patients learn "distancing," or dealing with such thoughts objectively and evaluating them, rather than blindly accepting them. Homework assignments can facilitate distancing: The patient records an automatic thought, and next to it he or she writes down a thought that counters the automatic thought, as the therapist might have done. According to Beck, certain basic themes soon emerge, such as being abandoned, as well as stylistic patterns of thinking, such as overgeneralization. The themes reflect the aforementioned rules, and the ultimate goal of therapy is to assist the patient to modify them.

Finally, cognitive therapy has been applied to a variety of psychological disorders with striking success. For example, studies from seven independent centers have compared the efficacy of cognitive therapy to antidepressant medication, a treatment of established efficacy. Comparisons of cognitive therapy to drugs have found cognitive therapy to be superior or equal to antidepressant medication. Further, follow-up studies indicate that cognitive therapy has greater long-term effects than drug therapy. Of special significance is the evidence of greater sustained improvement over time with cognitive therapy.

Cognitive therapy has been successfully applied to panic disorder, resulting in practically complete reduction of panic attacks after twelve to sixteen weeks of treatment. Additionally, cognitive therapy has been successfully applied to generalized anxiety disorder, eating disorders, and inpatient depression.

DEPRESSION AND COGNITIVE THERAPY

Cognitive theory and cognitive therapy originated in Beck's observation and treatment of depressed patients. Originally trained in psychoanalysis, Beck observed that his patients experienced specific types of thoughts, of which they were only dimly aware, that they did not report during their free associations. Beck noticed that these thoughts were frequently followed by an unpleasant effect. Further, he noted that as the patients examined and modified their thoughts, their mood began to improve.

At the time of the emergence of the cognitive model, the treatment world was dominated primarily by the psychoanalytic model (with its heavy emphasis on the unconscious processes) and to a lesser extent by the behavioral model (with its emphasis on the behavioral processes, to the exclusion of thought). The psychoanalytic model was under attack, primarily because of a lack of careful empirical support. In contrast, behavior therapists were actively demonstrating the efficacy of their approaches in carefully designed studies. Beck and his students began to develop and test cognitive procedures systematically, and they have developed an impressive body of research support for the approach.

SOURCES FOR FURTHER STUDY

Beck, Aaron T. *Cognitive Therapy and the Emotional Disorders.* New York: International Universities Press, 1976. An easy-to-read book that presents a general overview of the cognitive model and illustrates the cognitive model of different psychological disorders.

Beck, Aaron T., and Gary Emery. *Anxiety Disorders and Phobias: A Cognitive Perspective.* Reprint. New York: Basic Books, 1990. Presents the cognitive theory and model of anxiety disorders, as well as the clinical techniques used with anxious patients.

Beck, Aaron T., A. J. Rush, B. F. Shaw, and Gary Emery. *Cognitive Therapy of Depression.* Reprint. New York: Guilford Press, 1987. Presents the cognitive theory of depression and actual techniques used with depressed patients. Makes a theoretical contribution and serves as a clinical handbook on depression.

Burns, David D. *Feeling Good: The New Mood Therapy.* Rev. ed. New York: Avon, 1999. Readable introduction to the major concepts and techniques of cognitive therapy; written by one of Beck's students.

Emery, Gary, Steven D. Hollom, and Richard C. Bedrosian, eds. *New Directions in Cognitive Therapy: A Casebook.* New York: Guilford Press, 1981. Contains cases presented by major cognitive therapists. Focuses on the application of cognitive therapy to a wide range of presenting problems (such as loneliness and agoraphobia) as well as diverse populations.

Donald G. Beal

SEE ALSO: Cognitive Behavior Therapy; Cognitive Social Learning: Walter Mischel; Personal Constructs: George A. Kelly.

CONDITIONING

TYPE OF PSYCHOLOGY: Learning
FIELDS OF STUDY: Instrumental conditioning; Pavlovian conditioning

Conditioning and learning are roughly synonymous terms. Both refer to changes in behavior resulting from experience, but conditioning has a more specific meaning, referring to changes in behavior that are the direct result of learning relationships between environmental events. Two types of relationships are studied by learning psychologists. The first involves learning the relationship between environmental events that consistently occur together. The second involves learning the environmental consequences of behavior. These two learning scenarios correspond to classical and operant conditioning respectively.

KEY CONCEPTS
- behavioral approach
- conditioned stimulus (CS)
- conditioned response (CR)
- contiguity
- Law of Effect
- operant response (R)
- reinforcing stimulus (Sr)
- schedules of reinforcement
- shaping
- unconditioned stimulus (US)
- unconditioned response (UR)

Learning refers to any change in behavior or mental processes associated with experience. Traditionally psychologists interested in learning have taken a behavioral approach which involves studying the relationship between environmental events and resulting behavioral changes in detail. Though the behavioral approach typically involves studying the behavior of nonhuman subjects in controlled laboratory environments, the results that have been found in behavioral research have often found wide application and use in human contexts. Since the early twentieth century behavioral psychologists have extensively studied two primary forms of learning, classical and operant conditioning.

CLASSICAL CONDITIONING
Classical conditioning is also referred to as associative learning or Pavlovian conditioning, after its primary founder, the Russian physiologist Ivan Petrovich Pavlov (1849-1936). Pavlov's original studies involved examining digestion in dogs. The first step in digestion is salivation. Pavlov developed an apparatus that allowed him to measure the amount of saliva a dog produced when presented with food. Dogs do not need to learn to salivate when food is given to them—that is an automatic, reflexive response. However, Pavlov

noticed that, with experience, the dogs began to salivate before the food was presented, suggesting that new stimuli had acquired the ability to elicit the response. In order to examine this unexpected finding, Pavlov selected specific stimuli, which he systematically presented to the dog just before food was presented. The classic example is the ringing of a bell, but there was nothing special about the bell per se. Dogs do not salivate in response to a bell ringing under normal circumstances. What made the bell special was its systematic relationship to the delivery of food. Over time, the dogs began to salivate in response to the ringing of the bell even when the food was not presented. In other words, the dogs learned to associate the bell with food so that the response (salivation) could be elicited by either stimulus.

In classical conditioning terminology, the food is the unconditioned stimulus (US). It is unconditioned (or unlearned) because the animal naturally responds to it before the experiment has begun. The sound of the bell ringing is referred to as the conditioned stimulus (CS). It is not naturally effective in eliciting salivation—for it to be so, learning on the part of the subject is required. Salivating in response to food presentation is referred to as

Ivan Pavlov.
(Library of Congress)

the unconditioned response (UR), and salivating when the bell is rung is referred to as the conditioned response (CR). Though it would seem that saliva is saliva, it is important to differentiate the conditioned from the unconditioned response, because these responses are not always identical. More important, one is a natural, unlearned response (the UR), while the other requires specific learning experiences in order to occur (the CR).

Classical conditioning is not limited to dogs and salivation. Modern researchers examine classical conditioning in a variety of ways. What is important is the specific pairing of some novel stimulus (the CS) with a stimulus that already elicits the response (the US). One common experimental procedure examines eye blink conditioning in rabbits, where a brief puff of air to the eye serves as the US, and the measured response (UR) is blinking. A tone, a light, or some other initially ineffective stimulus serves as the CS. After many pairings in which the CS precedes the air puff, the rabbit will begin to blink in response to the CS in the absence of the air puff. Another common behavior that is studied in classical conditioning research is conditioned suppression. Here a CS is paired with an aversive US, such as a mild electric shock. Presentation of the shock disrupts whatever behavior the animal is engaged in at the time, and with appropriate pairing over time, the CS comes to do so as well. A final example that many humans can relate to is taste aversion learning. Here a specific taste (CS) is paired with a drug or procedure that causes the animal to feel ill (US). In the future, the animal will avoid consuming (CR) the taste (CS) associated with illness (US). Taste aversions illustrate the fact that all forms of conditioning are not created equal. To learn a conditioned eye blink or salivation response requires many CS-US pairings, while taste aversions are often learned with only one pairing of the taste and illness.

UNDERLYING FACTORS
Psychologists have long studied the factors that are necessary and sufficient for producing classical conditioning. One important principle is contiguity, which refers to events occurring closely together in space or time. Classical conditioning is most effective when the CS and US are contiguous, though precisely how closely together they must be presented depends upon the type of classical conditioning observed. Taste aversion conditioning, for example, will occur over much longer CS-US intervals than would be effective with other conditioning arrangements. Nevertheless, the sooner illness (US) follows taste (CS), the stronger the aversion (CR) will be.

Though seemingly necessary for classical conditioning, contiguity is not sufficient. A particularly clear demonstration of this fact is seen when the CS and US are presented at the exact same moment (a procedure called simultaneous conditioning). Though maximally contiguous, simultaneous conditioning is an extremely poor method for producing a CR. Furthermore, the order of presentation matters. If the US is presented before the CS, rather than afterward as is usually the case, then inhibitory conditioning will occur.

Inhibitory conditioning is seen in experiments in which behavior can change in two directions. For example, with a conditioned suppression procedure, inhibitory conditioning is seen when the animal increases, rather than decreases, its ongoing behavior when the CS is presented.

These findings have led modern researchers to focus on the predictive relationship between the CS and the UCS in classical conditioning. An especially successful modern theory of classical conditioning, the Rescorla-Wagner Model, suggests that CS's acquire associative strength in direct proportion to how much information they provide about the upcoming US. In addition to providing a quantitative description of the way in which CRs are learned, the Rescorla-Wagner model has predicted a number of counterintuitive conditioning phenomena, such as blocking and overshadowing. Taken as a whole, the newer theoretical conceptions of classical conditioning tend to view the learning organism less as a passive recipient of environmental events than as an active analyzer of information.

Does classical conditioning account for any human behaviors? At first glance, these processes might seem a bit simplistic to account for human behaviors. However, some common human reactions are quite obviously the result of conditioning. For instance, nearly everyone who has had a cavity filled will cringe at the sound of a dentist's drill, because the sound of the drill (CS) has been paired in the past with the unpleasant experience of having one's teeth drilled (US). Cringing at the sound of the drill would be a conditioned response (CR). Psychologists have found evidence implicating classical conditioning in a variety of important human behaviors, from the emotional effects of advertising to the functioning of the immune system to the development of tolerance in drug addiction.

OPERANT CONDITIONING

At about the same time that Pavlov was conducting his experiments in Russia, an American psychologist named Edward L. Thorndike (1874-1949) was examining a different form of learning that has come to be called instrumental or operant conditioning. Thorndike's original experiments involved placing cats in an apparatus he designed, which he called a puzzle box. A plate of food was placed outside the puzzle box, but the hungry cat was trapped inside. Thorndike designed the box so that the cat needed to make a particular response, such as moving a lever or pulling a cord, in order for a trap door to be released, allowing escape and access to the food outside. The amount of time it took the cat to make the appropriate response was measured. With repeated experience, Thorndike found that it took less and less time for the cat to make the appropriate response.

Operant conditioning is much different from Pavlov's classical conditioning. As was stated before, classical conditioning involves learning "what goes with what" in the environment. Learning the relationship changes behavior, though behavior does not change the environmental events themselves. Through experience, Pavlov's dogs began to salivate when the bell was rung, because the bell predicted food. However, salivating (the CR) did not cause the food to be delivered. Thorndike's cats, on the other hand, received no food until the appropriate response was made. Through experience, the cats learned about the effects of their own behavior upon environmental events. In other words, they learned the consequences of their own actions.

To describe these changes, Thorndike postulated the Law of Effect. According to the Law of Effect, in any given situation an animal may do a variety of things. The cat in the puzzle box could walk around, groom itself, meow, or engage in virtually any type of feline behavior. It could also make the operant response, the response necessary to escape the puzzle box and gain access to the food. Initially, the cat may engage in any of these behaviors and may produce the operant response simply by accident or chance. However, when the operant response occurs, escape from the box and access to the food follows. In operant conditioning terminology, food is the reinforcer, (Sr, or reinforcing stimulus) and it serves to strengthen the operant response (R) that immediately preceded it. The next time the animal finds itself in the puzzle box, its tendency to produce the operant response will be a bit stronger as a consequence of the reinforcement. Once the response is made again, the animal gains access to the food again—which strengthens the response further. Over time, the operant response is strengthened, while other behaviors that may occur are not strengthened and thus drop away. So, with repeated experience, the amount of time that it takes for the animal to make the operant response declines.

SKINNERIAN CONDITIONING

In addition to changing the strength of responses, operant conditioning can be used to mold entirely new behaviors. This process is referred to as shaping and was described by American psychologist B. F. Skinner (1904-1990), who further developed the field of operant conditioning. Suppose that the experiment's objective was to train an animal, such as a laboratory rat, to press a lever. The rat could be given a piece of food (Sr) each time it pressed the lever (R), but it would probably be some considerable time before it would do so on its own. Lever pressing does not come naturally to rats. To speed up the process, the animal could be "shaped" by reinforcing successive approximations of lever-pressing behavior. The rat could be given a food pellet each time that it was in the vicinity of the lever. The Law of Effect predicts that the rat would spend more and more of its time near the lever as a consequence of reinforcement. Then the rat may be required to make some physical contact with the lever, but not necessarily press it, in order to be rewarded. The rat would make more and more contact with the lever as a result. Finally, the rat would be required to make the full response, pressing the lever, in order to get food. In many ways, shaping resembles the childhood game of selecting some object in the room without saying what it is, and guiding guessers by saying "warmer" as they approach the object, and as they move away from it, saying nothing at all. Before long, the guessers will use the feedback to zero in on the selected object. In a similar manner, feedback in the form of reinforcement allows the rat to "zero in" on the operant response.

Skinner also examined situations where reinforcement was not given for every individual response but was delivered according to various schedules of reinforcement. For example, the rat may be required to press the lever a total of five times (rather than once) in order to get the food pellet, or the reinforcing stimulus may be delivered only when a response occurs after a specified period of time. These scenarios correspond to ratio and interval schedules. Interval and ratio schedules can be either fixed, meaning that the exact same rule applies for the delivery of each individual reinforcement, or variable, meaning that the rule changes from reinforcer to reinforcer. For example, in a variable ratio-five schedule, a reward may be given after the first five responses, then after seven responses, then after three. On average, each five responses would be reinforced, but any particular reinforcement may require more or fewer responses.

To understand how large an impact varying the schedule of reinforcement can have on behavior, one might consider responding to a soda machine versus responding to a slot machine. In both cases the operant response is inserting money. However, the soda machine rewards (delivers a can of soda) according to a fixed-ratio schedule of reinforcement. Without reward, one will not persist very long in making the operant response to the soda machine. The slot machine, on the other hand, provides rewards (delivers a winning payout) on a variable-ratio schedule. It is not uncommon for people to empty out their pockets in front of a slot machine without receiving a single reinforcement.

SUPERSTITIOUS PIGEONS
As with classical conditioning, exactly what associations are learned in operant conditioning has been an important research question. For example, in a classic 1948 experiment, Skinner provided pigeons with food at regular intervals regardless of what they were doing at the time. Six of his eight pigeons developed stereotyped (consistent) patterns of behavior as a result of the experiment despite the fact that the pigeons' behavior was not really necessary. According to the Law of Effect, some behavior would be occurring just prior to food delivery and this behavior would be strengthened simply by chance pairing with reinforcement. This would increase the strength of the response, making it more likely to occur when the next reward was delivered—strengthening the response still further. Ultimately, one behavior would dominate the pigeons' behavior in that experimental context. Skinner referred to this phenomenon as superstition. One need only observe the behavior of baseball players approaching the plate or basketball players lining up for a free-throw shot to see examples of superstition in human behavior.

Superstition again raises the issue of contiguity—simply presenting reinforcement soon after the response is made appears to strengthen it. However, later studies, especially a 1971 experiment conducted by J. E. R. Staddon and V. Simmelhag, suggested that it might not be quite that simple. Providing food rewards in superstition experiments changes a variety of responses, including natural behaviors related to the anticipation of food. In operant conditioning, animals are learning more than the simple contiguity of food and behavior; they are learning that their behavior (R) causes the delivery of food (Sr). Contiguity is important but is not the whole story.

In addition, psychologists have explored the question "What makes a reinforcer reinforcing?" That is to say, is there some set of stimuli that will "work" to increase the behaviors followed in every single circumstance? The answer is that there is not some set of rewards that will always increase behavior in all circumstances. David Premack was important in outlining the fact that reinforcement is relative, rather than absolute. Specifically, Premack suggested that behaviors in which an organism is more likely to engage serve to reinforce behaviors in which they are less likely to engage. In a specific example, he examined children given the option of playing pinball or eating candy. Some children preferred pinball and spent more of their time playing the game than eating the candy. The opposite was true of other children. Those who preferred pinball would increase their candy-eating behavior (R) in order to gain access to the pinball machine (Sr). Those who preferred eating candy would increase their pinball-playing behavior (R) in order to gain access to candy (Sr). Behaviors that a child initially preferred were effective in reinforcing behaviors that the child was less likely to choose—but not the other way around.

NEGATIVE CONSEQUENCES

Positive or rewarding outcomes are not the only consequences that govern behavior. In many cases, people respond in order to avoid negative outcomes or stop responding when doing so produces unpleasant events. These situations correspond to the operant procedures of avoidance and punishment. Many psychologists have advocated using reinforcement rather than punishment to alter behavior, not because punishment is necessarily less effective in theory but because it is usually less effective in practice. In order for punishers to be effective, they should be (among other things) strong, immediate, and consistent. This can be difficult to accomplish in practice. In crime, for example, many offenses may have occurred without detection prior to the punished offense, so punishment is not certain. It is also likely that an individual's court hearing, not to mention his or her actual sentence, will be delayed by weeks or even months, so punishment is not immediate. First offenses are likely to be punished less harshly than repeated offenses, so punishment gradually increases in intensity. In the laboratory, such a situation would produce an animal that would be quite persistent in responding, despite punishment.

In addition, punishment can produce unwanted side effects, such as the suppression of other behaviors, aggression, and the learning of responses to avoid or minimize punishing consequences. Beyond this, punishment requires constant monitoring by an external authority, whereas reinforcement typically does not. For example, parents who want to punish a child for having a messy room must constantly inspect the room to determine its state. The child certainly is not going to point out a messy room that will lead to punishment. On the other hand, if rewarded, the child will bring the neat room to the parents' attention. This is not to suggest that punishment should necessarily be abandoned as one tool for controlling behavior. Rather, the effectiveness of punishment, like reinforcement, can be predicted on the basis of laboratory results.

INTERACTIONS AND BIOLOGICAL CONSTRAINTS

Though the distinction between classical and operant conditioning is very clear in principle, it is not always so clear in practice. This makes sense if one considers real-life learning situations. In many circumstances, events in the environment are associated (occur together) in a predictable fashion, and behavior will have consequences. This can be true in the laboratory as well, but carefully designed experiments can be conducted to separate out the impact of classical and operant conditioning on behavior.

In addition, the effectiveness of both classical and operant conditioning is influenced by biological factors. This can be seen both in the speed with which classically conditioned taste aversions (as compared with other CRs) are learned and in the stimulation of natural food-related behaviors in operant superstition experiments. Related findings have demonstrated that the effects of rewarding behavior can be influenced by biology in other ways that may disrupt the conditioning process. In an article published in 1961, Keller and Marian Breland described their difficulties in applying the principles of operant conditioning to their work as animal trainers in the entertainment industry. They found that when trained with food reinforcement, natural behaviors would often interfere with the trained operant response—a phenomenon they called instinctive drift. From a practical point of view, their research suggested that to be successful in animal training, one must select operant responses that do not compete with natural food-related behaviors. From a scientific point of view, their research suggested that biological tendencies must be taken into account in any complete description of conditioning processes.

APPLICATIONS OF CONDITIONING TECHNOLOGY

Conditioning research serves as a valuable tool in the psychological exploration of other issues. In essence, conditioning technology provides a means for asking animals questions—a way to explore interesting cognitive processes such as memory, attention, reasoning, and concept formation under highly controlled laboratory conditions in less complex organisms.

Another area of research is the field of behavioral neuroscience, a field that combines physiological and behavioral approaches in order to uncover the neurological mechanisms underlying behavior. For example, the impact of various medications and substances on behavior can be observed by administering drugs as reinforcing stimuli. Animals will produce operant responses in order to receive the same drugs to which humans become addicted. However, in animals, the neurological mechanisms involved in developing addictions can be studied directly, using both behavioral and physiological experimental techniques in a way that would not be possible with human subjects because of ethical considerations.

In addition, the principles of classical and operant conditioning have been used to solve very real human problems in a variety of educational and therapeutic settings, a strategy called applied behavior analysis. The principles of operant conditioning have been widely applied in settings where some degree of control over human behavior is desirable. Token economies are situations in which specified behaviors, such as appropriate classroom behavior, are rewarded according to some schedule of reinforcement. The reinforcers are referred to as tokens because they need not have any rewarding value in and of themselves but can be exchanged for reinforcers at some later time. According to the principles of operant conditioning, people should increase the operant response in order to gain the reinforcers, and if the token economy is developed properly, that is exactly what occurs. If token economies sound rather familiar, it is for good reason. Money is an extremely potent token reinforcer for most people, who perform operant responses (work) in order to receive token reinforcers (money) that can later be exchanged for primary reinforcers (such as food, clothing, shelter, or entertainment).

Finally, learning principles have been applied in clinical psychology in an effort to change maladaptive behaviors. Some examples include a procedure called systematic desensitization, in which the principles of classical conditioning are applied in an effort to treat phobias (irrational beliefs), and social skills training, in which operant conditioning is used to enhance communication and other interpersonal behaviors. These are only two examples of useful applications of conditioning technology to treat mental illness. Such applications suggest the need for ongoing research into basic conditioning mechanisms. One must fully understand conditioning principles in order to apply them appropriately in the effort to understand and improve the human condition.

SOURCES FOR FURTHER STUDY

Domjan, Michael. *The Principles of Learning and Behavior.* 5th ed. Belmont, Calif.: Thomson/Wadsworth, 2003. An extremely useful and complete textbook presenting classical as well as up-to-date research in the areas of operant and classical conditioning.

Schwartz, Barry, ed. *Psychology of Learning: Readings in Behavior Theory.* New

York: W. W. Norton, 1984. A collection of reprinted articles on conditioning and learning.

Skinner, B. F. *Beyond Freedom and Dignity*. 1971. Reprint. Indianapolis, Ind.: Hackett, 2002. The influential B. F. Skinner outlines his philosophical views on conditioning and its importance in confronting world problems.

Linda R. Tennison

SEE ALSO: Behaviorism; Habituation and Sensitization; Learned Helplessness; Learning; Pavlovian Conditioning; Phobias; Reflexes.

CONSCIOUSNESS

TYPE OF PSYCHOLOGY: Consciousness
FIELDS OF STUDY: Cognitive processes; sleep; thought

Consciousness refers to a number of phenomena, including the waking state; experience; and the possession of any mental state. The phenomena of self-consciousness include proneness to embarrassment in social settings; the ability to detect one's own sensations and recall one's recent actions; self-recognition; awareness of awareness; and self-knowledge in the broadest sense.

KEY CONCEPTS
- awareness
- alternate state of consciousness
- developmental aspects of consciousness
- evolution of consciousness
- history of consciousness study

Many scientists have ignored the phenomena associated with consciousness because they deem it inappropriate for empirical investigation. However, there is clear evidence that this position is changing. Researchers in the fields of psychology, neurobiology, philosophy, cognitive science, physics, medicine, anthropology, mathematics, molecular biology, and art are now addressing major issues relating to consciousness. These researchers are asking such questions as what constitutes consciousness, whether it is possible to explain subjective experience in physical terms, how scientific methods can best be applied to the study of consciousness, and the neural correlates of consciousness.

Moreover, new methods of brain imaging have helped clarify the nature and mechanisms of consciousness, leading to better understanding of the relationship between conscious and unconscious processes in perception, memory, learning, and other domains. These and other questions have led to a growing interest in consciousness studies, including investigations of properties of conscious experience in specific domains (such as vision, emotion, and metacognition) and a better understanding of disorders and unusual forms of consciousness, as found in blindsight, synesthesia, and other syndromes.

HISTORY OF CONSCIOUSNESS STUDY

The definition of consciousness proposed by English philosopher John Locke (1632-1704)—"the perception of what passes in a man's own mind"—has been that most generally accepted as a starting point in understanding the concept. Most of the philosophical discussions of consciousness, however, arose from the mind-body issues posed by the French philosopher and mathematician René Descartes (1596-1650). Descartes raised the essential questions that, until recently, dominated consciousness studies. He asked whether the mind, or consciousness, is independent of matter, and whether consciousness is extended (physical) or unextended (nonphysical). He also inquired whether consciousness is determinative or determined. English philosophers such as Locke tended to reduce consciousness to physical sensations and the information they provide. European philosophers such as Gottfried Wilhelm Leibniz (1646-1716) and Immanuel Kant (1724-1804), however, argued that consciousness had a more active role in perception.

The nineteenth century German educator Johann Friedrich Herbart (1776-1841) had the greatest influence on thinking about consciousness. His ideas on states of consciousness and unconsciousness influenced the German psychologist and physiologist Gustav Theodor Fechner (1801-1887) as well as the ideas of Sigmund Freud (1856-1939) on the nature of the unconscious.

The concept of consciousness has undergone significant changes since the nineteenth century, and the study of consciousness has undergone serious challenge as being unscientific or irrelevant to the real work of psychology. Nineteenth century scholars had conflicting opinions about consciousness. It was either a mental stuff different from everyday material or a physical attribute like sensation. Sensation, along with movement, separates humans and other animals from nonsensate and immobile lower forms of life. Scholars viewed consciousness as different from unconsciousness, such as occurred in sleep or under anesthesia. Whatever the theory, these scholars generally employed the same method, that of introspection.

EXPERIMENTAL STUDY

It was the German psychologist Wilhelm Max Wundt (1832-1920) who began the experimental study of consciousness in 1879 when he established his research laboratory. Wundt saw the task of psychology as the study of the structure of consciousness, which extended well beyond sensations and included feelings, images, memory, attention, duration, and movement. By the 1920's, however, behavioral psychology had become the major force in psychology. John Broadus Watson (1878-1958) was the leader of this revolution. He wrote in 1913, "I believe that we can write a psychology and never use the terms consciousness, mental states, mind . . . imagery and the like." Between 1920 and 1950, consciousness was either neglected in psychology or treated as a historical curiosity. Behaviorist psychology led the way in rejecting mental states as appropriate objects for psychological study. The inconsistency of introspection as method made this rejection inevitable. Neurophysiologists also rejected consciousness as a mental state but allowed for the study of the biological underpinnings of consciousness. Thus, brain functioning became part of their study. The neural mechanisms of consciousness that allow an understanding between states of consciousness and the functions of the brain became an integral part of the scientific approach to consciousness. Brain waves—patterns of electrical activity—correlate with different levels of consciousness. These waves measure different levels of alertness. The electroencephalograph provides an objective means for measuring these phenomena.

Beginning in the late 1950's, however, interest in the subject of consciousness returned, specifically in those subjects and techniques relating to altered states of consciousness: sleep and dreams, meditation, biofeedback, hypnosis, and drug-induced states. When a physiological indicator for the dream state was found, a surge in sleep and dream research followed. The discovery of rapid eye movement (REM) helped to generate a renaissance in consciousness research. Thus, during the 1960's there was an increased search for "higher levels" of consciousness through meditation, resulting in a growing interest in the practices of Zen Buddhism and yoga from Eastern cultures.

This movement yielded such programs as transcendental meditation, and these self-directed procedures of physical relaxation and focused attention led to biofeedback techniques designed to bring body systems involving factors such as blood pressure or temperature under voluntary control. Researchers discovered that people could control their brain-wave patterns to some extent, especially the alpha rhythms generally associated with a relaxed, meditative state. Those people interested in consciousness and meditation established a number of "alpha training" programs.

Hypnosis and psychoactive drugs also received great attention in the 1960's. Lysergic acid diethylamide (LSD) was the most prominent of these substances, along with mescaline. These drugs have a long association with religious ceremonies in non-Western cultures. Fascination with the altered states of consciousness they induce led to an increased interest in research on consciousness. As the twentieth century progressed, the concept of consciousness began to come back into psychology. Developmental psychology, cognitive psychology, and the influence of cognitive philosophy each played a role in influencing the reintroduction of the concept, more sharply etched, into the mainstream of psychology.

JEAN PIAGET

Jean Piaget, the great developmental psychologist, viewed consciousness as central to psychological study. Therefore, he sought to find ways to make its study scientific. To do so, Piaget dealt in great detail with the meaning of the subject-object and mind-body problems. Piaget argued that consciousness is not simply a subjective phenomenon; if it were, it would be unacceptable for scientific psychology. Indeed, Piaget maintained that conscious phenomena play an important and distinctive role in human behavior. Moreover, he directed research to examine the way in which consciousness is formed, its origins, stages, and processes. Consciousness is not an epiphenomenon, nor can psychologists reduce it to physiological phenomena. For Piaget, consciousness involves a constructed subjective awareness. It is a developmentally constructed process, not a product. It results from interaction with the environment, not from the environment's action on it: "[T]he process of becoming conscious of an action scheme transforms it into a concept; thus becoming conscious consists essentially in conceptualization."

There are two relationships necessary for the understanding of consciousness. The first is that of subject and object. The second is the relationship between cognitive activity and neural activity. Both are essential to getting at the process of cognition and its dynamic nature.

MEMORY AND ALTERED STATES

A variety of studies and experiments have explored the effects of certain variables on consciousness. For instance, it is important to ascertain the way in which variables that increase memorability in turn influence metamemory. Results have been inconsistent. However, it was found that when experimenters directed subjects to remember some items and forget others, there was an increase in recalling those items that experimenters were directed to remember. There was, nevertheless, no effect on the accuracy of what was remembered.

Sleep and dreams, hypnosis, and other altered states have provided another intriguing area of study for those interested in consciousness. The relationship of naps to alertness later in the day has proved of great interest to psychologists. In one study, nine healthy senior citizens, seventy-four to eighty-seven years of age, experienced nap and no-nap conditions in two studies each. Napping was for one and one-half hours, from 1:30 to 3:00 P.M. daily. The no-nap condition prohibited naps and encouraged activity in that period. Various tests were used to measure evening activity as well as record sleep. Aside from greater sleep in the twenty-four-hour period for those who had the ninety-minute nap, there was no difference on any other measure.

The threat simulation theory of dreaming holds that dreams have a biological function to protect the dream self. This dream self behaves in a defensive fashion. An empirical test of this theory confirmed the predictions and suggests that the theory has wide implications regarding the functions of consciousness.

The study of consciousness, then, has elucidated understanding of perception, memory, and action, created advances in artificial intelligence, and illustrated the philosophical basis of dissatisfaction with the dualistic separation of mind and body. Electrical correlates of states of consciousness have been discovered as well as structures in the brain stem that regulate the sleep cycle. Other studies have looked at neural correlates in various states such as wakefulness, coma, the persistent vegetative state, the "locked-in" syndrome, akinetic mutism, and brain death. There are many other areas of consciousness in which neuroscience has made major advances.

An important problem neglected by neuroscientists is the problem of meaning. Neuroscientists are apt to assume that if they can see that a neuron's firing is roughly correlated with some aspect of the visual scene, such as an oriented line, then that firing must be part of the neural correlate of the seen line. However, it is necessary to explain how meaning can be expressed in neural terms as well as how the firing of neurons is connected to the perception of a face or person.

IMAGERY

Imagery is associated with memory, perception, and thought. Imagery occurs in all sensory modes. However, most work on imagery has neglected all but visual imagery. Concerns with imagery go back to the ancient Greek philosophers. Plato (c. 428-348 B.C.E.) and Aristotle (384-322 B.C.E.), for example, compared memory to a block of wax into which one's thoughts and perceptions stamp impressions. Aristotle gave imagery an important place in cognition and argued that people think in mental images. Early experimental psychologists, such as Wundt, carried on this notion of cognition.

Around 1901, Oswald Külpe (1862-1915) and his students at the University of Würzburg in Germany challenged these assumptions. However, these experiments employed introspective techniques, which Wundt and other attacked as being inconclusive. The controversy led to a rejection of mental imagery, introspection, and the study of consciousness itself. In the twentieth century, a movement toward seeing language as the primary analytical tool and a rejection of the old dominance of imagery came into fashion. The phenomenology of French philosopher and writer Jean-Paul Sartre (1905-1980) also led to a decline of interest in imagery.

A revival of research in imagery followed the cognitive science revolution of the 1960's and 1970's, contributing greatly to the rising scientific interest in mental representations. This revival stemmed from research on sensory deprivation and on hallucinogenic drugs. Studies in the role of imagery mnemonics also contributed to this reemergence of imagery studies.

CONCLUSION

As the concept of a direct, simple linkage between environment and behavior became unsatisfactory in the late twentieth century, the interest in altered states of consciousness helped spark new interest in consciousness. People are actively involved in their own behavior, not passive puppets of external forces. Environments, rewards, and punishments are not simply defined by their physical character. There are mental constructs involved in each of these. People organize their memories. They do not merely store them. Cognitive psychology, a new division of the field, has emerged to deal with these interests.

Thanks to the work of developmental psychologists such as Piaget, great attention is being given to the manner in which people understand or perceive the world at different ages. There are advances in the area of animal behavior, stressing the importance of inherent characteristics that arise from the way in which a species has been shaped to respond adaptively to the environment. There has also been the emergence of humanistic psychologists, concerned with the importance of self-actualization and growth. Clinical and industrial psychology have demonstrated that a person's state of consciousness in terms of current feelings and thoughts is of obvious importance. Although the role of consciousness was often neglected in favor of unconscious needs and motivations, there are clear signs that researchers are interested in emphasizing once more the nature of states of consciousness.

SOURCES FOR FURTHER STUDY

Brann, Eva T. H. *The World of the Imagination: Sum and Substance.* Savage, Md.: Rowman & Littlefield, 1991. Discusses the role of imagination in cognition.

Chalmers, David. *The Conscious Mind: In Search of a Fundamental Theory.* New York: Oxford University Press, 1996. Presents a clear summary of various theories of consciousness.

Greenfield, Susan A. *Journey to the Centers of the Mind.* New York: W. H. Freeman, 1995. This is a study of biological influences in cognition.

Libet, Benjamin. *Neurophysiology of Consciousness: Selected Papers and New Essays.* Boston: Birkhäuser, 1993. Clearly presents the role of neurophysiology in conscious thought.

Weiskrantz, Lawrence. *Consciousness Lost and Found.* New York: Oxford University Press, 1997. A study of modes of consciousness and the manner in which psychologists have rediscovered the importance of the concept.

Frank A. Salamone

SEE ALSO: Consciousness: Altered States; Dementia; Dreams; Thought: Study and Measurement.

CONSCIOUSNESS: ALTERED STATES

TYPE OF PSYCHOLOGY: Consciousness
FIELD OF STUDY: Cognitive processes

The investigation of altered states of consciousness began in psychology with the recognition that consciousness is not a fixed, unvarying state but is in a continual state of flux. Consciousness can be altered by many chemical and nonchemical means, and there is some evidence to indicate that certain altered states are necessary for normal psychological functioning.

KEY CONCEPTS
- biofeedback
- circadian rhythm
- electroencephalogram (EEG)
- hypnagogic and hypnopompic states
- hypnosis
- meditation
- psychoactive drugs
- restricted environmental stimulation (RES)

The great psychologist William James, in his 1890 textbook *The Principles of Psychology*, made the following now-famous observation regarding states of consciousness: "Our normal waking consciousness, rational consciousness as we call it, is but one special type of consciousness, whilst all about it, parted from it by the filmiest of screens, there lie potential forms of consciousness entirely different." James went on to say that the understanding of human psychological functioning would never be complete until these alternate states were addressed. Most psychologists would now acknowledge that a person's normal waking consciousness is readily subject to changes. These changes are referred to as altered states of consciousness. What constitutes a genuine altered state and how many such states may exist are both subjects of some controversy.

States of consciousness have always been central to the attempt to understand human nature. For example, every society of which any record exists has possessed both chemical and nonchemical means of altering consciousness.

From a historical point of view, Sigmund Freud (1856-1939) may have done more than any other theorist to stimulate interest in states of consciousness. Freud's psychoanalytic theory of personality held that there were three primary levels of consciousness: consciousness, preconsciousness, and unconsciousness. The conscious level includes mental activities of which one is unaware. The preconscious level consists of mental material of which one is currently unaware but that can be voluntarily recalled—roughly equivalent to memory. The unconscious level, which held the greatest interest for Freud, contains thoughts, feelings, memories, and drives that are blocked from awareness because they are unpleasant or arouse anxiety. In addition to his interest in these three levels of consciousness, Freud's interest in altered states at various points in his career was manifested in investigations of cocaine, hypnosis, and the analysis and interpretation of dreams.

In the early twentieth century, with the growth of behaviorism (which insisted that in order to be a science, psychology should confine itself to investigating only objective, observable behavior), the study of altered states of consciousness fell out of favor. Events in the larger culture during the 1960's and 1970's, however, helped stimulate interest in altered states within psychology. During this period, efforts to expand consciousness by means of drugs, meditation, Eastern religious practice, and new ways of relating to oneself and others led to the active study of altered states of consciousness. The attempts of psychologists to study altered states of experience will perhaps be viewed in the future as a landmark in the development of psychology as a science. The willingness of psychology to explore the novel realms that altered states represent may help to expand the understanding of both consciousness and reality.

VARIATIONS IN CONSCIOUSNESS

Physiological psychologist Karl Pribram lists the following states of consciousness: states of ordinary perceptual awareness; states of self-consciousness; dream states; hypnagogic and hypnopompic states (the transition states, characterized by vivid dreamlike imagery, that occur as one goes into and comes out of sleep); ecstatic states (such as the orgiastic experience); socially induced trance or trancelike states; drug-induced states; social role states; linguistic states (for example, a multilingual person thinking in one, rather than another, language); translational states (as when one linguistic universe is being recorded or translated in another); ordinary transcendental states (such as those experienced by an author in the throes of creative composition); extraordinary transcendental states that are achieved by special techniques; other extraordinary states (such as those that allow "extrasensory awareness"); meditational states; dissociated states, as in the case of pathological multiple personality; and psychomotor states manifest in temporal-lobe epilepsies. To that list could be added the following additional states: sleep; the hyperalert state, characterized by increased vigilance while one is awake; the lethargic state, characterized by dulled, sluggish mental activity; states of hysteria, with intense feeling and overpowering emotion; regressive states, such as senility; daydreaming with rapidly occurring thoughts that bear little relation to the external environment; coma; sleep deprivation; sensory overload or deprivation; and prolonged strenuous exercise. This list is by no means exhaustive.

Some of these states clearly represent greater degrees of alteration of the "normal" consciousness than others. There is, however, no universal agreement on what constitutes the normal state of consciousness. Charles Tart and other authors have suggested that what is usually called "normal" consciousness is not a natural, given state but a construction based mainly on cultural values and inputs. In any case, some altered states of consciousness are experienced on a daily basis by everyone, while others are much more rare and may require great effort or special circumstances to achieve.

INFLUENCES ON ALTERED CONSCIOUSNESS

Some alterations in conscious functions are induced by daily changes in biological rhythms. Bodily events that occur in roughly a twenty-four-hour cycle are referred to as circadian rhythms, from the Latin *circa* ("about") and *dies* ("day"). It is thought that these cycles are created by natural events, such as the light-dark cycle, and by other cues in the daily routine, such as mealtimes. The sleeping-waking cycle is the major circadian rhythm, but there are others, such as fluctuations in body temperature. This daily temperature cycle appears to be directly related to levels of mental activity. When all external cues are removed, circadian rhythms extend to about twenty-five hours. As a result of prolonged isolation, the cycle can become completely distorted, with periods of up to forty hours of waking followed by periods of up to twenty-two hours of sleep. When the change is gradual in this way, the individual has a distorted sense of time and believes that he or she is experiencing normal periods of sleep and waking. Abrupt changes in circadian rhythms, as when one crosses several time zones, are what lead to that sleepy, uncomfortable feeling known as jet lag.

In addition to biological rhythms, there are other regular daily variations in consciousness. On the way to sleep each night, people enter a kind of "twilight" period known as the hypnagogic state. The state of consciousness that is entered immediately before waking is called the hypnopompic state. In both these states, one is partially asleep and partially continuing to process environmental stimuli. Both are characterized by vivid imagery, and many people have reported creative insight during these periods.

STAGES OF SLEEP

Sleep itself is not a unified state but consists of five distinct stages: one stage of rapid eye movement (REM) sleep and four stages of nonrapid eye movement (NREM) sleep. During a typical night's sleep, one moves in and out of these stages four or five times. REM sleep is primarily associated with periods of dreaming. Sleeping subjects awakened during a period of REM sleep report having just experienced a dream about 80 percent of the time, compared with less than 10 percent when NREM sleep is interrupted. Psychologists are still unclear on exactly why humans need to sleep, but the need for periods of REM sleep might be part of the reason. When sleeping subjects are deprived of REM sleep (and their NREM sleep is undisturbed), they often show many of the symptoms of not having slept at all. Also, when later given the opportunity for uninterrupted sleep, they spend a greater percentage of time in the REM stage, as if making up for the lost REM sleep (this is referred to as the REM-rebound effect). The REM-rebound effect is lessened if the individual is encouraged to engage in an increased amount of daydreaming, which indicates a possible connection between day and night dreams.

PSYCHOACTIVE DRUGS

The use of psychoactive drugs is a common method for altering consciousness. These drugs are chemical substances that act on the brain to create psychological effects and are typically classified as depressants, stimulants, narcotics (opiates), hallucinogens, or antipsychotics. Several drugs, such as nicotine, caffeine, and alcohol, are so much a part of the lifestyle in modern society that users may not even think of them as drugs. The use of many psychoactive drugs can lead to physical or psychological dependence or addiction, as the body/mind develops a physiological/psychological need for the drug. The body can also build up a tolerance for a drug, which means that higher and higher doses are necessary to produce the same effects. Once addiction has been established, discontinuing the use of the drug can lead to withdrawal symptoms, such as nausea, fever, convulsions, and hallucinations, among others, which can sometimes be fatal.

The type of altered state produced by a psychoactive drug depends on the class to which the drug belongs. Depressants, such as alcohol, barbiturates, and tranquilizers, depress central nervous system functioning and usually produce relaxation, anxiety reduction, and—eventually—sleep. Narcotics (opiates), such as heroin, morphine, and codeine, depress activity in some areas of the cortex but create excitation in others, producing feelings of euphoria and providing relief from pain. Stimulants, such as amphetamines, cocaine, caffeine, and nicotine, stimulate central nervous system activity, producing feeling of alertness and euphoria and lack of appetite. Hallucinogens, such as lysergic acid diethylamide (LSD), mescaline, and psilocybin, can produce hallucinations, delusions, exhilaration, and, in some cases, quasi-mystical experiences.

HYPNOSIS AND MEDITATION

Two popular nonchemical techniques for altering consciousness are hypnosis and meditation. Hypnosis was first discovered in the eighteenth century by Franz Mesmer, and its use has been marked by controversy ever since. An altered state is induced in hypnosis by the suggestive instructions of the hypnotist, usually involving progressive relaxation. The hypnotized subject often appears to be asleep but remains alert inside, exhibiting varying degrees of responsiveness to the suggestions of the hypnotist. Only about 10 percent of the population can enter the deepest hypnotic state, while another 10 percent cannot be hypnotized at all. The rest of the population can achieve some degree of hypnotic induction. Psychologists argue about whether hypnosis is a genuine altered state or simply a form of role playing.

There is less controversy regarding meditation as a true altered state. Since the mid-1960's, there has been extensive research on the physiological changes that occur during meditation. Some of the findings include a decrease in oxygen consumption of 16 percent during meditation (compared with an 8 percent drop during the deepest stage of sleep), a cardiac output decrease of 25 percent, and an average slowing of the heart rate by five beats per minute. During meditation, electroencephalogram (EEG) patterns are dominated by the alpha rhythm, which has been associated with relaxation. An EEG is a graphic recording of the electrical activity of brain waves. Researchers R. K. Wallace and Herbert Benson believed that there was sufficient physiological evidence to justify calling the meditative state a "fourth major state of consciousness" (along with waking, dreaming, and sleeping), which they termed a "wakeful, hypometabolic [reduced metabolic activity] state." Beginning meditators usually report feelings of relaxation and "ordinary thoughts," while advanced practitioners sometimes report transcendental experiences of "consciousness without content."

APPLICATIONS OF HYPNOSIS

Research on altered states of consciousness has led to many benefits. The analgesic properties of hypnosis were verified in research conducted by Ernest Hilgard at Stanford University. He found that hypnotic suggestion could be used to reduce or eliminate experimentally induced pain. Even though subjects were not consciously aware of the pain, Hilgard found that, with the right questions, he could uncover a "hidden observer," a dissociated aspect of the subject's conscious awareness that did monitor the feelings of pain. Hilgard reports that hypnotic relief from pain has been reported for the chronic pain of arthritis, nerve damage, migraine headaches, and cancer. For individuals who are unable to be anesthetized because of allergic reactions or fear of needles, hypnosis is often used as an effective substitute for the control of pain. It has been effectively applied in cases involving dental work, childbirth, burns, abdominal surgery, and spinal taps. Hypnotic suggestion has also been effective in reducing the nausea associated with cancer chemotherapy.

The use of hypnosis to recover forgotten memories is much more controversial. One dramatic phenomenon displayed with certain hypnotic subjects is age regression, in which the individual not only is able to recall vividly childhood memories but also seems to reenact behaviors from childhood, including body postures, voice, and handwriting characteristics of a given age. There is no way of knowing, however, whether this represents true recall or is simply a type of fantasy and role playing. Hypnosis has also been used to enhance the memories of crime witnesses in court proceedings. There is evidence, however, that actual recall does not become more accurate and that the witness may be unintentionally influenced by the suggestions of the hypnotist, which could lead to inaccuracies and distortions in the "remembered" events. For this reason, courts in many states automatically disqualify testimony obtained by means of hypnosis.

BENEFITS OF MEDITATION

Research on the physiological effects of meditation led to the application of meditative techniques as a treatment to combat stress-related illnesses. Meditators have often experienced significant decreases in such problems as general anxiety, high blood pressure, alcoholism, drug addiction, insomnia, and other stress-related problems. Researchers have also found that the scores of meditators on various psychological tests have indicated general mental health, self-esteem, and social openness. Many psychologists argue, however, that these effects are not unique to meditation and can be produced by means of other relaxation techniques. Meditation researcher Robert Ornstein has suggested that the long-term practice of meditation may induce a relative shift in hemispheric dominance in the brain from the left hemisphere, which is associated with such linear processes as language and logical reasoning, to the right hemisphere, which is associated with nonlinear processes such as music perception and spatial reasoning. Consistent with this idea are findings that meditators are better on certain right-hemispheric tasks such as remembering musical tones but worse on verbal problem-solving tasks that involve the left hemisphere.

BIOFEEDBACK

Early research on advanced meditators in India indicated that they could exhibit control over what are normally autonomic processes in the body—for example, speeding up or slowing down the heart rate at will, stopping the heart for up to seventeen seconds, controlling blood flow to different areas of the body, and controlling brain-wave patterns at will. At first, these results were met with skepticism, but it is now known that humans and animals can learn to control previously involuntary processes by using a technique known as biofeedback. Through biofeedback training, an individual who is connected to a special measuring device can monitor autonomic events such as blood pressure, skin temperature, and muscle tension. Having this information can allow the individual gradually to gain control over these autonomic processes. Biofeedback techniques have been applied to an enormous variety of clinical problems. EEG biofeedback, for example, has been used to train epileptics to emit brain-wave patterns that are incompatible with those that occur during brain seizures. Other disorders that have been successfully treated by means of biofeedback include cardiac disorders, high blood pressure, tension headaches, anxiety, and neuromuscular disorders such as cerebral palsy.

SENSORY DEPRIVATION

Other applications have grown out of research on altered states of consciousness produced by restricting sensory stimulation from the environment. Researchers in the 1950's completed extensive studies on the effects of prolonged sensory deprivation. Subjects placed in soundproof isolation chambers with translucent goggles to eliminate vision and padded arm tubes to minimize touch sensation often experienced negative psychological effects after about a day. Most subjects suffered from extreme boredom, slowed reaction time, and impaired problem-solving ability. Some subjects reacted to sensory deprivation by creating their own internally generated sights and sounds in the form of hallucinations. These results led to the institution of special procedures to help reduce the effects of sensory deprivation in certain occupations; for example, airline pilots on long night flights, astronauts living for prolonged periods in tiny space capsules, and individuals working in isolated weather stations. A controlled form of sensory deprivation, known as restricted environmental stimulation therapy (REST), has been used to reduce the effects of overarousal and hyperactivity. REST sessions usually involve floating in heavily salted warm water in a dark, soundproof tank. Most subjects find this floating sensation very pleasant, and there have been many reports of long-term reductions in high blood pressure and other stress-related problems.

ARGUMENT FOR STATE-SPECIFIC SCIENCES

Although traditional scientific methods are poorly suited to the study of consciousness, many beneficial tools that can be used to measure the physiological correlation of altered states, such as the electroencephalograph, have been developed as an outgrowth of the study of states of consciousness.

Psychologist Charles Tart suggested the creation of state-specific sciences. In reaching this conclusion, he argues that any particular state of consciousness (including ordinary waking) is a semiarbitrary construction—a specialized tool that is useful for some things but not for others and that contains large numbers of structures shaped by a particular group's value judgments. Thus, science is observation and conceptualization carried out within the highly selective framework provided by a culturally determined ordinary state of consciousness. Tart suggests that, as altered states of consciousness often represent radically different ways of organizing observations and reworking conceptualizations of the universe (including oneself), if the scientific method were applied to developing sciences within various states of consciousness, there would be sciences based on radically different perceptions, logics, and communications, and thus science as a whole would gain new perspectives that would complement the existing one.

Regardless of whether this suggestion is taken seriously, it is clear that the study of states of consciousness has achieved legitimacy in scientific psychology. The investigation so far has revealed that human consciousness is much more diverse and varied than many psychologists previously believed.

SOURCES FOR FURTHER STUDY

Flannagan, Owen J. *Dreaming Souls: Sleep, Dreams, and the Evolution of the Mind.* New York: Oxford University Press, 1999. A professor of philosophy, experimental psychology, and neurobiology proposes that dreams are an unplanned side effect of the evolution of a human mind designed to "have experiences." Reviews current research and theory on the nature and functions of dreaming as well as presenting his own thesis.

Hilgard, Ernest Ropiequet. *Divided Consciousness: Multiple Controls in Human Thought and Action.* Expanded ed. New York: John Wiley & Sons, 1986. A discussion of consciousness by one of the most respected experimental psychologists. Included are discussions on the hidden observer phenomenon in hypnosis and on other dissociation phenomena such as multiple personality, amnesia, and fugue states.

Hobson, J. Allen. *The Dream Drugstore: Chemically Altered States of Consciousness.* Cambridge, Mass.: MIT Press, 2001. Discusses the natural and voluntarily altered chemistry of the brain and its effects on human consciousness. Hobson addresses the modern reliance on antidepressants such as Prozac as well as the "recreational" drugs of underground culture and presents the possible connections between dreaming states, drug-induced states, and mental illnesses in a nonjudgmental fashion.

Ornstein, Robert Evan, ed. *The Nature of Human Consciousness.* San Francisco: W. H. Freeman, 1973. This anthology contains essays by many of the pioneers in the psychological study of altered states of consciousness, including Carl Jung, Roberto Assagioli, Arthur Deikman, and many others. Topics include meditative states, psychosynthesis, Sufism, and synchronicity.

_____. *The Psychology of Consciousness.* 2d rev. ed. New York: Penguin Books, 1986. This is considered a classic text on altered states of consciousness. It provides in-depth discussions of the psychology of meditation and the relationship of altered states to hemispheric differences in the brain.

Ward, Colleen A., ed. *Altered States of Consciousness and Mental Health: A Cross-cultural Perspective.* Thousand Oaks, Calif.: Sage, 1989. A collection of papers assessing the mental health value and use of altered states of consciousness from a non-Western perspective.

Wolman, Benjamin B., and Montague Ullman, ed. *Handbook of States of Consciousness.* New York: Van Nostrand Reinhold, 1986. This is an excellent sourcebook on psychological theory and research on altered states of consciousness. Discusses, in addition to the topics covered in this article, trance states, lucid dreams, ultradian rhythms, and many other subjects.

Oliver W. Hill, Jr.

SEE ALSO: Consciousness; Dementia; Dreams; Thought: Study and Measurement.

CREATIVITY AND INTELLIGENCE

TYPE OF PSYCHOLOGY: Intelligence and intelligence testing
FIELD OF STUDY: General issues in intelligence

Creativity and intelligence are two aspects of cognitive performance in humans. Creativity refers to having inventive, productive, and imaginative qualities; intelligence refers to having mental acuteness, the ability to understand, and the ability to act effectively to solve problems within one's environment. The areas of creativity and intelligence have provided insight into what it means to be gifted and talented.

KEY CONCEPTS
- analogy
- cognitive skills
- creativity
- giftedness
- intelligence
- problem solving
- problem solving by analogy

Creativity and intelligence are two areas of cognitive functioning and performance which have been examined by researchers, educators, and others. Creativity can be defined as a person's cognitive abilities in areas such as fluency, flexibility, originality, elaboration, visualization, metaphorical thinking, problem definition, and evaluation. Intelligence is defined as the ability to perform various mental tasks which include reasoning, knowledge, comprehension, memory, applying concepts, and manipulating figures. The study of creativity and intelligence has developed based on studies in cognitive, developmental, and educational psychology.

Given that psychology as a discipline may be defined as the systematic study of the mind and behavior, when one studies creativity and intelligence, one learns how to improve performance and lead those persons who are creative, gifted, and talented to new heights. Specifically, when one studies creativity, one gains information about students' abilities in imagination, discovery, and the ability to invent. When one studies intelligence, one gains information about students' abilities in logic, memory, and organization.

Creativity and intelligence have played a significant role in the history of psychology and an even greater role in the history of humankind. Progress in education is evident in at least three occurrences. First, interest in measuring individual differences has led to the development of tests to quantify creative and intellectual abilities. Second, attention to persons who have been identified as creative, gifted, talented, or highly intelligent has led to the development of special programs, learning experiences, and scholarships for these students. Third, the needs of these students have led to research on the students themselves. The results of numerous empirical studies have been published to aid parents, educators, and the gifted or creative individual in understanding the needs of those with special abilities.

Certain issues related to creativity and intelligence have evolved from discrepancies that have been found in obtaining relationships between creativity and intelligence. It is a mistake to lump creative and intelligent people together: Creative ability is not synonymous with intellectual ability. Many students who are very high in intelligence, as measured by a test, are not high in other intellectual functions, such as creativity. Many students who are high in creativity are not also high in intelligence.

DEFINING AND MEASURING CREATIVITY

Creativity refers to the process of being imaginative and innovative. A creative person is able to link existing information with new information in productive ways. Students who are creative may often be referred to as being gifted and talented. Charles F. Wetherall has listed many characteristics of gifted, talented, or creative students. Creative students, for example, have a keen sense of observation and a desire to improve their abilities, produce a variety of possible solutions to problems, are curious and original, have the characteristic of persistence, are comfortable with ambiguity, are able to work independently, are able to analyze and synthesize information, demonstrate compulsivity and an urgency to complete a task or execute an idea, and have multiple latent abilities. Thus, when one's existing knowledge and information combine in a unique way, a creative product or idea is formed.

Many others have sought to describe creativity. Characteristics of creative persons and creativity, according to Gary A. Davis and Sylvia Rimm, include valuing creative thinking, appreciating novel and far-fetched ideas, being open-minded and receptive to zany ideas, and being mentally set to produce creative ideas. Robert Sternberg describes creative people as those who have the ability and willingness to go beyond the ordinary limitations of themselves and their environment and to think and act in unconventional and perhaps dreamlike ways. Further, he states that creative people go beyond the unwritten canons of society, have aesthetic taste, and are inquisitive and intuitive. Major contributions have been made to many fields of endeavor as a result of creative enterprise.

Creativity has been studied through research that sought to examine personality and family issues related to creativity, the ecology of creativity, musical creativity, and creative ability in women. Research by Robert Albert that examined relationships between creativity, identity formation, and career choice led him to make six suggestions for parents and teachers to help students achieve maximally. This information would be beneficial both to students who are gifted and to those who are not. His suggestions include helping students experience emotions such as anger, joy, fear, and passion; teaching involvement rather than techniques to students; seeking to discover what people can do; allowing students to experience some novelty and flexibility; encouraging the students to ask the questions "What do I think?" "How do I think?" "What can I do?" and "How do I feel about it now that I have tried?"; and enhancing learning by being actively engaged with and taking chances with one another.

THEORIES OF INTELLIGENCE

Intelligence, according to Paul Kline, refers to a person's ability to learn, understand, and deal with novel situations. The intelligent person may be viewed as quick-witted, acute, keen, sharp, canny, astute, bright, and brilliant. Robert Sternberg, in *Intelligence Applied: Understanding and Increasing Your Intellectual Skills* (1986), describes intelligence as comprising a very wide array of cognitive and other skills; he does not see intelligence as a single ability.

After examining many theories of intelligence, Sternberg developed the triarchic (three-part) theory of intelligence. In the componential subtheory, the first part of the theory, intelligence is related to the internal world of the individual. For example, a person who is intelligent in this area obtains high scores on standardized tests and is excellent in analytical thinking. The second part of the theory, the experiential subtheory, specifies intelligence in situations. A person who is intelligent in handling novel tasks with creativity but who may not have the best standardized test scores is demonstrating intelligence in this area. In the third part of the theory, the contextual subtheory, intelligence is related to the external world of the individual. For example, a person who is able to achieve success when interacting on the job or when influencing other people is demonstrating contextual intelligence.

ROLE OF ANALOGIES

Characteristics of intelligent persons include greater preference for, more attention to, and highly developed abilities for dealing with novelty; an ability to process information rapidly; an ability to ignore irrelevant information; and an ability to solve problems accurately. Problem-solving ability in intelligence may be observed in a person's ability to complete many tasks successfully. Among these tasks would be a person's ability to solve analogies.

Analogies are statements of a relationship between words, concepts, or situations. Problem solving by analogy occurs when students attempt to use the conditions and solution to one problem to assist them in understanding the conditions and solutions of another problem. Put another way, students use the relationships they see in one context or situation to assist them in understanding relationships in another context or situation. Many educators believe that solving analogies helps students to concretize their thinking, gauge how they understand information, tap and develop a facility for visual thinking, exercise and nurture creative and critical thinking, clarify and organize unfamiliar subject matter, and synthesize instructional material. Past research has pointed to an ability to solve analogies as one of the best predictors of intellectual ability.

Intelligence has also been studied by examining the way in which students who have been identified as gifted (based on high intelligence test scores) solve problems. It was found that highly intelligent people are better able to separate relevant and irrelevant information.

ASSESSMENT TESTS

Both creativity and intelligence can be assessed by specialized tests designed for that purpose. One of the first people to examine the concept of intelligence in the United States was James McKeen Cattell (1860-1944). He is credited with the introduction of the use of the phrase "mental tests." After studying in Europe, Cattell developed and sought to refine tests which focused on the cognitive skills that he believed indicated intellectual ability: strength, reaction time, and sensory discrimination.

The first test to examine individual differences in intelligence was devised and published in France by Alfred Binet and Théodore Simon in 1905; it was called the Binet-Simon test. The Binet-Simon test was translated into English and went through a series of revisions by various people. The version of the Binet-Simon test most used in the United States is the Stanford-Binet, which was first published in 1916.

E. Paul Torrance developed the Torrance Tests of Creative Thinking. These tests seek to assess creativity as it relates to fluency, flexibility, originality, and elaboration. Each of these areas can be understood in the context of examples. Fluency in creativity is the ability one has to produce numerous original ideas that solve problems. For example, persons may demonstrate fluency when they can state multiple uses for a ballpoint pen. Flexibility in creativity is the ability to produce ideas that show a variety of approaches that may be used. Originality is the ability to create uncommon or unusual responses; for example, a unique or unconventional use of the ballpoint pen would be classified as original. Elaboration refers to a person's ability to add details to a basic idea. For example, if a common item such as a ballpoint pen is discussed in extreme and minute details that do not focus on obvious aspects of the pen, elaboration is being demonstrated.

Intelligence tests consist of standardized questions and tasks that seek to determine the mental age of a person or the person's relative capacity to solve problems and absorb new information. Intelligence tests try to measure students' capacity to learn separate from their actual academic achievement.

Intelligence tests are either group-administered or individually administered; in group testings, large numbers of students can be assessed at the same time. According to Miles Storfer, individual intelligence tests such as the Stanford-Binet and the Wechsler series provide a good approximation of most people's abilities in the cognitive skills that the tests are designed to measure. These cognitive skills include being able to solve problems well, reasoning clearly, thinking logically, having a good vocabulary, and knowing an abundance of information in many areas.

IMPLICATIONS FOR SCIENCE AND TECHNOLOGY

Creative discovery has led to many technological breakthroughs and innovations in science and industry. Technological breakthroughs and success in science and industry have been evident in the extensive research into creative activity conducted by W. J. Gordon. He provides some source material that points to the relationship between invention, discovery, and learning. Creativity and analogies have led to breakthroughs in a wide variety of technological fields.

One example of the many technological breakthroughs and innovations in science and industry presented by Gordon occurred in 1865. John Boyd Dunlop was trying to think of a way to help his son be more comfortable when riding his bicycle over cobblestone streets. While watering his garden, he noticed how the hose resisted his fingers when he pressed his hand more firmly around it. He made the connections between the elastic resistance of the hose and how this type of elasticity would make his son more comfortable when biking. His first successful tire was made from a piece of garden hose.

SOURCES FOR FURTHER STUDY

Albert, Robert S. "Identity, Experiences, and Career Choice Among the Exceptionally Gifted and Eminent." In *Theories of Creativity*, edited by Mark A. Runco and Robert S. Albert. Newbury Park, Calif.: Sage, 1990. This twelve-chapter book on creativity is a compilation of the expertise of persons who have studied creativity in areas such as anthropology, behavior, cognition, development, and ecology.

Davis, Gary A., and Sylvia B. Rimm. *Education of the Gifted and Talented.* 5th ed. Boston: Pearson, 2004. Presents various skills, behaviors, and characteristics of students who are gifted, talented, or creative. The abilities and skills involved in creative problem solving are explained in clear language. An excellent source to gain information on the educational needs of gifted, talented, or creative students.

Gordon, W. J. "Some Source Material in Discovery-by-Analogy." *Journal of Creative Behavior* 8, no. 4 (1974): 239-257. Focusing on an associative view of invention, discovery, and learning, Gordon cites thirty-eight examples of associative analogical connections which have triggered famous innovations and breakthroughs. A wide variety of technological fields are included. Interesting reading; gives the foundations of many items used in everyday life.

Kline, Paul. *Intelligence: The Psychometric View.* New York: Routledge, 1991. Provides a summary of studies focusing on the nature of intelligence and other human abilities. Topics include the history of the concept of intelligence and ways to measure intelligence. The definitions of statistical and technical terms are presented in a clear and readable fashion.

Simenton, Dean Keith. *Origins of Genius: Darwinian Perspectives on Creativity.* New York: Oxford University Press, 1999. Explores the source of creativity in Darwinian properties of variation and selection.

Steptoe, Andrew, ed. *Genius and the Mind: Studies of Creativity and Temperament.* New York: Oxford University Press, 1998. A collection of case study essays on the psychology of creative "geniuses" such as Wolfgang Amadeus Mozart; George Gordon, Lord Byron; and William Shakespeare.

Sternberg, Robert J. *Intelligence Applied: Understanding and Increasing Your Intellectual Skills.* Orlando, Fla.: Harcourt Brace Jovanovich, 1986. A training program based on the triarchic theory of intelligence that Sternberg has developed. Details effective strategies for solving various types of problems, including science insight problems and analogies. Exercises for practice are included.

Storfer, Miles D. *Intelligence and Giftedness: The Contributions of Heredity and Early Environment.* San Francisco: Jossey-Bass, 1990. Storfer presents information on the effects of nurture on intelligence, focusing on the nature and development of intellectual giftedness and the characteristics of intellectually gifted people. The concept of intelligence in different socioeconomic conditions, in enrichment programs, and in its varying types are highlighted in separate chapters. The factors that influence intelligence and giftedness are examined in detail.

Torrance, Ellis Paul. *Education and the Creative Potential.* Minneapolis: University of Minnesota Press, 1963. A compilation of seven papers and six experimental studies conducted by Torrance, who developed a test to measure creative thinking and conducted longitudinal studies on creativity. Contains information on topics such as developing creative potential in schoolchildren and factors that facilitate or inhibit creativity in children.

Weisberg, Robert W. *Creativity: Genius and Other Myths.* New York: W. H. Freeman, 1986. Weisberg discusses the behaviors, activities, and finished products of individuals who have been described as creative. Defines creativity by giving real-life examples and discusses the role that intense knowledge or expertise plays in creative problem solving.

Debra A. King-Johnson

SEE ALSO: Giftedness; Intelligence; Intelligence Tests; Learning.

CROWD BEHAVIOR

TYPE OF PSYCHOLOGY: Social psychology
FIELDS OF STUDY: Aggression; group processes; social motives

Crowd behavior is the study of how the behavior of people in groups differs from that of individuals. People in crowds often become much more focused on their social identity than on their own individual identity. As a result, they are much more influenced by the norms of the group.

KEY CONCEPTS
- bystander effect
- deindividuation
- diffusion of responsibility
- group norms
- social identity theory

Crowds are groups of people who are together for short periods of time. The study of crowd behavior examines the actions that people in a crowd perform and how these actions differ from the behavior of individuals acting alone. Crowd behavior became a focus of scholarly thought in the late nineteenth and early twentieth centuries in reaction to the social turmoil in Western Europe at that time. Italian criminologist Scipio Sighele (1868-1913) first wrote about crowd behavior. French psychologist Gustave Le Bon (1841-1931), the founder of crowd psychology, formalized and popularized the concept with his book *The Crowd*, published in 1895. Le Bon's ideas reached a wide audience and are said to have influenced German dictator Adolf Hitler and Italian dictator Benito Mussolini as well as psychologists. Because crowds have performed many senseless and destructive acts, both historically and recently, understanding crowd behavior remains extremely important for psychologists.

The term "crowd" refers to a wide spectrum of human gatherings, varying in their complexity and the intention with which people join them. Some crowds are casual; people come together by happenstance (as a group of pedestrians standing on a sidewalk.) These tend to be simple, disorganized groups of people who do not know one another and will probably not see one another again. Others are conventionalized—the people have all chosen a common activity (for example, watching a parade or a sporting event) and express excitement in standard ways (cheering). Some crowds are purposive, choosing to be together for a common goal, such as a rally or political protest. These groups are often highly cohesive and highly organized.

Because crowds differ so much in their composition, organization, and purpose, there is also considerable variation in typical crowd behavior. Popular and scholarly attention has tended to focus on the situations in which crowd behavior is considered problematic. In these situations, the crowd often has an unusual problem to solve rapidly (for example, how to respond to a hostile police force). The occurrence of riots and violence attest to the fact that these sorts of problems are not always solved constructively by crowds. Crowds, of course, are capable of behaving in positive ways as well.

UNDERLYING PSYCHOLOGICAL PROCESSES

Early theories of crowd behavior hypothesized that unruly crowds were made up of criminals or the mentally deficient. Proponents of this perspective assumed that crowd behavior could be explained by the makeup of the individual personalities of people in the crowd and that certain kinds of people were more likely to be found in a crowd. Le Bon provided a more psychological analysis of crowd behavior, recognizing that even people of high intelligence could become members of an unruly crowd. He believed that crowds transform people, obliterating their normal abilities to be rational and putting them in a hypnotic, highly suggestible state. Le Bon disapproved of crowd behavior in all forms. Consequently, in his book he painted an extremely negative picture of crowd behavior.

Modern social psychological research suggests that neither of these early viewpoints is a good description of the psychological forces underlying crowd behavior. Experimental research has determined that almost any individual could be influenced to behave in uncharacteristic ways under the right circumstances. Le Bon's perspective has also been greatly refined. Rather than relying on Le Bon's concepts of mass hypnosis and loss of rationality, modern researchers draw primarily from social identity theory to help explain crowd behavior. Social identity theory, originally developed by European psychologists Henri Tajfel and John Turner in the 1970's, posits that the individual derives an important part of his or her sense of identity from the groups to which he or she belongs. Groups such as one's family, school, or religion can all provide positive sources of identity.

Under some circumstances, crowds can become a source of identity as well. A key psychological mechanism through which crowds become a source of identity is deindividuation, the loss of a person's sense of identity and weakening of inhibitions, which occurs only in the presence of others. Being in a crowd is likely to lead to deindividuation for a number of reasons. First, crowds lead individuals to feel less accountable for their actions; the individual is less likely to be singled out and feels less personally responsible for any act the crowd commits. Crowds also focus attention away from the self, so one's own values and internal standards become less influential. Thus, in line with social identity theory, deindividuation leads someone to become focused on social identity rather than individual identity. When social identity is salient to an individual, that person becomes particularly susceptible to social influence. Group norms, or a group's standards and expectations regarding appropriate behavior, become especially important, and the individual is likely to conform strictly to those norms. In the short time frame of many crowd gatherings, the norm becomes whatever everyone else is doing.

Being amid a group of people, however, does not always lead one to become deindividuated, nor does it always lead to the ascendancy of social identity over individual identity. Often crowds do not engage in collective behavior at all. For example, on most city streets, pedestrians walking and milling about do not consider themselves to be part of a group and do not draw a sense of identity from the people around them.

Eugen Tarnow noted that these wide variations in the effect of crowds on individuals can be best understood by identifying two phases, an individual phase and a conforming phase. During the individual phase, people move freely about. At these times, individuals are not particularly aware of their membership in a crowd and are not particularly influenced by those around them. In the conforming phase, however, individuals in a crowd are highly aware of the group of which they are a part, and they show high levels of conformity. During this phase, the group norms heavily influence each individual's behavior. Crowds typically alternate between these two phases, sometimes acting collectively, sometimes individually. For example, at a sporting event, fans are sometimes talking to their friends about topics of individual interest. However, when points are scored by the home team, the crowd responds collectively, as part of social group. At these moments spectators are not responding as individuals but as members of the social group, "fans."

The behaviors that members of a crowd perform will thus depend upon how strongly the crowd becomes a source of social identity and the norms

The way in which individuals behave in a crowd has been a subject of increasing attention. (CLEO Photography)

for behavior that become established among the group. Because these factors vary considerably from group to group, crowds cannot be characterized as wholly negative or uniformly simplistic, as Le Bon described them.

THE VIOLENT CROWD

Violent and destructive acts are among the most studied forms of crowd behavior. Many historical examples, from the French Revolution of 1789 to the Los Angeles riots of 1992, attest to the destructive power of crowds. A crowd of deindividuated people will not become violent, however, unless a group norm of violence becomes established. In riots, for example, there is usually an identifiable precipitating event (for example, one person smashing a window) that introduces a norm of violence. If a critical mass of people immediately follows suit, a riot ensues. Other crowds, such as lynch mobs, have the norm of violence previously established by their culture or by the group's previous actions.

Further, there is some evidence to suggest that the way in which a crowd of people is viewed by authorities can escalate crowd conflicts. For example, in 1998, European psychologists Clifford Stott and Stephen Reicher interviewed police officers involved with controlling a riot in Great Britain. Their analysis revealed that while police officers recognize that crowds contain subgroups of more dangerous or less dangerous members, they tend to treat all group members as potentially dangerous. The police officers' negative expectations often translate into combative behavior toward all crowd members. By acting on their negative expectations, authority figures often elicit the very behaviors they hope to prevent. This often leads to increased violence and conflict escalation.

Much evidence suggests that there is a direct relationship between the degree of deindividuation and the extremity of a crowd's actions. For example, in 1986, Brian Mullen examined newspaper accounts of sixty lynchings occurring in the first half of the twentieth century. His analysis revealed that the more people in the mob, the more violent and vicious was the event. Similarly, Leon Mann found in his analysis of twenty-one cases of threatened suicides that crowds watching were more likely to engage in crowd baiting (encouraging the person to jump from a ledge or bridge) when crowds were large and when it was dark. On a more mundane level, sports players are more aggressive when wearing identical uniforms than when dressed in their own clothes. Any factor that increases anonymity seems to increase deindividuation and increase the power of social identity and thus increases the likelihood of extreme behavior.

In South Africa, psychological research on these phenomena has been presented in murder trials. People being tried for murder have argued that these psychological principles help explain their antisocial behavior. The use of psychological research findings for these purposes has sparked a great deal of controversy in the field.

THE APATHETIC CROWD

While crowds are most infamous for inciting people to rash action, sometimes crowds inhibit behavior. Research on helping behavior suggests that helping is much less likely to occur when there are many people watching. This well-established phenomenon, known as the bystander effect, was researched and described by American psychologists John Darley and Bibb Latane. In a typical experiment, participants overhear an "accident," such as someone falling off a ladder. Researchers observe whether participants go to help. Most people help when they are alone, but people are significantly less likely to help when they are with a crowd of other people. Darley and Latane argued that bystanders in a crowd experience a diffusion of responsibility. That is, each individual feels less personally responsible to act because each assumes that someone else will do so.

This phenomenon is exacerbated by the fact that in many situations, it is unclear whether an event is an emergency. For example, an adult dragging a screaming child out of a store could be a kidnapper abducting a child or a parent responding to a tantrum. Bystanders observe the reactions of others in the crowd to help them determine the appropriate course of action in an ambiguous situation. However, because the situation is ambiguous, typically each individual is equally confused and unsure. By waiting for someone else to act, bystanders convey the impression to others that they think nothing is wrong. Psychologists call this phenomenon pluralistic ignorance. People assume that even though others are behaving in exactly the same way as themselves (not acting), they are doing so for a different reason (knowing the situation is not an emergency). Thus, a social norm of inaction can also become established in a crowd.

THE PROSOCIAL CROWD

Despite the potential for great violence and destruction, most crowds that gather do so quite uneventfully. Further, sometimes crowd behavior is quite positive and prosocial. Research shows that sometimes deindividuation can lead to prosocial behavior. For example, nonviolent protests operate under an explicit norm of peaceful resistance and rarely lead to escalated violence on both sides.

The power of prosocial norms was also experimentally established in a 1979 study conducted by psychologists Robert Johnson and Leslie Downing. Johnson and Downing had participants dress in either nurse's apparel or a white robe and hood like those worn in the Ku Klux Klan. Some from each group had their individual identity made salient, while the rest did not. All participants were then given the opportunity to deliver an electric shock to someone who had previously insulted them. Among participants wearing the robes, those who were not identified delivered higher shock levels than those who were identified. Presumably these people were deindividuated and thus more strongly influenced by the violent cue of their costume. Of those in nurses' uniforms, the opposite was observed. Unidentified, deindividuated participants gave much less intense shocks than identified participants did. They were also more strongly influenced by the cues around them, but in this case the cues promoted prosocial action.

SOURCES FOR FURTHER STUDY

Coleman, A. M. "Crowd Psychology in South African Murder Trials." *American Psychologist* 46, no. 10 (1992): 1071-1079. This article describes the use of modern social psychological research on crowd behavior to argue for extenuating factors in murder trials. The ethical issues raised from psychological testimony are discussed.

Gaskell, G., and R. Benewick, eds. *The Crowd in Contemporary Britain.* London: Sage, 1987. An excellent, comprehensive discussion of crowd behavior and political responses to it, drawing on work from scholars in several social scientific disciplines.

Le Bon, Gustave. *The Crowd.* New Brunswick, N.J.: Transaction, 1995. First published in 1895, this classic work explores the nature of crowd behavior and the places in modern life where crowd behavior holds sway.

McPhail, Clark. *The Myth of the Madding Crowd.* New York: Aldine De Gruyter, 1991. Authored by one of the major modern researchers on crowd behavior, this book summarizes and critiques Gustave Le Bon and earlier crowd theorists and presents new formulations for understanding crowd behavior.

Mann, L. "The Baiting Crowd in Episodes of Threatened Suicide." *Journal of Personality and Social Psychology* 41, no. 4 (1981): 703-709. In this paper, Mann provides a fascinating analysis of the factors that make crowds more likely than individuals to bait potential suicides.

_____. "'The Crowd' Century: Reconciling Practical Success with Theoretical Failure." *British Journal of Social Psychology* 35, no. 4 (1996): 535-553. Discusses the limits of Gustave Le Bon's crowd psychology theory and explores why, despite these limits, Adolf Hitler and Benito Mussolini were able to use his theory so successfully to manipulate crowds.

Reicher, S. *Crowd Behavior.* New York: Cambridge University Press, 2002. Scholarly perspectives on crowd behavior.

Van Ginneken, Jaap. *Crowds, Psychology, and Politics, 1871-1899.* New York: Cambridge University Press, 1992. Provides a historical perspective on the development of the field of crowd psychology, showing how early theories were shaped by current political events.

Cynthia McPherson Frantz

SEE ALSO: Aggression; Groups; Helping.

Death and Dying

Type of psychology: Developmental psychology
Fields of study: Aging; classic analytic themes and issues; stress and illness

Death is a universal human experience that, for most of history, has been primarily the province of religion and philosophy. It has, however, increasingly been a concern of social scientists; perhaps, more than has been previously realized, death has important things to teach both scientists and laypersons about human existence.

Key concepts
- chronic illnesses
- death anxiety
- defense mechanisms
- denial
- five-stage theory
- syndrome

Although death is a universal phenomenon, it is a topic which has come late to psychology and the other social sciences. All people, including authors, scholars, and theologians, have dealt with death since before the beginning of recorded history. Handling death in a scientific way is, to a large extent, a product of the twentieth century.

The reasons for the scientific neglect of death are manifold. It is a complex idea and one against which most people build defense mechanisms (psychological strategies, generally unconscious, which the personality uses as a defense against anxiety). The scientist might argue that death is not an empirical fact (that is, one which relies on information that comes through the senses, as opposed to relying on logical or rational processes), in the sense that no one can experience death firsthand in order to study it or write about it. Sigmund Freud, the founder of psychoanalysis, said that no one can imagine his or her own death, and that does seem to be true; one who tries to imagine himself or herself dead is still around, in some sense, doing the imagining.

Some scholars have distinguished between the death state and the death event. The death state (what it is like to be dead) is essentially a religious or philosophical issue. It is not amenable to empirical study, although the impact of death on other people and the impact of thoughts about death while one is still alive can be studied. The death event, on the other hand, is, to some degree at least, a part of life. It is possible to study how, why, and where people die. It is possible to study the process of dying and to study grief and bereavement.

It has also become necessary, particularly in recent years, to ask difficult questions about death: questions about when physical death actually occurs, about humane treatment for the dying patient, about the so-called right to die, about children and the best way to answer their concerns about death, and about how best to help people deal with their grief. Most of these questions generally cannot be answered by science alone. Almost all deal with ethical, religious, and social issues as well as with scientific information.

It has been argued that Americans are "death-denying." Even though aspects of death are around all the time, Americans live most of the time as if death were not a reality. Ernest Becker argued in his classic book *The Denial of Death* (1973) that American lives are organized around the fear and denial of death. His often-convincing, although primarily philosophical, argument is augmented by research such as that of psychologists at Princeton University who studied undergraduates, most of whom did not admit having much conscious death anxiety (an emotional apprehension or vague fear caused by thinking about or facing the fact of death). Yet by a word-association test, measures of galvanic skin response (a biological electrical current in the skin assumed to be related to levels of psychological anxiety), and response latency (the time between the presentation of a stimulus word and the response from the subject), researchers collected data that clearly showed that these college students responded to words related to death with greater emotional intensity than to equivalent words drawn from other topic areas.

EMERGING UNDERSTANDING OF DEATH

If the United States is a death-denying society, it is nevertheless apparent that in the latter part of the twentieth century some people became willing to look at death more clearly; this is demonstrated in the behavioral and social sciences. In research, books, articles, and in many other ways, interest in death, dying, and closely related topics multiplied enormously.

In 1944 Erich Lindemann did a systematic study of the grief reactions of individuals who had lost a close relative; many of his subjects were relatives of those who died in the 1942 Cocoanut Grove nightclub fire in Boston that killed almost five hundred people. Lindemann was particularly interested in studying the differences between what he called "normal" grief and the "abnormal" reactions he saw in some of the survivors. He concluded from his study that acute grief is a definite syndrome (a combination of behaviors or symptoms which together may be signs of illness or pathology) with psychological and somatic symptomatology. In his description of normal grief, he said: "Common to all is the following syndrome—sensations of somatic distress occurring in waves lasting from 20 minutes to an hour, a feeling of tightness in the throat, choking with shortness of breath, need for sighing, an empty feeling in the abdomen, lack of muscular power, and an intense subjective distress described as tension or mental pain." Lindemann then pointed out the pathologies of grief, many of which are the intensification, elongation, or absence of the symptoms of normal grief.

Lindemann was a pioneer in the attempt to bring death into the arena of science, and since his time there have been thousands of studies, the creation of several organizations (such as the Association for Death Education and Counseling) and journals (such as *Omega*), and the publication of dozens of books (including textbooks) in the area of death and dying.

As an example of how science grows by building on the work of others, it was later found that Lindemann had not contacted his bereaved subjects soon enough to observe a stage of grief which seems to be almost universal: a period of shock, numbness, and denial in which the bereaved person acts as if nothing had happened for a few hours or even days—sometimes even longer in abnormal grief.

STAGES OF DYING

Evidence that many people were interested in the subject of death was the remarkable popularity of a book published in 1969. *On Death and Dying* was written by Elisabeth Kübler-Ross, a physician who had come to the United States from Switzerland. Perhaps the best-known aspect of Kübler-Ross's book, based on her informal research, was her outline of a series of stages which she had found many dying patients go through. She became convinced that modern medicine, in its efforts to keep the patient alive, treated dying patients in ways that were often inhumane. She found that very little was known about the psychology of the dying person; she pointed out that there were no courses on death and dying in medical schools or, for all practical purposes, anywhere else at the time.

Kübler-Ross interviewed several hundred persons who were dying of chronic illnesses—generally long-term illnesses, such as heart disease and cancer, which are the major causes of death in older Americans. She found that most dying patients go through five stages in the terminal period of their lives. The first stage is one of denial: "This is not really happening. Someone has made a mistake. I am not really going to die." In most people, the probable reality of the diagnosis eventually replaces the denial with a sense of anger: "Why me? Why now?" Generally, the anger is displaced onto the most available candidate—a physician, a family member, a nurse, God. The real object of the anger is death, but it is difficult to express anger toward an abstract and ill-defined concept. The third stage is one of bargaining: "If only I do not die, or at least if my life is extended, then I will change my ways." It generally becomes clear that the bargaining is not going to work, and the fourth stage is depression. Kübler-Ross describes it as "a sense of great loss." Losses of any kind are one of life's major difficulties, and death is the ultimate loss of everything. Finally, the fifth stage that Kübler-Ross observed is the stage of acceptance. This is not the same as saying that the patient now wants to die or is looking forward to death. Kübler-Ross describes this stage as "almost void of feelings." It is the acceptance of the inevitability of what is about to happen.

Kübler-Ross's five-stage theory has come under criticism. Edwin Shneidman, one of the first professionals to be called thanatologists because they specialize in working with the dying and the grieving, stated that in his experience he rarely sees the neat progression through the five stages that Kübler-Ross enumerates. Many others believe that the five-stage theory is too simplistic to describe the way things happen in the real world. (Kübler-Ross agrees that the five-stage theory does not apply to all dying people.) Undoubtedly, factors such as the length of the terminal illness, the religious beliefs of the dying person, the amount of support, and even the age of the patient may make a difference in the way people deal with their dying. Nevertheless, a framework such as the five stages, if not held too literally, seems to be a great aid for many who have to support or work with someone who is dying.

THE DEATH SYSTEM

Turning from the individual to the society, it is easy to see many places where death plays an important role in social life. Robert Kastenbaum has characterized this as the "death system." Just as society has many systems to deal with essential functions, such as the economic system, the educational system, and the transportation system, society must also deal with death on a daily basis. The death system would include, among other matters, all that is involved with the disposition of the dead body: the church or other religious organization, the funeral arrangements, the cemetery. A large number of people are involved, in one way or another, in this aspect of the death system. Although the funeral business has taken its share of criticism, some of it undoubtedly deserved, it fills a need that the majority of people in Western society have.

The death system also has other functions. Already noted is the care of the dying, which involves a large part of the health care system in the United States as well as family and friends and organizations such as hospice. One might also include in the death system the many aspects of society which are involved in trying to prevent death, from police officers to the national Centers for Disease Control to the hurricane warning center to the manufacturer of railroad crossing signals. Actually, few people in the United States do not have at least a peripheral connection to the death system. Many florists, for example, say that half or more of their business is providing flowers and wreaths for funerals and for cemetery plots.

MODERN RELATIONSHIPS WITH DEATH

Richard Kalish, among others, has pointed out a number of reasons for the interest in the study of death and dying. It is fairly easy to identify a number of factors that have increased concern about this topic. For example, more lives were lost in the twentieth century in warfare than in any other period of history. The presence of thermonuclear weapons continues to be a realistic concern for the peoples of the world. The increase in the number and influence of the elderly is also undoubtedly a factor. Most of the elderly die of heart disease, cancer, or other chronic illnesses in which dying takes place over a period of time. This has led to a different kind of acquaintance with death, in comparison to times not so long ago when death more commonly came as the result of a short acute illness.

Closely related to the previous point are the advances in medical technology which allow some people with chronic illnesses to be kept alive on life-support systems when their brains are no longer functioning. Because of such scientific advances, serious questions arise as to when death really occurs and as to what decisions ought to be made about that situation, legally, morally, and psychologically.

Undoubtedly, the impact of television has profoundly influenced society in its attitudes toward death and dying. For several decades, television has depicted death in both real-life and fictional situations. The effect of all this death on television (as well as in motion pictures) has yet to be studied or understood fully by psychologists or other social scientists.

A more sanguine reason for the increased interest in death and dying is that, perhaps, society is becoming more humane in its attempt to deal with these issues. There is a concern for "dying with dignity" and for a "good death" (the original meaning of the term "euthanasia"). The hospice movement has grown rapidly in the attempt to give the dying (particularly those dying from chronic illnesses) more choices about their dying and the opportunity to live out their final days in a way not so different from the way in which they lived the rest of their lives. Social scientists may be coming to realize that death has something important to teach humankind about human existence.

SOURCES FOR FURTHER STUDY

Becker, Ernest. *The Denial of Death.* 1973. Reprint. New York: Free Press, 1997. A strong book on the power of death both for the individual and within a culture. Written, to a large extent, from a psychoanalytic standpoint. Not easy to read without some background in psychology or anthropology.

Cohen-Almagor, Raphael. *The Right to Die with Dignity: An Argument in Ethics, Medicine, and the Law.* New Brunswick, N.J.: Rutgers University Press, 2001. An even-handed overview of the controversies surrounding physician-assisted suicide and the right to choose death in the face of terminal illness.

Feifel, Herman, ed. *The Meaning of Death.* New York: McGraw-Hill, 1965. One of the original books which stimulated interest in death and dying. Contains essays by writers such as Carl Jung, Paul Tillich, and Robert Kastenbaum, as well as articles reporting empirical studies. Generally reads well and contains myriad interesting and thoughtful ideas.

Kastenbaum, Robert. *Death, Society, and Human Experience.* Boston: Allyn & Bacon, 2000. A textbook for classes on the sociology of death and dying, bringing together perspectives from the humanities, social sciences, and psychology.

Kessler, David. *The Needs of the Dying: A Guide for Bringing Hope, Comfort, and Love to Life's Final Chapter.* New York: HarperCollins, 2000. Written by a leader in hospice care. Explains the common emotions and psychology of the dying and offers suggestions for dealing with death.

Kübler-Ross, Elisabeth. *On Death and Dying.* 1969. Reprint. New York: Scribner Classics Sons, 1997. A popular book which had a major impact on the general public. It reads well and is not only interesting but also of practical help to many who are dealing with the issue of dying.

Mitford, Jessica. *The American Way of Death.* 1963. Reprint. New York: Fawcett Crest, 1978. A polemical look at the funeral business. This book made many Americans aware of excesses and shoddy practices, which eventually led to a number of changes—some because of government regulation. Quite one-sided.

_____. *The American Way of Death Revisited.* New York: Alfred A. Knopf, 1998. Mitford's follow-up to her 1963 classic traces changes in the funeral industry over the intervening thirty-odd years. Ironically, a posthumous publication.

Tomer, Adrian, ed. *Death Attitude and Older Adults.* New York: Brunner/ Mazel, 2001. A collection of essays studying current practice in dealing with death from the perspectives of gerontology, thanatology, and general psychology.

James Taylor Henderson

SEE ALSO: Emotions; Stress-Related Diseases; Suicide.

DEMENTIA

TYPE OF PSYCHOLOGY: Cognition; memory; psychopathology
FIELDS OF STUDY: Aging; cognitive processes; depression; interpersonal
  relations; social perception and cognition; thought

Dementia is a chronic progressive brain disorder that may occur as a result of various events. Dementia is the loss of cognitive and social abilities to the degree that they interfere with activities of daily living (ADLs). Dementia may or may not be reversible.

KEY CONCEPTS
- activities of daily living (ADLs)
- cognition
- delirium
- depression
- memory loss
- pseudodementia

Dementia is usually characterized as a gradual, progressive decline in cognitive function that affects speech, memory, judgment, and mood. However, it may also be an unchanging condition that results from an injury to the brain. Initially individuals may be aware of a cognitive decline, but over time they cease to notice. The insidious and progressive nature of dementia may make early diagnosis difficult because cognitive changes may appear as only slight declines in memory, attention, and concentration or rare episodes of inconsistencies in behavior that are attributed to aging. Over time, increased confusion and irritability in unfamiliar environments, poor judgment, difficulty in abstract thinking, and personality changes may be seen.

Delirium is a transient alteration in mental status that is a common feature of dementia. Signs and symptoms of delirium develop over a short period of time. Once the underlying causes of delirium, such as medical problems, stress, or medications, are identified and ministered to, delirium can be reversed. Visual and auditory hallucinations, paranoia, and delusions of persecution may be observed. Memory loss is another symptom of dementia. People with dementia often forget how to perform activities of daily living (ADLs) that they have been performing for years, such as dressing, cleaning, and cooking. They may repeatedly ask the same questions, have the same conversations, forget simple words, or use incorrect words when speaking. They may become disoriented as to time and place and become lost in familiar surroundings. Problems with abstract thinking may make solving math problems and balancing a checkbook impossible. People with dementia may misplace items and be unable to find them because the items were put in unaccustomed places. Mood swings and drastic personality changes, such as sudden, unexpected swings from calm and happy states to tears and anger, are not uncommon in those with dementia.

Depression may be mistaken for dementia. Symptoms of depression include feelings of profound sadness, difficulty in thinking and concentrating, feelings of despair, and apathy. Severe depression brings with it an inability to concentrate and a poor attention span. As the person with dementia tries to conceal memory loss and cognitive decline, appetite loss, apathy, and feelings of uselessness may ensue. In combined dementia and depression, intellectual deterioration can be extreme. An older adult who is depressed may also show signs of confusion and intellectual impairment even though dementia is not present. These individuals are identified as having pseudodementia. Depression, alone or in combination with dementia, is treatable.

PREVALENCE AND IMPACT

Dementia may occur at all ages, but its incidence increases with advanced age. Dementia is most frequent in those older than seventy-five. There are an estimated 600,000 cases of advanced dementia in the United States, and milder degrees of altered mental status are very common in the elderly. The prevalence of dementia increases from 1 percent at age sixty to 40 percent at age eighty-five. The expense of long-term care at home or in a nursing facility has been estimated at $40 billion per year for people age sixty-five and older. The prevalence of dementia is expected to continue to increase as a result of increased life expectancy and an aging population of baby boomers. Many of the problems caused by dementia are due to memory loss.

CAUSES

Dementia may be reversible or irreversible. Reversible causes include brain tumors, subdural hematoma, slowly progressive or normal-pressure hydrocephalus; head trauma; endocrine conditions (such as hypothyroidism, hypercalcemia, hypoglycemia); vitamin deficiencies (of thiamin, niacin, or vitamin B_{12}); thyroid disease; ethanol abuse; infections; metabolic abnormalities; effects of medications; renal, hepatic, and neurological conditions; and depression. Irreversible dementia is more common in the elderly. Irreversible causes of dementia include diseases of the brain such as Alzheimer's, Parkinson's, Pick's, Creutzfeldt-Jakob, and Huntington's diseases; human immunodeficiency virus (HIV) infection; vascular dementia; and head trauma.

TYPES OF DEMENTIA

Alzheimer's disease is the most common form of dementia and is responsible for 50 percent of all dementias. No direct cause has been identified, but it is thought that viruses, environmental toxins, and family history are involved. Definitive diagnosis of Alzheimer's disease can only be made on autopsy when neurofibrillary tangles are found in the brain.

Vascular dementia generally affects people between the ages of sixty and seventy-five. It is estimated that 8 percent of individuals over sixty years old who have a stroke develop dementia within one year. Early treatment of hypertension and vascular disease may prevent further progression of dementia.

Parkinson's disease is an insidious, slow, progressive neurological condition that begins in middle to late life. It is characterized by tremor, rigidity, bradykinesia, and postural instability. Dementia is also present in 20 percent to 60 percent of those with Parkinson's disease. It is characterized by diminishing cognitive function, diminishing motor and executive function, and memory impairment.

Lewy body disease is similar to Alzheimer's disease. Visual hallucinations and Parkinson's-like features progress quickly. Lewy bodies are found in the cerebral cortex. Patients exhibit psychotic symptoms and have a sensitivity to antipsychotic medications.

Pick's disease and other frontal lobe dementias are rare and are identified by changes in personality and emotions, executive dysfunction, deterioration of social skills, inappropriate behavior, and language problems. Pick's disease is most common between ages fifty and sixty. It progresses rapidly and may be accompanied by apathy, extreme agitation, severe language difficulties, attention deficits, and inappropriate behavior. Pick's disease can only be confirmed on autopsy when Pick's inclusion bodies are found.

Another disorder that can lead to progressive dementia is Huntington's disease, a genetic disorder that usually occurs in middle age. The basal ganglia and subcortical structures in the brain are affected, causing spasticity in body movements. Personality, memory, intellect, speech, and judgment are altered.

Creutzfeldt-Jakob disease (spongiform encephalopathy) is a rare and fatal brain disorder caused by a virus that converts protein into infectious, deadly molecules. Early symptoms may be memory loss and changes in behavior. Creutzfeldt-Jakob disease progresses into mental deterioration, muscle spasms, weakness in the extremities, blindness, and coma.

RISK FACTORS AND DIAGNOSIS

Risk factors for dementia include a family history of dementia, head trauma, lower educational level, and gender (women are more prone than men to dementia). Alcohol and drug abuse, infections, cardiovascular disease, and head injuries are also causes for the development of dementia.

The criteria in the American Psychiatric Association's *Diagnostic and Statistical Manual of Mental Disorders: DSM-IV-TR* (rev. 4th ed., 2000) for the diagnosis of dementia require the presence of multiple cognitive deficits in addition to memory impairment. The diagnosis of dementia is based on cognitive deficits that are severe enough to cause impairment in occupational or social functioning and must represent a decline from a previous level of functioning. The nature and degree of impairment are variable and often depend on the particular social setting of the individual. Standardized mental status tests are a baseline for evaluation for dementia. Examples of

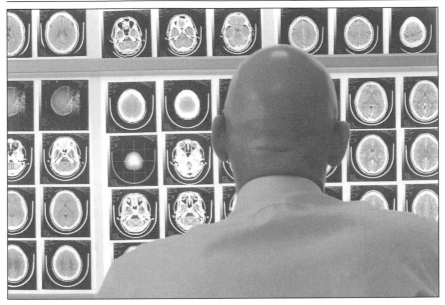

A computer tomography (CT) scan can sometimes identify the source of dementia. (Digital Stock)

some short tests are the Mini-Mental Status Test, the Blessed Information-Memory-Concentration Test, and the Short Portable Mental Status Questionnaire. A standardized mental status test score should be used to confirm the results of a history and physical examination. Standardized mental status tests should not be the single deciding factor for the diagnosis of dementia. Some tests such as blood evaluations, urinalysis, chest radiography, carotid ultrasound, Doppler flow studies, electroencephalogram, lumbar puncture, and computed tomography (CT) scans of the head are done in relation to the presenting symptoms.

TREATMENT

The goals of treating dementia are improving mental function and maintaining the highest level of function possible. Many families care for family members with dementia at home. A structured home environment and established daily routines are important as the person with dementia begins to experience difficulty learning and remembering new activities. Establishing simple chores to enhance a sense of usefulness, such as watering plants, dusting, and setting the table, are helpful. It is essential to provide a safe home environment. This includes maintaining uncluttered surroundings and removing potentially dangerous items such as matches, lighters, knives, scissors, and medications. In later stages of dementia, stoves, ovens, and other cooking items may need to be disabled to prevent fires. Clocks, calendars, television, magazines, and newspapers are good ways to help to keep those with dementia oriented. As functioning decreases, nursing home placement may be necessary.

It is important that the families who care for members with dementia at home are made aware of community services that can assist them in locating support groups and social service agencies to access day care, counseling, home, day, respite care, and group therapy services.

Pharmaceutical Therapies

Nerve growth factor, antioxidant therapy, and other drugs are being investigated for the management of dementia. Psychotrophic medications such as carbamazepine, desipramine, haloperidol, lorazepam, and thioridazine are used to control symptoms of agitation, anxiety, confusion, delusions, depression, and hallucinations in patients with dementia. Unfortunately, some of the medications used to improve patients' quality of life may not work, may worsen memory deficits, or cause neurological effects such as irreversible tremors (tardive diskinesia).

It is important to reduce cerebrovascular risk factors such as hypertension, diabetes, smoking, hyperlipidemia, and coronary artery disease in patients with vascular dementia. Dementia resulting from neurologic conditions (Parkinson's disease, normal-pressure hydrocephalus, brain lesions, carotid artery disease) requires a neurological workup. Dementia related to a hereditary condition requires referral for genetic counseling.

Sources for Further Study

Epstein, David, and James Gonnor. "Dementia in Elderly: An Overview." *Generations* 23, no. 3 (1999): 9-17. Presents an overview of various types of dementia and their treatments.

Rabins, Peter V., Constantine G. Lyketsos, and Cynthia Steele. *Practical Dementia Care.* New York: Oxford University Press, 1999. Written primarily for medical professionals. Covers definitions, evaluation, diseases causing dementia, care for the patient and the family, treatment options, terminal care, and ethical and legal issues.

Schindler, Rachel. "Late-Life Dementia." *Geriatrics* 55, no. 10 (2000): 55-57. Discusses American Psychiatric Association guidelines for detecting and treating dementia.

Teitel, Rosette, and Marc Gordon. *The Handholder's Handbook: A Guide to Caregivers of People with Alzheimer's or Other Dementias.* New Brunswick, N.J.: Rutgers University Press, 2001. A guide to practical and emotional issues for caregivers of dementia patients. Chapters provide checklists of topics that caregivers should deal with or cover as they adjust to their role.

Sharon Wallace Stark

See also: Aging: Cognitive Changes; Alzheimer's Disease; Brain Structure; Parkinson's Disease; Support Groups.

DEPRESSION

TYPE OF PSYCHOLOGY: Psychopathology
FIELD OF STUDY: Depression

The study of depression has focused on biological underpinnings, cognitive concomitants, stress and coping style precursors, and interpersonal context.

KEY CONCEPTS
- bipolar disorder
- major depressive episode
- manic episode
- unipolar depression

Almost everyone gets "down in the dumps" or has "the blues" sometimes. Feeling sad or dejected is clearly a normal part of the spectrum of human emotion. This situation is so common that a very important issue is how to separate a normal blue or down mood or emotion from an abnormal clinical state. Most clinicians use measures of intensity, severity, and duration of these emotions to separate the almost unavoidable human experience of sadness and dejection from clinical depression.

Depression is seen in all social classes, races, and ethnic groups. It is so pervasive that it has been called the common cold of mental illness in the popular press. It is approximately twice as common among women as it is among men. Depression is seen among all occupations, but it is most common among people in the arts and humanities. Famous individuals such as American president Abraham Lincoln and British prime minister Winston Churchill had to cope with depression; Churchill called the affliction "the black dog." More recently, United States senator Thomas Eagleton and astronaut Edwin "Buzz" Aldrin were known to have bouts of serious depression.

Of all problems that are mentioned by patients at psychological and psychiatric clinics, some form of depression is most common. It is estimated that approximately 25 percent of women in the United States will experience at least one significant depression during their lives. Contrary to a popular misconception that depression is most common among the elderly, it is actually most common in twenty-five- to forty-four-year-olds. About 10 percent of the college population report moderate depression, and 5 percent report severe depression. Suicidal thoughts are common in depressive clients. In long-term follow-up, it has been found that approximately 15 percent of depressed individuals eventually kill themselves. Alternatively viewed, approximately 60 percent of suicides are believed to be caused by depression or by depression in association with alcohol abuse. As has been vividly portrayed in the media, teenage suicide in the United States is increasing at an alarming rate.

The role of family or genetic factors in depression was addressed long ago by Robert Burton in *The Anatomy of Melancholy* (1621), in which he noted that the "inbred cause of melancholy is our temperature, in whole or part, which we receive from our parents" and "such as the temperature of the father is, such is the son's, and look what disease the father had when he begot him, his son will have after him." More than 350 years later, the role of family factors in depression was addressed in a major collaborative study in the United States. In what was called the National Institute of Mental Health Collaborative Study of the Psychobiology of Depression, a large number of standardized instruments were developed to assess prevalence and incidence of depression, life histories, psychosocial stressors, and outcome of depression. The family members of depressed persons were assessed along with the depressed individual. It was found that bipolar depression was largely confined to relatives of individuals with bipolar disorder. Unipolar depression, however, was common among relatives of both unipolar- and bipolar-depressed individuals. The different patterns of familial transmission for bipolar and unipolar disorders strengthen the general conviction that these two disorders should be kept distinct from each other.

One explanation for increased vulnerability to depression in close relatives of depressed individuals is an inherited deficiency in two key compo-

The loss of a life partner is a source of intense grief and may trigger depression in the survivor. (PhotoDisc)

nents of brain chemistry: norepinephrine and serotonin, both of which are neurotransmitters. If depressions could be reliably subtyped according to the primary neurotransmitter deficiency, the choice of antidepressant medication would logically follow. Research is conflicting, however, on whether there is one group of depressed individuals who are low in norepinephrine and normal in serotonin and another group of depressives who are low in serotonin and normal in norepinephrine. Future developments in the study of neurotransmitters may have practical implications for the matching of particular pharmacotherapy interventions with particular types of depression. Evidence does indicate that for many depressed patients, substantial alteration in neurotransmitter activity occurs during their depression. This altered activity may directly mediate many of the disturbing symptoms of depression.

COGNITIVE AND STRESS THEORIES

A different approach to understanding depression has been put forward by cognitive theorists. According to Aaron Beck, in *Cognitive Therapy and the Emotional Disorders* (1976), cognitive distortions cause many, if not most, of a person's depressed states. Three of the most important cognitive distortions are arbitrary inference, overgeneralization, and magnification and minimization. Arbitrary inference refers to the process of drawing a conclusion from a situation, event, or experience when there is no evidence to support the conclusion or when the conclusion is contrary to the evidence. For example, an individual concludes that his boss hates him because she seldom says positive things to him. Overgeneralization refers to an individual's pattern of drawing conclusions about his or her ability, performance, or worth based on a single incident. An example of overgeneralization is an individual concluding that he is worthless because he is unable to find his way to a particular address (even though he has numerous other exemplary skills). Magnification and minimization refer to errors in evaluation that are so gross as to constitute distortions. Magnification refers to the exaggeration of negative events; minimization refers to the underemphasis of positive events.

According to Beck, there are three important aspects of these distortions or depressive cognitions. First, they are automatic—that is, they occur without reflection or forethought. Second, they appear to be involuntary. Some patients indicate that these thoughts occur even though they have resolved not to have them. Third, the depressed person accepts these thoughts as plausible, even though others would not view them in the same manner.

While there is ample empirical support for the association of depression and negative cognitive factors such as cognitive distortions, irrational beliefs, and negative statements about oneself, research that demonstrates the ability of cognitive variables to predict subsequent depression is just beginning. It appears that a cognitive vulnerability plays a role in symptom formation for at least some individuals and in the maintenance of ongoing episodes of depression for many, if not all, depressed persons.

Yet another approach to understanding depression focuses on stress and coping. James Coyne, in a 1991 article, suggests that depression may be understood as a failure to cope with ongoing life problems or stressors. It has been hypothesized that coping effectively with problems and stressors can lessen the impact of these problems and help prevent them from becoming chronic. Depressed patients show slower recovery if they display poor coping skills. Avoidance coping strategies appear to be particularly likely in depression and are one example of poor coping. Depressed persons also show elevated levels of emotion-focused coping strategies, such as wishful thinking, distancing, self-blame, and isolation. These strategies also tend to be ineffective. While most forms of coping are impaired during an episode of depression, only self-isolation, an interpersonal avoidance strategy, appears to be an enduring coping style of persons vulnerable to depression. Thus, coping processes appear to change for the worse during an episode of depression, and poor coping helps to maintain the episode. In particular, depressed persons appear likely to avoid problem situations and to engage in strategies with a low likelihood of resulting in problem resolution or an enhanced sense of personal control.

Interpersonal approaches to understanding depression are related to stress and coping models but highlight the interpersonal environment as particularly important in depression. There is considerable evidence that low levels of social support are related to depression. Perhaps the relationship between social support and depression results from the fact that depressed persons do not seek social support; however, there is also evidence that poor social support leads to or maintains depressive symptomatology. In particular, evidence links the absence of close relationships with the development of depressive symptomatology. Accordingly, the work on general social support and depression can be seen as pointing in the direction of direct consideration of intimate relationships and their role in depression. Because the strongest family ties are usually in the marital relationship, it is natural to look to the marital relationship for particularly powerful opportunities to provide social support. Indeed, there is considerable evidence of an association between marital discord and depression. It had been expected by some that the association between marital discord and depression would be greater for women than men; however, it is generally equivalent between sexes. Indeed, the risk of having a major depressive episode is approximately twenty-five times higher for both men and women if they are in a discordant marital relationship than if they are in a harmonious marital relationship.

TREATMENT METHODS
There are a number of ways to understand depression, and each approach appears to have something to offer. Given the distressing nature of depression, it is not surprising that these differing approaches have led to several effective ways of treating depression.

Pharmacological interventions for unipolar depression have sometimes been held to normalize a genetically determined biochemical defect; the evidence, however, does not support this extreme biological characterization of unipolar depression. Yet neurotransmitters may directly mediate many of the behaviors affected in depression (for example, sleep, appetite, and pleasure), and neurotransmitter level and activity are disturbed as a concomitant of many episodes of depression. Hence, the use of antidepressant agents that influence neurotransmitter level or activity should be helpful in reducing or eliminating symptoms of depression even if the disturbance in neurotransmitter level or activity is itself the result of environmental or cognitive changes. In addition, there is considerable direct evidence that antidepressants can be useful in treating depression in many cases. In controlled trials, both more recently developed and older forms of antidepressants provided improvement rates of 66 to 75 percent, in contrast to placebos, which showed improvement rates of 30 to 60 percent. Exactly for whom they will work, however, and exactly how or why they work are still not entirely clear.

A second effective approach to the treatment of depression can be found in cognitive therapy. It has become clear that altering cognitions and behavior in a cognitive behavioral format can relieve an ongoing episode of depression and may reduce the likelihood of relapse further than the use of psychopharmacology alone. Thus, cognitive processes are, at a minimum, reasonable targets of intervention in the treatment of many depressed patients. In addition, cognitive therapy appears to work well at decreasing depressive symptomatology even in the context of ongoing marital discord. Thus, for many depressed patients, interventions targeted at altering dysfunctional, negative automatic thoughts are likely to be useful.

Finally, interpersonal psychotherapy (IPT) has been developed by Gerald Klerman. This successful approach emphasizes abnormal grief, interpersonal disputes, role transitions, loss, and interpersonal deficits as well as social and familial factors. Results of a large, multicenter collaborative study conducted by the National Institute of Mental Health (NIMH) indicated that IPT can work as well as antidepressant medication for many depressed patients. In addition, earlier research indicated that IPT can improve the social functioning of depressed patients in a manner not typically produced by antidepressant medications alone. Given the interpersonal problems which are often part of a depressive episode, these improvements in social functioning and interpersonal environment appear to be particularly important for depressed persons. In a related development, marital therapy has been tested as a treatment for depressed persons who are maritally discordant, and it appears to be successful.

FROM MELANCHOLY TO PROZAC
The identification of depression as a recognizable state has a very long history. Clinical depression was described as early as the eighth century B.C.E.

in the biblical descriptions of Saul. During the fourth century B.C.E., Hippocrates coined the term "melancholy" to describe one of the three forms of mental illness he recognized. Later, Galen attempted to provide a biochemical explanation of melancholy based on the theory of "humors." Indeed, repeated descriptions and discussions of depression are present from classical times through the Middle Ages and into modern times.

The first comprehensive treatment of depression in English was provided by Timothy Bright's *Treatise of Melancholia* (1586). In 1621 Robert Burton provided his own major work on depression, *The Anatomy of Melancholy.* Most of the credit for developing the modern understanding of affective disorders, however, is given to Emil Kraepelin, a German psychiatrist. It was in Kraepelin's system that the term "depression" first assumed importance.

Since classical times, there has been debate about whether depression is best considered an illness or a response to an unhappy situation. Indeed, it is obvious to the most casual observer that sadness is a normal response to unhappy events. Even now, there is less than complete agreement on when fluctuations in mood should be considered pathological and when they are within normal limits. To help resolve this problem, diagnostic criteria have been developed, and structured interview procedures are often used to determine whether a particular individual should be considered depressed.

In the American Psychiatric Association's *Diagnostic and Statistical Manual of Mental Disorders: DSM-IV-TR* (rev. 4th ed., 2000), a common diagnostic tool, unipolar depression is divided into the categories Dysthymic Disorder, Major Depressive Disorder-Single Episode, and Major Depressive Disorder-Recurrent, while bipolar depression is divided into Bipolar I Disorder, Bipolar II Disorder, Cyclothymic Disorder, and Bipolar Disorder Not Otherwise Specified (NOS). In most articles, the term "depression" refers to unipolar depression only. Because unipolar depression is much more common than bipolar depression, it is likely that it will continue to attract a larger share of research attention in the future.

Throughout history, models of depression have become increasingly sophisticated, progressing from Hippocrates' theory that depression was produced by an excess of black bile to modern biochemical, cognitive, coping, stress, and interpersonal models. In the future, even more sophisticated models of depression may provide guidance for the next great challenge facing clinical psychology: reversing the trend in Western societies toward ever-increasing rates of depression.

SOURCES FOR FURTHER STUDY

Beach, Stephen R. H., E. E. Sandeen, and K. D. O'Leary. *Depression in Marriage.* New York: Guilford Press,, 1990. Summarizes the literature on basic models of depression. Provides the basis for understanding the important role of marriage in the etiology, maintenance, and treatment of depression.

Beck, Aaron T. *Cognitive Therapy and the Emotional Disorders.* 1976. Reprint.

New York: New American Library, 1979. Clearly lays out the basics of the cognitive model of depression. An important start for those who wish to understand the cognitive approach more thoroughly.

Burns, David D. *Feeling Good: The New Mood Therapy.* Rev. ed. New York: Avon Books, 1999. Provides a very entertaining and accessible presentation of the cognitive approach to depression. Presents basic results and the basics of cognitive theory as well as a practical set of suggestions for getting out of a depression.

Coyne, James C., ed. *Essential Papers on Depression.* New York: New York University Press, 1986. Includes representatives of every major theoretical position advanced between 1900 and 1985. Each selection is a classic presentation of an important perspective. This source will acquaint the reader with the opinions of major theorists in their own words.

Coyne, James C., and G. Downey. "Social Factors and Psychopathology: Stress, Social Support, and Coping Processes." *Annual Review of Psychology* 42 (1991): 401-426. This influential essay ties together stress and coping with interpersonal processes to provide a deeper understanding of the nature of depression. Also provides an account of advances in the way both depression and interpersonal processes related to depression may be studied.

Kleinman, Arthur, and Byron Good. *Culture and Depression.* Berkeley: University of California Press, 1985. This exceptional volume examines the cross-cultural research on depression. Anthropologists, psychiatrists, and psychologists attempt to address the diversity that exists across cultures in the experience and expression of depression.

Paykel, Eugene S. *Handbook of Affective Disorders.* 2d ed. New York: Guilford Press, 1992. Provides comprehensive coverage of depression, mania, and anxiety in relation to depression. Includes detailed descriptions of symptoms, assessment procedures, epidemiology, and treatment procedures.

Solomon, Andrew. *The Noonday Demon: An Atlas of Depression.* New York: Charles Scribner's Sons, 2000. Solomon, who suffered serious depression, provides an insightful investigation of the subject from perspectives of history, psychology, literature, psychopharmacology, law, and philosophy.

Stahl, Stephen M. *Essential Psychopharmacology of Depression and Bipolar Disorder.* New York: Cambridge University Press, 2000. Coverage of the rapidly expanding options in drug treatments for depression.

Stephen R. H. Beach

SEE ALSO: Abnormality: Psychological Models; Bipolar Disorder; Clinical Depression; Cognitive Behavior Therapy; Cognitive Therapy; Death and Dying; Drug Therapies; Emotions; Mood Disorders; Suicide.

DEVELOPMENT

TYPE OF PSYCHOLOGY: Developmental psychology
FIELDS OF STUDY: Adolescence; behavioral and cognitive models; infancy and childhood

Developmental theories allow psychologists to manage and understand the enormous body of data on behavioral development from infancy through old age. Theories of development focus on many different issues and derive from many perspectives and periods in history. All, however, are concerned with explaining stability and change in human behavior as individuals progress through their lives.

KEY CONCEPTS
- behaviorism
- emergent process
- heuristic
- "organic lamp" theory
- psychodynamic theory

Developmental theory has changed greatly over time. The theories of societies at various times in history have emphasized different aspects of development. The Puritans of the sixteenth and seventeenth centuries, for example, focused on the moral development of the child; they believed that Original Sin was inherent in children and that children had to be sternly disciplined in order to make them morally acceptable. In contrast to this view was the developmental theory of the eighteenth century French philosopher Jean-Jacques Rousseau, who held that children were born good and were then morally corrupted by society. Sigmund Freud (1856-1939) was interested in psychosexual development and in mental illness; his work therefore focused on these areas. John B. Watson (1878-1958), B. F. Skinner (1904-1990), and Albert Bandura (born 1925) worked during a period when the major impetus in psychology was the study of learning; not surprisingly, this was the focus of their work.

As developmental theorists worked intently within given areas, they often arrived at extreme positions, philosophically and scientifically. For example, some theorists focused upon the biology of behavior; impressed by the importance of "nature" (genetic or other inherited sources) in development, they may have neglected "nurture" (learning and other resources received from parents, the world, and society). Others focused upon societal and social learning effects and decided that nurture was the root of behavior; nature has often been relegated to subsidiary theoretical roles in physiological and anatomical development. Similar conflicts have arisen concerning developmental continuity or discontinuity, the relative activity or passivity of children in contributing to their own development, and a host of other issues in the field.

These extreme positions would at first appear to be damaging to the understanding of development; however, psychologists are now in a position to evaluate the extensive bodies of research conducted by adherents of the various theoretical positions. It has become evident that the truth, in general, lies somewhere in between. Some developmental functions proceed in a relatively stepwise fashion, as Jean Piaget (1896-1980) or Freud would hold; others are much smoother and more continuous. Some development results largely from the child's rearing and learning; other behaviors appear to be largely biological. Some developmental phenomena are emergent processes (any process of behavior or development that was not necessarily inherent in or predictable from its original constituents) of the way in which the developing individual is organized, resulting from both nature and nurture in intricate, interactive patterns that are only beginning to be understood. These findings, and the therapeutic and educational applications that derive from them, are only comprehensible when viewed against the existing corpus of developmental theory. This corpus, in turn, owes its existence to the gradual construction and modification of developmental theories of the past.

THEORETICAL QUESTIONS AND PROPERTIES

Theoretical perspectives on development derive from a wide variety of viewpoints. Although there are numerous important theoretical issues in development, three questions are central for most theories. The first of these is the so-called nature-nurture question, concerning whether most behavioral development derives from genetics or from the environment. The second of these issues is the role of children in their own development: Are children active contributors to their own development, or do they simply and passively react to the stimuli they encounter? Finally, there is the question of whether development is continuous or discontinuous: Does development proceed by a smooth accretion of knowledge and skills, or by stepwise, discrete developmental stages? Current perspectives within developmental psychology represent very different views on these issues.

Useful developmental theories must possess three properties. They must be parsimonious, or as simple as possible to fit the available facts. They must be heuristically useful, generating new research and new knowledge. Finally, they must be falsifiable, or testable: A theory that cannot be tested can never be shown to be right or wrong. Developmental theories can be evaluated in terms of these three criteria.

PSYCHODYNAMIC THEORIES

Arguably, the oldest developmental theoretical formulation in use is the psychodynamic model, which gave rise to the work of Erik Erikson (1902-1994), Carl Jung (1875-1961), and, as its seminal example, the theory of Sigmund Freud. Freud's theory holds that all human behavior is energized by dynamic forces, many of which are consciously inaccessible to the individual. There are three parts to the personality in Freud's formulation: the id, which emerges first and consists of basic, primal drives; the ego, which finds realistic ways to gratify the desires of the id; and the superego, the individual's moral conscience, which develops from the ego. A primary energizing force for development is the libido, a psychosexual energy that invests itself in different aspects of life during the course of development. In the first year of life (Freud's oral stage), the libido is invested in gratification through oral behavior, including chewing and sucking. Between one and three years of age (the anal stage), the libido is invested in the anus, and the primary source of gratification has to do with toilet training. From three to six years, the libido becomes invested in the genitals; it is during this phallic stage that the child begins to achieve sexual identity. At about six years of age, the child enters latency, a period of relative psychosexual quiet, until the age of twelve years, when the genital stage emerges and normal sexual love becomes possible.

Freud's theory is a discontinuous theory, emphasizing stage-by-stage development. The theory also relies mainly on nature, as opposed to nurture; the various stages are held to occur across societies and with little reference to individual experience. The theory holds that children are active in their own development, meeting and resolving the conflicts that occur at each stage.

The success of psychodynamic theory has been questionable. Its parsimony is open to question: There are clearly simpler explanations of children's behavior. The falsifiability of these ideas is also highly questionable because the theories are quite self-contained and difficult to test. Psychodynamic theory, however, has proven enormously heuristic—that is, having the property of generating further research and theory. Hundreds of studies have set out to test these ideas, and these studies have significantly contributed to developmental knowledge.

BEHAVIORIST THEORIES

In contrast to psychodynamic theories, the behaviorist theories pioneered by John B. Watson and B. F. Skinner hold that development is a continuous process, without discrete stages, and that the developing child passively acquires and reflects knowledge. For behaviorists, development results from nurture, from experience and learning, rather than from nature. The most important extant behaviorist theory is the social learning theory of Albert Bandura, which holds that children learn by watching others around them and imitating others' actions. For example, Bandura demonstrated that children were far more inclined to commit violent acts (toward a toy) if someone else, particularly an adult, committed the acts first. The children were especially disposed to imitate if they perceived the acting individual as powerful or as rewarded for his or her violent actions.

ORGANIC LAMP THEORIES

The behaviorist theories are relatively parsimonious and heuristic. They are also testable, and it has been shown that, although many of the findings of the behaviorists have stood the test of time, there are developmental findings that do not fit this framework. To understand these findings, one must turn to the so-called organic lamp theories. This term comes from the fact that within these theories, children are seen as active contributors to their own development, and certain developmental processes are held to be emergent: As fuel combusts to produce heat and light in a lamp, hereditary and environmental factors combine in development to produce new kinds of behavior. This framework was pioneered by Kurt Goldstein and Heinz Werner, but the most significant extant organic lamp theory is the cognitive development theory of Jean Piaget.

PIAGET'S CONTRIBUTIONS

Piaget's theory involves a discontinuous process of development in four major stages. The sensorimotor stage (birth to two years) is followed by the preoperational stage (two to seven years), the concrete operational stage (seven years to adolescence), and the formal operational stage (adolescence to adulthood). During the sensorimotor stage, the child's behavior is largely reflexive, lacking coherent conscious thought; the child learns that self and world are actually different, and that objects exist even when they are not visible. During the preoperational stage, the child learns to infer the perspectives of other people, learns language, and discovers various concepts for dealing with the physical world. In the concrete operational stage, the ability to reason increases, but children still cannot deal with abstract issues. Finally, in formal operations, abstract reasoning abilities develop. The differences between the stages are qualitative differences, reflecting significant, discrete kinds of behavioral change.

Piaget's theory is not entirely accurate; it does not apply cross-culturally in many instances, and children may, under some experimental circumstances, function at a higher cognitive level than would be predicted by the theory. In addition, some aspects of development have been shown to be more continuous in their nature than Piaget's ideas would indicate. Yet Piaget's formulation is relatively parsimonious. The various aspects of the theory are readily testable and falsifiable, and the heuristic utility of these ideas has been enormous. This theory has probably been the most successful of the several extant perspectives, and it has contributed significantly to more recent advances in developmental theory. This progress includes the work of James J. Gibson, which emphasizes the active role of the organism, embedded in its environment, in the development of perceptual processes; the information processing theories, which emphasize cognitive change; and the ethological or evolutionary model, which emphasizes the interplay of developmental processes, changing ecologies, and the course of organic evolution.

MODERN-DAY APPLICATIONS

Developmental theory has been important in virtually every branch of medicine and education. The psychoanalytic theories of Sigmund Freud were the foundation of psychiatry and still form a central core for much of modern psychiatric practice. These theories are less emphasized in modern clinical psychology, but the work of Freud, Erikson, Jung, and later psychodynamicists is still employed in many areas of psychotherapy.

The behavioristic theories have proved useful in the study of children's learning for educational purposes, and they have considerable relevance for social development. An example is seen in the area of media violence. Bandura's work and other research stemming from social learning theory has repeatedly demonstrated that children tend to imitate violent acts that they see in real life or depicted on television and in other media, particularly if the individuals who commit these acts are perceived as powerful or as rewarded for their actions. Although this is disputed, especially by the media, most authorities are in agreement that excessive exposure to televised violence leads to real-world violence, largely through the mechanisms described by social learning theorists. Social learning theory has contributed significantly to an understanding of such topics as school violence, gang violence, and violent crime.

INTERPLAY OF NATURE VERSUS NURTURE

The organic lamp views have provided developmentalists with useful frameworks against which to understand the vast body of developmental data. Work within the Piagetian framework has shown that both nature and nurture contribute to successful development. One cannot, for example, create "superchildren" by providing preschoolers with college-level material. In general, they are simply not ready as organisms to cope with the abstract thinking required. On the other hand, the work of researchers on various Piagetian problems has shown that even very young children are capable of complex learning.

Organic lamp theory has demonstrated the powerful interplay between biological factors and the way in which children are raised. An example is seen in the treatment of Down syndrome, a chromosomal condition that results in mental retardation. The disorder occurs when there are three chromosomes, rather than two, at the twenty-first locus. Clearly, this is a biological condition, and it was believed to be relatively impervious to interventions that come from the environment. It has now been shown, however, that children afflicted with Down syndrome develop much higher intelligence when raised in an intellectually stimulating environment, as opposed to the more sterile, clinical, determined environments typically employed in the past. The child's intellect is not entirely determined by biology; it is possible to ameliorate the biological effects of the syndrome by means of environmental intervention. This type of complex interplay of hereditary and environmental factors is the hallmark of applied organic lamp theory.

The most important application of developmental theory generally, however, lies in its contribution to the improved understanding of human nature. Such an understanding has considerable real-world importance. For example, among other factors, an extreme faith in the nature side of the nature-nurture controversy led German dictator Adolf Hitler to the assumption that entire races were, by their nature, inferior and therefore should be exterminated. His actions, based on this belief, led to millions of human deaths during World War II. Thus, one can see that developmental theories, especially if inadequately understood, may have sweeping applications in the real world.

SOURCES FOR FURTHER STUDY

Gollin, Eugene S., ed. *Developmental Plasticity: Behavioral and Biological Aspects of Variations in Development.* New York: Academic Press, 1981. Excellent coverage of important theoretical issues in modern developmental psychology. Accessible to college or graduate students with some background in psychology or biology.

Lerner, Richard M. *On the Nature of Human Plasticity.* New York: Cambridge University Press, 1984. Insightful discussion of modern theory in developmental psychology and some historic antecedents. Emphasis on biological issues. Accessible to advanced students, graduate students, or professionals.

Miller, Patricia H. *Theories of Developmental Psychology.* 4th ed. New York: Worth, 2002. Excellent, comprehensive treatment of developmental theory. Describes extant theories in detail and discusses commonalities and dissimilarities. Accessible to the layperson with some background in psychology.

Piaget, Jean. *Biology and Knowledge.* Chicago: University of Chicago Press, 1971. This is a seminal summary of Piagetian theory that contains more general information and information concerning theory construction than do Piaget's other, more specific works. Readily accessible to the college student or the advanced high school student.

Shaffer, David Reed. *Developmental Psychology: Childhood and Adolescence.* 6th ed. Belmont, Calif.: Wadsworth, 2001. Good general textbook on developmental psychology with an excellent basic treatment of theoretical issues in development. Accessible to the college or high school student.

Siegler, Robert S. *Emerging Minds: The Process of Change in Children's Thinking.* New York: Oxford University Press, 1996. Proposes a methodology of describing change as children's cognitive processes evolve.

Matthew J. Sharps

SEE ALSO: Adolescence: Cognitive Skills; Aging: Cognitive Changes; Attachment and Bonding in Infancy and Childhood; Behaviorism; Cognitive Development: Jean Piaget; Ego Psychology: Erik Erikson; Gender-Identity Formation; Psychosexual Development.

Developmental Disabilities

Type of psychology: Developmental psychology
Fields of study: Childhood and adolescent disorders; cognitive
   development; infancy and childhood; organic disorders

Developmental disabilities are conditions that result in substantial functional limitations. They manifest themselves in childhood and persist throughout the life span, requiring a continuum of medical, educational, and social services.

Key concepts
- activities of daily living (ADLs)
- individual education plan (IEP)
- individual family service plan (IFSP)
- medically fragile
- mental retardation
- pervasive developmental disorder (PDD)

The concept of developmental disabilities was first introduced in the Developmental Disabilities Services and Facilities Construction Act of 1970. Subsequently, the Developmental Disabilities Assistance and Bill of Rights Act of 1990 defined developmental disabilities. The term "developmental disability" means a severe, chronic disability of a person five years of age or older that is attributable to a mental or physical impairment or a combination of both. The disability must manifest itself before the person reaches the age of twenty-two and be expected to continue indefinitely. It results in substantial functional limitations in three or more areas of major life activity, including self-care, receptive and expressive language, learning, mobility, self-direction, capacity for independent living, and economic self-sufficiency. The inclusion of the requirement of substantial functional limitations in three or more major life areas forms the basis for provision of services to individuals with severe impairments.

   The American Psychiatric Association does not use the term "developmental disabilities." However, it does identify pervasive developmental disorders (PDD) in its diagnostic manual. The description of these disorders and their manifestations in many ways overlaps the definition of developmental disabilities.

   The terms "developmental disabilities" and "mental retardation" are often used as if they were synonymous. However, there are important distinctions as well as areas of overlap. The President's Committee on Mental Retardation uses the definition developed and used by the American Association on Mental Retardation and generally understood by the Arc-USA (a national organization for people with mental retardation and related developmental disabilities and their families). Developmental disabilities include more disabilities than those encompassed under mental retardation.

Developmental disabilities comprise severe and chronic disabilities, while mental retardation includes a large number of individuals functioning at the mild level of cognitive impairment who require little or no support in adulthood. However, mental retardation does account for 70 percent of the people who are developmentally disabled. The term "medically fragile" is sometimes used to describe those vulnerable individuals whose complex medical needs can seriously compromise their health status.

POSSIBLE CAUSES

There are a multitude of etiologies for developmental disabilities. The cause can be prenatal, perinatal, or postnatal. Risk factors for developmental disabilities can be biological, environmental, or a combination of both. Genetics plays a role in conditions such as Tay-Sachs disease and other inborn errors of metabolism, Klinefelter's syndrome, Fragile X syndrome, and Down syndrome, that typically lead to developmental disability. Genetic causes may be chromosomal abnormalities, single gene defects, or multifactorial disorders. For example, autism appears to have a genetic component that interacts with developmental factors.

A number of conditions in the prenatal environment may increase the likelihood that a child will be born with the potential for a developmental disability. Fetal alcohol syndrome, for example, is completely preventable if pregnant women do not drink alcohol. Women who have sufficient amounts of folic acid in their diets reduce the risk of having a child with a neural tube defect that can result in a developmental disability.

Smoking during pregnancy, use of certain drugs such as cocaine or heroin, poor maternal nutrition, and extremes of maternal age greatly increase the chances of fetal brain damage or premature delivery and low birth weight. Babies with low birth weights are three times more likely than normal-weight babies to have developmental disabilities. Approximately 61 percent of premature infants have a developmental disability of some kind.

Children may later be at risk through environmental causes such as lead poisoning, inadequate nutrition, infections, nonstimulating environments, abuse, neglect, and traumatic brain injury.

DIAGNOSING DEVELOPMENTAL DISABILITIES

Developmental disabilities are defined in terms of what an individual can or cannot do rather than in terms of a clinical diagnosis. They affect the typical processes in a child's growth, particularly the maturation of the central nervous system. For this reason, early identification is important. The potential exists for an improved outcome if children are provided with education and habilitation. Prenatal diagnostic techniques may be appropriate for at-risk pregnancies. If a fetus is known to be affected, the physician is better able to plan the delivery and for special care during the newborn period.

Newborn screening is another way in which to identify conditions that can result in developmental disabilities if untreated. The Apgar test is ad-

DSM-IV-TR CRITERIA FOR PERVASIVE DEVELOPMENTAL DISORDERS

ASPERGER'S DISORDER (DSM CODE 299.80)

Qualitative impairment in social interaction, manifested by at least two of the following:

- marked impairment in use of multiple nonverbal behaviors (eye-to-eye gaze, facial expression, body postures, gestures)
- failure to develop peer relationships appropriate to developmental level
- lack of spontaneous seeking to share enjoyment, interests, or achievements with others
- lack of social or emotional reciprocity

Restricted, repetitive, and stereotyped patterns of behavior, interests, and activities, manifested by at least one of the following:

- preoccupation with one or more stereotyped and restricted patterns of interest abnormal in either intensity or focus
- apparently inflexible adherence to specific, nonfunctional routines or rituals
- stereotyped and repetitive motor mannerisms (hand or finger flapping, complex whole-body movements)
- persistent preoccupation with parts of objects

Symptoms cause clinically significant impairment in social, occupational, or other important areas of functioning

No clinically significant general delay in language

No clinically significant delay in cognitive development or development of age-appropriate self-help skills, adaptive behavior (other than in social interaction), and curiosity about environment

Criteria for another specific pervasive developmental disorder or schizophrenia not met

AUTISTIC DISORDER (DSM CODE 299.00)

Six or more criteria from three lists

1) Qualitative impairment in social interaction, manifested by at least two of the following:

- marked impairment in use of multiple nonverbal behaviors
- failure to develop peer relationships appropriate to developmental level
- lack of spontaneous seeking to share enjoyment, interests, or achievements with others
- lack of social or emotional reciprocity

2) Qualitative impairments in communication, manifested by at least one of the following:

- delay in, or total lack of, development of spoken language, not accompanied by attempts to compensate through alternative modes of communication such as gesture or mime

- in individuals with adequate speech, marked impairment in ability to initiate or sustain conversation
- stereotyped and repetitive use of language or idiosyncratic language
- lack of varied, spontaneous make-believe play or social imitative play appropriate to developmental level

3) Restricted, repetitive, and stereotyped patterns of behavior, interests, and activities, manifested by at least one of the following:

- preoccupation with one or more stereotyped and restricted patterns of interest abnormal in either intensity or focus
- apparently inflexible adherence to specific, nonfunctional routines or rituals
- stereotyped and repetitive motor mannerisms
- persistent preoccupation with parts of objects

Delays or abnormal functioning in at least one of the following areas, with onset prior to age three:

- social interaction
- language as used in social communication
- symbolic or imaginative play

Symptoms not better explained by Rett's Disorder or Childhood Disintegrative Disorder

CHILDHOOD DISINTEGRATIVE DISORDER (DSM CODE 299.10)

Apparently normal development until at least age two, with age-appropriate verbal and nonverbal communication, social relationships, play, and adaptive behavior

Clinically significant loss of previously acquired skills before age ten in at least two of the following areas:

- expressive or receptive language
- social skills or adaptive behavior
- bowel or bladder control
- play
- motor skills

At least two of the following abnormalities of functioning:

- qualitative impairment in social interaction (impairment in nonverbal behaviors, failure to develop peer relationships, lack of social or emotional reciprocity)
- qualitative impairments in communication (delay or lack of spoken language, inability to initiate or sustain conversation, stereotyped and repetitive use of language, lack of varied make-believe play)
- restricted, repetitive, and stereotyped patterns of behavior, interests, and activities, including motor stereotypies and mannerisms

Symptoms not better explained by another specific pervasive developmental disorder or schizophrenia

(continued)

DSM-IV-TR Criteria for Pervasive Developmental Disorders — *continued*

Rett's Disorder (DSM code 299.80)

Apparently normal prenatal and perinatal development, apparently normal psychomotor development through first five months after birth, and normal head circumference at birth

Onset of all the following after the period of normal development:

- deceleration of head growth between five and forty-eight months of age
- loss of previously acquired purposeful hand skills between five and thirty months of age, with the subsequent development of stereotyped hand movements
- loss of social engagement early in course (although often social interaction develops later)
- poorly coordinated gait or trunk movements
- severely impaired expressive and receptive language development, with severe psychomotor retardation

Pervasive Developmental Disorder Not Otherwise Specified (DSM code 299.80)

ministered by the medical staff in the delivery room at one minute, five minutes, and, if there are complications, at ten and fifteen minutes after birth. It measures the effects of various complications of labor and birth and determines the need for resuscitation. The test assesses physical responsiveness, development, and overall state of health using a scale of five items rated from 0 to 2. A low Apgar score at birth can signal the potential for a developmental disability.

Measurement of head circumference is a useful tool for predicting whether an infant is likely to have a neurodevelopmental impairment such as microcephaly. A blood test screening can be done for phenylketonuria (PKU), congenital hypothyroidism, galactosemia, maple syrup urine disease, homocystinuria, and biotinidase deficiency. Early detection of these conditions and appropriate intervention may reduce the severity of the resulting disability.

An older child can be referred to a developmental pediatrician for assessment of a developmental disability if the child has not attained expected age-appropriate developmental milestones, exhibits atypical development or behavior, or regresses to a previous level of development. Correcting for prematurity in developmental testing is necessary. An instrument commonly used is the Denver Developmental Screening Test. The more severely affected a child is, the clearer is the diagnosis, as an individual's failure to meet developmental milestones may represent a short-term problem that resolves over time as the child "catches up." Even readily identifiable indicators of potential disability do not always result in expected delays.

Related issues such as feeding, elimination, and cardiorespiratory problems; pressure sores; and infection control are also considered as part of the diagnosis. Screening for lead poisoning or psychological testing may be recommended.

At whatever age the person is referred, a multidisciplinary evaluation attempts to establish a baseline of the present level of performance, including both skills and deficits. Activities of daily living (ADLs) such as bathing, eating, and dressing are widely used in assessing this population. Needing assistance with ADLs becomes an important criterion for determining eligibility for public and private disability benefits. An appraisal is made of those deficits that can be remedied and those that require accommodation. The predictive accuracy of the diagnosis improves with the individual's age.

Language development is another predictor variable. Individuals with developmental disabilities may have little or no apparent intent to communicate and may not understand that they can affect their environment through communication. Though developmental disabilities, by definition, are severe, it is possible that a child not previously identified could be detected by routine public school prekindergarten screening.

THE DEVELOPMENTALLY DISABLED POPULATION
The Administration on Developmental Disabilities of the United States Department of Health and Human Services estimates that there are four million Americans with developmental disabilities. Data specific to the incidence and prevalence of developmental disabilities are difficult to obtain because of the various etiologies present in this population. Conditions which often fall under the umbrella of developmental disabilities include mental retardation, autism, epilepsy, spinal cord injury, sensory impairment, traumatic brain injury, and cerebral palsy.

Though developmental disabilities can be associated with neurological damage, many of the conditions resulting in a developmental disability do not result in lowered intellectual functioning. Persons with developmental disabilities are estimated to comprise 1.7 to 1.8 percent of the population. This percentage has risen markedly since the mid-1970's for two reasons: increased life span for older individuals with disabilities and a greater number of children and adolescents surviving conditions that previously would have been fatal. The number of students diagnosed with autism has grown dramatically, from approximately 5,500 in the 1991-1992 school year to nearly 55,000 in 1998-1999.

Between 200,000 and 500,000 people in the United States over the age of sixty may have some form of developmental disability. Some of these individuals present special problems as they age. Those with epilepsy appear to be at greater risk for osteoporosis, while those with Down syndrome seem to begin the aging process earlier than others.

TREATMENT OPTIONS

The person with a developmental disability needs a combination of interdisciplinary services that are individually planned and coordinated and are of lifelong duration or extended duration throughout the life cycle. Because the causes and manifestations of developmental disabilities are so varied, each affected person is unique and requires an individualized approach to treatment and training. Each disability has specific needs that must be addressed and accommodations that must be provided.

When a defect has been identified prenatally, fetal treatment may be possible in order to prevent developmental disability. Some inborn errors of metabolism respond to vitamin therapy given to the mother. Bone marrow transplants and fetal surgery have also been performed.

Services for children from birth to two years of age provide special education as well as access to specialists in the areas of speech and physical therapy, psychology, medicine, and nursing. Assistive technology, physical adaptations, and case management are also offered. Medical management, monitoring, and consultation may be the responsibility of a developmental pediatrician.

Early intervention may be home-based, or the child can be enrolled in a center with a low child-to-teacher ratio. In either case, an Individual Family Service Plan (IFSP) is developed which includes a statement of the child's present level of development, the family's concerns, priorities, and resources, major outcomes to be achieved, and the specific early intervention services to be provided; identification of the coordinator responsible for implementing the plan; and procedures for transition to preschool.

Among the equipment used in treating the child may be positioning devices, wheelchairs, special car restraints, amplification devices, and ambulation aids. Some children may require gastronomy tubes, tracheostomy tubes, cardiorespiratory monitors, nasogastric tubes, ventilators, bladder catheters, splints, or casting. They may be placed on antiepileptic medication, antispasticity drugs, antireflux medications, antibiotics, respiratory medications, or medications to influence mood and behavior.

The Individuals with Disabilities Education Act mandates comprehensive educational services for children from three through twenty-one years of age. Services are offered in a continuum of settings that are individually determined. These settings may include hospitals, residential facilities, separate day schools, homes, and public schools. Children are ideally placed in what the law refers to as the least restrictive environment. An Individual Education Plan (IEP) replaces the IFSP.

ADLs are a prime focus of the educational program. The goal is to promote independence in such areas as eating, drinking, dressing, using the toilet, grooming, and tool use, which, in turn, fosters self-esteem.

Facilitating language acquisition and communicative intent are critical to any intervention program. Many developmentally disabled individuals will need numerous stimulus presentations before acquiring a rudimentary vocabulary. For those children who continue to be nonverbal, alternative communication systems such as sign language, use of pictures, and communication boards are introduced to enable communicative interaction. Computers with interface devices such as switches or touch-sensitive screens may be introduced to children with cerebral palsy.

Children with developmental disabilities exhibit challenging behaviors more often than typically developing children. After previously unrecognized medical conditions are ruled out as causes, positive behavioral supports at home and in school or traditional behavior management programs aim to produce comprehensive change in those challenging behaviors. Drugs that affect central nervous system function can also be helpful in treating disruptive behaviors.

Newer treatment approaches include neurodevelopmental therapy and sensory integration therapy. Neurodevelopmental therapy is widely used by physical and occupational therapists. It emphasizes sensorimotor experience to facilitate normal movement and posture in young developmentally disabled children with cerebral palsy or other, related disorders. Sensory integration is a normal process in which the child's central nervous system organizes sensory feedback from the body and the environment and makes appropriate adaptive responses. Sensory integration therapy uses controlled sensory input to promote those adaptive responses.

Adults with developmental disabilities are living longer than ever before. Most have the ability to live happy, productive lives in their communities. One component of treatment is transition planning. The Developmental Disabilities Act of 1984 emphasizes the importance of employment of persons with developmental disabilities and offers guidelines for providing supported employment services. Other transition issues include sexuality, social integration, recreation, and community residential options. Medical and physical care plans are necessary because long-term consequences of therapeutic interventions may occur. Movement disorders can result from the prolonged use of neuroleptic medications, while bone demineralization may be caused by the chronic use of certain anticonvulsants.

HISTORY OF TREATMENT

Services for people now referred to as having a developmental disability began in the United States in 1848 in Boston. The philosophy of early schools was to cure the "deviant." However, by 1877 a unidisciplinary medical model replaced the educational model and emphasized providing shelter and protection to this population. Later, the interest in Mendelian genetics led to a change in focus to protecting society from those whose disabilities were considered hereditary. By 1926, twenty-three states had laws requiring mandatory sterilization of the developmentally disabled on the books, and between 1925 and 1955 more than fifty thousand involuntary sterilizations were performed in the United States. In the 1950's, parents began to organize opportunities for individuals with developmental disabilities within public school systems.

Treatment evolved from the medical model to a multidisciplinary approach in which a physician consulted with other experts. Later, an interdisciplinary model emerged in which professionals from each discipline gathered to discuss their individual assessments and decide jointly on a plan of care. More recently, a transdisciplinary approach has been developed in which professionals, along with the individual concerned and his or her family, work together equally to identify needs, plan care, implement interventions, and evaluate progress.

Though the term "developmental disabilities" was not used in it, PL 94-142, the Education for All Handicapped Children Act of 1975, mandated a free, appropriate, public education for children who could be considered developmentally disabled. The Education of the Handicapped Act Amendments of 1986 extended early intervention services under the auspices of the public schools to identified children three to five years of age and those at risk for developmental disabilities. This legislation was reauthorized as the Individuals with Disabilities Education Act (IDEA) of 1990. Guarantees of equal protection under the law were extended to adults with developmental disabilities by the Americans with Disabilities Act (ADA) of 1990.

The years since 1970 have been a period of remarkable growth and achievement in services for individuals with developmental disabilities. Cultural, legal, medical, and technological advances have occurred. Services now include protection and advocacy systems under the auspices of state councils on developmental disabilities; university centers involved in education, research, and direct service; training in self-determination; and family supports. At the heart of this growth has been a transformation from a system of services provided primarily in institutions to one provided primarily in local communities. There has been a movement away from segregation and toward integration following what has been called the principle of normalization.

SOURCES FOR FURTHER STUDY

Batshaw, Mark L., ed. *Children with Disabilities.* 5th ed. Baltimore: Paul H. Brooks, 2002. A primer on developmental disabilities for educators, therapists, psychologists, social workers, health care professionals, and child advocates. Families can find useful information on medical and rehabilitation aspects of developmental disabilities.

Copeland, Mildred E., and Judy R. Kimmel. *Evaluation and Management of Infants and Young Children with Developmental Disabilities.* Baltimore: Paul H. Brookes, 1989. The authors present clear and concise descriptions of selected developmental disabilities, illustrated with photographs and sketches. Discussion of assessment and management is geared to teachers and parents.

Dowrick, Peter W. "University-Affiliated Programs and Other National Resources." In *Handbook of Developmental Disabilities*, edited by Lisa A. Kurtz, Peter W. Dowrick, Susan E. Levy, and Mark L. Batshaw. Gaithersburg,

Md.: Aspen, 1996. Provides a listing of referral sources by region and by state.

Roth, Shirley P., and Joyce S. Morse, eds. *A Life-Span Approach to Nursing Care for Individuals with Developmental Disabilities.* Baltimore: Paul H. Brookes, 1994. Though written for nurses, this book gives the general reader a foundation of information regarding developmental disabilities from a quality-of-life perspective.

Gabrielle Kowalski

SEE ALSO: Autism; Mental Retardation.

DIAGNOSIS

TYPE OF PSYCHOLOGY: All
FIELDS OF STUDY: All

Diagnosis is a process whereby an assessor evaluates symptoms and signs of illness or abnormality in order to be able to determine the type of problem present. This can be done using interviews, observation, and formal testing instruments or procedures.

KEY CONCEPTS
- assessment
- associated features
- course
- criteria
- differential diagnosis
- interviewing
- screening
- signs
- symptoms

The word "diagnosis" is derived from two Greek roots: *dia*, which means "to distinguish," and *gnosis*, which means "knowledge." It is most often understood to be a noun, but from the perspective of a psychologist or a person assessing an afflicted individual, it is seen as a process whereby one understands the condition of the person affected. It is also important to remember that diagnosis is not a one-time event but is ongoing. For example, diagnoses may shift. Changes can be noted in terms of signs (the observable indications of mental health problems) and symptoms (the problems reported by clients indicating their discomfort, notice of changes, or abnormality in their way of being). In some ways, diagnosis has no discrete end but consists of different observation points in time when the progress of a disorder is evaluated.

SCREENING

The goal of diagnosis is to arrive at information that can be communicated and used to aid in the treatment of the person with the mental or physical health problem. In the United States, mental health diagnoses are typically based on the framework presented in the American Psychiatric Association's *Diagnostic and Statistical Manual of Mental Disorders* (DSM), which is updated periodically. In order to be diagnosed with a particular mental disorder, individuals go through a systematic evaluation to determine whether they satisfy the diagnostic criteria, the conditions necessary to qualify for a disorder, as described in the DSM.

Often, this process begins when individuals or their relatives notice symptoms and seek the consultation of a professional. At that time, the professional will begin a series of systematic inquiries, ruling possible conditions in and out of consideration, in order to determine how best to proceed with further diagnostic work. In some cases, a preliminary step called screening may be undertaken. Screening is a relatively brief procedure in which the signs and symptoms that have the highest association with specific mental health conditions are asked about in order to determine whether a more thorough evaluation is necessary.

Typically, screening results in a person being placed into one of two categories: possibly having the condition of concern or mostly likely not having the condition. Those individuals in the former category receive more thorough evaluations. Those who are judged as unlikely to have the condition do not receive more thorough evaluations immediately but instead may be invited to continue their own observations of symptoms or to begin another path of diagnostic inquiry.

For those performing the screening, the primary goal is to identify those individuals who may have the problem. It is also important, however, not to rule out individuals for further evaluation who might actually have the condition but do not appear to do so during the screening. In technical terms, the first group is known as true positives: individuals who are screened as likely to have the condition and who actually have it. The second group is known as false negatives: individuals who are screened as not having the condition but actually do have it.

Screening tests increase in their usefulness if they are not overly sensitive and do not produce too many false positives: people who screen positive but who actually do not have the condition. It is important to minimize false positives because some diagnostic procedures, such as magnetic resonance imaging (MRI), are expensive. Additionally, some diagnostic procedures can be invasive, such as injection dye procedures used to observe different organ systems in action. Minimizing false positives in screening saves money for health care providers and, more important, saves potential pain, suffering, and anxiety for individuals.

Finally, screening also increases in usefulness when it can effectively identify true negatives: individuals who are screened as not having the problem and who, in fact, do not. The sooner these individuals are identified, the more quickly they can be considered for other diagnostic possibilities.

ASSESSMENT

In general, screening is important because it is often brief and can be applied to a large number of people with little effort, saving expensive time on evaluation and yet efficiently identifying individuals most likely to have a formal mental health condition. It is much less costly than the next step in a diagnostic workup after being screened as positive: the process of assessment, a lengthier process in which detailed information is gathered in a systematic way about the patient's probable condition. Assessment procedures may include formal diagnostic interviewing, in which the psychologist or clinician asks a step-by-step series of questions to get a clear picture of what the symptoms are and how they developed. Interviewing can be used to assess not only the individual affected but also family members or significant others, as sometimes these individuals have valuable information related to the history or development of the symptoms. These informants can also be helpful if the individual is not able or willing to speak about or to describe the condition.

Assessment procedures may also include the use of questionnaires, surveys, or checklists about symptoms. They may include observation by the psychologist in interpersonal interactions or under certain other conditions. They may also include formal medical tests, such as blood tests, urine toxicology, and tests of psychomotor performance.

Overall, assessment procedures seek to reveal the course of the symptoms present or how they have changed over time. Assessment also seeks to show how the most prominent symptoms relate to one another and to less prominent symptoms. This is particularly important to a process called differential diagnosis, in which disorders that may appear alike in some features are diagnostically separated from one another in order to determine if one or more conditions are present.

If, in the process of assessment, it is found that the number, severity, and duration of the individual's symptoms and signs meet the diagnostic criteria, or standards of required evidence to warrant a diagnosis, then a diagnosis is rendered. If the signs and symptoms are all manifest but fall short of being present in the right number, severity, or duration, then the condition might be thought of as subclinical. This would mean that although the symptoms do not meet the formal criteria necessary to warrant a diagnosis, they are problematic and may still require some clinical observation and attention.

Finally, sometimes a client may have one disorder that is clearly present but also has what might be called leftover symptoms that do not seem to fit. In some cases, these symptoms may be what are known as associated features, or symptoms associated with disorders but not part of the disorder in a formal diagnostic way. For example, many people who suffer from agoraphobia also experience symptoms of depression. In some cases, these individuals also qualify for a diagnosis of depression. In other cases, they are experiencing depressed mood as a consequence of having agoraphobia, and the depression is an associated feature. Once these aspects of a diagnosis are understood, the information can be put to use.

IMPORTANCE

Diagnoses are important because of the information that they convey. They are important in facilitating effective communication among professionals as well as for effective treatment planning. The diagnostic terminology of the DSM allows professionals to communicate clearly with one another about their clients' conditions. This communication helps to direct clients to the proper treatment and also ensures continuity of care when clients switch treatment providers. For example, a client who is traveling or is outside his or her regular locale may need assistance and seek out another health care provider. The new provider would be greatly aided in helping the client by communication with the regular provider about the individual and his or her condition. A proper assignment could then be reached to create a useful treatment strategy.

On another level, standard diagnoses are useful because they also allow for important communication between clinicians and researchers in psychology. This is most true when new symptoms are emerging and the need arises for developing new treatment strategies. When the mental health community uses the same language about signs and symptoms in the study of specific conditions, medical and psychological knowledge can advance much more efficiently.

More practically, diagnostic information is important to treatment because diagnostic information is needed to justify treatment financially. When a client meets formal diagnostic criteria for a disorder, the health care provider can administer services and justify the treatment to insurance agencies and others interested in the financial management of mental health problems. Diagnoses may also help such agencies to discover trends in which treatments work and where disorders tend to be developing (the focus of the field of epidemiology) or to recognize gaps in services, such as when people with certain disorders suddenly disappear from the mental health care system.

Even more important, however, standard diagnoses and thorough diagnostic procedures allow for good communication among professionals, their clients, and the families of those affected by mental illness. Communicating diagnostic information effectively to the client and family members or significant others is likely to help with the management of the problem. The better that all involved understand the symptoms and prognosis (expectations for the effects of the condition on future functioning), the more likely everyone is to assist with treatment compliance. Further, it can be very helpful to families to learn that their loved ones have formal diagnoses. Mental health conditions can create chaos and misunderstanding, and improvements in relationships may occur if families and significant others are able to place problematic symptoms in perspective. Rather than attributing symptomatic behavior to personal irresponsibility or problems of character, family members and friends can see the symptoms as reflecting the illness. Although this understanding does not make everything perfect, it may help facilitate a more effective problem-solving strategy for the affected person and his or her significant others.

CONTEXT

Diagnosis is a process most often associated with a visit to a primary care physician. However, professionals of many types gather diagnostic information and render diagnoses. Psychiatrists and psychologists predominate in the area of mental health diagnoses, but social workers, educational counselors, substance abuse counselors, criminal justice workers, social service professionals, and those who work with the developmentally disabled also gather mental health diagnostic information and use it in their work.

Over time, the process of assessment has been separated from the actual diagnostic decision, so that assistants and helpers may be the ones gathering and organizing the symptom-related information in order to present it to the expert diagnostician who has the authority to render the diagnosis. This shift has occurred as a matter of financial necessity in many cases, as it is more expensive to use experts for time-intensive information gathering than it is to use such assistants. Increasing effort has also been focused on developing more accurate diagnostic screening and assessment instruments to the same end. If time can be saved on assessment by using screening, so that only very likely cases receive full symptom assessment, then valuable medical resources will be saved. Further, if paper-and-pencil or other diagnostic procedures can be used to better describe symptoms in a standardized manner, then even the time of diagnostic assistants can be saved.

On one hand, such advances may allow more people to be treated in an efficient manner. On the other hand, some complain that people can fall through the cracks and be missed on a screening, and consequently continue to suffer. This situation may be particularly likely for individuals who are not often included in the research upon which the screening instruments are designed, such as women and minorities. Similarly, others suggest that these processes put too much paper between the client and the health care provider, creating barriers and weakening therapeutic relationships.

In considering cultural practices and understandings of the doctor-patient relationship, this effect is even more important, as many cultural groups see the social nature of this relationship as a critical piece of the treatment interaction. While efficiency and saving money are important, it must be recognized that those goals are culturally bound and are choices that are being made. They are not the only way for the art and science of diagnosis to proceed.

It is also important for diagnosticians to recognize cultural differences in terms of the way in which symptoms are experienced, expressed, and understood. For some, mental health disorders may be seen as expressions of underlying spiritual problems; for others, they may be seen as disharmonies among elements in the universe or environment; and for others, they may be seen as extensions of physical problems. Each of these perspectives is a valid way of understanding such conditions, and it is only good training that includes attention to cultural variation in diagnostic procedures and practice that will allow diagnosticians to function effectively.

It should also be noted that culture is not limited to a client's racial background or ethnicity; it also varies by characteristics such as gender, age, sexual orientation, socioeconomic status, and locale. Increasingly, diagnosticians are being forced to grapple with such diversity so as to improve diagnostic procedures and client care. Such characteristics are important to diagnosis not only because of differences in perspectives on illness but also because of differences in the prevalence of illnesses in various groups. This distinction is particularly important when considering medical conditions that might be associated with psychological disorders. In some cases, medical problems may mimic psychiatric disorders; in other cases, they may mask, or cover up, such disorders. Because some disorders are more common in certain populations—such as among women, people of color, and elders—knowledge of such prevalence is important to the process of differential diagnosis.

Culture is also an important consideration in diagnosis because the information gathered is transmitted socially. Knowledge of diagnoses is exchanged among professionals, researchers, clients, and their families. Diagnoses have social meaning and can result in those carrying the diagnosis being stigmatized. As crucial differences exist in the degree of stigmatization in different cultures, the delivery of such important mental health information deserves thoughtful consideration, good planning, and follow-up to ensure that all parties involved are properly informed.

SOURCES FOR FURTHER STUDY

American Psychiatric Association. *Diagnostic and Statistical Manual of Mental Disorders: DSM-IV-TR.* Rev. 4th ed. Washington, D.C.: Author, 2000. The standard text outlining the major mental health disorders diagnosed in the United States.

Beutler, Larry E., and Mary L. Malik. *Rethinking the DSM: A Psychological Perspective.* Washington, D.C.: American Psychological Association, 2002. Offers some critiques of the DSM, the dominant diagnostic framework used in the United States.

Castillo, Richard J. *Culture and Mental Illness: A Client-Centered Approach.* Pacific Grove, Calif.: Brooks/Cole, 1997. Discusses how cultural issues fit into the diagnostic process and the understanding of mental health and illness.

Seligman, Linda. *Diagnosis and Treatment Planning in Counseling.* 2d ed. New York: Plenum Press, 1996. Connections between diagnosis and treatment planning are highlighted in this text, with case examples for illustration.

Shea, Shawn Christopher. *Psychiatric Interviewing: The Art of Understanding—A Practical Guide for Psychiatrists, Psychologists, Counselors, Social Workers, and Other Mental Health Professionals.* 2d ed. Philadelphia: W. B. Saunders, 1998. The skills of interviewing as a means of establishing a therapeutic relationship and the basis for forming diagnostic impressions are reviewed from a perspective that is useful for a variety of mental health practitioners. Also allows nonprofessionals to see how interviewing is structured and leads to diagnoses.

Simeonsson, Rune J., and Susan L. Rosenthal, eds. *Psychological and Developmental Assessment: Children with Disabilities and Chronic Conditions.* New

York: Guilford Press, 2001. This text focuses on issues important to the diagnosis of mental health and other behavioral disorders in children.

Trzepacz, Paula T., and Robert W. Baker. *Psychiatric Mental Status Examination.* New York: Oxford University Press, 1993. The mental status examination is one of the foundations of any psychiatric diagnosis. This book describes these procedures for assessing the appearance, activity level, mood, speech, and other behavioral characteristics of individuals under evaluation.

Nancy A. Piotrowski

See also: Madness: Historical Concepts; Psychopathology; Survey Research: Questionnaires and Interviews.

Domestic Violence

Type of psychology: Psychopathology
Fields of study: Adulthood; aggression

Domestic violence refers to all forms of abuse which occur within families, including child abuse, elder abuse, and spouse abuse. The term came into common usage in the 1970's to emphasize wife abuse. Domestic violence is explained by several psychologically based theories which in turn propose different solutions.

Key concepts
- battered woman syndrome
- cycle of violence
- domestic violence
- family systems theory
- feminist psychological theory
- learning theory
- post-traumatic stress disorder
- psychoanalytic theory
- systems theory
- wife abuse

Domestic violence is difficult to measure because there are no agreed-upon standards as to what it is. In addition, most domestic violence occurs in private, and victims are reluctant to report it because of shame and fear of reprisal. Its scope is also difficult to determine, and society's reluctance to acknowledge it results in only estimated numbers of rapes, robberies, and assaults committed by family members and other relatives, such as spouses, former spouses, children, parents, boyfriends, and girlfriends.

In the 1970's, publicity about domestic violence, and more specifically wife abuse, made the public aware that many women did not live in peace and security in their own homes. Through the usage of the terms "abuse," "woman abuse," "battering," "partner abuse," "spouse abuse," "intimate violence," "family violence" and "relationship violence," feminists made the public aware of the problem. As a result of the publicity, women were identified as the most likely victims of domestic violence.

The selection of a name for the behavior will have implications for treatment choices. In addition, the term "domestic violence" removes the issue from a societal perspective, which condones, reinforces, and perpetuates the problem. Domestic violence minimizes the role of gender and places the relationship in the dominant spot. As a result, the choice of a name offers varying perspectives, which differentially view the persons involved, the nature of the problem, and possible solutions.

Abused women in a domestic violence situation are confronted with several types of abuse, namely economic abuse, physical abuse, psychological/

emotional abuse, and sexual abuse. Economic abuse results when the financial resources to which a woman is legally entitled are not accessible to her. Examples of economic abuse include being prevented from seeking employment even if qualified to do so, as well as being denied access to needed education, which would aid the woman in securing better employment.

Physical abuse is the major way that abusive men control the behavior of women. Abused women have likened psychological or emotional abuse to brainwashing. Little research has been done on this type of abuse because it is difficult to record. The abused woman is terrorized, isolated, and undermined by her abuser. Psychological or emotional abuse allows men to avoid the legal effects of physical abuse, because they can frighten women without touching them. Five common emotional abuse methods include isolation, humiliation and degradation, "crazy-making" behavior, threats to harm the woman or those she loves, and suicidal and homicidal threats.

Sexual violence was reported by 33 percent to 59 percent of the battered women in a study by Angela Browne published in 1987. Since 1992, it has been legal throughout the United States for a woman to charge her husband with rape. Historically, rape was thought of as intercourse forced on someone other than the wife of the accused. As a result, a woman could not legally accuse her husband of rape.

Possible Causes

Four theories, each of which has a psychological basis, attempt to explain wife abuse. Each of the theories has a unique perspective regarding the causes of wife abuse. The four theories are family systems theory, feminist psychological theory, learning theory, and psychoanalytic theory.

The first theory, family systems theory, includes the application of systems theory to all current family therapy approaches. Systems theory stresses mutual influences and reciprocal relationships between the individual members and the whole, as well as vice versa. In family systems theory, abuse is seen as a feature of the relationship between the abused wife and her husband. Underlying the abusive behavior, both the abused wife and her husband have a frail sense of self. When they marry or establish a relationship, a battering routine or system unfolds. Several factors lead the man to have a drive for power and control over the woman. These factors include social conditions, the need for control, intimacy fears, and lack of awareness of his own conflicts regarding dependency. The abused woman, in turn, has a limited range of coping behaviors, dependency conflicts, a history of childhood family violence, and other psychosocial traits which are similar to those of the man. Change is prevented from occurring, and the dysfunctional interpersonal behavior patterns continue as a result of the unwritten expectations that control these behaviors. Change is blocked by the use of violent behavior.

The second theory, feminist psychological theory, is based on the work of American feminist psychologist Lenore Walker. She believes that the behaviors of abused women are coping behaviors developed as a result of living in a brutal environment.

Walker first theorized the concept of learned helplessness as used in relation to abused women. The abused woman can do nothing to stop the violence. The woman's chief concern is survival. However, survival comes with consequences. Several of the consequences include passively giving in to her abuser, becoming an observer of her own abuse through the process of disassociation, and waiting for days to seek medical care because she may distort the reality of the abuse. In addition, women's helplessness is reinforced by society in two ways. First, women learn to respond passively to abuse through gender-role socialization. Second, women's ability to control their lives is thwarted through the interrelated effects of sexism, discrimination, and poverty.

Walker has described a cycle of violence that unfolds in the individual relationship. The woman yields to the batterer's demands in the first stage in order to keep small episodes from increasing. However, over time these small episodes increase and accumulate. The woman also begins to withdraw from family and friends because she does not want them to know what is going on as the family tension increases. As time passes, the woman withdraws from the batterer as well, because she realizes that her efforts to prevent further development of the violence are futile. The batterer, in turn, becomes more and more angry because he fears that he is losing control of his wife. He then explodes, in the second stage. The third stage quickly follows; The batterer is characterized as being placid, and there is a pause in the abusive behaviors. The man promises the woman that he will change, brings her gifts, and is extremely regretful. He changes back into the man she originally loved and is at his most defenseless state.

In order to explain the behaviors of women who have been frequently abused, Walker developed the theory of the battered woman syndrome, which she sees as a variant of post-traumatic stress disorder (PTSD). The key behaviors of anxiety, cognitive distortion, and depression can on one hand help a woman to survive her abuse. On the other hand, they can interfere with her ability to change her life situation by using appropriate methods.

The third theory is learning theory, incorporating both social learning theory and cognitive behavioral therapy. Social learning theorists stress the occurrence of modeling and the reinforcements received for abusive behavior. Cognitive behavioral theorists stress the internalization of beliefs that support abusive behavior. Boys may internalize the belief that they should be in charge by learning abusive behaviors from male role models, ranging from their fathers to media stars. Girls internalize the belief that they are helpless and weak by learning passively from their role models. Later adult behaviors are hindered by the earlier learned behaviors and internalized messages.

The fourth theory, psychoanalytic theory, focuses on intrapersonal pathology. This theory argues that the early life experiences of abused women and abusive men shape the particular pathological personality. The battered woman develops beliefs and behaviors that are dysfunctional in adulthood, although they are based in childhood experiences with cruel persons. The women do not resist the abuse. They submit to the abuse because they fear offending the stronger male and also because they think of themselves as deserving abuse. The women choose abusive men and may even touch off the abusive behavior because of their strong feelings of worthlessness. Passive-aggressive, psychopathic, obsessive-compulsive, paranoid, and sadistic are some of the labels given to violent men who have experienced severe and traumatic childhood abuse episodes themselves. Men learn that violence gets them what they want and also allows them to feel good about themselves, in spite of their childhood experiences of abuse both as victims and as observers.

DIAGNOSING DOMESTIC VIOLENCE

Six factors have been identified as increasing a woman's chances of being in an abusive relationship: age, alcohol use, childhood experience with violence, race, relationship status, and socioeconomic factors.

A person's risk of being abused or being an abuser increases among adolescents. Research has discovered high levels of abuse among dating couples. However, the rate of violence among dating couples falls below that of couples who are married or cohabitating if controlled for age.

Clinical samples in which women are asked to describe their husbands' drinking patterns have provided the basis for the opinion that men beat their wives when they are drunk. Researchers have found that from 35 percent to 93 percent of abusers are problem drinkers. Better controlled studies have found that in only 25 percent of the cases was either partner drinking at the time of the abuse.

Individuals are more likely to be an abused woman or an abusive man if they were abused as a child. It is less clear that a relationship exists between witnessing wife abuse as a child and experiencing it as an adult. Researchers have found that men are more likely to become adult abusers if they observed domestic violence as boys. The data are inconclusive regarding a woman's chance of being abused if she observes domestic violence as a child. Men who observed domestic violence between their parents are three times more likely to abuse their wives. Sons of the most violent parents have a rate of wife abuse 1,000 percent greater than sons of nonviolent parents.

African American and Latino families have above-average rates of wife abuse. Abuse rates for African Americans are four times the rate of white Americans and twice the rate of other minorities. There are twice as many Latina women abused as non-Latina white women. Socioeconomic factors can explain these differences. According to data from a 1980 survey, African Americans earning $6,000 to $11,999 annually (approximately 40 percent of all African American respondents) had higher rates of wife abuse than comparably earning white Americans, while they had lower rates than white Americans in all other socioeconomic levels. When age, economic deprivation, and urban residence are controlled, then the differences between Latina and non-Latina white Americans vanish.

Legally married couples have half the amount of violence as cohabiting couples. It is felt that cohabiting couples may allow conflict to escalate because they are less invested in the relationship, more likely to struggle over autonomy and control issues, and more isolated from their social networks.

Domestic violence is more common in families with fewer economic resources, though it is found in all socioeconomic levels. Higher rates of wife abuse have been found in families in which the man works in a blue-collar job or is unemployed or underemployed and the family lives at the poverty level.

THE ABUSED POPULATION

Male partners severely assault more than 1.5 million married and cohabitating women each year. Of women treated in hospital emergency rooms, 22 percent to 35 percent are there because of symptoms related to abuse. Approximately 20 percent to 25 percent of all women are abused at least once by a male partner. Victims of boyfriends tend to be young (sixteen to twenty-four years old), while victims of current or former spouses are likely to be older (twenty to thirty-four years old). Women in families with incomes over $50,000 are four times less likely to be abused than are women in families with annual incomes of less than $20,000.

Marital counseling is sometimes prescribed to identify dysfunctional patterns. (PhotoDisc)

TREATMENT OPTIONS

The four theories of domestic abuse also provide several treatment options for the psychologist. Family systems theory prescribes marital counseling to bring about change in the marital system and to identify dysfunctional patterns. Partners are each responsible for changing the way they relate to each other and for the specific behaviors that contribute to the violence.

Walker describes three levels of intervention in terms of feminist psychological theory. Primary prevention changes the social conditions that directly and indirectly contribute to the abuse of women. Examples would include eliminating rigid gender-role socialization and reducing levels of violence in society. Secondary intervention encourages women to take control of their lives and to break the cycle of violence. Examples include crisis hot lines as well as financial and legal assistance. A shelter where the women will slowly regain their ability to make decisions for themselves and where they will be safe is an example of tertiary intervention. At this level, women have been totally victimized and are unable to act on their own.

Learning theory stresses that the partners be given opportunities to learn and be rewarded for a new range of actions and underlying beliefs. It is felt that intervention should teach the partners how they have learned and been rewarded for their present behaviors. As a result, the intervention moves beyond a pathological framework. Other approaches, mainly from a cognitive-behavioral perspective, strive to change dysfunctional thoughts, teach new behaviors, and eliminate the abuse. This approach works with couples and with abusive men in a group.

Psychoanalytic theory stresses long-term, corrective, individual psychotherapy. The end result of the therapy would be to help the abused woman to break the cycle of violence. She would learn to avoid choosing men who re-create her familiar and unhappy childhood by their violent behavior.

HISTORY OF TREATMENT

Domination of women by men has a long history. Early Roman law gave men absolute power over their wives. However, it is not clear if they had the power to put their wives to death. Physical force was their chief means of control. As the Roman Empire declined, men's right to control women continued to be supported by church doctrine.

The "rule of thumb" was born in English common law, which stated that men had the right to beat their wives as long as the weapon they used was "a rod no bigger than their thumb." Early U.S. judicial decisions supported the right of men to beat their wives. The government's hands-off policy and the legal sanction to a husband's right to control the behavior of his wife were the two major impacts of the court rulings. The first wave of feminists in the nineteenth century briefly exposed the existence of wife abuse and made some efforts to criminalize it. This state of affairs continued until the 1970's, when the second wave of feminism exposed the public to the abuse that many women experienced in their own homes. The battered women's movement identified two key concerns: first, to create a society that no longer accepted domestic violence and second, to provide safe, supportive shelter for all women who were abused.

SOURCES FOR FURTHER STUDY

Ammerman, Robert T., and Michel Hersen, eds. *Assessment of Family Violence: A Clinical and Legal Sourcebook.* 2d ed. New York: John Wiley & Sons, 1999. Leading figures in the field of family violence review a decade of research and examine strategies and measures relevant to assessment of the problem. They also comment on treatment planning and legal requirements. Other areas of concern include epidemological models, intervention planning, and standards of practice.

Browne, Angela. *When Battered Women Kill.* New York: Free Press, 1987. A study based on interviews with 250 physically abused women, 42 of whom had killed their batterers, shows how "romantic idealism" drives the early stages of the abusive relationship. Obsessive "love" continues along with the abuser's need to control the woman physically. Coping and survival strategies of the battered women are presented.

Buttell, Frederick P. "Moral Development Among Court-Ordered Batterers: Evaluating the Impact of Treatment." *Research on Social Work Practice* 11, no. 1 (2001): 93-107. Court-ordered participants in a cognitive-behavioral group treatment program for batterers were studied regarding changing their levels of moral reasoning. The control group consisted of thirty-two adult men with an average age of thirty-two years, 84 percent of whom African American, who were ordered into a standard group treatment program. The major finding was that the current treatment program was ineffectual in changing batterers' moral reasoning.

Goetting, Ann. *Getting Out: Life Stories of Women Who Left Abusive Men.* New York: Columbia University Press, 1999. Sixteen women shared their stories with the author, who organized them into seven categories, including women of privileged backgrounds, children, two-timing batterers, family and friends to the rescue, shelter life, positive workings of the system, and the impacts of loss and death. A very readable book.

Gondolf, Edward W., and Robert J. White. "Batterer Program Participants Who Repeatedly Reassault: Psychopathic Tendencies and Other Disorders." *Journal of Interpersonal Violence* 16, no. 4 (2001): 361-380. Psychopathic tendencies were studied in 580 men from four batterers' programs. The men had assaulted their partners many times in spite of arrests for domestic violence and being referred to batterer counseling programs. The major conclusion was that men who had abused their partners many times were no more likely to have a psychopathic disorder than other men.

Jones, Loring, Margaret Hughes, and Ulrike Unterstaller. "Post-traumatic Stress Disorder (PTSD) in Victims of Domestic Violence: A Review of the Research." *Trauma Violence and Abuse* 2, no. 2 (2001): 99-119. An analysis of data from the literature focusing on the interplay between post-traumatic stress disorder (PTSD) and being a battered woman. The authors identified three major objectives of the study as well as seven major findings, chief of which is that PTSD symptoms are consistent with the symptoms of battered women.

Krishman, Satya P., Judith C. Hilbert, and Dawn Van Leeuwen. "Domestic Violence and Help-Seeking Behaviors Among Rural Women: Results from a Shelter-Based Study." *Family and Community Health* 24, no. 1 (2001): 28-38. A study conducted on a sample of predominantly Latino women living in rural communities that focused on their help-seeking behaviors, including those at a rural domestic violence shelter. One major finding was that a high percentage of the Latino subjects had thought about or attempted suicide.

Pellauer, Mary. "Lutheran Theology Facing Sexual and Domestic Violence." *Journal of Religion and Abuse* 2, no. 2 (2000): 3-48. The author argues that Martin Luther was theologically ambivalent on the issues of wife battering and child abuse and seemed to be confused between the ideas of sexuality and sexual violence. She ends her essay with a review of the themes for a Lutheran response to domestic violence, as well as making several recommendations for action based on further analysis of Luther's writings and teachings.

Smith, Darcy M., and Joseph Donnelly. "Adolescent Dating Violence: A Multisystemic Approach of Enhancing Awareness in Educators, Parents, and Society." *Journal of Prevention and Intervention in the Community* 21, no. 1 (2001): 53-64. Mental health professionals have hesitated to report that adolescents are the fastest growing at-risk segment of the population. One in eight high school students and one in five college students will be involved in abusive relationships. In 1993, six hundred teenage girls were murdered by their boyfriends. Prevention and treatment strategies are also presented.

Walker, Lenore E. *The Battered Woman Syndrome.* 2d ed. New York: Springer, 1999. A readable volume in which the author reports the results of a research project to identify key psychological and sociological factors that make up the battered woman syndrome. In addition, she tested eight specific theories about battered women and also gathered relevant data about battered women.

Carol A. Heintzelman

SEE ALSO: Aggression.

Dreams

TYPE OF PSYCHOLOGY: Cognition; consciousness
FIELDS OF STUDY: Classic analytic themes and issues; cognitive processes; sleep; thought

Dreams are the series of images, thoughts, and feelings that occur in the mind of the sleeping person. Dreams are usually confused with waking reality while they are occurring. Distinctive neurological phenomena are associated with the production of dreams, and diverse psychological experiences are conveyed in dreaming.

KEY CONCEPTS

- D-sleep
- latent content
- manifest content
- NREM sleep
- REM sleep
- S-sleep
- sleep mentation

Humans spend roughly one-third of their lives sleeping, and laboratory research indicates that at least a third of the sleep period is filled with dreaming. Thus, if a person lives seventy-five years, he or she will spend more than eight of those years dreaming. People throughout the millennia have pondered the meaning of those years of dreaming, and their answers have ranged from useless fictions to psychological insights.

Some of the earliest known writings were about dreams. The *Epic of Gilgamesh*, written around 3500 B.C.E., contains the first recorded dream interpretation. An Egyptian document dating to the Twelfth Dynasty (1991-1786 B.C.E.) called the Chester Beatty Papyrus (after its discoverer) presented a system for interpreting dreams. The biblical book of Genesis, attributed to Moses, who is claimed to have lived between 1446 and 1406 B.C.E., records a dream of Abimelech (a contemporary of Abraham and Sarah) from a period that appears to antedate the Twelfth Dynasty. Other classics of antiquity, such as the *Iliad* and *Odyssey* of Homer (c. 725 B.C.E.), the *Republic* of Plato (427-347 B.C.E.), and *On the Senses and Their Objects*, written by Aristotle (384-322 B.C.E.), grappled with discerning the meaning of dreams. Artemidorus Daldianus (c. second century C.E.) provided a comprehensive summary of ancient thinking on dreams in his famous book, *Oneirocritica* (the interpretation of dreams).

To understand dreaming, it must be distinguished from related phenomena. If the person is fully awake and perceives episodes departing from natural reality, the person is said to have experienced a vision. Experiencing an unintended perceptual distortion is more properly called a hallucination. A daydream is a purposeful distortion of reality. In the twilight realm of dreamlike imagery occurring just before falling asleep or just before becoming fully awake, hypnagogic or hypnopompic reverie, respectively, are said to occur. Dreams occur only in the third state of consciousness—being fully asleep. Another distinction is needed to differentiate between the two types of psychological phenomena that occur when a person is in this third realm of consciousness. Dreams have the attributes of imagery, temporality (time sequence), confusion with reality, and plot (an episode played out). Those subjective experiences that occur during sleep and are lacking in these attributes can be labeled as sleep mentation.

TYPES OF DREAMS

Just as there are different types of dreamlike experiences, there are different kinds of dreams. While there will be shortcomings in any effort toward classifying dreams, some approximate distinctions can be made in regard to sleep stage, affect (feelings and emotions), reality orientation, and dream origin.

When people fall asleep, brain activity changes throughout the night in cycles of approximately ninety minutes. Research with the electroencephalograph (which records electrical activity) has demonstrated a sequence of four stages of sleep occurring in these cycles. The first two stages are called D-sleep (desynchronized EEG), which constitutes essential psychological rest—consolidation of memories and processing of thoughts and emotions. The other two stages, which constitute S-sleep (synchronized EEG), are necessary for recuperation from the day's physical activity—physical rest. S-sleep usually disappears during the second half of a night's sleep. Dreaming occurs in both S-sleep and D-sleep but is much more likely to occur in D-sleep.

A further distinction in the physiology of sleep is pertinent to the type of dreaming activity likely to occur. During stage one sleep there are often accompanying rapid eye movements (REM) that are not found in other stages of sleep. Researchers often distinguish between REM sleep, where these ocular movements occur, and non-REM (NREM) sleep, in which there is an absence of these eye movements. When people are aroused from REM sleep, they report dreams a majority of the time—roughly 80 percent—as opposed to a minority of the time—perhaps 20 percent—with NREM sleep. Furthermore, REM dreams tend to have more emotion, greater vividness, more of a plot, a greater fantastical quality, and episodes that are more likely to be recalled and with greater clarity.

The prevalence of affect in dreams is linked with people's styles of daydreaming. Those whose daydreams are of a positive, uplifting quality tend to experience the greatest amount of pleasant emotionality in their dreams. People whose daydreams reflect a lot of anxiety, guilt, and negative themes experience more unpleasant dreams. While most dreams are generally unemotional in content, when there are affective overtones, negative emotions predominate about two-thirds of the time. Unpleasant dreams can be categorized into three types. Common nightmares occur in REM sleep and are caused by many factors, such as unpleasant circumstances in life, daily stresses, or traumatic experiences. Common themes are being chased, falling, or reliving an aversive event. Night terrors are most likely to occur in stage four sleep and are characterized by sudden wakening, terror-stricken reactions, and disorientation that can last several minutes. Night terrors are rarely recollected. An extreme life-threatening event can lead to post-traumatic stress disorder (PTSD). Recurring PTSD nightmares, unlike other nightmares and night terrors, are repetitive nightmares in which the sufferer continues to relive the traumatic event. Furthermore, PTSD nightmares can occur in any stage of sleep.

DREAMS AND REALITY

The reality level of dreams varies in terms of time orientation and level of consciousness. Regarding time orientation, dreams earlier in the night contain more themes dealing with the distant past—such as childhood for an adult—while dreams closer toward waking up tend to be richer in content and have more present themes—such as a current concern. The future is emphasized in oneironmancy, the belief that dreams are prophetic and can warn the dreamer of events to come.

The unconscious mind contains material that is rarely accessible or completely inaccessible to awareness. The personal unconscious may resurrect dream images of experiences that a person normally cannot voluntarily recall. For example, a woman may dream about kindergarten classmates about whom she could not remember anything while awake. The psychologist Carl Jung proposed that dreams could sometimes include material from the collective unconscious—a repository of shared human memories. Thus, a dream in which evil is represented by a snake may reflect a universal human inclination to regard snakes as dangerous.

When waking reality, rather than unconscious thoughts, intrude upon dreaming, lucid dreams occur. Lucid dreams are characterized by the dreamer's awareness in the dream that he or she is dreaming. Stephen LaBerge's research has revealed that lucid dreams occur only in REM sleep and that people can be trained to experience lucidity, whereby they can exercise some degree of control over the content of their dreams.

ORIGINS AND SIGNIFICANCE

Theories about the origins of dreams can be divided into two main categories: naturalistic and supernaturalistic. Proponents of naturalistic theories of dreaming believe that dreams result from either physiological activities or psychological processes. Aristotle was one of the first people to offer a physiological explanation for dreams. His basic thesis was that dreams are the afterimages of sensory experiences. A modern physiological approach to dreaming was put forth in the 1970's by J. Allan Hobson and Robert McCarley. According to their activation-synthesis theory, emotional and visual areas of the brain are activated during REM sleep, and the newly alerted frontal lobe tries to make sense of this information plus any other sensory or physiological activity that may be occurring at that time. The result is that ongoing activity is synthesized (combined) into a dream plot. For example, a man enters REM sleep and pleasant memories of playing in band during school are evoked. Meanwhile, the steam pipes in his bedroom are banging. The result is a dream in which he is watching a band parade by with the booming of bass drums ringing in his ears. Hobson does not believe that, apart from fostering memories, dreams have any psychological significance.

Plato believed that dreams do have psychological significance and can reveal something about the character of people. More recent ideas about the psychological origins of dreams can be divided into symbolic approaches that emphasize the hidden meanings of dreams and cognitive perspectives that stress that dreaming is simply another type of thinking and that no deep, hidden motives are contained in that thinking. The most famous symbolic approach to dreaming was presented by Sigmund Freud in his book *The Interpretation of Dreams* (1900). For Freud, the actual dream content is meaningless. It hides the true meaning of the dream, which must be interpreted. David Foulkes, in *Dreaming: A Cognitive-Psychological Analysis* (1985), proposed a contrary perspective. His cognitive approach to dreaming states that dreams are as they are remembered and that it is meaningless to search for deep meanings. Foulkes proposes that randomly activated memories during sleep are organized into a comprehensible dream by a "dream-production system."

The final category of dreams represents the most ancient explanation—dreams may have a supernatural origin. Often connected with the supernatural approach is the belief that God or supernatural beings can visit a person in a dream and heal that person of physical illnesses. This belief is called dream incubation and was widely practiced by the ancient Greeks beginning around the sixth century B.C.E. Several hundred temples were dedicated to helping believers practice this art. Spiritual healing, not physical healing, is the theme presented in the numerous references to dreaming in the Bible: more than one hundred verses in nearly twenty chapters. The Bible presents a balanced picture of the origins of dreams. God speaks through dreams to Abimelech in the first book of the Old Testament (Genesis 20:6) and to Joseph in the first book of the New Testament (Matthew 1:20). However, Solomon (Ecclesiastes 5:7) and Jeremiah (23:25-32) warn that many dreams do not have a divine origin.

DREAM CONTENT

Dream content varies depending on stage of sleep and time of night. Research has also revealed that characteristics of the dreamer and environmental factors can influence the nature of dreams.

Three human characteristics that influence dreams are age, gender, and personality. It has been found that children are more likely to report dreams (probably because they experience more REM sleep), and their dreams are reported to have more emotional content, particularly nightmarish themes.

Elderly people report more death themes in their dreams. Male dreams have more sexual and aggressive content than female dreams, which have more themes dealing with home and family. Women report that they dream of their mothers and babies more when they are pregnant. Introverts report more dreams and with greater detail than extroverts. Psychotic individuals (those with severe mental disorders), depressed people, and those whose occupations are in the creative arts (musicians, painters, and novelists) report more nightmares. Schizophrenics and severely depressed people provide shorter dream reports than those of better mental health. It is also reported that depressed people dream of the past more than those who are not depressed.

Environmental factors occurring before and during sleep can shape the content of dreams. What people experience prior to falling asleep can show up in dreams in blatant, subtle, or symbolic forms. People watching movies that evoke strong emotions tend to have highly emotional dreams. In fact, the greater the emotionality of a daily event, the greater the probability that the event will occur in a dream during the subsequent sleep period. Those who are wrestling mentally with a problem often dream about that problem. Some have even reported that the solutions to their problems occurred during the course of dreaming. The German physiologist Otto Loewi's Nobel Prize-winning research with a frog's nerve was inspired by a dream he had. Sometimes events during the day show up in a compensatory form in dreams. Those deprived of food, shelter, friends, or other desirables report an increased likelihood of dreaming about those deprivations at night.

Events occurring during sleep can be integrated into the dream plot as well. External stimuli such as temperature changes, light flashes, and various sounds can be detected by the sleeping person's senses and then become part of the dream. However, research indicates that sensory information is only infrequently assimilated into dreams. Internal stimulation from physiological activities occurring during sleep may have a greater chance of influencing the nature of dreams. Dreams about needing to find a bathroom may be caused in part by a full bladder. Similarly, nighttime activation of the vestibular system (which controls the sense of balance), the premotor cortex (which initiates movements), and the locus coeruleus (which plays a role in inhibiting muscles during sleep so that dreams are not acted out) perhaps can stimulate the production of dreams about falling, chasing, or being unable to move, respectively.

DREAM INTERPRETATION

There is a plethora of books about dream interpretation offering many different, and often contradictory, approaches to the subject. With so many different ideas about what dreams mean, it is difficult to know which approach is more likely to be successful.

A few principles increase the probability that a dream interpretation approach will be valid. First, the more dream content recalled, the better the opportunity to understand its meaning. Most people remember only bits and pieces of their dreams, and serious efforts to interpret dreams require serious efforts by people to remember their dreams. Second, the more a theme recurs in a series of dreams, the greater the likelihood that the theme is significant. Dream repetition also helps in interpretation: Content from one dream may be a clue to the meaning of other dreams. Finally, the focus of dream interpretation should be the dreamer, not the dream. In order to understand the dream, one must spend time and effort in knowing the dreamer.

There are many scholarly approaches to dream interpretation. Three theories are particularly noteworthy due to their influence on the thinking of other scholars and their utility for clinical application. Each perspective emphasizes a different side of the meaning of dreams.

Sigmund Freud proposed that dreams are complementary to waking life. His basic thesis was that many wishes, thoughts, and feelings are censored in waking consciousness due to their unsuitability for public expression and are subsequently pushed down into the unconscious. This unconscious material bypasses censorship in dreaming by a process in which the hidden, "true" meaning of the dream—the latent content—is presented in a disguised form—the manifest content. The manifest content is the actual content of the dream that is recalled. To interpret a dream requires working through the symbolism and various disguises of the manifest content in order to get to the true meaning of the dream residing in the latent content. For example, Jane's manifest content is a dream in which she blows out candles that surround a gray-headed man. The candles might symbolize knowledge, and the gray-headed man may represent her father. The latent content is that Jane resents her father's frequent and interfering advice. Thus, blowing out the candles represents Jane's desire to put an end to her father's meddling.

Carl Jung proposed that dreams could be understood at different levels of analysis and that the essential purpose of dreams was compensatory. By compensatory, Jung meant that dreams balance the mind by compensating for what is lacking in the way a person is living life. For example, the timid Christian who is afraid to speak up for his or her beliefs with atheistic colleagues dreams of being a bold and eloquent evangelist. Jung believed that four levels of analysis could be used to help dreamers gain insight into their dreams. His general rule guiding the use of these levels is that recourse to analysis at deeper levels of consciousness is only warranted if the dream cannot be adequately understood from a more surface level of examination. To illustrate, a man has a dream in which he steps into a pile of manure. At the conscious level of analysis, it may be that he is dreaming about a recent experience—no need to posit symbolic interpretations. Looking into his personal unconscious, an image from his childhood may be evoked. Recourse to the cultural level of consciousness would examine what manure symbolizes in his culture. It could be a good sign for a farmer in an agrarian world but a bad sign for a politician in an industrialized society. In some cases, it may be necessary to look at the dream from the perspective of the collective unconscious. Manure might be an ancient, universal image that symbolizes fertility. Could the man be questioning whether or not he wants to be a father?

Zygmunt Piotrowski developed a theory of dream interpretation based on projective techniques. For Piotrowski, in a dream about another person, that person may actually represent a facet of the dreamer's own mind. The more the dream figure is like the dreamer and the closer the proximity between the figure and the dreamer in the dream, the greater the likelihood the dreamer is projecting him- or herself (seeing in others what is really in the self) into that dream figure. For instance, a woman may dream she is walking with her closest friend but that friend is ignoring everything she is saying to her. An interpretation according to Piotrowski's system could be that the dreamer is actually dealing with the fact that she is not a good listener.

Dreams may be complementary, compensatory, or projective, useless fictions, avenues of insight, or products of the brain. Many credible answers have been proposed, but it is hard to believe that there is a single explanation for every instance of dreaming. Perhaps the best answer is that dreams reveal many different things about many different dreamers—biologically, psychologically, socially, and spiritually.

SOURCES FOR FURTHER STUDY

Dement, William C. *The Promise of Sleep.* New York: Random House, 1999. One of the pioneers in sleep research presents a comprehensive overview of sleep for the general public. Chapters 13 and 14 specifically deal with dreaming, while research pertinent to dreaming is also found in other chapters.

Farthing, G. W. *The Psychology of Consciousness.* Englewood Cliffs, N.J.: Prentice Hall, 1992. In a scholarly book emphasizing research on various aspects of consciousness, Farthing examines dreaming in three chapters and related phenomena in two other chapters.

Freud, Sigmund. *The Interpretation of Dreams.* Translated by Joyce Crick, edited by Ritchie Robertson. New York: Oxford University Press, 1999. This is the classic book that outlined Freud's theory of the mind and revolutionized thinking about dreams.

Hall, James A. *Patterns of Dreaming.* Boston: Shambhala, 1991. Hall looks at dream interpretation from a Jungian perspective with an emphasis on clinical application. This intellectually sound book contains excellent historical background and well-rounded coverage of different approaches toward dream interpretation, including a brief look at Piotrowski's system.

Kallmyer, J. D. *Hearing the Voice of God Through Dreams, Visions, and the Prophetic Word.* Harre de Grace, Md.: Moriah Press, 1998. This book is an excellent source for a spiritual examination of dreaming.

Paul J. Chara, Jr.

SEE ALSO: Analytical Psychology: Carl Jung; Consciousness: Altered States; Psychoanalytic Psychology and Personality: Sigmund Freud; Sleep.

DRIVES

TYPE OF PSYCHOLOGY: Motivation
FIELD OF STUDY: Motivation theory

A drive is a state influenced by an animal's need; the animal is motivated to reduce tension or to seek a goal. Drive theory is concerned with the nature of the internal forces that compel an animal to behave.

KEY CONCEPTS
- drive
- drive reduction
- law of effect
- need
- reinforcement

One goal of science is to understand, predict, or manipulate natural events. A scientist may start by observing an event of interest and measuring it as precisely as possible to detect any changes. In experimental research, scientists systematically manipulate various other events to see whether the event of interest also varies. In survey research, various events are measured to see whether they vary with the event of interest. Understanding is achieved when the relationship between the event of interest (the dependent variable) and other events (independent variables) is established. One can then predict or manipulate the event of interest. A theory provides a guideline to organize the variables into a system based upon common properties. To a psychologist, the dependent variable is the behavior of all animals and humans. The independent variable (also called a determinant) may be any other variable related to behaviors. Psychological research aims to discover the determinants of certain behavior; some of them are motivational variables. The field of motivation examines why particular behavior occurs, why it is so strong, and why it is so persistent.

A drive is a process related to the source of behavioral energy originating from within the body that is created by disturbances in homeostasis (a state of systemic equilibrium). A homeostatic imbalance creates a state of need for certain stimuli from the environment which can restore the balance. For example, abnormal body temperature and hyperosmolality of the body fluid (electrolyte concentration outside cells that is higher than that of the intracellular fluid, resulting in cell dehydration) are disturbances in homeostasis. The homeostatic balance can be restored through two means. Physiological means such as vasodilation, sweating, and panting serve to reduce body temperature; concentration of electrolytes in the urine by the kidneys reduces hyperosmolality. Second, behavioral means such as taking off clothes, turning on an air conditioner, and drinking cold liquid lower body temperature; drinking water would also result in reducing the hyperosmolality. One may examine a case of homeostatic imbalance in detail to illustrate how the two means function to restore the balance.

When the body fluid volume is reduced (hypovolemia) because of loss of blood or of body fluid from intense sweating, the body responds immediately by vasoconstriction, reducing urine volume (through vasopressin release), and conserving sodium (through aldosterone release). Those are physiological means that will restore the blood pressure and prevent circulatory failure. Eventually, however, the body must get back the lost fluid from the environment via behavior (seeking water and drinking) to achieve long-lasting homeostasis. The physiological means are immediate and effective, but they are only stopgap measures. Behavior is the means with which the animal interacts with its environment to get back the lost resource.

DRIVE, REINFORCEMENT, AND LEARNING

The concept of drives is very important to the theories of Clark L. Hull, a neobehaviorist. According to Hull, a drive has at least two distinct functions as far as behavioral activation is concerned. Without drives there could be no reinforcement and thus no learning, because drive reduction is the reinforcement. Without drives there could be no responses, for drives activate behavioral potentials into performance. Drive theory maintains that a state named "drive" (or D) is a necessary condition for behavior to occur; however, D is not the same as the bodily need. D determines how strongly and persistently a behavior will occur; it connects the need and behavior. This distinction between need and drive is necessary because, while the state of need serves as the source of behavior, the intensity of behavior is not always related to the intensity of need. Need can be defined as a state of an organism attributable to deprivation of a biological or psychological requirement, related to a disturbance in the homeostatic state.

There are cases in which the need increases but behavior does not, or in which the need remains but behavior is no longer manifested. Prolonged deprivation, for example, may not result in a linear or proportional increase in behavior. A water-deprived animal may stop drinking even before cellular dehydration is restored to the normal state; the behavior is changing independently of homeostatic imbalance. Cessation of behavior is seen as being attributable to drive reduction.

Hull uses D to symbolize drive and sHr (H is commonly used to denote this, for convenience) to symbolize a habit which consists of an acquired relationship between stimulus (S) and response (R). It represents a memory of experience in which certain environmental stimuli and responses were followed by a reward. An effective reward establishes an S-R relationship; the effect is termed reinforcement. One example of an H would be an experience of maze stimuli and running that led to food. H is a behavioral potential, not a behavior. Food deprivation induces a need state that can be physiologically defined; then D will energize H into behavior. The need increases monotonically with hours of deprivation, but D increases only up to three days without food. A simplified version of the Hullian formula for a behavior would be "behavior = HD," or "performance = behavioral potential energizer." The formula indicates that learning, via establishing behavioral potential, and D, via energizing the potential, are both necessary for performance to occur. This is a multiplicative relationship; that is, when either H or D is zero, a specific performance cannot occur.

ROLE OF FREUD'S ID

Sigmund Freud proposed, in his psychoanalytical approach to behavioral energy, that psychic energy is the source of human behaviors. The id is the reservoir of instinctual energy presumed to derive directly from the somatic processes. This energy is unorganized, illogical, and timeless, knowing "no values, no good or evil, no morality," according to Freud in 1933. The id operates according to the pleasure principle, using the primary process to discharge its energy as soon as possible, with no regard for reality. When the discharge is hindered by reality, however, the ego handles the situation according to the reality principle, using a secondary process to pursue realistic gratification. The ego mediates between the id on one hand and reality on the other.

Freud thus conceptualized the id to be the energy source and the ego to manage behavior in terms of reality. Learning is manifested in the way the ego manages behavior for gratification under the restriction of the environment and the superego. In this model, the drive is seen as the energizer of behavior. The similarity between the Freudian and Hullian concepts of drive is obvious. Food deprivation would generate homeostatic imbalance, which is the somatic process, and the need, which is similar to the energy of the id. The organism cannot obtain immediate gratification because of environmental constraints to obtain food, so behavior is generated to negotiate with the environment. Drive is much like the ego because it energizes the behavioral potentials into behaviors to seek reality gratification, which is equivalent to drive reduction. The concept of pleasure and behavioral changes commonly appears in various theories that incorporate a subtle influence of Freudian thought.

DEPRIVATION AND INCENTIVE MOTIVES

In one classic experiment, Carl J. Warden studied the persistence of behavior as a function of various sources, including the strength of a drive, using an apparatus called a Columbia obstruction box. He demonstrated that a rat without food would cross an electrified grid to reach a goal box that held food. When the rat was immediately brought back from the goal box to the start box, it would cross the grid again and again. The number of grid crossings was positively related to the number of days without food for up to three days. From the fourth day without food, however, the number of crossings slowly decreased. When baby rats were placed in the goal box, a mother rat would cross the grid repeatedly. When a male or female rat was placed in the goal box, a rat of the opposite sex would cross repeatedly. The number of crossings by the male rat was positively related to the duration it spent without a female companion.

These animals were all manifesting the effect of different drives: hunger, maternal instinct, or sex. It was shown that the maternal drive was associated with the greatest number of crossings (twenty-two times in twenty minutes), followed by thirst (twenty times), hunger (seventeen), female sex drive (fourteen), male sex drive (thirteen), and exploration (six). Warden demonstrated that various internal forces, created by deprivation and hormonal state, and external forces, created by different goal objects, together determine the grid-crossing behavior. The level of deprivation induces drive motivation; the reward in the goal box induces incentive motivation. In this example, the focus is on drive motivation.

If one were to place a well-trained rat into a maze, it might or might not run to the goal box. Whether it would run, how fast it would run, and how well (in terms of errors) it would run would depend upon whether the subject were food-deprived. With food deprivation, the well-trained rat would run to the goal box with few errors. If it had just been fed, it would not run; it would simply wander, sniff at the corner, and go to sleep. The environmental stimulus (the maze) is the same; the rat's behavior is different because the internal force—the drive created by food deprivation—is different. A need state produces D, and D then triggers behavior. The behavior that will occur is determined jointly by the past experience of learning, which is termed H, as well as stimuli, S, from the environment. An inexperienced rat, without the H of maze running, will behave differently from a well-trained rat in a maze. D is an intervening variable: It connects need and behavior, so one must consider both the source (need) and the consequence (behavior) to define D. When D is zero, there will be no maze running, no matter how well-trained the rat is. On the other hand, if there is no H (training), the proper maze-running behavior will not occur, no matter how hungry the rat is. An animal must be exposed to a maze when hungry to learn to negotiate the various turns on the way to the goal box containing food. Without food deprivation (and the resultant D), the animal would not perform, even if it could; one cannot tell whether an animal has the knowledge to run the maze until one introduces a D variable. H is a potential of behavior, and D makes the potential into the observable reality of performance. Motivation turns a behavior on.

These ideas can be applied to countless real-life examples. If a person is not very good at playing tennis (has a low H), for example, no matter how motivated (high D) he is, he will not be able to beat a friend who is an expert at the game. If a person is very good at tennis (high H) but does not feel like playing (low D), perhaps because of a lack of sleep, she will not perform well. The same situation would apply for taking a test, delivering a speech, or running a marathon.

PUZZLE-BOX LEARNING

In another experiment involving drive, Edward L. Thorndike put a cat into a puzzle box. The cat attempted to get out via various behaviors (mewing, scratching, and so on). By chance, it stepped on a plate that resulted in the door opening, allowing the cat to escape. The cat was repeatedly returned to the box, and soon it would escape right away by stepping on the plate; other, useless behaviors were no longer manifested. The source of D in this case was the anxiety induced by confinement in the box, which could be measured by various physiological changes, such as heart rate and hormonal levels. Escaping would make the anxiety disappear; D is reduced. D reduction results in an increase in the probability that the behavior immediately preceding it (stepping on the plate) will recur. Thorndike describes this puzzle-box learning as trial and error, implying a blind attempt at various means of escape until one happens to work. He states that a "satisfying effect" will create repetition, calling this the law of effect; the essence of the satisfying effect appears to be drive reduction. A five-stage learning cycle is then com-

Edward L. Thorndike.
(Library of Congress)

plete: It consists of need, drive, behavior, drive reduction, and behavior repetition.

CENTRAL MOTIVE STATE

The question of how a habit (H) is formed and how it is stored in the brain is a lively research topic in the psychobiology of learning, memory, and cognition, as well as in neuropsychology, which deals with learning deficit and loss of memory. Drive and reinforcement are important variables that determine whether learning will succeed and whether past learning will be manifested as behaviors. Research on hunger and thirst forms one subfield of psychobiology.

If D is the common energizer of various behaviors, then all sources of D—hunger, thirst, sex, mothering, exploration—should have something in common physiologically. The so-called central motive state is hypothesized to be such a state. It is known that arousal is common to the sources of D. Research involves biological delineation of the sources of D; researchers are studying the mechanisms of hunger, for example. There has been insufficient attention paid to the physiological processes by which hunger may motivate various behaviors and by which drive reduction would serve as a reinforcement in learning. Extreme lack of motivation can be seen in some depressed and psychotic patients, which results both in a lack of new learning and in a lack of manifesting what is already known. The neuronal substrates of this "lack of energy" represent one problem under investigation in the area of drive and motivation.

SOURCES FOR FURTHER STUDY

Amsel, Abram. *Mechanisms of Adaptive Behavior: Clark Hull's Theoretical Papers, with Commentary.* New York: Columbia University Press, 1984. An annotated collection of Hull's theoretical work on drives and behavior.

Bolles, Robert C. *Theory of Motivation.* 2d ed. New York: Harper & Row, 1975. This standard text in motivation reviews the concepts of motivation and drive and present pros and cons of the drive concept.

Freud, Sigmund. *New Introductory Lectures on Psychoanalysis.* Translated and edited by James Strachey. New York: W. W. Norton, 1989. Freud's 1933 work explains his theory of the workings of the id, ego, and superego. His concept of behavioral energy is described in this book.

Hull, Clark Leonard. *Principles of Behavior.* 1943. Reprint. New York: Appleton-Century-Crofts, 1966. This bible of the Hullian neobehavioristic theory delineates the concepts of D and H and the philosophical bases of behavioral study. The theory has excited many students into studying psychology.

Pfaff, Donald W., ed. *The Physiological Mechanisms of Motivation.* New York: Springer-Verlag, 1982. Various authors describe the physiological substrates of different sources of drive and motivation in terms of the nervous system, hormones, and body fluid parameters.

Stellar, James R., and Eliot Stellar. *The Neurobiology of Motivation and Reward.* New York: Springer-Verlag, 1985. Eliot Stellar, one of the best-known theorists in biopsychology of motivation, along with his son, describes how biological antecedents of motivation can be found to explain various behavior.

Warden, Carl John. *Animal Motivation: Experimental Studies on the Albino Rat.* New York: Columbia University Press, 1931. This was the first research attempting to compare different sources of drive using various reward substances.

Sigmund Hsiao

SEE ALSO: Hunger; Instinct Theory; Motivation; Thirst.

Drug Therapies

DATE: The 1950's forward

TYPE OF PSYCHOLOGY: Biological bases of behavior; psychopathology; psychotherapy

FIELDS OF STUDY: Anxiety disorders; depression; models of abnormality; nervous system; organic disorders; personality disorders; schizophrenias; sexual disorders; stress and illness; substance abuse

Psychotropic drugs have revolutionized the treatment of mental illness. Many disorders, including anxiety, depression, and schizophrenia, may be treated effectively with these modern drugs. However, the use of psychotropic drugs has created new problems, both for individuals and for society.

KEY CONCEPTS
- antianxiety drugs
- antidepressant drugs
- antipsychotics
- mood stabilizers
- neurotransmitters
- psychopharmacology
- psychostimulants
- psychotropic

Based on the rapidly increasing body of chemical knowledge developed during the late nineteenth century, interest in drug therapy in the early twentieth century was high. Researchers experimented with insulin, marijuana, antihistamines, and lithium with varying success. The term "psychopharmacology," the study of drugs for the treatment of mental illness, dates to 1920. Before 1950, no truly effective drug therapies existed for mental illness. Physicians treated mentally ill patients with a combination of physical restraints, blood-letting, sedation, starvation, electric shock, and other minimally effective therapies. They used some drugs for treatment, including alcohol and opium, primarily to calm agitated patients.

In 1951 French scientist Paul Charpentier synthesized chlorpromazine (brand name Thorazine) for use in reducing surgical patients' anxiety and the prevention of shock during surgery. Physicians noted its calming effect and began to use it in psychiatry. Previously agitated patients with schizophrenia not only became calmer, but their thoughts also became less chaotic and they became less irritable. Chlorpromazine was truly the first effective psychotropic drug (that is, a drug exerting an effect on the mind) and is still used today.

The discovery of chlorpromazine ushered in a new era in the treatment of psychiatric illness. Pharmaceutical companies have developed and introduced dozens of new psychotropic drugs. Many long-term psychiatric treatment facilities have closed, and psychiatrists have released the vast majority of their patients into community-based mental health care. Many patients with mental health problems are treated on an outpatient basis, with brief hospitalizations for stabilization in some cases. Treatment goals are no longer simply to sedate patients or to protect themselves and others from harm but to provide them with significant relief from their symptoms and to help them function productively in society. As scientific knowledge about the brain and its function increases, researchers are able to create drugs targeting increasingly specific areas of the brain, leading to fewer adverse side effects.

This psychotherapeutic drug revolution has had some negative consequences, however. Drug side effects range from the annoying to the life threatening. Community mental health treatment centers have not grown in number or received funding sufficient to meet the needs of all the patients released from long-term care facilities. Many mentally ill patients have fallen through the cracks of community-based care and live on the streets or in shelters for the homeless. In addition, some physicians and patients have come to expect a "pill for every ill" and fail to use other, equally or more effective treatment methodologies. Researchers estimate that 15 percent of the population of the United States receives a prescription for a psychotropic drug each year, greatly adding to the nation's health care costs. The majority of these prescriptions are written by generalist physicians rather than by psychiatrists, raising concerns about excessive or inappropriate prescribing. Some people abuse these drugs, either by taking their medications in excess of the amount prescribed for them or by obtaining them illicitly. Studies have shown that prescription drug abuse causes more injuries and deaths than abuse of all illicit drugs combined. Feminist scholars have pointed out that physicians tend to prescribe psychotropic drugs more readily for women than for men.

Despite the negative effects, psychotropic drugs are extremely important in the provision of health care, not only for those people traditionally thought of as mentally ill but also for people with chronic pain, serious medical illness, loss and grief, and those who have experienced traumatic events.

HOW PSYCHOTROPIC DRUGS WORK

To understand how these mind-affecting drugs work, it is necessary to understand a little of how the brain works. The brain is made up primarily of neurons (nerve cells) that form circuits controlling thoughts, emotions, physical activities, and basic life functions. These nerve cells do not actually touch one another but are separated by gaps called synapses. An electrical impulse moves along the neuron. When it reaches the end, it stimulates the release of chemicals called neurotransmitters into the synapse. These chemicals then fit into receptors on the next neuron and affect its electrical impulse. The neurotransmitters act by either causing the release of the electric impulse or inhibiting it so the neuron does not fire. Any neurotransmitter left in the synapse is then reabsorbed into the original neuron. This process is called reuptake.

Problems can arise from either too much or too little neurotransmission. Too much transmission may occur when the neuron fires in the absence of a stimulus or when too many neurotransmitters attach to the receptors on the far side of the synapse (the postsynaptic receptors). Too little transmission can occur when too few neurotransmitters attach to these postsynaptic receptors. The primary neurotransmitters involved in mental illnesses and their treatment are dopamine, serotonin (5-HT), norepinephrine, and gamma-aminobutyric acid (GABA).

ANTIDEPRESSANT DRUGS

Some scientists believe that depression is caused by insufficient norepinephrine, serotonin, or dopamine in the synapse. Others theorize that depression has to do with the number and sensitivity of postsynaptic receptors involved in the neuron's response. Drugs for the treatment of depression come in four major classes: the monoamine oxidase inhibitors (MAOIs), the tricyclic antidepressants, the selective serotonin reuptake inhibitors (SSRIs), and "other." None of these drugs is addictive, although patients need to be weaned from them slowly to avoid rebound depression or other adverse effects.

MAOIs were the first modern antidepressants. Monoamine oxidase is an enzyme that breaks down serotonin, norepinephrine, and dopamine. Inhibiting the enzyme increases the supply of these neurotransmitters. MAOI drugs available in the United States include phenelzine and tranylcypromine. These drugs are not used as commonly as are the other antidepressants, mostly because of their side effects. However, they are used when other treatments for depression fail. In addition, they may be used to treat narcolepsy, phobias, anxiety, and Parkinson's disease. Common side effects include drowsiness, fatigue, dry mouth, and dizziness. They may also cause orthostatic hypotension (a drop in blood pressure when arising) and sexual dysfunction. Most important, the MAOIs interact with tyramine-containing foods, such as hard cheese, red wine, and smoked or pickled fish. Consuming these foods along with an MAOI can cause a hypertensive crisis in which the patient's blood pressure rises to potentially deadly levels. Patients taking MAOIs must also avoid other drugs which stimulate the nervous system to avoid blood pressure emergencies.

The tricyclic antidepressants were introduced in 1958. They all inhibit the reuptake of neurotransmitters but differ in which neurotransmitter is involved. Some affect primarily serotonin, some norepinephrine, and some work equally on both. Tricyclics commonly available in the United States include amitriptyline, imipramine, doxepin, desipramine, nortriptyline, amoxapine, protriptyline, and clomipramine. Primarily used for depression, these drugs may also be helpful in the treatment of bed-wetting, agoraphobia (fear of being out in the open) with panic attacks, obsessive-compulsive personality disorder, chronic pain, nerve pain, and migraine headaches.

An important treatment issue is that it takes two to three weeks of tricyclic therapy before the depressed patient feels much improvement in mood and energy. During this time, the side effects, which include dry mouth, blurred vision, constipation, urinary retention, orthostatic hypotension, weight gain, sexual dysfunction, cardiac problems, and jaundice, tend to be the most bothersome, leading patients to abandon the treatment before it becomes effective. Another important treatment issue is that tricyclic antidepressants are highly lethal in overdose. Some of the tricyclics are highly sedating and so may be useful in patients who are having difficulty sleeping. On the other hand, a patient who is already feeling sluggish and sleepy may benefit from a tricyclic that is less sedating. Any antidepressant may precipitate mania or hypomania in a patient with a predisposition to bipolar (manic-depressive) disorder. Elderly patients may be at increased risk for falls or confusion and memory impairment when taking tricyclics and should be started on very low doses if a tricyclic is indicated.

The newer selective SSRIs have several advantages over the tricyclics: They are much less lethal in overdose, are far safer for use among the elderly, and do not cause weight gain. They work, as the name implies, by decreasing serotonin reuptake, thereby increasing the amount of neurotransmitter available at the synapse. Like the tricyclics, SSRIs may need to be taken for several weeks before a patient notices significant improvement in mood and energy level. SSRIs available in the United States include fluoxetine (Prozac), sertraline (Zoloft), fluvoxamine (Luvox), paroxetine (Paxil), trazodone (Desyral), nafazodone (Serzone), and venlafaxine (Effexor). In addition to depression, the SSRIs are used for treatment of bulimia nervosa and obsessive-compulsive disorder. Possible side effects include nausea, diarrhea, nervousness, insomnia, anxiety, and sexual dysfunction.

Other drugs used in the treatment of depression include mianserin, maprotiline, and bupropion. The mechanisms by which these drugs work are not clear, but they may be useful in patients for whom the other antidepressants do not work or are contraindicated.

MOOD STABILIZERS

Some patients who have depression also have episodes of elevated mood and erratic, uncontrolled behavior. These patients are diagnosed with bipolar disorder, formerly known as manic-depression. The underlying cause for this disorder is unknown, but there is a strong genetic predisposition. Evidence suggests the condition is due to overactivity of the neurotransmitters. Treatment for bipolar disorder consists of mood-stabilizing drugs. These drugs control not only the "highs" but also the episodes of depression.

Lithium is a naturally occurring mineral that was observed to calm agitated behavior in ancient Egypt. Its usefulness as a mood stabilizer was first scientifically established in the 1940's and it was approved in 1970 for use in the United States. It is effective not only in stabilizing the mood during a manic episode but also in the prevention of future episodes. A significant problem with the use of lithium is that the dose at which it becomes effective is quite close to the dose which produces toxicity, characterized by drowsiness, blurred vision, staggering, confusion, irregular heart beat, seizures, and coma. Patients taking lithium must therefore have blood drawn on a regular basis in order to determine drug levels. Patients who have poor kidney function should not take lithium because it is excreted primarily through the urine. Lithium's side effects include nausea, diarrhea, tremor of the hands, dry mouth, and frequent urination.

Drugs usually used for the treatment of seizures may also help stabilize mood in bipolar patients, usually at lower doses than would be used for seizure control. These include carbamazepine, divalproex, gabapentin, lamotrigine, and topiramate. It is believed that these drugs increase the amount of GABA at the synapse. GABA has a calming or inhibitory effect on the neurons. Side effects of these medications include dizziness, nausea, headaches, and visual changes.

PSYCHOSTIMULANTS

Attention-deficit hyperactivity disorder (ADHD) is found in both children and adults. Children with ADHD have difficulties at school because of impulsivity and inattention. The underlying cause of ADHD is extremely complex, and the ways in which drugs used to treat it work are equally complex. The most successful treatments are with drugs that actually stimulate the central nervous system. Drug therapy is most effective when combined with behavioral treatments. The most commonly used psychostimulants are methylphenidate and pemoline, but amphetamines are sometimes used as well. Formerly, depressed patients were treated with amphetamines and similar compounds; occasionally this use is still found. These stimulant drugs do improve school performance; however, they may cause growth retardation in both height and weight. They may also cause insomnia and nervousness. Importantly, these drugs may be abused, leading ultimately to addiction, paranoia, and severe depression during withdrawal.

ANTIANXIETY DRUGS

These drugs are central nervous system depressants. Many of these antianxiety drugs or anxiolytics are, in higher doses, also used as sedative-hypnotics, or calming and sleep-inducing drugs. They seem to act by enhancing the effect of GABA in the brain. The earliest of these depressant drugs included chloroform, chloral hydrate, and paraldehyde, and they were used for anesthesia and for sedation.

Barbiturates were introduced in Germany in 1862 and were widely used for treatment of anxiety and sleep problems until the 1960's. Barbiturates are still available today, including pentobarbital, secobarbital, amobarbital, and phenobarbital. Their major adverse effect is respiratory depression, particularly when used in combination with alcohol, another central nervous system depressant. With the advent of the safer benzodiazepines, use of the barbiturates has declined steadily.

Benzodiazepines are used for two major problems: anxiety and insomnia. Anxiety disorders appropriate for this kind of treatment include generalized anxiety disorder, panic disorder, obsessive-compulsive disorder, phobic disorder, and dissociative disorder. The benzodiazepines commonly used for anxiety include alprazolam, chlordiazepoxide, clonazepam, clorazepate, diazepam, lorazepam, and oxazepam. For most of these disorders, however, behavioral, cognitive, group, and social therapy, or one of these therapies plus medication, are more effective than medication alone. Benzodiazepines used for insomnia include estazolam, flurazepam, midazolam, quazepam, temazepam, and triazolam. Benzodiazepines may also be used to prevent the development of delirium tremens during alcohol withdrawal. Patients become tolerant to the effects of these drugs, meaning they have the potential for physical dependency and addiction. In addition, benzodiazepines interact with many other drugs, including alcohol. Their use should be limited to brief periods of time, particularly in the treatment of insomnia. Long-term treatment for anxiety should be monitored carefully by the health care provider. Elderly people are more likely than younger people to suffer adverse effects (such as confusion or falls) from benzodiazepine use.

Another drug developed for treatment of anxiety is buspirone. Propranolol and atenolol, usually used to treat high blood pressure, are useful in treating stage fright or performance anxiety, and clonidine, another blood pressure medication, is successfully used in treatment of anxiety. Nonbenzodiazepine sleep agents include zolpidem and zaleplon.

ANTIPSYCHOTIC DRUGS

Formerly known as "major tranquilizers" or "neuroleptics," the antipsychotic drugs have revolutionized the treatment of schizophrenia and other psychoses. The underlying cause of psychosis is not known, but it is thought to be related to the neurotransmitter dopamine. Most of the antipsychotics block the dopamine receptors in the brain. The older antipsychotic drugs include thorazine, thioridazine, perphenazine, trifluoperazine, fluphenazine, thiothixene, and haloperidol. These older drugs treat the so-called positive symptoms of schizophrenia—hallucinations and delusions—but they have little effect on the "negative" symptoms—withdrawal, poor interpersonal relationships, and slowing of the body's movement. They also have multiple serious side effects including severe muscle spasm, tremor, rigidity, shuffling gait, stupor, fever, difficulty speaking, blood pressure changes, restlessness, and involuntary movements of the face, trunk, arms, and legs. Some of these are treatable using other drugs, but some are neither treatable nor reversible.

In an effort to overcome these problems, newer antipsychotics have been developed. The first of these was clozapine, which was successful in treating about one-third of the patients who did not respond to other antipsychotic drugs. While it had fewer of the serious side effects listed above, a small percentage of patients experience a severe drop in the white blood cells, which puts them at risk for serious infection. For this reason, patients on clozapine must be followed with frequent blood counts. Other newer antipsychotics include risperidone, olanzapine, and quetiapine. In addition to fewer of the serious side effects, the newer antipsychotics seem to have some effect on the negative symptoms.

Sources for Further Study

Breggin, David, and Peter Cohen. *Your Drug May Be Your Problem: How and Why to Stop Taking Psychiatric Drugs.* Cambridge, Mass.: Perseus, 2000. A controversial book making an important argument that too many people are taking psychiatric medications and suffering serious side effects from those drugs. The authors give specifics about how to withdraw from drugs safely.

Drummond, Edward H. *The Complete Guide to Psychiatric Drugs: Straight Talk for Best Results.* New York: John Wiley & Sons, 2000. Covers the state of knowledge about psychiatric illness, what medications may be helpful, how to decide whether medication might be useful, managing side effects, and nondrug therapies.

Gorman, Jack M. *The Essential Guide to Mental Health: The Most Comprehensive Guide to the New Psychiatry for Popular Family Use.* New York: St. Martin's Press, 1998. Covers psychiatric illness, how to search for a psychiatrist, drugs, and over-the-counter remedies.

_____. *Essential Guide to Psychiatric Drugs.* 3d ed. New York: St. Martin's Press, 1997. Contains detailed descriptions of the psychiatric medications available in the United States, including uses, adverse effects, cost, dosages, and research findings. Written in a straightforward style for the layperson but also useful to clinicians.

Healy, David. *The Creation of Psychopharmacology.* Cambridge, Mass.: Harvard University Press, 2002. Details the discovery and development of psychiatric medications, the extremely profitable partnership between psychiatrists and the large pharmaceutical companies, and the frightening consequences for today's culture and society.

Kramer, Peter D. *Listening to Prozac: A Psychiatrist Explores Antidepressant Drugs and the Remaking of the Self.* New York: Penguin, 1997. An examination of the growing use of drugs in the treatment of mental illness, with discussion of the implications of this practice, both positive and negative.

Olson, James. *Pharmacology Made Ridiculously Simple.* 2d ed. Miami: MedMaster, 2001. A brief and straightforward explanation of the general principles of pharmacology. Enhanced by excellent diagrams and tables.

Rebecca Lovell Scott

See also: Cognitive Behavior Therapy; Cognitive Therapy; Psychotherapy: Goals and Techniques.

EATING DISORDERS

TYPE OF PSYCHOLOGY: Psychopathology
FIELD OF STUDY: General constructs and issues

Eating disorders include a group of eating and weight disturbances, including anorexia nervosa, bulimia nervosa, and binge-eating disorder, associated with underlying psychological problems.

KEY CONCEPTS
- anorexia nervosa
- binge-eating disorder
- bulimia nervosa
- eating disorder
- obesity

Eating disorders were identified as early as ancient Roman times, when banqueters gorged themselves, then induced vomiting. Some of the early Christian saints were anorexic. However, eating disorders only emerged as an area of social and medical concern in the second half of the twentieth century.

Persons with eating disorders have a distorted body image and unrealistic ideas about weight. Although such disorders are found primarily among young, middle- to upper-middle-class, well-educated Caucasian women, eating disorders increasingly affect and may be overlooked in men, older women, and persons of color. No single factor appears to be the cause of eating disorders, with social, cultural, psychological, genetic, biological, and physical factors all playing a part. Treatment may include hospitalization for nutritional monitoring and for stabilization in persons with serious medical complications or who are at risk for suicide. Regardless of the setting, treatment is best carried out by a multidisciplinary team, including a primary care physician or psychiatrist, a psychotherapist, a nutritionist, and, if appropriate, a family therapist.

Eating disorders are best thought of as problems involving body weight and distorted body image on a continuum of severity. The most serious is anorexia nervosa, a disorder characterized by weight loss greater than or equal to 15 percent of the body weight normal for the person's height and age. Bulimia nervosa is usually found in persons of normal weight and is characterized by consumption of large amounts of food followed by self-induced vomiting, purging with diuretics or laxatives, or excessive exercise. Binge-eating disorder, found usually in persons with some degree of overweight, is characterized by the consumption of large amounts of food without associated vomiting or purging. Other, milder, forms of eating disorders are at the least serious end of the continuum. Obesity may or may not be part of this continuum, depending on the presence or absence of underlying psychological problems. About one-third of obese persons have binge-eating disorder.

POPULATION AT RISK

Women constitute 90 percent of people diagnosed with eating disorders—eight million adolescent and young adult women in the United States alone. The majority of these are Caucasian (95 percent) and from middle- to upper-middle-class backgrounds. Research in the latter part of the twentieth century indicated that adolescent and young adult women were most likely to be affected; however, these disorders are now found in girls as young as nine and in older women. By the end of the twentieth century, eating disorders were also increasingly identified in women from other ethnic and socioeconomic groups. These disorders are most likely underreported in men and seem to affect gay men disproportionately. Also at risk are men with certain professions or avocations such as jockeys, dancers, body builders, and wrestlers, in which weight and body shape are an issue.

CAUSES OF EATING DISORDERS

No single cause has been identified for eating disorders. However, nearly all eating disorders begin with dieting to lose weight. Because these disorders are found almost exclusively in the developed world, where food is plentiful and where thinness in women is idealized, it appears that social and cultural

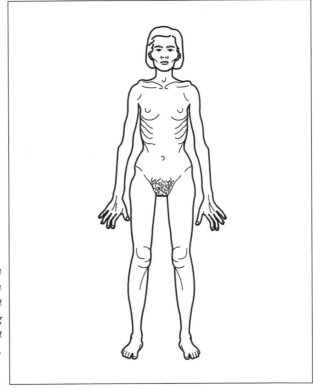

Anorexia nervosa is a body-image disorder in which fear of being fat results in undereating and other behaviors that lead to emaciation and, if unchecked, death. (Hans & Cassidy, Inc.)

factors are important contributors. Some theorists believe that cultural values of independence and personal autonomy, rather than interdependence and the importance of human relationships, contribute to eating pathology. Still others point to the changing and contradictory societal expectations about the roles of women as a contributing factor.

Studies suggest a genetic predisposition to eating disorders, particularly in those persons who engage in binge eating and purging behaviors. Their family histories typically include higher than expected numbers of persons with mood disorders and substance abuse problems. Dysfunctions in the pathways for the substances that transmit messages in the brain, the neurotransmitters, are thought to play a role in the development and maintenance of eating disorders, although these dysfunctions are not sufficient to explain the entire problem by themselves. The psychological theories about the causes of eating disorders postulate that individuals with underlying feelings of powerlessness or personal inadequacy attempt to cope by becoming preoccupied with their body's shape and size. Finally, the incidence of sexual abuse is higher among persons with eating disorders, particularly bulimia nervosa, than among those in the general population.

Eating disorders seem to develop in three stages. Stage 1 involves the period from the time a child is conceived until the onset of a particular behavior that precipitates the eating disorder. During this stage, individual psychological, personal, and physical factors, plus family, social, and cultural factors, place the person at increased risk. Individual risk factors include a personal history of depression, low self-esteem, perfectionism, an eagerness to please others, obesity, and physical or sexual abuse. Family risk factors include a family member with an eating disorder or a mood disorder and excessive familial concern for appearance and weight. Social and cultural issues include emphasis on the cultural ideal of excessive thinness, leading to dissatisfaction with the body and dieting for weight loss. Young women who are dancers, runners, skaters, gymnasts, and the like may be particularly susceptible to this kind of cultural pressure.

Stage 2 involves the factors which actually precipitate the eating disorder. Some identified precipitating factors include onset of puberty, leaving home, new relationships, death of a relative, illness, adverse comments about weight and body appearance, fear of maturation, the struggle for autonomy during the midteen years, and identity conflicts.

Stage 3 involves the factors which perpetuate the eating disorder. These can be cognitive distortions, interpersonal events, or biological changes related to starvation.

Associated Medical Problems

Women with anorexia nervosa stop menstruating. Anorexics may also have abdominal pain, constipation, and increased urination. The heart rate may be slow or irregular. Many develop downy, dark body hair (lanugo) over normally hairless areas. They may have bloating after eating and swelling of the feet and lower legs. Low levels of potassium and sodium and other imbalances in the body's electrolytes can lead to cardiac arrest, kidney failure, weakness, confusion, poor memory, disordered thinking, and mood swings. The death rate for anorexics is high: About 5 percent will die within eight years of being diagnosed and 20 percent within twenty years.

Self-induced vomiting can lead to erosion of tooth enamel, gum abscesses, and swelling of the parotid glands in front of the ear and over the angle of the jaw. About one-third of women with bulimia have abnormal changes in their menstrual cycles. Some bulimics consume so much food in such a short period of time that their stomachs rupture. More than 75 percent of these individuals die. Use of ipecac and laxatives can lead to heart damage. Symptoms include chest pain, skipped heartbeats, and fainting, and these heart problems can lead to death. In addition, bulimics are at increased risk for ulcers of the stomach and small intestine and for inflammation of the pancreas.

One commonly overlooked problem is the "female athletic triad," a combination of disordered eating, loss of menstruation, and osteoporosis. This can lead to fractures and permanent loss of bone minerals.

ANOREXIA NERVOSA

The diagnosis of anorexia nervosa is made in persons who have lost 15 percent or more of the body weight that is considered normal for their height and age and who have an intense and irrational fear of gaining weight. Even with extreme weight loss, anorexics perceive themselves as overweight. Their attitude toward food and weight control becomes obsessive and they frequently develop bizarre or ritualistic behaviors around food, such as chewing each bite a specific number of times. Anorexics minimize the seriousness of their weight loss and are highly resistant to treatment.

The two basic types of anorexia nervosa are the restricting type and the binge-eating/purging type. The restricting type is characterized by an extremely limited diet, often without carbohydrates or fats. This may be accompanied by excessive exercising or hyperactivity. Up to half of anorexics eventually lose control over their severely restricted dieting and begin to engage in binge eating. They then induce vomiting, use diuretics or laxatives, or exercise excessively to control their weight. People who are in the binge-eating/purging group are at greater risk for medical complications.

As the weight loss in either type reaches starvation proportions, anorexics become more and more preoccupied with food; they may hoard food or steal. They also experience sleep abnormalities, loss of interest in sex, and poor concentration and attention. In addition, they slowly restrict their social contacts and become more and more socially isolated. In general, anorexics of the binge-eating/purging type are likely to have problems with impulse control and may engage in substance abuse, excessive spending, sexual promiscuity, and other forms of compulsive behavior. This group is also more likely to attempt suicide or to hurt themselves than others with eating disorders.

BULIMIA NERVOSA

Persons who have bulimia nervosa are similar in behavior to the subset of anorexics who binge and purge, but they tend to maintain their weight at or near normal for their age and height. They intermittently have an overwhelming urge to eat, usually associated with a period of anxiety or depression, and can consume as many as 15,000 calories in a relatively short period of time, typically one to two hours. Binge foods are usually high calorie and easy to digest, such as ice cream. The binge eating provides a sense of numbing of the anxiety or relief from the depression. Failing to recognize that they are full, bulimics eventually stop eating because of abdominal pain, nausea, being interrupted, or some other non-hunger-related reason. At that point, psychological stress again increases as they reflect on the amount they have eaten. Most bulimics then induce vomiting, but some use laxatives, diuretics, severe food restriction, fasting, or excessive exercise to avoid gaining weight.

Bulimics tend to be secretive, binge eating and purging when alone. These episodes may occur only a few times a week or as often as several times a day. As with binge-eating/purging anorexics, bulimics are likely to abuse alcohol and other drugs, make suicidal gestures, and engage in other kinds of impulsive behavior such as shoplifting. Because of the electrolyte imbalances and other adverse consequences of repeated vomiting or the use of laxatives or diuretics, bulimics are at risk for multiple serious medical complications which, if uncorrected, can lead to death.

BINGE-EATING DISORDER

The American Psychiatric Association has developed provisional criteria for binge-eating disorder in order to study this disorder more completely. The criteria include compulsive and excessive eating at least twice a week for six months without self-induced vomiting, purging, or excessive exercise. That is, binge-eating disorder is bulimia nervosa without the compensatory weight-loss mechanisms. For this reason, most binge eaters are slightly to significantly overweight. In addition to the eating problems, many binge eaters experience relationship problems and have a history of depression or other psychiatric disorders.

OTHER EATING DISORDERS

Anorexia and bulimia nervosa and binge-eating disorder have strict diagnostic criteria set forth by the American Psychiatric Association. However, these three do not cover the entire spectrum of disordered eating patterns. Those people who induce vomiting after consuming only a small amount of food, for example, or those who chew large amounts of food and spit it out rather than swallow it, do not fit the diagnosis of bulimia. For such persons, a diagnosis of "Eating Disorder, Not Otherwise Specified" is used.

PREVALENCE OF EATING DISORDERS

Anorexia nervosa is the rarest of the eating disorders, affecting fewer than 1 percent of adolescent and young women (that is, women ages thirteen to twenty-five) and a tiny proportion of young men. Bulimia nervosa, on the other hand, affects up to 3 percent of teenage and young adult women and about 0.2 percent of men. Even more of this age group, probably 5 percent, suffer from binge-eating disorder. In obese patients, fully one-third meet the criteria for this disorder. Binge eating is the most common eating disorder in men, although more women actually have this disorder. Eating Disorders, Not Otherwise Specified, are even more common.

TREATMENT

Treatment of persons with eating disorders can take place in an inpatient or an outpatient setting. Hospitalization is indicated for patients with severe malnutrition, serious medical complications, an increased risk of suicide, and those who are unable to care for themselves or have failed outpatient treatment.

The first step in the treatment of anorexics must be restoring their body weight. This may require hospitalization. A system of carefully structured rewards for weight gain is often successful. For example, the gain of a target amount of weight may be tied to being allowed to go outside or having visits from friends. Once the anorexic is nutritionally stabilized, individual, family, cognitive-behavioral, and other therapies are indicated to address issues specific to the individual.

The first step in the treatment of bulimics is a comprehensive medical evaluation. Bulimics are less likely than anorexics to require hospitalization. As with anorexia nervosa, treatment includes individual, family, and cognitive-behavioral therapies. In addition, group therapy may be helpful. Cognitive-behavioral therapies are effective in the treatment of bulimia nervosa. Patients are taught to recognize and analyze cues that trigger the binge-purge cycle. Once analyzed, they are taught to reframe these thoughts, feelings, and beliefs to more adaptive and less destructive ones, thus altering the cycle.

Outpatient care should be carefully coordinated among a multidisciplinary team: an experienced health care practitioner to monitor the patient's medical condition, a therapist to address psychological and emotional issues, a family therapist to deal with control and other issues within the family, and a nutritionist to develop and monitor a sensible meal plan.

Medications may be a helpful adjunct in some cases, particularly in those eating-disordered patients who have an additional psychiatric diagnosis such as major depression or obsessive-compulsive disorder. Simply gaining weight usually improves mood in anorexics, but antidepressants (particularly the selective serotonin-reuptake inhibitors or SSRIs) may help not only with depression but also with the obsessive-compulsive aspects of the anorexic's relationship with food.

Several different antidepressants (including monoamine oxidase inhibitors, the tricyclics amitriptyline and desipramine, and high-dose fluoxetine, an SSRI) are associated with fewer episodes of binge eating and purging in bulimic patients, in addition to their use in treating anxiety and depression. These drugs have not been studied extensively in the treatment of binge-eating disorder, however.

PREVENTION OF EATING DISORDERS

Preventive measures should include education about normal body weight for height and techniques used in advertising and the media to promote an unrealistic body image. Parents, teachers, coaches, and health care providers all play a role in prevention. Parents, coaches, and teachers need to be educated about the messages they give to growing children about bodies, body development, and weight. In addition, they need to be aware of early signs of risk. Health care providers need to include screening for eating disorders as a routine part of care. Specific indicators include dieting for weight loss associated with unrealistic weight goals, criticism of the body, social isolation, cessation of menses, and evidence of vomiting or laxative or diuretic use.

SOURCES FOR FURTHER STUDY

Battegay, Raymond. *The Hunger Diseases.* Northvale, N.J.: Jason Aronson, 1997. Addresses the emotional hunger that, the author contends, underlies all eating disorders, from anorexia to obesity.

Bruch, Hilde. *The Golden Cage: The Enigma of Anorexia Nervosa.* Reprint. Cambridge, Mass.: Harvard University Press, 2001. A classic work by a pioneer in the field of eating disorders. Portrays the development of anorexia nervosa as an attempt by a young woman to attain a sense of control and identity. Discusses the etiology and treatment of anorexia from a modified psychoanalytic perspective.

Brumberg, Joan J. *Fasting Girls: The History of Anorexia Nervosa.* Rev. ed. New York: Vintage, 2000. Outlines the history of anorexia nervosa. Examines the syndrome from multiple perspectives while leaning toward a cultural and feminist perspective. A well-researched and very readable work.

Gordon, Richard. *Eating Disorders: Anatomy of a Social Epidemic.* 2d rev. ed. New York: Blackwell, 2000. A survey of current clinical practice in dealing with eating disorders as well as thorough coverage of their history and social context.

Hirschmann, Jane R., and Carol H. Munter. *When Women Stop Hating Their Bodies: Freeing Yourself from Food and Weight Obsessions.* New York: Fawcett, 1997. Follow-up to the authors' *Overcoming Overeating* (1988) reviews the psychological basis for compulsive eating and provides alternative strategies to persons who have an addictive relationship with food. Presents convincing arguments against dieting and proposes that self-acceptance, physical activity, and health are more appropriate long-term solutions to the problem of overeating.

Sacker, Ira M., and Marc A. Zimmerman. *Dying to Be Thin: Understanding and Defeating Anorexia Nervosa and Bulimia.* Updated ed. New York: Warner Books, 2001. A practical approach, written by two medical doctors, to understanding the sources and causes of eating disorders and how to overcome them. Includes a guide to resources, treatment clinics, and support groups.

Rebecca Lovell Scott

SEE ALSO: Anxiety Disorders; Depression; Hunger; Obsessive-Compulsive Disorder.

Ego Psychology
Erik Erikson

DATE: The late 1930's forward
TYPE OF PSYCHOLOGY: Personality
FIELD OF STUDY: Personality theory

Ego psychology, pioneered by Erikson, Heinz Hartmann, Erich Fromm, Harry Stack Sullivan, and Karen Horney, provided a significant new reformation to the personality theory of Freudian psychoanalysis. Erikson's theory of the growth of the ego throughout the life cycle provided an especially important contribution to this movement.

KEY CONCEPTS
- ego
- id
- psychoanalysis
- psychosocial
- unconscious

Ego psychology emerged in the late 1930's as a reform movement within psychoanalysis. Psychoanalysis, as developed by Sigmund Freud in the previous three decades, was an innovative approach to understanding psychological life. Freud developed the methodology and vocabulary to focus on the meaningfulness of lived experience. For Freud, the true meaning of an experience was largely unconscious. Dreams, slips of the tongue or pen, and symptoms provided examples of such unconscious layers of meaning. In psychoanalytic terminology, beneath the level of the conscious ego, there is an unconscious substructure (the id). Freud used the metaphor of an iceberg to relate these two levels, indicating that the conscious level is analogous to the small, visible tip of an iceberg that shows above the water, whereas the unconscious level is like its large, underwater, invisible mass. The ego, this small surface level of the personality, "manages" one's relations with the world beyond the psyche. The id, in contrast, is "intrapsychic" in the sense that it is not in a relation with the "outer" world beyond the psyche. Rather, the id draws its energy from the biological energy of the instinctual body (such as instincts for sex and aggression). In this traditional psychoanalytic theory, then, the conscious level of the person is rooted in, and motivated by, an unconscious level, as psychological life is ultimately rooted in biological forces.

Freudian psychoanalysis advanced psychology by legitimating the study of the meaningfulness of human actions, but it did so at the price of conceiving of conscious, worldly experience as being only a surface, subtended by unconscious, biological forces, mechanisms cut off from worldly involvement. By the late 1930's, some psychoanalysts had concluded this was too steep a price to pay. The first to formulate these objections systematically was Heinz Hartmann, whose writings between 1939 and 1950 advanced the argument for the autonomy of the ego as a structure of the personality independent of the domination of the unconscious id. It was Hartmann who gave to this protest movement the name "ego psychology."

In the next generation of analysts, this movement found its most articulate voices: Erich Fromm, Harry Stack Sullivan, Karen Horney, and Erik Erikson. Writing from the 1940's through the 1980's, all contributed independently to a perspective that grants to the ego a status much more significant than its role in Freudian psychoanalysis. For them, it is people's relations with the world (and not their subterranean biological energy) that is the most important aspect of their psychological life. For this reason, these psychologists have also sometimes been known as the "social" or "interpersonal" analysts. While all four have unquestionably earned their enduring international reputations, Erikson became the most well known, on account of his formulation of a powerful and comprehensive developmental theory to account for the growth of the ego throughout life.

Freud had asserted that the ego was a weak aspect of the personality, whereas Hartmann posited a strong ego. However, there are wide individual differences in ego strength. Erikson demonstrated how ego strength emerges across stages of a person's development and showed that its particular growth depends on the quality, at each stage, of a person's relations with the world and with other people.

ERIKSON'S SHIFT TO THE PSYCHOSOCIAL LEVEL

Freud had also sketched a developmental theory for psychoanalysis. Built upon his view of the primacy of the intrapsychic id and its bodily source of energy, this theory focused on psychosexual development. For Freud, "sexual" means more than the usual notion of genital sexuality; it is a more general dynamic expression of bodily energy that manifests itself in different forms at different developmental stages. The adult (genital) stage of sexuality, reached at puberty, is the culmination and completion of one's psychosexual development. Preceding that development, Freud saw four pregenital stages of psychosexual development: the oral stage, the anal stage, the phallic stage, and the latency stage. Hence, for this theory of psychosexual development, each stage is centralized as a stage by a particular expression of sexual or erogenous energy. In each stage there is a particular mode of the bodying forth of this energy as desire, manifested by the unique bodily zone that becomes the erogenous zone of that specific stage. It is seen as erogenous because of that bodily zone's capacity to be especially susceptible to stimulation or arousal, such that it becomes the prime source of bodily satisfaction and pleasure at that stage.

Erikson concluded that this psychosexual level was a valid but incomplete portrait of development. More than other proponents of ego psychology, he sought to work with Freud's emphasis on the bodily zones while striving to include that vision within a larger, more encompassing framework. Erikson theorized that each bodily mode correlated with a psychological modality, one that implicated the person's developing ego relations with the world. In particular, he emphasized one's relations with other people as the most important "profile" of the world. He saw the psychosexual meaning of the various bodily zones grounded by changes in the person's social existence at each stage. For that reason, Erikson named his approach a theory of psychosocial development and argued that the growth of the ego could not be reduced to changes in bodily energies. He demonstrated how the psychosexual dimension always implied a key human relation at the heart of each stage, and so the interpersonal could not be reduced to some intrapsychic cause but was itself the basis for the actual development of that stage.

The significance of this shift from the psychosexual level of development to the psychosocial one was enormous, but it can best be appreciated in the context of its depiction of each of the particular stages. One other impact was also strikingly noteworthy. Whereas Freud's theory of psychosexual development saw the process as coming to an end with the person's arrival at the genital stage (with puberty), Erikson realized that the growth of the ego in psychosocial development does not end there but continues in subsequent stages throughout the person's life. In that way, he also transformed developmental psychology from its origins as merely a child psychology into a truly life-span psychology, a revision now widely accepted.

STAGES OF DEVELOPMENT
Erikson specified eight stages of psychosocial development over the course of the life cycle. He saw these unfolding not in a linear sense but epigenetically; that is, in such a way that each stage builds upon those that came before. The first four of these stages are those of childhood, and here Erikson accepts Freud's delineation but adds a psychosocial dimension to each.

The first stage of development (roughly the first year of life) Freud termed the oral stage, naming it (as he did with each stage) after that region of the body seen to be the erogenous zone of that stage. For Freud, the baby's psychosexuality expresses itself primarily through the erogenous power of the mouth and lips. Certainly babies' tendency to mouth almost anything they can get hold of indicates a certain erotic appeal of orality at this time.

However, for Erikson, this bodily expression is not the foundational one. Rather, orality is a wider theme. The essence of this oral pleasure is the satisfaction of "taking in" the world. Such taking in is not restricted to the mouth. Babies take in with their eyes, their ears, their fingers—in every way possible. Orality, as taking in, is not merely a bodily zone but a psychological modality of relating to the world. This world-relation also implicates another person. For a quite helpless baby to be able to get or take in, there must be another person there giving (typically a parent). This psychological modality, in other words, is already essentially and profoundly interpersonal. As a result, it is the quality of this interpersonal relationship with the "mothering ones" that will provide the basis of the baby's growth at this stage. If the parents (as the face of the world) are dependably there for the baby, the baby will come to be able to count on their omnipresent beneficence.

With such experience, the baby develops a sense of "basic trust"— Erikson's term for the ego growth of this first stage. Basic trust implies a certain relation with the world: specifically, one in which the person can relax and take his or her own ongoingness for granted. Once trust is gained, such a person can face the uncertainties to come with the secure confidence that, whatever may happen, he or she will be fine. In contrast, if the baby does not encounter a trustworthy world at this stage, he or she will be unable to develop this core sense of basic trust. The baby will, instead, be overwhelmed by the experience of "basic mistrust"—the anxiety that accompanies the lurking, ever-present possibility of threat, that edge of anonymous malevolence. Then, full openness to the world is always constricted by the need for the self-preservation of the ego.

Freud identified the second psychosexual stage (roughly the period from age one to three) as the anal stage, on account of the pleasure available by the new ability of the child to control eliminative functioning—what is colloquially called toilet training. Here again, Erikson reexamined this bodily mode and discovered, at the heart of it, a psychosocial dynamic. The issue of control in mastering the processes of elimination involves two kinds of action: retention (of feces or urine) until one gets to the toilet, and then elimination (once one is at the toilet).

Erikson recognized that this interplay between retention and elimination is more than merely the organ mode of sphincter control. Rather, it manifests a more basic psychological modality: the interplay between holding on and letting go. It is not only with regard to the eliminative functions that this dynamic gets played out in this stage. Most important, it is in the social arena, with one's parents, that toddlers grow this new capacity to exercise control. Even toilet training itself is an exquisitely interpersonal interaction of the child with the parental "trainers."

It is not only toilet training that distinguishes children's quest for control at this stage. In many ways the child is now striving for a new encounter with others. Securely grounded now by the sense of basic trust gained in the previous stage, children are ready to move from a relationship of dependence to one of independence. Even being able to stand up on their own two feet evinces this new relationship. From a newfound delight in the power of speaking the word "no!" to the appearance of strong preferences in everything from clothes to food, and most evidently in their emotional reactions to the denial of these preferences, toddlers are asserting a declaration of independence. Though the consequent contest of wills with the parents can be difficult, ultimately the child learns both to have autonomy and to recognize its social limits. This growth of autonomy is the key gain of this second stage, as the ego grasps its radical independence from the minds or control of others. If the child does not have the opportunity to develop this experience, the consequence would be to develop a crippling sense of shame and self-doubt instead.

The third stage of psychosexual development (ages three through six) is Freud's phallic stage, because the child's sexual organs become the erogenous zone at this time. Freud did not mean to imply that children experience their sexuality in the sense of adult, genital sexuality; there is no experience of orgasms and no interest in intercourse at this time. Rather, for Freud, the sex organs become erogenous on account of their power to differentiate gender. Hence, the classic psychoanalytic themes of penis envy and castration anxiety are rooted in this stage as well as the Oedipal conflict—children's imaginal working out of their now gender-based relations with their parents.

For Erikson, it is not the genitals as bodily organs that are the source of such anxiety or envy. Rather, they symbolize social roles. As a result, in a sexist culture, it would be no wonder that a girl may envy the greater psychosocial status enjoyed by the boy. Correlatively, the boy would experience the anxiety of losing his newfound gender-based potency. Here again, Erikson finds a profound interpersonal dynamic at work. This new positing of oneself is not done only in the child's fantasy life. The ego at this stage is growing new capacities to engage the world: the ability to use language, more fine locomotor activity, and the power of the imagination. Through these developing capacities, children can thrust themselves forth with a new sense of purpose. On the secure basis of trust and autonomy, they can now include initiative in their world relations, supported by their parents as encouraging prototypes. On the other hand, the parents can so stigmatize such projects of initiative that children may instead become convinced that they manifest their badness. In such cases, feelings of guilt can overwhelm their sense of initiative, as they become crippled by guilt not only for what they have done but also for who they are as initiating beings.

Freud identified the fourth psychosexual stage as the latency stage (ages seven to twelve) because psychosexuality was not manifest at that time. It had become latent, or driven underground, by the conclusion of the Oedipal conflict. For Freud, psychosexual development is arrested at this stage and must await the eruption of puberty to get started again. Erikson sees in this stage a positive growth in the child's ego. Once more, changes in psychosocial relations lead the way. The child goes off to school, and to a wider world beyond the immediate family circle, to encounter the world beyond the imaginal realm: a place in which actual accomplishments await the application of actual skills. Rather than being satisfied with imagining hitting a home run, the child now strives to actually hit the ball. It is, in other words, a time for the development of skills, techniques, and competencies that will enable one to succeed at real-world events. Sports, games, school, bicycling, camping, collecting things, taking care of pets, art, music, even doing chores now offer children arenas to test their growing capacity to learn the ways of the world.

At the heart of this learning process are teachers, not only professionals but learned others of many kinds. The child becomes a student to many experts, from coaches to Cub Scout leaders to the older boy next door who already knows about computers. Even sports heroes or characters in books with whom the child has no personal contact can emerge as profoundly valuable teachers, opening the world and showing the way to mastery of it. This is what Erikson means by a sense of industry, which is for him the key egoic gain of this stage. If children's efforts are not encouraged and cultivated, however, they can instead find their industrious tendency overwhelmed by a sense of inferiority and inadequacy.

PSYCHOSOCIAL STAGES OF LATER CHILDHOOD

It is when the child arrives at Freud's fifth stage that the psychosexual and psychosocial theories must part from their previous chronological company. Freud's fifth stage is the genital stage: the completion of psychosexual development. With puberty, the person attains the same capacities and erogenous orientation as an adult and thus becomes as mature, psychosexually speaking, as any adult. For Erikson's theory, however, the onset of puberty does not mark the completion of psychosocial development, which continues throughout life, but only its next stage: adolescence (ages twelve to twenty-one). Once more, the changing bodily zone implicates a changing social existence, for puberty is more than a merely chemical or hormonal change. More than the body, it is the whole person who is transformed by this flood of new issues and possibilities. This eruption provokes questions that had been taken for granted before. "Who am I becoming? Who am I to be?" appear, in small and large ways. The new adolescent must confront such new questions when on a date, at a party, or even when deciding what to wear to school each day. In other words, the adolescent ego has now developed a self-reflective loop, in which its own identity is now taken as an issue to be formed, a task that it must resolve for itself.

The formation of ego-identity can be an especially acute challenge in modern culture, where the traditional embeddedness in extended families and communities is often no longer available to provide the network of identifications with which to resolve these questions. Instead, adolescent peer groups become the key psychosocial relationship for this stage. These reference groups offer the adolescent the prospect of trying on a new identity by embracing certain subgroup values, norms, and perspectives. This experimental phase is an acting "as if"—as if the person were who they are trying out to be.

Optimally, adolescents will have the latitude to assume and discard prospective identities within the fluidity of what Erikson called a psychosocial moratorium—a time out from having to bear the same weight of consequences for their choices that an adult would. For example, pledging a lifetime commitment to a boyfriend at thirteen does not, in fact, entail the same level of commitment that a marriage would; nor does deciding to major in accounting upon arriving at college actually bind one to follow through with a lifetime career as an accountant. With sufficient opportunity to explore and try out various tentative choices, adolescents will, optimally, conclude this stage by arriving at a more clarified sense of their own values and sense of direction. If this is not achieved, adolescents will either be left with a feeling of identity diffusion or have prematurely foreclosed on a possible identity that does not fit.

PSYCHOSOCIAL STAGES OF ADULTHOOD

Beyond adolescence, Erikson also identified three psychosocial stages of adulthood: early adulthood, middle age, and old age. The first, roughly the period of one's twenties and thirties, begins with the person's moving out from under the insulating protection of the adolescent psychosocial moratorium. One's choices (of marriage, career, family) cease to be "as if"; they are now profoundly real commitments with long-term impact. Making such commitments is not only a momentary event (such as saying "I do") but requires devoting oneself to living an ongoing and open-ended history. This new situation inaugurates the next psychosocial development, which Erikson names the crisis of intimacy versus isolation. Intimacy here has a broader range than its connotation of sexual relations: It encompasses the capacity to relate to another with fullness and mutuality. To be fully open with and to another person entails obvious risks—of being misunderstood or rejected—but with it comes the enormous gain of true love. To experience the closeness, sharing, and valuing of the other without boundaries is the hallmark of an infinite relationship (infinite, that is, not necessarily in duration but in depth). The relationship with a loved other is the evident psychosocial context of this growth. If it does not occur, then the early adult will come to experience instead a deep sense of isolation and loneliness. This consequence can accrue either through the failure to enter into a relationship or through the failure, within a relationship, to achieve intimacy. Some of the most terrible afflictions of isolation at this stage are within those marriages so lacking in intimacy that the couple are essentially isolated even though living together.

Beginning around age forty, a further stage of adult psychosocial development begins: middle age. The situation has once again changed. People are no longer merely starting out on their adulthood but have by now achieved a place in the adult world. Typically, if they are going to have a family, they have got it by now; if a career, they are well launched by now. Indeed, middle age, the period from forty to sixty-five, marks the attainment of the height of a person's worldly powers and responsibilities. Whatever worldly mountain one is going to climb in this lifetime, it is during middle age that one gets as high up it as one will go. The arrival at this new position opens the door to the next stage of development. Now the psychosocial growth will involve one's social relations with the next generation, centered on the issue of generativity versus stagnation. The long plateau of middle age offers the opportunity to become helpful to those who follow along that upward climb. These are, most immediately, one's own children but also include the next generation in the community, on the job, in the profession, in the whole human family. The middle-aged adult is in the position of being the teacher, the mentor, the instituter, the creator, the producer—the generator. Having arrived at the peak of one's own mountain, one no longer need be so concerned about placating someone else and so is able now fully to be oneself. To be an original, the middle-aged adult can also originate in the truest sense: to give of oneself to those who, following along behind, need that help. In this way, the person grows the specific ego-strength of care: an extending of oneself to others in an asymmetric way, giving without expectation of an equal return, precisely because one can. The failure to grow in this way results in stagnation—the disillusioned boredom of a life going nowhere. Some middle-aged adults, trying futilely to ward off this gnawing feeling of stagnation, hide behind desperate efforts of self-absorption, what Erikson called "treating oneself as one's one and only child."

By the late sixties, a variety of changes mark the onset of the final stage of psychosocial development: old age. Retirement, becoming a grandparent, declining health, and even the increasingly frequent death of one's own age-mates precipitate a new issue into the forefront: one's own mortality. While people at every age know they are mortal, this knowledge has no particular impact on one's life when one is younger because it is then so easily overlooked. In contrast, by old age, this knowledge of one's mortality is now woven into the very fabric of one's everyday life in a way that it can no longer be evaded by imagining it postponed until some distant, abstract future.

American society tends to avoid really confronting one's being-towards-death. Some psychologists have gone so far as to say that death has replaced sex as the primary cultural taboo, hidden in hospital rooms and code words ("passed on," "put to sleep," "expired"). Fearing death, people find it very hard to grow old. If one is not available to the growth opportunities of this stage, one is likely to sink instead into despair—a feeling of regret over a life not lived. Often even one's despair cannot be faced and is then hidden beneath feelings of disgust and bitterness: a self-contempt turned outward against the world.

Erikson points out that this final stage of life offers the opportunity for the ultimate growth of the ego. To embrace one's mortality fully allows one to stand open-eyed at the edge of one's life, a perspective from which it becomes possible to really see one's life as a whole. One can then see, and own, one's life as one's own responsibility, admitting of no substitutes. It is this holistic vision of one's life that Erikson calls integrity: the full integration of the personality. It is in this vision that people can actually realize that their own lives are also integrated with life as a whole, in a seamless web of interconnections. Thus, the ego finally finds its ultimate, transpersonal home within the whole of being. It is this perspective that opens the door to wisdom, the final growth.

SOURCES FOR FURTHER STUDY

Coles, Robert. *Erik H. Erikson: The Growth of His Work.* Boston: Little, Brown, 1970. A fine blend of Erikson's biography with his major ideas.

_____, ed. *The Erik Erikson Reader.* New York: W. W. Norton, 2000. A collection of Erikson's most influential and accessible writings.

Erikson, Erik H. *Childhood and Society.* 1950. Reprint. New York: Norton, 1993. A wide-ranging compilation of Erikson's studies of development, clinical practice, cross-cultural analyses, and psychohistory. His most accessible and popular book.

_____. *Gandhi's Truth: On the Origins of Militant Nonviolence.* 1970. Reprint. New York: Norton, 1993. Erikson's application of his developmental theory to the life of Mahatma Gandhi. This book won the Pulitzer Prize.

_____. *Identity and the Life Cycle.* 1959. Reprint. New York: Norton, 1980. Erikson's view of human development, with particular emphasis on ego identity and its formation in adolescence.

_____. *The Life Cycle Completed.* Extended version. New York: W. W. Norton, 1997. Erikson's final book, examining the life cycle from the viewpoint of the final stage.

Friedman, Lawrence. *Identity's Architect: A Biography of Erik H. Erikson.* New York: Simon & Schuster, 1999. A thorough and balanced biography of Erikson, written by an author who interviewed his subject extensively in the last years of his life.

Hartmann, Heinz. *Essays on Ego Psychology.* New York: International Universities Press, 1964. A collection of Hartmann's foundational essays on the autonomy of the ego.

Yankelovich, Daniel, and William Barrett. *Ego and Instinct.* New York: Vintage, 1971. An original contribution to the dialogue of Freudian psychoanalysis and ego psychology on the question of human nature.

Christopher M. Aanstoos

SEE ALSO: Personality Theory; Psychoanalytic Psychology; Psychoanalytic Psychology and Personality: Sigmund Freud.

EMOTIONS

TYPE OF PSYCHOLOGY: Emotion
FIELD OF STUDY: Motivation theory

Emotion is a basic aspect of human functioning. Emotions are personal experiences that arise from a complex interplay among physiological, cognitive, and situational variables. Theories and measurement of emotion allow psychologists to understand diverse expressions of behavior, and they form the cornerstone of many approaches to the treatment of psychological problems.

KEY CONCEPTS
- cognitive appraisal
- emotional intensity
- primary emotions
- psychosomatic disorders
- secondary emotions
- state emotion
- trait emotion
- visceral responses

An emotion is a valenced experience that is felt with some degree of intensity, involves a person's interpretation of the immediate situation, and is accompanied by learned and unlearned physical responses. Emotions are transitory states, and they have five characteristics. First, emotions are experiences, not specific behaviors or thoughts. Although thoughts can sometimes lead to emotions, and behaviors can sometimes be caused by emotions, an emotion is a personal experience. Second, an emotional experience has "valence," meaning that the emotion has a positive or negative quality. Because emotions have valence, they often motivate people toward action. People tend to seek activities, situations, and people that enhance their experience of positive emotional states, and they tend to avoid situations that are connected with the experience of negative emotions.

Third, emotions involve cognitive appraisals. That is, one's interpretation of the immediate situation influences which emotion is experienced. For example, a child may experience either joy or fear when being chased, depending on whether the child interprets the chase as playful or dangerous. Fourth, emotions involve physical responses. Physical responses may be internal, such as changes in heart rate, blood pressure, or respiration (called visceral responses); physical responses can also be external, such as facial expressions. In addition, the bodily responses that characterize emotions are partly reflexive (unlearned) and partly learned. An increase in heart rate is a reflexive response that accompanies intense fear. That which a person fears, however, and his or her accompanying bodily response may be the product of learning; crying when afraid is an emotional expression that is subject to learning experiences. Fifth, emotions can vary in intensity: Anger can become rage, amusement can become joy, and fear can be heightened to a state of terror.

Psychologist Robert Plutchik contends that there are eight innate, primary emotions: joy, anticipation, anger, disgust, sadness, surprise, fear, and acceptance. Like the colors of a color wheel, primary emotions can combine to produce secondary emotions: surprise plus sadness can produce disappointment; anger plus disgust can produce contempt; and fear plus surprise can produce awe. Because each primary emotion can vary in intensity, and each level of intensity for one emotion can combine with some other level of intensity of another emotion, the total number of possible emotions runs to the hundreds. Although many psychologists agree that there exist primary emotions, there is no way that a person could distinguish such a large number of personal emotional experiences. Moreover, psychologists have not even attempted to measure such an unwieldy array of secondary emotions.

State and Trait Emotions
Nevertheless, psychologists have developed numerous assessment instruments to study common emotions. (An assessment instrument is a method used to measure some psychological quality.) Because there are so many different emotions, the study of emotion requires the development of specific methods that can accurately measure each of the common emotions. The most popular method of measuring an emotion is a self-report questionnaire in which a person answers questions relevant to a particular emotion. When measuring emotions, researchers make a distinction between "state" and "trait" emotion. An emotional state refers to what a person is experiencing at the moment. If one is interested in assessing how anxious someone currently is, one might use a questionnaire that asks the person to respond to several anxiety-related statements, using a scale from 1 ("not at all") to 5 ("very much"). Some examples of relevant statements are "I feel tense," "I feel nervous and shaky inside," "My heart is beating rapidly," and "I feel a sense of foreboding." The higher the total score on the questionnaire, the more anxiety the person is experiencing at the moment.

Trait emotion refers to how often an emotion is experienced. An "anxious person" is someone who frequently experiences the state of anxiety. Moreover, one would call someone a "hostile person" if one determined that he or she frequently exhibits states of anger. Examples of statements that assess trait anxiety are "I frequently become tense," "I often feel afraid for no apparent reason," "I am bothered by dizzy spells," and "I tend to worry a lot."

Assessment Measures
Psychologists have developed numerous questionnaires to assess emotions. There are self-report measures to assess anxiety, anger, guilt, happiness, and

hopelessness, to name a few. In addition to measures of specific emotions, researchers have developed methods for assessing emotional intensity. Emotional intensity refers to the strength with which a person experiences both positive and negative emotions. It has been found that people who are emotionally intense report a feeling of well-being as "exuberance, animated joyfulness, and zestful enthusiasm." On the other hand, people who score low on a measure of emotional intensity experience a state of well-being as "serenity, contentment, tranquil calmness, and easygoing composure."

In addition to the use of self-report measures of emotion, psychologists often use physiological measures. Using sophisticated biological measuring instruments, psychologists are able to assess emotional arousal by measuring, for example, heart rate, skin sweating, respiration, blood pressure, and muscle tension. By examining the amount these measures change in response to a stimulus, researchers are able to infer emotional arousal. For example, it has been found that people who have the type of personality that puts them at risk for heart attacks show greater increases in blood pressure when trapped in a traffic jam, in comparison to those people who have personality characteristics that do not predispose them to heart attacks. In this instance, the psychologist uses the measure of blood pressure to infer a negative emotion, such as anger or frustration.

One question that arises when using physiological measures to assess emotions is whether each emotion has a specific pattern of physiological responses. For example, blood pressure appears to be particularly responsive to anger-inducing situations. People's heart rates, however, increase during emotional states of excitement, anxiety, anger, and sexual arousal. For this reason, researchers may use multiple measures of emotion, assessing self-reports of emotion while physiological responses are being recorded. Another way of assessing emotions is by direct observation of overt behavior. Approach behavior can indicate acceptance, and avoidance behavior can reflect fear or disgust. In addition, facial expressions have been used to assess various emotional states.

POLYGRAPHS

When researchers developed means for measuring visceral responses and discovered that these responses are associated with emotions, it was not long before the possibility of detecting lies was raised. The use of a polygraph to detect lying is based on the assumption that people will feel anxious or guilty when asked a question that has personal, emotional significance to past deeds. The polygraph tester measures and compares physiological responses to both control questions and relevant questions to infer lying. For example, if a person is suspected of murdering John Smith on May 16, the tester may ask the control question: "Have you ever hurt someone?" Because everyone has hurt someone at one time or another, and probably feels guilty about it, some level of emotional response will be registered in changes in heart rate and respiration. The relevant question is "Did you kill John Smith on May

16?" Supposedly, the innocent person will show a greater emotional response to the control question than the relevant question. The perpetrator of the crime should show a greater emotional response to the relevant question because of its extreme emotional significance.

The use of polygraph testing is surrounded by controversy. Although some liars can be detected, if a perpetrator does not feel guilty about the crime—or does not believe that the polygraph can measure lying—he or she will not show the expected response to the critical questions about the crime. In addition, research has shown that some innocent people will become so anxious when asked "relevant" questions that they are mistakenly viewed as guilty. The American Psychological Association has expressed grave concern over the validity of polygraph testing. The U.S. Congress has outlawed the use of preemployment testing to predict who might, for example, steal inventory. Despite the reservations of the American Psychological Association, however, security agencies and defense industries are allowed to use polygraph testing.

CLINICAL APPLICATIONS AND THEORY

The development of theories of emotion and of methods for measuring emotions has wide application in the field of clinical psychology. Many psychological disorders are defined by emotional problems. People with phobias exhibit excessive anxiety in situations that offer little or no possibility of harm. Strong fears of water, heights, insects, closed spaces, flying, and social situations are common examples of phobias. Theories of emotion provide a framework within which clinicians can understand the development of phobias. Measures of anxiety can be used to help diagnose those people who suffer from phobias.

Depression is another example of a psychological disorder that has a strong emotional component. Twenty percent of women and 10 percent of men will experience a major depression at some time in their lives. This complex disorder is manifested by distorted thinking (such as self-critical thinking), physical difficulties (such as fatigue), and an array of emotions. Some of the emotional symptoms of depression include sadness, anxiety, and guilt. Thus, when psychologists assess the emotional aspects of depression, they use questionnaires that include items that address several different emotions.

Not only does the study of emotion help psychologists to understand psychological disorders, but methods of treatment have also been developed based on the understanding of emotion. For example, psychological research has shown that emotional responses, such as anxiety, can be learned. Consequently, treatment strategies have been developed to help people unlearn their anxiety reactions. As a result, many people who suffer from simple phobias can be treated effectively in a short period of time. Theories of emotion that examine the relation between thinking and emotion have led to therapies to alleviate depression. Aaron Beck has shown that the sadness, anxiety, and guilt that accompany depression can be treated by helping people change their styles of thinking.

Another area within clinical psychology that has benefited by the increasing understanding of emotion is psychosomatic disorders. A psychosomatic disorder (also called a psychophysiological disorder) is an abnormal physical condition brought about by chronic negative emotions. Ulcers, hypertension, headaches, and arthritis are examples of conditions that can be brought about or worsened by negative emotions. The emotions that are most often implicated in the development of psychosomatic disorders are anger and anxiety. For example, researchers have discovered that prolonged anxiety induced by internal conflict can cause ulcers in susceptible people. In addition, researchers now have evidence that chronic hostility is a risk factor for the development of heart disease.

Social psychologists study the influence of social factors on behavior. Theories of emotion have been a focus of social psychologists because one's experience of emotion is in part determined by the immediate situation, and the immediate situation often includes the behavior of others. Indeed, Stanley Schachter, a social psychologist, is responsible for the development of a theory of emotion that underscores the importance of one's cognitive appraisal of the social context in determining the emotion that one experiences. For example, when people experience physiological arousal, their own emotional experience will most likely be consistent with their interpretation of the social context. If they are with a happy person, they will experience happiness; if they are in the presence of an angry person, they will experience anger. Theories of emotion have also increased understanding of many social phenomena, such as aggression and interpersonal attraction.

EMOTION RESEARCH

For centuries, philosophers and psychologists have recognized the importance of understanding personality differences based on the type and degree of emotional expression. In the fifth century B.C.E., the Greek physician Hippocrates classified people on the basis of emotional temperament. The view that people differ in temperament remains today. Arnold Buss and Robert Plomin have hypothesized that newborns differ in their susceptibility to distress, fear, and anger. Everyday descriptions of people as "happy-go-lucky," "stoic," and "volatile" represent the tendency to group people according to characteristic styles of emotional expression. Clinical psychologists speak of the "hysterical personality" as exhibiting excessive emotional lability and the "schizoid personality" as showing emotional indifference toward others.

Theologians have traditionally approached emotion as representing the dark side of human nature. What elevates humans above other animals has been thought to be the capacity to overcome passion with reason. Even this seemingly archaic view of emotion has its counterpart in modern psychology. Psychoanalysts help people gain control of their feelings through understanding the unconscious roots of their emotions. Cognitive therapists attempt to alleviate emotional dysfunctions by teaching clients to "think more rationally."

The modern era of research on emotion can be traced to Charles Darwin's 1872 book *The Expression of the Emotions in Man and Animals*. Darwin believed that emotional displays evolved as a means of communication and had adaptive significance for the survival of the species. Indeed, there is some scientific support for the assertion that emotional expressions are basic biological responses: Newborn infants show expressions of emotion that closely match the expressions of adults; all infants, including those born deaf and blind, exhibit similar facial expressions in similar situations; very young babies can tell the difference between different emotional expressions; and there is considerable similarity in the expression of emotions across diverse cultures.

In the second half of the twentieth century, psychologists made important advances in formulating theories of emotions and devising assessment instruments to measure emotions. Scientists have arrived at the point where they recognize many of the fundamental aspects of emotion: the nervous system, thought, behavior, and the immediate situation. The challenge for the future is to map the intricate interplay among these variables and achieve a thorough understanding of this basic facet of human functioning.

SOURCES FOR FURTHER STUDY

Barlow, David H. *Anxiety and Its Disorders*. 2d ed. New York: Guilford Press, 2001. In the early part of the book, the author reviews basic aspects of emotion. The remainder is devoted to the emotion of anxiety and how anxiety forms the basis of many clinical disorders. Some of the disorders addressed are panic disorder, obsessive-compulsive disorder, phobias, and post-traumatic stress disorder. A very comprehensive treatment of anxiety disorders. Barlow takes a strong research orientation and presents the material at a college level.

Bernstein, Douglas A., Stewart Alison Clarke, and Louis A. Penner. *Psychology*. 5th ed. New York: Houghton Mifflin, 1999. Presents an introduction to the topic of emotion. Covers a wide range of areas: definition of emotion, physiology of emotion, major theories, social aspects of emotion, and facial expressions. The authors do not assume that the reader has any background in psychology, and they write in a clear, concise manner, providing interesting examples and graphics.

Corcoran, Kevin J., and Joel Fischer. *Adults*. Vol. 2 in *Measures for Clinical Practice: A Sourcebook*. 3d ed. New York: Free Press, 2000. Reprints more than one hundred self-report assessment instruments. An excellent source for learning how researchers measure emotions, and can be used should one want to conduct a study. This book, however, does not include some of the most commonly used questionnaires for measuring emotions.

Ekman, Paul, and Richard J. Davidson, eds. *The Nature of Emotion: Fundamental Questions*. New York: Oxford University Press, 1997. The editors asked twenty-four leading theorists in the field of the psychology of emotions to answer the same twelve questions on their subject. Areas of agreement and disagreement are highlighted, along with a summary chapter at the end.

Laurence Grimm

SEE ALSO: Clinical Depression; Personality: Psychophysiological Measures; Phobias.

ENDOCRINE SYSTEM

TYPE OF PSYCHOLOGY: Biological bases of behavior
FIELD OF STUDY: Endocrine system

Behavior, by definition, includes physiological events which are responses to internal and external stimuli; the endocrine system, through the action of hormones and in co-operation with the nervous system, plays a necessary role in bringing about these reactions in animals and humans.

KEY CONCEPTS
- adrenal glands
- biopsychology
- endocrine system
- ethology
- hormone
- hypothalamus
- pituitary gland

Curiosity about behavior, both animal and human, is of long standing. The suspicion that substances in the body contribute to behavior also has a long history. During the fifth century B.C.E., Hippocrates suggested, in his humoral theory, that personality was determined by four body fluids: phlegm, black bile, yellow bile, and blood. The dominance of one or another of the fluids was associated with a behavior pattern. A proportionate distribution of the fluids resulted in a balanced personality. This theory has contributed terms such as phlegmatic, sanguine, bilious, and good- or bad-humored to describe personality types and states of mind.

Aristotle (384-322 B.C.E.) is reported to have performed castration experiments on both fowl and men in order to alter behavior. He believed that something produced by the testes caused typically male behavior. Several nineteenth century researchers continued the study of the connection between the testes and male reproductive behavior. In 1849, Arnold Adolphe Berthold initiated a series of experiments on cockerels. He removed the testes from six birds and noted their loss of "male" behavior. Testes were transplanted into the abdomens of half the castrated birds. Successful transplantation restored the typical male crowing and combativeness.

During the late nineteenth and early twentieth centuries, the sciences became more organized. Interest in behavior and its causes continued. The science of ethology, which focuses on animal behavior, came into existence. In the early 1900's, John B. Watson founded a branch of psychology that became known as behavior science. This area of psychology concentrated on human behavioral studies. Eventually, ethology and behavior science contributed to biopsychology, a new branch of psychology which incorporates and applies data from neuroscience, genetics, endocrinology, and physiology in the quest for biological explanations of behavior. Biopsychology embraces several subdivisions. Physiological psychology focuses on nervous system and endocrine system research. Psychopharmacology specializes in the effects of drugs on the nervous system and, ultimately, on behavior. The development of therapeutic drugs is a goal of this discipline. The neuropsychologist studies the effects of brain damage on behavior. Psychophysiology differs from physiological psychology in that the psychophysiologist uses only human subjects, while the physiological psychologist experiments on laboratory animals, especially rats.

Early research in physiological psychology focused on the nervous system, but it soon became evident that the endocrine system also influenced behavior and that the effects of the two systems were interrelated contributors to behavior. The endocrine system essentially consists of ductless glands that produce chemical substances called hormones. The hormones elicit physiological reactions, either locally or at some distant target site. When acting at a distance, the hormones travel to the site by way of the circulatory system.

Hans Selye, a Canadian scientist, proposed a direct connection between the endocrine system and behavior. In 1946, he described physiological events that were triggered by stress. This set of bodily changes became known as the general adaptation syndrome. The syndrome involved the mobilization of the autonomic nervous system, the adrenal glands, and the anterior lobe of the pituitary.

As research continued, data on the role of the endocrine system in determining behavior began to accumulate. Researchers continue to look to the endocrine system to provide clues about the causes of psychiatric diseases and the efficacy of hormone therapy in treating the diseases, as well as in altering behavior patterns.

INVERTEBRATES

Among most invertebrates (animals without backbones), endocrine glands are not in evidence. Specialized cells known as neurosecretory cells serve as endocrine tissue. The cells, which resemble neurons (the functional cells of the nervous system) are hormone producers. In invertebrate animals such as the hydra and planaria, the secretions (hormones) of the neurosecretory cells seem to influence growth and may be the underlying cause of the tremendous powers of regeneration possessed by the animals. There are indications that the development of sexuality, the laying of eggs, and the release of sperm may be under hormonal control in these animals. Attempts to establish the link between hormones and invertebrate behavior when the hormones are produced by neurosecretory cells have inherent problems. A common method of studying hormone influence involves removal of the secreting organ, which causes a hormone deficit. Changes in physiology or behavior are observed. A hormone is then provided to the animal to see if the original condition can be restored. Use of this method is complicated by the difficulty in removing all the functioning neurosecretory cells. In addition, the cells regenerate rapidly. This prevents an accurate assessment of the effects of hormone deficit.

Hormone effects are observable and measurable in the more developed invertebrates such as the *Arthropoda*. Studies carried out on insects and crustaceans indicate the presence of both neurosecretory cells and endocrine glands. Among the behaviors and activities controlled by the hormones released from either the cells or the glands are molting, sexual differentiation, sexual behavior, water balance, and diapause. Because arthropods are encased in an outer skeletal structure, it is necessary for the animals to shed their outer structure in order to grow. During the growth years, the animals go through cycles of shedding the outer skeleton—or molting—growing, and reforming an outer coat. There is evidence that insects are under hormonal control when they enter a state of diapause, or arrested behavior in adverse times.

VERTEBRATES

All vertebrates (animals with backbones) have a well-developed and highly organized endocrine system. The system consists of the following glands: the pituitary, the pineal, the thyroid, the thymus, the pancreas, a pair of adrenals (each adrenal actually acts as two glands—the adrenal cortex produces unique hormones and functions independently of the adrenal medulla), a pair of parathyroids, and a pair of ovaries or testes. Endocrine tissue in the gastrointestinal tract readies the system for the digestive process. During a pregnancy, the placental tissue assumes an endocrine function. Although the kidneys do not produce a hormone directly, they release an enzyme which converts a blood protein into a hormone that stimulates red blood cell production.

All vertebrates have a pituitary. The pituitary is a small, round organ found at the base of the brain. This major endocrine gland interacts with the hypothalamus of the nervous system. Together, they control behavior. The hypothalamus receives information about physiological events in the body by monitoring the composition of the blood. In turn, the hypothalamus signals the pituitary by either a nerve impulse or a chemical messenger. The pituitary responds by releasing or ceasing to release hormones that will have a direct effect on physiology or will stimulate other endocrines to release their hormones in order to alter the physiological event and influence behavior. The endocrine system exerts its effects on a biochemical level.

The human endocrine system is typical of vertebrate endocrine systems and their effect on behavior, although certain hormones may have a more pronounced and obvious effect in other vertebrates. For example, melanocyte-stimulating hormone, which is generated by the anterior lobe of the pituitary, greatly increases skin pigmentation in amphibians. This creates a protective coloration. In humans, the darkening effect is not achieved unless excessive hormone is administered. The protective function is not apparent. There are enough similarities among human and animal endocrine functions and

GLANDS OF THE ENDOCRINE SYSTEM

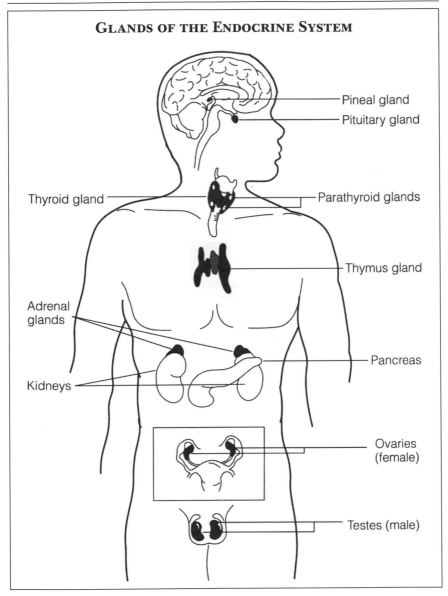

(Hans & Cassidy, Inc.)

effects, however, to warrant the use of data from both ethology and human behavioral studies in determining the biological bases for behavior.

INFLUENCE ON REPRODUCTIVE BEHAVIOR

The influence of the endocrine system on behavior has been studied on many levels. Much of the work has been done on animals; laboratory rats have been the most frequently used subjects. There is, however, a growing body of information on hormonal effects on a variety of human behaviors, including reproductive and developmental behavior, reaction to stress, learning, and memory. Studies carried out in reproductive and developmental biology on both animal and human subjects have substantiated the belief that hormones influence mating behavior, developmental events including sexual differentiation, and female and male sexuality.

Castration experiments have linked the testes with a male mating behavior pattern in animals. The sexually active male animal aggressively seeks and attempts to mount the female, whether she is receptive or not. The castrated male retains the ability to mount a female but loses the aggressiveness and does not persistently pursue females. The male may assume the more submissive female behavior and even engage in homosexual encounters. Normally, the release of reproductive hormones in the male is noncyclic, whereas in the female it is cyclic. Castrated animals begin to exhibit the female, cyclic pattern of hormone release. The hormonal influence is confirmed by administering androgens (male hormones) to the castrated animals. Male mating behavior and the noncyclic release of hormones returns.

The presence of male hormones has an effect on the female cycle and sexual receptivity. Pheromones are substances secreted on the body of one individual which influence the behavior of another. These chemical messengers function during mate attraction, territoriality, and episodes of fear. Their existence and functions are well documented throughout the animal kingdom, especially among insects and mammals. In experiments using rats, it was shown that the pheromones act in conjunction with male hormones in bringing the female to a state of receptivity. The urine of noncastrated male rats contains androgens. When a male rat is introduced into a cage of sexually inactive females, the male sends off chemical signals by way of pheromones and the androgen-containing urine. The result is the accelerated onset of estrus, or sexual receptivity, on the part of the females. Castrated males produce pheromones but do not have androgens in the urine. When castrated males are introduced into a cage of inactive females, the estrous cycle is not affected.

All female mammals, with the exception of monkeys, apes, and humans, experience estrus. Under hormonal control, the female is receptive to the male once or twice a year, when her eggs are available for fertilization. This period of receptivity is known as the estrous phase, or heat. Research shows that the particular female hormone which induces estrus is progesterone.

HORMONAL INFLUENCES
The work done by researchers in developing contraceptives clarified the role of hormones in the functioning of the human female reproductive system. The system operates in a monthly cycle during which ovarian and uterine changes occur under hormonal control. These hormones do not affect a woman's receptivity, which is not limited to fertile periods.

Testosterone derivatives known as anabolic steroids are illegally used by some athletes in an attempt to increase muscularity, strength, and performance. While both sexes do experience the desired effects, long-term, high-dosage usage has undesirable consequences. This is particularly true in women, who begin to exhibit a deepening of the voice, a male body shape, and increased body and facial hair. Both men and women can become sterile. Psychotic behaviors and states such as depression and anger have been recorded.

Developmental biologists indicate that hormones exert their influence as early as six or seven weeks into embryonic development. At this point, undifferentiated tissue with the potential of developing into either a female or a male reproductive system will develop into a male system in the presence of testosterone and into a female system in its absence. There is some evidence that the embryonic hormones have an effect on the developing brain, producing either a male or female brain. Functionally, this may account for the cyclic activity of female reproductive hormones and the noncyclic activity of the male. A few anatomical differences between male and female brains have been observed in both rats and humans. In the hypothalamus of the brain, there are cell bodies called nuclei. In rats and in humans, these nuclei are larger in males than in females.

Learning and memory can be experimentally affected by hormones. Experiments reveal that chemicals which resemble adrenocorticotropic hormone (ACTH) can extend the memory time of rats. Rats, stimulated by electric shock and provided with an avoidance possibility such as moving into another chamber of a cage or climbing a pole in the center of the cage, were administered ACTH-like molecules. The treated rats were able to remember the appropriate reaction to the stimulus for a longer period of time than the untreated rats. In other experiments, rats in a maze were administered vasopressin, a posterior pituitary hormone, which increased their frequency in selecting the correct pathway through the maze.

The effect of vasopressin on human memory is not as clearly defined. There have been positive results with schizophrenic patients and patients with alcohol-induced amnesia. In these cases, memory has been enhanced to a limited degree. There is no solid evidence that learning and memory in humans will be greatly improved by the administration of vasopressin.

Areas such as eating disorders, psychotic behavior, hormone therapy, behavior modification, and biological clocks and rhythms challenge the physiological psychologist to further research to test hormonal influences.

Sources for Further Study

Bioscience 33 (October, 1983). The entire issue is devoted to the effects of hormones on behavior. Includes an article on invertebrates in general, followed by articles on fish through primates. Written in nonesoteric language.

Brennan, James F. *History and Systems of Psychology.* 5th ed. Englewood Cliffs,

N.J.: Prentice-Hall, 1997. Readable presentation of the history and development of psychology. Covers the highlights of the discipline from the time of ancient Greece. Good background material for those not well grounded in psychology and interesting reading for those with a historical leaning.

Donovan, Bernard T. *Hormones and Human Behaviour.* New York: Cambridge University Press, 1985. An excellent compilation of the information available on hormones and behavior up to 1985. Uses technical language, but one who reads on a high-school level and has had some exposure to science will find the book informative and interesting. Focuses on the pituitary, the gonads, and the adrenals, and their effect on human behavior.

Drickamer, Lee C., Stephen H. Vessey, and Elizabeth Jakob. *Animal Behavior.* 5th ed. New York: McGraw-Hill, 2001. Intended for undergraduate students who are interested in animal behavior. Of particular interest is chapter 10, which deals with hormones and behavior. Presents a clear explanation of the endocrine system and the mechanism of hormone action. Avoids highly technical language. The effect of hormones on behavior of invertebrates and vertebrates is well illustrated with many interesting examples from the animal world.

Highnam, Kenneth Charles, and Leonard Hill. *The Comparative Endocrinology of the Invertebrates.* 2d ed. Baltimore: University Park Press, 1977. Various types of invertebrate endocrine systems are described in this book. Although the book was published in 1977, it is a valuable source of information, especially on the insect and crustacean hormones. Technical language is used but is clearly explained in laypersons' terms. Drawings and charts contribute to the understanding of the material.

Pinel, John P. J. *Biopsychology.* 4th ed. Boston: Allyn & Bacon, 1999. A textbook intended for use by undergraduate college students. There are two chapters of particular interest. Chapter 1 defines the position of biopsychology within the larger field of psychology, delineates the subdivisions of biopsychology, and describes the type of research carried out in each area. An account of research involving the human reproductive hormones and their effects is found in chapter 10. Both chapters are interesting and well written. The author makes use of good examples, drawings, and charts.

Rosemary Scheirer

SEE ALSO: Emotions; Hormones and Behavior; Memory: Animal Research; Stress: Physiological Responses.

EXPERIMENTATION

INDEPENDENT, DEPENDENT, AND CONTROL VARIABLES

TYPE OF PSYCHOLOGY: Psychological methodologies
FIELDS OF STUDY: Experimental methodologies; methodological issues

The scientific method involves the testing of hypotheses through the objective collection of data. The experiment is an important method of data collection in which the researcher systematically controls multiple factors in order to determine the extent to which changes in one variable cause changes in another variable. Only the experimental method can reveal cause-effect relationships between the variables of interest.

KEY CONCEPTS
- control group
- control variables
- dependent variable
- ecological validity
- experiment
- field experiment
- hypothesis
- independent variable
- random assignment

Psychology is typically defined as the science of behavior and cognition and is considered a research-oriented discipline, not unlike biology, chemistry, and physics. To appreciate the role of experimentation in psychology, it is useful to view it in the context of the general scientific method employed by psychologists in conducting their research. This scientific method may be described as a four-step sequence starting with identifying a problem and forming a hypothesis. The problem must be one suitable for scientific inquiry. Questions concerning values, such as whether rural life is "better" than city life, are more appropriate for philosophical debate than scientific investigation. Questions better suited to the scientific method are those that can be answered through the objective collection of facts—for example, "Are children who are neglected by their parents more likely to do poorly in school than children who are well treated?" The hypothesis is the tentative guess, or the prediction regarding the question's answer, and is based upon other relevant research and existing theory. The second step, and the one with which this article is primarily concerned, is the collection of data (facts) in order to test the accuracy of the hypothesis. Any one of a number of methods might be employed, including simple observation, survey, or experimentation. The third step is to make sense of the facts that have been accumulated by subjecting them to careful analysis; the fourth step is to share any significant findings with the scientific community.

RESEARCH APPROACHES

In considering step two, the collection of data, it seems that people often mistakenly use the words "research" and "experiment" interchangeably. A student might ask whether an experiment has been done on a particular topic when, in fact, the student really wants to know if *any* kind of research has been conducted in that area. All experiments are examples of research, but not all research is experimental. Research that is nonexperimental in nature might be either descriptive or correlational.

Descriptive research is nearly self-explanatory; it occurs when the researcher wants merely to characterize the behaviors of an individual or, more likely, a group. For example, one might want to survey the students of a high school to ascertain the level of alcohol use (alcohol use might be described in terms of average ounces consumed per student per week). One might also spend considerable time observing individuals suffering from, for example, infantile autism. A thorough description of their typical behaviors could be useful for someone investigating the cause of this disorder. Descriptive research can be extremely valuable, but it is not useful when researchers want to investigate the relationship between two or more variables (things that vary, or quantities that may have different values).

In a correlational study, the researcher measures how strongly the variables are related, or the degree to which one variable predicts another variable. A researcher who is interested in the relationship between exposure to violence on television (variable one) and aggressive behavior (variable two) in a group of elementary school children could administer a survey asking the children how much violent television they view and then rank the subjects from high to low levels of this variable. The researcher could similarly interview the school staff and rank the children according to their aggressive behavior. A statistic called a correlation coefficient might then be computed, revealing how the two variables are related and the strength of that relationship.

CAUSE AND EFFECT

Correlational studies are not uncommon in psychological research. Often, however, a researcher wants even more specific information about the relationships among variables—in particular, about whether one variable causes a change in another variable. In such a situation, experimental research is warranted. This drawback of the correlational approach—its inability to establish causal relationships—is worth considering for a moment. In the hypothetical study described above, the researcher may find that viewing considerable television violence predicts high levels of aggressive behavior, yet she cannot conclude that these viewing habits cause the aggressiveness. After all, it is entirely possible that aggressiveness, caused by some unknown factor, prompts a preference for violent television. That is, the causal direction is unknown; viewing television violence may cause aggressiveness, but the inverse (that aggressiveness causes the watching of violent television programs) is also feasible.

As this is a crucial point, one final illustration is warranted. What if, at a certain Rocky Mountain university, a correlational study has established that high levels of snowfall predict low examination scores? One should not conclude that something about the chemical composition of snow impairs the learning process. The correlation may be real and highly predictive, but the causal culprit may be some other factor. Perhaps, as snowfall increases, so does the incidence of illness, and it is this variable that is causally related to exam scores. Maybe, as snowfall increases, the likelihood of students using their study time for skiing also increases.

Experimentation is a powerful research method because it alone can reveal cause-effect relationships. In an experiment, the researcher does not merely measure the naturally occurring relationships between variables for the purpose of predicting one from the other; rather, he or she systematically manipulates the values of one variable and measures the effect, if any, that is produced in a second variable. The variable that is manipulated is known as the independent variable; the other variable, the behavior in question, is called the dependent variable (any change in it depends upon the manipulation of the independent variable). Experimental research is characterized by a desire for control on the part of the researcher. Control of the independent variable and control over extraneous variables are both wanted. That is, there is a desire to eliminate or hold constant the factors (control variables) other than the independent variable that might influence the dependent variable. If adequate control is achieved, the researcher may be confident that it was, in fact, the manipulation of the independent variable that produced the change in the dependent variable.

CONTROL GROUPS

Returning to the relationship between television viewing habits and aggressive behavior in children, suppose that correlational evidence indicates that high levels of the former variable predict high levels of the latter. Now the researcher wants to test the hypothesis that there is a cause-effect relationship between the two variables. She decides to manipulate exposure to television violence (the independent variable) to see what effect might be produced in the aggressiveness of her subjects (the dependent variable). She might choose two levels of the independent variable and have twenty children watch fifteen minutes of a violent detective show, while another twenty children are subjected to thirty minutes of the same show.

If an objective rating of playground aggressiveness later reveals more hostility in the thirty-minute group than in the fifteen-minute group, she still cannot be confident that higher levels of television violence cause higher levels of aggressive behavior. More information is needed, especially with regard to issues of control. To begin with, how does the researcher know that it is the violent content of the program that is promoting aggressiveness? Perhaps it is the case that the more time they spend watching television, regardless of subject matter, the more aggressive children become.

This study needs a control group: a group of subjects identical to the experimental subjects with the exception that they do not experience the independent variable. In fact, two control groups might be employed, one that watches fifteen minutes and another that watches thirty minutes of nonviolent programming. The control groups serve as a basis against which the behavior of the experimental groups can be compared. If it is found that the two control groups aggress to the same extent, and to a lesser extent than the experimental groups, the researcher can be more confident that violent programming promotes relatively higher levels of aggressiveness.

The experimenter also needs to be sure that the children in the thirty-minute experimental group were not naturally more aggressive to begin with. One need not be too concerned with this possibility if one randomly assigns subjects to the experimental and control groups. There are certainly individual differences among subjects in factors, such as personality and intelligence, but with random assignment (a technique for creating groups of subjects across which individual differences will be evenly dispersed) one can be reasonably sure that those individual differences are evenly dispersed among the experimental and control groups.

Subject Variables

The experimenter might want to control or hold constant other variables. Perhaps she suspects that age, social class, ethnicity, and gender could also influence the children's aggressiveness. She might want to make sure that these subject variables are eliminated by either choosing subjects who are alike in these ways or by making sure that the groups are balanced for these factors (for example, equal numbers of boys and girls in each group). There are numerous other extraneous variables that might concern the researcher, including the time of day when the children participate, the length of time between television viewing and the assessment of aggressiveness, the children's diets, the children's family structures (single versus dual parent, siblings versus only child), and the disciplinary styles used in the homes. Resource limitations prevent every extraneous variable from being controlled, yet the more control, the more confident the experimenter can be of the cause-effect relationship between the independent and dependent variables.

Influence of Rewards

One more example of experimental research, this one nonhypothetical, will further illustrate the application of this methodology. In 1973, Mark Lepper, David Greene, and Richard Nisbett tested the hypothesis that when people are offered external rewards for performing activities that are naturally enjoyable, their interest in these activities declines. The participants in the study were nursery school children who had already demonstrated a fondness for coloring with marking pens; this was their preferred activity when given an opportunity for free play. The children were randomly assigned to one of three groups. The first group was told previously that they would receive a "good player award" if they would play with the pens when later given the opportunity. Group two received the same reward but without advance notice; they were surprised by the reward. The last group of children was the control group; they were neither rewarded nor told to expect a reward.

The researchers reasoned that the first group of children, having played with the pens in order to receive a reward, would now perceive their natural interest in this activity as lower than before the study. Indeed, when all groups were later allowed a free play opportunity, it was observed that the "expected reward" group spent significantly less time than the other groups in this previously enjoyable activity. Lepper and his colleagues, then, experimentally supported their hypothesis and reported evidence that reward causes interest in a previously pleasurable behavior to decline. This research has implications for instructors; they should carefully consider the kinds of behavior they reward (with gold stars, lavish praise, high grades, and so on) as they may, ironically, be producing less of the desired behavior. An academic activity that is enjoyable play for a child may become tedious work when a reward system is attached to it.

CRITICISMS

While most would agree that the birth of psychology as a science took place in Leipzig, Germany, in 1879, when Wilhelm Wundt established the first laboratory for studying psychological phenomena, there is no clear record of the first use of experimentation. Regardless, there is no disputing the attraction that this method of research has had for many psychologists in the twentieth century. Psychologists clearly recognize the usefulness of the experiment in investigating potential causal relationships between variables. Hence, experimentation is employed widely across the subfields of psychology, including developmental, cognitive, physiological, clinical, industrial, and social psychology.

This is not to say that all psychologists are completely satisfied with experimental research. It has been argued that an insidious catch-22 exists in some experimental research that limits its usefulness. The argument goes like this: Experimenters are motivated to control rigorously the conditions of their studies and the relevant extraneous variables. To gain such control, they often conduct experiments in a laboratory setting. Therefore, subjects are often observed in an artificial environment, engaged in behaviors that are so controlled as to be unnatural, and they clearly know they are being observed—which may further alter their behavior. Such research is said to be lacking in ecological validity or applicability to "real-life" behavior. It may show how subjects behave in a unique laboratory procedure, but it tells little about psychological phenomena as displayed in everyday life. The catch-22, then, is that experimenters desire control in order to establish that the independent variable is producing a change in the dependent variable, and the more such control, the better; however, the more control, the more risk that the research may be ecologically invalid.

FIELD EXPERIMENTS

Most psychologists are sensitive to issues of ecological validity and take pains to make their laboratory procedures as naturalistic as possible. Additionally, much research is conducted outside the laboratory in what are known as field experiments. In such studies, the subjects are unobtrusively observed (perhaps by a confederate of the researcher who would not attract their notice) in natural settings such as classroom, playground, or workplace. Field experiments, then, represent a compromise in that there is bound to be less control than is obtainable in a laboratory, yet the behaviors observed are likely to be natural. Such naturalistic experimentation is likely to continue to increase in the future.

Although experimentation is only one of many methods available to psychologists, it fills a particular need, and that need is not likely to decline in the foreseeable future. In trying to understand the complex relationships among the many variables that affect the way people think and act, experimentation makes a valuable contribution: It is the one methodology available that can reveal unambiguous cause-effect relationships.

SOURCES FOR FURTHER STUDY

Barber, Theodore Xenophon. *Pitfalls in Human Research.* New York: Pergamon Press, 1976. It is useful to learn from the mistakes of others, and Barber provides an opportunity by describing ten categories of likely errors in designing and conducting research. This is not a long book (117 pages), and it is enjoyable reading, especially the specific accounts of flawed research.

Carlson, Neil R. *Psychology: The Science of Behavior.* 5th ed. Upper Saddle River, N.J.: Prentice Hall, 1999. The second chapter of this introductory psychology text may be the most reader-friendly reference in this bibliography. Titled "The Ways and Means of Psychology," it provides a brief introductory overview of the scientific method, experimental and correlational research, and basic statistics; it is well suited for the novice. Colorful graphics, a concluding summary, and a list of key terms are all helpful.

Hearst, Eliot, ed. *The First Century of Experimental Psychology.* Hillsdale, N.J.: Lawrence Erlbaum, 1979. Primarily for the student interested in the history of experimental psychology. This is a 693-page book; while most of the fourteen chapters are devoted to specific topics in psychology such as emotion, development, and psychopathology, the final chapter by William Estes provides an excellent overview of experimental psychology and considers some broad, profound issues.

Shaughnessy, John J., and Eugene B. Zechmeister. *Research Methods in Psychology*. 6th ed. New York: McGraw-Hill, 2002. This is one of a number of textbooks that discuss psychological research in the light of the scientific method. It is fairly accessible, has a thorough and competent description of experimentation, and considers some ethical issues. Glossary, index, and references are all provided.

Stern, Paul C., and Linda Kalof. *Evaluating Social Science Research*. 2d ed. New York: Oxford University Press, 1996. A clearly written, nonthreatening book for the early to middle-level college student. The focus of the author is on encouraging the critical analysis of research; to this end, case-research examples are presented for examination. End-of-chapter exercises are included to aid the student in integrating information.

Mark B. Alcorn

SEE ALSO: Animal Experimentation.

FIELD THEORY
KURT LEWIN

TYPE OF PSYCHOLOGY: Personality
FIELDS OF STUDY: Motivation theory; personality theory; social perception and cognition

Lewin's field theory maintains that behavior is a function of the life space, or psychological reality, of the individual. Individuals are motivated to reduce tensions that arise in this life space. Lewin's theory can be used to understand a wide range of everyday behavior and to suggest strategies for addressing social problems, such as the reduction of prejudice and the resolution of social conflicts.

KEY CONCEPTS
- life space
- locomotion
- quasi-stationary equilibrium
- region of life space
- tension

Kurt Lewin was a theorist of everyday life. His field theory attempts to explain people's everyday behavior, such as how a waiter remembers an order, what determines the morale and productivity of a work group, what causes intergroup prejudice, how a child encounters a new environment, or why people eat the foods that they do.

For Lewin, what determines everyday behavior is the "life space" of the individual. The life space represents the psychological reality of the individual; it is the totality of all psychological facts and social forces that influence an individual at a given time and place. For example, the life space of a child entering a novel domain is, for the most part, undifferentiated, and thus results in exploration on the part of the child. On the other hand, the life space of an employee at work may be well differentiated and populated with demands from the employer to produce more goods, from coworkers to follow a production norm, and from home for more income. There might, additionally, be physical needs to slow down.

EVOLUTION OF LEWIN'S THEORY

Field theory was born on the battlefields of World War I. Lewin served as a soldier in the German army. His first published article was titled "The War Landscape," and it described the battlefield in terms of life space. The soldier's needs determined how the landscape was to be perceived. When the soldier was miles from the front, the peaceful landscape seemed to stretch endlessly on all sides without direction. As the war front approached, the landscape took on direction, and peaceful objects such as rocks and trees became elements of battle, such as weapons and places to hide.

After the war, Lewin took an academic appointment at the Psychological

Institute of Berlin, where he served on the faculty with Gestalt psychologists Wolfgang Köhler and Max Wertheimer. While at the institute, Lewin further developed his field theory and conducted the first program of experimental social psychological research exploring topics such as memory for interrupted tasks, level of aspiration, and anger. His work derived as much from field theory as it did from his curiosity about the social world. For example, research on memory for interrupted tasks began when he and his students wondered why a waiter could remember their rather lengthy order but would forget it immediately after the food was served. In field theory terms, noncompleted tasks (such as the waiter's recall before delivering the order) were recalled better because they maintained a tension for completion compared to completed tasks, for which this tension is resolved.

As the Nazi Party rose to power in Germany, Lewin correctly perceived that his own Jewish life space and that of his family were becoming progressively more threatened and intolerable. Like many Jewish intellectuals of the time, Lewin emigrated to the United States; he obtained a number of visiting appointments until he established the Center for Group Dynamics at the Massachusetts Institute of Technology in 1944. Lewin's American research was much more applied than his work in Europe, and it concentrated particularly on social problems such as prejudice and intergroup conflict—perhaps as a result of his own experience of prejudice as a Jew in Germany.

Before his death in 1947, Lewin helped train the first generation of American students interested in experimental social psychology, including such notables as Leon Festinger, Harold Kelley, Stanley Schachter, and Morton Deutsch. As a result, Lewin's intellectual legacy pervades the field of experimental social psychology. Today, first-, second-, third-, and even fourth-generation Lewinian social psychologists continue to carry on his research legacy by investigating topics of long-standing interest to Lewin, such as prejudice, achievement, organizational behavior, social cognition, and the reduction of cognitive tensions or dissonance and by attempting to explain how individuals construe their environments and how those environments affect behavior.

LIFE SPACE REGIONS

The concept of life space is usually divided into two parts: person and environment. These two parts can be differentiated further into regions. A region is any major part of the life space that can be distinguished from other parts and is separated by more or less permeable boundaries. For example, regions differentiated within the person might consist of needs, goals, hopes, and aspirations of the individual, whereas the differentiation of the environment might consist of profession, family, friendships, social norms, and taboos.

Locomotion, or behavior and change in the life space, is determined by the differentiation of regions in the life space and by the forces for change emanating from each region. Often, in any given life space, there are opposing or conflicting forces. For example, a boss may want to increase productivity as much as possible, whereas coworkers may seek to limit production to levels obtainable by all workers. According to Lewin, these tensions, or opposing social forces, provide the motivation for behavior and change in the life space. Tension can be resolved by any number of activities, including reconfiguring the life space either physically (for example, getting a new job) or mentally (for example, devaluing either the boss's or coworkers' opinions); performing a substitute task that symbolically reduces tension (for example, performing different tasks of value to the boss); or finding the "quasi-stationary equilibrium," or position where all opposing forces are equal in strength (for example, performing at a level between boss's and coworkers' recommendations).

COMPARISON WITH BEHAVIORISM AND PSYCHOANALYSIS

It is useful to compare Lewin's field theory with the two other major theories of the time: behaviorism and psychoanalysis. Lewin's field theory can be summarized by the equation $B = f(P,E)$, or, "Behavior is a function of person and environment." In other words, behavior is function of the life space of a total environment as perceived by the individual. In psychoanalytic thought, behavior is a function of the history of the individual. For example, past childhood experience is supposed to have a direct impact on current psychological processes. In contrast, Lewin's theory is ahistorical. Although the individual's past may influence that person's approach and construal of the psychological field, its influence is only indirect, as behavior is a function of the current and immediate life space.

Lewin's field theory differs from behaviorism on at least two key dimensions. First, Lewin emphasized the subjectivity of the psychological field. To predict and understand behavior successfully, a therapist needs to describe the situation from the viewpoint of the individual whose behavior is under consideration, not from the viewpoint of an observer. Second, Lewin's theory emphasizes that behavior must be understood as a function of the life space or situation as a whole. In other words, behavior is motivated by the multitude of often interdependent forces affecting an individual, as opposed to one or two salient rewards or reinforcers that may be present.

ROLE IN SOCIAL CHANGE

Lewin's field theory has had many applications, particularly in the area of social change. Lewin's approach to solving social problems was first to specify, in as much detail as possible, the life space of the individual involved. Next, he would identify the social forces affecting the individual. Finally, Lewin would experiment with changing these social forces or adding new ones to enact social change. Two applications of field theory performed by Lewin and his associates serve as good examples. One deals with changing food preferences and the other with the reduction of intergroup conflicts and prejudice.

During World War II, there was a shortage of meat, an important protein source in the United States. As part of the war effort, Lewin was assigned the task of convincing Americans to eat sweetbreads—certain organ meats, which many Americans find unappetizing—to maintain protein levels. Lewin began by first describing the consumption channel, or how food reaches a family's table. At the time, housewives obtained food from either a garden or a grocery store and then moved it to the table by purchasing it, transporting it home, storing it in an icebox or pantry, and then preparing it. At each step, Lewin identified forces that kept the gatekeeper—in this case, the housewife—from serving sweetbreads. Such forces might have included the belief that family members would not eat sweetbreads, inexperience with the selection and preparation of sweetbreads, or inherently distasteful aspects of the food.

In attempting to remove and redirect these forces, Lewin experimented with two approaches, one successful and the other not. In the unsuccessful case, Lewin presented housewives with a lecture detailing the problems of nutrition during the war and stating ways of overcoming obstacles in serving sweetbreads; he discussed ways to prepare sweetbreads, provided recipes, and indicated that other women had successfully served sweetbreads for their families with little complaint. Only 3 percent of the housewives hearing this lecture served sweetbreads. From Lewin's perspective, such a lecture was ineffective because it did not involve the audience and arouse the level of tension needed to produce change. Lewin's second method was a group discussion. The housewives were asked to discuss how they could persuade "housewives like themselves" to serve sweetbreads. This led to a discussion of the obstacles that the housewife might encounter, along with ways of overcoming these obstacles (just as in the lecture). Such a discussion was effective because it created tension for the housewife: "I just told everyone why they should and how they could eat sweetbreads, and I am not currently serving them myself." After this group discussion, 32 percent (an almost elevenfold increase) of the housewives involved served sweetbreads.

CONFLICT AND PREJUDICE

Lewin approached the problem of intergroup conflict and racial prejudice by describing the life spaces of the members of the conflicting parties. For example, Lewin saw the life space of many minority group members (such as religious and racial minorities) as full of obstacles and barriers which restrict movement in the life space. The life space of the majority member often consigned the minority member to a small and rigidly bounded region (for example, a ghetto). By isolating minority group members, majority group members can develop unrealistic perceptions or stereotypes of the out-group. Such life spaces are very likely to result in intergroup conflict.

The field theory analysis of racial prejudice suggests that one way to reduce intergroup conflict is to remove obstacles and increase the permeability of intergroup barriers. In the later part of his career, Lewin established the Commission on Community Interrelations as a vehicle for discovering ways of removing intergroup barriers. Lewin and his colleagues discovered some of the following successful techniques for promoting intergroup harmony: enacting laws that immediately removed barriers, such as racial quotas limiting the number of Jews who could attend certain universities; immediate hiring of blacks as sales personnel, thereby increasing the permeability of intergroup boundaries by making contact between group members more likely; responding directly to racial slurs with a calm appeal based on American traditions and democracy to provide a countervailing force to the slur; promoting meetings of warring groups in a friendly atmosphere as a means of breaking down group boundaries; and immediately integrating housing as a successful way of promoting racial harmony.

SOURCES FOR FURTHER STUDY

Bar-Gal, David, Martin Gold, and Miriam Lewin, eds. *The Heritage of Kurt Lewin: Theory, Research, and Practice.* New York: Plenum Press, 1992. Published with the Society for the Psychological Study of Social Issues. Includes a bibliography.

De Rivera, Joseph, comp. *Field Theory as Human-Science: Contributions of Lewin's Berlin Group.* New York: Gardner Press, 1976. An English translation of research conducted by Lewin and his students when Lewin was at the University of Berlin.

Lewin, Kurt. *A Dynamic Theory of Personality.* New York: McGraw-Hill, 1959. Lewin's first major English work, consisting of a translation of many of his first papers published in Germany.

_____. "Group Decision and Social Change." In *Readings in Social Psychology,* edited by Theodore M. Newcomb and Eugene L. Hartley. New York: Holt, 1958. Describes how Lewin changed food preferences during World War II, providing an excellent example of how to apply field theory to practical problems.

_____. *Resolving Social Conflicts; and, Field Theory in Social Science.* Washington, D.C.: American Psychological Association, 1997. A reprint of two of Lewin's most influential works, collecting his major papers discussing practical problems of modern society such as prejudice and group conflict. Provides excellent examples of how to apply field theory to social problems.

Marrow, Alfred Jay. *The Practical Theorist: The Life and Work of Kurt Lewin.* New York: Teachers College Press, 1977. This definitive biography of Lewin, written by one of his students, describes the life of Lewin and provides a glimpse of the personality behind field theory.

Wheelan, Susan A., Emmy A. Pepitone, and Vicki Abt, eds. *Advances in Field Theory.* Thousand Oaks, Calif.: Sage, 1990. A collection of essays addressing issues in field theory such as managing social conflict, self-help groups, field theory and the construction of social problems, and academic sex discrimination.

Anthony R. Pratkanis and Marlene E. Turner

SEE ALSO: Groups; Motivation.

GENDER-IDENTITY FORMATION

TYPE OF PSYCHOLOGY: Developmental psychology
FIELDS OF STUDY: Cognitive development; infancy and childhood

Gender-identity formation refers to the complex processes through which children come to incorporate their gender into their behavior, attitudes, and self-understanding. This includes the development of an inner sense of one's femaleness or maleness; the acquisition of knowledge about cultural expectations for females and males; and the development of attitudes, interests, and behavior that reflect these expectations.

KEY CONCEPTS
- gender constancy
- gender identity
- gender schema
- sex role
- sex-role socialization
- sex typing

The first question that is usually asked about a newborn baby is whether it is a boy or a girl. The single fact of the child's gender has enormous implications for the course of his or her entire life. Gender-identity formation refers to the complex processes through which children incorporate the biological and social fact of their gender into their behavior, attitudes, and self-understanding.

This area includes ideas about two major, interrelated processes: gender-identity development and sex typing. The term "gender-identity development," used in its narrower sense, refers to the process through which children come to label themselves cognitively as boys or girls and to have an inner sense of themselves as male or female. "Sex typing," also called gender-role acquisition, refers to the processes through which children learn what is expected of members of their gender and come to exhibit primarily those personality traits, behaviors, interests, and attitudes.

CULTURAL CONTEXTS

Social-learning theorists such as Walter Mischel have described mechanisms of learning through which children come to exhibit sex-typed behavior. Boys and girls often behave differently because they are rewarded and punished for different behaviors. In other words, they receive different conditioning. In addition, children's behavior becomes sex typed because children observe other males and females regularly behaving differently according to their gender, and they imitate or model this behavior.

Parents are especially important in the process of learning one's gender role, both as models for gender-appropriate behavior and as sources of rewards or reinforcement. Because parents become associated with positive experiences (such as being fed and comforted) early in life, children learn to look to them and other adults for rewards. Parents and other adults such as teachers often react differentially to gender-typed behaviors, rewarding gender-appropriate behavior (for example, giving praise or attention) and punishing gender-inappropriate behavior (for example, frowning, ignoring, or reprimanding).

As children become more involved with their peers (children their own age), they begin to influence one another's behavior, often strongly reinforcing traditional gender roles. The fact that children are usually given different toys and different areas in which to play based on their gender is also important. Girls are given opportunities to learn different behaviors from those of boys (for example, girls learn nurturing behavior through playing with dolls) because they are exposed to different experiences.

Using what is called a cognitive developmental perspective, Lawrence Kohlberg described developmental changes in children's understanding of gender concepts. These changes parallel the broad developmental changes in the way children's thinking is organized, first described by Jean Piaget and Barbel Inhelder. Children mature naturally through stages of increasingly complex cognitive organization. In the area of understanding gender, the first stage is the acquisition of a rudimentary gender identity, the ability to categorize oneself correctly as a boy or a girl.

Children are able to apply correct gender labels to themselves by about age three. At this stage, young children base gender labeling on differences in easily observable characteristics such as hairstyle and clothing, and they do not grasp the importance of genital differences in determining gender. As children's thinking about the physical world becomes more complex, so does their understanding of gender. Gradually, by about age seven, children enter a second stage and acquire the concept known as gender constancy.

GENDER CONSTANCY
Gender constancy refers to the understanding that gender is a stable characteristic that cannot change over time and that is not altered by superficial physical transformations such as wearing a dress or cutting one's hair. As children come to see gender as a stable, important characteristic of themselves and other people, they begin to use the concept consistently to organize social information. They learn societal expectations for members of each gender by watching the actions of the people around them.

Kohlberg proposed that children use their developing knowledge of cultural gender expectations to teach themselves to adopt culturally defined gender roles (self-socialization). He argued that children acquire a strong motive to conform to gender roles because of their need for self-consistency and self-esteem. A young boy says to himself, "I am a boy, not a girl; I want to do boy things, play with boy toys, and wear boy clothes."

Children hold more rigid gender stereotypes before they acquire gender constancy (ages two through seven); once gender constancy is achieved, they become more flexible in their adherence to gender roles. As children enter adolescence, their thinking about the world again enters a new stage of development, becoming even more complex and less rigid. As a result, they may be able to achieve what Joseph Pleck has called "sex-role transcendence" and to choose their interests and behaviors somewhat independent of cultural gender-role expectations.

GENDER SCHEMA

Gender-schema theory is a way of explaining gender-identity formation, which is closely related to the cognitive developmental approach. The concept of a schema or a general knowledge framework comes from the field of cognitive psychology. Sandra Bem proposed that each person develops a set of gender-linked associations, or a gender schema, as part of a personal knowledge structure. This gender schema filters and interprets new information, and as a result, people have a basic predisposition to process information on the basis of gender. People tend to dichotomize objects and attributes on the basis of gender, even including qualitites such as color, which has no relevance to biological sex.

Bem proposed that sex typing develops as children learn the content of society's gender schema and as they begin to link that schema to their self-concept or view of themselves. Individuals vary in the degree to which the gender schema is central to their self-concept; it is most central to the self-concept of highly sex-typed individuals (traditionally masculine males or traditionally feminine females).

GENDER IDENTITY DISORDER

Ideas about gender-identity formation have important implications for child rearing and education. Most parents want to help their child identify with and feel positive about his or her gender. Those few children who fail to develop a clear inner sense of themselves as male or female consistent with their biological sex may have significant social adjustment difficulties; they are sometimes given psychological treatment for a condition called gender-identity disorder.

According to the American Psychiatric Association's *Diagnostic and Statistical Manual of Mental Disorders: DSM-IV-TR* (rev. 4th ed., 2000), gender-identity disorder is defined by a strong and persistent cross-gender identification. In a child, it is manifested by such features as repeated statements of the desire to be, or insistence that he or she is, the other gender; preference for or insistence on wearing stereotypical clothing of the opposite sex; strong and persistent preference for cross-sex roles in make-believe play or fantasies of being the other gender; an intense desire to participate in the stereotypical games of the opposite sex; and a strong preference for playmates of the other sex. A boy with this disorder may assert that his penis is disgusting or will disappear, or that it would be better not to have one. He may show an aversion toward rough-and-tumble play and reject male stereotypical toys, games, and activities. A girl with this disorder may reject urinat-

Gender-role acquisition refers to the processes through which children learn what is expected of members of their gender and come to exhibit primarily those personality traits and interests. (CLEO Photography)

ing in a sitting position, assert that she has or will grow a penis, claim that she does not want to grow breasts or to menstruate, or show a marked aversion toward feminine clothing.

Adults who continue to have a gender identity that is inconsistent with their biological sex may desire surgery and hormonal treatments to change their sex. This rare condition, called transsexualism, is more common among biological males than females. Although many people have interests, personality characteristics, or sexual preferences commonly associated with the other gender, they are not transsexuals; their inner sense of their gender is consistent with their biological sex.

GENDER EQUALITY

Often parents and educators want to help children avoid becoming strongly sex typed. They do not want children's options for activities, interests, and aspirations to be limited to those traditionally associated with their gender. Adopting strongly sex-typed interests may be especially problematic for girls because the traditional female role and the qualities associated with it (that is, emotionality, nurturance, and dependence) tend to be devalued in American culture. Traditionally masculine interests and behaviors are usually tolerated in girls before puberty; it is all right to be a "tomboy." Traditionally feminine interests and behaviors, however, tend to be vigorously discouraged in boys; it is not acceptable to be a "sissy."

Considerable research has focused on whether and how socializing agents, including parents, teachers, peers, and media such as children's books and television, reinforce gender stereotypes and teach children to exhibit sex-typed behaviors. Researchers have been concerned both with how gender roles are modeled for children and with how sex-typed behavior is rewarded. A study by Lisa Serbin and her colleagues carried out in the 1970's is an example. These researchers observed teachers' interactions with children in a preschool setting and recorded their observations in a standardized way. They found that teachers gave more attention to girls when they were physically close to them than when they were farther away; however, teachers' attention to boys did not vary with the child's proximity. This finding suggests that teachers reinforce girls more than boys for "dependent" behavior without necessarily meaning to do so.

Parents often report that they try to treat their children the same regardless of their gender. Many of the most powerful influences parents exert result from behaviors of which they are probably unaware. Research studies have shown that parents consistently interact differently with male and female children in areas such as engaging in gross motor play (for example, running, jumping, throwing), encouraging children's sex-typed play (particularly discouraging doll play among boys), demanding effort and giving help with problem-solving tasks, and allowing children to have independence and freedom from supervision.

Children's peers have been shown to play an important role in sex-role socialization. Particularly in early childhood, when children's gender concepts tend to be far more rigid than those of adults, peers may be the source of misinformation (for example, "girls can't be doctors; girls have to be nurses") and of strong sanctions against behavior that is inconsistent with one's gender role.

Laboratory studies have shown that exposure to gender stereotypes in books and on television tends to have a measurable effect on children's sex-typed behavior. For example, children are more likely to play with a "gender-inappropriate" toy after reading a story in which a child of their gender played with that toy. In addition, these media may be important in the development of a child's gender schema because they provide a rich network of information and associations related to gender. Extensive studies of the gender-related content of children's books and children's television were conducted in the 1970's, and this led to reform efforts by some textbook publishers and television producers.

One influential study by a group called Women on Words and Images published in 1975 analyzed the contents of 134 grade-school readers and found gender-stereotypic portrayals of male and female characters, gender-stereotypic themes, and male dominance to be the rule. Boys outnumbered girls as major characters by five to two; in 2,760 stories examined, only three mothers were shown working outside the home. Systematic studies of children's television have produced similar results.

FREUDIAN THEORY

Psychologists have been interested in gender-identity formation since the work of Sigmund Freud and other early psychoanalytic theorists in the beginning of the twentieth century. Since the early 1970's, however, there has been a major shift in thinking about this topic, largely as a result of the women's movement. Early work in this area considered sex typing to be a healthy and desirable goal for children. Since the 1970's, much research has been based on the assumption that rigid adherence to traditional gender roles is restrictive and undesirable.

Freud's theory of psychosexual development was the first to attempt to explain gender-identity formation. Freud believed that sex-typed behavior results primarily from girls identifying with (wanting to be like) their mothers and boys identifying with their fathers. However, he believed that during infancy both boys and girls form strong sexual feelings for their mothers and identify with them. Thus, Freud tried to explain how boys come to identify with their fathers and how girls transfer their sexual feelings to their fathers.

Freud believed that the discovery that girls and women do not have penises leads the three- to five-year-old boy to develop great fear that he will lose his own penis (castration anxiety). As a result, the boy begins to identify with his father out of fear that the father will take away his penis. He gives up his identification with his mother and suppresses his sexual feelings toward her. For a little girl, the same discovery leads to penis envy and to blaming her mother for her lack of this desired organ. Because of her disappointment, she transfers her sexual feelings from her mother to her father, and she fantasizes that her father will give her a penis substitute—a baby.

Freud's theory was an important inspiration for much of the work done on gender identity prior to the late 1960's. Since that time, however, developmental psychologists have not often used Freud's theory because most of its concepts rely on the idea of unconscious forces that cannot be evaluated scientifically.

Freud's idea that "anatomy is destiny"—that profound psychological differences between the sexes are inevitable—met with strong criticism with the rise of the women's movement. The issue of the relative importance of biological, genetic factors (or "nature") compared with experiential, social factors (or "nurture") in gender-identity formation has been a major source of controversy in psychology. Most psychologists acknowledge a role for both nature and nurture in forming differences in the behavior of boys and girls. Psychologists are interested in understanding the ways in which inborn capacities (such as cognitive organization) interact with environmental experiences in forming a person's identity as a male or a female.

The twentieth century experienced a great upheaval in thinking about gender roles, and this has been mirrored by changes in psychological research and theory about gender. The growing scientific understanding of gender identity may help to form future societal attitudes as well as being formed by them.

SOURCES FOR FURTHER STUDY

Abbott, Tina. *Social and Personality Development.* New York: Routledge, 2002. An introductory psychology textbook. Part 2 covers gender and gender identity development.

Bem, Sandra Lipsitz. *The Lenses of Gender: Transforming the Debate on Sexual Inequality.* New Haven, Conn.: Yale University Press, 1993. Discusses theories about gender relations through the lenses of androcentrism (taking male experience for the norm), gender polarization (placing male and female experience at opposite ends of a cultural spectrum, with nothing in between), and biologic essentialism (using biological differences to account for cultural realities).

Butler, Judith. *Gender Trouble.* Reprint. New York: Routledge, 1999. The tenth anniversary reprint of this classic work on gender formation and transgression in American society.

Fast, Irene. *Gender Identity: A Differentiation Model.* Hillsdale, N.J.: Lawrence Erlbaum, 1984. Reviews theories in the light of Freudian psychoanalytic theory.

Kimmel, Michael. *The Gendered Society.* New York: Oxford University Press, 2001. Examines gender from the positions of difference (placing "male" and "female" on a spectrum rather than opposite ends of a pole) and dominance (arguing that gender inequality causes the perception of gender difference, which in turn is used to justify inequality).

Unger, Rhoda K., ed. *Handbook of the Psychology of Women and Gender.* New York: John Wiley & Sons, 2001. A clinical and research handbook covering major theories, trends, and advances in the psychology of women and gender. Emphasizes multicultural issues and the impact of gender on physical and mental health.

Lesley A. Slavin

SEE ALSO: Development; Hormones and Behavior; Personality Theory; Psychoanalytic Psychology and Personality: Sigmund Freud; Women's Psychology: Karen Horney; Women's Psychology: Sigmund Freud.

GIFTEDNESS

Type of psychology: Developmental psychology; intelligence and
   intelligence testing
Fields of study: Ability tests; cognitive development; general issues in
   intelligence; intelligence assessment

Giftedness refers to a capability for high performance in one or more areas of accomplishment. The focus on giftedness as a human capability has led to efforts to identify giftedness early in life, to develop special programs of instruction for gifted children and adolescents, and to design counseling interventions to help gifted learners realize their potentials.

Key concepts
- asynchronous development
- child prodigies
- gifted education program
- intelligence test scores
- Marland definition
- precociousness
- prodigious savants
- standardized test scores
- talent

Modern studies of giftedness have their origin in the work of Lewis Terman at Stanford University, who in the 1920's used intelligence test scores to identify intellectually gifted children. His minimal standard for giftedness was an intelligence quotient (IQ) of 140 on the Stanford-Binet Intelligence Test, a number at or above which only 1 percent of children are expected to score. (The average IQ score is 100.) Terman and his associates identified more than fifteen hundred children in California as gifted, and follow-up studies on "the Terman gifted group" were conducted throughout these children's later lives. Although individuals in the gifted group tended to achieve highly in school and in their careers, they were not greatly different from average scorers in other ways. Terman's research dispelled the myths that high scorers on IQ tests were, as a group, socially maladjusted or "burned out" in adulthood. They were high achievers and yet normal in the sense that their social relationships were similar to those of the general population.

By the time the Terman gifted group reached retirement age, it was clear that the study had not realized the hope of identifying eminence. None of the children selected had, as adults, won a Nobel Prize, although two children who were rejected for the study later did so (physicist Luis Alvarez and engineer William Shockley). High IQ scores did not seem to be characteristic of artistic ability. Apparently, an IQ score of 140 or above as a criterion for giftedness in children was not able to predict creative accomplishments in later life.

Studies conducted in the 1950's under the direction of Donald Mac-Kinnon at the University of California at Berkeley tended to confirm this conclusion. Panels of experts submitted the names of whomever they believed to be the most creative architects, mathematicians, and research scientists in the United States. Then these individuals were invited to take part in assessments, including measurement of their intelligence through the Wechsler Adult Intelligence Scale. The IQ scores of these highly creative individuals ranged from 114 to 145, averaging around 130, significantly below Terman's criterion for giftedness. No one knows how these adults would have scored on the Stanford-Binet test as children, or how creative adults in other domains would have scored, but the results confirmed that a score of 140 on an intelligence test is not a prerequisite for outstanding creative accomplishment.

More recent studies have cast light on the importance of nurture in the development of a broader range of talent. A team of researchers at the University of Chicago headed by Benjamin Bloom investigated the lives of 120 talented adults in six fields: piano, sculpture, swimming, tennis, mathematics, and research neurology. They found that in most cases, accomplishments on a national or international level by the time an individual has reached the age of forty had their origin not in a prodigious gift but in child-centered homes. The child's early experiences of the field were playful, rewarding, and supported by parents. Rapid progress was due to a work ethic instilled by parents ("always do your best") and by increasingly expert and selective teachers, whom parents sought out. Bloom's findings did not exactly contradict those of Terman (no testing was done), but they suggested that nurture and motivation play the lead and supporting roles in the development of a wide range of talent.

Just what general ability IQ tests measure remains uncertain, but increasingly, psychologists and educators have conceptualized giftedness as a function of specialized capabilities and potential for performance in specific fields such as mathematics, biology, dance, or visual arts. A definition of giftedness first offered in a 1971 report to the Congress of the United States by Sidney Marland, then commissioner of education, indicates a much broader concept of giftedness than high IQ scores have been found to measure. "Gifted and talented children are those identified by professionally qualified persons who, by virtue of outstanding abilities, are capable of high performance." He continued,

> Children capable of high performance include those with demonstrated achievement or potential ability in any of the following areas, singly or in combination:
> 1. general intellectual ability
> 2. specific academic aptitude

3. creative or productive thinking
4. leadership ability
5. visual or performing arts
6. psychomotor ability.

This definition of giftedness, known after its author as the Marland definition, does not distinguish giftedness from talent and includes performance capabilities that are sometimes related only distantly to performance on an IQ test. Nevertheless, the legacy of the Terman study of giftedness is that high IQ test scores remain one among several ways for psychologists and educators to identify intellectual giftedness among children in the general population. Giftedness in academic, creative, leadership, artistic, and psychomotor domains, however, is generally identified in other ways.

IDENTIFICATION OF GIFTEDNESS

Different percentages of the general population have been identified as gifted, depending on the definition of giftedness. Terman's use of IQ scores of 140 or above identified 1 percent of scorers as gifted. The current common indicator of intellectual giftedness is a score of 130 or above on a standardized, individually administered intelligence test, which is achieved by the top 2.5 percent of scorers. By the broader Marland definition, some form of which has been enacted through legislation by most states that have mandated gifted education programs, a minimum of 3 to 5 percent of school children are estimated to be gifted. Other definitions would identify as many as 10 to 15 percent of schoolchildren as gifted, or as many as 15 to 25 percent in a talent pool. Gifted and talented students receiving services in schools in the United States constitute about 6 percent of all children who are enrolled.

By almost any definition, giftedness is very difficult to identify during infancy. Most researchers would agree that giftedness has a biological foundation, but whether this foundation exists as a general or a specific capability is unknown. One of the earliest indicators of many forms of giftedness is precociousness, or unusually early development or maturity. During preschool years, precociousness can generalize across several domains, such as the use of logic with an extensive vocabulary, or it can be more specialized, such as drawing realistic pictures of animals or objects, or picking out a tune by ear on a musical instrument. Development does not seem to proceed in all areas at the same pace, however, so a young child may develop early in one or two areas but still behave in many ways like other children of the same age. Because of such asynchronous development, parents should not assume that a child who can master the moves of checkers at four years of age, for example, will accept losing a game any better than the average four-year-old.

A surprising number of gifted children are their parents' only children or first-borns, but this fact only reveals that their precocious development is due, at least in part, to learning from the models in their early environment who are adults rather than age-mates. As Bloom's study suggested, parents or other adult caretakers provide opportunities, resources, and encouragement to learn. Whatever reading ability a child may have, for example, can be nurtured by adults who read both to her and around her, who provide appropriate materials to read, and who show interest in the child's spontaneous efforts to read.

A child who is developing a talent early often will tend to rehearse it spontaneously, or call for repeated performance or for explanation by the parent (or other model) to review or understand what the child wants to learn. An eight-year-old, for example, might draw a whimsical but easily recognizable portrait of a parent's face while watching cartoons. A nine-year-old might play a competent if not yet masterful game of chess with the school principal, who then asks the child to explain certain moves, and so on. The products and performances of gifted children in elementary school are often similar to the products and performances of skilled but less gifted adolescents. For this reason, gifted children are often bored when instruction is designed for their age level rather than for an advanced level and rapid pace of learning.

By the school years, children's giftedness can be assessed reliably in ways other than observation of precociousness. Assessment usually begins with nomination by a teacher, parent, group of peers, or possibly the child himself or herself to identify who is gifted. Some psychologists have argued that nominations by those who know children well can be sufficient for placement in a gifted education program or a set of services beyond those normally provided by the regular school program, in order to help gifted children realize their potentials.

Teacher nominations cannot be the sole indicator of who is gifted, however, because studies have shown them to miss about half of all gifted children. Nominations by teachers and others are often supported by academic marks during the previous year, and these evidences of achievement are often supplemented by standardized test scores. These scores can result from individual or group assessments of intelligence, school ability, cognitive abilities, academic aptitudes or achievements, and creative or productive thinking abilities. Because tests themselves have been found to identify only half of all gifted children, test scores are sometimes supplemented by scores from other types of instruments (such as checklists), ratings of portfolios or performances, or interviews to complete the assessment process. No single assessment technique or instrument has been found to identify satisfactorily all types of giftedness in the Marland definition. Underrepresentation of African American, Latino, and American Indian children in gifted education programs in the United States remains largely a problem of identification.

INSTRUCTION OF GIFTED CHILDREN AND ADOLESCENTS
Eligibility for a gifted education program may be decided as a result of the process of identification, but the design of a program of instruction for each

child is often a separate set of decisions, sometimes requiring further assessments. It must be decided whether a child who is nearing the end of first grade but who has performed at the seventh-grade level on a standardized achievement test should be promoted to a much higher grade next year. An adolescent who is writing commercial music, and who is successfully performing it on weekends, might be allowed to leave school during the day to make a recording. The programming decisions to be made are as diverse as the talents of the children themselves.

It is not surprising, then, that no single strategy for teaching gifted children has been found to be the best. Rather, broad strategies of intervention can be classified as modifications in curriculum content or skills and modifications in school environment. Either of these strategies might be formalized by means of a written plan or contract, which is an agreement between individuals, such as the learner, the teacher, and (when relevant) others, including the gifted education teacher or the parent(s). Parents have the right to refuse special services for their children, but few do.

Children who display advanced cognitive skills at an early age may need additional educational opportunities to maximize their potential. (CLEO Photography)

Modifications in curriculum content for gifted students might include content acceleration (such as early admission, grade skipping or "telescoping" two years into one); content enrichment (materials to elaborate on basic concepts in standard program); content sophistication (more abstract or fundamental considerations of basic concepts); and content novelty (such as units on highly specialized topics). Modifications in skills include training in component skills of problem solving; various forms of problem solving (such as creative, cooperative, or competitive); and development of creativity. A program for the first-grader who is performing on achievement tests at the seventh-grade level, for example, might call for placement in a higher grade level (grade skipping), although which grade level to place the child in would have to be determined using teacher observations, interview results, and diagnostic tests.

Possible modifications in the school environment include provisions for enrichment in the regular classroom (such as access to special equipment); a consultant teacher (who helps the classroom teacher develop lessons); a resource room (or "pullout" program); mentoring (often by a professional in the community); independent study (often a special project); special-interest classes (such as creative writing); special classes (such as advanced placement biology); and special schools (such as a statewide math and science school). A program for the musically creative adolescent might incorporate mentoring by a music professional, who would report to the school on a regular basis about work completed by the adolescent at a recording studio or while otherwise away from school during school hours.

Of all of these modifications, teachers and parents seem to be most concerned about content acceleration, particularly if it involves grade skipping. As long as children are not socially and emotionally "hurried" by adults to achieve early, research suggests that the impact of content acceleration is positive. Most children who spend all or part of the school day with older children have ample opportunities to socialize with age-mates (if they wish) after school, on weekends, and in their neighborhoods. Being gifted can imply a preference for working alone or with older children, but it does not imply being lonely, particularly for those who are moderately gifted.

Individualized education programs (IEPs) are especially important for highly gifted children, such as child prodigies, who have either an extremely high IQ (180 or above) or expertise in a domain-specific skill by age ten; prodigious savants, formerly known as *idiots savants*, who have an IQ below 70 but expertise in a domain-specific skill (such as calendar calculating); and gifted children with disabilities. Children with disabilities (some of them multiple disabilities) may represent several percent of those who are gifted. In the United States, an IEP for these children is mandated by law. The importance of an individual program is evidenced by the case of Helen Keller, whose home tutoring not only resulted in the development of her intellectual abilities but also enabled her later accomplishments as an advocate for the blind throughout the world.

COUNSELING GIFTED LEARNERS

Beginning in the 1920's, Leta Hollingworth at Columbia University investigated characteristics of children who scored over 180 on the Stanford-Binet test. Her study of twelve children (eight boys and four girls) suggested that despite their overall adjustment, children who were highly intellectually gifted tended to encounter three challenges not encountered by most other children. The first was a failure to develop work habits at school because of a curriculum paced for much less capable learners. The second was difficulty in finding satisfying companionship because of their advanced interests and abilities in relation to their age-mates. The third was vulnerability to frustration and depression because of a capacity to understand information on an adult level without sufficient experience to know how to respond to it.

Hollingworth suggested that the problem of work habits could be addressed by a combination of acceleration and enrichment. The problem of loneliness could be solved by training gifted children in social games—such as checkers or chess—that could be played by people of any age, and the problems of frustration and depression by careful adult supervision and patience. Research has tended to confirm that the problems Hollingworth identified often need to be addressed, not only in cases of extreme precociousness but, to a lesser extent, in the lives of many people identified as gifted.

If underachievement by a gifted child has its source in an unchallenging or otherwise inappropriate educational program, the recommended action is to assess strengths and weaknesses (a learning disability may be the problem), then design a more appropriate program or place the child in one that already exists. If the source of underachievement is low self-esteem, the home environment may be unlike that found by Bloom to nurture talent. In this case, family counseling can often reverse underachievement.

To help a gifted child with peer relations, group counseling with other gifted children can be particularly beneficial. Not only can group members share their experiences of being gifted, but they can establish and maintain friendships with those who have similar (or sometimes quite different) exceptionalities. Group sessions can be both therapeutic and developmental.

At least some of the emotional challenges facing gifted children develop from their emotional sensitivity and excitability. Because parents and siblings often share these characteristics, the stage is set for conflict. What is surprising is that conflict does not create unhappiness more often. In the main, gifted people report satisfaction with their home lives. If tensions in the home arise more often than average, the parents of gifted children and the children themselves may need to develop more effective conflict resolution strategies and higher levels of self-understanding. Developmental counseling can assist parents and children in making these changes.

SOURCES FOR FURTHER STUDY

Bloom, Benjamin S., ed. *Developing Talent in Young People.* New York: Ballantine, 1985. A landmark study of the environmental influences which shape talent.

Colangelo, Nicholas, and Gary A. Davis, eds. *Handbook of Gifted Education.* 2d ed. Boston: Allyn & Bacon, 1997. A valuable collection of chapters for those with some background knowledge of gifted education.

Gallagher, James, and Shelagh Gallagher. *Teaching the Gifted Child.* 4th ed. Boston: Allyn & Bacon, 1994. A general overview of strategies for teaching gifted learners.

MacKinnon, Donald W. *In Search of Human Effectiveness.* Buffalo, N.Y.: Creative Education Foundation, 1978. A technical but readable account of an intensive effort to assess adult creativity.

Marland, Sidney P. *Education of the Gifted and Talented.* Washington, D.C.: Government Printing Office, 1972. Many current definitions of giftedness have their origin in this report, which is accessible in the Educational Resource Information Center (ERIC) collection as document Nos. ED056243 (Volume 1, *Report to the Congress of the United States*) and ED056244 (Volume 2, *Background Papers*).

Shurkin, Joel N. *Terman's Kids: The Groundbreaking Study of How the Gifted Grow Up.* Boston: Little, Brown, 1992. A highly readable summary of Terman's findings, set in a modern perspective by a journalist.

Silverman, Linda K. *Counseling the Gifted and Talented.* Denver, Colo.: Love, 1993. Describes the personal and emotional characteristics of gifted children, their home lives, and the challenges of raising them. Recommended reading for parents as well as professionals.

Winner, Ellen. *Gifted Children: Myths and Realities.* New York: Basic Books, 1996. Responds to nine myths about gifted children with a balance of case studies and research evidence. Recommended especially for those interested in the nature and nurture of unusually gifted children.

John F. Wakefield

SEE ALSO: Creativity and Intelligence; Intelligence; Intelligence Tests; Learning.

GROUPS

TYPE OF PSYCHOLOGY: Social psychology
FIELD OF STUDY: Group processes

The structure and function of groups have stimulated a large quantity of research over the years. What groups are, how groups form, and the positive and negative effects of groups on individuals are the primary areas of research that have provided insights into social behavior.

KEY CONCEPTS
- deindividuation
- density
- group formation
- identity
- self-attention
- social support

In any newspaper, one is likely to find several captivating stories that highlight the powerful negative influence that groups can exert on individuals. For example, one may recall the tragic violence exhibited by British sports fans at the international soccer matches in Belgium in the spring of 1985. One may also consider the one-man crime wave of Fred Postlewaite. For twenty years, Postlewaite engaged in a cross-country vandalism spree against the Sigma Alpha Epsilon college fraternity, which had rejected him in his youth.

There are equally dramatic instances of the powerful positive influences of groups. When the Spy Run Creek in Fort Wayne, Indiana, began to flood its banks in 1982, a group of the community's youths voluntarily participated in efforts to hold back its rising waters. There was also the rescue of four-year-old Michelle de Jesus, who had fallen from a subway platform into the path of an onrushing train. Everett Sanderson, a bystander, leapt down onto the tracks and flung the child into the crowd above. After he failed in his attempt to jump back to the platform, he was pulled up to safety at the last instant by bystanders.

These real-life events are noteworthy because they illustrate the universality of groups and the various ways that groups influence individual behavior. Although everyone can attest the prevalence of groups and the power that they can wield over individuals, several characteristics of groups are not as well defined. Several questions remain as to what groups are, how groups form, what groups look like, and the disadvantages and advantages of group membership. In spite of these questions, psychologists have come to understand many aspects of groups and the ways in which they influence individual behavior.

DEFINITION AND FORMATION OF GROUPS

The members of Congress who compose the House of Representatives of the United States are a group. The urban committee deciding how to allocate budgetary resources for unwed mothers in a particular city is a group. The members of a car pool sharing a ride to the train station every day are a group. The family seated around the dinner table at home in the evening is a group. The acting troupe performing *Hamlet* is a group. There are other examples of groups, however, that may be a little less obvious. All the unwed mothers in an urban area might be considered a group. A line of people waiting to buy tickets to a Broadway show might be thought of as a group. People eating dinner at the same time in a diner might even be considered a group. The people in the audience who are watching an acting troupe perform could behave as a group.

There are several ways in which people come to join the groups to which they belong. People are born into some groups. Several types of groupings are influenced in large part by birth: family, socioeconomic status, class, race, and religion. Other groups are formed largely by happenstance: for example, a line of the same people waiting for the 8:05 ferry every day. Some groups, however, are determined more clearly by intentional, goal-oriented factors. For example, a group of people at work who share a concern for well-being, health, and fitness may decide to form an exercise and nutrition group. Students interested in putting on a concert might decide to form a committee to organize bake sales, car washes, and fund drives in order to raise the money needed to achieve this goal. Finally, group memberships are sometimes created or changed as an effort toward self-definition or self-validation. For example, one can try to change one's religion, political orientation, professional associations, friendships, or family in an effort to enhance how one feels about oneself—or how others feel about one. An individual searching for a positive self-definition may join a country club, for example, to benefit from the social status acquired from such group membership.

STAGES OF GROUP DEVELOPMENT

Although there are countless underlying reasons for someone's membership in a given group, the work of Bruce Tuckman suggests that groups progress through a relatively consistent series of stages or phases in their development. Forming refers to a phase of coming together and orientation. Group members become acquainted with one another and define the requirements of group membership as well as the tasks to be performed. Storming refers to a phase of polarization and conflict. During this phase, group members deal with disagreements, compete for attractive positions within the group, and may become dissatisfied with other group members or the group as a whole. Norming refers to a phase when conflicts are solved and group members arrive at agreements regarding definitions of tasks and the requirements of group membership. Performing refers to the phase when group members concentrate on achieving their major task and strive toward shared goals. Finally, for some groups, adjourning refers to the disbanding or dissolution of the group after task completion.

For example, consider a special task force created to search for a missing child. During the forming stage, the members of this group will volunteer for, or be appointed to, the group. Although the general goals and definition of the group may have been established with the decision to implement such a task force, a storming phase would occur that would lead the group members into the sometimes difficult task of defining specific procedures of operation, responsibilities of particular task force members, a functional hierarchy, and so on. The norming phase would represent the resolution of the polarizations that emerged during the storming phase, as the committee proceeded to establish an agenda, a decision structure, and a means of implementing decisions. During the performing phase, the task force would actually perform the tasks agreed upon during the norming phase. Having finished its task, the group would then be adjourned.

GROUP TOPOGRAPHY

The topography of a group refers to its physical features. This includes such elements as the size of the group, the composition of the group, and the relationships between the various members of the groups. These topographical features of groups have been the focus of countless studies.

One obvious physical feature that could vary from one group to another is size. Some scholars have categorized group types in terms of size. For example, some researchers have found it useful to distinguish between small primary groups (from two to twenty group members), small nonprimary groups (from three to a hundred members), large groups (one thousand to ten thousand members), and largest groups (ten thousand-plus members). While such classifications may be interesting, the realities of everyday groups are typically more modest than such grand schemes would suggest. In a large number of settings, naturally occurring, free-forming groups typically range in size from two to seven persons, with a mean of about three. There are certainly exceptions to this rule of thumb; for example, most audiences watching theater troupes are considerably larger than three people. Nevertheless, most of the groups in which people interact on a day-to-day basis are relatively small. The size of a group tends to set the stage for many other topographical features of group life.

VARIATIONS IN GROUP COMPOSITION

The number of relationships possible in a group, according to James H. S. Bosard, is a direct consequence of the size of the group: the larger the group, the larger the number of possible relationships the individual might find within the group. It is possible to express the precise mathematical function relating the number of possible relationships between individuals in a group and group size (N): This function is represented by the formula

$(N^2-N)/2$. For example, if the group is made of Tom and Dick, there is only one possible relationship between members of the group (Tom-Dick). If the group is made up of the three people Tom, Dick, and Harry, there are three possible relationships (Tom-Dick, Tom-Harry, and Dick-Harry). If the group is made up of seven people, there are twenty-one possible relationships between individuals; if there are ten people in the group, there are forty-five possible relationships between individuals.

Thus, groups have the potential to become increasingly complex as the number of people in the group increases. There are many possible consequences of this increasing complexity. For one thing, it becomes increasingly harder to pay an equal amount of attention to everyone in the group as it increases in size. Brian Mullen and colleagues state that the person in the group who talks the most is paid the most attention, and in turn is most likely to emerge as the leader of the group; this effect (sometimes referred to as the "blabbermouth" theory of leadership) increases as the size of the group increases. It also becomes increasingly difficult to get to know everyone in the group and to spend equal amounts of time with everyone in the group as the group increases in size.

SIMPLIFYING GROUP COMPLEXITY

People in groups may tend toward a convenient simplification of this inevitable complexity. Scholars have long recognized the tendency for group members to divide other group members into groups of "us" and "them" rather than to perceive each person as a distinct entity. Groups can often be divided into perceptually distinct, smaller groups. For example, a committee might be composed predominantly of elderly members, with only one or a few young members. The general tendency is for people to focus their attention on the smaller group. The reason for this is that the smaller group seems to "stand out" as a perceptual figure against the background of the larger group. Thus, the youthful member of an otherwise elderly committee is likely to attract a disproportionate amount of attention from the committee members.

Not only will the members of the larger group pay more attention to the smaller group, but the members of the smaller group will do so as well. Thus, the members of the smaller group will become more self-attentive, more aware of themselves and their behavior. On the other hand, the members of the larger group become less self-attentive, or, as Ed Diener contends, more deindividuated—less aware of themselves and their behavior. For example, the single woman in a group of mechanical engineers that are otherwise men will quickly stand out. The male mechanical engineers may tend to think of that one distinct individual in terms of her status as a woman. Moreover, the lone woman may become more sensitive than usual about her behavioral transgressions of the norms guiding sexual roles in an all-male working environment.

IMPLICATIONS FOR SOCIAL BEHAVIOR

Thus, group composition has been demonstrated to predict the extent to which people pay attention to and are aware of, themselves and specific facets of themselves, and to predict a variety of social behaviors including participation in religious groups, bystander intervention in emergencies, worker productivity, stuttering in front of an audience, and conformity.

For example, an analysis of the participation of congregation members in their religious groups documented the powerful effect of group composition on behavior of group members. As the size of the congregation increased relative to the number of ministers, the congregation members were less likely to participate in the group (in terms of activities such as attending worship services, becoming lay ministers, or "inquiring for Christ"). In this instance, becoming "lost in the crowd" impaired the normal self-regulation behaviors necessary for participation. Alternatively, analysis of the behavior of stutterers in front of an audience also documented the powerful effects of group composition on the behavior of group members. As the size of the audience increased relative to the number of stutterers speaking, the verbal disfluencies (stuttering and stammering) of the speakers increased. In this instance, becoming the center of attention exaggerated the normal self-regulation behaviors necessary for speech, to the point of interfering with those behaviors. Group composition's effects of making the individual lost in the crowd or the center of attention are not inherently good or bad; positive or negative effects depend on the context.

Studying group dynamics, such as the reactions of an audience, can yield important psychological information. (CLEO Photography)

GROUP DENSITY

Another facet of the topography of the group that is related to group size is density. Density refers to the amount of space per person in the group (the less space per person, the higher the density). Doubling the number of people in the group meeting in a room of a given size will decrease by one-half the amount of space available for each member of the group. Alternatively, halving the number of people in the group will double the amount of space available per person. Thus, in a room of a given size, density is directly linked to the size of the group. This particular approach to density is called social density, because it involves a change in density by manipulation of the social dimension (group size). One could also manipulate the physical dimension (room size), rendering a change in what is called spatial density. Thus, halving the size of the room will halve the amount of space available to each group member.

Density has been demonstrated to influence a variety of social behaviors. People have been found to report feeling more anxious, more aggressive, more unpleasant, and, understandably, more crowded as a function of density. An analysis of the effects of "tripling" in college dormitories illustrates these types of effects. As a cost-cutting measure, colleges and universities will often house three students in a dormitory room that was initially constructed for two (hence, tripling). Tripling has been demonstrated to lead to an increase in arguments among the roommates, increased visits to the student health center, decreased grades, and increased overall dissatisfaction.

ROLE IN BEHAVIOR AND IDENTITY

Groups exert sometimes dramatic, sometimes subtle influences on behavior. These influences are sometimes beneficial and sometimes detrimental. An understanding of the effect of groups on the individual sets the stage for a deeper understanding of many facets of social life. One of the reasons for the formation or joining of groups is the definition of the self. On a commonly used questionnaire that requires a person to respond twenty times to the question "Who am I?," people tend to respond with references to some sort of group membership, be it family, occupation, hobby, school, ethnic, religious, or neighborhood. Groups help establish one's identity, both for one's own benefit and for the benefit of others with whom one interacts.

COSTS OF GROUP MEMBERSHIP

Belonging to groups has its price, however; as discussed at length by Christian Buys, one's very membership in a group may carry with it hidden costs, risks, or sacrifices. A more complete understanding of groups requires a consideration of this aspect of membership in a group. Attaining certain types of rewards may be incompatible with belonging to a group. For example, the goal of completing a difficult and complicated task may be facilitated by belonging to a group of coworkers who bring the varied skills and knowledge required for successful task completion. Yet one group member's goal of always being the center of attention, or of needing to feel special and unique, may have to be subverted if the group is to perform the task for which it formed. What the individual wants or needs may sometimes be displaced by what the group needs.

Moreover, the deindividuation (an individual's loss of self-awareness, resulting in a breakdown in the capacity to self-regulate) fostered by groups breaks down the individual's ability to self-regulate. Research has demonstrated the state of deindividuation to increase the (simulated) electric shocks people will deliver to other people in experiments, to increase the use of profanity, and to increase stealing among Halloween trick-or-treaters. The paradigmatic illustration of the negative effects of deindividuation is the lynch mob. An analysis of newspaper accounts, conducted by Brian Mullen, of lynch mob atrocities committed in the United States over a sixty-year period showed that the savagery and atrocity of the mob toward its victim(s) increased as the size of the mob increased relative to the number of its victims.

GROUP MEMBERSHIP BENEFITS

As discussed by Lynn Anderson, just as there are costs involved in belonging to a group, there are also benefits that accrue from group membership. Although the negative aspects of group membership may capture one's attention more forcefully, the positive aspects are no less common or important. A complete understanding of the purpose of groups requires a consideration of the positive side of belonging to a group. A considerable amount of evidence has documented the physiological, attitudinal, and health effects of social support systems. For example, people who belong to a varied and tight social support network have been found to be in better physical health and to be better able to resist stress than those lacking such support. As examples, one might consider the effects of such popular support groups as Alcoholics Anonymous and Mothers Against Drunk Driving as well as lesser known support groups that deal with specific issues such as loss and bereavement. These groups provide the imperative psychological function of allowing their members a new avenue for coping with their problems.

Perhaps the most notable effects of the group on self-definition and identity are observed when these taken-for-granted benefits are taken away. The woman who has defined herself in terms of her marital status can find her identity cast adrift after a divorce. Similarly, foreign-exchange students often report dislocation or disorientation of identity immediately upon their return home. After months or years of trying to establish a new identity based on new friends, new social contexts, or new groups, that new identity is now inappropriate and out of place in their old social context.

SOURCES FOR FURTHER STUDY

Brown, Rupert, ed. *Group Processes: Dynamics Within and Between Groups.* 2d rev. ed. New York: Basil Blackwell, 2000. This is a readable treatment of theories and research on group processes, with a particular emphasis on British and European contributions. A variety of compelling and relevant social issues are covered, such as social conformity, crowd behavior, group productivity, and ethnic prejudice.

Canetti, Elias. *Crowds and Power.* Translated by Carol Stewart. 1962. Reprint. New York: Noonday Press, 1998. This is a classic historical discussion of the effects of crowds on individuals and societies. Such avenues of group behavior are described as open and closed crowds, invisible crowds, baiting crowds, and feast crowds.

Forsyth, Donelson R. *Group Dynamics.* 3d ed. Belmont, Calif.: Wadsworth, 2000. This thorough volume provides access to a wide-ranging review of evidence regarding all aspects of group processes.

Mullen, Brian, and George R. Goethals, eds. *Theories of Group Behavior.* New York: Springer-Verlag, 1987. This comprehensive edited volume considers several theories of group behavior in order to expand fully on the phenomenon. Classic as well as modern and controversial theories are described by several of the social psychologists who originally formulated the accounts.

Turner, John C., et al. *Rediscovering the Social Group: A Self-Categorization Theory.* Oxford, England: Basil Blackwell, 1987. A sophisticated in-depth treatment of a new theory of behavior in groups. This theoretical approach integrates a vast amount of data and sets the stage for further research in group behavior.

Tara Anthony and Brian Mullen

SEE ALSO: Affiliation and Friendship; Support Groups.

HABITUATION AND SENSITIZATION

TYPE OF PSYCHOLOGY: Learning
FIELD OF STUDY: Biological influences on learning

Habituation, a form of behavior modification, is a decrease in behavioral response that results from repeated presentation of a stimulus. Sensitization is a heightened behavioral response that results from a stronger stimulus.

KEY CONCEPTS
- adaptation
- innate
- learning
- neuron
- neurotransmitter
- opponent process theory
- stimulus
- synapse

Habituation and sensitization are the two most fundamental and widespread forms of learning in the animal kingdom. According to ethologists, learning is any modification in behavior that results from previous experience, in some way involves the nervous system, and is not caused by development, fatigue, or injury. More advanced forms of learning include association, perceptual or programmed learning, and insight. The two simplest (nonassociative) forms of learning are habituation and sensitization. These two processes can be characterized as behavioral modifications that result from repeated presentation of simple environmental stimuli.

Habituation is a decrease in response to repeated presentation of a stimulus—an environmental cue that can potentially modify an animal's behavior via its nervous system. One of the most widely cited examples of this kind of learning involves the startle response exhibited by nestling birds in response to potential predators such as hawks. A young duck, for example, will exhibit an innate startle response whenever a hawk-shaped model or silhouette is passed overhead. With repeated presentation of the model, however, the intensity of the bird's response will decline as the animal becomes habituated, or learns that the stimulus bears no immediate significance.

Common throughout the animal kingdom and even among some groups of protozoans, habituation is important for preventing repeated responses to irrelevant environmental stimuli that could otherwise overwhelm an organism's senses and interfere with other critical tasks. In the case of a nestling bird, there is a clear advantage to an alarm response in the presence of a potential predator; however, a continued fixed response would result in an unnecessary expenditure of energy and distraction from other important activities such as feeding.

In identifying a habituation response, it is necessary to distinguish between true habituation and sensory adaptation and fatigue. These latter two phenomena involve a waning in responsiveness that is caused by temporary insensitivity of sense organs or by muscle fatigue and thus are not considered forms of learning. In contrast, habituation results in a drop in responsiveness even though the nervous system is fully capable of detecting a signal and eliciting a muscle response.

In contrast to habituation, sensitization is the heightened sensitivity (or hypersensitivity) that results from initial or repeated exposure to a strong stimulus. Examples of sensitization include the increased sensitivity of humans to soft sounds following exposure to a loud, startling noise such as a gunshot, or the increased responsiveness and sensitivity of a laboratory animal to mild (usually irrelevant) tactile stimulation after an electric shock. Sensitization increases an organism's awareness and responsiveness to a variety of environmental stimuli, thereby preparing it for potentially dangerous situations.

COMPARISON OF RESPONSES

At first glance, habituation and sensitization seem to be opposite behavioral responses—one a decrease in responsiveness and the other an increase—but, in fact, they are physiologically different processes, each with its own set of unique characteristics.

At the physiological level, the two responses are determined by contrasting neurological processes that take place in different parts of the nervous system. Habituation is thought to take place primarily in the reflex arc (or SR) system, which consists of short neuronal circuits between sense organs and muscles. In contrast, sensitization is assumed to occur in the state system, or that part of the nervous system that regulates an organism's state of responsiveness. The SR system controls specific responses, whereas the state system determines an organism's general level of readiness to respond. The interaction between habituation and sensitization and these systems determines the exact outcome of a response. At the cellular level, habituated sensory neurons produce fewer neurotransmitters on the postsynaptic membrane, while sensitized neurons are stimulated by other neurons to increase neurotransmitter production and hence responsiveness of the nerves. Thus, while their ultimate neurological effects are somewhat opposite, the mechanisms by which such effects are achieved are quite different.

Other important differences between habituation and sensitization include contrasting recovery times, opposite patterns of stimulus specificity, and differences in responsiveness to stimulus intensity. Sensitization is generally characterized by a short-term or spontaneous recovery, as are some cases of habituation. In certain situations, however, recovery from habituation may take several days, and even then it may result in incomplete or less intense responses.

In comparison to sensitization, habituation is usually elicited by very specific sign stimuli such as certain colors, shapes, or sounds. Thus, even after complete habituation to one stimulus, the organism will still respond fully to a second stimulus. Sensitization, on the other hand, can be characterized as a more generalized response, one in which a single stimulus will result in complete sensitization to a variety of stimuli. Such fundamental differences between these two learning processes reflect differences in their function and survival value. It is a clear advantage to an organism to increase its general awareness to a variety of stimuli (such as occurs in sensitization) once it is alarmed. A similar generalized pattern of habituation, however, would shut down the organism's sensitivity to many important stimuli and possibly put the organism in danger.

A final important difference between habituation and sensitization is the manner in which the two processes are affected by stimulus strength. Habituation is more likely to occur if the repeated stimulus is weak, and sensitization will occur when the stimulus is strong.

These various characteristics have important survival implications, especially for species that rely on stereotypic responses to avoid predation and other life-threatening situations. They ensure that the response is elicited in a timely fashion, that the animal is returned to a normal state in a relatively short period of time, and that the animal is not overwhelmed with sensory input.

Aplysia Research

Habituation and sensitization have been studied in a variety of contexts and in a number of organisms, from simple protozoans (such as *Stentor*) to human subjects. Such studies have focused on the adaptive significance of these simple learning processes, their neurological control, and the range of behavioral responses that result from interaction between these two forms of learning.

One particular organism in which the neurological basis of habituation and sensitization has been extensively studied is the marine slug *Aplysia*. Eric Kandel and his associates at Columbia University showed that when the mantle of this organism is prodded, the slug quickly withdraws its gills into a central cavity. After repeated prodding, it learns to ignore the stimulus; that is, it becomes habituated. Conversely, when the slug is stimulated with an electric shock, its sensitivity to prodding increases greatly, and it withdraws its gills in response to even the slightest tactile stimulation (that is, it becomes sensitized).

Because *Aplysia* possesses only a few, large neurons, it is an excellent organism in which to study the physiological basis of learning. Capitalizing on this unique system, Kandel and his colleagues have been able to establish the neurological changes that accompany simple forms of learning. In the case of habituation, they have shown that repeated stimulation interferes with calcium ion channels in the nerve which, under normal circumstances, causes synaptic vesicles to release neurotransmitters, which in turn relay a nervous impulse between two neurons. Thus, habituation results in a blocking of the chemical signals between nerves and thereby prevents gill withdrawal.

When *Aplysia* is stimulated (or sensitized) by an electric shock, an interneuron (a closed nerve circuit contained within one part of the nervous system) stimulates the sensory neuron by opening calcium ion channels, increasing neurotransmitter production, and promoting gill withdrawal. Thus, the proximate neurological changes that take place during sensitization and habituation are nearly opposite, but they are achieved by very different neurological circuits.

STUDIES OF THE SUCKING REFLEX

A second area in which habituation and sensitization responses have been the subject of extensive investigation is the sucking reflex exhibited by human infants. When the cheeks or lips of a young child are touched with a nipple or finger, the infant will automatically begin sucking. In a study designed to explore how various stimuli affect this reflex, it was shown that babies respond much more vigorously to a bottle nipple than to the end of a piece of rubber tubing. In addition, repeated presentation of a bottle nipple causes an increase in sucking response, whereas repeated stimulation with rubber tubing causes a decrease in sucking. The sensitized or elevated response to a rubber nipple is a result of activation of the state system, which increases the baby's awareness and readiness to respond. Sensitization, however, does not occur when the baby is stimulated with rubber tubing, and instead the child habituates to this stimulus.

ROLE IN EMOTIONAL REACTIONS

In addition to influencing simple innate behaviors such as sucking reflexes and withdrawal responses, habituation is believed to be responsible for a number of more complex emotional reactions in humans. Explanations for the effects of habituation on emotions are derived primarily from the opponent process theory of motivation.

The opponent process theory holds that each emotional stimulation (or primary process) initiated by an environmental stimulus is opposed by an internal process in the organism. The emotional changes that actually occur in the organism are predicted to result from the net effect of these two processes. The opponent process detracts from the primary process, and summation of the two yields a particular emotional response. It is hypothesized that when the organism is repeatedly stimulated, the primary process is unaffected, but the opponent process is strengthened, which results in a net reduction in the overall emotional response. In other words, repeated presentation of an emotion-arousing stimulus results in habituation in the emotional response, primarily as a result of the elevated opponent response.

An increase in drug tolerance which results from repeated usage of a drug is best explained by this kind of habituation. Habitual users of alcohol, caffeine, nicotine, or various opiate derivatives must consume greater quantities of such drugs each time they are ingested in order to achieve the same emotional stimulation. Thus, with repeated usage, there is a decline in the overall emotional response. This decline in the euphoric effects of a drug is primarily the result of an increase in the opponent process, which can be characterized as the negative effects of the drug. This is presumably why habitual users experience severe physiological problems (for example, headaches or delirium tremens) upon termination of a drug.

Similar patterns of habituation have also been suggested to explain the human emotional responses associated with love and attachment and the extreme feelings of euphoria derived from various thrill-seeking activities such as skydiving. Thus, while habituation and sensitization are simple forms of learning, they may be involved in a variety of more complex behaviors and emotions as well.

INTERACTION OF LEARNING AND INSTINCT

Studies of habituation and sensitization have been especially helpful in clarifying the physiological and genetic mechanisms that control various forms of learning. Such investigations have also shown that habituation and sensitization are widespread phenomena with tremendous adaptive significance throughout the animal kingdom.

Ethologists, in marked contrast with psychologists (especially behaviorist psychologists), historically have emphasized the importance of underlying physiological mechanisms in the regulation of various behavioral phenomena. Traditionally, they argued that many forms of behavior are not only genetically determined, or innate, but further constrained by the physiological hardware of the organism. They held that psychologists completely ignored these factors by focusing on only the input and output of experiments. Psychologists, on the other hand, have maintained that nearly all forms of behavior are influenced in some way by learning. These contrasting views, which developed largely as a result of different experimental approaches, eventually gave way to a more modern and unified picture of behavior.

One area of research that greatly facilitated this unification was the study of habituation and sensitization. By discovering the chemical and neurological changes that take place during these simple forms of learning, neurobiologists succeeded in demonstrating how the physiological environment is modified during the learning process and that such modifications are remarkably similar throughout the animal kingdom. Thus, it became quite clear that an understanding of proximate physiological mechanisms was central to the study of behavior and learning.

In addition, other studies on sensitization and habituation helped establish the generality of these processes among various groups of animals. They showed that simple forms of learning can occur in nearly all major animal phyla, and that these learning processes often result in modification of simple innate behaviors as well as a variety of more complex responses. From these and other studies, it was soon evident that learning and instinct are not mutually exclusive events but two processes that work together to provide animals with maximum adaptability to their environment. The kind of learning that occurs during habituation and sensitization allows animals to modify simple, fixed behaviors in response to repeated exposure to environmental stimuli. Habituation allows an organism to filter irrelevant background stimuli and prevent sensory overload and interference of normal activities critical to its survival. Sensitization helps increase an organism's awareness of stimuli in the face of potentially dangerous situations.

These two forms of learning represent important behavioral adaptations with tremendous generality in the animal kingdom. Even in humans, a variety of seemingly complex behaviors can be attributed to interactions between sensitization and habituation and the simple neurological changes that accompany them.

SOURCES FOR FURTHER STUDY

Domjan, Michael. *Principles of Learning and Behavior.* 5th ed. Belmont, Calif.: Thomson/Wadsworth, 2003. Provides a complete treatment of the psychological basis and mechanisms of learning. Chapter 3 is devoted entirely to habituation and sensitization, and it provides several specific examples of these processes in both human and animal subjects. Includes many original data tables and graphs and a thorough review of the literature.

Grier, James W. *Biology of Animal Behavior.* 2d ed. New York: McGraw-Hill, 1992. This college-level text provides comprehensive treatment of the study of animal behavior. Clearly written and well illustrated; should provide a good introduction for the layperson. Six chapters are devoted to the physiological control of behavior, and one chapter deals entirely with learning and memory.

McFarland, David, ed. *The Oxford Companion to Animal Behavior.* Rev. and enlarged ed. New York: Oxford University Press, 1987. Intended as a reference guide, this comprehensive survey of behavior was written by a team of internationally known biologists, psychologists, and neurobiologists. It contains more than two hundred entries covering a variety of topics. Provides a detailed summary of various forms of learning, including habituation and sensitization. The index provides cross-references organized by both subject and species lists.

Manning, Aubrey, and Marian Stamp Dawkins. *An Introduction to Animal Behavior.* 5th ed. New York: Cambridge University Press, 1998. A concise handbook offering a light introduction to many general aspects of animal behavior and learning. Provides a discussion on stimulus filtering, an entire chapter on the physiological basis of behavior and motivation, and a complete summary of various forms of learning. Well researched, clearly written, and effectively illustrated.

Raven, Peter H., and George B. Johnson. *Biology.* 6th ed. Boston: McGraw-

Hill, 2002. Chapter 56 of this general text on the science of biology offers an excellent first introduction to the general concepts of ethology and animal behavior. Includes a brief summary of learning and detailed coverage of habituation, sensitization, and conditioning in *Aplysia*. A concise summary, suggestions for additional reading, and review questions appear at the end of each chapter.

Shepherd, Gordon Murray. *Neurobiology.* 3d ed. New York: Oxford University Press, 1997. This somewhat advanced college-level volume on neurobiology offers an in-depth account of the physiological basis of learning and memory. A portion of chapter 30 is devoted to the neurological changes associated with habituation and sensitization. Detailed diagrams, data summaries, and complete literature reviews are provided.

Michael A. Steele

SEE ALSO: Conditioning; Learning; Motivation; Pavlovian Conditioning; Reflexes.

HELPING

TYPE OF PSYCHOLOGY: Developmental psychology; motivation; personality; social psychology
FIELD OF STUDY: Prosocial behavior

Theories of helping behavior have attempted to explain why people offer physical and psychological assistance to others in both emergency and nonemergency situations. These theories have considered the roles of physiological arousal, judgments of costs and rewards, mood states, and attributions of responsibility in influencing helping behavior.

KEY CONCEPTS
- arousal cost-reward model
- attributions about responsibility
- mood and helping
- norm of reciprocity
- prosocial behavior
- self-help groups
- spirituality

Helping involves assisting, in some way, another person or animal in need. Helping behaviors can take a variety of forms. Some, such as carrying a book for a friend, require little effort. Others, such as jumping into a frozen lake to rescue a drowning stranger, are life-threatening. To explain helping behavior, researchers have studied many variables and have developed theories to organize them and account for their interrelationships.

AROUSAL COST-REWARD MODEL

In 1981, Jane Allyn Piliavin, John Dovidio, Samuel Gaertner, and Russell Clark introduced the "arousal cost-reward" model. This model assumes that witnessing the need or distress of another person is physiologically arousing. When one attributes the source of one's arousal to another person's distress, the arousal is sometimes experienced as emotionally unpleasant, and one becomes motivated to reduce it.

According to the arousal cost-reward model, a person will choose to engage in the arousal-decreasing response associated with the fewest net costs. Net costs are based on two types of rewards and costs associated with the helping situation: costs for not helping and rewards and costs for helping. Costs for not helping occur when no assistance is given and may include experiences such as feeling troubled because someone in need is continuing to suffer, or receiving criticism from others for being callous. Costs for helping are direct negative outcomes that the potential helper might experience after offering help, such as loss of time, embarrassment, or injury. Helping, however, can also be associated with positive outcomes such as praise, gratitude, and feelings of self-worth.

Piliavin and her colleagues suggest that both types of costs influence the decision to help. When net costs are low, as the costs for not helping increase, helping in the form of direct intervention becomes more likely. If net costs for helping are high, however, direct intervention is unlikely regardless of potential costs for not helping. In this latter situation, a person may give indirect assistance (for example, by calling someone else to help). Alternatively, the person may deny responsibility for helping, reinterpret the situation as one in which help is not needed, or try to leave the scene altogether.

ATTRIBUTIONS OF RESPONSIBILITY

Philip Brickman and his colleagues argue that when one sees a person in need, one makes attributions about how responsible that person is for the problem he or she faces and also about how much responsibility that person should take for its solution. These attributions, in turn, influence one's judgment about who one thinks is best suited to deliver help, and, if one decides to offer help oneself, they influence its form. One may be most likely to offer direct assistance if one attributes little responsibility to that person for solving the problem—as when a child is lost in a shopping mall. In contrast, if one judges a person to be responsible for solving his or her problem, as when a friend has a nasty boss, one may offer encouragement and moral support but not directly intervene. Thus, who one thinks should provide the remedy—oneself, experts, or the person who needs the help—depends on attributions that one makes about responsibility.

MOOD

One's mood may also influence one's decision to help someone who is in need. In general, people experiencing a positive mood, such as happiness, are more likely to offer help than are those in neutral moods. Using quantitative procedures for summarizing the results of thirty-four experimental studies, Michael Carlson, Ventura Charlin, and Norman Miller concluded that the best general explanation for why positive moods increase helpfulness is that they heighten sensitivity to positive reinforcement or good outcomes. This sensitivity includes both thinking more about good outcomes for oneself and increased thought about the goodness of behaving prosocially. This general summary incorporates many explanations that have been proposed for the relation between positive moods and helping, among them the mood maintenance and social outlook explanations.

Mood maintenance argues that one behaves more helpfully when happy because doing so prolongs one's good mood. The social outlook explanation points instead to the fact that positive moods are often the consequences of another person's behavior (for example, being given a compliment). Such actions by others trigger thoughts about human kindness, cooperativeness, and goodness. These thoughts, if still present when someone asks for help, make a person more likely to respond positively.

The effects of bad moods on helpfulness are more complex. Carlson and Miller also quantitatively summarized the effects found in forty-four studies concerned with the impact of various mood-lowering events on helpfulness. These studies included such diverse procedures for inducing negative moods as having subjects repeat depressing phrases, view unpleasant slides, imagine sad experiences, and fail at a task. Two factors can apparently account for most of the findings on negative moods and helping. The first is whether the target of the mood-lowering event is the self or someone else; the second is whether the self or an outside force is responsible for the mood-lowering event. When one is responsible for imposing a mood-lowering event on another person and therefore feels guilty, helping is very likely. When one is responsible for an event that lowers one's own mood (as when one engages in self-harm) or when one witnesses another person impose a mood-lowering event on someone else (that is, when one experiences empathy), a positive response to a subsequent request for help is more likely but not as much so as in the first case. In contrast, when someone else is responsible for one's own negative mood—when one has been victimized—one's helpfulness tends to be inhibited.

THEORETICAL EXPLANATIONS

These explanations can be applied to a wide range of helping situations—reactions to both physical and psychological distress, situations in which helping appears to be determined by a rational consideration of costs and rewards, and situations in which the help offered seemingly is irrational and very costly.

One study on which the arousal cost-reward model was based suggests how consideration of costs and rewards might affect the decision to offer direct physical assistance. In this study, a man feigned collapse on the floor of a New York subway a few minutes after boarding the train and remained there until help was given. In some cases, the man smelled of alcohol and carried an alcohol bottle wrapped in a paper bag, giving the impression that drunkenness had caused his fall. In other instances, the man carried a cane, suggesting that he had fallen because of a physical impairment. Although many people offered assistance in both conditions, more people helped the man with the cane than the man who appeared to be drunk.

The different amounts of assistance in the two conditions may result from differences in perceived net costs. Potential helpers may have expected greater costs when the man looked drunk than when he appeared to be disabled. Helping a drunk may require more effort and be more unpleasant than helping someone with a physical impairment. It may also be less intrinsically and extrinsically rewarding than helping someone with a physical impairment. Finally, costs for not helping may be lower in the case of the drunk than for the man with the cane. The drunk may be perceived as "only drunk" and therefore not really needy. Thus, the finding that more people helped the man with the cane is consistent with the hypothesis that helping increases as the net costs associated with the helping response decrease.

Although considerations of costs and rewards are important, it would be unrealistic to think that helping only occurs when net costs are low. People may engage in very costly helping behaviors when physiological arousal is especially high, such as in clear, unambiguous emergencies. The actions of an unknown passenger aboard an airplane that crashed into a frozen river illustrate this point. As a helicopter attempted to pull people out of the water to safety, this passenger repeatedly handed the lowered life ring to other, more seriously injured passengers, even though these acts of heroism eventually cost him his life.

Much research on helpfulness has asked, When do people help? It is also important, however, to look at what type of help is given and how the person in need is expected to react to offers of assistance. The Brickman model, involving attributions of responsibility for the problem and its solution, does this. It also looks at more everyday forms of helping. According to Brickman, if one attributes responsibility for both the problem and its solution to the person in need, one is applying the moral model of helping. With this orientation, one may have the tendency to view the person in need as lazy and undeserving of help. In the subway example, people may not have helped the fallen drunk because they made such attributions. Although people who apply the moral model may not give direct assistance, they may sometimes support and encourage the person's own effort to overcome the problem.

If one sees people as responsible for their problem but not for its solution, then one is applying the enlightenment model. Criminals are held responsible for violating the law but are jailed because they are judged incapable of reforming themselves, and jail is believed to be rehabilitating as well as punishing. Discipline from those in authority is seen as the appropriate helping response, and submission to it is expected from the person receiving the "assistance."

The medical model applies when the person is seen as responsible for neither the problem nor its solution. This orientation is often taken toward the ill. Such situations call for an expert whose recommendations are to be accepted and fulfilled.

In the final combination of attributions of responsibility for a problem and its solution, the compensatory model, the person is not held responsible for having caused the problem. The problem may be judged to be caused by factors beyond the person's control, such as when an earthquake occurs. In this model, however, the person is held responsible for solving the problem. Helpers may provide useful resources but are not expected to take the initiative for a solution. In the case of an earthquake, the government may offer low-interest loans for rebuilding, but victims must decide whether to apply for one and rebuild their homes.

HISTORICAL BACKGROUND

Concern with helping behavior has its roots in early philosophy. Thinkers such as Aristotle, Socrates, Niccolò Machiavelli, and Thomas Hobbes debated whether humans are by nature good or bad, selfish or selfless. Most empirical psychological research on the topic, however, was not initiated until after the 1950's. This was probably not coincidental. Many people were concerned with the atrocities of World War II and, in the United States, with rising crime rates. In response, psychologists not only began to investigate human cruelty but also gave increased attention to what could be done to offset it. Similarly, the emergence of the Civil Rights movement, with its emphasis on cooperation and harmony, probably further propelled the study of prosocial behavior. The term "prosocial behavior," or behavior intended to benefit other people, is sometimes used synonymously with "helping" and is sometimes meant to be a larger category that includes helping.

Early studies of helping behavior examined situational variables that influence the decision to help someone who is in physical distress. The arousal cost-reward model and the subway experiment characterize this type of work. Also important during this period were Alvin Gouldner's theorizing on the norm of reciprocity and subsequent empirical investigation of the norms governing helping behavior, such as Leonard Berkowitz's work in the 1960's. As social psychologists explored situational variables that influence helping, developmental psychologists examined the emergence of positive social behavior in children. Some, such as Jean Piaget and Lawrence Kohlberg, postulated distinct stages of moral development. Others focused on how people who model helping behavior influence children's subsequent behavior.

EXTENSIONS OF THE EARLIER RESEARCH

While research continues in all these areas, other questions also attract interest. Studies of people's responses to others' physical distress have been extended by research on how people respond to someone in psychological distress. Similarly, researchers have extended their interests in the potential helper to examine how the person in need of help is affected by seeking and receiving it.

Also important in understanding helping behavior has been the study of personality and how individuals differ in their tendency to help. Some of this work is related to research on norms, in that it looks at whether people develop a personal set of rules or standards which govern their helping behavior. Another approach, adopted by Margaret Clark and Judson Mills, has looked at how the relationship between the help requester and the help giver influences helpfulness. Research on helping now incorporates many different influences on the helping process, from individual to social to developmental factors. In the process, the applicability of the research findings has grown and has given rise to a broader understanding of the types of helping behavior that may occur, when they may occur, who might engage in them, and why.

SOURCES FOR FURTHER STUDY

Batson, Charles Daniel. *The Altruism Question: Toward a Social-Psychological Answer.* Hillsdale, N.J.: Lawrence Erlbaum, 1991. Discusses altruism and empathy from a social psychological perspective and addresses the debate about whether or not altruism is merely self-serving egoism. Also discusses altruistic motivation and personality. Batson is highly regarded for his many experimental studies of helping behavior.

Blumenthal, David R. *The Banality of Good and Evil: Moral Lessons from the Shoah and Jewish Tradition.* Washington, D.C.: Georgetown University Press, 1999. The author is a theologian who reviews social, psychological, child developmental, and personality research in the presentation of his ideas regarding the ordinariness of good and evil. The book is a study of the behavior, character, and motivation of people who rescued or protected Jews in Nazi Europe. The commentary on what it means to be a moral human is often moving. This book is especially important in light of the Christian bias in much of the helping and prosocial research literature. Very highly recommended.

Clark, Margaret S., ed. *Prosocial Behavior.* Newbury Park, Calif.: Sage Publications, 1991. Focuses on the broad area of positive social behaviors and therefore includes discussions of altruism as well as chapters on helping. Two chapters deal with the development of prosocial behavior. Also noteworthy is a chapter that covers aspects of help-seeking behavior. A chapter on moods and one on the arousal cost-reward model are included as well.

Derlega, Valerian J., and Janusz Grzelak, eds. *Cooperation and Helping Behavior: Theories and Research.* New York: Academic Press, 1982. The first chapter provides a nontechnical discussion of the similarities and differences between the related issues of helping and cooperation, while also serving as an introduction to later chapters. Chapters on helping discuss the arousal cost-reward model and extend the model to show how help seekers may be influenced by cost/reward considerations.

Oliner, Pearl M., and Samuel P. Oliner. *Toward a Caring Society: Ideas into Action.* Westport, Conn.: Praeger, 1995. The Oliners are social scientists affiliated with the Altruistic Personality and Prosocial Behavior Institute. They offer guidelines for promoting caring behavior in families, in schools, at work, and in religious organizations based on careful consideration of a variety of sources, including the literature on altruism, helping, and prosocial behavior. They present caring, or the assumption of responsibility for the welfare of others, as a way to redress an overly individualistic and materialistic culture. Many poignant and inspiring narrative excerpts are included.

Rushton, J. Philippe, and Richard M. Sorrentino, eds. *Altruism and Helping Behavior: Social, Personality, and Developmental Perspectives.* Hillsdale, N.J.: Lawrence Erlbaum, 1981. Covers, as the title implies, three main areas. Under developmental issues, varied topics such as the influence of television and the role of genetics (sociobiology) are covered. Also includes a discussion of moods and a model of how norms may influence helping.

Schroeder, David A., Louis A. Penner, John F. Dovidio, and Jane A. Piliavin. *The Psychology of Helping and Altruism: Problems and Puzzles.* New York: McGraw-Hill, 1995. Good review of the research literature. Includes discussions of the relationships among biology, personality, and social learning as they relate to prosocial behavior. The reciprocity involved in seeking and giving help is also discussed. The book is intended for upper-level undergraduate and graduate students.

Staub, Ervin, Daniel Bar-Tal, Jerzy Karylowski, and Janusz Reykowski, eds. *Development and Maintenance of Prosocial Behavior: International Perspectives on Positive Morality.* New York: Plenum Press, 1984. This set of twenty-four chapters from various researchers focuses not only on helping but also on other positive behaviors such as cooperation, generosity, and kindness. Covers a range of topics, from developmental aspects of prosocial behavior to the effects of help seeking and help receiving to applications of knowledge about helping behavior. A unique aspect of this book is its consideration of research done in many different countries.

Tiffany A. Ito and Norman Miller; updated by Tanja Bekhuis

SEE ALSO: Aggression; Crowd Behavior; Moral Development.

HOMOSEXUALITY

TYPE OF PSYCHOLOGY: Motivation
FIELDS OF STUDY: Attitudes and behavior; interpersonal relations; physical
   motives

Sexuality is one of the most complex and individual attributes of the human psyche.
There are four types of theories with regard to the development of sexual orientation,
but none seems sufficient to explain the huge diversity to be found in sexual expression
across ages and cultures.

KEY CONCEPTS
- androgyny
- gay
- homophobia
- homosexual
- lesbian
- pedophile
- transsexual
- transvestite

Theories on the origin and development of homosexual orientation can be
categorized into four groups: psychoanalytic, biological, social learning, and
sociobiological theories. Psychoanalytic theories are based on the Freudian
model of psychosexual stages of development, developed by Austrian psychiatrist Sigmund Freud. According to this model, every child goes through
several stages, including the "phallic stage," during which he or she learns to
identify with his or her same-sex parent. For boys, this is supposed to be particularly difficult, as it requires redefining the strong bond that they have
had with their mother since birth. According to Freudian theorists, homosexuality is an outcome of the failure to resolve this developmental crisis: If a
boy's father is absent or "weak" and his mother is domineering or overpro-
tective, the boy may never come to identify with his father; for a girl, having a
"cold" or rejecting mother could prevent her from identifying with the female role.

THEORETICAL MODELS
Research has found that homosexuals are, in fact, more likely to feel an inability to relate to their same-sex parent than are heterosexuals and to report that the same-sex parent was "cold" or "distant" during their childhood.
Some studies have suggested, however, that this psychological distance between parent and offspring is found mostly in families with children who
show cross-gender behaviors when very young and that the distancing is
more likely to be a result of preexisting differences in the child than a cause
of later differences.

Biological theories have suggested that homosexuality is genetic, a result of hormone levels different from those found in heterosexuals, or is a result of prenatal maternal effects on the developing fetus. Although there may be genes that predispose a person to become homosexual under certain circumstances, no specific genes for homosexuality have been identified. Similarly, there are no consistent differences between levels of hormones in homosexual and heterosexual adults. The possibility remains that subtle fluctuations of hormones during critical periods of fetal development may influence brain structures which regulate sexual arousal and attraction.

Social-learning models suggest that homosexual orientation develops as a response to pleasurable homosexual experiences during childhood and adolescence, perhaps coupled with unpleasant heterosexual experiences. Many boys have homosexual experiences as part of their normal sexual experimentation while growing up. According to the model, some boys will find these experiences more pleasurable or successful than their experiments with heterosexuality and will continue to seek homosexual interactions. Why only certain boys find their homosexual experiences more pleasurable than their heterosexual experiences could be related to a variety of factors, including the child's age, family dynamics, social skills, and personality. Young girls are less likely to have early homosexual experiences but may be "turned off" from heterosexuality by experiences such as rape, abuse, or assault.

Sociobiological models are all based on the assumption that common behaviors must have evolved because they were somehow beneficial, or related to something beneficial, which helped the individuals who performed them to pass their genes to the next generation. From this perspective, homosexuality seems incongruous, but because it is so common, researchers have tried to find out how homosexual behavior might, in fact, increase a person's ability to pass on genes to subsequent generations. Theorists have come up with three possible explanations—the parental manipulation model, the kin selection model, and the by-product model.

The parental manipulation model suggests that homosexuals do not directly pass on more of their genes than heterosexuals but that their parents do. According to this model, parents subconsciously manipulate their child's development to make him or her less likely to start a family; in this way, the adult child is able to contribute time, energy, and income to brothers, sisters, nieces, and nephews. In the end, the parents have "sacrificed" one child's reproduction in exchange for more grandchildren—or, at least, for more indulged, more evolutionarily competitive grandchildren.

The kin selection model is similar, but in it, the homosexual individual is not manipulated but sacrifices his or her own reproduction willingly (although subconsciously) in exchange for more nieces and nephews (that is, more relatives' genes in subsequent generations). According to this model, individuals who are willing to make this sacrifice (no matter how subconscious) are either those who are not likely to be very successful in heterosexual interactions (and are thus not actually making much of a sacrifice) or those who have a particular attribute that makes them especially good at helping their families. As an analogy, theorists point out how, through much of human history, reproductive sacrifice in the form of joining a religious order often provided income, protection, or status for other family members.

The by-product model suggests that homosexuality is an inevitable outcome of evolved sex differences. According to this model, the facts that, overall, men have a higher sex drive than women and that, historically, many societies have allowed polygyny (where one man has more than one wife) will result in many unmated males who still have an urge to satisfy their high sex drive. Thus, men will become (or will at least act) homosexual when male partners are easier to find than female partners. This model is the one most likely to explain "facultative homosexuality," that is, homosexual behavior by people who consider themselves basically heterosexual.

SOCIAL CONTEXTS

Prior to the gay liberation movement of the 1970's, homosexuality was classified as a mental disorder. In the 1970's, however, when psychiatrists were revising the American Psychiatric Association's *Diagnostic and Statistical Manual of Mental Disorders* (DSM), they removed homosexuality from the list of illnesses. The third edition of the manual (DSM-III), published in 1980, reflected this change. Homosexuality is not associated with disordered thinking or impaired abilities in any way. Therefore, counseling or therapy for the purpose of changing sexual orientation is not recommended. Even when sought, such therapy is rarely successful. On the other hand, many gays, especially adolescents, find benefit from counseling in order to find information, support, and ways to cope with their sexuality.

For men, sexual orientation seems to be fixed at an early age; most gay men feel that they were always homosexual, just as most heterosexual men feel they were always heterosexual. In women, however, sexual orientation is less likely to be fixed early; some women change from a heterosexual to homosexual orientation (or vice versa) in adulthood. In such cases, sexual orientation is better seen as a choice than as an acting out of something preexisting in the psyche, and often such changes are made after a woman has left an unhealthy or abusive relationship or has experienced some other sort of emotional or psychological awakening that changes her outlook on life. In these cases, counseling for the sake of changing sexual orientation per se is not recommended, but it may be appropriate for the woman to seek help dealing with the other changes or events in her life. Most women in this circumstance find that a same-sex, even lesbian, therapist is most helpful, because she will be likely to empathize with her client.

Many women who change sexual orientation in midlife already have children, and many who are lesbian from adolescence choose to have children by artificial insemination or by having intercourse with a male friend. Often, such women have found a lack of support for their parenting and sometimes experience legal problems retaining custody rights of their children. Gay men, too, have had difficulty retaining parental rights or becoming foster or adoptive parents.

Psychological research shows, however, that homosexuals are as good at parenting as heterosexuals and that they are as effective at providing role models. Homosexuals are more likely than heterosexuals to model androgyny—the expression of both traditionally masculine and traditionally feminine attributes—for their children. Some research has shown that an androgynous approach is healthier and more successful in American society than sticking to traditionally defined roles. For example, sometimes women need to be assertive on the job or in relationships, whereas traditionally, men were assertive and women were passive. Similarly, men are less likely to experience stress-related mental and physical health problems if they learn to express their emotions, something only women were traditionally supposed to do.

Neither modeling androgyny nor modeling homosexuality is likely to cause a child to become homosexual, and children raised by homosexual parents are no more likely to become homosexual than children raised by heterosexual parents. Similarly, modeling of androgyny or homosexuality by teachers does not influence the development of homosexuality in children and adolescents. Having an openly homosexual teacher may be a stimulus for a gay child to discover and explore his or her sexuality, but it does not create that sexuality.

Other variations in adult sexual expression, sometimes associated with or confused with homosexuality, are transvestism and transsexuality. Transvestism occurs when a person enjoys or is sexually excited by dressing as a member of the opposite sex. Some gay men enjoy cross-dressing, and others enjoy acting feminine. The majority of homosexuals, however, do not do either; most transvestites are heterosexual. Transsexuality is different from both homosexuality and transvestism; it is categorized by a feeling that one is trapped in a body of the wrong sex. Transsexuality, unlike homosexuality or transvestism, is considered a mental disorder; it is officially a form of gender dysphoria—gender confusion. Transsexuals may feel as though they are engaging in homosexual activity if they have sexual relations with a member of the opposite sex. Some transsexuals decide to cross-dress and live as a member of the opposite sex. They may have hormone treatments or surgery to change legally into a member of the opposite sex. Transsexuality, unlike homosexuality or transvestism, is very rare.

THE HOMOSEXUAL SPECTRUM

The word "homosexual" is usually used in everyday language as a noun, referring to someone who is sexually attracted to, and has sexual relations with, members of the same sex. As a noun, however, the word is misleading, because few people who call themselves homosexual have never engaged in heterosexual activity. Similarly, many people who call themselves heterosexual have at some time engaged in some sort of homosexual activity. Therefore, many sex researchers (sexologists) use a seven-point scale first devised for the Alfred Kinsey surveys in the 1940's, ranging from 0 (exclusively heterosexual) to 6 (exclusively homosexual). Others prefer to use the words "heterosexual" and "homosexual" as adjectives describing behaviors rather than as nouns.

Homosexual behavior has been documented in every society that sexologists have studied; in many societies it has been institutionalized. For example, the ancient Greeks believed that women were spiritually beneath men and that male-male love was the highest form of the emotion. In Melanesian societies, homosexual activity was thought to be necessary in order for young boys to mature into virile, heterosexual adults. Homosexuality as an overall preference or orientation is harder to study, but it is thought that between 5 percent and 10 percent of adult males, and between 2 percent and 4 percent of females, have a predominantly homosexual orientation.

NEGATIVE CULTURAL STEREOTYPES

In Western, Judeo-Christian culture, homosexual behavior has long been considered taboo or sinful. Thus, in the United States and other predominantly Christian cultures, homosexuality has been frowned upon, and homosexuals have been ostracized, being seen as perverted, unnatural, or sick. In 1974, however, the American Psychiatric Association determined that homosexuality was not indicative of mental illness. In contrast to early twentieth century studies of homosexuals who were either psychiatric patients or prison inmates, later studies of a representative cross-section of people showed that individuals with a homosexual orientation are no more likely to suffer from mental illness than those with a heterosexual orientation.

In spite of these scientific data, many heterosexuals (especially men) still harbor negative feelings about homosexuality. This phenomenon is called homophobia. Some of this fear, disgust, and hatred is attributable to the incorrect belief that many homosexuals are child molesters. In fact, more than 90 percent of pedophiles are heterosexual. Another source of homophobia is the fear of acquired immunodeficiency syndrome (AIDS). This deadly, sexually transmitted disease is more easily transmitted through anal intercourse than through vaginal intercourse and thus has spread more rapidly among homosexuals than heterosexuals. Education about safe sex practices, however, has dramatically reduced transmission rates in homosexual communities.

Sexologists have not been able to avoid the political controversies surrounding their field, making the study of a difficult subject even harder. Research will continue, but no one should expect fast and simple explanations. Sexuality, perhaps more than any other attribute of the human psyche, is personal and individual. Questions about sexual orientation, sexual development, and sexual behavior are all complex; it will take a long time to unravel the answers.

SOURCES FOR FURTHER STUDY

Baird, Vanessa. *The No-Nonsense Guide to Sexual Diversity.* New York: Verso, 2001. A wide-ranging survey of cultural attitudes toward homosexuality throughout the world and over time. Provides a country-by-country survey of laws concerning homosexuality and addresses the rise in opposition to sexual nonconformism among religious fundamentalists of all stripes.

Bell, Alan P., and Martin Weinberg. *Homosexualities: A Study of Diversity Among Men and Women.* New York: Simon & Schuster, 1978. This official Kinsey Institute publication presents the methods and results of the most extensive sex survey to focus specifically on homosexual behavior. Presents descriptions of homosexual feelings, partnerships, and lifestyles, based on intensive interviews with more than fifteen hundred men and women.

Brookey, Robert Alan. *Reinventing the Male Homosexual: The Rhetoric and Power of the Gay Gene.* Bloomington: Indiana University Press, 2002. Discusses recent attempts to identify a genetic component to sexual orientation and the cultural effect of such research on gay identity.

Dean, Tim, and Christopher Lane, eds. *Homosexuality and Psychoanalysis.* Chicago: University of Chicago Press, 2001. Reviews the often conflicted relationship between psychoanalytic theory and homosexuality. Covers the attitudes toward homosexuality found in the writings of Sigmund Freud, Melanie Klein, Wilhelm Reich, Jacques Lacan, and Michel Foucault, among others.

Garnets, Linda, and Douglas C. Kimmel, eds. *Psychological Perspectives on Lesbian and Gay Male Experiences.* New York: Columbia University Press, 1993. A collection of essays focusing on gay identity development, gender differences, ethnic and racial variation, long-term relationships, adult development, and aging.

Koertge, Noretta, ed. *Nature and Causes of Homosexuality: A Philosophic and Scientific Inquiry.* New York: Haworth Press, 1982. This volume is the third in an ongoing monograph series titled Research on Homosexuality, each volume of which was originally published as an issue of the *Journal of Homosexuality.* All volumes are valuable, although somewhat technical. This one is a good place to start; others cover law, psychotherapy, literature, alcoholism, anthropology, historical perspectives, social sex roles, bisexuality, and homophobia.

Tripp, C. A. *The Homosexual Matrix.* 2d ed. New York: McGraw-Hill, 1987. For those who want to read for pleasure as well as for information. Tripp covers fact, culture, and mythology, both historical and modern. A good representative of the "gay liberation" era books on homosexuality, most of the text is as valid as when it was written (though it clearly does not cover post-AIDS changes in homosexual culture and behavior).

Whitham, Frederick L. "Culturally Invariable Properties of Male Homosexuality: Tentative Conclusions from Cross-Cultural Research." *Archives of*

Sexual Behavior 12 (1983): 40. Unlike much of the cross-cultural literature on homosexuality, this article focuses specifically on cross-cultural prevalence and attributes of those with a homosexual orientation, rather than on the institutionalized and ritual forms of homosexual behavior found in many non-Western cultures.

Linda Mealey

SEE ALSO: Adolescence: Sexuality; Attraction Theories; Gender-Identity Formation; Sexual Variants and Paraphilias.

Hormones and Behavior

Type of psychology: Biological bases of behavior
Fields of study: Auditory, chemical, cutaneous, and body senses;
endocrine system

Hormones are chemical messengers, usually of protein or steroid content, that are produced in certain body tissues and that target specific genes in the cells of other body tissues, thereby affecting the development and function of these tissues and the entire organism. By exerting their influences on various parts of the body, hormones can affect behavior.

Key concepts
- endocrine gland
- hormone
- human growth hormone (HGH)
- hypothalamus
- melatonin
- oxytocin
- pheromone
- pituitary
- steroid
- vasopressin

Cell-to-cell communication among the trillions of cells that make up multicellular animals relies primarily upon the specialized tissues of the nervous and endocrine systems. These two systems are intricately connected, with the former having evolved from the latter during the past five hundred million years of animal life. The endocrine system consists of specialized ductless glands located throughout the animal body that produce and secrete hormones directly into the bloodstream. Hormones are chemical messengers that usually are composed of protein or steroid subunits. The bloodstream transports the hormones to various target body tissues, where the hormones contact cell membranes and trigger a sequence of enzyme reactions which ultimately result in the activation or inactivation of genes located on chromosomes in the cell nucleus.

A gene is a segment of a chromosome that is composed of deoxyribonucleic acid (DNA). The DNA nucleotide sequence of the gene encodes a molecule of messenger ribonucleic acid (mRNA) which, in turn, encodes a specific protein for the given gene. If the control sequence of a gene is activated, then ribonucleic acid (RNA) and protein will be produced. If the control sequence of a gene is inactivated, then RNA and protein will not be produced. Hormones target the genes in specific cells to start or stop the manufacture of certain proteins. Within cells and the entire organism, proteins perform important functions. Therefore, hormones control the production of proteins by genes and, as a result, control many activities of the entire animal.

The nervous system, which in vertebrate animals has evolved to become more elaborate than the endocrine system, consists of billions of neurons (nerve cells) that conduct electrical impulses throughout the body. Neurons transmit information, contract and relax muscles, and detect pressures, temperature, and pain. Neuron networks are most dense in the brain (where there are one hundred billion neurons) and spinal cord, where much of the electrical information is centralized, relayed, and analyzed. Neurons must communicate electrical information across the gaps, or synapses, which separate them. To accomplish this goal, the transmitting neuron releases hormones called neurotransmitters, which diffuse across the synapse to the receiving neuron, thereby instructing the receiving neuron to continue or stop the conduction of the electrical message. There are many different types of neurotransmitters, just as there are many different types of regular hormones.

NERVOUS SYSTEM-ENDOCRINE SYSTEM INTERACTIONS

The link between the nervous and endocrine systems lies in two glands located between the cerebrum and the brain stem, the hypothalamus and the hypophysis (the pituitary gland). Electrical impulses from neurons in the cerebral cortex may activate the hypothalamus to release hormones that activate the hypophysis to release its hormones, which in turn activate or inactivate other endocrine glands throughout the body. These glands include the thyroid, parathyroids, thymus, pancreas, adrenals, and reproductive organs. This entire system operates by negative feedback homeostasis so that, once information is transferred and specific bodily functions are achieved, nervous or hormonal signals travel back to the hypothalamus to terminate any further action.

Animal behavior occurs as a result of the actions of the nervous and endocrine systems. There is a complex interplay among these two body systems, the environment, and an individual's genetic makeup in terms of the cause-and-effect, stimulus-response events that constitute behavior. An animal receives external information via its special senses (eyes, ears, nose, mouth) and somatic sense organs (touch, pain, temperature, pressure). This external information travels along sensory neurons toward the brain and spinal cord, where the information is analyzed and a motor response to the external stimulus is initiated. Some of these motor responses will be directed toward the sense organs, locomotory muscles, and organs such as the heart and intestines. Other impulses will be directed toward the hypothalamus, which controls body cycles such as all endocrine system hormones, heart rate, sleep-wake cycles, and hunger.

When the hypothalamus releases the hormone corticoliberin, the pituitary gland (the hypophysis) releases the hormones thyrotropin (which activates the thyroid gland), prolactin (which stimulates milk production in the female breast), and growth hormone (which triggers growth in children and metabolic changes in adults). When the thyroid gland is activated, hormones such as thyroxine and triiodothyronine are released to accelerate cellular metabolism, an event which may occur in certain situations such as stress or fight-or-flight encounters.

If the pituitary gland releases adrenocorticotropic hormone (ACTH), the adrenal glands will be activated to release their hormones. The adrenal cortex produces and secretes a variety of hormones, such as aldosterone, which regulates the blood-salt balance directly and blood pressure indirectly; cortisol, which accelerates body metabolism; and androgens, or sex hormones. All of these are steroid hormones, which are involved in rapidly preparing the body for strenuous performance. Even more pronounced are the effects of the adrenal medulla, which produces and secretes the hormone neurotransmitters epinephrine and norepinephrine; these two hormones accelerate heart, muscle, and nerve action as well as stimulate the release of fat and sugar into the bloodstream for quick energy, all of which are extremely important for spontaneous activity such as fighting with or fleeing from enemies. The control of sugar storage and release from the liver by the pancreatic hormones insulin and glucagon also are important in this process.

THE EFFECTS OF HORMONES ON BEHAVIOR

The study of hormones and their effects upon individual and group behaviors is of immense interest to psychologists. Hormones represent the biochemical control signals for much of animal and human behaviors. Understanding precisely how hormones affect individuals, both psychologically and physiologically, could be of great value in comprehending many different human behaviors, in treating abnormal behaviors, and in helping individuals to cope psychologically with disease and stress. The hormonal control of behavior in humans and in many other animal species has been extensively studied, although much research remains to be performed. Hormones have been clearly linked to reproductive behavior, sex-specific behavioral characteristics, territoriality and mating behaviors, physiological responses to certain external stimuli, and stress.

The pineal gland, located in the posterior cerebrum, releases the hormone melatonin, which regulates the body's circadian rhythms and possibly its sexual cycles as well. Melatonin is normally synthesized and secreted beginning shortly after dusk throughout the night and ending around dawn. It thus corresponds with the individual's normal sleep-wake cycle. Melatonin may play an important role in humans adapting to shift work. It is promoted as a nutritional supplement to help people get a good night's sleep.

HORMONES AND REPRODUCTION

The most extensive research involving hormonal effects on behavior has been conducted on reproductive behavior. Among the most powerful behavior-

Hormones control a variety of behaviors in humans and animals, such as maternal imprinting. (Digital Stock)

influencing hormones are the pituitary gonadotropins luteinizing hormone (LH) and follicle-stimulating hormone (FSH). These two hormones target the reproductive organs of both males and females and stimulate these organs to initiate sexual development and the production of sexual steroid hormones—estrogen and progesterone in females, testosterone in males. These sex hormones are responsible not only for the maturation of the reproductive organs but also for secondary sexual characteristics such as male aggression and female nesting behavior.

Reproductive patterns vary from species to species in occurrence, repetition of occurrence, and behaviors associated with courtship, mating, and caring for young. The achievement of reproductive maturity and reproductive readiness in a given species is subject to that species' circadian rhythm, a phenomenon regulated by hormones released from the hypothalamus, hypophysis, and pineal gland. These three endocrine glands are influenced primarily by the earth's twenty-four-hour rotation period and the twenty-eight-day lunar cycle. Furthermore, genetically programmed hormonal changes at specific times during one's life cycle also play a major role in the occurrence of reproductive behaviors.

In female vertebratesm, LH, FSH, and estrogen are responsible for the maturation of the ovaries, the completion of meiosis (chromosome halving) and the release of eggs for fertilization, and secondary sexual characteristics. The secondary sexual characteristics involve physiological and closely related behavioral changes. In bird species, these changes include the construction of a nest and receptivity to dominant males during courtship rituals. In mammals, these same hormones are involved in female receptivity to dominant males during courtship. Physiological changes in mammals include the deposition of fat in various body regions, such as the breasts and buttocks, and increased vascularization (more blood vessel growth) in the skin. Females of most mammal and bird species go into heat, or estrus, one or several times per year, based on hormonally regulated changes in reproductive organs. Human females follow a lunar menstrual cycle in which LH, FSH, estrogen, and progesterone oscillate in production rates. These hormonal variations influence female body temperature and behavior accordingly.

Male sexual behavior is controlled predominantly by testosterone produced in the testicles and male androgens produced in the adrenal cortex. These steroid hormones cause muscle buildup, increased hair, and aggressive behavior. As a consequence, such steroids are often used (illegally) by athletes to improve their performance. In a number of mammal and bird species, elevation of sex steroids causes increased coloration, which serves both as an attractant for females and as an antagonistic signal to competitor males. The aggressive behavior that is stimulated by the male sex steroid hormones thus plays a dual role in courtship and mating rituals and in territorial behavior, phenomena which are tightly linked in determining the biological success of the individual.

Pheromones are hormones released from the reproductive organs and skin glands. These hormones target the sense organs of other individuals and affect the behavior of these individuals. Sex pheromones, for example, attract males to females and vice versa. Other pheromones enable a male to mark his territory and to detect the intrusion of competitor males into his territory. Others enable an infant to imprint upon its mother. Such hormones number in the hundreds, but only a few dozen have been studied in detail. Pheromones released by males serve as territorial markers, as is evidenced by most mammalian males spraying urine on objects in their own territory. Exchanges of pheromones between males and females are important stimulants for courtship and mating. In some species, the release of pheromones—or even the sight of a potential mate—will trigger hormonally controlled ovulation in the female. Furthermore, in several species, such as elephant seals and lions, the takeover of a harem by a new dominant male, a process that usually involves the killer of the previous male's offspring, stimulates the harem females to ovulate. The diversity of reproductive behaviors that is regulated by hormones seems to be almost as great as the number of species.

HORMONES AND STRESS

The fight-or-flight response is a hormonally controlled situation in which the body must pool all of its available resources within a relatively short time span. The detection of danger by any of the special senses (sight, smell, hearing) triggers the hypothalamus to activate the pituitary gland to release adrenocorticotropic hormone, which causes the adrenal gland to release its highly motivating hormones and neurotransmitters. Many body systems are subsequently affected, especially the heart and circulatory system, the central nervous system, the digestive system, and even the immune system. One reason the fight-or-flight response is of major interest to psychologists is its link to stress.

Stress is overexcitation of the nervous and endocrine systems. It is caused by the body's repeated exposure to danger, excessive physical exertion, or environmental pressures that affect the individual psychologically. Stress is a major problem for humans in a fast-paced technological society. The physiological and behavioral manifestations of stress are very evident. There is considerable evidence that stress is associated with heart disease, cancer, weakened immune systems, asthma, allergies, accelerated aging, susceptibility to infections, learning disorders, behavioral abnormalities, insanity, and violent crime.

The demands that are placed upon individuals in fast-paced, overpopulated societies are so great that many people exhibit a near-continuous fight-or-flight response. This response, in which the body prepares for maximum physical exertion in a short time span, is the physiological basis of stress. It is not intended to be maintained for long periods of time; if it is not relieved, irreparable effects begin to accumulate throughout the body, particularly within the nervous system. Medical psychologists seek to understand the hormonal basis of physiological stress in order to treat stress-prone individuals.

HORMONES AND AGING

Another hormone that greatly influences human behavior and development is human growth hormone (HGH). This hormone is produced by the anterior pituitary (adenohypophysis) gland under the control of the hypothalamus. HGH production peaks during adolescence, corresponding to the growth spurt. While it is produced throughout life, it declines with age in all species studied to date. In humans, HGH production tends to drop quickly beginning in the thirties so that by age sixty, HGH production is only about 25 percent of what it was earlier in life, and it continues to decline until death. The decrease in HGH production with age has been tied to thinning of skin and wrinkle formation, muscle wasting, sleep problems, cognitive and mood changes, decreased cardiac and kidney function, lessening of sexual performance, and weakening of bones, contributing to osteoporosis. Nutritional supplements including the amino acids arginine, lysine, and glutamine are being investigated as growth hormone releasers, thought to decrease signs of aging. Their use remains controversial.

HORMONE TREATMENT OF HEALTH PROBLEMS

The ultimate goals of hormone studies are to arrive at an understanding of the physiological basis of behavior and to develop treatments for behavioral abnormalities. Synthetic hormones can be manufactured in the laboratory. Their mass production could provide solutions to many psychological problems such as stress, deviant behavior, and sexual dysfunction. Synthetic hormones already are being used as birth control mechanisms aimed at fooling the female body's reproductive hormonal systems.

Ongoing research focuses on the importance of many hormones, especially on understanding their functions and how they might be used in the treatment of common disorders. Two hormones produced by the hypothalamus and released by the posterior pituitary (neurohypophysis) gland are vasopressin (antidiuretic hormone) and oxytocin. Vasopressin keeps the kidneys from losing too much water and helps maintain the body's fluid balance. Variants of vasopressin which decrease blood pressure, identified by Maurice Manning, may lead to a new class of drugs to control high blood pressure. Oxytocin induces labor by causing uterine contractions and also promotes the production of milk for breastfeeding. Manning and Walter Chan are working to develop oxytocin receptor antagonists that may be used to prevent premature births.

THE PAST, PRESENT, AND FUTURE OF HORMONES

The activities of all living organisms are functionally dependent upon the biochemical reactions that make up life itself. Since the evolution of the first eukaryotic cells more than one billion years ago, hormones have been utilized in cell-to-cell communication. In vertebrate animals (fish, amphibians, reptiles, birds, and mammals), endocrine systems have evolved into highly complicated nervous systems. These nervous systems are even evident in the invertebrate arthropods (crustaceans, spiders, and so on), especially among the social insects, such as ants. The endocrine and nervous systems are intricately interconnected in the control of animal physiology and behavior.

Psychologists are interested in the chemical basis of human behavior and therefore are interested in human and mammalian hormones. Such hormones control a variety of behaviors, such as maternal imprinting (in which an infant and mother bond to each other), courtship and mating, territoriality, and physiological responses to stress and danger. Animal behaviorists and psychologists study the connection between hormones and behavior in humans, primates, and other closely related mammalian species. They identify similarities in behaviors and hormones among a variety of species. They also recognize the occurrence of abnormal behaviors, such as antisocial behavior and sexual deviance, and possible hormonal imbalances that contribute to these behavioral anomalies.

While the biochemistry of hormones and their effects upon various behaviors have been established in considerable detail, numerous behaviors that are probably under hormonal influence have yet to be critically analyzed. Among them are many subtle pheromones that affect a person's interactions with other people, imprinting pheromones that trigger attraction and bonding between individuals, and hormones that link together a variety of bodily functions. These hormones may number in the hundreds, and they represent a challenging avenue for further research. Unraveling the relationships between hormones and behavior can enable researchers to gain a greater understanding of the human mind and its link to the rest of the body and to other individuals. These studies offer potential treatments for behavioral abnormalities and for mental disturbances created by the physiologically disruptive effects of drug use, a major problem in American society. They also offer great promise in the alleviation of stress, another major social and medical problem.

SOURCES FOR FURTHER STUDY

Campbell, Neil A., Jane B. Reece, and Laurence G. Mitchell. *Biology.* 6th ed. San Francisco: Benjamin Cummings, 2002. This introductory biology text presents an exhaustive overview of biology. Unit 7, dealing with animal form and function, gives an overview of the endocrine system, along with a discussion of its effects on reproduction, development, and behavior.

James, Vivian, ed. "Hormones and Sport Symposium." *Journal of Endocrinology* 170 (2001). This special issue is devoted to the effects of hormones on sporting activity. The coverage within the issue focuses on the role of hormones in sports as well as the problems in attempting to eliminate potentially problematic drug abuse by athletes.

Manning, Aubrey. *An Introduction to Animal Behavior.* 4th ed. Reading, Mass.: Addison-Wesley, 1992. This concise, thorough survey of animal behavior theory and research employs hundreds of experimental studies to describe major aspects of the subject. Chapter 2, "The Development of Behavior," discusses the roles of hormones in animal development and social behavior. Chapter 4, "Motivation," is an extensive study of animal drives and motivations as influenced by hormones, pheromones, and environmental stimuli.

Martini, Frederic H., E. F. Bartholomew, and K. Welch. *The Human Body in Health and Disease.* Upper Saddle River, N.J.: Prentice Hall, 2000. This college-level text outlines the structure and function of the endocrine system and demonstrates its interrelationship with the nervous system and its effects on behavior. Well-written and illustrated.

Nelson, Randy J. *An Introduction to Behavioral Endocrinology.* 2d ed. Sunderland, Mass.: Sinauer Associates, 2000. This text covers hormones and behavior in historical perspective, knowledge in cell and molecular biology and behavior, present and future research in the field.

Raven, Peter H., and George B. Johnson. *Biology.* 6th ed. Boston: McGraw-Hill, 2002. An introductory survey of biology for the beginning student. It contains beautiful illustrations and photographs. Describes the endocrine systems of human and mammals, the major hormones produced by each endocrine gland, and the effects of these hormones upon the body.

Sherwood, Lauralee. *Human Physiology: From Cells to Systems.* 5th ed. Belmont, Calif.: Thomson/Brooks/Cole, 2004. This college physiology text outlines the functioning of the endocrine glands and the hormones that they produce. Two chapters focus on endocrinology, highlighting the effects of hormones on behavior.

Wallace, Robert A., Gerald P. Sanders, and Robert J. Ferl. *Biology: The Science of Life.* 4th ed. New York: HarperCollins, 1999. This introduction to biology for the beginning student exhausts the subject, but it does so by providing a wealth of information, constructive diagrams, and beautiful photographs dealing with human hormones and their effects upon the body.

David Wason Hollar, Jr.; updated by Robin Kamienny Montvilo

SEE ALSO: Emotions; Endocrine System; Nervous System; Stress.

HUMANISTIC TRAIT MODELS
GORDON ALLPORT

TYPE OF PSYCHOLOGY: Personality
FIELDS OF STUDY: Humanistic-phenomenological models; personality
theory

Allport's humanistic trait model explains how a person's unique personal characteristics provide a pattern and direction to personality. It reveals the limitations of psychological theories that focus only on general rules of human behavior and provides insight into how to conduct in-depth study of individual dispositions.

KEY CONCEPTS
- cardinal disposition
- central dispositions
- common traits
- functional autonomy
- idiographic or morphogenic study
- nomothetic study
- personal dispositions
- proprium
- secondary dispositions

The humanistic trait model of Gordon Allport (1897-1967) was based on his profound belief in the uniqueness of every personality, as well as his conviction that individuality is displayed through dominant personal characteristics that provide continuity and direction in a person's life. He saw personality as dynamic, growing, changing, and based on one's perception of the world. Like other humanists, Allport believed that people are essentially proactive, or forward moving; they are motivated by the future and seek tension and change rather than sameness. In addition, each individual possesses a set of personal dispositions that define the person and provide a pattern to behavior.

Allport's approach is different from those of other trait theorists who have typically sought to categorize personalities according to a basic set of universal, essential characteristics. Allport referred to such characteristics as common traits. Instead of focusing on common traits that allow for comparisons among many people, Allport believed that each person is defined by a different set of characteristics. Based on his research, he estimated that there are four thousand to five thousand traits and eighteen thousand trait names.

FUNCTIONAL AUTONOMY AND PERSONAL DISPOSITIONS
Most personality theorists view adulthood as an extension of the basic motives present in childhood. Consistent with his belief that personality is

always evolving, Allport believed that the motivations of adulthood are often independent of the motivations of childhood, and he referred to this concept as functional autonomy. For example, a person who plays a musical instrument during childhood years because of parental pressure may play the same instrument for relaxation or enjoyment as an adult. Although not all motives are functionally autonomous, many adult activities represent a break from childhood and are based on varied and self-sustaining motives.

According to this perspective, personality is based on concrete human motives that are represented by personal traits or dispositions. Human traits are seen as guiding human behavior, but they must also account for wide variability within a person's conduct from situation to situation. As a result, Allport distinguished between different types and levels of traits or dispositions. Common traits represent those elements of personality that are useful for comparing most people within a specific culture, but they cannot provide a complete profile of any individual person. In contrast, personal dispositions represent the true personality, are unique to the person, and represent subtle differences among persons.

Three kinds of personal dispositions exist: cardinal dispositions, central dispositions, and secondary dispositions. When a person's life is dominated by a single, fundamental, outstanding characteristic, the quality is referred to as a cardinal disposition. For example, Adolf Hitler's cruelty and Mahatma Ghandhi's pacifism are examples of cardinal dispositions. Central dispositions represent the five to ten important qualities of a person that would typically be discussed and described in a thorough letter of recommendation. Finally, secondary dispositions are characteristics that are more numerous, less consistently displayed, and less important than central dispositions.

THREE ASPECTS OF THE PROPRIUM

Allport referred to the unifying core of personality, or those aspects of the self that a person considers central to self-identity, as the proprium. During the first three to four years of life, three aspects of the proprium emerge. The sense of a bodily self involves awareness of body sensations. Self-identity represents the child's knowledge of an inner sameness or continuity over time, and self-esteem reflects personal efforts to maintain pride and avoid embarrassment. Self-extension emerges between the fourth and sixth year of life; this refers to the child's concept of that which is "mine," and it forms the foundation for later self-extensions such as career and love of country. The self-image, which also emerges between ages four and six, represents an awareness of personal goals and abilities as well as the "good" and "bad" parts of the self. The ability to see the self as a rational, coping being emerges between ages six and twelve and represents the ability to place one's inner needs within the context of outer reality. Propriate striving often begins in adolescence and focuses on the person's ability to form long-term goals and purposes. Finally, the self as knower represents the subjective self and one's ability to reflect on aspects of the proprium.

IDIOGRAPHIC RESEARCH

From this humanistic trait framework, human personality can only be fully understood through the examination of personal characteristics within a single individual. The emphasis on individuality has significant implications for the measurement of personality and for research methods in psychology. Most psychological research deals with standardized measurements and large numbers of people, and it attempts to make generalizations about characteristics that people hold in common. Allport referred to this approach as nomothetic. He contrasted the study of groups and general laws with idiographic research, or approaches for studying the single person. Idiographic research, which is sometimes referred to as morphogenic research, includes methods such as autobiographies, interviews, dreams, and verbatim recordings.

One of Allport's famous studies of the individual appears in *Letters from Jenny* (1965), a description of an older woman's personality that is based on the analysis of approximately three hundred letters that she wrote to her son and his wife. Through the use of personal structure analysis, statistical analysis, and the reactions of various trained judges, Allport and his colleagues identified eight clusters of characteristics, including the following: artistic, self-centered, aggressive, and sentimental. Through revealing the central dispositions of a single individual, this study provided increased insight about all people. It also demonstrated that objective, scientific practices can be applied to the study of one person at a time.

PERSONAL ORIENTATIONS

Allport preferred personality measures designed to examine the pattern of characteristics that are important to a person and that allow for comparison of the strengths of specific characteristics within the person rather than with other persons. The *Study of Values* (3d ed., 1960), which was developed by Allport, Philip Vernon, and Gardner Lindzey, measures a person's preference for the six value systems of theoretical, economic, social, political, aesthetic, and religious orientations. After rank ordering forty-five items, the individual receives feedback about the relative importance of the six orientations within himself or herself. Consistent with the emphasis on uniqueness, the scale does not facilitate comparisons between people. Although the language of this scale is somewhat outdated, it is still used for value clarification and the exploration of career and lifestyle goals.

Allport's research also focused on attitudes that are influenced by group participation, such as religious values and prejudice. Through the study of churchgoers' attitudes, he distinguished between extrinsic religion, or a conventional, self-serving approach, and intrinsic religion, which is based on internalized beliefs and efforts to act upon religious beliefs. Allport and his colleagues found that extrinsic churchgoers were more prejudiced than intrinsic religious churchgoers; however, churchgoers who strongly endorsed both extrinsic and intrinsic religion were even more prejudiced than either extrinsic or intrinsic religious church attenders. Allport also examined cultural, family, historical, and situational factors that influence prejudice.

AMALGAMATION OF APPROACHES

Allport provided theoretical and research alternatives at a time when a variety of competing approaches, including humanistic, psychoanalytic, and behavioral perspectives, were seeking preeminence in psychology. Allport found many existing theories to be limiting, overly narrow, and inadequate for describing the wide variations in human personality. As a result, he proposed an eclectic approach to theory that combined the strengths of various other perspectives. Instead of emphasizing a single approach, Allport thought that personality can be both growth-oriented and proactive, as well as reactive and based on instinctual processes. Through an eclectic approach, he hoped that the understanding of personality would become more complete.

Allport was also concerned that many of the existing theories of his time, especially psychoanalytic theories, virtually ignored the healthy personality. In contrast to Sigmund Freud, Allport strongly emphasized conscious aspects of personality and believed that healthy adults are generally aware of their motivations. Unlike Freud's notion that people are motivated to reduce the tension of instinctual drives, he believed that people seek the kind of tension that allows them to grow, develop goals, and act in innovative ways.

TRAIT APPROACHES

Like humanistic theorists Carl Rogers and Abraham Maslow, Allport identified vital characteristics of mature persons. His list of the characteristics of mature persons overlaps substantially with Maslow's enumeration of the qualities of self-actualizing persons and Rogers's definition of the "person of tomorrow." Allport's list includes extension of the sense of self (identifying with events and persons outside oneself), emotional security, realistic perception, insight and humor, and a unifying philosophy of life.

Allport developed his theory at a time when other trait approaches that were based on nomothetic study were gaining prominence. Whereas Allport emphasized individual uniqueness, Raymond Cattell identified twenty-three source traits, or building blocks of personality, and Hans Eysenck identified three primary dimensions of extroversion, neuroticism, and psychoticism. Within the nomothetic tradition, more recent researchers have reexamined earlier nomothetic trait theories and have identified five primary common dimensions of personality: surgency (active/dominant persons versus passive/submissive persons), agreeableness (one's warmth or coldness), conscientiousness (one's level of responsibility or undependability), emotional stability (unpredictability versus stability), and culture (one's intellectual understanding of the world). Allport would have found these efforts to identify basic dimensions of personality to have limited usefulness for defining and understanding individual personality styles.

Recent criticisms of trait approaches that emphasize universal characteristics of people indicate that these approaches underestimate the role of situations and human variability and change across different contexts. Furthermore, those approaches that focus on general traits provide summaries and demonstrate trends about behavior but do not provide explanations for behavior.

The awareness that general trait approaches are inadequate for predicting behavior across situations has led to a resurgence of interest in the types of idiographic research methods proposed by Allport. Approaches to personality have increasingly acknowledged the complexity of human beings and the reality that individuals are influenced by a wide array of features that are often contradictory and inconsistent. Allport's emphasis on the scientific study of unique aspects of personality provided both the inspiration and a general method for examining the singular, diverse variables that define human beings.

SOURCES FOR FURTHER STUDY

Allport, Gordon W. "An Autobiography." In *A History of Psychology in Autobiography*, edited by Edwin Garrigues Boring and Gardner Lindzey. Vol. 5. New York: Appleton-Century-Crofts, 1967. Allport provides an interesting account of his life, including an encounter with Sigmund Freud.

_____. *Becoming: Basic Considerations for a Psychology of Personality*. Reprint. New Haven, Conn.: Yale University Press, 1967. A short, straightforward, clear statement of Allport's basic assumptions about personality. The author attempts to provide the basic foundation for a complete personality theory and emphasizes the importance of both open-mindedness and eclecticism in the study of personality.

_____. *Pattern and Growth in Personality*. New York: Holt, Rinehart and Winston, 1967. This textbook is the most complete account of Allport's personality theory. It includes extensive descriptions of Allport's approach to personality and individuality, personality development, the structure of the personality, the characteristics of the mature personality, and methods of personality assessment.

Allport, Gordon W., Philip E. Vernon, and Gardner Lindzey. *Study of Values*. 3d ed. Boston: Houghton Mifflin, 1960. A scale that measures a person's preference for six value orientations: religious, theoretical, economic, aesthetic, social, or political values. The personal ordering of these values provides a framework for reflecting upon and understanding the values that make up one's philosophy of life. The language is outdated and gender-biased, but the book represents one application of Allport's work.

Evans, Richard I. *Gordon Allport: The Man and His Ideas.* New York: Praeger, 1981. This book is based on a series of dialogues with Allport that focus on his unique contributions and his vision of the future of personality psychology. Also includes a discussion and evaluation of Allport's ideas by three distinguished psychologists who studied under his direction.

Maddi, Salvatore R., and Paul T. Costa. *Humanism in Personology: Allport, Maslow, and Murray.* Chicago: Aldine-Atherton, 1972. This volume compares the work of Allport with the contributions of two other humanistic personality theorists. Although the theories of these three differ substantially, they share an emphasis on human uniqueness, a faith in human capabilities, and a view of people as proactive, complex, and oriented toward the future.

Masterson, Jenny (Gove) [pseud.]. *Letters from Jenny.* Edited and interpreted by Gordon W. Allport. New York: Harcourt, Brace & World, 1965. An example of idiographic or morphogenic study of the personality. After studying 301 letters from an older woman to her son and his wife, Allport grouped her characteristics into eight clusters that correspond to the number of central dispositions that he proposed make important elements of personality.

Peterson, Christopher. *Personality.* 2d ed. San Diego, Calif.: International Thomson, 1992. This text on personality contains three chapters that summarize, compare, and evaluate various trait approaches along the following dimensions: theory, research, and applications. Describes major criticisms of trait approaches and discusses the practical implications of trait theories.

Carolyn Zerbe Enns

SEE ALSO: Psychoanalytic Psychology and Personality: Sigmund Freud.

HUNGER

TYPE OF PSYCHOLOGY: Motivation
FIELD OF STUDY: Physical motives

The psychological bases of hunger play an important role in the external and internal mediating forces that can affect and modify the physiological aspects of hunger.

KEY CONCEPTS
- appetite
- bingeing
- deprivation
- eating disorders
- external cues
- homeostasis
- hypothalamus
- primary motives
- satiety
- set point

Primary motives are generated by innate biological needs that must be met for survival. These motives include hunger, thirst, and sleep. Hunger has been studied extensively, yet there is still uncertainty as to exactly how this drive works. A large body of research about the physiological analysis of hunger has led to the identification of important differences between physical hunger and psychological hunger.

Physical hunger theories assume that the body's physiological mechanisms and systems produce hunger as a need and that when this need is satisfied, the hunger drive is, for the time being, reduced. Psychologists have developed models and theories of hunger by analyzing its boundaries and restraint or regulation. The early findings on hunger regulation mechanisms emphasized the biological state of the individual and the control of an individual over the hunger drive. If a person experiences hunger, consumption of food will continue until it is terminated by internal cues. This is referred to as regulation.

The individual learns to avoid hunger by reacting to the internal cues of satiety or fullness. The satiety boundary is characterized by feelings of fullness ranging from satisfaction to uncomfortable bloating. The normal eater learns to avoid transgression far or often into this latter zone. Beyond the reaction to internal cues is a zone of indifference, in which the body is not subject to biological cues. Instead, hunger is influenced by social, cognitive, and psychological cues. These cues may be external or internalized but do not rely on satiety cues for restraint.

Eating past the point of satiety is referred to as counterregulation or, more commonly, as binge eating or compulsive eating. Because the inhibitors of hunger restraint are not physiological in this zone, the restraint and dietary boundaries are cognitively determined. The physical hunger mechanisms may send signals, but quite ordinary ideas such as "being hungry" and "not being hungry" must be interpreted or received by the individual. The person must learn to distinguish between bodily sensations that indicate the need for food and the feelings that accompany this need, such as anxiety, boredom, loneliness, or depression.

Thus, there are both internal cues and external cues that define hunger and lead an individual to know when to eat and how much to eat. External cues as a motive for eating have been studied extensively, particularly in research on obesity and eating disorders such as binge behavior and compulsive overeating. External cues include enticing smells, locations such as restaurants or other kinds of social settings, and the social environment—what other people are doing. When external cues prevail, a person does not have to be hungry in order to feel hungry.

CHILDREN'S HUNGER

The awareness of hunger begins very early in life. Those infants who are fed on demand, whose cries of hunger determine the times at which they are fed, are taught soon after they can feed themselves that their eating must conform to family rules about when, what, and how much to eat in order to satisfy their hunger. Infants fed on a schedule learn even earlier to conform to external constraints and regulations regarding hunger. Throughout life, responding to hunger by feeding oneself is nourishing both physiologically and psychologically. Beginning in infancy, the sequences of getting hungry and being fed establish the foundations of the relationship between the physiological need or drive and the psychological components of feelings such as affiliation, interaction, calm, and security when hunger is satisfied.

In preschool and early school years, when children are integrating themselves into their social world, food acceptance and cultural practices are learned. Prior to the peer group and school environment, the family and media are usually the main vehicles of cultural socialization of the hunger drive. According to social learning theory, these agents will play an important role in the child's learning to interpret his or her level of hunger and in subsequent eating patterns, both directly and indirectly. The modeling behavior of children is also related to hunger learning.

Experiences of hunger and satiety play a central role in a person's relationship to hunger awareness, eating, and food. Some dispositions that influence hunger and eating behavior are long-term (fairly stable and enduring), while other habits and attitudes may fluctuate. There are numerous theories about the relation between the hunger drive and other factors such as genetic inheritance and activity level.

HUNGER AND THE BRAIN

A strictly physiological analysis claims that an individual's responses to hunger are caused by the brain's regulation of body weight. If the body goes below its predetermined "set point," internal hunger cues are initiated to signal the need for food consumption. External restraints, such as attempts to live up to ideal cultural thinness standards, also affect behavior and may result in restrained eating in order to maintain a body weight below the body's defined set point.

The idea of a body set point is rooted in the work of physiologist Claude Bernard (1813-1878), a pioneer in research based on the concept of homeostasis, or system balance in the body. Homeostasis has played a fundamental role in many subsequent investigations regarding the physiology of hunger and the regulatory systems involved in hunger satisfaction. Inherent in the set-point theory is the concept of motivation, meaning that an organism is driven physiologically and behaviorally toward maintenance of homeostasis and the body's set point and will adapt to accommodate the systems involved in maintenance.

In addition, there appear to be two anatomically and behaviorally distinct centers located in the hypothalamus, one regulating hunger and the other regulating satiety. The area of the hypothalamus responsible for stimulating eating behavior is the lateral hypothalamus. The ventromedial hypothalamus is the area responsible for signaling the organism to stop eating. The

Hunger is a physiological response, but eating is a learned behavior.
(CLEO Photography)

lateral hypothalamus is responsible for establishing a set point for body weight.

In comparing hunger and satiety sensation differences, increased hunger and disturbed satiety appear to be two different and quite separate mechanisms. Imbalance or dysfunction of either the hunger mechanism or the satiety sensation can lead to obesity, overeating, binge eating, and other eating disorders. It appears that the way hunger is experienced accounts, in part, for its recognition. Whether hunger is experienced in context with other drives or becomes a compulsive force that dominates all other drives in life is a complex issue.

The prevalence of eating disorders and the multitude of variables associated with hunger drives and regulation have provided psychologists with an opportunity to examine the ways in which hunger might take on different meanings. To a person who is anorexic, for example, hunger may be a positive feeling—a state of being "high" and thus a goal to seek. To others, hunger may produce feelings of anxiety, insecurity, or anger. In this case, a person might eat before feeling hunger to prevent the feelings from arising. People's ability to experience hunger in different ways provides psychologists with two types of hunger, which are commonly referred to as hunger and appetite.

Hunger and appetite are not the same. Actual physical need is the basis of true hunger, while appetite can be triggered by thought, feeling, or sensation. Physical need can be separate from psychological need, although they may feel the same to the person who is not conscious of the difference. Compulsive eaters are often unable to recognize the difference between "real" hunger and psychological hunger, or appetite. While psychological hunger can be equally as motivating a need as stomach hunger, appetite (or mouth hunger) is emotionally, cognitively, and psychologically based thus cannot be fed in the same way. Stomach hunger can be satisfied by eating, whereas "feeding" mouth hunger must involve other activities and behaviors, as food does not ultimately seem to satisfy the mouth type of hunger.

THE CULTURAL CONTEXT OF HUNGER

One approach to increasing understanding of hunger and its psychological components is to examine hunger in its cultural context. In American culture, the experience of hunger is inextricably tied to weight, eating, body image, self-concept, social definitions of fatness and thinness, and other factors which take the issue of hunger far beyond the physiological facts. Historian Hillel Schwartz has traced the American cultural preoccupation with hunger, eating, and diet by examining the cultural fit between shared fictions about the body and their psychological, social, and cultural consequences. Hunger becomes a broader social issue when viewed in the context of the culture's history of obsession with dieting, weight control, and body image. The personal experience of hunger is affected by the social and historical context.

Eating disorders such as anorexia, bulimia, and compulsive overeating provide evidence of the complex relationship between the physiological and psychological components of hunger. Obesity has also been examined using medical and psychological models. The etiology of hunger's relationship to eating disorders has provided insight, if not consensus, by investigating the roles of hereditary factors, social learning, family systems, and multigenerational transmission in hunger as well as the socially learned eating patterns, food preferences, and cultural ideals that can mediate the hunger drive. Body image, eating restraint, and eating attitudes have been assessed by various methods. The focus of much of the research on hunger beyond the early animal experiments has been eating disorders. The findings confirm that hunger is more than a physiological need and is affected by a multitude of variables.

HUNGER REGULATION

The desire to regulate hunger has resulted in a wide variety of approaches and techniques, including professional diet centers, programs, and clinics; self-help books and magazines; diet clubs and support groups; self-help classes; and "diet doctors." Many people have benefited from psychotherapy in an effort to understand and control their hunger regulation mechanisms. Group therapy is one of the most successful forms of psychotherapy for food abusers. Types of group therapy vary greatly and include leaderless support groups, nonprofessional self-help groups such as Overeaters Anonymous, and groups led by professional therapists.

Advantages of group support for hunger regulation include the realization that one is not alone. An often-heard expression in group therapy is "I always thought I was the only person who ever felt this way." Other advantages include group support for risk taking, feedback from different perspectives, and a group laboratory for experimenting with new social behaviors. Witnessing others struggling to resolve life issues can provide powerful motivation to change. Self-help and therapy groups also offer friendship and acceptance. Creative arts therapies are other forms of psychotherapy used by persons seeking to understand and control their hunger regulation mechanisms. Creative therapy may involve art, music, dance, poetry, dreams, and other creative processes. These are experiential activities, and the process is sometimes nonverbal.

A more common experience for those who have faced the issue of hunger regulation is dieting. Despite the high failure rate of diets and weight-loss programs, the "diet mentality" is often associated with hunger regulation. Robert Schwartz studied the elements of the diet mentality, which is based on the assumption that being fat is bad and being thin is good. Dieting often sets up a vicious cycle of failure, which deflates self-esteem, thus contributing to shame and guilt, and leads to another diet. The diet mentality is self-defeating. Another key element to the diet mentality is the mechanism of self-deprivation that comes from not being allowed to indulge in certain foods and the accompanying social restrictions and isolation that dieting creates. Dieting treats the symptom rather than the cause of overeating.

Numerous approaches to hunger regulation share a condemnation of the diet mentality. Overcoming overeating; understanding, controlling, and recovering from addictive eating; and being "thin-within" are approaches based on addressing hunger regulation from a psychological perspective rather than a physiological one. These approaches share an emphasis on the emotional and feeling components of hunger regulation. They encourage the development of skills to differentiate between stomach hunger and mind hunger—that is, between hunger and appetite—and thereby to learn to recognize satiety as well as the reasons for hunger.

Behavior modification consists of a variety of techniques that attempt to apply the findings and methods of experimental psychology to human behavior. Interest in applying behavioral modification to hunger regulation developed as a result of the research on external cues and environmental factors that control the food intake of individuals. By emphasizing specific training in "stimulus control," behavior modification helps the individual to manage the environmental determinants of eating.

The first step in most behavior modification programs is to help the patient identify and monitor activities that are contributing to the specific behavior. In the case of an individual who overeats, this could involve identifying such behaviors as frequent eating of sweets, late evening snacking, eating huge meals, or eating in response to social demands. Because most people have more than one stimulus for eating behavior, the individual then observes situational stimuli: those that arise from the environment in which eating usually takes place. Once the stimuli are identified, new behaviors can be substituted—in effect, behavior can be modified.

MODELS OF HUNGER

Early scientific interest in hunger research was dominated by medical models, which identified the physiological mechanisms and systems involved. One of the earliest attempts to understand the sensation of hunger was an experiment conducted in 1912, in which a subject swallowed a balloon and then inflated it in his stomach. His stomach contractions and subjective reports of hunger feelings could then be simultaneously recorded. When the recordings were compared to the voluntary key presses that the subject made each time he experienced the feeling of hunger, the researchers concluded that it was the stomach movements that caused the sensation of hunger. It was later found, however, that an empty stomach is relatively inactive and that the stomach contractions experienced by the subject were an experimental artifact caused by the mere presence of the balloon in the stomach.

Further evidence for the lack of connection between stomach stimuli and feelings of hunger was provided in animal experiments which resulted in differentiating two areas of the hypothalamus responsible for stimulating eating behavior and signaling satiety—the "start eating" and "stop eating" centers.

Psychologist Stanley Schachter and his colleagues began to explore the psychological issues involved in hunger by emphasizing the external, non-physiological factors involved. In a series of experiments in which normal-weight and overweight individuals were provided with a variety of external eating cues, Schachter found that overweight subjects were more attentive to the passage of time in determining when to eat and were more excited by the taste and sight of food than were normal-weight persons. More recently, the growth of the field of social psychology has provided yet a different perspective on hunger, one that accounts for the situational and environment factors which influence the physiological and psychological states. For example, psychologists have examined extreme hunger and deprivation in case studies from historical episodes such as war, concentration camps, and famine in the light of the more recent interest in the identification and treatment of eating disorders.

There does not appear to be a consistent or ongoing effort to develop an interdisciplinary approach to the study of hunger. Because hunger is such a complex drive, isolating the factors associated with it poses a challenge to the standard research methodologies of psychology such as the case study, experiment, observation, and survey. Each methodology has its shortcomings, but together the methodologies have produced findings which clearly demonstrate that hunger is a physiological drive embedded in a psychological, social, and cultural context.

Viewing hunger as a multidimensional behavior has led to an awareness of hunger and its implications in a broader context. Changing dysfunctional attitudes, feelings, thoughts, and behaviors concerning hunger has not always been seen as a choice. Through continued psychological research into the topic of hunger—and increasing individual and group participation in efforts to understand, control, and change behaviors associated with hunger—new insights continue to emerge that will no doubt cast new light on this important and not yet completely understood topic.

SOURCES FOR FURTHER STUDY

Arenson, Gloria. *A Substance Called Food.* 2d ed. Boston: McGraw-Hill, 1989. Presents a variety of perspectives on eating: the psychological, the physiological, and the transpersonal. Particularly useful in providing self-help advice and treatment modalities. Examines the compulsiveness of food addiction and sees behavior modification as a means of addressing the addictive behavior.

Battegay, Raymond. *The Hunger Diseases.* Northvale, N.J.: Jason Aronson, 1997. Addresses the emotional hunger that, the author contends, underlies all eating disorders, from anorexia to obesity.

Hirschmann, Jane R., and Carol H. Munter. *When Women Stop Hating Their Bodies: Freeing Yourself from Food and Weight Obsessions.* New York: Fawcett,

1997. A follow-up to the authors' *Overcoming Overeating* (1988). Reviews the psychological bases for compulsive eating and provides alternative strategies to persons who have an addictive relationship with food. Presents arguments against dieting and proposes that self-acceptance, physical activity, and health are more appropriate long-term solutions to the problem of overeating.

Nisbett, Richard E. "Hunger, Obesity, and the Ventromedial Hypothalamus." *Psychological Review* 79, no. 6 (1972): 433-453. Based on research which differentiated the two areas of the hypothalamus that involve hunger: the "start eating" and "stop eating" mechanisms. Explains the idea of "set point," or the body mechanism which regulates homeostasis. This article is a classic in the field of hunger because it explains the physiological location of hunger and the important role of the hypothalamus.

Schachter, Stanley, and Larry P. Gross. "Manipulated Time and Eating Behavior." *Journal of Personality and Social Psychology* 10, no. 2 (1968): 98-106. Schachter's experiments provide the basis for attention to, and recognition of the importance of, external, nonphysiological factors affecting hunger. This article was one of the first to address the psychological components of hunger by examining the external triggers to eating.

Schwartz, Hillel. *Never Satisfied: A Cultural History of Diets, Fantasies, and Fat.* New York: Free Press, 1986. Schwartz, a historian, looks at diets and eating from the perspective of American social and cultural history. Examines how "shared fictions" about the body fit with various reducing methods and fads in different eras.

Schwartz, Robert. *Diets Don't Work.* 3d ed. Oakland, Calif.: Breakthru, 1996. Practical "how-to" guide to dismantling the diet mentality. This book is a good, basic, and sensible guide for taking stock of the self-defeating weight-loss attitudes and behaviors prevalent in temporary diets versus long-term attitudinal and behavior strategies for permanent weight control.

Tribole, Evelyn, and Elyse Resch. *Intuitive Eating: A Recovery Book for the Chronic Dieter.* 5th ed. New York: St. Martin's Press, 1996. Advocates listening to authentic hunger cues and avoiding emotion-based overeating.

Robin Franck

See also: Drives; Eating Disorders; Thirst.

IDENTITY CRISES

TYPE OF PSYCHOLOGY: Developmental psychology
FIELDS OF STUDY: Adolescence; adulthood

Identity crises are the internal and external conflicts faced by the adolescent/young adult when choosing an occupation and coming to terms with a basic ideology. Development of a personal identity is a central component of psychosocial maturity.

KEY CONCEPTS
- identity
- identity confusion/diffusion
- identity status
- negative identity
- psychosocial maturity
- psychosocial moratorium

Identity crises are an integral phase in human development. According to ego psychologist Erik Erikson (1902-1994), successful resolution of the identity crisis is contingent on the earlier resolution of the crises associated with infancy and childhood, such as trust, autonomy, initiative, and industry. Further, the extent to which the conflict surrounding identity is resolved will influence how the individual will cope with the crises of adulthood.

According to Erikson's model of the human life cycle, an identity crisis is one of the psychosocial conflicts faced by the adolescent. In Erikson's model, which was published in the 1960's, each age period is defined by a certain type of psychosocial crisis. Adolescence is the life stage during which acquiring an identity presents a major conflict. Failure to resolve the conflict results in identity confusion/diffusion—that is, an inadequate sense of self.

Identity implies an existential position, according to James Marcia, who construes identity as a self-structure composed of one's personal history, belief system, and competencies. One's perception of uniqueness is directly related to the development of this self-structure. A somewhat similar position has been taken by Jane Kroger, who views the identity crisis as a problem of self-definition. The resulting identity is a balance between self and others. Erikson defines identity as the belief that one's past experiences and identity will be confirmed in the future—as exemplified in the choice of a career. Identity is a composite of one's sexuality, physical makeup, vocation, and belief system. Identity is the pulling together of who one is and who one can become, which involves compositing one's past, present, and future. It is a synthesis of earlier identifications. Successfully resolving the identity crisis is contingent on the interactions that the adolescent/young adult has with others. Erikson contends that interacting with others provides the needed feedback about who one is and who one ought to be. These interactions with others enable the adolescent/young adult to gain a perspective of self that includes an evaluation of his or her physical and social self. Identity acquisition is cognitive as well as social.

CONDITIONS FOR IDENTITY CRISIS
From Erikson's perspective, as discussed in a 1987 article by James Cote and Charles Levine, four conditions are necessary for an identity crisis: Puberty has been reached; the requisite cognitive development is present; physical growth is nearing adult stature; and societal influences are guiding the person toward an integration and resynthesis of identity. The dialectics of society and personality, implicit in the last condition, are given the most attention by Erikson, according to Cote and Levine, because the other three conditions are part of normative development. Developmental levels of the individual and societal pressures combine to elicit an identity crisis, but Cote and Levine note that timing of this crisis is contingent on factors such as ethnicity, gender, socioeconomic status, and subculture, as well as personality factors (for example, authoritarianism or neuroticism) and socialization practices. The severity of the identity crisis is determined by the extent to which one's identity portrayal is interfered with by the uncertainty inherent in moving toward self-definition and unexpected events.

PSYCHOLOGICAL MORATORIUM
An integral part of the identity crisis is the psychological moratorium, a time during which society permits the individual to work on crisis resolution. During this moratorium, the adolescent/young adult has the opportunity to examine societal roles, career possibilities, and values, free from the expectation of commitments and long-term responsibilities. Although some individuals choose to remain in a moratorium indefinitely, Erikson contends that there is an absolute end to the recognizable moratorium. At its completion, the adolescent/young adult should have attained the necessary restructuring of self and identifications so that he or she can find a place in society which fits this identity.

Based on Erikson's writings, Cote and Levine identify two types of institutionalized moratoria: the technological moratorium, which is highly structured, and the humanistic moratorium, which is less highly structured. The technological moratorium is the product of the educational system, which is charged by society with socializing youth to fit in adult society. Individuals in this moratorium option experience less difficulty in resolving the identity crisis because they move into occupations and societal roles for which they have been prepared with significantly less intrapsychic trauma in accepting an ideology. The school takes an active role in easing this transition by providing vocational and academic counseling for students, facilitating scheduling so that students can gain work experience while enrolled in school, and encouraging early decision making as to a future career.

The identity crisis for individuals in the humanistic moratorium is more stressful and painful and of longer duration than for those in the technological moratorium. The focal concern of the adolescent/young adult in the humanistic moratorium is humanistic values, which are largely missing from the technological moratorium. There is more variability in this concern for humanistic values, which is reflected in the moratorium that is chosen and the commitments that are made. These conditions elicit an alternation between progressive and regressive states, with the individual making commitments at one time and disengaging at another. The character Holden Caulfield in J. D. Salinger's classic novel *The Catcher in the Rye* (1951) is an example of this type of identity problem. More extreme identity confusion is found among individuals in this moratorium. According to Cote and Levine, social support is often lacking, which hinders formation of a stable identity. Family and community support is especially important for these individuals. Yet these are the adolescents/young adults who, because their lifestyle departs from the societal mold, are often ostracized and denied support. Individuals may promote a cause of some type. Those who choose a humanistic moratorium are more likely to be intellectual, artistic, antiestablishment, and ideologically nonconforming. After a time, some of these individuals accept technological values and roles.

Individuals whose identity seeking is not influenced by technological or humanistic moratoria face a rather different situation. Some remain in a constant state of flux, in which choices are avoided and commitments are lacking. Others take on a negative identity by accepting a deviant lifestyle and value system (for example, delinquency or gang membership). In this instance, the negative elements of an identity outweigh the positive elements. This type of identity crisis resolution occurs in an environment which precludes normative identity development (for example, excessively demanding parents, absence of an adequate role model).

IDENTITY STATUS PARADIGM

Erikson's writings on identity crises have been responsible for an extensive literature consisting of conceptual as well as empirical articles. Perhaps the most widely used application is Marcia's identity status paradigm, in which he conceptualized and operationalized Erikson's theory of identity development in terms of several statuses which result from exploration and commitment. By 1988, more than one hundred empirical studies had been generated from this paradigm, according to a review by Cote and Levine. The identity status paradigm provides a methodological procedure for determining identity statuses based on resolution of an identity crisis and the presence of commitments to an occupation and an ideology.

According to the Marcia paradigm, an ego identity can be one of several statuses consisting of achievement, foreclosure, moratorium, or diffusion. An achievement status indicates resolution of the identity crisis and firm commitments to an occupation and an ideology. In a foreclosure status, one has formed commitments but has not experienced a crisis. The moratorium status denotes that an identity crisis is being experienced, and no commitments have been made. The diffusion status implies the absence of a crisis and no commitments. Much of the research has focused on identifying the personality characteristics associated with each of these statuses. Other studies have examined the interactional patterns as well as information-processing and problem-solving strategies. Achievement and moratorium statuses seek out, process, and evaluate information in their decision making. Foreclosures have more rigid belief systems and conform to normative standards held by significant others, while those in the diffusion status delay decision making. Significant differences have been found among the statuses in terms of their capacity for intimacy, with diffusions scoring lowest, followed by foreclosures. Achievement and moratorium statuses have a greater capacity for intimacy.

PARENTAL SOCIALIZATION AND FEMALE IDENTITY

One area of research that continues to attract attention is parental socialization patterns associated with crisis resolution. The findings to date reveal distinctive parental patterns associated with each status. Positive but somewhat ambivalent relationships between parents and the adolescent/young adult are reported for achievement status. Moratorium-status adolescents/young adults also seem to have ambivalent relationships with their parents, but they are less conforming. Males in this status tend to experience difficulty in separating from their mothers. Foreclosures view their parents as highly accepting and encouraging. Parental pressure for conformity to family values is very evident. Diffusion-status adolescents report much parental rejection and detachment from parents, especially from the father. In general, the data from family studies show that the same-sex parent is an important figure in identity resolution.

An interest in female identity has arisen because different criteria have been used to identify identity status based on the Marcia paradigm. Attitudes toward premarital sexual relations are a major content area in status determination. The research in general shows that achievement and foreclosure statuses are very similar in females, as are the moratorium and diffusion statuses. This pattern is not found for males. It has been argued by some that the focal concerns of females, in addition to concerns with occupation and ideology, involve interpersonal relationships more than do the concerns of males. Therefore, in forming a self-structure, females may examine the outside world for self-evaluation and acceptance in addition to the internal examination of self which typically occurs in males. The effect of an external focus on identity resolution in females is unknown, but this type of focus is likely to prolong the identity crisis. Further, it is still necessary to determine the areas in which choices and commitments are made for females.

NEGATIVE IDENTITY

The concept of negative identity has been used frequently in clinical settings to explain antisocial acts and delinquency in youth as well as gang-related behavior. A 1988 study by Randall Jones and Barbara Hartman found that the use of substances (for example, cigarettes, alcohol, and other drugs) was higher and more likely in youths of identity-diffusion status. Erikson and others have argued that troubled youths find that elements of a negative identity provide them with a sense of some mastery over a situation for which a positive approach has been continually denied them. In the examples cited, deviant behavior provided both this sense of mastery and an identity.

Role in Understanding Adolescents

The identity crisis is the major conflict faced by the adolescent. Erikson's theories about the identity crisis made a major contribution to the adolescent literature. Marcia's reconceptualization of ego identity facilitated identity research and clinical assessment by providing a methodological approach to identity development and the psychological concomitants of identity. As a result, the study of identity and awareness of the psychological impact on the individual become major research areas and provided a basis for clinical intervention.

The concept of identity crises originated with Erikson, based on the clinical experiences which he used to develop a theory of ego identity development. Explication of this theory appeared in his writings during the 1950's and 1960's. Erikson's theory of the human life cycle places identity resolution as the major crisis faced by the adolescent. The success of this resolution is determined by the satisfactory resolution of crises in the stages preceding adolescence.

Identity formation is a major topic in most textbooks on adolescence, and it is a focal concern of practitioners who treat adolescents with psychological adjustment problems. Until the appearance of Erikson's writings, the field of adolescence was mostly a discussion of physical and sexual development. His focus on psychosocial development, especially the emergence of a self-structure, increased immeasurably the understanding of adolescent development and the problems faced by the adolescent growing up in Western society. As Cote and Levine noted, identity is a multidimensional construct consisting of sociological perspectives, specifically the social environment in which the individual interacts, as well as psychological processes. Thus, a supportive social environment is critical to crisis resolution. The absence of this supportive environment has frequently been cited as an explanation for identity problems and the acquisition of a negative identity.

Temporal Considerations

It is important to realize that identity has a temporal element as well as a lifelong duration. That is, identity as a personality characteristic undergoes transformations throughout the life cycle. While crisis resolution may be achieved during adolescence/young adulthood, this self-structure is not permanent. Crises can reemerge during the life span. The midlife crises of middle adulthood, written about frequently in the popular press, are often viewed as a manifestation of the earlier identity crisis experienced during adolescence/young adulthood.

The outlook for identity crises is difficult to forecast. The psychological moratorium will continue to be an important process. Given the constant change in American society, the moratorium options available for youth may be more restricted, or more ambiguous and less stable. This scenario is more probable for humanistic moratoria as society moves toward more institutional structure in the form of schools taking on increased responsibility for the socialization of children and youth. The provision of child care before and after school is one example of the school's increased role. The erosion which has occurred in family structure presents another problem for identity crisis resolution.

SOURCES FOR FURTHER STUDY

Cote, James E., and Charles Levine. "A Critical Examination of the Ego Identity Status Paradigm." *Developmental Review* 8 (June, 1988): 147-184. Critiques the Marcia identity-status paradigm and notes several areas of divergence from Erikson's conceptualization theory of identity. Advances the argument for an interdisciplinary approach to understanding identity and identifies several questions about identity crises that need to be considered.

_____. "A Formulation of Erikson's Theory of Ego Identity Formation." *Developmental Review* 7 (December, 1987): 209-218. A comprehensive review of Erikson's theory of ego identity and the role of psychological moratoria in the resolution of identity crises. Discusses Erikson's concepts of value orientation stages and the ego-superego conflict over personality control. Offers criticisms of Erikson's work and suggests cautions for the researcher.

Erikson, Erik Homburger. *Childhood and Society.* Reprint. New York: W. W. Norton, 1993. The thirty-fifth anniversary edition. A presentation of case histories based on Erikson's clinical experiences as well as a discussion of Erikson's life-cycle model of human development. One section of the book is devoted to an examination of youth and identity. Clinical studies are used to illustrate the problems youth face in identity resolution.

_____. *Identity, Youth, and Crisis.* Reprint. New York: W. W. Norton, 1994. A theoretical discussion of ego identity formation and identity confusion, with special attention given to issues such as womanhood or race and identity. Erikson relies heavily on his vast clinical experiences to illustrate the concepts that he discusses. The life cycle as it applies to identity is examined from an epigenetic perspective.

Kroger, Jane. *Identity in Adolescence.* 2d ed. New York: Routledge, 1996. A presentation of identity development as conceptualized by Erikson and others. Each approach is criticized, and the empirical findings generated by the approach are summarized. The first chapter of the book is devoted to an overview of identity from a developmental and sociocultural perspective. The final chapter presents an integration of what is known about identity.

Marcia, James E. "Identity in Adolescence." In *Handbooks of Adolescent Psychology*, edited by Joseph Adelson. New York: John Wiley & Sons, 1980. A discussion of the identity statuses developed by Marcia, based on a paradigm derived from Erikson's conceptualization of ego identity. Reviews the research literature on personality characteristics, patterns of interaction, developmental studies, identity in women, and other directions in identity research. Ends with a discussion of a general ego-developmental approach to identity.

Joseph C. LaVoie

SEE ALSO: Adolescence: Cognitive Skills; Development; Ego Psychology: Erik Erikson; Gender-Identity Formation; Psychoanalytic Psychology; Self.

IMPRINTING

TYPE OF PSYCHOLOGY: Learning
FIELDS OF STUDY: Biological influences on learning; endocrine system

Imprinting is an endogenous, or inborn, animal behavior by which young mammals and birds learn specific, visible physical patterns to associate with important concepts such as the identification of one's mother, navigation routes, and danger. The phenomenon, which relies primarily upon visual cues and hormonal scents, is of high survival value for the species possessing it.

KEY CONCEPTS
- conditioning
- critical period
- endogenous behavior
- ethology
- exogenous behavior
- imprinting
- pheromone
- plasticity
- visual cues
- vocal cues

Imprinting is an important type of behavior by which an animal learns specific concepts and identifies certain objects or individuals that are essential for survival. Imprinting events almost always occur very early in the life of an animal, during critical periods or time frames when the animal is most sensitive to environmental cues and influences. The phenomenon occurs in a variety of species, but it is most pronounced in the homeothermic (warm-blooded) and socially oriented higher vertebrate species, especially mammals and birds.

Imprinting is learned behavior. Most learned behavior falls within the domain of exogenous behavior, or behavior that an animal obtains by its experiences with fellow conspecifics (members of the same species) and the environment. Imprinting, however, is predominantly, if not exclusively, an endogenous behavior, which is a behavior that is genetically encoded within the individual. An individual is born with the capacity to imprint. The animal's cellular biochemistry and physiology will determine when in its development it will imprint. The only environmental influence of any consequence in imprinting is the object of the imprint during the critical period. Ethologists, scientists who study animal behavior, debate the extent of endogenous and exogenous influences upon animal behavior. Most behaviors involve a combination of both, although one type may be more pronounced than the other.

The capacity for an animal to imprint is genetically determined and, therefore, is inherited. This type of behavior is to the animal's advantage for critical situations that must be correctly handled the first time they occur. Such behaviors include the identification of one's parents (especially one's mother), the ability to navigate, the ability to identify danger, and even the tendency to perform the language of one's own species. Imprinting behaviors generally are of high survival value and hence must be programmed into the individual via the genes. Biological research has failed to identify many of the genes that are responsible for imprinting behaviors, although the hormonal basis of imprinting is well understood. Most imprinting studies have focused upon the environmental signals and developmental state of the individual during the occurrence of imprinting.

MATERNAL IMPRINTING

These studies have involved mammals and birds, warm-blooded species that have high social bonding, which seems to be a prerequisite for imprinting. The most famous imprinting studies were performed by the animal behaviorists and Nobel laureates Konrad Lorenz (1903-1989) and Nikolaas Tinbergen (1907-1988). They and their many colleagues detailed analyses of imprinting in a variety of species, in particular waterfowl such as geese and ducks. The maternal imprinting behavior of the newborn gosling or duckling upon the first moving object that it sees is the most striking example of imprinting behavior.

The maternal imprint is the means by which a newborn identifies its mother and the mother identifies its young. In birds, the newborn chick follows the first moving object that it sees, an object that should be its mother. The critical imprinting period is within a few hours after hatching. The chick visually will lock on its moving mother and follow it wherever it goes until the chick reaches adulthood. The act of imprinting not only allows for the identification of one's parents but also serves as a trigger for all subsequent social interactions with members of one's own species. As has been established in numerous experiments, a newborn gosling that first sees a female duck will imprint on the duck and follow it endlessly. Upon reaching adulthood, the grown goose, which has been raised in the social environment of ducks, will attempt to behave as a duck, even to the point of mating. Newborn goslings, ducklings, and chicks can easily imprint on humans.

In mammals, imprinting relies not only visual cues (specific visible physical objects or patterns that an animal learns to associate with certain concepts) but also on physical contact and smell. Newborn infants imprint upon their mothers, and vice versa, by direct contact, sight, and smell during the critical period, which usually occurs within twenty hours following birth. The newborn and its mother must come into direct contact with each other's skin and become familiarized with each other's smell. The latter phenomenon involves the release of special hormones called pheromones from each individual's body. Pheromones trigger a biochemical response in the body of the recipient individual, in this case leading to a locked identification pattern for the other involved individual. If direct contact between

Konrad Lorenz. (The Nobel Foundation)

mother and infant is not maintained during the critical imprinting period, then the mother may reject the infant because she is unfamiliar with its scent. In such a case, the infant's life would be in jeopardy unless it were claimed by a substitute mother. Even in this situation, the failure to imprint would trigger subsequent psychological trauma in the infant, possibly leading to aberrant social behavior in later life.

BIRD MIGRATION AND DANGER RECOGNITION
Although maternal imprinting in mammal and bird species represents the best-documented studies of imprinting behavior, imprinting may be involved in other types of learned behavior. In migratory bird species, ethologists have attempted to explain how bird populations navigate from their summer nesting sites to their wintering sites and back every year without error. Different species manage to navigate in different fashions. The indigo bunting, however, navigates via the patterns of stars in the sky at night. Indigo bunting chicks imprint upon the celestial star patterns for their sum-

mer nesting site during a specific critical period, a fact that was determined by the rearrangement of planetarium stars for chicks by research scientists.

Further research studies on birds also implicate imprinting in danger recognition and identification of one's species-specific call or song. Young birds of many species identify predatory birds (for example, hawks, falcons, and owls) by the outline of the predator's body during flight or attack and by special markings on the predator's body. Experiments also have demonstrated that unhatched birds can hear their mother's call or song; birds may imprint on their own species' call or song before they hatch. These studies reiterate the fact that imprinting is associated with a critical period during early development in which survival-related behaviors must become firmly established.

HUMAN IMPRINTING

Imprinting is of considerable interest to psychologists because of its role in the learning process for humans. Humans imprint in much the same fashion as other mammals. The extended lifetime, long childhood, and great capacity for learning and intelligence make imprinting in humans an important area of study. Active research on imprinting is continually being conducted with humans, primates, marine mammals (such as dolphins, whales, and seals), and many other mammals as well as with a large variety of bird species. Comparisons among the behaviors of these many species yield considerable similarities in the mechanisms of imprinting. These similarities underscore the importance of imprinting events in the life, survival, and socialization of the individual.

With humans, maternal imprinting occurs much as with other mammals. The infant and its mother must be in direct contact during the hours following birth. During this critical period, there is an exchange of pheromones between mother and infant, an exchange that, to a large extent, will bond the two. Such bonding immediately following birth can occur between infant and father in the same manner. Many psychologists stress the importance of both parents being present at the time of a child's delivery and making contact with the child during the critical hours of the first day following birth. Familiarization is important not only for the child but for the parents as well because all three are imprinting upon one another.

Failure of maternal or paternal imprinting during the critical period following birth can have drastic consequences in humans. The necessary, and poorly understood, biochemical changes that occur in the bodies of a child and parent during the critical period will not occur if there is no direct contact and, therefore, no transfer of imprinting pheromones. Consequently, familiarization and acceptance between the involved individuals may not occur, even if intense contact is maintained after the end of the critical period. The psychological impact upon the child and upon the parents may be profound, perhaps not immediately, but in later years. Studies on this problem are extremely limited because of the difficulty of tracing cause-and-effect relationships over many years when many behaviors are involved. There is some evidence, however, which indicates that failure to imprint may be associated with such things as learning disabilities, child-parent conflicts, and abnormal adolescent behavior. Nevertheless, other cases of imprinting failure seem to have no effect, as can be seen in tens of thousands of adopted children. The success or failure of maternal imprinting in humans is a subject of considerable importance in terms of how maternal imprinting affects human behavior and social interactions in later life.

Different human cultures maintain distinct methods of child rearing. In some cultures, children are raised by family servants or relatives from birth onward, not by the actual mother. Some cultures wrap infants very tightly so that they can barely move; other cultures are more permissive. Child and adolescent psychology focuses attention upon early life experiences that could have great influence upon later social behavior. The success or failure of imprinting, along with other early childhood experiences, may be a factor in later social behaviors such as competitiveness, interaction with individuals of the opposite sex, mating, and maintenance of a stable family structure. Even criminal behavior and psychological abnormalities may be traceable to such early childhood events.

EXPERIMENTS

Imprinting studies conducted with mammal and bird species are much easier because the researcher has the freedom to conduct controlled experiments that test many different variables, thereby identifying the factors that influence an individual animal's ability to imprint. For bird species, a famous experiment is the moving ball experiment. A newly hatched chick is isolated in a chamber within which a suspended ball revolves around the center of the chamber. The researcher can test not only movement as an imprinting trigger but also other variables, such as critical imprinting time after hatching, color as an imprinting factor, and variations in the shape of the ball as imprinting factors. Other experiments involve switching eggs between different species (for example, placing a duck egg among geese eggs).

For mammals, imprinting has been observed in many species, such as humans, chimpanzees, gorillas, dolphins, elephant seals, wolves, and cattle. In most of these species, the failure of a mother to come into contact with its newborn almost always results in rejection of the child. In species such as elephant seals, smell is the primary means by which a mother identifies its pups. Maternal imprinting is of critical importance in a mammalian child's subsequent social development. Replacement of a newborn monkey's natural mother with a "doll" substitute leads to irreparable damage; the infant is socially and sexually repressed in its later life encounters with other monkeys. These and other studies establish imprinting as a required learning behavior for the successful survival and socialization of all birds and nonhuman mammals.

BIOLOGY AND BEHAVIOR

Animal behaviorists and psychologists attempt to identify the key factors that are responsible for imprinting in mammalian and avian species. Numerous factors, including vocal cues (specific sounds, frequency, and language that an animal learns to associate with certain concepts) and visual cues probably are involved, although the strongest two factors appear to be direct skin contact and the exchange of pheromones that are detectable by smell. The maternal imprinting behavior is the most intensively studied imprinting phenomenon, though imprinting appears to occur in diverse behaviors such as mating, migratory navigation, and certain forms of communication.

Imprinting attracts the interest of psychologists because it occurs at critical periods in an individual's life; because subsequent developmental, social, and behavioral events hinge upon what happens during the imprinting event; and because imprinting occurs at the genetic or biochemical level. Biochemically, imprinting relies upon the production and release of pheromones, molecules that have a specific structure and that can be manufactured in a laboratory. The identification and mass production of these pheromones could possibly produce treatments for some behavioral abnormalities.

As an endogenous (instinctive) form of learning, imprinting relies upon the highly complex nervous and endocrine systems of birds and mammals. It also appears limited to social behavior, a major characteristic of these species. The complex nervous systems involve a highly developed brain, vocal communication, well-developed eyes, and a keen sense of smell. The endocrine systems of these species produce a variety of hormones, including the pheromones that are involved in imprinting, mating, and territoriality. Understanding the nervous and endocrine regulation of behavior at all levels is of major interest to biological and psychological researchers. Such studies may prove to be fruitful in the discovery of the origin and nature of animal consciousness.

Imprinting may be contrasted with exogenous forms of learning. These other learning types include conditioning, in which individuals learn by repeated exposure to a stimulus, by association of the concept stimulus with apparently unrelated phenomena and objects, or by a system of reward and punishment administered by parents. Other exogenous learning forms include habituation (getting used to something) and trial and error. All learned behaviors are a combination of endogenous and exogenous factors.

SOURCES FOR FURTHER STUDY

Beck, William S., Karel F. Liem, and George Gaylord Simpson. *Life: An Introduction to Biology*. 3d ed. New York: HarperCollins, 1991. Introduction to biology for the beginning student. Contains a clear text, many strong diagrams and illustrations, and beautiful photographs. Contains a thorough discussion of animal behavior, famous experiments, and various types of animal learning, including imprinting, and describes the studies of Konrad Lorenz and others.

Klopfer, Peter H., and Jack P. Hailman. *An Introduction to Animal Behavior: Ethology's First Century.* 2d ed. Englewood Cliffs, N.J.: Prentice-Hall, 1974. An excellent and well-organized introduction to the history of animal behavior research. Presents major themes and models and cites many important studies. Two chapters discuss instinctive and learned aspects of behavioral development.

Manning, Aubrey, and Marian Stamp Dawking. *An Introduction to Animal Behavior.* 5th ed. New York: Cambridge University Press, 1998. Concise, detailed, and thorough presentation of animal behavior research. Encompasses all major behavioral theories and supporting experiments. Includes a good discussion of imprinting studies, particularly with reference to maternal imprinting, and describes the biological bases behind imprinting and other behaviors.

Raven, Peter H., and George B. Johnson. *Biology.* 6th ed. Boston: McGraw-Hill, 2002. A strong presentation of all aspects of biology for the beginning student. Includes excellent diagrams and illustrations. Summarizes the major theories and classic experiments of animal behavior research, including imprinting studies.

Wallace, Robert A., Gerald P. Sanders, and Robert J. Ferl. *Biology: The Science of Life.* 3d ed. New York: HarperCollins, 1991. An outstanding book for beginning students that describes all major concepts in biology with great clarity, using numerous examples, good illustrations, and beautiful photographs. Discusses behavioral research, including studies of maternal imprinting.

Wilson, Edward Osborne. *Sociobiology: The New Synthesis.* Cambridge, Mass.: The Belknap Press of Harvard University Press, 2000. A comprehensive study of sociobiology, a perspective which maintains that animal behavior is a driving force in animal species evolution. The author, a prominent entomologist, is a leading proponent of this controversial theory, which he defends with hundreds of case studies. Describes the biological basis of behavior during all stages of animal development.

David Wason Hollar, Jr.

SEE ALSO: Hormones and Behavior; Instinct Theory; Learning; Reflexes.

INDIVIDUAL PSYCHOLOGY
ALFRED ADLER

TYPE OF PSYCHOLOGY: Personality
FIELDS OF STUDY: Personality theory; psychodynamic and neoanalytic
   models

Individual psychology is the personality theory that was developed by Adler after he broke from Freudian psychoanalytical ideas. Adler emphasized the importance of childhood inferiority feelings and stressed psychosocial rather than psychosexual development.

KEY CONCEPTS
- compensation
- inferiority
- masculine protest
- private logic
- social interest
- style of life

Individual psychology is the name of the school of personality theory and psychotherapy developed by Alfred Adler (1870-1937), a Viennese general-practice physician turned psychiatrist. The term "individual" has a dual implication: It implies uniqueness (each personality exists in a person whose distinctiveness must be appreciated); also, the personality is an indivisible unit that cannot be broken down into separate traits, drives, or habits which could be analyzed as if they had an existence apart from the whole.

The essence of a person's uniqueness is his or her style of life, a unified system which provides the principles that guide everyday behavior and gives the individual a perspective with which to perceive the self and the world. The style of life is fairly stable after about age six, and it represents the individual's attempt to explain and cope with the great problem of human existence: the feeling of inferiority.

ROLE OF INFERIORITY
According to Adler, all people develop a feeling of inferiority. First of all, they are born children in an adult world and realize that they have smaller and weaker bodies, less knowledge, and virtually no privileges. Then people start to compare themselves and realize that there are other people their own age who are better athletes, better scholars, more popular, more artistically talented, wealthier, more socially privileged, more physically attractive, or simply luckier. If one allows the perception of one's own self-worth to be influenced by such subjective comparisons, then one's self-esteem will be lowered by an inferiority complex.

Adler believed that because one's style of life is largely determined early in life, certain childhood conditions make individuals more vulnerable to feelings of inferiority. For example, children born into poverty or into ethnic groups subjected to prejudice may develop a heightened sense of inferiority. Those children with real disabilities (learning or physical disabilities, for example) would also be more susceptible to devaluing their own worth, especially when others are excessively critical or mocking.

ROLE OF EARLY FAMILY LIFE

Adler looked inside the family for the most powerful influences on a child's developing style of life. Parents who treat a child harshly (through physical, verbal, or sexual abuse) would certainly foster feelings of inferiority in that child. Similarly, parents who neglect or abandon their children contribute to the problem. (Adler believed that such children, instead of directing their rage outward against such parents, turn it inward and say, "There must be something wrong with me, or they would not treat me this way.") Surprisingly, Adler also believed that those parents who pamper their children frustrate the development of positive self-esteem, for such youngsters conclude that they must be very weak and ineffectual in order to require such constant protection and service. When such pampered children go out into the larger world and are not the recipients of constant attention and favors, their previous training has not prepared them for this; they rapidly develop inferior feelings.

The impact of the family on the formulation of one's style of life also includes the influence of siblings. Adler was the first to note that a child's birth order contributes to personality. Oldest children tend to be more serious and success-oriented, because they spend more time with their parents and identify more closely with them. When the younger children come along, the oldest child naturally falls into a leadership role. Youngest children are more likely to have greater social skills and be creative and rebellious. Regardless of birth order, intense sibling rivalries and comparisons can easily damage the esteem of children.

INDIVIDUAL INTERPRETATION OF CHOICE

Adler was not fatalistic in discussing the possible impact on style of life of these congenital and environmental forces; he held that it is neither heredity nor environment which determines personality but rather the way that individuals interpret heredity and environment. These two things furnish only the building blocks out of which the individual fashions a work of art: the style of life. People have (and make) choices, and this determines their own development; some people, however, have been trained by life to make better choices than others.

All individuals have the capacity to compensate for feelings of inferiority. Many great athletes were frail children and worked hard to develop their physical strength and skills. Some great painters overcame weak eyesight;

great musicians have overcome poor hearing. Given proper encouragement, people are capable of great accomplishments.

DEVELOPMENT OF SOCIAL INTEREST

The healthy, normal course of development is for individuals to overcome their feelings of inferiority and develop social interest. This involves a feeling of community, or humanistic identification, and a concern with the well-being of others, not only one's own private feelings. Social interest is reflected in and reinforced by cooperative and constructive interactions with others. It starts in childhood, when the youngster has nurturing and encouraging contacts with parents, teachers, and peers.

Later, the three main pillars of social interest are friends, family, and career. Having friends can help overcome inferiority, because it allows one to be important in the eyes of someone else. Friends share their problems, so one does not feel like the only person who has self-doubt and frustration. Starting one's own family reduces inferiority feeling in much the same way. One feels loved by spouse and children, and one is very important to them. Having an occupation allows one to develop a sense of mastery and accomplishment and provides some service to others or to society at large. Therefore, those people who have difficulty establishing and maintaining friendships, succeeding as a spouse or parent, or finding a fulfilling career will have less opportunity to develop a healthy social interest and will have a greater susceptibility to lingering feelings of inferiority.

PRIVATE LOGIC

The alternatives to developing social interest as a way of escaping from feelings of inferiority are either to wallow in them or to explain them away with private logic. Private logic is an individual's techniques for coping with the feeling of inferiority by unconsciously redefining himself or herself in a way not compatible with social interest. Such individuals retreat from meaningful interpersonal relationships and challenging work because it might threaten their precariously balanced self-esteem. Private logic convinces these individuals to seek a sham sense of superiority or notoriety in some way that lacks social interest.

One such approach in private logic is what Adler termed masculine protest (because Western patriarchal culture has encouraged such behavior in males and discouraged it in females). The formula is to be rebellious, defiant, even violent. Underlying all sadism, for example, is an attempt to deny weakness. The gangster wants more than money, the rapist more than sex: They need a feeling of power in order to cover up an unresolved inferiority feeling.

USE IN CHILD DEVELOPMENT STUDIES

Adler's theory, like Sigmund Freud's psychoanalysis and B. F. Skinner's radical behaviorism, is a flexible and powerful tool for understanding and guiding human behavior. The first and foremost applications of individual psychology have been in the areas of child rearing, education, and guidance. Because the first six years of life are formative, the contact that children have during this time with parents, teachers, siblings, and peers will influence that child's later decisions in the direction of social interest or private logic. Adlerians recommend that parents and teachers be firm, fair, and, above all, encouraging. One should tell children that they can overcome their disabilities and praise every progress toward accomplishment and social interest. One should avoid excessive punishments, for this will only convince children that others are against them and that they must withdraw into private logic.

After World War I, the new Social Democratic government of Austria gave Adler the task of developing a system of youth guidance clinics throughout the nation. Each child age six to fourteen was screened, then counseled, if necessary. In the 1920's, the rates of crime and mental disorders among young people declined dramatically.

USE IN ELDER STUDIES

A second example of the applicability of Adler's theory occurs at the other end of the life cycle: old age. Late life is a period in which the incidence of mental disorders, especially depression, increases. This can be understood in terms of diminished opportunity to sustain social interest and increased sources of inferiority feeling.

Recall that social interest has three pillars: career, friends, and family. Traditionally, one retires from one's career at about age sixty-five. Elders who do not develop satisfying new activities (especially activities which involve a sense of accomplishment and contribution to others) adjust poorly to retirement and tend to become depressed. Old friends die or move into retirement communities. Sometimes it is harder to see and talk with old friends because of the difficulty of driving or using public transportation as one ages, or because one or one's friends become hard of hearing or experience a stroke that impairs speech. By far the greatest interpersonal loss in later life is the loss of a spouse. When adult children move away in pursuit of their own lives, this may also give an elder the perception of being abandoned.

Conditions that can rekindle old feelings of inferiority abound in later life. Real physical inferiorities arise. The average elder reports at least two of the following chronic conditions: impaired vision, impaired hearing, a heart condition, stroke, or arthritis. The United States is a youth- and body-oriented culture that worships physical attractiveness, not wrinkles and fat. Some elders, especially those who have had the burdens of long-term illness, feel inferior because of their reduced financial resources.

USE IN STUDYING PREJUDICE

A third area of application is social psychology, especially the study of prejudice. Gordon Allport suggested that those who exhibit racial or religious prejudice are typically people who feel inferior themselves: They are trying to feel better about themselves by feeling superior to someone else. Typically, prejudice against African Americans has been greatest among whites of low socioeconomic status. Prejudice against new immigrants has been greatest among the more poorly skilled domestic workers. Another example of prejudice would be social class distinctions. The middle class feels inferior (in terms of wealth and privilege) to the upper class. Therefore, the middle class responds by using its private logic to demean the justification of wealth: "The rich are rich because their ancestors were robber barons or because they themselves were junk bond traders in the 1980's." The middle class feels superior to the lower class, however, and again uses private logic to justify and legitimize that class distinction: "The poor are poor because they are lazy and irresponsible." In order to solidify its own identity as hardworking and responsible, the middle class develops a perception of the poor that is more derogatory than an objective analysis would permit.

The most telling application of the theory of individual psychology to prejudice occurred in the first part of the twentieth century in Germany. The rise of Nazi anti-Semitism can be associated with the humiliating German defeat in World War I and with the deplorable conditions brought about by hyperinflation and depression. Adolf Hitler first blamed the Jews for the "November treason" which brought about the defeat of the German army. (This private logic allowed the German people to believe that their defeated army would have achieved an all-out victory at the front had it not been for the Jewish traitors back in Berlin.) All the problems of capitalism and social inequality were laid at the feet of Jewish financiers, and every fear of rabble-rousing Communists was associated with Jewish radicals. Because everything bad, weak, cowardly, or exploitive was labeled "Jewish," non-Jewish Germans could believe that they themselves were everything good. The result of the institutionalization of this private logic in the Third Reich led to one of the most blatant examples of masculine protest that humankind has witnessed: World War II and the Holocaust.

USE IN INTERPERSONAL RELATIONS

A fourth application is associated with business management and sales. Management applies interpersonal relations to subordinates; sales applies interpersonal relations to prospective customers. Adler's formula for effective interpersonal relations is simple: Do not make the other person feel inferior. Treat workers with respect. Act as if they are intelligent, competent, wise, and motivated. Give subordinates the opportunity and the encouragement to do a good job, so that they can nurture their own social interest by having a feeling of accomplishment and contribution. Mary Kay Ash, the cosmetics magnate, said that she treated each of her employees and distributors as if each were wearing a sign saying "make me feel important." A similar strategy should apply to customers.

FREUD'S INFLUENCE

The idea of the inferiority complex bears some similarity to the writings of many previous thinkers. Nineteenth century French psychologist Pierre Janet came closest by developing a theory of perceived insufficiency as a root of all neurosis. American psychologist William James spoke of an innate craving to be appreciated. Adler's emphasis on the individual's capacity for compensation (a defense mechanism for overcoming feelings of inferiority by trying harder to excel) and on masculine protest has parallels in the writings of philosopher Friedrich Nietzsche.

The optimistic, simplified, psychosocial approach of Alfred Adler can only be understood as a reaction to the pessimistic, esoteric, psychosexual approach of Sigmund Freud. Adler was a respected general practitioner in Vienna. He heard his first lecture on psychoanalysis in 1899 and was fascinated, although he never regarded himself as a student or disciple of Freud. He was invited to join the Vienna Psychoanalytic Society, and did so in 1902, but he was never psychoanalyzed himself. By the end of the decade, he had become president of the society and editor of its journal. As Adler's own theories developed, and as he voiced them within the psychoanalytic association, Freud became increasingly defensive.

Adler came to criticize several underpinnings of psychoanalytic theory. For example, he suggested that the Oedipus complex was merely the reaction of a pampered child, not a universal complex. Adler saw dysfunctional sexual attitudes and practices as a symptom of the underlying neurosis, not as its underlying cause. When Adler would not recant his heresy, the Vienna Psychoanalytic Society was split into a Freudian majority and an Adlerian minority. For a brief period, the Adlerians retained the term "psychoanalysis," only later defining their school as individual psychology.

Freud's influence on Adler can be seen in the emphasis on the importance of early childhood and on the ideas that the motives that underlie neurosis are outside conscious awareness (private logic) and that it is only through insight into these motives that cure can be attained. It is largely in Adler's reaction against Freud, however, that Adler truly defined himself. He saw Freud as offering a mechanistic system in which individuals merely react according to instincts and their early childhood environment; Adler believed that individuals have choices about their futures. He saw Freud as emphasizing universal themes that are rigidly repeated in each patient; Adler believed that people fashion their unique styles of life. Adler saw Freud as being focused on the intrapsychic; Adler himself emphasized the interpersonal, social field.

While Freud's personality theory has been the best remembered, Adler's has been the most rediscovered. In the 1940's, holistic theorists such as Kurt Lewin and Kurt Goldstein reiterated Adler's emphasis on the individual's subjective and comprehensive approach to perceptions. In the 1960's, humanistic theorists such as Abraham Maslow and Carl Rogers rediscovered Adler's emphasis on individuals overcoming the conditions of their childhood and striving toward a self-actualization and potential to love. In the 1980's, cognitive theorists such as Albert Ellis, Aaron Beck, and Martin E. P. Seligman emphasized how individuals perceive and understand their situation as the central element underlying psychopathology.

STRENGTHS AND WEAKNESSES

An evaluation of individual psychology must necessarily include some enumeration of its weaknesses as well as its strengths. The positives are obvious: The theory is easy to comprehend, optimistic about human nature, and applicable to the understanding of a wide variety of issues. The weaknesses would be the other side of those very strengths. If a theory is so easy to comprehend, is it not then simplistic or merely a reformulation of common sense? This may explain why so many other theorists "rediscovered" Adler's ideas throughout the twentieth century. If a theory is so optimistic about human potential, can it present a balanced view of human nature? If a theory is flexible and broad enough as to be able to explain so much, can it be precise enough to explain anything with any depth? Although everything in individual psychology fits together as a unified whole, it is not always clear what the lines of reasoning are. Does excessive inferiority feeling preclude the formulation of social interest, or does social interest assuage inferiority feeling? Does inferiority feeling engender private logic, or does private logic sustain inferiority feeling? At different times, Adler and Adlerians seem to argue both sides of these questions. The Achilles heel of individual psychology (and of psychoanalysis) is prediction. If a given child is in a situation that heightens feelings of inferiority, will that child overcompensate effectively and develop social interest as an adult, or will private logic take over? If it does, will it be in the form of self-brooding or masculine protest?

Although the fuzziness of Adlerian concepts will preclude individual psychology from being a major force in academic psychology, it is safe to predict that future theorists will again rediscover many of Alfred Adler's concepts.

SOURCES FOR FURTHER STUDY

Adler, Alfred. *The Practice and Theory of Individual Psychology.* New York: Routledge, 1999. One in Routledge's International Library of Psychology series, reprinting classic, milestone works on psychology. Adler's own introduction to his work.

Bottome, Phyllis. *Alfred Adler: A Biography.* New York: G. P. Putnam's Sons, 1939. This classic biography was written only two years after Adler's death. It gives much insight into the man and his theory, but the book is a bit too laudatory.

Dreikurs, Rudolf. *Fundamentals of Adlerian Psychology.* 1950. Reprint. Chicago: Alfred Adler Institute, 1989. The author was an Adlerian disciple who became the leader of the Adlerian movement in the United States after World War II. His simple style and straightforward advice are in keeping with the style of Adler himself. Dreikurs's expertise was in the area of child development.

Ganz, Madelaine. *The Psychology of Alfred Adler and the Development of the Child.* New York: Routledge, 1999. Another in Routledge's International Library of Psychology series. A well-organized introduction to Adler's theories.

Mozak, Harold, and Michael Maniacci. *A Primer of Adlerian Psychology: The Analytic-Behavioral-Cognitive-Psychology of Alfred Adler.* New York: Brunner/Mazel, 1999. An introduction aimed at students, with summary and review questions at the end of each chapter.

Sweeney, Thomas. *Adlerian Counseling: A Practitioner's Approach.* 4th ed. Philadelphia: Taylor & Francis, 1998. Provides a practical overview of Adler's individual psychology. Written for practicing mental health professionals.

T. L. Brink

See also: Cognitive Psychology; Ego Psychology: Erik Erikson; Psychoanalytic Psychology; Psychoanalytic Psychology and Personality: Sigmund Freud.

Industrial/Organizational Psychology

Type of psychology: Social psychology
Fields of study: Group processes; motivation theory; social perception and cognition

Industrial/organizational psychology applies psychological research methods and theories to issues of importance in work organizations. From its beginnings as psychology applied to a few personnel topics, it has expanded to deal with almost all aspects of work, changing as they have.

Key concepts
- experimentation
- fairness in work settings
- field research
- industrial psychology
- organizational psychology
- scientific method

Industrial/organizational psychology (often shortened to I/O psychology) is a somewhat deceptive title for the field. Even when industrial psychology alone was used to label it, practitioners were involved with issues and activities far beyond solving industrial problems—for example, designing procedures for selecting salespeople, advertising methods, and reducing accidents on public transportation. "Organizational" suggests the application of knowledge to organizations, but the intended meaning is closer to "the study of forces that influence how people and their activities at work are organized."

In colleges and universities, I/O psychology is a long-recognized discipline. Graduate programs leading to the M.A. and, more commonly, Ph.D. degrees in this field are most typically offered within psychology departments, sometimes in collaboration with departments of business; occasionally they are offered by business departments alone. In most cases, students working toward graduate degrees in I/O psychology first study a wide range of psychological topics, then study in even greater detail those that make up the I/O specialty. The study of research methods, statistical tools for evaluating findings, motivation, personality, and so on forms a base from which psychological testing, interviewing, job analysis, and performance evaluation are studied in depth.

Evolution of Study

Psychologists were certainly not the first to study work settings and suggest changes, or even the first to apply the scientific method to the enterprise. For example, Frederick Winslow Taylor and Frank Gilbreth were industrial engineers who considered workers not too different from cogs in the machines also involved in industry. Their "time and motion" studies sought to discover how workers could most efficiently carry out their parts of the enterprise. Although their conclusions are often now cited as examples of inhumane manipulation of workers for companies' benefits, Taylor and Gilbreth envisioned that both workers and employers were to gain from increases in efficiency. Not surprisingly, most of what industrial engineering studied was appropriated by industrial psychology and remains part of I/O psychology—usually under the designations "job design" and "human factors engineering" in the United States, or the designation "ergonomics" elsewhere.

Early psychologists had an advantage over the others studying and offering advice about work. They were popularly identified as people experts, and for the many problems thought to be based on human characteristics or limitations, their expertise was acknowledged, even while it was very modest. The advantage of being expected to make valuable contributions was put to good use, and within the first two decades of the twentieth century, industrial psychology became a recognized discipline with the ability to deliver most of what was expected of it.

Ironically, wars materially aided the early development of industrial and organizational psychology. World War I provided psychologists unprecedented opportunities to try intelligence testing on a very large scale and to develop and implement a very large personnel program. Robert Yerkes directed the intelligence testing of more than one million men between 1917 and 1919, and Walter Dill Scott and Walter Van Dyke Bingham interviewed and classified more than three million men before the war ended.

Testing, interviewing, and classification were also part of industrial psychologists' efforts during World War II, and many other lines of research and application were also pursued. Human factors engineering, which emphasized machine design tailored to the people who would use the device, was greatly advanced by the necessity that people be able to control aircraft and other sophisticated weapons.

Following each war, some of the psychologists who had successfully worked together chose to continue to do so. Major consulting firms grew out of their associations and remain a source of employment for many I/O psychologists.

METHODS OF RESEARCH
Industrial/organizational psychology borrowed much from many other areas of psychology during its growth and has retained the strong research orientation common to them, along with many of the research methods each has developed and many of the findings that each has generated. Bringing psychological methods to work settings where experts from many other disciplines are studying some of the same problems results in conflicts, but it also produces a richness of information beyond the scope of any one of the disciplines.

In most cases, the most feasible approach to data collection for I/O psychologists is field research, an approach in which evidence is gathered in a "natural" setting, such as the workplace. (By contrast, laboratory research involves an artificial, contrived setting.) Systematic observation of ongoing work can often give a psychologist needed information without greatly disturbing the workers involved. Generally, they will be told that data are being gathered, but when the known presence of an observer likely would change what is being studied, unobtrusive methods might be used. Information from hidden cameras, or observations from researchers pretending to be workers and actually engaging in whatever must be done, can be used when justified.

Again studying within the actual work setting, I/O psychologists may sometimes take advantage of natural experiments, situations in which a change not deliberately introduced may be studied for its effect on some important outcome. If, for example, very extreme, unseasonable temperatures resulted in uncontrollably high, or low, temperatures in an office setting, a psychologist could assess the effects on employee discomfort, absenteeism, or productivity.

Still studying within the actual work setting, an I/O psychologist may arrange a quasi-experiment, a situation in which the researcher changes some factor to assess its effect while having only partial control over other factors that might influence that change. For example, the psychologist might study the effects of different work schedules by assigning one schedule to one department of a company, a second schedule to a second department, and a third schedule to a third department. The departments, the people, and the differences in the work itself would prevent the strategy from being a true experiment, but it still could produce some useful data.

An experiment, as psychology and other sciences define it, is difficult to arrange within work settings, but it may be worth the effort to evaluate information gathered by other methods. In the simplest form of experiment, the researcher randomly assigns the people studied into two groups and, while holding constant all other factors that might influence the experiment's outcome, presents some condition (known as an independent variable) to one group of subjects (the experimental group) and withholds it from another (the control group). Finally, the researcher measures the outcome (the dependent variable) for both groups.

Carrying out a true experiment almost always requires taking the people involved away from their typical activities into a setting obviously designed for study (usually called the laboratory, even though it may bear little resemblance to a laboratory of, say, a chemist). The need to establish a new, artificial setting and the need to pull workers away from their work to gather information are both troublesome, as is the risk that what is learned in the laboratory setting may not hold true back in the natural work setting.

Correlational methods, borrowed from psychometrics, complement the observational and experimental techniques just described. Correlation is a mathematical technique for comparing the similarity of two sets of data (literally, to determine their co-relation). An important example of the I/O psychologist's seeking information on relationships is found in the process of hiring-test validation, answering the question of the extent to which test scores and eventual work performance are correlated. To establish validity, a researcher must demonstrate a substantial relationship between scores and performance, evidence that the test is measuring what is intended.

APPLICATIONS IN THE WORKPLACE

Industrial/organizational psychology, as the term implies, focuses on two broad areas; Linda Jewell and Marc Siegall, in their *Contemporary Industrial/Organizational Psychology* (3d ed., 1998), demonstrate this by their arrangement of topics. Industrial topics include testing; job analysis and evaluation; recruitment, selection, and placement of applicants; employee training and socialization; evaluation of employee job performance; job design; working conditions; health and safety; and motivation. Organizational topics include a company's social system and communication, groups within organizations, leadership, and organizational change and development. Topics of overlap of the two areas include absenteeism, turnover, job commitment, job satisfaction, employee development, and quality of work life.

Testing in I/O psychology most often is done to assess peoples' aptitudes or abilities as a basis for making selection, placement, or promotion decisions about them. It may also be used for other purposes—for example, to judge the quality of training programs. The tests used range from ones of general aptitude (IQ, or intelligence quotient, tests) through tests of specific aptitudes, interests, and personality, although use of IQ and personality tests remains controversial. Aptitude for success in academically related activity (as might be related to one's IQ) is often of only modest importance in work settings, but the folk wisdom "the best person is the most intelligent person" can lead to giving IQ tests routinely to applicants. Personality is a troublesome concept within psychology. Tests of it can be useful to clinicians working with mental health issues but are rarely useful as bases for employment-related decisions. When outcomes from personality testing are specific enough to be useful—for example, when they reveal serious personality problems—the same information is usually obtainable from reviews of work history or from interviews.

Along with other procedures related to making decisions about people in work settings, testing is often targeted as being unfair to some groups—for example, African Americans or women. If the use of a particular test results in decision making that even suggests unfair discrimination, companies must have available solid evidence that this is not the case, if they choose to continue using the test.

Job analysis determines what tasks must be carried out in a job. It serves as the major basis for deciding what skills successful job applicants must have or what training to provide newly hired workers. The evaluation of job performances of individual employees must be based on what they should be doing, revealed by job analysis. Dismissal, retention, promotion, and wage increases may all be related to job analysis information. It is also a basis for job evaluation, the determining of what is appropriate pay for the job, although evaluation often must also be based on the availability of applicants, average wages in a geographic area, and other factors.

Recruiting, selecting, and placing refer to sequential steps in filling positions. Although some companies can let prospective employees come to them, many prefer actively to seek applicants. Recruiting may involve little more than announcing that a position is open or as much as sending trained representatives to find promising people and encourage them to apply for work. At least two considerations make vigorous recruiting attractive. First, it is often possible for companies to reduce training costs greatly by finding applicants who are already proficient. Second, when minority-group employees are needed to achieve fair balance in an organization, recruiting can often focus on members of ethnic minorities or women.

Although training may be unnecessary if a company is able to hire already-skilled people, training is generally advantageous after hiring and periodically over a worker's tenure. Promotion may be based on success in training, or training may follow promotion based on other considerations. Although "training" suggests the development or enhancement of job skills, it often also includes socialization, the bringing of new employees into the "family" of the company and the teaching of values, goals, and expectations that extend beyond carrying out a specific work assignment. Job design, working conditions, health and safety, and motivation are usually given separate chapters in texts, but often in work settings they must be considered as a set. For example, if a job, as designed, forces or even encourages workers to put their health or safety at risk, their working conditions are unsatisfactory, and when they recognize the nature of the situation, their motivation is likely to be impaired.

LEGAL AND ETHICAL REQUIREMENTS

When industrial psychologists of the early twentieth century recommended hiring or promotion, designed training, or carried out any other of their responsibilities, they had only to satisfy their employers' demands. Since the late 1960's, I/O psychologists have also had to satisfy legal and ethical requirements pertaining to a host of problem areas such as racism, sexism, age discrimination, and discrimination against the handicapped. More than good intentions are necessary here. The psychologists must work to balance the societal demands for fairness in work settings (the basing of decisions about workers' hiring, salary, promotion, and so on entirely on work-relevant considerations and not on race, sex, age, or other personal characteristics) and the practical interests of employers, sometimes having to endure criticism for even the most ingenious of solutions.

For example, if an employer finds the company must increase its number of Latino workers, vigorous recruiting is an excellent first step, yet it may prove expensive enough to aggravate the employer. If recruiting is not successful because would-be applicants doubt the employer's sincerity, both they and the employer will be unhappy. If recruiting is successful in generating interest, but many interested individuals are unqualified, providing them special training could be a reasonable solution. Applicants might feel it degrading, however, to be required to undergo more training than others before them, or the employer might balk at the extra cost involved.

The first industrial psychologists needed little more than solid training in their discipline to achieve success. Their successors need, beyond training in a discipline that has enlarged enormously, the talents of diplomats.

SOURCES FOR FURTHER STUDY

Anderson, Neil, Deniz S. Ones, and Handan Kepir Sinangil, eds. *Handbook of Industrial, Work, and Organization Psychology.* 2 vols. Thousand Oaks, Calif.: Sage, 2002. Volume 1 focuses on industrial psychology theories, techniques, and methods. Volume 2 offers specific case studies in topics such as motivation, leadership, organizational justice, and organizational development and change.

Hilgard, Ernest Ropiequet. *Psychology in America: A Historical Survey.* San Diego, Calif.: Harcourt Brace Jovanovich, 1987. Chapter 19, "Industrial and Organizational Psychology," is a definitive review of about eighty years of the field's advancement from a promising application of the new "scientific psychology" to a major subdiscipline of modern psychology. The subject is also covered in some of Hilgard's other chapters (for example, those on intelligence, on motivation, and on social psychology).

Jewell, Linda N., and Marc Siegall. *Contemporary Industrial/Organizational Psychology.* 3d ed. Belmont, Calif.: Wadsworth, 1998. A text for an introductory college course offering excellent coverage of the discipline's topics. Written for students majoring in business as much as for those majoring in psychology. A book that almost anyone can understand.

Rogelberg, Steven, ed. *Blackwell Handbook of Research Methods in Industrial and Organizational Psychology.* New York: Blackwell, 2002. A comprehensive overview of the field, useful to beginners and experts alike. Addresses both practical and theoretical issues of industrial psychology.

Rosenzweig, Mark R., and Lyman W. Porter, eds. *Annual Review of Psychology.* Stanford, Calif.: Annual Reviews. Most volumes of this highly respected series contain a chapter or two on I/O psychology, indexed under "Personnel-Organizational Psychology." Each volume also contains a chapter title index for at least the previous decade, making location of particular topics reasonably easy.

Harry A. Tiemann, Jr.

SEE ALSO: Motivation.

INSTINCT THEORY

TYPE OF PSYCHOLOGY: Motivation
FIELDS OF STUDY: Biological influences on learning; motivation theory

Until behaviorism, which rejected instincts, became the dominant theoretical model for psychology during the early decades of the twentieth century, instinct theory was often used to explain both animal and human motivation. As behaviorism faded, aspects of instinct theory returned to psychology—modernized, but still recognizable as parts of the oldest theory of motivation.

KEY CONCEPTS
- behaviorism
- instinct
- motivation
- reflex
- scientific method
- tropism

When instinct theory was incorporated into the new scientific psychology of the late nineteenth century, it was already centuries old. In its earliest form, instinct theory specified that a creature's essential nature was already established at birth and that its actions would largely be directed by that nature. A modern restatement of this notion would be that, at birth, creatures are already programmed and that they must operate according to their programs.

Charles Darwin's theory of evolution through natural selection, first published in 1859, led to great controversy in the late nineteenth and early twentieth centuries. It also fostered speculation that, if humans were evolved from earlier forms and were therefore more closely related to other animals than had once been believed, humans might have instincts—inherited behaviors—as other animals were observed to have. William McDougall was one of the main early instinct theorists; he suggested a list of human instincts in 1908 that included such varied behaviors as repulsion, curiosity, self-abasement, and gregariousness. Many researchers came up with their own lists of human instincts; by the 1920's, more than two thousand had been suggested.

A computer program can be printed out and studied, but an instinct in the original sense cannot so easily be made explicit. At best, it can be inferred from the behavior of an animal or person after other explanations for that behavior have been discounted. At worst, it is simply assumed from observing behavior. That a person has, for example, an instinct of argumentativeness could be assumed from the person's arguing; arguing is then "explained" by declaring that it comes from an instinct of argumentativeness. Such circular reasoning is unacceptable in scientific analyses, but it is very common in some early scientific (and many modern, popular) discussions of instinct.

VARIATIONS IN THEORY

As is often the case with ideas that have long been believed by both scientists and the public, instinct theory has separated into several theories. The earliest form was accepted by Aristotle, the ancient Greek philosopher and scientist. He wrote in his *Politics* that "a social instinct is implanted in all men by nature" and stated that "a man would be thought a coward if he had no more courage than a courageous woman, and a woman would be thought loquacious if she imposed no more restraint on her conversation than the good man." The first comment declares an inherent quality of people; the second, inherent qualities of men and women. Very likely, Aristotle's beliefs were based on observation of people around him—a good beginning but not a sufficient basis for making factual comments about people in general.

Aristotle's views were those of a scientist of his day. Centuries later, a scientist would not hold such views, but a layperson very well might. Over the many centuries since Aristotle expressed his views on instinct theory, "popular" versions of it have been more influential than the cautious versions offered by later scientists.

HISTORIC MISINTERPRETATIONS

Modern science reaches conclusions based, to the greatest extent possible, on evidence gathered and interpreted along lines suggested by theories. Traditional instinct theory is especially weak in suggesting such lines; usually it put early psychologists in the position of trying to support the idea that instinct had caused a behavior by demonstrating that nothing else had caused it. Rather than supporting one possibility, they were attempting to deny dozens of others. Even worse, they were forcing thought into an "either-or" pattern rather than allowing for the possibility that a behavior may be based on inherited influences interacting with learned ones.

For example, to try to evaluate the possibility that people are instinctively afraid of snakes, one could begin by finding a number of people afraid of snakes, followed by an attempt to discount all the ways in which those individuals might have learned their fear—that they had never been harmed by a snake, never been startled, never been told that snakes are dangerous, and so on. The task is all but impossible, almost guaranteeing that a researcher will conclude that there are several ways that the fear could have been learned, so there is no need for an instinct explanation. The fact that people who fear snakes can learn not to fear them can be offered as further evidence that they had learned their original fear—not a particularly compelling argument.

When behaviorism became the predominant theoretical stance of psychology in the 1920's, the problems with instinct as an explanation of motivation were "resolved" simply by sidestepping them. Instincts were discarded as unscientific, and other concepts—such as needs, drives, and motives—were substituted for them. Psychology's dropping of the term "instinct" from its jargon did not eliminate, either for lower animals or for people, the behaviors it had originally labeled. Dropping the term did, however, separate even further the popular views of instinct from the scientific ones.

REEMERGENCE OF "HUMAN NATURE" RESEARCH

Instinct theory's purpose in psychology's infancy was the same as it had once been in the distant past: to explain motivation of a variety of species, from the simplest creatures up through humans. Unfortunately, it had also served other purposes in the past, purposes which often proved unwelcome to early behavioral scientists. To declare people superior to other animals, or men superior to women, or almost any target group better or worse than another was not a goal of psychology.

Worse than the heritage of centuries of misuse of the concept of instinct, however, was the accumulation of evidence that instincts (as originally defined, as completely unlearned behavior) were limited to simple creatures and were virtually nonexistent in people. Psychology and related sciences virtually eliminated instinct as a motivational concept for decades, yet they could not avoid bringing back similar notions. The term "instinct" was gone, but what it tried to explain was not. For example, social psychologists, working in the 1940's to find alternatives to the belief that aggression is instinctive in humans, proposed that frustration (goal blocking) is a major cause. When pressed to explain why frustration led to aggression, many indicated that this is simply part of human nature. Some years later, it was demonstrated that the presence of some sort of weapon during a frustrating experience enhanced the likelihood of aggression, apparently through a "triggering effect." Instinct as a concept was not invoked, but these ideas came very close.

Even closer was the work of another group of scientists, ethologists, in their explanations of some animal behaviors. Evaluating what might be thought a good example of instinct in its earliest definition, a duckling following its mother, they demonstrated that experience with a moving object is necessary. In other words, learning (but learning limited to a very brief period in the duckling's development) led to the behavior. Many other seemingly strong examples of instinct were demonstrated to be a consequence of some inner predisposition interacting with environmental circumstances. A new, useful rethinking of the ancient instinct concept had begun.

INSTINCTIVE INFLUENCES

A 1961 article by Keller and Marian Breland suggested that instinct should still be a part of psychology, despite its period of disgrace. In training performing animals, the scientists witnessed a phenomenon they termed "instinctive drift." (It is interesting to note that although other terms, such as "species-specific behavior," were at that time preferred to "instinct," the Brelands stated their preference for the original label.) Instinctive drift refers to the tendency of a creature's trained behavior to move in the direction of inherited predispositions.

The Brelands tried to teach pigs to place coins in a piggy bank; they found that although the pigs could easily be taught to pick up coins and run toward the bank, they could not be stopped from repeatedly dropping and rooting at them. Raccoons could be taught to drop coins in a container but could not be stopped from "dipping" the coins in and rubbing them together, a drift toward the instinctive washing of food. Several other species presented similar problems to their would-be trainers, all related to what the Brelands willingly called instinct.

Preparedness is another example of an instinct/learning relationship. Through conditioning, any creature can be taught to associate some previously neutral stimuli with a behavior. Dogs in Ivan Pavlov's laboratory at the beginning of the twentieth century readily learned to salivate at the sound of a bell, a signal that food would appear immediately. While some stimuli can easily serve as signals for a particular species, others cannot. It seems clear that animals are prepared by nature for some sorts of learning but not others. Rats can readily be trained to press a lever (a bar in a Skinner box) to obtain food, and pigeons can readily be trained to peck at something to do so, but there are some behaviors that they simply cannot learn to serve that purpose.

Conditioned taste aversion is yet another example of an instinctive influence that has been well documented by modern psychology. In people and other animals, nausea following the taste of food very consistently leads to that taste becoming aversive. The taste/nausea combination is specific; electric shock following a taste does not cause the taste to become aversive, nor does a visual stimulus followed by nausea cause the sight to become aversive. Researchers theorize that the ability to learn to detect and avoid tainted food has survival value, so it has become instinctive.

LIMITATIONS AND MISUSE OF THEORY

In popular use, belief in instincts has confused and hurt people more than it has enlightened or helped them. Instinct theory often imposes a rigid either-or form on people's thinking about human motivation. That is, people are encouraged by the notion of instinct to wonder if some behavior—aggression, for example—is either inherent in people or learned from experience.

Once one's thoughts are cast into such a mold, one is less likely to consider the strong likelihood that a behavior has multiple bases, which may be different from one person to the next. Instead of looking for the many possible reasons for human aggression—some related to inherent qualities and some related to learned qualities—one looks for a single cause. Often, intently focusing on one possibility to the exclusion of all others blinds people to the very fact that they are doing so. Searching for "the" answer, they fail to recognize that their very method of searching has locked their thinking onto a counterproductive track.

Instinct theory has been invoked to grant humans special status above that of other animals. Generally, this argument states that humans can reason and rationally control their actions, while lower animals are guided solely by instincts. At best, this argument has been used to claim that humans are especially loved by their god. At worst, the idea that lower animals are supposedly guided only by instinct was used by philosopher René Descartes to claim that animals are essentially automatons, incapable of actually feeling pain, and that therefore they could be vivisected without anesthesia.

Instinct theory has also been used to support the claim that some people are more worthy than other people. Those with fewer "base instincts," or even those who by their rationality have overcome them, are supposedly superior. Acceptance of such ideas has led to very real errors of judgment and considerable human suffering. For example, over many centuries, across much of the world, it was believed that women, simply by virtue of being female, were not capable of sufficiently clear thinking to justify providing them with a formal education, allowing them to own property, or letting them hold elected office or vote. Anthropologist Margaret Mead, in her 1942 book *And Keep Your Powder Dry: An Anthropologist Looks at America*, reports reversal of the claim that women inherently lack some important quality. Young women in her classes, when told the then-prevailing view that people had no instincts and therefore that they had no maternal instinct became very upset, according to Mead, believing that they lacked something essential. Many minority racial or ethnic groups have suffered in similar fashion from claims that, by their unalterable nature, they are incapable of behaving at levels comparable to those in the majority.

Instinct theory has been used to suggest the absolute inevitability of many undesirable behaviors, sometimes as a way of excusing them. The ideas that philandering is part of a man's nature or that gossiping is part of a woman's are patently foolish uses of the concept of instinct.

SOURCES FOR FURTHER STUDY

Birney, Robert Charles, and Richard C. Teevan. *Instinct: An Enduring Problem in Psychology*. Princeton, N.J.: Van Nostrand, 1961. A collection of readings intended for college students. Contains fourteen articles, ranging from William James's 1887 discussion of instinct to Frank Beach's 1955 "The Descent of Instinct," in which Beach traces the idea of instinct from the time of the ancient Greeks up to the 1950's and concludes that "the instinct concept has survived in almost complete absence of empirical validation."

Breland, Keller, and Marian Breland. "The Misbehavior of Organisms." *American Psychologist* 16 (November, 1961): 681-684. In the process of training performing animals, the Brelands were forced to contend with inherited behaviors of their pupils. This article alerted a generation of psychologists to the possibility that instinct had been inappropriately eliminated from their thinking. The writing is clear and amusing, and the article should be fairly easy to locate; most college and university libraries will have the journal.

Cofer, Charles Norval, and M. H. Appley. *Motivation: Theory and Research.* New York: John Wiley & Sons, 1964. Long regarded as a classic on the topic of motivation, this book includes (in chapter 2, "Motivation in Historical Perspective") thirty-two pages of material that traces instinct through the centuries. Chapter 3, "The Concept of Instinct: Ethological Position," discusses ways the once discredited concept was returning to psychology in the early 1960's.

Hilgard, Ernest Ropiequet. *Psychology in America: A Historical Survey.* San Diego, Calif.: Harcourt Brace Jovanovich, 1987. The material Hilgard covers is often complex, but his clear organization and writing make it accessible to most readers. Material related to instinct in several chapters (for example, those on motivation, comparative psychology, and social psychology) can help a reader gain further background on instinct's place in psychology.

Mead, Margaret. *And Keep Your Powder Dry: An Anthropologist Looks at America.* 1942. Reprint. New York: Berghahn Books, 2000. The classic by Mead on Western contemporary cultures.

Watson, John Broadus. *Behaviorism.* 1924. Reprint. New Brunswick, N.J.: Transaction, 1998. The fifth chapter of Watson's popular presentation of the new psychology he was sponsoring ("Are There Any Human Instincts?") nicely illustrates how behaviorism handled instinct. This chapter contains Watson's famous declaration, "Give me a dozen healthy infants, well-formed, and my own specified world to bring them up in and I'll guarantee to take any one at random and train him to become any type of specialist I might select. . . . " Watson's writing is still charming, but his position is today mainly a curiosity.

Weiten, Wayne. *Psychology: Themes and Variations.* 6th ed. Belmont, Calif.: Thomson/Wadsworth, 2004. Introductory psychology texts all have some coverage of instinct's return to psychology and, more important, describe how several other concepts have been introduced to deal with topics with which instinct was once inappropriately linked. Weiten's text is one of the best: easy and interesting to read, yet strong in its coverage of scientific psychology.

Harry A. Tiemann, Jr.

SEE ALSO: Aggression; Behaviorism; Conditioning; Drives; Imprinting; Learning; Motivation; Reflexes.

INTELLIGENCE

TYPE OF PSYCHOLOGY: Intelligence and intelligence testing
FIELDS OF STUDY: General issues in intelligence; intelligence assessment

Intelligence is a hypothetical concept, rather than a tangible entity, that is used by psychologists and other scientists to explain differences in the quality and adaptive value of the behavior of humans and, to some extent, animals. Its meaning and the theoretical models used to explore it are as varied as the field of psychology itself.

KEY CONCEPTS
- cognitive psychology
- correlation
- factor
- factor analysis
- heritability

The idea that human beings differ in their capacity to adapt to their environments, to learn from experience, to exercise various skills, and to succeed at various endeavors has existed since ancient times. Intelligence is the attribute most often singled out as responsible for successful adaptations. Up to the end of the nineteenth century, notions about what constitutes intelligence and how differences in intelligence arise were mostly speculative. In the late nineteenth century, several trends converged to bring about an event that would change the way in which intelligence was seen and dramatically influence the way it would be studied. That event, which occurred in 1905, was the publication of the first useful instrument for measuring intelligence, the Binet-Simon scale, which was developed in France by Alfred Binet and Théodore Simon.

Although the development of intelligence tests was a great technological accomplishment, it occurred, in a sense, somewhat prematurely, before much scientific attention had been paid to the concept of intelligence. This circumstance tied the issue of defining intelligence and a large part of the research into its nature and origins to the limitations of the tests that had been devised. In fact, the working definition of intelligence that many psychologists have used either explicitly or implicitly in their scientific and applied pursuits is the one expressed by Edwin Boring in 1923, which holds that intelligence is whatever intelligence tests measure. Most psychologists realize that this definition is redundant and inadequate in that it erroneously implies that the tests are perfectly accurate and able to capture all that is meant by the concept. Nevertheless, psychologists and others have proceeded to use the tests as if the definition were true, mainly because of a scarcity of viable alternatives.

The general public has also been led astray by the existence of "intelligence" tests and the frequent misuse of their results. Many people have come to think of the intelligence quotient, or IQ, not as a simple score achieved on a particular test, which it is, but as a complete and stable measure of intellectual capacity, which it most definitely is not. Such misconceptions have led to an understandable resistance toward and resentment of intelligence tests.

CHANGING DEFINITIONS

Boring's semifacetious definition of intelligence may be the best known and most criticized one, but it is only one among many that have been offered. Most experts in the field have defined the concept at least once in their careers. Two of the most frequently cited and influential definitions are the ones provided by Alfred Binet himself and by David Wechsler, author of a series of "second-generation" individual intelligence tests that overtook the Binet scales in terms of the frequency with which they are used. Binet believed that the essential activities of intelligence are to judge well, to comprehend well, and to reason well. He stated that intelligent thought is characterized by direction, knowing what to do and how to do it; by adaptation, the capacity to monitor one's strategies for attaining a desired end; and by criticism, the power to evaluate and control one's behavior. In 1975, almost sixty-five years after Binet's death, Wechsler defined intelligence, not dissimilarly, as the global capacity of the individual to act purposefully, to think rationally, and to deal effectively with the environment.

In addition to the testing experts (psychometricians), developmental, learning, and cognitive psychologists, among others, are also vitally interested in the concept of intelligence. Specialists in each of these subfields emphasize different aspects of it in their definitions and research.

Representative definitions were sampled in 1921, when the *Journal of Educational Psychology* published the views of fourteen leading investigators, and again in 1986, when Robert Sternberg and Douglas Detterman collected the opinions of twenty-four experts in a book titled *What Is Intelligence? Contemporary Viewpoints on Its Nature and Definition*. Most of the experts sampled in 1921 offered definitions that equated intelligence with one or more specific abilities. For example, Lewis Terman equated it with abstract thinking, which is the ability to elaborate concepts and to use language and other symbols. Others proposed definitions that emphasized the ability to adapt or learn. Some definitions centered on knowledge and cognitive components only, whereas others included nonintellectual qualities, such as perseverance.

In comparison, Sternberg's and Detterman's 1986 survey of definitions, which is even more wide ranging, is accompanied by an organizational framework consisting of fifty-five categories or combinations of categories under which the twenty-four definitions can be classified. Some theorists view intelligence from a biological perspective and emphasize differences across species or the role of the central nervous system. Some stress cognitive aspects of mental functioning, while others focus on the role of motivation and goals. Still others, such as Anne Anastasi, choose to look upon intelligence as a quality that is inherent in behavior rather than in the individual.

Another major perspective highlights the role of the environment, in terms of demands and values, in defining what constitutes intelligent behavior. Throughout the 1986 survey, one can find definitions that straddle two or more categories.

A review of the 1921 and 1986 surveys shows that the definitions proposed have become considerably more sophisticated and suggests that, as the field of psychology has expanded, the views of experts on intelligence may have grown farther apart. The reader of the 1986 work is left with the clear impression that intelligence is such a multifaceted concept that no single quality can define it and no single task or series of tasks can capture it completely. Moreover, it is clear that in order to unravel the qualities that produce intelligent behavior, one must look not only at individuals and their skills but also at the requirements of the systems in which people find themselves. In other words, intelligence cannot be defined in a vacuum.

New intelligence research focuses on different ways to measure intelligence and on paradigms for improving or training intellectual abilities and skills. Measurement paradigms allow researchers to understand ongoing processing abilities. Some intelligence researchers include measures of intellectual style and motivation in their models.

FACTOR ANALYSIS

The lack of a universally accepted definition has not deterred continuous theorizing and research on the concept of intelligence. The central issue that has dominated theoretical models of intelligence is the question of whether it is a single, global ability or a collection of specialized abilities. This debate, started in England by Charles Spearman, is based on research that uses the correlations among various measures of abilities and, in particular, the method of factor analysis, which was also pioneered by Spearman. As early as 1904, Spearman, having examined the patterns of correlation coefficients among tests of sensory discrimination and estimates of intelligence, proposed that all mental functions are the result of a single general factor, which he later designated g.

Spearman equated g with the ability to grasp and apply relations. He also allowed for the fact that most tasks require unique abilities, and he named those s, or specific, factors. According to Spearman, to the extent that performance on tasks was positively correlated, the correlation was attributable to the presence of g, whereas the presence of specific factors tended to lower the correlation between measures of performance on different tasks.

By 1927, Spearman had modified his theory to allow for the existence of an intermediate class of factors, known as group factors, which were neither as universal as g nor as narrow as the s factors. Group factors were seen as accounting for the fact that certain types of activities, such as tasks involving the use of numbers or the element of speed, correlate more highly with one another than they do with tasks that do not have such elements in common.

Factor-analytic research has undergone explosive growth and extensive variations and refinements in both England and the United States since the 1920's. In the United States, work in this field was influenced greatly by Truman Kelley, whose 1928 book *Crossroads in the Mind of Man* presented a method for isolating group factors, and L. L. Thurstone, who by further elaboration of factor-analytic procedures identified a set of about twelve factors that he designated as the "primary mental abilities." Seven of these were repeatedly found in a number of investigations, using samples of people at different age levels, that were carried out by both Thurstone and others. These group factors or primary mental abilities are verbal comprehension, word fluency, speed and accuracy of arithmetic computation, spatial visualization, associative memory, perceptual speed, and general reasoning.

ORGANIZATIONAL MODELS

As the search for distinct intellectual factors progressed, their number multiplied, and so did the number of models devised to organize them. One type of scheme, used by Cyril Burt, Philip Vernon, and others, is a hierarchical arrangement of factors. In these models, Spearman's g factor is placed at the top of a pyramid, and the specific factors are placed at the bottom. In between, there are one or more levels of group factors selected in terms of their breadth and arranged according to their interrelationships with the more general factors above them and the more specific factors below them.

In Vernon's scheme, for example, the ability to change a tire might be classified as a specific factor at the base of the pyramid, located underneath an intermediate group factor labeled mechanical information, which in turn would be under one of the two major group factors identified by Vernon as the main subdivisions under g—namely, the practical-mechanical factor. The hierarchical scheme for organizing mental abilities is a useful device that is endorsed by many psychologists on both sides of the Atlantic Ocean. It recognizes that very few tasks are so simple as to require a single skill for successful performance, that many intellectual functions have some common elements, and that some abilities play a more pivotal role than others in the performance of culturally valued activities.

Another well-known scheme for organizing intellectual traits is the structure-of-intellect (SOI) model developed by J. P. Guilford. Although the SOI is grounded in extensive factor-analytic research conducted by Guilford throughout the 1940's and 1950's, the model goes beyond factor analysis and is perhaps the most ambitious attempt to classify systematically all the possible functions of the human intellect. The SOI classifies intellectual traits along three dimensions—namely, five types of operations, four types of contents, and six types of productions, for a total of 120 categories $(5 \times 4 \times 6)$. Intellectual operations consist of what a person actually does (for example, evaluating or remembering something), the contents are the types of materials or information on which the operations are performed (for example, symbols, such as letters or numbers), and the products are the form in which the contents are processed (for example, units or relations).

Not all the 120 categories in Guilford's complex model have been used, but enough factors have been identified to account for about 100 of them, and some have proved very useful in labeling and understanding the skills that tests measure. Furthermore, Guilford's model has served to call attention to some dimensions of intellectual activity, such as creativity and interpersonal skills, that had been neglected previously.

COMPETENCE AND SELF-MANAGEMENT

Modern theorists in the area of intelligence have tried to avoid the reliance on factor analysis and existing tests that have limited traditional research and have tried different approaches to the subject. For example, Howard Gardner, in his 1983 book *Frames of Mind: The Theory of Multiple Intelligences*, starts with the premises that the essence of intelligence is competence and that there are several distinct areas in which human beings can demonstrate competence. Based on a wide-ranging review of evidence from many scientific fields and sources, Gardner designated seven areas of competence as separate and relatively independent "intelligences." In his 1993 work *Multiple Intelligences*, Gardner revised his theory to include an eighth type of intelligence. This set of attributes is comprised of verbal, mathematical, spatial, bodily/kinesthetic, musical, interpersonal, intrapersonal, and naturalist skills.

Another theory is the one proposed by Robert Sternberg in his 1985 book *Beyond IQ: A Triarchic Theory of Human Intelligence*. Sternberg defines intelligence, broadly, as mental self-management and stresses the "real-world," in addition to the academic, aspects of the concept. He believes that intelligent behavior consists of purposively adapting to, selecting, and shaping one's environment and that both culture and personality play significant roles in such behavior. Sternberg posits that differences in IQ scores reflect differences in individuals' stages of developing the expertise measured by the particular IQ test, rather than attributing these scores to differences in intelligence, ability, or aptitude. Sternberg's model has five key elements: metacognitive skills, learning skills, thinking skills, knowledge, and motivation. The elements all influence one another. In this work, Sternberg claims that measurements derived from ability and achievement tests are not different in kind; only in the point at which the measurements are being make.

INTELLIGENCE AND ENVIRONMENT

Theories of intelligence are still grappling with the issues of defining its nature and composition. Generally, newer theories do not represent radical departures from the past. They do, however, emphasize examining intelligence in relation to the variety of environments in which people actually live rather than to only academic or laboratory environments. Moreover, many investigators, especially those in cognitive psychology, are more interested in breaking down and replicating the steps involved in information processing and problem solving than they are in enumerating factors or settling on a single definition of intelligence. These trends hold the promise of moving the work in the field in the direction of devising new ways to teach people to understand, evaluate, and deal with their environments more intelligently instead of simply measuring how well they do on intelligence tests. In their 1998 article "Teaching Triarchically Improves School Achievement," Sternberg and his colleagues note that teaching or training interventions can be linked directly to components of intelligence. Motivation also plays a role. In their 2000 article "Intrinsic and Extrinsic Motivation," Richard Ryan and Edward Deci provide a review of modern thinking about intrinsic and extrinsic motivation. The authors suggest that the use of motivational strategies should promote student self-determination.

The most heated of all the debates about intelligence is the one regarding its determinants, often described as the "nature-nurture" controversy. The "nature" side of the debate was spearheaded by Francis Galton, a nineteenth century English scientist who had become convinced that intelligence was a hereditary trait. Galton's followers tried to show, through studies comparing identical and nonidentical twins raised together and raised apart and by comparisons of people related to each other in varying degrees, that genetic endowment plays a far larger role than the environment in determining intelligence. Attempts to quantify an index of heritability for intelligence through such studies abound, and the estimates derived from them vary widely. On the "nurture" side of the debate, massive quantities of data have been gathered in an effort to show that the environment, including factors such as prenatal care, social-class membership, exposure to certain facilitative experiences, and educational opportunities of all sorts, has the more crucial role in determining a person's level of intellectual functioning.

Many critics, such as Anastasi (in a widely cited 1958 article entitled "Heredity, Environment, and the Question 'How?'") have pointed out the futility of debating how much each factor contributes to intelligence. Anastasi and others argue that behavior is a function of the interaction between heredity and the total experiential history of individuals and that, from the moment of conception, the two are inextricably tied. Moreover, they point out that, even if intelligence were shown to be primarily determined by heredity, environmental influences could still modify its expression at any point. Most psychologists now accept this "interactionist" position and have moved on to explore how intelligence develops and how specific genetic and environmental factors affect it.

Sources for Further Study

Fancher, Raymond E. *The Intelligence Men: Makers of the IQ Controversy.* New York: W. W. Norton, 1985. Presents the history of the various debates on intelligence in a highly readable fashion. The lives and ideas of the pioneers in the field, such as Alfred Binet and Francis Galton, are described in some detail.

Gardner, Howard. *Frames of Mind: The Theory of Multiple Intelligences.* 2d ed. New York: Basic Books, 1993. Gardner's description of the talents he designates as "intelligences" and explanation of the reasons for his selections provide a fascinating introduction to many of the most intriguing aspects of the field, including the extremes of prodigies and prodigious savants.

_____. *Multiple Intelligences: Theory into Practice.* New York: Basic Books, 1993. Gardner's update of his original theory of multiple intelligences adds an eighth intelligence to the set.

Guilford, Joy Paul. *The Nature of Human Intelligence.* New York: McGraw-Hill, 1967. Guilford describes the foundation of his theory of the structure of the intellect and in the process reviews the history of research into and theorizing about intelligence. This volume is an important contribution to the field.

Ryan, R. M., and E. L. Deci. "Intrinsic and Extrinsic Motivation." *Contemporary Educational Psychology* 25 (2000): 54-67. Reviews contemporary thinking on the subject.

Sternberg, Robert J. *Successful Intelligence.* New York: Plume, 1997. A book aimed at the layperson, describing Sternberg's theory of triarchic intelligence and its practical applications.

_____. *The Triarchic Mind: A New Theory of Human Intelligence.* New York: Penguin Books, 1989. Sternberg reviews and criticizes the limitations of traditional views of intelligence and presents his own variations on that theme. The book is addressed to a general audience and contains intellectual exercises aimed at enhancing the reader's performance on cognitive tests.

Sternberg, Robert J., Torff, B., and E. L. Grigorenko. "Teaching Triarchically Improves School Achievement." *Journal of Educational Psychology* 90 (1998): 374-384. A review of practical application of Sternberg's theory of triarchic intelligence.

Vernon, Philip Ewart. *Intelligence: Heredity and Environment.* San Francisco: W. H. Freeman, 1979. Presents a thorough and thoughtful review of research on both sides of the "nature-nurture" debate on the development of intelligence. The issue of racial differences in intelligence is also discussed at length.

Susana P. Urbina; updated by Ronna F. Dillon

SEE ALSO: Cognitive Psychology; Creativity and Intelligence; Giftedness; Intelligence Tests; Logic and Reasoning; Mental Retardation; Race and Intelligence.

Intelligence Tests

Type of psychology: Intelligence and intelligence testing
Fields of study: Ability tests; intelligence assessment

Individual intelligence tests are used by psychologists to evaluate a person's current cognitive ability and prior knowledge. The intelligence testing movement has a long history, including the development of numerous group and individual tests to measure one aspect of a person's overall intelligence, which frequently changes over time.

Key concepts
- age norm
- cognition
- intelligence
- intelligence quotient (IQ)
- mentally gifted
- mentally handicapped
- percentile
- performance tests
- sensorimotor tests
- verbal tests

Although means for measuring mental ability date as far back as 2000 B.C.E., when the ancient Chinese administered oral tests to determine a candidate's fitness for carrying out the tasks of civil administration, the modern intelligence test has its origins in the nineteenth century, when Jean-Étienne-Dominique Esquirol drew a clear distinction between mentally deranged people ("lunatics") and mentally retarded people ("idiots"). Esquirol believed that it was necessary to devise a means of gauging "normal" intelligence so that deviations from an agreed-upon norm could be ascertained, and he pointed out that intellectual ability exists on a continuum extending from idiocy to genius. His work coincided with studies in Europe and the United States that were designed to develop a concept of "intelligence" and to fashion a means of testing this capacity. Work done by Sir Francis Galton in the United Kingdom on hereditary genius, by James McKeen Cattell in the United States on individual differences in behavior, and by Hermann Ebbinghaus in Germany on tests of memory, computation, and sentence completion culminated in the 1905 Binet-Simon scale, created by Alfred Binet and Théodore Simon. It was the first practical index of intelligence measurement as a function of individual differences. This test was based on the idea that simple sensory functions, which had formed the core of earlier tests, are not true indicators of intelligence and that higher mental processes had to be included.

THE BINET TESTS

Binet, a psychologist and educator, founded the first French psychological laboratory. He was a pioneer in the study of individual differences in abilities and introduced intelligence tests that were quickly accepted and widely used in Europe and the United States. His work stemmed from a commission from the minister of education in Paris, who gave him the task of devising a way to distinguish between idiocy and lunacy, as Esquirol had defined them, and normal intelligence, so that handicapped students could be given special instruction. Binet and Simon used many items that had been developed by earlier examiners; the key advances they made were to rank items in order of difficulty and to register results in terms of age-based cognitive development. Their scale reflected the idea that intelligence was a combination of faculties—judgment, practical sense, and initiative—and contained measures related to memory, reasoning ability, numerical facility, and object comparison.

Binet and Simon's work demonstrated the feasibility of mental measurement, assessing intelligence for the first time in general terms rather than measuring its component parts. Binet revised the test in 1908, and another revision was published in 1911, the year of his death. Advances in his basic design led to the development of tests that could be used for all children (not only those considered mentally limited) in assessing their "mental quotient," a ratio adapted by Lewis Terman of Stanford University. It was obtained by dividing mental age (as determined through scores on a test) by chronological age. Terman renamed it the intelligence quotient (IQ), and his 1916 version of the Binet-Simon scale became known as the Stanford-Binet test, the most common intelligence test administered in the United States during the twentieth century. It was revised and updated in 1937, 1960, 1972, and 1986, when a point-scale format was introduced for the first time.

THE WECHSLER TESTS

Binet's test depended on an age scale; that is, the questions which were answered correctly by a majority of ten-year-old children were assigned to the ten-year age level of intelligence. A more sophisticated version of the test devised by Robert Yerkes depended on a point scale for scoring; this format was fully developed by David Wechsler. While the Binet-Terman method used different tests for different age groups, Wechsler worked toward a test to measure the same aspect of behavior at every age level. The goal of his test was to measure intelligence in a holistic (encompassing the larger whole of personality) fashion that did not depend on the verbal skills that the Stanford-Binet tests required. Wechsler thought of intelligence as a multifaceted complex of skills, the total of an effective intellectual process; he wanted his test to show the way intelligent people behaved as a consequence of an awareness of the results of their actions. He thought that those actions would be more rational, worthwhile (in terms of social values), and meaningful than those of less intelligent people.

Wechsler's first test (the Wechsler-Bellevue Intelligence Scale) was published in 1939, and it awarded points for each answer depending on the level of sophistication of the response. The test consisted of six verbal subjects (information, comprehension, arithmetic, similarities, vocabulary, and digit span) and five performance subtests (picture completion, picture arrangement, block design, object assemblies, and digit symbols). The division into verbal and performance skills permitted the calculation of three intelligent quotients: a verbal IQ based on the sum of the verbal tests, correlated with norms of age, a performance IQ based on the sum of performance tests, and a full-scale IQ derived from the sum of all the answers. The test was standardized on a sample of adults, and it could be used to test individuals who had linguistic or sensorimotor handicaps. The pattern of scores on the separate tests could also be used to diagnose learning disability or, in some situations, clinical disorder or dysfunction.

The original test was limited by the sample used for standardization, but the 1955 Wechsler Adult Intelligence Scale (WAIS) provided a basis for testing adults from the ages of sixteen to seventy-five. Further revision in the standard scale (including the WAIS-R, 1981) updated the test to coincide with changes in cultural experience. In addition, a Wechsler Intelligence Scale for Children (WISC) was designed to cover ages five to fifteen in 1949 and was revised (WISC-R) in 1974 to cover ages six to sixteen. In 1991, another revision (WISC-III) was introduced. Subsequent modifications also led to a test suitable for preschool children, the Wechsler Preschool and Primary Scales of Intelligence (WPPSI) of 1967, which covered ages four to six and a half and included mazes, animal figures, and geometric designs. This test was revised in 1981 (WPPSI-R) to extend its range over three years to seven years, three months. Further adjustments have also been made to account for a candidate's sociocultural background in a test called the System of Multicultural Pluralistic Assessment (SOMPA, 1977).

Recent definitions of intelligence have resulted in further development of testing instruments. Raymond Cattell's proposal that intelligence could be divided into two types—fluid (or forming) and crystallized (fixed)—led to a test that used figure classification, figure analysis, and letter and number series to assess the essential nonverbal, relatively culture-free aspects of fluid intelligence; it used vocabulary definition, abstract word analogies, and general information to determine the skills that depend on exposure to cultural processes inherent in crystallized intelligence. Other theories, such as Jean Piaget's idea that intelligence is a form of individual adaptation and accommodation to an environment, led to the development of a test which measures mental organization at successive ages.

USES OF INTELLIGENCE ASSESSMENT

There was a tendency at various times during the twentieth century to regard intelligence assessment as an answer to questions of placement and classification in almost every area of human experience. The most effective and scientifically valid uses of tests, however, have been in predicting performance in scholastic endeavor, in revealing disguised or latent ability to assist in career counseling, in determining the most appropriate developmental programs for handicapped or mentally handicapped individuals, in locating specific strengths and weaknesses in an individual, in measuring specific changes associated with special programs and forms of therapy, and in comparing a child's mental ability with that of other children observed in a similar situation to establish a profile of cognitive skills.

One of the most widespread and effective uses of intelligence tests is the determination of possible problems in a child's course of basic education. As reported by Lewis Aiken in *Assessment of Intellectual Functioning* (1987), a typical case involved an eight-year-old boy with a suspected learning disability. He was given the WISC-R test in 1985, and his full-scale IQ was figured to be 116, placing him in the high average classification. This provided an assessment of general intelligence and scholastic aptitude. His verbal IQ was 127, placing him in the ninety-seventh percentile, indicative of exceptional verbal comprehension. This suggested that he could reason very well, learn verbal material quickly, and process verbal information effectively. His performance IQ of 98 placed him in the average category, but the magnitude of the difference between his verbal and performance IQs is very unusual in children of his age. It pointed to a need for additional interpretive analysis as well as further study to reveal the reasons behind the discrepancy. Close scrutiny of the test results showed that low scores on the arithmetic, digit span, and coding subtests might indicate a short attention or memory span, poor concentration, or a lack of facility in handling numbers. While no absolute conclusions could be drawn at this point, the results of the test could be used in conjunction with other procedures, observation, and background information to determine an appropriate course of action.

INTELLIGENCE AND GUIDANCE

Another common use of an intelligence test is to help an examinee determine specific areas of ability or aptitude which might be useful in selecting a career route. As reported in Aiken, a college senior was given the Otis-Lennon School Ability Test (O-LSAT, Advanced Form R) just before her twenty-second birthday. She planned to enroll in a program in a graduate business school and work toward an M.B.A. degree. The O-LSAT is designed to gauge general mental ability, and it includes classification, analogy, and omnibus (a variety of items to measure different aspects of mental functioning) elements. The omnibus includes verbal comprehension, quantitative reasoning, and the ability to follow directions.

The examinee was able to complete the test in thirty-five minutes and used the remaining allotted time to check her answers. Her raw score (number of items answered correctly) was 64 (out of 80), her school ability index was 116—which approximated her IQ—and her percentile rank among candidates in the 18-plus range was 84. These scores were in the average range for college seniors, indicating an overall intellectual ability that could be classified as "high average" in terms of the general population. Of the sixteen items answered incorrectly, a superficial analysis pointed toward some difficulty with nonverbal reasoning, but no conclusions could be reached without further examination in this area. There was no significant pattern of errors otherwise, and the random distribution offered no additional guide to areas of weakness. The initial conclusion that was drawn from the test was that a career in business was appropriate and that with hard work and the full application of her intellectual abilities, she would be able to earn an M.B.A. at a reputable university.

A particularly important application of intelligence assessment is the identification and guidance of a child with advanced intellectual abilities. In a case reported in Jerome M. Sattler's *Assessment of Children* (1988), a three-year-old boy was tested repeatedly from that age until his sixth birthday. This procedure required the implementation of the Stanford-Binet Form L-M, the WPPSI, and the Peabody Individual Achievement Test (PIAT) for grade equivalents. The Stanford-Binet scores were 127 (at age three), 152, 152, and 159+ (with a linear extrapolation to 163). During his first test he was anxious and did not give long verbal responses, but the range of his scores indicated a very superior classification. He did not cooperate with the examiner on the WPPSI vocabulary and animal subtests (the examiner believed that he was not interested), but his performance at age four placed him in the superior range. On the PIAT, he was consistently above average, earning a grade equivalent above 4.0 at the age of six, with a grade equivalent of 7.4 (his highest score) in mathematics; the average grade equivalent for age six is 1.0.

As Sattler points out, the case illustrates "a number of important principles related to testing and assessment." In the largest sense, it illustrates the way different tests measuring general intelligence may yield different results (although all pointed toward superior mental development). The same test may also yield different scores at different age levels. The child's motivation (among other factors) may also play an important part in his results. More specifically, because the boy showed more interest in reading at age three and mathematics at age six, the test could not be considered a useful predictor of later interest, although an interest in solving perceptual-logical problems remained consistent throughout. Finally, because the parents had kept a detailed record of the boy's early development in a baby book, the rich history recorded there was corroborated by the test results which reaffirmed their initial suspicions that the boy was unusually gifted. During his first year in school, he tended to play alone and had frequent minor tantrums which affected his performance in school subjects. When he became accustomed to the social process of school life, however, he was able to demonstrate the ability that his parents had observed at home and that the initial tests validated.

DEFINITIONS OF INTELLIGENCE

While intelligence tests of some sort appeared in human history as early as the Old Testament book of Judges (7:3-7, 12:6), which indicates that early Jewish society used questions and observations in personnel selection, the intelligence test as it is known today can be traced to Renaissance Europe. In 1575, the Spanish physician Juan Huarte wrote *Examen de Ingenios*, a treatise concerning individual differences in mental ability with suggestions for appropriate tests. His work, and that of other investigators and theorists, was the result of the rise of a middle class with aspirations to productive employment. Previously, the aristocracy had controlled everything, and fitness for a position was determined by lineage. Once this monarchical rule began to break down, other means were necessary for determining who was fit for a particular occupation and what might be the most productive use of a person's abilities. When it became apparent that royal blood was no guarantee of competence, judgment, or mental acuity, the entire question of the origins of intelligence began to occupy members of the scientific community. For a time, the philosophy of empiricism led scientists toward the idea that the mind itself was formed by mental association among sense impressions, and sensorimotor tests were particularly prominent. As the results of these tests failed to correlate with demonstrations of mental ability (such as marks in school), however, other means were sought to measure and define intelligence. The interest in intelligence testing in the nineteenth century was an important aspect of the development of psychology as a separate scientific discipline, and the twin paths of psychometric (that is, the quantitative assessment of an individual's attributes or traits) and statistical analysis on one hand and philosophical conjecture concerning the shape and operation of the mind on the other were joined in experimentation concerning methods of assessing intelligence.

From their first applications in France as a diagnostic instrument, intelligence tests have been used to help psychologists, educators, and other professionals plan courses of action to aid individuals suffering from some mental limitation or obstacle. This role has been expanded to cover the full range of human intellectual ability and to isolate many individual aspects of intelligence in myriad forms. The profusion of tests has both complicated and deepened an understanding of how the mind functions, and the continuing proposition of theories of intelligence through the twentieth century resulted in an increasingly sophisticated battery of tests designed to assess and register each new theory.

MODERN TESTING

In addition, technological developments, particularly the growing use of computers, permit a wider use of flexible testing in which the decision about what item or task to present next depends on the previous answer. Computers are also useful in "number crunching," so that such basic components of a test system as norms, derived scores, and reliability and validity coefficients (the basic statistical material behind the calculation of scores) can be assembled more quickly and efficiently. Computers also make it possible to administer tests at multiple sites simultaneously when an individual examiner's presence is not necessary. Nevertheless, the human capacity for judgment and analysis in the interpretation of results remain crucial to test procedures.

Intelligence testing is likely to continue as a primary means of predicting educational or vocational performance, but tests designed to measure the mind in terms of its ability to process information by shifting strategies in response to a changing environment are likely to become more prevalent. The proliferation of more detailed, separate sets of norms for different groups (age, sex, ethnic origin, and so on) is likely to continue. Also, the relationship between intelligence per se and behavioral attitudes that seem to resemble aptitude rather than personality measures is part of the heredity-environment controversy that will continue. Finally, advances in studies on the neurophysiological bases of intelligence will be reflected in tests responsive to a growing understanding of the biochemical aspects of cognition. As an operating principle, though, professionals in the field will have to be guided by a continuing awareness that intelligence testing is only one aspect of understanding a person's total behavior and that the limitations involved in the measuring process must be understood to avoid incorrect or inappropriate diagnoses that might prove harmful to an individual.

Howard Gardner postulated a theory of intelligence which focuses on a symbol system approach that combines both factor analytic and information processing methodology. He included seven dimensions of intelligence: verbal and linguistic, mathematical and logical, visual and spatial, body and kinesthetic, musical and rhythmical, interpersonal, intrapersonal, and environmental. The concept of types of intelligence is not new. L. L. Thurstone developed a test of eight scales named the Primary Mental Abilities test. Edward L. Thorndike identified several types of intelligence: abstract, social, and practical. Sternberg used informational processing and cognitive theory in his model of intelligence and identified three different types of information processing components: metacomponents, performance components, and knowledge acquisition components. He saw metacomponents as the higher-order control processes used to oversee the planning, monitoring, and evaluation of task performance.

SOURCES FOR FURTHER STUDY

Gardner, Howard. *Multiple Intelligences: The Theory in Practice.* New York: Basic Books, 1993. Gardner discusses his theory of multiple intelligences, which takes into consideration the psychological, biological, and cultural dimensions of cognition.

Goldstein, Gerald, and Michael Hersen, eds. *Handbook of Psychological Assessment.* 3d ed. New York: Pergamon, 2000. There are a series of chapters on assessment of intelligence as well as on psychometric foundations of testing.

Jensen, Arthur. *The "G" Factor: The Science of Mental Ability.* Westport, Conn.: Praeger, 1998. The author discusses the structure of intelligence.

Kampaus, Randy W. *Clinical Assessment of Child and Adolescent Intelligence.* 2d ed. Boston: Allyn & Bacon, 2001. A good overview of intelligence tests used with children and adolescents.

Sternberg, Robert J., ed. *Handbook of Intelligence.* New York: Cambridge University Press, 2000. The writers discuss the history and theory of intelligence, the development of intelligence, and the biology of intelligence.
Leon Lewis and James R. Deni; updated by Robert J. Drummond

SEE ALSO: Intelligence; Race and Intelligence; Survey Research: Questionnaires and Interviews.

LANGUAGE

TYPE OF PSYCHOLOGY: Cognition; language
FIELDS OF STUDY: Cognitive processes; thought

Language is a system of arbitrary symbols that can be combined in conventionalized ways to express ideas, thoughts, and feelings. Various theories and models have been constructed to study, describe, and explain language acquisition, language processing, and its relation to thought and cognition.

KEY CONCEPTS
- displacement
- grammar
- language faculty
- linguistic relativity
- morphology
- phonology
- pragmatics
- semantics
- syntax
- universal grammar

Language is a system of arbitrary symbols that can be combined in conventionalized ways to express ideas, thoughts, and feelings. Language has been typically seen as uniquely human, separating the human species from other animals. Language enables people of all cultures to survive as a group and preserve their culture. The fundamental features of human language make it extremely effective and very economical. Language uses its arbitrary symbols to refer to physical things or nonphysical ideas; to a single item or a whole category; to a fixed state or to a changing process; to existent reality or to nonexistent fiction; to truths or to lies.

Language is systematic and rule-governed. Its four component subsystems are phonology, semantics, grammar, and pragmatics. The phonological system uses phonemes (the smallest speech sound units capable of differentiating meanings) as its building blocks to form syllables and words through phonemic rules. For example, /m/ and /n/ are two different phonemes because they differentiate meaning as in /mēt/ (meat) versus /nēt/ (neat), and "meat" has three phonemes of /m/, /ē/, and /t/ placed in a "lawful" order in English to form one syllable. The semantic system makes language meaningful. It has two levels: Lexical semantics refers to the word meaning, and grammatical semantics to the meaning derived from the combinations of morphemes (the smallest meaning units) into words and sentences. "Beds," for example, has two morphemes, "bed" as a free morpheme means "a piece of furniture for reclining or sleeping," and "s" as a bound morpheme means "more than one."

The grammatical system includes morphology and syntax. Morphology specifies rules to form words (for example, prefixes, suffixes, grammatical morphemes such as "-ed," and rules to form compound words such as "blackboard"). Syntax deals with rules for word order in sentences (such as, "I speak English," but not "I English speak"). Furthermore, the syntax of human language has four core elements, summarized in 1999 by Edward Kako as discrete combinatorics (each word retains its general meaning even when combined with other words), category-based rules (phrases are built around word categories), argument structure (the arguments or the participants involved in an event, labeled by verbs, are assigned to syntactic positions in a sentence), and closed-class vocabulary (the grammatical functional words, such as "the," "on," or "and," are usually not open to addition of new words).

The fourth subsystem in human language is the pragmatic system. It involves rules to guide culture-based, appropriate use of language in communication. For example, people choose different styles (speech registers) that they deem appropriate when they talk to their spouses versus their children. Other examples include the use of contextual information, inferring the speaker's illocutionary intent (intended meaning), polite expressions, conversational rules, and referential communication skills (to speak clearly and to ask clarification questions if the message is not clear).

Language is creative, generative, and productive. With a limited number of symbols and rules, any language user is able to produce and understand an unlimited number of novel utterances. Language has the characteristic of displacement; that is, it is able to refer to or describe not only items and events here and now but also items and events in other times and places.

LANGUAGE ACQUISITION AND DEVELOPMENT

Views on language acquisition and development are diverse. Some tend to believe that language development follows one universal path, shows qualitatively different, stagelike shifts, proceeds as an independent language faculty, and is propelled by innate factors. Others tend to believe in options for different paths, continuous changes through learning, and cognitive prerequisites for language development.

UNIVERSAL PATHWAY IN LANGUAGE DEVELOPMENT. Stage theories usually suggest a universal path (an invariant sequence of stages) for language development. A typical child anywhere in the world starts with cooing (playing with the vowel sounds) at two to three months of age, changes into babbling (consonant-vowel combinations) at four to six months, begins to use gestures at nine to ten months, and produces first words by the first birthday. First word combinations, known as telegraphic speech (content word combinations with functional elements left out, such as "Mommy cookie!") normally appear when children are between 1.5 and 2.5 years. Meanwhile, rapid addition of new words results in a vocabulary spurt. Grammatical rules are being figured out, as seen in young children's application of regular grammatical rules to irregular exceptions (called overregularization, as in "I hurted my finger"). Later on, formal education promotes further vocabulary growth, sentence complexity, and subtle usages. Language ability continues to improve in early adulthood, then remains stable. It generally will not decline until a person reaches the late sixties.

DIFFERENT PATHWAYS IN LANGUAGE DEVELOPMENT. Although the universal pattern appears true in some respects, not all children acquire language in the same way. Analyses of young children's early words have led psychologists to an appreciation of children's different approaches to language. In her 1995 book *Individual Differences in Language Development,* Cecilia Shore analyzed the different pathways of two general styles (sometimes termed analytic versus holistic) in the four major language component areas.

In early phonological development, holistic babies seem to attend to prosody or intonation. They tend to be willing to take risks to try a variety of sound chunks, thus producing larger speech units in sentencelike intonation but with blurred sounds. Analytic babies are phonemic-oriented, paying attention to distinct speech sounds. Their articulation is clearer.

In semantic development, children differ not only in their vocabulary size but also in the type of words they acquire. According to Katherine Nelson (cited in Shore's work), who divided children's language acquisition styles into referential versus expressive types, the majority of the referential babies' first words were object labels ("ball," "cat") whereas many in the expressive children's vocabulary were personal-social frozen phrases ("Don't do dat"). In Shore's opinion, the referential babies are attracted to the referential function of nouns and take in the semantic concept of object names; the expressive children attend more to the personal-social aspect of language and acquire relational words, pronouns, and undifferentiated communicative formulaic utterances.

Early grammatical development shows similar patterns. The analytical children are more likely to adopt the nominal approach and use telegraphic grammar to combine content words but ignore the grammatical inflections (such as the plural "-s"). The holistic children have a tendency to take the pronominal approach and use pivot-open grammar to have a small number of words fill in the frame slots (for instance, the structure of "allgone [. . .] " generates "allgone shoe," "allgone cookie," and so on). The units of language acquisition might be different for different children.

In the area of pragmatic development, children may differ in their understanding of the primary function of language. Nelson has argued that the referential children may appreciate the informative function of language and the expressive children may attend to the interpersonal function of language. The former are generally more object-oriented, are declarative, and display low variety in speech acts, whereas the latter are more person-oriented, are imperative, and display high variety in speech acts.

Convenient as it is to discuss individual differences in terms of the two general language acquisition styles (analytic versus holistic), it does not mean that the two are necessarily mutually exclusive—children actually use both strategies, although they might use them to different extents at different times and change reliance patterns over time.

THEORIES OF LANGUAGE DEVELOPMENT

With an emphasis on language performance (actual language use in different situations) rather than language competence (knowledge of language rules and structure), learning theories contend that children learn their verbal behavior (a term suggested by the behaviorist B. F. Skinner in 1957 to replace the vague word of "language") primarily through conditioning and imitation, not maturation. Classical conditioning allows the child to make associations between verbal stimuli, internal responses, and situational contexts to understand a word's meaning. It also enables the child to comprehend a word's connotative meaning—whether it is associated with pleasant or unpleasant feelings. Operant conditioning shapes the child's speech through selective reinforcement and punishment. Adults' verbal behaviors serve as the environmental stimuli to elicit the child's verbal responses, as models for the child to imitate, and as the shaping agent (through imitating their children's well-formed speech and recasting or expanding their ill-formed speech).

Nevertheless, learning theories have difficulty explaining many phenomena in language development. Imitation cannot account for children's creative yet logical sayings, such as calling a gardener "plantman," because there are no such models in adult language. Shaping also falls short of an adequate explanation, because adults do not always correct their children's mistakes, especially grammatical ones. Sometimes they even mimic their children's cute mistakes. Furthermore, residential homes are not highly controlled laboratories—the stimulus-response-consequence contingencies are far from perfect.

THE NATIVIST PERSPECTIVE. The nativist perspective, turning to innate mechanisms for language development, has the following underlying assumptions: language is a human-species-specific capacity; language is "unlearnable," because it is impossible for a naïve and immature child to figure out such a complex linguistic system from an imperfect, not very consistent, highly opaque, and frequently ambiguous language environment; and there is a common structural core in all human languages. In 1965, linguist Noam Chomsky posited an innate language-acquisition device (LAD), with the "universal grammar" residing in it, to explain children's rapid acquisition of any language and even multiple languages. LAD is assumed to be a part of the brain, specialized for processing language. Universal grammar is the innate knowledge of the grammatical system of principles and rules expressing the essence of all human languages. Its transformational generative grammar consists of rules to convert the deep structure (grammatical classes and their relationships) to surface structure (the actual sentences said) in the case of production, or vice versa in the case of comprehension.

Equipped with this biological endowment, children need only minimal language exposure to trigger the LAD, and their innate knowledge of the universal grammar will enable them to extract the rules for the specific language(s) to which they are exposed.

Evidence for the nativist perspective can be discussed at two levels: the linguistic level (language rules and structure) and the biological level. At the linguistic level, people are sensitive to grammatical rules and linguistic structural elements. For example, sentences in the active voice are processed more quickly than sentences in the passive voice, because the former type is closer to the deep structure and needs fewer transformation steps than the latter type. "Click insertion" studies (which insert a "click" at different places in a sentence) and "interrupted tape" studies (which interrupt a tape with recorded messages at different points) have shown a consistent bias for people to recall the click or interruption position as being at linguistic constituent boundaries, such as the end of a clause. After a sentence has been processed, what remains in memory is the meaning or the gist of the sentence, not its word-for-word surface structure, suggesting the transformation from the surface structure to the deep structure. Around the world, the structure of creolized languages (invented languages), including the sign languages invented by deaf children who have not been exposed to any language, is similar and resembles early child language. Young children's early language data have also rendered support. In phonology, habituation studies show that newborns can distinguish between phonemes such as /p/ and /b/. Most amazingly, they perceive variations of a sound as the same if they come from the same phoneme but different if they cross the boundary into a different phoneme (categorical speech perception). In semantics, babies seem to know that object labels refer to whole objects and that a new word must mean the name of a new object. If the new word is related to an old object whose name the child already knows, the word must mean either a part or a property of that object (the mutual exclusivity hypothesis). In the domain of grammar, Dan Isaac Slobin's 1985 cross-cultural data have shown that young children pay particular attention to the ends of words and use subject-object word order, probably as a function of their innate operating principles. By semantic bootstrapping, young children know that object names are nouns and that action words are verbs. By syntactic bootstrapping, they understand a word's grammatical class membership according to its position in a sentence. Even young children's mistaken overregularization of grammatical rules to exceptions demonstrates their success in rule extraction, as such mistaken behavior is not modeled by adults.

THE NEURAL STOREHOUSE. At the biological level, human babies seem to be prepared for language: They prefer the human voice to other sounds and the human face to other figures. Some aspects of the language developmental sequence appear to be universal—even deaf children start to coo and babble at about the same ages as hearing children, despite of their lack of language input, and later develop sign combinations that are very similar to telegraphic speech. Children's language environment is indeed quite chaotic, yet it takes them only four to five years to speak their mother tongue like an adult without systematic, overt teaching. Furthermore, a critical or sensitive period seems to exist for language acquisition. Young children are able to pick up any language or a second language effortlessly, with no accent or grammatical mistakes. After puberty, people generally have to exert great efforts to learn another language, and their pronunciation as well as grammar typically suffers. Reinforced language teaching in postcritical years was not successful in the cases of "Victor" (a boy who had been deserted in the wild) and "Genie" (a girl who had been confined in a basement). Edward Kako's 1999 study, a careful analysis of the linguistic behavior of a parrot, two dolphins, and a bonobo, led him to conclude that no nonhuman animals, including the language-trained ones, show all of the properties of human language in their communication, although he respectfully acknowledges all the achievements in animal language training. Language is unique to human beings.

Although the neural storehouse for the universal grammar has not been pinpointed yet, cognitive neuroscience has delivered some supportive evidence. Infants' brains respond asymmetrically to language sounds versus nonlanguage sounds. Event-related potentials (ERPs) have indicated localized brain regions for different word categories in native English speakers. Research suggests possible specific brain structures that had registered a detailed index for nouns. Brain studies have confirmed the left hemisphere's language specialization relative to the right hemisphere, even among very young infants. Broca's area and Wernicke's area are housed in the left hemisphere. Damage to Broca's area results in Broca's aphasia, with a consequence of producing grammatically defective, halting, telegramlike speech. When Wernicke's area is damaged, speech fluency and grammatical structure are spared but semantics is impaired. This linguistic lateralization pattern and the linguistic consequences of brain injuries are also true of normal and aphasic American Sign Language users.

However, the nativist perspective is not immune to criticism. The universal grammar cannot adequately explain the grammatical diversity in all human languages. The growth spurts in brain development do not correspond to language development in a synchronized manner. The importance of social interaction, contextual factors, and formal education for knowledge and pragmatic usage of complex rules, subtle expressions, speech acts and styles has been neglected in nativist theories.

Dissatisfied with this nature-nurture dichotomy, interactionist theories try to bring the two together. They recognize the reciprocal influences, facilitating or constraining, dependent or modifying, among multiple factors from the biological, cognitive, linguistic, and social domains. For instance, the typical prenatal and postnatal mother-tongue environment will eventually wean the infants' initial ability to differentiate the speech sounds of any language and, at the same time, sharpen their sensitivity to their native language. Deaf children's babbling does not develop into words as does that of hearing children. Babies deprived of the opportunity of social interaction, as seen in the cases of "Victor" and "Genie," will not automatically develop a proper language. It is in the dynamic child-environment system that a child acquires language.

LANGUAGE AND COGNITION

COGNITIVE DEVELOPMENT AND LANGUAGE ACQUISITION.
Cognitive theorists generally believe that language is contingent on cognitive development. The referential power in the arbitrary symbols assumes the cognitive prerequisite of understanding the concepts they signify. As a cognitive interactionist, Jean Piaget believed that action-based interaction with the world gave rise to the formation of object concepts, separation of self from the external world, and mental representation of reality by mental images, signs, and symbols (language). Language reflects the degree of cognitive maturity. For example, young children's immature egocentric thought (unable to understand others' perspectives) is revealed in their egocentric speech (talking to self)—children seem to show no realization of the need to connect with others' comments or to ascertain whether one is being understood. Older children's cognitive achievements of logical thinking and perspective-taking lead to the disappearance of egocentric speech and their use of socialized speech for genuine social interaction. Although language as a verbal tool facilitates children's interaction with the world, it is the interaction that contributes to cognitive development. Piaget gave credit to language only in the later development of abstract reasoning by adolescents.

In L. S. Vygotsky's social-functional interactionist view, language and cognition develop independently at first, as a result of their different origins in the course of evolution. Infants use practical/instrumental intelligence (intelligence without speech) such as smiling, gazing, grasping, or reaching, to act upon or respond to the social world. Meanwhile, the infants' cries and vocalizations, though they do not initially have true communicative intent (speech without thinking), function well in bringing about adults' responses. Adults attribute meaning to infants' vocalizations and thus include the babies in the active communicative system, fostering joint attention and intersubjectivity (understanding each other's intention). Such social interactions help the infants eventually complete the transition from nonintentional to intentional behavior and to discover the referential power of symbols, thus moving on to verbal thinking and later to meaningful speech. Externalized speech (egocentric speech) is a means for the child to monitor and guide his or her own thoughts and problem-solving actions. This externalized functional "conversation with oneself" (egocentric speech) does not disappear but is internalized over time and becomes inner speech, a tool for private thinking. Thus, in Vygotsky's theory, language first develops independently of cognition, then intersects with cognition and contributes significantly to cognitive development thereafter. Language develop-

DSM-IV-TR Criteria for Language Disorders

Expressive Language Disorder (DSM code 315.31)

Scores from standardized measures of expressive language development substantially below those from standardized measures of nonverbal intellectual capacity and receptive language development

May be manifested by the following:
- markedly limited vocabulary
- errors in tense
- difficulty recalling words
- difficulty producing sentences with developmentally appropriate length or complexity

Expressive language difficulties interfere with academic or occupational achievement or with social communication

Criteria for Mixed Receptive-Expressive Language Disorder or a pervasive developmental disorder are not met

If mental retardation, speech-motor or sensory deficit, or environmental deprivation is present, language difficulties exceed those usually associated with these problems

Mixed Receptive-Expressive Language Disorder (DSM code 315.32)

Scores from a battery of standardized measures of receptive and expressive language development substantially below those from standardized measures of nonverbal intellectual capacity

Symptoms include those for Expressive Language Disorder as well as difficulty understanding words, sentences, or specific types of words (such as spatial terms)

Receptive and expressive language difficulties interfere significantly with academic or occupational achievement or with social communication

Criteria for a pervasive developmental disorder are not met

If mental retardation, speech-motor or sensory deficit, or environmental deprivation is present, language difficulties exceed those usually associated with these problems

ment proceeds from a global, social functional use (externalized speech) to a mature, internalized mastery (inner speech), opposite to what Piaget suggested.

LINGUISTIC RELATIVITY. Linguistic relativity refers to the notion that the symbolic structure and use of a language will shape its users' way of thinking. The Sapir-Whorf hypothesis, also known as linguistic determinism, is a strong version. According to anthropologist John Lucy, writing in 1997, all the variations of linguistic relativity, weak or strong, share the assumption that "certain properties of a given *language* have consequences for patterns of *thought* about *reality*. . . . Language embodies *an interpretation* of reality and language can *influence* thought about that reality." Many researchers have tested these claims. Lera Boroditsky, for example, in a 2001 study examined the relationship between spatial terms used to talk about time and the way Mandarin Chinese speakers (using vertical spatial metaphors) and English speakers (using horizontal spatial metaphors) think about time. The findings suggested that abstract conceptions, such as time, might indeed be subject to the influence from specific languages. On the other hand, the influence between language and thought might be more likely bidirectional than unidirectional. Many examples from the Civil Rights movement or the women's movement, such as the thought of equality and bias-free linguistic expressions, can be cited to illustrate the reciprocal relationships between the two.

LANGUAGE FACULTY AS A MODULE. There are debates over whether language is a separate faculty or a part of general cognition. Traditional learning theories are firm in the belief that language is a learned verbal behavior shaped by the environment. In other words, language is not unique in its own right. By contrast, nativist theorists insist on language being an independent, innate faculty. Chomsky even advocates that, being one of the clearest and most important separate modules in the individual brain, language should be viewed internally from the individual and therefore be called internal language or "i-language," distinct from "e-language" or the external and social use of language. Nativists also insist on language being unique to humans, because even higher-order apes, though they have intelligence (such as tool using, problem solving, insights) and live a social life, do not possess a true language.

The view of language as an independent faculty has received support from works in cognitive neuroscience, speech-processing studies, data associated with aphasia (language impairment due to brain damage), and unique case studies. Specific word and grammatical categories seem to be registered in localized regions of the brain. Some empirical studies have suggested that lexical access and word-meaning activation appear to be autonomic (modular). As noted, Broca's aphasia and Wernicke's aphasia display different language deficit symptoms. In 1991, Jeni Yamada reported the case of Laura, a retarded woman with an IQ score of just 41 when she was in her twenties. Her level of cognitive problem-solving skill was comparable to that of a preschooler, yet she was able to produce a variety of grammatically sophisticated sentences, such as "He was saying that I lost my battery powered watch that I loved; I just loved that watch." Interestingly, Laura's normal development in phonology, vocabulary, and grammar did not protect her from impairment in pragmatics. In responding to the question, "How do you earn your money?," Laura answered, "Well, we were taking a walk, my mom, and there was this giant, like, my mother threw a stick." It seems that some components of language, such as vocabulary and grammar, may function in a somewhat autonomic manner, whereas other parts, such as pragmatics, require some general cognitive capabilities and social learning experiences.

Cognitive psychologists hold that language is not a separate module but a facet of general cognition. They caution people against hasty acceptance of brain localization as evidence for a language faculty. Arshavir Blackwell and Elizabeth Bates (1995) have suggested an alternative explanation for the agrammaticality in Broca's aphasia: Grammatical deficits might be the result of a global cognitive resource diminution, rather than just the damaged Broca's area. In 1994, Michael Maratsos and Laura Matheny criticized the inadequate explanatory power of the language-as-a-faculty theory pertaining to the following phenomena: comprehension difficulties in Broca's aphasia in addition to grammatical impairment; semantically related word substitutions in Wernicke's aphasia; the brain's plasticity or elasticity (the flexibility of other parts of the brain adapting to pick up some of the functions of the damaged parts); and the practical inseparability of phonology, semantics, syntax, and pragmatics from one another.

Some information-processing models, such as connectionist models, have provided another way to discuss language, not in the traditional terms of symbols, rules, or cognitive capacity but in terms of the strengths of the connections in the neural network. Using computer modeling, J. L. McClelland explains that knowledge is stored in the weights of the parameter connections, which connect the hidden layers of units to the input units that process task-related information and the output units that generate responses (performance). Just like neurons at work, parallel-distributed processing, or many simultaneous operations by the computer processor, will result in self-regulated strength adjustments of the connections. Over extensive trials, the "learner" will go through an initial error period (the self-adjusting, learning period), but the incremental, continual change in the connection weights will give rise to stagelike progressions. Eventually, the machine gives rulelike performance, even if the initial input was random, without the rules having ever been programmed into the system. These artificial neural networks have successfully demonstrated developmental changes or stages in language acquisition (similar to children's), such as learning the past tense of English verbs. As a product of the neural network's experience-driven adjustment of its connection weights, language does not need cognitive prerequisites, or a specific language faculty in the architecture (the brain). Although emphasizing learning, these models are not to prove the tabula rasa (blank slate) assumption of traditional behaviorism, either, because even small variations in the initial artificial brain structure can make qualitative differences in language acquisition. The interaction between the neural structure and environment (input cues and feedback patterns) is further elaborated in dynamic systems models. For example, Paul van Geert's dynamic system, proposed in 1991, is an ecosystem with heuristic principles modeled after the biological system in general and the evolutionary system in particular. The system space consists of multiple growers or "species" (such as vocabulary and grammatical rules) in interrelated connections. Developmental outcome depends on the changes of the components in their mutual dependency as well as competition for the limited internal and external resources available to them.

CONCLUSION

As Thomas M. Holtgraves said in 2002, "It is hard to think of a topic that has been of interest to more academic disciplines than language." Language can be analyzed at its pure, abstract, and symbolic structural level, but it should also be studied at biological, psychological, and social levels in interconnected dynamic systems. Continued endeavors in interdisciplinary investigations using multiple approaches will surely lead to further understanding of language.

SOURCES FOR FURTHER STUDY

Blackwell, Arshavir, and Elizabeth Bates. "Inducing Agrammatic Profiles in Normals: Evidence for the Selective Vulnerability of Morphology Under Cognitive Resource Limitation." *Journal of Cognitive Neuroscience* 7, no. 2 (1995): 228-257. Raises caution about the interpretation of agrammatic aphasia as evidence for a grammar module and proposes global resource diminution as an alternative explanation.

Boroditsky, Lera. "Does Language Shape Thought? Mandarin and English Speakers' Conceptions of Time." *Cognitive Psychology* 43, no. 1 (2001): 1-22. Three empirical studies to test the Whorfian hypothesis of language's ability to shape speakers' abstract conceptions.

Chomsky, Noam. *Aspects of the Theory of Syntax.* Cambridge, Mass.: MIT Press, 1965. Explains the innate universal grammar and how the transformational grammar works to map the deep structures to surface structures.

_____. "Language from an Internalist Perspective." In *The Future of the Cognitive Revolution,* edited by David Johnson and Christina E. Erneling. New York: Oxford University Press, 1997. Explains why the author insists on language being modular.

Daniels, Harry, ed. *An Introduction to Vygotsky.* New York: Routledge, 1996. A collection of articles about Soviet psychologist L. S. Vygotsky's theoretical position on thought and speech.

Gleason, Jean Berko, and Nan E. Bernstein, eds. *Psycholinguistics.* 2d ed. Fort Worth, Tex.: Harcourt Brace College Publishers, 1998. Contributors discuss language users' knowledge, the biological bases of human communicative behavior, speech perception and production, word meaning, sentence and discourse processing, language acquisition, reading comprehension, and bilingualism.

Holtgraves, Thomas M. *Language as Social Action: Social Psychology and Language Use.* Mahwah, N.J.: Lawrence Erlbaum, 2002. An interdisciplinary review of the literature that treats language as social action, most relevant to the areas of social psychology, cognitive psychology, and communication.

Kako, Edward. "Elements of Syntax in the Systems of Three Language-Trained Animals." *Animal Learning & Behavior* 27, no. 1 (1999): 1-14. A systematic analysis of the language performance of a parrot, two dolphins, and a bonobo against four criteria of syntax.

Lloyd, Peter, and Charles Fernyhough, eds. *Lev Vygotsky: Critical Assessments, Volume II: Thought and Language.* New York: Routledge, 1999. Vygotsky's views on thought and language (verbal self-regulation, private speech, and play) are introduced, contrasted to Piagetian views, and tested in studies.

Lucy, John A. "Linguistic Relativity." *Annual Review of Anthropology* 26 (1997): 291-312. A review of the history of the linguistic relativity hypothesis and various approaches to testing the hypothesis.

McClelland, J. L. "A Connectionist Perspective on Knowledge and Development." In *New Approaches to Process Modeling*, edited by Tony Simon and Graeme S. Halford. Hillsdale, N.J.: Lawrence Erlbaum, 1995. Discusses the applicability of a connectionist approach to the rulelike progression of behavior.

Matatsos, Michael, and Laura Matheny. "Language Specificity and Elasticity: Brain and Clinical Syndrome Studies." *Annual Review of Psychology* 45 (1994): 487-516. A review of module theories of language and alternative explanations based on clinical studies involving language speakers and signers.

Piaget, Jean. *The Language and Thought of the Child.* Translated by Marjorie and Ruth Gabain. Reprint. New York: Routledge, 2002. Explains the qualitative differences in children's egocentric speech and socialized speech and their relationship to thought, with child language data.

Shore, Cecilia M. *Individual Differences in Language Development.* Vol. 7 in *Individual Differences and Development*, edited by Robert Plomin. Thousand Oaks, Calif.: Sage, 1995. Discusses the individual differences in phonological, lexical, grammatical, and pragmatic development of young children aged one to three years.

Van Geert, Paul. "A Dynamic Systems Model of Cognitive and Language Growth." *Psychological Review* 98, no. 1 (1991): 3-53. A dynamic system model analogized to the evolutional system explains how the components in cognitive and language systems mutually support or compete for limited internal and external resources for growth.

Yamada, Jeni E. *A Case for the Modularity of Language.* Cambridge, Mass.: MIT Press, 1991. A case report of Laura, whose vocabulary and grammar seemed to have developed independently of her rather low cognitive abilities.

Ling-Yi Zhou

SEE ALSO: Brain Structure; Speech Disorders.

Learned Helplessness

Type of psychology: Learning
Fields of study: Cognitive learning; critical issues in stress; problem solving

The concept of learned helplessness, first observed in laboratory animals, has been applied to humans in various situations; in particular, it has been applied to depression. The idea holds that feelings of helplessness are often learned from previous experience; therefore, it should also be possible to unlearn them.

Key concepts
- attribution
- helplessness
- learning
- personality
- self-concept

The concept of learned helplessness originated with experiments performed on laboratory dogs by psychologist Martin E. P. Seligman and his colleagues. Seligman noticed that a group of dogs in a learning experiment were not attempting to escape when they were subjected to an electric shock. Intrigued, he set up further experiments using two groups of dogs. One group was first given electric shocks from which they could not escape. Then, even when they were given shocks in a situation where they could avoid them, most of the dogs did not attempt to escape. By comparison, another group, which had not first been given inescapable shocks, had no trouble jumping to avoid the shocks. Seligman also observed that, even after the experiment, the dogs that had first received the unavoidable shocks seemed to be abnormally inactive and had reduced appetites.

After considerable research on the topic, Seligman and others correlated this "learned" helplessness and depression. It seemed to Seligman that when humans, or other animals, feel unable to extricate themselves from a highly stressful situation, they perceive the idea of relief to be hopeless and they give up. The belief that they cannot affect the outcome of events no matter what force they exert on their environment seems to create an attitude of defeat. Actual failure eventually follows, thereby reinforcing that belief. It seems that the reality of the situation is not the crucial factor: What matters is the perception that the situation is hopeless.

ATTRIBUTIONAL STYLE QUESTIONNAIRE

As research continued, however, Seligman discovered that exposure to uncontrollable negative situations did not always lead to helplessness and depression. Moreover, the results yielded no explanation of the loss of self-esteem frequently seen in depressed persons. To refine their ability to predict helpless attitudes and behavior, Seligman and his colleagues developed a measuring mechanism called the attributional style questionnaire. It involves twelve hypothetical events, six bad and six good.

Subjects involved in testing are told to imagine themselves in the situations and to determine what they believe would be the major cause of the situation if it were to happen to them. After subjects complete the test, their performance is rated according to stability versus instability, globality versus specificity, and externality versus internality. An example of stable, global, internal perceptions would be a feeling of stupidity for one's failure; an unstable, specific, and external perception might consider luck to be the cause of the same situation. The questionnaire has been used by some industries and corporations to identify people who may not be appropriate for certain positions requiring assertiveness and a well-developed ability to handle stress. The same questionnaire has also been used to identify individuals who may be at high risk for developing psychosomatic disorders so that early intervention can be implemented.

Perhaps the primary significance of learned helplessness is its model of how a person's perception of a life event can influence the person's behavior—and can therefore affect his or her life and possibly the lives of others. Seligman believes that the way people perceive and explain the things that happen to them may be more important than what actually happens. These perceptions can have serious implications for a person's mental and physical health.

PERCEPTIONS OF HELPLESSNESS

The human mind is so complex, and the cognitive process so unknown, that perception is one of the most confusing frontiers facing social scientists. Why do people perceive situations as they do—often as events far different from the ones that actually transpired? If a person is convinced that an event occurred the way he or she remembers it, then it becomes that person's reality. It will be stored that way and may be retrieved that way in the future—perhaps blocking opportunities for positive growth and change because the memory is based on an inaccurate perception.

If children are taught that they are "stupid" because they cannot understand what is expected of them, for example, then they may eventually stop attempting to understand: They have learned that their response (trying to understand) and the situation's outcome are independent of each other. If such helpless feelings are reinforced, the individuals may develop an expectation that no matter what they do, it will be futile. They will then develop a new feeling—helplessness—which can be generalized to a new situation and can interfere with the future. Various studies have indeed shown that many people have been "taught" that, no matter what their response, the outcome will be the same—failure—so there is no reason to bother to do anything.

ROLE IN VICTIMIZATION

One example of this can be demonstrated in the area of victimized women and children. Halfway houses and safe houses are established in an attempt to both protect and retrain battered women and children. Efforts are made to teach them how to change their perceptions and give them new feelings of potency and control. The goal is to teach them that they can have an effect on their environment and have the power to administer successful positive change. For many women, assertiveness training, martial arts classes, and seminars on how to make a strong positive statement with their self-presentation (such as their choice of clothes) become matters of survival.

Children, however, are in a much more vulnerable situation, as they must depend on adults in order to survive. For most children in the world, helplessness is a reality in many situations: They do not, in fact, have much control over what happens to them, regardless of the response they exhibit. Adults, whether they are parents, educators, church leaders, or older siblings, have the responsibility of being positive role models to help children shape their perceptions of the world. If children are allowed to express their feelings, and if their comments are listened to and considered, they can see that they do have some power over their environment and can break patterns of learned helplessness.

A therapist has described "Susan," a client who as a youngster had lived with the belief that if she argued or asserted her needs with her parents they would leave her. She became the "perfect" child, never arguing or seeming to be ungrateful; in the past, if she had, her parents would often get into a fight and one would temporarily leave. Susan's perception was that if she asserted her needs, she was abandoned; if she then begged the parent who remained to tell the absent parent that she was sorry and would never do it again, that parent would return. In reality, her parents did not communicate well and were using their child as an excuse to get angry and leave. The purpose was to punish the other adult, not to hurt the child.

When Susan became an adult, she became involved with a man who mistreated her, both physically and emotionally, but always begged forgiveness after the fact. She always forgave him, believing that she had done something wrong to deserve his harsh treatment in the first place. At her first session with a therapist, she was reluctant to be there, having been referred by a women's shelter. She missed her second session because she had returned to her lover, who had found her at the shelter. Eventually, after a cycle of returns to the shelter, the therapist, and her lover, Susan was able to break free and begin the healing process, one day at a time. She told the therapist repeatedly that she believed that no matter what she did, the outcome would always be the same—she would rather be with the man who abused her but paid attention to her than be alone. After two difficult years of concentrating on a new perception of herself and her environment, she began to experience actual power in the form of positive effectiveness on her life. She became able to see old patterns before they took control and to replace them with new perceptions.

Another example of the power that perceptions of helplessness can have concerns a man ("John") who, as a young boy, was very attached to his father and used to throw tantrums when his father had to leave for work. John's mother would drag him to the kitchen and hold his head under the cold water faucet to stop his screaming; it worked. The child grew up with an impotent rage toward his mother, however, and disappointment in his father for not protecting him. He grew up believing that, no matter how he made his desires known, his feelings would be drowned, as they had been many years before. As a teenager, John grew increasingly violent, eventually getting into trouble; he did not realize that his family was dysfunctional and did not have the necessary skills to get better.

John was never able to believe in himself, even though—on raw rage and little confidence—he triumphed over his pain and terror to achieve an advanced education and black belt in the martial arts. He even developed a career teaching others how to gain power in their lives and how to help nurture the spirit of children. Yet after all this, he still does not have much confidence in his abilities. He is also still terrified of water, although he forces himself to swim.

MIND-BODY RELATIONSHIP

Research has provided validity for the suspected link between how a person perceives and influences his or her environment and that person's total health and effectiveness. There has been evidence that the mind and body are inseparable, that one influences the other even to the point of breakdown or healing. Leslie Kamen, Judith Rodin, and Seligman have corroborated the idea that how a person explains life situations (a person's explanatory style) seems to be related to immune system functioning. Blood samples were taken from a group of older persons who had been interviewed about life changes, stress, and health changes. Those whose interviews revealed a pessimistic or depressive explanatory style had a larger percentage of suppressor cells in their blood. Considering the idea that suppressor cells are believed to undermine the body's ability to fight tumor growth, these discoveries suggest a link between learned helplessness (as revealed by attitude and explanatory style) and susceptibility to diseases.

Studies have also been conducted to determine whether learned helplessness and explanatory style can predict illness. Results, though inconclusive, suggest that a person's attitude and perception of life events do influence physical health some twenty to thirty years later and can therefore be a valuable predictor and a tool for prevention. Particularly if an illness is just beginning, a person's psychological state may be crucial to healing.

NEW RESEARCH DIRECTIONS

The concepts of helplessness and hopelessness versus control over life situations are as old as humankind. The specific theory of learned helplessness, however, originated with the experiments conducted by the University of Pennsylvania in the mid-1960's by Seligman, Steven F. Maier, and J. Bruce Overmier. The idea that helplessness could be learned has opened the door to many exciting new approaches to disorders formerly considered personality or biologically oriented, such as psychosomatic disorders, victimization by gender, depression, and impaired job effectiveness.

The idea that people actually do have an effect on their environment is of tremendous importance to those suffering from depression. Most such people mention a general feeling of hopelessness, which makes the journey out of this state seem overwhelming; the feeling implies that one is powerless over one's reactions and behavior. Research-based evidence has shown that people do have the power to influence their perceptions of their environment and, therefore, change their reactions to it.

If the research on perception and learned helplessness is accurate, a logical next step is to find out how explanatory style originates and how it can be changed. Some suspected influences are how a child's first major trauma is handled, how teachers present information to be learned (as well as teachers' attitudes toward life events), and parental influence. Perhaps the most promising aspect of the research on learned helplessness is the idea that what is learned can be unlearned; therefore, humans really do have choices as to their destiny and quality of life. Considerable importance falls upon those who have a direct influence on children, because it is they who will shape the attitudes of the future.

SOURCES FOR FURTHER STUDY

Applebee, Arthur N. *The Child's Concept of Story, Ages Two to Seventeen.* Reprint. Chicago: University of Chicago Press, 1989. An innovative approach and eight thought-provoking chapters give this book an edge on some of the classics in this field. The author examines the use of language and how perceptions can be influenced by it. Demonstrates an adult's and child's sense of story as well as the responses of adolescents. The author shows how perceptions are easily manipulated by skillful use of phrasing. There are three appendices: a collection of analysis and data, elements of response, and a thorough supplementary table.

Bammer, Kurt, and Benjamin H. Newberry, eds. *Stress and Cancer.* Toronto: Hogrefe, 1981. This edited group of independently written chapters presents thirteen different perspectives from a variety of professionals working in the field of cancer and stress. Well written; achieves its goal without imposing editorial constraints. Perception of events is emphasized as a major determinant of healing. Excellent resources.

Coopersmith, Stanley. *The Antecedents of Self Esteem.* 1967. Reprint. Palo Alto, Calif.: Consulting Psychologists Press, 1981. Emphasizes the importance of limits and boundaries of permissible behavior in the development of self-esteem. Discusses the mirror-image idea of humans emulating society as it develops through the parent/child relationship. There are four very helpful measuring devices in the appendix.

Peterson, Christopher, Steven F. Maier, and Martin E. P. Seligman. *Learned Helplessness: A Theory for the Age of Personal Control.* New York: Oxford University Press, 1995. Summarizes the theory and application of the theory of learned helplessness, focusing on personal control as a tool for overcoming the condition.

Seligman, Martin E. P. *Helplessness: On Depression, Development, and Death.* 1975. Reprint. New York: W. H. Freeman, 1992. This easily read and understood book was written by the master researcher in the field of learned helplessness. Covers such areas as anxiety and unpredictability, education's role in emotional development, experimental studies, and how perception influences everyday life. Excellent references. Highly recommended for anyone interested in the topic.

Frederic Wynn

SEE ALSO: Conditioning; Depression; Learning.

LEARNING

TYPE OF PSYCHOLOGY: Biological bases of behavior; learning; motivation
FIELDS OF STUDY: Biological influences on learning; instrumental
   conditioning; Pavlovian conditioning; problem solving

Learning refers to a change in behavior as a result of experience. Learning is studied in a variety of species in an attempt to uncover basic principles. There are two major types of learning: classical (Pavlovian) conditioning and operant (instrumental) conditioning. Exposure to uncontrollable aversive events can have detrimental effects on learning. Consequences can be successfully used to develop a variety of behaviors, including even random, unpredictable performance. Learning produces lasting changes in the nervous system.

KEY CONCEPTS
- classical conditioning
- contingency
- law of effect
- learned helplessness
- operant conditioning
- shaping

Learning has been of central interest to psychologists since the emergence of the field in the late 1800's. Learning refers to changes in behavior that result from experiences. The term "behavior" includes all actions of an organism, both those that are directly observable, such as typing at a keyboard, and those that are unobservable, such as thinking about how to solve a problem. Psychologists studying learning work with a variety of species, including humans, rodents, and birds. Nonhuman species are studied for a variety of reasons. First, scientists are interested in fundamental principles of learning that have cross-species generality. Second, the degree of experimental control that can be obtained with nonhumans is much higher than with humans. These controlled conditions make it more likely that any effect that is found results from the experimental manipulations, rather than some uncontrolled variable. Third, studying the learning of nonhumans can be helpful to animals. For example, a scientist might need to know the best way to raise an endangered giant condor to maximize its chances of survival when introduced to the wild.

There are two major types of learning. Classical conditioning (also called Pavlovian conditioning, after Russian physiologist Ivan Pavlov) involves transfer of control of reflexes to new environmental stimuli. For example, a glaucoma test at an optometrist's office used to involve a puff of air being delivered into the patient's eyes, which elicited blinking. After this experience, putting one's head into the machine would elicit blinking; the glaucoma-testing machine would elicit the reflex of blinking, before the air puff was delivered.

Operant conditioning, also called instrumental conditioning, involves the regulation of nonreflexive behavior by its consequences. American psychologist Edward Thorndike was a pioneer in the study of operant conditioning, publishing his work about cats escaping from puzzle boxes in 1898. Thorndike observed that over successive trials, movements that released a latch, allowing the animal to get out of the box and get some food, became more frequent. Movements not resulting in escape became less frequent. Thorndike called this the Law of Effect: responses followed by satisfaction would be strengthened, while responses followed by discomfort would be weakened. The study of operant conditioning was greatly extended by American behaviorist B. F. Skinner, starting in the 1930's.

Beginning in the 1960's, American psychologists Martin Seligman, Steven Maier, J. Bruce Overmier, and their colleagues discovered that the controllability of events has a large impact on future learning. Dogs exposed to inescapable electric shock became passive and failed to learn to escape shock in later situations in which escape was possible. Seligman and colleagues called this phenomenon "learned helplessness" because the dogs had learned that escape was not possible and gave up. The laboratory phenomenon of learned helplessness has been applied to the understanding and treatment of human depression and related conditions.

In the 1970's, some psychologists thought the use of rewards (such as praise or tangible items) was harmful to motivation, interest, and creativity. Beginning in the 1990's, however, American Robert Eisenberger and Canadian Judy Cameron, conducting research and analyzing previous studies, found that rewards generally have beneficial impacts. Rewards appear to have detrimental effects only when they are given regardless of how the person or animal does. Furthermore, the work of Allen Neuringer and colleagues has shown that, contrary to previous thinking, both people and animals can learn to behave in random, unpredictable ways.

The changes in behavior produced by learning are accompanied by changes in physiological makeup. Learning is associated with changes in the strength of connections between neurons (nerve cells in the brain), some quite long-lasting. Eric R. Kandel and his colleagues have documented the changes in physiology underlying relatively simple learning in giant sea snails, progressing to more complex behaviors in mammals. Similar physiological changes accompany learning in a variety of organisms, highlighting the continuity of learning across different species.

CLASSICAL CONDITIONING

Classical conditioning was first systematically investigated by Ivan Pavlov in the late 1800's and early 1900's. Classical conditioning involves the transfer of control of an elicited response from one stimulus to another, previously neutral, stimulus. Pavlov discovered classical conditioning accidentally while investigating digestion in dogs. A dog was given meat powder in its mouth to elicit salivation. After this process had been repeated a number of times, the dog would start salivating before the meat powder was put in its mouth. When it saw the laboratory assistant, it would start to salivate, although it had not initially salivated at the sight. Pavlov devoted the rest of his long career to the phenomenon of classical conditioning.

In classical conditioning, a response is initially elicited by an unconditioned stimulus (US). The US is a stimulus that elicits a response without any prior experience. For example, the loud sound of a balloon bursting naturally causes people to blink their eyes and withdraw from the noise. The response that is naturally elicited is called the unconditioned response (UR). If some stimulus reliably precedes the US, then over time it, too, will come to elicit a response. For example, the sight of an overfull balloon initially does not elicit blinking of the eyes, but if the sight of the balloon reliably precedes the loud noise that comes when it bursts, people eventually come to blink and recoil at the sight of an overfull balloon. The stimulus with the new power to elicit the response is called the conditioned stimulus (CS), and the response elicited by the CS is called the conditioned response (CR).

Classical conditioning occurs with a variety of behaviors and situations. For example, a person who was stung by a wasp in a woodshed may now experience fear on approaching the woodshed. In this case, the building becomes a CS eliciting the CR of fear because the wasp's sting (the US) elicited pain and fear (the UR) in that place. To overcome the classical conditioning, the person would need to enter the woodshed repeatedly without incident. If the woodshed was no longer paired with the painful sting of the wasp, over time the CR would extinguish.

Many phobias are thought to arise through classical conditioning. One common successful treatment is systematic desensitization, in which the person, through progressive steps, gradually faces the feared object or situation until the fear CR extinguishes. Classical conditioning has been recognized as the culprit in food aversions developed by people receiving chemotherapy treatments for cancer. In this case, the food becomes a CS for illness (the CR) by being paired with the chemotherapy treatment (the US) that later elicits illness (the UR). Using more advanced principles of classical conditioning learned through research with nonhumans, people are now able to reduce the degree of aversion that occurs to regular meals, thus preventing the person from developing revulsions to food, which would further complicate the treatment of the cancer by introducing potential nutritional problems.

OPERANT CONDITIONING

Operant conditioning (also called instrumental conditioning) involves the regulation of voluntary behavior by its consequences. Thorndike first systemically studied operant conditioning in the late 1800's. He placed cats in puzzle boxes and measured the amount of time they took to escape to a waiting bowl of food. He found that with increasing experience, the cats escaped more quickly. Movements that resulted in being released from the box, such as stepping on a panel or clawing a loop in a string, became more frequent, whereas movements that were not followed by release became less frequent. This type of operant learning is called "trial-and-error learning," because there is no systematic attempt made to teach the behavior. Instead, the organism makes many mistakes, which become less likely over time, and sometimes hits on the solution, which then becomes more likely over time.

B. F. Skinner, beginning in the 1930's, greatly extended and systematized the study of operant conditioning. One of his major contributions was to invent an apparatus called the operant chamber, which provided a controlled environment in which behavior was automatically recorded. In the operant chamber, an animal, such as a rat, would be able to make an arbitrary response, such as pressing a small lever on the side of the chamber with its paws. The apparatus could be programmed to record the response automatically and provide a consequence, such as a bit of food, to the animal. There are several advantages to this technique. First, the chamber filters out unplanned sights and sounds that could disturb the animal and affect ongoing behavior. Second, the animal is free to make the response at any time, and so response rate can vary over a wide range as a result of any experimental manipulations. This range means that response rate is a sensitive measure to detect the effects of changes the experimenter makes. Third, the automatic control and recording means that the procedure can be repeated exactly the same way in every experimental session and that the experimenter's ideas about what should happen cannot influence the outcome. The operant conditioning chamber is used extensively today in experiments investigating the learning of a variety of species from different perspectives.

One major technique to teach new behavior is called shaping. Shaping refers to providing a consequence for successive approximations to a desired response. For example, to teach a child to tie shoelaces, a parent might start by crossing the laces, forming the loops and crossing them, and having the child do the last part of pulling the loops tight. The parent would then praise the child. The parent could then gradually have the child do more and more of the task, until the whole task is successfully completed from the start. This type of approach ensures that the task is never too far out of reach of the child's current capabilities. Shaping takes place when young children are learning language, too. At first, parents and other caregivers are overjoyed at any approximation of basic words. Over time, however, they require the sounds to be closer and closer to the final, precisely spoken performance. Shaping can be used to teach a wide variety of behaviors in humans and nonhumans. The critical feature is that the requirement for the reward is gradually increased, in pace with the developing skill. If for some reason the behavior deteriorates, then the requirement can be lowered until the person is once again successful, then proceed again through increasing levels of difficulty. In order for any consequence to be effective, it should occur immediately after the behavior and every time the behavior occurs.

REINFORCERS AND PUNISHERS

In operant conditioning, there are four basic contingencies that can be used to modify the frequency of occurrence of nonreflexive behavior. A contingency refers to the relation between the situation, a behavior, and the consequence of the behavior. A reinforcer is a consequence that makes a behavior more likely in the future, whereas a punisher is a consequence that makes a behavior less likely in the future. Reinforcers and punishers both come in both positive and negative forms. A positive consequence is the presentation of a stimulus or event as a result of the behavior, and a negative consequence is the removal of a stimulus or event as a result of the behavior. Correctly used, the terms "positive" and "negative" refer only to whether the event is presented or removed, not whether the action is judged good or bad.

A positive reinforcer is a consequence that increases the future likelihood of the behavior that produced it. For example, if a parent were to praise a child at dinner for eating properly with a fork, and as a result the child used the fork properly more often, then praise would have served as a positive reinforcer. The vast majority of scientists studying learning recommend positive reinforcement as the best technique to promote learning. One can attempt to increase the desired appropriate behavior through positive reinforcement, rather than focusing on the undesired or inappropriate behavior. If the appropriate behavior becomes more frequent, then chances are that the inappropriate behavior will have become less frequent as well, due to the fact that there are only so many things that a person can do at one time.

A negative reinforcer is a consequence that increases the future likelihood of the behavior that removed it. For example, in many cars, a buzzer or bell sounds until the driver puts on the seatbelt. In this case, putting on the seatbelt is negatively reinforced by the removal of the noise. Another example of negative reinforcement occurs when a child is having a tantrum in a grocery store until given candy. The removal of the screaming would serve as a negative reinforcer for the parent's behavior: In the future when the child was screaming, the parent would probably be more likely to give the child candy. Furthermore, the parent is providing positive reinforcement for screaming by presenting a consequence (candy) for a behavior (screaming) that makes the behavior more likely to occur in similar situations in the future. This example should make clear that reinforcement is defined in terms of the presentation or removal of an event increasing the likelihood of a behavior in the future, not in terms of intentions or opinions. Most parents would not consider the behavior inadvertently created and maintained in this way to be "positive."

Positive punishment refers to the presentation of an event that decreases the likelihood of the behavior that produced it. For example, if a person touches a hot stove, the pain that ensues makes it much less likely that the person will touch the stove under those conditions in the future. In this case, the behavior (touching the stove) produces a stimulus (pain) that makes the behavior less frequent. Negative punishment, on the other hand, refers to the removal of an event that decreases the likelihood of the behavior that produced it. For example, if a birdwatcher walking through the woods makes a loud move that causes all of the birds to fly away, then the watcher would be less likely to move like that in the future. In this way, watchers learn to move quietly to avoid disturbing the birds they are trying to observe.

Negative reinforcement, positive punishment, and negative punishment all involve what is called aversive control. An aversive stimulus is anything that an organism will attempt to escape from or try to avoid if possible. Aversive control refers to learning produced through the use of an aversive stimulus. For example, parents sometimes use spanking or hitting in an attempt to teach their child not to do something, such as hitting another child. This type of approach has been shown to have a number of undesirable outcomes, however. One problem is that the appropriate or desired alternative behavior is not taught. In other words, the child does not learn what should be done instead of what was done. Another problem is that the use of aversive stimuli can produce aggression. Humans and nonhumans alike often respond to painful stimuli with an increased likelihood of aggression. The aggression may or may not be directed toward the person or thing that hurt them. Additionally, the use of aversive control can produce avoidance—children who have been spanked or hit may try to stay away from the person who hurt them. Furthermore, through observation, children who have been spanked may be more likely to use physical harm to others as an attempted solution when they encounter conflict. Indeed, corporal punishment (the use of spanking or other physical force intended to cause a child to experience pain, but not injury, for the purpose of correction) has been linked to many undesirable outcomes for children, some of which extend well into adulthood. Beginning in the 1970's, American psychologist Murray Straus and his colleagues investigated the impact of corporal punishment on children. Their findings indicated that the use of corporal punishment is associated with an increase in later antisocial behavior, a decrease in cognitive development relative to children who are not spanked, and an increased likelihood of spousal abuse as an adult, in addition to several other detrimental outcomes.

LEARNED HELPLESSNESS

As Seligman, Maier, and Overmier discovered, exposure to uncontrollable aversive events can have profound impacts on future learning, a phenomenon called "learned helplessness." In learned helplessness, an organism that has been exposed to uncontrollable aversive events later has an impaired ability to learn to escape from aversive situations and even to learn new, unrelated behaviors. The phenomenon was accidentally discovered in laboratory research with dogs. Seligman and his colleagues found that dogs that were exposed to electrical shocks in a harness, with no possibility of escape, later could not learn to escape shocks in a shuttle box in which they had only to jump to the other side. Disturbingly, they would lie down and whimper, not even trying to get away from the completely avoidable shocks. Dogs that had not been exposed to the uncontrollable shocks learned to escape in the shuttle box rapidly. More important, dogs exposed to the same number and pattern of shocks, but with the ability to turn them off, also had no trouble learning to escape in the shuttle box. In other words, it was the exposure to uncontrollable shocks, not just shocks, that produced the later deficit in escape learning. Moreover, the dogs that had been exposed to uncontrollable aversive events also had difficulties learning other, unrelated, tasks. This basic result has since been found many times with many different types of situations, species, and types of aversive events. For example, learned helplessness has been shown to occur in dogs, cats, mice, rats, gerbils, goldfish, cockroaches, and even slugs. Humans show the learned helplessness phenomenon in laboratory studies as well. For example, people exposed to an uncontrollable loud static noise later solved fewer anagrams (word puzzles) than people exposed to the same amount and pattern of noise but who could turn it off.

Learned helplessness has major implications for the understanding and treatment of human depression. Although certainly the case with people is more complex, animals that have developed learned helplessness in the laboratory show similarities to depressed people. For example, they have generalized reduced behavioral output. Similarly, researchers discovered early on that learned helplessness in rats could be prevented by treatment with antidepressant medication. Furthermore, exposure to uncontrollable aversive events produces deficiencies in immune system function, resulting in greater physical ailments, in both animals and people. In people, serial combinations of uncontrollable aversive events, such as sudden and unexpected loss of a spouse or child, being laid off from a job, or losing a home to fire, can result in the feeling that one is powerless and doomed. These feelings of helplessness can then produce changes, such as decreased interest in life and increased illness, which further compound the situation. Fortunately, there are effective treatments for learned helplessness. One solution already mentioned is antidepressant medication, which may work in part because it overcomes the physiological changes produced by the helpless experience. Additionally, therapy to teach effective coping and successful learning experiences can reverse learned helplessness in people and laboratory animals.

LEARNED CREATIVITY AND VARIABILITY

Beginning in the 1970's, some psychologists began to criticize the use of rewards to promote learning. Tangible rewards, as well as praise and attention, they argued, could interfere with creativity, problem-solving ability, motivation, and enjoyment. Fortunately, these concerns were allayed in the 1990's by careful research and examination of previous research, most notably that

Children can learn to be creative in their drawing; creativity was formerly thought to be outside the domain of learning.
(EyeWire)

of Eisenberger and Judy Cameron. Together, they analyzed the results of more than one hundred published studies on the effects of rewards and found that in general, rewards increase interest, motivation, and performance. The only situation in which rewards had detrimental effects was when they were offered independently of performance. In other words, giving "rewards" regardless of how the person does is bad for morale and interest.

Furthermore, several aspects of performance previously thought to be beyond the domain of learning, such as creativity and even randomlike behavior, have been demonstrated to be sensitive to consequences. Children can learn to be creative in their drawing, in terms of the number of novel pictures drawn, using rewards for novelty. Similarly, as shown by the work of American psychologist Allen Neuringer and his colleagues, people and animals alike can learn to engage in strings of unpredictable behavior that cannot be distinguished from the random sort of outcomes generated by a random number generator. This finding is particularly interesting given that this novel behavior has been found to generalize to new situations, beyond the situation in which the learning originally occurred. Learned variability has been demonstrated in dolphins, rats, pigeons, and humans, including children with autism. Learning to be creative and to try new approaches has important implications for many aspects of daily life and problem solving.

BIOLOGICAL BASES OF LEARNING

The features of learning do not occur in a vacuum: They often produce lasting, physiological changes in the organism. The search for the physical underpinnings of learning has progressed from relatively basic reflexes in relatively simple organisms to more complex behaviors in mammals. Beginning in the 1960's, Eric R. Kandel and his colleagues started to examine simple learning in the large sea snail *Aplysia*. This snail was chosen as a model to study physiological changes in learning because its nervous system is relatively simple, containing several thousand neurons (nerve cells) compared to the billions of neurons in mammals. The neurons are large, so researchers can identify individual cells and monitor them for changes as learning progresses. In this Nobel Prize-winning work, Kandel and colleagues outlined many of the changes in the degree of responsiveness in connections between neurons that underlie classical conditioning processes. The same processes have been observed in other species, including mammals, and the work continues to expand to more complex behavior. This research shows the commonality in learning processes across species and emphasizes the progress in understanding the physical basis that underlies learning.

SOURCES FOR FURTHER STUDY

Branch, Marc N., and Timothy D. Hackenberg. "Humans Are Animals, Too: Connecting Animal Research to Human Behavior and Cognition." In *Learning and Behavior Therapy*, edited by William O'Donohue. Boston: Allyn & Bacon, 1998. The authors explain the relevance of work with nonhumans to humans. Includes a discussion of the effects of explicit rewards on motivation and the phenomenon of learning without awareness. This book chapter is clearly written and understandable to the interested nonprofessional reader.

Carroll, Marilyn E., and J. Bruce Overmier, eds. *Animal Research and Human Health: Advancing Human Welfare Through Behavioral Science*. Washington, D.C.: American Psychological Association, 2001. Contains descriptions of the application of research with animals to a variety of human conditions, including anxiety, stress, depression, drug abuse, aggression, and a variety of areas of learning. Also contains a section on the ethics of using animals in behavioral research and a list of additional readings.

Eisenberger, Robert, and Judy Cameron. "The Detrimental Effects of Reward: Myth or Reality?" *American Psychologist* 51, no. 11 (1996): 1153-1166. This journal article in the publication of the American Psychological Association provides an analysis of over one hundred studies and finds that rewards generally are not detrimental, but are in fact beneficial, to motivation, interest, and enjoyment of a task. Although the article contains advanced statistical techniques, they are not critical to the understanding of the findings.

Mazur, James E. *Learning and Behavior.* Upper Saddle River, N.J.: Prentice Hall, 2001. This best-selling introduction to the topic of learning and behavior assumes no prior knowledge of psychology. The reading is straightforward though sometimes challenging as it covers the basics of classical and operant conditioning, biological bases of learning and behavior, and applications to complex human learning situations.

Overmier, J. Bruce, and V. M. LoLordo. "Learned Helplessness." In *Learning and Behavior Therapy*, edited by William O'Donohue. Boston: Allyn & Bacon, 1998. Scholarly, complete discussion of the history of research in learned helplessness, thorough description of the phenomenon, up to current controversies and debates in this area. Contains information on the physiological underpinnings of learned helplessness and the application of this research to human depression. Includes large reference section with classic papers in this area of research.

Seligman, Martin E. P. *Learned Optimism.* New York: Pocket Books, 1998. This book by one of the pioneers in the area describes the basic research underlying the proposed therapeutic approach to address problems with learned helplessness. Contains scales to assess the reader's degree of optimism and scientifically based recommendations to change problematic behavior. Written for a broad audience.

Skinner, B. F. *Science and Human Behavior.* Reprint. New York: Classics of Psychiatry & Behavioral Sciences Library, 1992. This classic work by Skinner was designed to bring the study of human learning to a wide audience. Describes the application of science to human problems. Reviews basic learning principles before discussing their application to a variety of wide ranging human issues.

Straus, Murray A., and Denise A. Donnelly. *Beating the Devil out of Them: Corporal Punishment in American Families and Its Effects on Children.* New Brunswick, N.J.: Transaction, 2001. This thought-provoking book by one of the foremost experts on family violence is written for a broad audience. Discusses the prevalence of spanking and other forms of corporal punishment. Outlines the short-term and long-term impacts of spanking on children, including increased aggression, criminality, and depression. Includes a discussion of benefits of alternative child-rearing strategies.

Amy L. Odum

SEE ALSO: Cognitive Development: Jean Piaget; Giftedness; Imprinting; Intelligence; Language; Learning Disorders; Logic and Reasoning; Memory; Mental Retardation; Pavlovian Conditioning; Race and Intelligence; Thought: Study and Measurement.

Learning Disorders

Type of psychology: Psychopathology
Field of study: Childhood and adolescent disorders

Learning disorders (LD) comprise the disorders usually first diagnosed in infancy, childhood, or adolescence. Because the condition affects the academic progress of approximately 5 percent of all public school students in the United States, it has attracted the attention of clinicians, educators, and researchers from varied disciplines. Substantial progress has been made in the assessment and diagnosis of learning disorders but questions regarding etiology, course, and treatment of the disorder continue to challenge investigators.

Key concepts
- disorder of written expression
- dyslexia
- learning disabilities
- learning disorder not otherwise specified
- mathematics disorder
- phonological processing
- reading disorder

Learning disorders (LD) is a general term for clinical conditions that meet three diagnostic criteria: An individual's achievement in an academic domain (such as reading) is substantially below that expected given his or her age, schooling, and level of intelligence; the learning disturbance interferes significantly with academic achievement or activities of daily living that require specific academic skills; and if a sensory deficit (such as blindness or deafness) is present, the learning difficulties are in excess of those usually associated with it. The American Psychiatric Association's *Diagnostic and Statistical Manual of Mental Disorders: DSM-IV-TR* (rev. 4th ed., 2000) specifies four subcategories of learning disorders: Reading Disorder, Mathematics Disorder, Disorder of Written Expression, and Learning Disorder Not Otherwise Specified (NOS). The criteria for the first three specific learning disorders are the same except for the academic domain affected by the disorder. The fourth subcategory is reserved for disorders involving learning the academic skills that do not meet the criteria for any specific learning disorder. Included are problems in all three academic domains (reading, mathematics, written expression) that together significantly interfere with academic achievement even though academic achievement as measured on standardized tests does not fall substantially below what is expected given the individual's chronological age, intelligence quotient (IQ), or age-appropriate education.

A variety of statistical approaches are used to produce an operational definition of "substantially below" academic achievement. Despite some controversy about its appropriateness, the most frequently used approach defines "substantially below" as a discrepancy between achievement and IQ of more than two standard deviations (SD). In cases where an individual's performance on an IQ test may have been compromised by an associated disorder in linguistic or information processing, an associated mental disorder, a general medical condition, or the individual's ethnic or cultural background, a smaller discrepancy (between one and two SDs) may be acceptable.

Differential diagnosis involves differentiating learning disorders from normal variations in academic achievement, scholastic difficulties due to lack of opportunity, poor teaching, or cultural factors, and learning difficulties associated with a sensory deficit. In cases of pervasive developmental disorder or mild mental retardation, an additional diagnosis of learning disorder is given if the individual's academic achievement is substantially below the expected level given the individual's schooling and intelligence.

The term "learning disorders" was first applied to a clinical condition meeting these three criteria in the *Diagnostic and Statistical Manual of Mental Disorders* (4th ed., DSM-IV), published in 1994. Earlier editions of the DSM used other labels such as "learning disturbance," a subcategory within special symptom reactions in DSM-II (1968). In DSM-III (1980) and DSM-III-R (1987), the condition was labeled "Academic Skills Disorders" and listed under "Specific Developmental Disorders"; furthermore, the diagnosis was based only on "substantially below" academic achievement, and the disorder was classified as an Axis II rather than an Axis I or clinical condition. The LD condition is also known by names other than those used in the psychiatric nomenclature, most frequently as "learning disabilities," which is defined as a disorder in one or more of the basic psychological processes involved in understanding or in using spoken or written language, which may manifest itself in an imperfect ability to listen, think, speak, read, write, spell, or do mathematical calculations in children whose learning problems are not primarily the result of visual, hearing, or motor handicaps, mental retardation, emotional disturbance, or environmental, cultural, or economic disadvantage. Learning disabilities is the term used in P.L. 94-142, the Education for All Handicapped Children Act of 1975, and in P.L. 101-476, the Individuals with Disabilities Education Act. Specific learning disorders are also referred to by other names, such as dyslexia (Reading Disorder), dyscalculia (Mathematics Disorder), or dysgraphia (Disorder of Written Expression). Empirical evidence about prevalence, etiology, course of the disorder, and intervention comes mainly from subjects identified as having dyslexia or learning disabilities.

PREVALENCE

Prevalence rates for learning disorders vary, depending on the definitions and methods of determining the achievement-intelligence discrepancy. According to the American Psychiatric Association, estimates range from 2 percent to 10 percent for the general population, and 5 percent for public school students in the United States. The prevalence rate for each specific learning disorder is more difficult to establish because many studies simply report the total number of learning disorders without separating them according to subcategory. Reading disorder is the most common, found in 4 percent of school-age children in the United States. Approximately four out of five cases of LD have Reading Disorder alone or in combination with Mathematics Disorder or Disorder of Written Expression. About 1 percent of school-age children have Mathematics Disorder, one out of five cases of LD. Disorder of Written Expression alone is rare; it is usually associated with Reading Disorder.

Studies based on referrals to school psychologists or clinics reported that more males than females manifested a learning disorder. However, studies employing careful diagnostic assessment and strict application of the criteria have found more equal rates for males and females. LD often coexists with another disorder, usually language disorders, communication disorders, attention-deficit hyperactivity disorder (ADHD), or conduct disorder.

ETIOLOGY

There is strong empirical support for a genetic basis of Reading Disorder or dyslexia from behavior genetic studies. John C. DeFries and his colleagues indicate that heredity can account for as much as 60 percent of the variance in Reading Disorders or dyslexia. As for the exact mode of genetic transmission, Lon R. Cardon and his collaborators, in two behavior genetic studies, identified chromosome 6 as a possible quantitative trait locus for a predisposition to develop Reading Disorder. The possibility that transmission occurs through a subtle brain dysfunction rather than autosomal dominance has been explored by Bruce Pennington and others.

The neurophysiological basis of Reading Disorders has been explored in studies of central nervous dysfunction or faulty development of cerebral dominance. The hypothesized role of central nervous dysfunction has been difficult to verify despite observations that many children with learning disorders had a history of prenatal and perinatal complications, neurological soft signs, and electroencephalograph abnormalities. In 1925, neurologist Samuel T. Orton hypothesized that Reading Disorder or dyslexia results from failure to establish hemispheric dominance between the two halves of the brain. Research has yielded inconsistent support for Orton's hypothesis and its reformulation, the progressive lateralization hypothesis. However, autopsy findings of cellular abnormalities in the left hemispheres of dyslexics that were confirmed in brain imaging studies of live human subjects have reinvigorated researchers. These new directions are pursued in studies using sophisticated brain imaging technology.

Genetic and neurophysiological factors do not directly cause problems in learning the academic skills. Rather, they affect development of neuropsychological, information-processing, linguistic, or communication abilities, producing difficulties or deficits that lead to learning problems. The most promising finding from research on process and ability deficits concerns phonological processing—the ability to use phonological information (the phonemes or speech sounds of one's language)—in processing oral and written language. Two types of phonological processing, phonological awareness and phonological memory (encoding or retrieval), have been studied extensively. Based on correlational and experimental data, there is an emerging consensus that a deficit in phonological processing is the basis of reading disorder in a majority of cases.

ASSESSMENT

Assessment refers to the gathering of information in order to attain a goal. Assessment tools vary with the goal. If the goal is to establish the diagnosis, assessment involves the individualized administration of standardized tests of academic achievement and intelligence that have norms for the child's age and, preferably, social class and ethnicity. To verify that the learning disturbance is interfering with a child's academic achievement or social functioning, information is collected from parents and teachers through interviews and standardized measures such as rating scales. Behavioral observations of the child may be used to supplement parent-teacher reports. If there is visual, hearing, or other sensory impairment, it must be determined that the learning deficit is in excess of that usually associated with it. The child's developmental, medical, and educational histories and the family history are also obtained and used in establishing the differential diagnosis and clarifying etiology.

If LD is present, the next goal is a detailed description of the learning disorder to guide treatment. Tools will depend upon the specific type of learning disorder. For example, in the case of dyslexia, E. Wilcutt and Pennington suggest that the achievement test given to establish the achievement-intelligence discrepancy be supplemented by others such as the Gray Oral Reading Test (GORT-III), a timed measure of reading fluency as well as reading comprehension. Still another assessment goal is to identify the neuropsychological, linguistic, emotional, and behavioral correlates of the learning disorder and any associated disorders. A variety of measures exist for this purpose. Instrument selection should be guided by the clinician's hypotheses, based on what has been learned about the child and the disorder. Information about correlates and associated disorders is relevant to setting targets for intervention, understanding the etiology, and estimating the child's potential response to intervention and prognosis.

In schools, identification of LD involves a multidisciplinary evaluation team including the classroom teacher, a psychologist, and a special education teacher or specialist in the child's academic skill deficit (such as reading). As needed, input may be sought from the child's pediatrician, a speech therapist, an audiologist, a language specialist, or a psychiatrist. A thorough assessment should provide a good description of the child's strengths as well as weaknesses that will be the basis of effective and comprehensive treat-

DSM-IV-TR Criteria for Learning Disorders

Mathematics Disorder (DSM code 315.1)

Mathematical ability, as measured by individually administered standardized tests, substantially below that expected given chronological age, measured intelligence, and age-appropriate education

Disorder interferes significantly with academic achievement or activities of daily living requiring mathematical ability

If a sensory deficit is present, mathematical difficulties exceed those usually associated with it

Reading Disorder (DSM code 315.00)

Reading achievement, as measured by individually administered standardized tests of reading accuracy or comprehension, substantially below that expected given chronological age, measured intelligence, and age-appropriate education

Disorder interferes significantly with academic achievement or activities of daily living requiring reading skills

If a sensory deficit is present, reading difficulties exceed those usually associated with it

Disorder of Written Expression (DSM code 315.2)

Writing skills, as measured by individually administered standardized tests or functional assessments of writing skills, substantially below those expected given chronological age, measured intelligence, and age-appropriate education

Disorder interferes significantly with academic achievement or activities of daily living requiring the composition of written texts (such as writing grammatically correct sentences and organized paragraphs)

If a sensory deficit is present, writing difficulties exceed those usually associated with it

Learning Disorder Not Otherwise Specified
(DSM code 315.9)

---

ment plans for both the child and the family. In school settings, these are called, respectively, an Individual Educational Plan (IEP) an
d an Individual Family Service Plan (IFSP).

TREATMENT

Most children with LD require special education. Depending upon the disorder's severity, they may learn best in a one-on-one setting, small group, special class, or regular classroom plus resource room tutoring.

Treatment of LD should address both the disorder and associated conditions or correlates. Furthermore, it should include assisting the family and school in becoming more facilitative contexts for development of the child with LD. Using neuropsychological training, psychoeducational methods, behavioral or cognitive-behavioral therapies, or cognitive instruction, singly or in combination, specific interventions have targeted the psychological process dysfunction or deficit assumed to underlie the specific learning disorder; a specific academic skill such as word attack; or an associated feature or correlate such as social skills. Process-oriented approaches that rose to prominence in the 1990's are linguistic models aimed at remediating deficits in phonological awareness and phonological memory, and cognitive models which teach specific cognitive strategies that enable the child to become a more efficient learner. Overall, treatment or intervention studies during the last two decades of the twentieth century and at the beginning of the twenty-first century are more theory-driven, built on prior research, and rigorous in methodology. Many studies have shown significant gains in target behaviors. Transfer of training, however, remains elusive. Generalization of learned skills and strategies is still the major challenge for future treatment research. As the twenty-first century begins, LD remains a persistent or chronic disorder.

SOURCES FOR FURTHER STUDY

American Psychiatric Association. *Diagnostic and Statistical Manual of Mental Disorders: DSM-IV-TR.* Rev. 4th ed. Washington, D.C.: Author, 2000. Provides a detailed description of the diagnostic criteria, associated features and disorders, and differential diagnosis. It also describes the course of the disorder and familial pattern, if any, for the specific learning disorders.

Brown, F. R., III, H. L. Aylward, and B. K. Keogh, eds. *Diagnosis and Management of Learning Disabilities.* San Diego, Calif.: Singular Publishing Group, 1996. A multidisciplinary group of contributors provide a comprehensive yet detailed view of diagnosis, assessment, and treatment of learning problems. Because of its clarity and scope, this is recommended as an introductory text.

Lyon, G. Reid. "Treatment of Learning Disabilities." In *Treatment of Childhood Disorders,* edited by E. J. Mash and L. C. Terdal. New York: Guilford Press, 1998. This chapter gives an excellent description of treatment models and reviews the research on their respective efficacies.

Sternberg, R. J., and Louise Spear-Swerling, eds. *Perspectives on Learning Disabilities.* Boulder, Colo.: Westview Press, 1999. This sophisticated presentation and critique of biological, cognitive, and contextual approaches to learning disabilities is highly recommended for graduate students and professionals.

Felicisima C. Serafica

SEE ALSO: Attention-Deficit Hyperactivity Disorder (ADHD); Brain Structure; Intelligence; Intelligence Tests; Language; Logic and Reasoning; Memory; Speech Disorders.